The World Disorder

Luiz Alberto Moniz Bandeira

The World Disorder

US Hegemony, Proxy Wars, Terrorism
and Humanitarian Catastrophes

 Springer

Luiz Alberto Moniz Bandeira†
Emeritus professor for History
University of Brasília
St. Leon-Rot, Germany

Translator: Américo Lucena Lage

ISBN 978-3-030-03203-6   ISBN 978-3-030-03204-3   (eBook)
https://doi.org/10.1007/978-3-030-03204-3

Library of Congress Control Number: 2018965208

Original edition: Luiz Alberto Moniz Bandeira: *A desordem mundial. O espectro da total dominação: guerras por procuração, terror, caos e catástrofes humanitárias.* Published by Civilização Brasileira 2017. © Luiz Alberto Moniz Bandeira. All rights reserved. Translated from the Brazilian edition by Américo Lucena Lage.

This Springer imprint is published by the registered company Springer Nature Switzerland AG
The registered company address is: Gewerbestrasse 11, 6330 Cham, Switzerland

"In war, too, the discretionary power of the Executive is extended; its influence in dealing out offices, honors, and emoluments is multiplied; and all the means of seducing the minds, are added to those of subduing the force, of the people. The same malignant aspect in republicanism may be traced in the inequality of fortunes, and the opportunities of fraud, growing out of a state of war, and in the degeneracy of manners and of morals engendered by both. No nation could preserve its freedom in the midst of continual warfare."

—James Madison, *4th president of the United States (1809–1817)*[1]

"Militarism, a common feature of breakdown and disintegration, is frequently effective in increasing a society's command both over other the living societies and over the inanimate forces of nature."

—Arnold J. Toynbee.[2]

"War is a racket. It always has been. It is possibly the oldest, easily most profitable, surely the most vicious. It is the only one international in scope. It is the only one in which the profits are reckoned in dollars and the losses in lives."

—General Smedley Darlington Butler.[3]

---

[1]MADISON, James. "Political Observations", April 20, 1795. In: _____. *Letters and Other Writings of James Madison*. vol. 4. Philadelphia: J. B. Lippincott & Co., 1865, p. 491.

[2]TOYNBEE, Arnold J. *A Study of History*. Abridgement of vols. I–VI. London/New York/Toronto: Geoffrey Cumberlege/Oxford University Press, 1951, p. 364.

[3]BUTLER, General Smedley Darlington. *War Is a Racket*. Dragon Nikolic (Editor), 2012, p. 1.

To His Highness,
Dom Duarte, Duke of Braganza,
Head of the Royal House of Portugal,
my friend.

And, as always, to Margot, my adored wife,
whose care still keeps me on this earth,
and Egas, our son, our pride.

Foreword: Erosion of US Democracy and International Disorder

The great disorder Luiz Alberto Moniz Bandeira writes about in this book is the disorder of international relations and the internal confusion in which the United States is immersed. It is the disorder mainly in Eastern Europe, particularly in Ukraine, and in the Middle East. Its main cause is the United States itself and the decay of democracy in that country. This superpower continues to export democracy to the rest of the world, however, even if this has to be done through war, while at the same time its own democracy, which after the Second World War was the most advanced in the world, declines internally.

And this notable historian of modernity tells us that democracy has indeed started to erode in the United States. No longer does it ensure the fundamental rights of individuals, arbitrarily detaining, torturing, or simply assassinating them if they are considered terrorists or enemies. The rationale for this is the "war on terror"; the real reasons are the great power's determination to occupy the domestic market of other countries with its financing and direct investments and its reluctance in accepting the emergence of other powers that are not under its sphere of influence.

But Moniz Bandeira does not remain on the theoretical plane. On the contrary, he dives into practice quoting document after document and interview after interview, which he gathered to write *The Global Disorder*. For him, what happened in the United States was a process of *"mutazione dello Stato"* from democracy to oligarchy, the dictatorship of financial capital. This is linked to the increasing domestic inequality since the 1980s and the increasing competition from developing countries to become exporters of manufactured goods and services, particularly China and India. Instead of accepting a multipolar world, in which the United States would be the main actor for a long time, they adopted policies that make the world more insecure and chaotic.

São Paulo, Brazil   Luiz Carlos Bresser-Pereira
March 2016

Foreword: Learning from Contemporary History

Professor Moniz Bandeira has produced yet another great work. In his academic humility, he has asked me to write its foreword, which is understandable. I am part of its chain of thought and methodology.

The method is the heart of the matter, which in my view will necessarily include:

1. Having an in-depth knowledge of the relevant history
2. Learning the structuring and permanent lessons from it
3. Looking for the economic root of all causes
4. Developing the theory of imperialism, of dependence, and of war
5. Understanding pure geopolitics and the "geopolitics of interests"
6. Practicing the analysis of the contradictory
7. Being free, thinking freely, whatever the cost, wanting to go further.

This work goes looking for the roots of the contemporary global disorder. To a certain extent, it is a genealogical study, since the discovery of the causes of the unbalance follows a process equivalent to genetic decoding. The characteristics are not lost in the causality; they remain in the DNA of the effects. The brilliant and irreverent idea of unearthing American "fascism" through this method produces effects that would have been unthinkable. Neutral interests don't exist, nor have they ever existed. And for interests moving billions of dollars, this is even more evident. The transnational capitalist dialectic has created not only NATO, but the Cold War. For what? It is laid out in this admirable work. What repercussions did these macro-processes have for individuals and social classes. This is also explained. How was the plutocracy structured based on this, domestically speaking, but especially in the international context? You'll need to read what is written. This system is a system of circular causality, self-sustaining, continuous, and overwhelming. It led to the crisis of 2007/2008, which many had foreseen. And how did the "fascist" American DNA survive after September 11? What happened with the invasion of Iraq? And what about Guantanamo? How did the fascism-enabling facts defeat the safeguards and liberal ideals of the "founding fathers"?

In the dialectic logic, we need to understand the contradictory, i.e., the antitheses, or the threats to this system, hence the inevitability of the concerted reference to

Russia, Iran, North Korea, and China, faced with the expansion of NATO and the new shape of Western imperialism. This is why the debacles of the USSR, Ukraine, Georgia, Afghanistan, the Middle East, and Africa are connected.

One of the points I stress mostly arises from the American ignorance regarding its opponents. This historic and repeated inability to understand others (friend and foe) anthropologically and sociologically was and remains one of the main Achilles' heels of the West in general and of the United States in particular. This inability leads it to make successive mistakes, for which the solution is to throw money (uselessly) at the problems it has created. Today, it calls on the private sector to pay for the war off the books and outside congress' control. The diplomats are the politicians underwriting agreements that are barely met.

The return to history, in the final parts of the book, makes all sense in this method. The method proposes the eternal return to critical history, geopolitics, and political theory. The difficulty lies in really doing this. Something professor Moniz Bandeira does masterfully.

This book represents another milestone in the explanation of the evil that is befalling us. And it creates the roots to see what awaits us.

I would like to thank my friend Moniz Bandeira for this sublime lesson, as well as for the lessons of resistance, of freedom, of strength, of struggle, of gallantry, nobility of spirit, of resistance against everything and everyone, "ça ira."

I want to congratulate Brazil for the work of this immortal scholar. Blessed is the nation with such a child.

Lisbon, Portugal   António C. A. de Sousa Lara
February 2016

Preface

The World Disorder is an offshoot of my other works *The Second Cold War* and *Formation of the American Empire*. Together they make up a *corpus*. I've always understood that political science, economics, and history intersect, one depending on the other, reciprocally influencing and blending with each other.

Since I've worked for the press when I was young and taught political communication as political scientist at the Catholic University of Rio de Janeiro, I took it upon myself to confront and carefully cross-check the most diverse information, assessing the plausibility of events and scraping off the ideological varnish so often covering the news so as to manage and manipulate popular perceptions. This is why I applied the strictest rigor in the research for this work, just as in my other works, verifying all details of events in the press of the most diverse countries, reading statements and speeches from statesmen and official documents from several governmental and/or international bodies, sanding off the ideological manipulation, the false conscience (*falsches Bewusstsein*),[4] and taking, as Thucydides taught (Athens, 460 B.C.-Thrace, 398 B.C.?), that which is most clear, real, and truthful, stripped of its mythological dress.[5]

In the development of this work, I have obviously relied on the collaboration of many people, some of whom have asked me not to mention their names for safety reasons. Nevertheless, I must thank my friends, His Royal Highness Dom Duarte, Duke of Bragança; the ambassadors Samuel Pinheiro Guimarães, Frederico Meyer, and Cesário Melantonio; and the professors António de Sousa Lara, of the Higher Institute of Social and Political Sciences (ISCSP) at the University of Lisbon, Paulo Fernando de Moraes Farias, of the Department of African Studies and Anthropology at the University of Birmingham, Michael Löwy, of the Centre National de Recherches Scientifiques (CNRS) in Paris, Tulio Vigevani, Professor Emeritus at the Universidade Estadual Paulista, Alberto Justo Sosa, founder and member of the

---

[4]Karl Marx & Friedrich Engels, 1981, pp. 26–27 and 40.

[5]Thucydides, 1952, pp. 104–195.

Comisión Directiva de AMERSUR ONG in Buenos Aires, Theotônio dos Santos, Coordinator of the Unesco Chair and Network—Universidad de las Naciones Unidas—on the global economy, Rio de Janeiro, and Gilberto Calcagnotto, sociologist, former researcher at GIGA—Institut für Lateinamerika-Studien, in Hamburg, and my right-hand man in Germany.

Their generous collaboration—information, suggestions, proofreading of texts, etc.—doesn't imply their absolute agreement or an acceptance of my comments and conclusions. For those, I alone am responsible.

Acknowledgement

Author "Luiz Alberto Moniz Bandeira" died on November 10, 2017 in the age of 81 years after a long chronical illness. M. A. Gilberto Calcagnotto is the corresponding trustee and he can be reached in calcagnottogilb@aol.com.

St. Leon-Rot, Germany   Luiz Alberto Moniz Bandeira
February 2016

Contents

About the Author

Luiz Alberto Vianna de Moniz Bandeira, Baron von São Marcos (by Portugal), graduated in juridical sciences and also holds a Ph.D. in political science from the University of São Paulo. He was a professor at the *Escola de Sociologia e Politica de São Paulo*. In 1976, he received grants from, among other institutions, the Ford Foundation, to conduct research in Argentina, Uruguay, and Paraguay on Brazil's historical role in the Rio de la Plata Basin. From 1977 through 1979, he extended this research project to the United States and Europe, thanks to a postdoctoral fellowship awarded by the Social Science Research Council and the Joint Committee on Latin American Studies of the American Council of Learned Societies in New York. He held the Chair of History of Brazilian Foreign Policy in the Department of History at the University of Brasília. He was awarded the Juca Pato Prize and named as Brazilian Intellectual of 2005 for the book *Formação do Império Americano (Da Guerra contra a Espanha à Guerra no Iraque)*. He was subsequently awarded an honorary doctorate by UniBrasil in Curitiba and by the Federal University of Bahia. Moniz Bandeira has been invited to lecture in many countries around the world. He was an Under-Secretary in Rio de Janeiro's State Government, being its representative in the federal capital, Brasília, from 1991 through 1994 and a cultural attaché at the Consulate-General of Brazil in Frankfurt am Main from 1996 through 2002. Luiz Alberto de Vianna Moniz Bandeira has been awarded, among others, the Cross of Merit by Germany and the Gran-Cross of Baron of Rio Branco, by Brazil. He died on November 10, 2017 after a long chronical illness at the age of 81 years in St. Leon-Rot/Germany, leaving not only his wife and his son, but also the whole scientific community. Nevertheless, he lives on in his more than 20 books analysing within a dialectical and historic approach current political developments worldwide.

Chapter 1
Introduction: The United States, the Middle East, Syria, and Ukraine—A Dialectical Approach on Recent History

From there come the much-knowing maidens,
three from the sea that lies under the tree:
one was named Urdh,
another Verdhandi
—they carved in wood—and Skuld the third;
they laid down the law, they chose lives
for the children of men, people's fates.
"Völuspá (The Prophecy of the Seeress)" ("*Davon kommen*
Frauen, vielwissende,/ Drei aus dem See dort unterm Wipfel./
Urdh heißt die eine, die andre Verdhandi:/ Sie schnitten
Stäbe; Skuld hieß die dritte./ Sie legten Lose, das Leben
bestimmten sie/ Den Geschlechtern der Menschen, das
Schicksal verkündend."
"*Völuspá* (The Prophecy of the Seeress)" is part of the *Edda*
Mayor, which gathers Scandinavian poems written in the
tenth and eleventh centuries. *"Der Seherin Gesicht." Die*
Edda—Götterdichtung Spruchweisheit Heldensängen der
Germanen. Munique: Dietrich Gelbe Reihe, 2004, p. 35.
"Valans Spådom." Eddan—De Nordiska Guda—Och
Hjältesångerna. Stockholm: Norstedrs Förlag, 1998, p. 8.
The maidens are *Die Nornen*, the goddesses of destiny (*die*
Schicksalgottheiten). In Germanic mythology (*West- und*
Nordgermanisch) they appear in three personifications. Urður
or Udhr or Wyrd is the *Norn* of what was, of everything that
happened and is happening, and shapes what is to become,
destiny. Verðandi or Verdhandi, becoming, is the *Norn* of
what is, representing the present moment of change; and
Skuld (Should) is the *Norn* of what should be, the future, the
necessity. These three *Nornen* don't represent, schematically,
the past, the present and the future, as they are sometimes
interpreted. They act as one.).

An ancestor of mine, the philosopher Antonio Ferrão Moniz de Aragão (1813–1887), who was a disciple of Auguste Comte (1798–1857) and one of the first to bring positivism to Brazil, wrote that "for an in-depth knowledge of history,

© Springer Nature Switzerland AG 2019
L. A. Moniz Bandeira, *The World Disorder*,
https://doi.org/10.1007/978-3-030-03204-3_1

we must not be satisfied with the chronological classification of facts," but "compare the sequence of events in different nations and the progress of civilization in every age."[1] According to his teachings, "historical facts analyzed and understood this way can be placed in a vast system in which they are all connected to each other through all manner of relations, enabling us to lift ourselves to an even more important study, which is the explanation of these facts through the investigation of their causes...."[2]

Capitalism—with its process of global accumulation and expansion—has cast a web over all industrialized, agricultural, precapitalist, and noncapitalist regions of the world, entangling them economically and politically in a global whole, in a system of communicating vessels. It made societies interdependent, despite and/or as a result of their varying degrees of progress and civilization. The world economy is therefore a higher reality, not a set, a sum, or a web of national economies. And political science needs to study the ontogeny of the state in the oppressive accumulation process of capitalist power, which not only negates itself through quantitative and qualitative mutations but also nullifies this negation in the course of history and the evolution of the world economy. This historical and dialectical approach is the only way to reach and understand the intimate nature of a social and political phenomenon (*Phänomen*), its essential and structural determination, and not merely its accidentality, the epiphenomena of circumstance (*Begleiterscheinungen*).

Coincidence does not exist. Causality, however, does. Facts occur for some cause that often is not known. They are linked in their evolution. And as in nature, some links intertwine but don't generate another movement, that would cut the chain of necessity and prevent the determination of the infinite chain of history. This lesson comes from Titus Lucretius Carus (*ca*. 99 BC–*ca*. 55 BC), in his work *De Rerum Natura*.[3] As Hegel eloquently puts it, understanding the flow of events and their unfolding in the future requires, therefore, knowledge of the past, as the real substance of the present, in which possibilities and contingencies are emerging to suppress (*aufheben*) and preserve (*aufheben/aufbewahren*) the inherent contradictions of the historic process.[4] In Germanic and Nordic mythology, time is indivisible. The past remains alive and unfolds in the present, which flows continuously as mighty reality. Fernand Braudel understood very well that "l'histoire est une dialectique de la durée; par elle, grâce à elle, elle est étude du social, et donc de passé, et donc aussi du présent, l'un et l'autre inséparable."[5]

Economic, social, and political phenomena result from quantitative and qualitative mutations, even when they appear spontaneous, emerging from multiple, complex, endless, linked, and intertwined causes. There is a reciprocal relationship of

---

[1] Antônio Ferrão Moniz de Aragão, 1871, p. 378 passim.

[2] *Ibidem*, p. 378.

[3] "*Denique si semper motu conectitur omnis/ et vetere exoritur < motus > novus ordine certo/nec declinando faciunt primordia motus/principium quoddam, quod fati foedera rumpat,/ex infinito ne causam causa sequatur* [...]." Vrs—251–255, in: Don Fowler, 2002, p. 10.

[4] George Wilhelm Friedrich Hegel, 1990, pp. 198–203, 241–244.

[5] Fernand Braudel, 1969, pp. 104–105.

action and reaction between events, which is why we have to study them in all their ontological dimensions, from new and different angles. For history evolves ad infinitum, not in a straight line, but in a spiral, sometimes curving, folding on itself, and jumping to alternate lines. As the capitalist economy globalized ever further, intertwining and grouping all regions and countries, entangling them in one asymmetric, irregular, complex, and yet interdependent whole, social and political events have almost always been directly or indirectly interconnected. And the osmosis is even more pronounced in international politics, according to domestic conditions and the different structures of institutions and states, which changed with the evolution of productive forces.

The *putsch* that brought down President Viktor Yanukovych in Kiev on February 22, 2014, with the open support of the American State Department, occurred while the conflict in Syria was raging, after President Barack Obama took on the mantle of universal dictator, saying that President Bashar al-Assad "must step out," "must go out." The same thing he had told President Muammar Gaddafi before Libya was bombed and destroyed in 2011. Washington's support to the coup in Ukraine and to the opposition in the armed struggle against Bashar al-Assad's regime was not meant to establish a democracy in any of these two countries. President Viktor Yanukovych was legally and legitimately elected, and his government was not a dictatorship. Despite being dictatorial, president Bashar al-Assad's regime was secular and constitutionally guaranteed religious freedoms and women's rights. But despite being distinct and far away from each other, these two events merged. Their background was the same.

After the debacle of the Soviet Union, the United States presented itself—with all the arrogance of its triumphalism of its god-given exceptionalism—as the one and only center of world power. And they didn't treat "Russia seriously as a great power," Professor Henry Kissinger remarked[6] in an interview to the magazine *The National Interest*, stressing that a *"new foreign-policy view" had emerged in the Republican party, which* "was more missionary; it emphasized that America had a mission to bring about democracy—if necessary, by the use of force," with a kind of "intolerance toward opposition."[7] This trend had characterized both the extreme right and the extreme left, "and they changed sides occasionally," he added.

Democracy imposed by force will never be a real democracy but a *fake democracy* to be wielded by financial capital and big corporations. The ingredients of totalitarianism, which can almost always be traced back to Wall Street, therefore resemble those nurturing Germany's *Nationalsozialismus* (Nazism) and expansionist drive under Adolf Hitler in the 1930s. And as Kissinger emphasized, since the defeat of Germany and Japan in 1945, the United States had fought in five wars,

---

[6]Jacob Heilbrunn, "The Interview: Henry Kissinger." The National Interest, September/October 2015. Available at <http://nationalinterest.org/print/feature/the-interview-henry-kissinger-13,615>.

[7]*Ibidem.*

"started with great enthusiasm," but the "hawks" "did not prevail at the end."[8] They lost all five. The problem—as Kissinger pointed out—stems from the United States' refusal to learn from experience. Policy is essentially being made "by an ahistorical people," since schools no longer teach history as a sequence of events but in terms of "themes without context" put in an "entirely new context."[9]

After remarking that when you read Muslim battalions fighting in Ukraine "all sense of proportion was lost," and when the journalist Jacob Heilbrunn observed "that's a disaster, obviously," professor Henry Kissinger replied: "To me, yes. It means that breaking Russia has become an objective."[10] Indeed, the purpose of conservatives and the "hawks" of the Democratic Party, including President Obama, who got himself elected in a dove's dress, was to actually break up Russia, starting with its Muslim periphery. This had been the old strategy of the geopolitical scholar Zbigniew Brzezinski, former adviser to President Jimmy Carter, who believed Islamic fundamentalism was an important ideological weapon not only to prevent communist influence from spreading in the Middle East, Africa, and the Indian Ocean but also to incite the Asian republics of the Soviet Union to revolt against the government in Moscow.[11] But President Obama could not even isolate Russia, a country of enormous geographic proportions and with huge reserves of natural resources, especially energy, a *pivotal country* in Eurasia.

The journalist Jacob Heilbrunn then pointed to "the return, at least in Washington, D.C., of the neo-conservatives and liberal 'hawks' determined to break the back of the Russian Government," to which Henry Kissinger, whom he interviewed in July 2015, replied: *"Until they face the consequences."*[12] The problem with the wars America had been waging since 1945, he argued, had been its inability to link strategy with what was possible in the internal scenario. *"The hawks did not prevail at the end"*—said Kissinger. And hence the fiascos were the consequence.

In 2014, President Putin knew perfectly well that Islamic units were involved in Ukraine and that special forces of the United States and other countries were training 400–1000 Chechens in the fields of Tunisia and Turkey, headed by the terrorists Omar al-Shishani, Saifullah al-Shishani, and Amir Muslim, Uzbeks, and other jihadists from the North Caucasus.[13] He declared he would fight the terrorists in Syria before he would have to fight them in Russia inside his own territory, once they

---

[8]*Ibidem.*

[9]*Ibidem.*

[10]*Ibidem.*

[11]Zbigniew Brzezinski, 1986, p. 226; Luiz Alberto Moniz Bandeira, 2014, pp. 396–402.

[12]Jacob Heilbrunn, "The Interview: Henry Kissinger." The National Interest, September/October 2015. Available at <http://nationalinterest.org/print/feature/the-interview-henry-kissinger-13,615>.

[13]Murad Batal al-Shishani, "Islamist North Caucasus Rebels Training a New Generation of Fighters in Syria." Terrorism Monitor, v. 12, February 3, 2014. Available at: <http://www.jamestown.org/programs/tm/single/?cHash=ae2a2cd5f15746b0534e5bb000c9ceff&tx_ttnews[tt_news]=41927#. VolBKVJ0f_A-Guido Steinberg>; Guido Steinberg, "A Chechen al-Qaeda? Caucasian Groups Further Internationalise the Syrian Struggle." Stiftung Wissenschaft und Politik: German Institute

returned. And from its very beginning, the war in Syria had been a hybrid proxy war, with on the one side Syria, Russia, and—with boots on the ground—Iran and on the other Qatar, Saudi Arabia, and Turkey, funding and arming the terrorists of the most diverse Sunni groups and nationalities, Da'ish (acronym for al-Dawla al-Islamiya fil Iraq wa al-Sham) or ISIS/ISIL (the English acronym for the Islamic State in Iraq) and al-Sham (Levant/Greater Syria),[14] a dissident group of al-Qa'ida, and with all the support (including logistics and intelligence) from the United States and its NATO vassals. Everything pointed to the fact that the neocons and liberal hawks, the *lobbies* of the war industry—represented by such senators as John McCain—and of financial capital, all nestled in Washington, pretended to expand the transnational war to the Islamic periphery of Russia.

Moscow had long realized the threat. In the reception of new ambassadors on November 26, 2015, President Putin said more than 100 thousand acts of terror were committed throughout the world in the 2000s and that its victims had been people of various nationalities and religions, with more than 32,000 victims in 67 countries only in 2014.[15] He then referred to the *"passive position"* of a number of governments, which were often in direct collusion with the terrorists, contributing to the rise of this *"terrible phenomenon"* known as the Islamic State. He added that such governments "not only cover up the terrorists, their illicit trafficking in oil, people, drugs, works of art and arms, but also benefit from it, making hundreds of millions, even billions of dollars."[16] He repeated the accusation he had made during the 70th session of the General Assembly of the United Nations, by warning that it was "equally irresponsible to manipulate extremist groups to achieve political goals, hoping to get rid or eliminate them later."[17]

And a few months later, the neocons and liberal hawks in Washington who had been so keen "to break the back of the Russian government" had to "face the consequences," as Professor Kissinger had foreseen.[18] The Russian military intervention in Syria subverted the oblique game being played by the always disingenuous President Obama. It changed the balance of power in Syria and throughout the

---

for International and Security Affairs (SWP). SWP Comments, June 30, 2014, pp. 1–7. Available at: <https://www.swp-berlin.org/fileadmin/contents/products/comments/2014C31_sbg.pdf>.

[14]Al-Sham, in Arabic, means the Levant/Greater Syria and was used during the Great Caliphate, in the seventh century, to define the entire region between the Mediterranean, the Euphrates, and Asia Minor, covering the Aegean Sea, the Black Sea, and Egypt.

[15]"Presentation of foreign ambassador's letters of credence: Vladimir Putin received letters of credence from 15 foreign ambassadors. By tradition, the ceremony marking the official start of the ambassador's mission in the Russian Federation took place in the Grand Kremlin Palace's Alexander Hall" President of Russia. The Kremlin, Moscow. November 26, 2015. Available at: <http://en.kremlin.ru/events/president/news/50786>.

[16]*Ibidem.*

[17]"Vladimir Putin in the plenary meeting of the 70th session of the UN General Assembly in New York." *New York, Presidential Executive Office* 2015. Available at: <http://en.kremlin.ru/events/president/news/50385>.

[18]*Ibidem.*

Middle East, with Russia reemerging as a superpower in the international scenario vis-à-vis the United States and the European Union and in close political and economic alliance with China. A report from the Office of Naval Intelligence (ONI) published by the US Naval Institute reflected the shock and alarm within the American military world with the more advanced and modern Russian military naval and air power, demonstrated with the supersonic 3 M-14 T Kalibr NK (Klub-N) VLS cruise missiles fired from corvettes and destroyers in the Caspian Sea and from submarines in the Mediterranean against targets in Syria, flying over 900 miles (1448 km), as well as with the devastating air strikes by Sukhoi Su-34 s and other jets.[19] According to some analysts, the 3 M-14 T Kalibr NI missiles exceeded their American counterparts in technological capabilities.[20] And Gustav Gressel of the European Council on Foreign Relations noted that President Putin had demonstrated the rapid transformation promoted in the Russian armed forces both with the reintegration of Crimea and the intervention in Syria, making it more professional and agile, ready to fight, react, attack, and deploy abroad.[21]

With the attacks carried out with Russian fighter jets and naval units against the fortifications and installations from Da'ish or the Islamic State, the forces of the Syrian Arab Army and Iran could intensify their land offensive and reconquer a great part of the country's territory. In just 4 days—from December 25 to 29, 2015—the Russian air force used 164 sorties to shatter around 556 terrorist fortifications in the provinces of Aleppo, Idlib, Latakia, Hama, Homs, Damascus, Deir ez-Zor, and Raqqa.[22] Three important plateaus in Kabbani and Sirmaniyah also fell under the control of Assad's forces.[23] And Russia made progress deploying the more powerful

---

[19]"Document Office of Naval Intelligence Report on Russian Navy: The following is the Office of Naval Intelligence (ONI) report, The Russian Navy: A Historic Transition. U.S. Naval Institute." *USNI News.htm*, December 18, 2015. Available at <http://news.usni.org/2015/12/18/document-office-of-naval-intelligence-report-on-russian-navy>.

[20]Steven Lee Myers & Eric Schmitt, "Russian Military Uses Syria as Proving Ground, and West Takes Notice." *The New York Times*, October 14, 2015. Available at: <http://www.nytimes.com/2015/10/15/world/middleeast/russian-military-uses-syria-as-proving-ground-and-west-takes-notice.html?_r=0>; Catrin Einhorn & Hannah Fairfield & Tim Wallace, "Russia Rearms for a New Era." *The New York Times*, Thursday, December 24, 2015. Available at: <http://www.nytimes.com/interactive/2015/12/24/world/asia/russiaarming.html?hp&action=click&pgtype=Homepage&clickSource=story-heading&module=photo-spot-region&region=top-news&WT.nav=top-news>.

[21]Gustav Gressel, "Russia's post-Cold War borders. Russia's Quiet Military Revolution, and What It Means For Europe." *European Council on Foreign Relations (ECFR)*, 143, pp. 1–17. Available at: <http://www.ecfr.eu/page/-/Russias_Quiet_Military_Revolution.pdf>; Catrin Einhorn &, Hannah Fairfield & Tim Wallace, "Russia Rearms for a New Era." *The New York Times*, Thursday, December 24, 2015. Available at: <http://www.nytimes.com/interactive/2015/12/24/world/asia/russiaarming.html?hp&action=click&pgtype=Homepage&clickSource=story-heading&module=photo-spot-region&region=top-news&WT.nav=top-news>.

[22]"International Military Review—Syria-Iraq battlespace, Dec. 29, 2015." *International Military Review*, December 29, 2015. Available at: <http://southfront.org/international-military-review-syria-iraq-battlespace-dec-29-2015/>.

[23]*Ibidem.*

S-400 s antiaircraft/antimissile defense system, installed in Khmeimim, encroaching ever further on the border between Syria and Turkey in order to prevent any other ambush from Ankara.

I am writing this introduction in the midst of political events that are still taking shape, transforming themselves as the clouds in the sky. The beheading of the Shiite cleric Sheik Nimr al-Nimr, along with 47 others accused of terrorism, on January 2, 2016, by the Wahhabi tyranny in Riyadh, was probably meant to escalate tensions in the Middle East, especially with Iran, to unforeseeable dimensions, at a time when Da'ish was losing ground in Syria and in Iraq, unable to crush the Houthis (Shiite sect) or occupy Sana'a, the capital, and the west of Yemen. The UN High Commissioner for Human Rights, Zeid Ra'ad Al Hussein, declared that the execution in a single day of 47 prisoners, almost a third of the total number of death sentences (157) in 2015 in Saudi Arabia, and especially of Sheikh Nimr Al-Nimr or any other individual who hadn't committed any crime, should be seen "*as most serious*" under the international law of human rights.[24]

Saudi Arabia is the most corrupt and despotic country in the Middle East, where the freedoms of expression, assembly, and association have been most drastically repressed, where any opinion contrary to Wahhabism is persecuted and where critics and peaceful dissidents are incarcerated and executed.[25] And this is the country that has allied itself with the United States, enjoying more than four decades of support for its pernicious policy to destroy all secular, although sometimes dictatorial, regimes in the region. Between October 2010 and October 2014, Washington signed more than US$90 billion worth in contracts with the tyranny in Riyadh for the supply of aircraft and the most diverse weapon systems, according to the Congressional Research Service.[26] In *Timon of Athens,* William Shakespeare already wrote: "*Gold? yellow, glittering, precious gold? [...] Thus much of this will make black*

[24]"Zeid deplores mass execution of 47 people in Saudi Arabia." *United Nations of the Human Rights- Office of the High Commissioner for Human Rights.* Geneva, January 3, 2016. Available at: <http://www.ohchr.org/EN/NewsEvents/Pages/Media.aspx?IsMediaPage=true&LangID=E>.

[25]"Arábia Saudita—Reino da Arábia Saudita—Chefe de Estado e de governo: Rei Abdullah bin Abdul Aziz Al Saud. 62." *O Estado dos Direitos Humanos no Mundo: Anistia Internacional.* Informe 2014/15, pp. 63–64. Available at: <https://anistia.org.br/wp-content/uploads/2015/02/Informe-2014-2015-O-Estado-dos-Direitos-Humanos-no-Mundo.pdf>.

[26]Christopher M. Blanchard (Specialist in Middle Eastern Affairs), "Saudi Arabia: Background and U.S. Relations." *Congressional Research Service—Informing legislative debate since 2014. September 8, 2015. 7-5700* www.crs.gov -RL33533. Available at: <http://fas.org/sgp/crs/mideast/RL33533.pdf>. Accessed on January 8, 2014; Dan Lamothe, "How U.S. weapons will play a huge role in Saudi Arabia's war in Yemen." *The Washington Post,* March 26, 2015. Available at: <https://www.washingtonpost.com/news/checkpoint/wp/2015/03/26/how-u-s-weapons-will-play-a-large-role-in-saudi-arabias-war-in-yemen/>; Natasha Mozgovaya, "U.S. Finalizes $30 Billion Weapons Deal With Saudi Arabia: White House says agreement—under which 84 F-15 fighter jets will be sold to the kingdom, will help U.S. economy and strengthen regional security." *Há'aretz,* December 29, 2011. Available at: <http://www.haaretz.com/middle-east-news/u-s-finalizes-30-billion-weapons-deal-with-saudi-arabia-1.404461>.

white, foul fair, wrong right, base noble, old young, coward valiant."[27] And so for Washington, the black gold—oil for arms—transformed the most despotic regime in the Middle East in its fairest and most exuberant democracy, where human rights were strictly followed. President Obama would never tell the king he "must step out," "must go", as he had done with Colonel Gaddafi and Bashar al-Assad. On the contrary, he armed him with the most modern war material produced in the United States. And Britain, France, and Germany did the same. But according to the assessment of the Bundesnachrichtendienst (BND), the German intelligence service, Saudi Arabia represented a risk of becoming the greatest destabilizing force in the Middle East.

The beheading of Sheikh Nimr Al-Nimr occurred at a time when Iran was being integrated into the fuel markets with the lifting of sanctions by the United States and when Saudi Arabia, whose budget depended for 75% on oil revenues, was mired in a severe economic and financial crisis, with an alarming deficit of 14.5% of its GDP expected for 2016 due to the precipitous drop in the price of oil, forcing King Salmān ibn 'Abd al-'Azīz Al Sa'ūd to begin cutting all subsidies on electricity, water, and the construction of roads, buildings, and other infrastructure works.

There would be consequences, especially after angry mobs burned down the Saudi embassy in Iran, probably without the government trying to intervene, which served as justification for the Wahhabi tyranny in Riyadh to cut relations with the Shiite government in Tehran and align itself with the other Sunni countries. The execution of Sheikh Nimr Al-Nimr, therefore, was possibly also meant to modify the economic and geopolitical confrontation, accentuating the secular sectarian nature— sunnis *vs.* shiites—to drive a wedge between Iran and other Muslim countries and hinder its participation in peace talks about Syria and Yemen. The provocation by the Saudi monarchy had begun when its fighter jets pounded the civilian population of Yemen and reached the Iranian embassy in Sana'a.[28]

But events are still unfolding, and we must rely on written and oral sources, on a corporate media that is not always reliable and prone to serve as a complement in modern warfare, using strategic communication offensives, serving as outlets for *psy-ops* (*psychological operations*), misinformation, and counter information, deliberately or semi-deliberately spreading subliminal lies or cover-ups emanating from intelligence services or other government bodies of obscure and ambiguous origins (activists, NGOs). At the heart of this phenomenon lie the distortion, manufacture, and falsification of facts—corrupting words like democracy—and the omission of news in order to manipulate public opinion and produce strategic effects.[29] News agencies today, therefore, almost always operate and reflect the psychology of the corporate, economic, and political interests of advertisers and governments, the

---

[27]William Shakespeare, 1975, p. 761.

[28]"Iran accuses Saudis of hitting Yemen embassy." *BBC*: *Middle East*, January 7, 2016. Available at: <http://www.bbc.com/news/world-middle-east-35251917>.

[29]Nick Davies, 2008, pp. 214, 230–231, 241–243; Udo Ulfkotte, 2014, pp. 43–46, 146–150.

dominant position of the major industrial powers, influencing the press of other countries who buy their services.

The Meikite archbishop of Aleppo, Jean-Clément Jeanbart, during the Night of Witnesses organized each year by Aid to the Church in Need, said that "the European media have not ceased to suppress the daily news of those who are suffering in Syria and they have even justified what is happening in our country by using information without taking the trouble to verify it." In addition, he told reporters that the West continued its silence about the atrocities committed by the armed opposition, while denigrating the Syrian government and its president. And he added: "Bashar al-Assad has many defects, but you have to realize he has many good points as well." "Schools are free, hospitals too, mosques and churches pay no taxes, what government in the region does things like that? Be honest! Remember too that if we prefer today to support the government, it's because we fear the installation of a Sunni theocracy that would deprive us of the right to live on our own lands."[30] And according to the Apostolic Vicar of Aleppo, the Franciscan Georges Abou Khazen, appointed by Pope Francis, the people of the city saw the military operation by Russia as their salvation, "a real effort to fight terrorism and promote peace."[31]

[30]Charlotte D'ornellas (Journaliste indépendante), "La sainte colère de l'archevêque d'Aleppo. Les médias européens n'ont cessé d'étouffer le quotidien de ceux qui souffrent en Syrie." *Boulevard Voltaire*, Available at: <http://www.bvoltaire.fr/charlottedornellas/sainte-colere-de-larcheveque-dalep,235328>; *Idem*. "Aleppo, la collera del vescovo" *La Stampa*, February 3, 2016. Available at: <http://www.lastampa.it/2016/02/03/blogs/san-pietro-e-dintorni/aleppo-la-collera-del-vescovo-kXa49OUOjrxEj6lr2CjsUI/pagina.html?zanpid=2132932023625905153/>; *Idem*. "Aleppo, na ira de um Bispo" Fratres in Unum.Com—Ecce quam bonum et quam incundum habitare fratres in unum. February 11, 2016. By Marco Tosatti—*La Stampa* | Translation: Gercione Lima. Available at: <http://fratresinunum.com/>.

[31]Ruth Gledhill, "Russian action in Syria offers hope, claims Catholic bishop." *Christian Today*, February 19, 2016. Available at: <http://www.christiantoday.com/article/russian.action.in.syria.offers.hope.claims.catholic.bishop/80213.htm>; "'Russian operation in Syria is our salvation'—top Syrian Catholic bishop to RT." *RT*, February 18, 2016. Available at: <https://www.rt.com/news/332922-aleppo-bishop-russia-support/>.

Chapter 2
The US Republic and Its Transformation into an Oligarchic Tyranny

2.1 Nazi-Fascism and the Phenomenon of *Mutazione dello Stato*

As a phenomenon, Nazi-Fascism is not peculiar to Italy and Germany. Under different forms, it threatened and spread to other European countries, such as Portugal and Spain, between the 1920s and the outbreak of Second World War (1939–1945).[1] What happened in these countries was similar to what Niccolò Machiavelli (1469–1527) called *mutazione dello stato (mutatio rerum, commutatio rei publicae)*, when the *res publica*, a state, transforms itself into a tyranny in the name of freedom, with or without violence.[2] The political phenomenon of the twentieth century called Nazi-Fascism could and can occur in modern states when and where the oligarchy and financial capital are no longer capable of maintaining balance in society through the normal means of repression, disguised in the classical forms of democratic legality. Depending on the specific conditions of time and place, Nazi-Fascism will assume different characteristics and colors, but its essence will remain: a peculiar type of regime that places itself above society, sustained by a system of acts of force, with the atrophy of civil liberties and the institutionalization of the counterrevolution through a perpetual domestic and international war. The goal is to establish and/or maintain a world order subordinate to its national principles and interests, and favorable to its security and national prosperity.

---

[1] Luiz Alberto Moniz Bandeira, 1969, p. 7.

[2] "[...] *Mutazione che si fanno dalla vita libera alla tirannica, e per contrario, alguna se ne faccia con sangue, alguna senza* [...]." Niccoló Machiavelli, 2013, pp. 491–492; Hannah Arendt, 1965, pp. 35–36.

© Springer Nature Switzerland AG 2019
L. A. Moniz Bandeira, *The World Disorder*,
https://doi.org/10.1007/978-3-030-03204-3_2

2.2   The Wall Street Plot Against Franklin D. Roosevelt's Administration in 1933

During the Great Depression, following the collapse of the Wall Street stock market on Black Friday in October 1929, certain financial and industrial groups conspired to fund and arm Army veterans, under the mantle of the American Legion. Their mission was to march on the White House, arrest Franklin D. Roosevelt (1933–1945), and put an end to his New Deal policies.[3] This conspiracy involved 24 of America's richest and most powerful families, such as the Morgans, Robert Sterling Clark, the DuPonts, the Rockefellers, the Mellons, J. Howard Pew and Joseph Newton Pew of the company Sun Oil, Remington, Anaconda, Bethlehem, Goodyear, Bird's Eye, Maxwell House, Heinz Schol, and Prescott Bush. The goal was to install a fascist dictatorship inspired by Italy and Hitler's incipient project in Germany.[4]

2.3   The Accusation of General Smedley D. Butler and the McCormack-Dickstein Committee

The Wall Street Plot was aborted, however. Major General (r) Smedley Darlington Butler (1881–1940), who the big businessmen had tried to co-opt, denounced the conspiracy to the reporter Paul French of the *Philadelphia Record* and the *New York Evening Post*. And on March 20, 1934, the House of Representatives adopted Resolution 198, brought to the floor by the Democratic representatives John W. McCormack (Massachusetts) and Samuel Dickstein (New York), creating the House Un-American Activities Committee (HUAC).

During his testimony before the McCormack-Dickstein Committee, Major General Smedley D. Butler, twice awarded the Medal of Honor for separate acts of exceptional heroism, said that the fascist coup would rely on a private army of 500,000 veterans and other people and that it had been outlined by the businessmen Gerard C. MacGuire (1897–1935), attorney of the brokerage Grayson M-P. Murphy

---

[3]The *New Deal* President Roosevelt promoted in order to recover the United States from the Great Depression, caused by the *crash* of 1929, consisted of economic and social reforms aimed at reducing and ending unemployment and poverty. Some of its main measures were the Social Security Act, the US Housing Authority, the Farm Security Administration, and the Fair Labor Standards Act, which set maximum working hours and minimum wages for most categories of workers.

[4]"McCormack-Dickstein Committee". US House of Representatives, Special Committee on Un-American Activities, Investigation of Nazi Propaganda Activities and Investigation of Certain Other Propaganda Activities United States Congress. Available at: <http://www.archives.gov/legislative/guide/house/chapter-22-select-propaganda.html>; Barbara Lamonica, "The Attempted Coup against FDR". *PROBE,* March/April 1999 issue (Vol. 6 n° 3). Available at: <http://www.ctka.net/pr399-fdr.html>; Arthur M. Schlesinger Jr., 2003, pp. 83–86.

& Co., and William Doyle, former commander of the American Legion, one of the most powerful fascist organizations in the United States.[5] They had offered him, at first, US$100,000 to command the uprising against President Roosevelt.[6] He refused.

Lieutenant Colonel James E. Van Zandt, commander of the organization Veterans of Foreign Wars (VFW), confirmed he had refused to participate in the plot, as did Captain Samuel Glazier of the CCC Camp in Elkridge, Maryland. The latter told the McCormack-Dickstein Committee, under oath, that Jackson Martindell, a financier connected with the investment banks, had invited him to train 500,000 civilian soldiers.[7]

The documents of the McCormack-Dickstein Committee inquiry have been declassified,[8] but with several sections extensively redacted, including the testimony from General (r) Smedley D. Butler, as it implicated in the plot several directors of financial corporations and executives of important industrial groups, such as the Guaranty Trust, Grayson Murphy, JPMorgan, Irénée du Pont, from the DuPont Company, and Lammot du Pont, owner of the arms manufacturer Remington Arms Co., who was investing heavily in fascist Italy and had created the Black Legion, a sort of Klux Klux Klan, and the American Liberty League, organized in 1934, in opposition to President Franklin D. Roosevelt's administration and the New Deal policies.[9]

None of them were prosecuted. There was a cover up to safeguard the image of the United States as a democracy, its myth of "exceptionality," the country where no

---

[5]George Seldes, *Facts and Fascism*. New York: In Fact Inc., 5th Edition, 1943, pp. 105–114; Denton, Sally. *The Plots against the President—FDR, a Nation in Crisis, and the Rise of the American Right*. New York: Bloomsbury Press, 2012, pp. 192–197.

[6]Barbara Lamonica, "The Attempted Coup against FDR". *PROBE*, March/April 1999 issue (Vol. 6, no. 3). Available at: <http://www.ctka.net/pr399-fdr.html>; Sally Denton, 2012, p. 54.

[7]Katie L. Delacenserie, & (professor) James W. Oberly, & Eau Claire Wisconsin, "Wall Street's Search for a Man on a White Horse: The Plot to Overthrow Franklin Delano Roosevelt". For Presentation to History 489. University of Wisconsin- Eau Claire. Spring 2008, p. 29; "The Business Plot (Takeover of the White House) 1933". January 10, 2009. Available at: <http://www.abovetopsecret.com/forum/thread426623/pg1>.

[8]"Investigation of un-American propaganda activities in the United States. Hearings before a Special Committee on Un-American Activities, House of Representatives, Seventy-fifth Congress, third session-Seventy-eighth Congress, second session, on H. Res. 282, to investigate (1) the extent, character, and objects of un-American propaganda activities in the United States; (2) the diffusion within the United States of subversive and un-American propaganda that is instigated from foreign countries or of a domestic origin and attacks the principle of the form of government as guaranteed by our Constitution; and (3) all other questions in relation thereto that would aid Congress in any necessary remedial legislation". *United States Congress House. Special Committee on Un-American Activities (1938–1944).* Volume: Appendix pt. 7. Washington, U.S. Govt. Printing Office. National Archive. Available at: <https://archive.org/stream/investigationofu07unit/investigationofu07unit_djvu.txt>.

[9]Jules Archer, 2007, pp. 20–34.

coup had ever taken place.[10] The McCormack-Dickstein Committee excluded from its report many of the more embarrassing names implicated by Gerald MacGuire and confirmed by General Smedley D. Butler. As later revealed, some of these names included Alfred E. Smith (1873–1944), the Democratic presidential candidate in 1928; General Hugh S. Johnson (1882–1942), head of the National Recovery Administration; and General Douglas MacArthur (1880–1964), Chief of Staff of the Army and the likely commander of the White House assault,[11] in addition to several other military officers who were aware of the plot.[12] President Roosevelt also didn't order the arrest of any businessman, such as the previously cited Irénée du Pont, Lammot du Pont II, or William Knudsen, CEO of General Motors. He feared provoking a new crash in Wall Street and worsening the depression in which the United States had been mired since 1929.[13]

The corporate press in the United States also paid little attention to the episode. The journalist George Seldes pointed out that "of all the hypocrisies of American journalism the greatest is the claim of a free press."[14] Instead, it was a profit-making scheme that attacked workers on behalf of free enterprise. In the midst of the depression caused by the crash of 1893, the American historian Henry B. Adams already noted that

> The press is the hired agent of a monied system, and set up for no other purpose than to tell lies where its interests are involved. One can trust nobody and nothing. As far as my observation goes, society is today more rotten than at any time within my personal knowledge. The whole thing is one vast structure of debt and fraud.[15]

The documents of the McCormack-Dickstein Committee, deposited in the National Archive of the United States, remained secret and were only completely declassified in 2001, when two old German Jews, Kurt Julius Goldstein (1914–2007), then 87 years old, and Peter Gingold (1916–2006), survivors of the Holocaust, filed a lawsuit against the Bush family in the United States. They demanded US$40 billion for the slave labor they had to perform in the Auschwitz

---

[10]Although the United States have not experienced actual military coups because of its cultural and political traditions and its highly developed capitalism, four of its presidents have been assassinated as a result of plots to change the government: Abraham Lincoln (1865), James Garfield (1881), William McKinley (1901), and John F. Kennedy (1963). Another five suffered attempts of their lives but escaped. Andrew Jackson (1835), Franklin D. Roosevelt as president elect (1933), Harry S. Truman (1950), Gerald Ford (1975), and Ronald Reagan (1981).

[11]Sally Denton, 2012, pp. 1, 31–32, 191.

[12]Clayton Cramer, "An American Coup d'État?" *History Today*, vol. 45, issue: 11, 1995. Available at: <http://www.historytoday.com/clayton-cramer/american-coup-detat>; "An attempted American coup d'État: 1934". *What Really Happened—The History the Government hopes you don't learn*. Available at: <http://whatreallyhappened.com/WRHARTICLES/coup.htmlDouglasa>.

[13]Charles Higham, 1983, pp. 162–165.

[14]George Seldes, 1943, pp. 244–245.

[15]*Letters of Henry Adams (1892–1918)*—Edited by Worthington Chauncey Ford—Boston/Nova York: Houghton Mifflin Company, 1938, vol. II, p. 99. Available at: <http://archive.org/stream/lettersofhenryad008807mbp/lettersofhenryad008807mbp_djvu.txt>.

concentration camp for the companies of the Thyssen group.[16] Judge Rosemary Mayers Collyer dismissed the case, with the specious claim that it could not continue under the principle of "state sovereignty," that is, because George W. Bush, grandson of Prescott Bush, Fritz Thyssen's partner, was president of the United States and therefore enjoyed immunity. Later, she would receive her reward. President George W. Bush appointed her to the District Court of Columbia and the United States Foreign Intelligence Surveillance Court.

2.4 Big Business: The Prescott Bush Family and the Transfer of Resources to Hitler

It was no news that the Bush family had been involved in money laundering and transfers to Nazis in Germany. On July 31, 1941, the *New York Herald-Tribune*[17] reported that the Union Banking Corporation (UBC), of which Prescott Bush was a director in the United States, had sent US$3 million in 1933 to the *Nationalsozialistische Deutsche Arbeiterpartei* (NSDAP) led by Adolf Hitler.[18] Sidney Warburg, in *Hitler's Secret Backers*, and Antony C. Sutton, in *Wall Street and the Rise of Hitler*, estimated that until 1933, UBC had transferred the total sum of US$32,000,000 to "Nazi bigwigs" in Germany.[19] And after the documents in the National Archive had been declassified, the British newspaper *The Guardian* confirmed Prescott Bush's financial involvement with the architects of Nazism, in his capacity as director and shareholder of UBC, which represented Fritz Thyssen's interests in New York.[20]

In fact, Prescott Bush (1895–1972), father to President Herbert Walker Bush (1989–1993) and grandfather to President George W. Bush, had been director of the Union Banking Corp. (UBC), a subsidiary of the *Bank voor Handel en Scheepvaart NV*, linked to the United Steel Works conglomerate (*Vereinigte Stahlwerke* [United

---

[16]Ben Aris (Berlin) & Duncan Campbell, (Washington), "How Bush's grandfather helped Hitler's rise to power". *The Guardian*, September 25, 2004.

[17]Facsimile available at: <http://www.fleshingoutskullandbones.com/P.Bush-Union_Banking/NYTH.html#>.

[18]Michael Kranish, "Prescott Bush & Nazis", *Boston Globe*, July 4, 2001. The Mail Archive, available at: <https://www.mail-archive.com/ctrl%40listserv.aol.com/msg71122.htm>; *Idem*. "Powerful alliance aids 'Bushes' rise". (Part One), *Boston Globe*, April 22, 2001; *Idem*. "Triumph, troubles shape generations". (Part Two), *Boston Globe*, April 23, 2001; *Bushology Interactive*: *2000–2004—The Bush dynasty*. Available at: <http://www.moldea.com/bushology3.html>.

[19]Sidney Warburg, 1995, pp. 14–16 and 44–47; Antony C. Sutton, 2011, pp. 25–30, 132.

[20]Ben Aris, (Berlin) & Duncan Campbell (Washington), "How Bush's grandfather helped Hitler's rise to power." *The Guardian*, September 25, 2004; "Documents: Bush's Grandfather Directed Bank Tied to Man Who Funded Hitler", October 17, 2003. Associated Press. Available at: <http://www.foxnews.com/story/2003/10/17/documents-bush-grandfather-directed-bank-tied-to-man-who-funded-hitler/>.

Steel Works Corporation or German Steel Trust]). And both the bank and the steel industry were part of the conglomerate owned by Fritz Thyssen (1873–1951) and his brother, Heinrich Thyssen-Bornemisza (1875–1947), according to the report of the Office of Alien Property Custodian, dated October 5, 1942.[21] Prescott Bush also owned a share in the Consolidated Silesian Steel Company (CSSC), which exploited the mineral reserves of Silesia on the German-Polish border and used slave labor in concentration camps, including Auschwitz. The publicly available documents, however, don't make clear whether Prescott Bush and UBC still had ties with the CSSC in 1942, when Thyssen's archives in the United States were seized after the declaration of war between the two countries on December 11, 1941.[22]

According to Webster Griffin Tarpley and Anton Chaitkin, authors of the biography of former President George H. W. Bush, his father, Prescott Bush, as director of the family businesses, played a central role in Hitler's financing and armament.[23] He received US$1.5 million for his share in UBC.[24] This capital allowed his son, George H. W. Bush, to set up the firms Bush-Overbey Oil Development Co. and Zapata Petroleum, later called Harbinger Group Inc., bringing together several companies to explore oil in the Gulf of Mexico and Cuba. According to an internal CIA memorandum of November 29, 1975, George H. W. Bush founded Zapata Petroleum with the collaboration of Thomas J. Devine, who stepped down from his senior CIA position to engage in private business. As wildcatter he possessed vast knowledge of the location of large oil reserves in various regions.[25]

The sympathy for Nazi-Fascism didn't fade after the failed plot against President Franklin D. Roosevelt's administration. Communism was feared in Wall Street, especially since the early 1930s. Fascism, however, was admired as avant-garde.[26] For a long time, several Catholic, evangelical, and even Jewish bankers did business with the Nazi regime, granting it about US$7 billion in credit in that decade.[27] Jewish bankers rationalized this by saying antisemitism seemed fine for them under the Nazi regime because it targeted the poor, refugees, and workers.[28] And in 1936, 148 of the 919 board members of the stock exchange were Jewish (according to the 1936 inventory published by *Fortune* magazine).[29] With reason, Harvard Professor

---

[21]"Documents: Bush's Grandfather Directed Bank Tied to Man Who Funded Hitler." October 17, 2003. Quoted.

[22]Available at: <http://www.theguardian.com/world/2004/sep/25/usa.secondworldwar/print>.

[23]Webster Griffin Tarpley & Anton Chaitkin, 1982, pp. 28–34; Ben Aris, (Berlin) & Duncan Campbell (Washington), "How Bush's grandfather helped Hitler's rise to power." *The Guardian*, September 25, 2004.

[24]"Looking behind the Bushes—Great moments in a great American family." *The Progressive Review. An Online Journal of Alternative News & Information.* Available at: <http://prorev.com/bush2.htm>.

[25]Russ Baker & Jonathan Z. Larsen, "CIA Helped Bush Senior in Oil Venture". *Real News Project*, January 8, 2007. Available at: <http://www.ctka.net/zapata.html>.

[26]Sally Denton, 2012, p. 54.

[27]George Seldes, 1943, pp. 154–155.

[28]*Ibidem*, p. 154.

[29]*Ibidem*, p. 155.

Gaetano Salvermini (1873–1957) told reporter Joseph Philip that he believed "almost 100% of American Big Business" sympathized with the philosophy driving Hitler and Mussolini because of its method to coerce labor.[30]

The bankers Winthrop Aldrich, CEO of Chase National Bank, and Henry Mann, of the National City Bank, were received by Hitler in Germany in August and September 1933. And despite Hitler's ideas and antisemitism, they expressed their willingness to "work with him" to the American ambassador in Berlin (1933–1938), William E. Dodd (1869–1940).[31] According to the historian Arthur M. Schlesinger Jr., former adviser to president John F. Kennedy (1961–1963), fascism in the United States was not merely a disease of the lower middle class.[32] The dream cherished by the big businessmen from Wall Street still remained murky and shrouded in confusion.[33] In 1934, William Randolph Hearst (1863–1951),[34] the media tycoon of the *San Francisco Examiner*, *The New York Journal*, and many other newspapers (approximately 28), magazines, and radio stations, visited Berlin, was received by Hitler, and, upon returning to the United States, wrote that the Führer was "certainly an extraordinary man." He then set out to advertise the Nazi regime, writing of its "great policy, the great achievement" of saving Germany from communism.[35]

On November 28, 1935, the American Ambassador in Berlin, William E. Dodd, wrote in his diary that the businessman Thomas J. Watson (1874–1956), president and CEO of International Business Machines (IBM), who enjoyed a wage of US $1000 per day, visited him and told him that "if big business insists on defeating democracy in the United States there will be a revolution which may lose business men all they have."[36] IBM, however, which in Germany was known as Deutsche Hollerith Maschinen Gesellschaft, or Dehomag, also cooperated with Hitler's regime. In addition to other equipment, it used its subsidiaries to supply the machines that enabled the slaughter of millions of Jews in Treblinka and several other concentration camps.[37] And Thomas J. Watson received the *Großkreuz des Deutschen Adlerordens* [Grand Cross of the Order of the German Eagle], although he returned it in 1940.[38]

---

[30] *Ibidem*, p. 46.

[31] William E Dodd Jr. & Martha Dodd (Editors), 1943, pp. 35 and 45.

[32] Arthur M. Schlesinger Jr., 1960, p. 82.

[33] Antony C. Sutton, 2002, pp. 167–172.

[34] William Randolph Hearst was played by Orson Welles in the film *Citizen Kane*, produced in 1941. This film, directed by Welles, is considered one of the masterpieces of cinema.

[35] *Ibidem*, pp. 84–86.

[36] William E. Dodd, Jr. & Martha Dodd (Editors), 1943, p. 288.

[37] Edwin Black, "How IBM Helped Automate the Nazi Death Machine in Poland" Week of March 27-April 2, 2002 [Posted on March 26, 2002]. Available at: <http://emperors-clothes.com/analysis/ibm.htm>; Edwin Black is the author of the book *IBM and the Holocaust: The Strategic Alliance between Nazi Germany and America's Most Powerful Corporation*.

[38] Gesche Sager, "Henry Ford und die Nazis—Der Diktator von Detroit." *Spiegel Online*, July 29, 2008. Available at: <http://www.spiegel.de/einestages/henry-ford-und-die-nazis-a-947358.html>.

On December 30, 1935, Major Truman Smith (1913–2007), military attaché of the United States in Berlin (1935–1939), informed Ambassador William E. Dodd that Germany was "one military camp."[39] At the end of 1937, Germany's air force, the Luftwaffe, had 175–225 squadrons. At the same time, Hitler maintained an immense army, was building a huge fleet of submarines, continued his rocket development program, and installed numerous textile and synthetic gasoline plants.[40] In 1935, Douglas Miller, the acting commercial attaché, predicted that "in 2 years Germany will be manufacturing oil and gas enough out of soft coal for a long war, the Standard Oil Company of New York furnishing millions of dollars to help."[41] Indeed, in collaboration with I.G. Farben, the Rockefellers' Standard Oil had been producing oil, gasoline and synthetic rubber for Nazi Germany from bituminous coal through the hydrogenation process since 1933, which allowed Adolf Hitler to ignite the Second World War with the invasion of Poland in 1939.[42] Standard Oil's headquarters in Switzerland worked independently, since it was in a neutral country, and in 1942 the company requested authorization to continue selling oil to Germany, this time from the fields it operated in Romania.[43] That same year, its subsidiary, the West India Oil Company, which had been founded to refine oil in Cuba and the Caribbean, shipped oil to Germany through the company Cia Argentina Comercial de Pesquería, based in Buenos Aires.

On August 29, 1936, Ambassador William E. Dodd remarked that Hitler was the "absolute master" of 60 million people in Germany, that Benito Mussolini was the "master" of 42 million in Italy leading other countries down the path of dictatorship, and that in the United States, the "capitalists are pressing in the same Fascist direction, supported by capitalists in England."[44]

In a letter to President Roosevelt, Ambassador Dodd wrote:

At the present moment more than a hundred American corporations have subsidiaries here or cooperative understandings. The DuPonts have three allies in Germany that are aiding in the armament business. Their chief ally is the I. G. Farben Company, a part of the Government which gives 200,000 marks a year to one propaganda organization operating on American opinion. Standard Oil Company (New Jersey sub-company) sent US$2,000,000 here in December 1933 and has made US$500,000 a year helping Germans make Ersatz gas for war purposes; but Standard Oil cannot take any of its earnings out of the country except in goods. They do little of this, report their earnings at home, but do not explain the facts. The International Harvester Company president told me their business here, in Germany, rose 33% a year (arms manufacture, I believe), but they could take nothing out. Even our airplanes people have secret arrangement with Krupps. General Motor Company and Ford

---

[39]William E. Dodd Jr. & Martha Dodd (Editors), 1943, pp. 299–300.

[40]Truman Smith, 1984, pp. 117, 143.

[41]William E. Dodd Jr. & Martha Dodd (Editors), pp. 299–300.

[42]Antony C. Sutton, 2002, pp. 67–76; Joseph Borkin, 1978, pp.76–94.

[43]Charles Higham, 1983, pp. 54–55; George Seldes, 1943, pp. 252–253.

[44]William E. Dodd Jr. & Martha Dodd (Editors), 1943, pp. 352–353.

do enormous businesses [sic] here through their subsidiaries and take no profits out. I mention these facts because they complicate things and add to war dangers.[45]

Later, he told the press:

A clique of U.S. industrialists is hell-bent to bring a fascist state to supplant our democratic government and is working closely with the fascist regime in Germany and Italy. I have had plenty of opportunity in my post in Berlin to witness how close some of our American ruling families are to the Nazi regime. Certain American industrialists had a great deal to do with bringing fascist regimes into being in both Germany and Italy. They extended aid to help Fascism occupy the seat of power, and they are helping to keep it there.[46]

Large corporations in the United States not only opposed President Roosevelt's administration, they also cooperated, decisively, with the rise and consolidation of Adolf Hitler's tyranny, as they had done before with Benito Mussolini. Several banking houses in Wall Street, including the Bank of America (Forbes), Dillon, Read & Co., Harris Bank, Morgan Bank, Guaranty Trust, and Chase Manhattan Bank, invested in Germany and profited from the Nazi regime, as did the corporations Standard Oil (New Jersey), Dupont, Dow Chemical, General Motors (GM), General Electric (A.E.G.), Vacuum Oil Company, and Ford Motors Company. Henry Ford (1863–1947), author of the book *The International Jew: The World's Problem* (1920), had been funding the Nazi party NSDAP since the 1920s, and he also sent his personal money—about 10,000 or 20,000 mark (*Reichmarks*)—to Adolf Hitler, which he kept doing every year through Swiss or Swedish banks as a birthday present until April 20, 1944.[47] The two found themselves in their hatred of the Jews. And when he celebrated his 75th birthday on July 30, 1938, Henry Ford was honored in Cleveland with the *Großkreuz des Deutschen Adlerordens* by the German Ambassador in the United States, Karl Kapp, an honor also bestowed to Benito Mussolini and Francisco Franco, dictator of Spain.

The investments of American corporations in Germany during the Nazi regime had reached approximately US$475 million by the time of the attack on Pearl Harbor on December 7, 1941.[48] Six days later, President Roosevelt reactivated the Trading With the Enemy Act (TWEA) of October 6, 1917, and in 1942, Washington

---

[45]"William E. Dodd to Franklin D. Roosevelt." Franklin D. Roosevelt Presidential Library and Museum—Great Britain/German Diplomatic Files—Box 32—Folder Titles List Dodd->FDR 10/19/36. Germany: William E. Dodd: 1936–38 (i300) Index. Available at: <http://docs.fdrlibrary.marist.edu/psf/box32/a300l02.html>.

[46]Dodd interview: Federated Press, January 7, 1938. *Apud* George Seldes, 1943, pp. 122–123; Sheldon Drobny, "Bob Novak Thinks Prescott Bush Was A Liberal." *Huffington Post*, July 27, 2007. Available at: <http://www.huffingtonpost.com/sheldon-drobny/bob-novak-thinks-prescott_b_58119.html>.

[47]George Seldes, 1943, pp. 135–138; Gesche Sager, "Henry Ford und die Nazis—Der Diktator von Detroit". *Spiegel Online*, July 29, 2008. Available at: <http://www.spiegel.de/einestages/henry-ford-und-die-nazis-a-947358.html>.

[48]Jacques R. Pauwels, "Profits über Alles! American Corporations and Hitler". *Global Research*, May 15, 2014—*Global Research*, June 8, 2004. *Centre for Research on Globalization*. Available at: <http://www.globalresearch.ca/profits-ber-alles-american-corporations-and-hitler/4607>.

determined the closure and seizure of the assets from the Union Banking Corp., a subsidiary of the Bank voor Handel en Scheepvaart NV, linked to the United Steel Works conglomerate (Vereinigte Stahlwerke [United Steel Works Corporation]). But even during the Second World War (1939–1945), many American corporations, including Mack Truck, Phillips Petroleum, Standard Oil of California, and Firestone Tires, continued to do business clandestinely with the Nazi regime through sub-sidiaries in Switzerland and Sweden. Others, such as Ford, with a share of 52% in Ford-Werke in Cologne, and General Motors, owner of the truck, land mine, torpedo detonator, and ballistic rocket manufacturer Adam Opel AG, kept subsidiaries with facilities in Rüsselsheim (Hesse) and Brandenburg.[49] In 1944, General Motors was still importing products from Germany in Sweden.[50] Hitler had not confiscated any of the subsidiaries from American corporations—Ford and GM—but he systemat-ically put them under the jurisdiction of the Reich and ordered their custody as the property of the enemy.

Meanwhile, the National City Bank and Chase National Bank maintained their ties with the Bank für Internationalen Zahlungsausgleich (BIZ) or Bank for Interna-tional Settlements, which continued its operations in Basel, Switzerland, under the law of neutrality, mediating business with the Axis countries. Between 1940 and 1946, this bank was chaired by Thomas H. McKittrick (1889–1970), an American citizen, but it was controlled by prominent officials of the Nazi regime, including Walter Funk, Minister for Economic Affairs (1938–1945), and Emil Johann Rudolf Puhl, director and vice president of the Reichsbank of Germany. In 1944, BIZ accepted the transfer of the gold the Nazis had plundered from the Jews in various countries, who were exterminated in the gas chambers of Auschwitz, Majdanek, Treblinka, Belzec, Chelmno, and Sobibor with the toxic Zyklon B, composed of hydrocyanic acid, chlorine, and nitrogen, and supplied by the powerful conglomer-ate of the chemical industry I. G. Farben.[51] The gold was melted and marked with a date prior to the Second World War in order to disguise its origin and to be used by the Nazi leaders, who were facing defeat in war.

---

[49]Edwin Black, "The Nazi Party: General Motors & the Third Reich". Jewish Virtual Library. American-Israeli Cooperative Enterprise. Available at: <http://www.jewishvirtuallibrary.org/jsource/Holocaust/gm.html>; Jacques R. Pauwels, "Profits über Alles! American Corporations and Hitler". *Global Research*, May 15, 2014 -*Global Research*, June 8, 2004. Centre for Research on Globalization. Available at: <http://www.globalresearch.ca/profits-ber-alles-american-corpora tions-and-hitler/4607>.

[50]Charles Higham, 1983, p. 176.

[51]Joseph Borkin, 1978, pp. 121–123 and 205; Paul Joseph Watson, "Former Nazi Bank to Rule the Global Economy". *Prison* Planet.com, April 30, 2010/In Featured Stories, Old Infowars Posts Style. Available at: <http://www.infowars.com/former-nazi-bank-to-rule-the-global-economy/>.

Chapter 3
The Military-Industrial Complex in the West and the Opposing Power Sphere in the East

3.1 Spheres of Influences After the Second World War: Free World Versus Iron Curtain

Germany and Italy were defeated on the battlefields of Europe during the Second World War, which claimed the lives of 420 thousand US soldiers. The Soviet Union lost between 18 million and 24 million people (civilian and military), the equivalent to 13.6–14.2% of its population, estimated to be around 168.5 million in the first half of the 1940s. The western democracies, however, incorporated many elements of Nazi-Fascism into their ideological arsenal, i.e., elements of a totalitarian state, especially in the context of the Cold War, which broke out with the rise of the Soviet Union as superpower. And so the fascist-style, but peculiar, dictatorships in Portugal and Spain remained untouchable and began receiving the support from the United States, France, and Great Britain as part of the so-called Free World, in opposition to the *Iron Curtain*, the term coined by Winston Churchill, Prime Minister of Great Britain, at the outbreak of the Cold War. The Soviet Union spread this curtain from Stettin in the Baltic to Trieste in the Adriatic, splitting the continent with behind it the old states of Central and Eastern Europe.[1]

Until then, the United States had formally rejected the concepts of spheres of influence and balance of power, defending an era of peace based on the collective security of the UN, open to democratic nations.[2] In 1947, however, it induced the countries of Latin America to sign the Inter-American Treaty of Reciprocal Assistance (Treaty of Rio de Janeiro), and in 1948, it led the creation of the Organization of American States, which could be traced back to the former International Union of American Republics (1889–1890). Just as the Soviet Union would not accept the

---

[1]"Winston Churchill's *Iron Curtain Speech*—Winston Churchill presented his *Sinews of Peace*, (the *Iron Curtain Speech*), at Westminster College in Fulton, Missouri on March 5, 1946". *History Guide*. Available at: <http://www.historyguide.org/europe/churchill.html>.
[2]Stephen E. Ambrose, 1985, pp. 63–64.

© Springer Nature Switzerland AG 2019
L. A. Moniz Bandeira, *The World Disorder*,
https://doi.org/10.1007/978-3-030-03204-3_3

election of an anti-communist government in the "people's democracies" of Eastern Europe, the United States began encouraging military coups in Latin America and recognizing and cultivating "friendly relations with the worst dictatorships on the right." This analysis came from the Brazilian embassy in Washington, headed by Ambassador Roberto Campos.[3] "From the perspective of military sectors in Washington, such governments are much more useful to the interests of the continental security than constitutional systems," he stressed.[4] Nelson Rockefeller also regarded them "the major force for constructive social change in the American Republic." These military dictatorships, inspired by the National Security Doctrine, were similar to that special type of regime in a permanent state of counterrevolution, resting on the principle of absolute state power, placed above the individual and in a continuous war against an internal enemy: the communist subversion represented by unions, strikes etc., threatening the safety of the *Free World*.[5] And the security of the *Free World* meant protecting the interests of the *Free Market*, business, and American banks against any nationalist threat identified with communism. This was the corner stone of the policies of all American administrations—be they Republican or Democrat—vis-à-vis Latin America.[6]

3.2   NATO's "To Keep the Americans In, the Russians Out and the Germans Down"

The United States also pulled the countries of Western Europe into its sphere of influence through the creation of the North Atlantic Treaty Organization (NATO), on April 4, 1949, as a collective defense system, "a necessary mechanism," according to General Dwight Eisenhower. Only 6 years later did the Soviet Union involve the countries under its domain militarily, when it signed the Treaty of Warsaw (Treaty of Friendship, Cooperation, and Mutual Assistance) on May 4, 1955, with the Central and Eastern European countries.[7] NATO, however, encompassed a multiple purpose: "keep the Americans in, the Russians out and the Germans down,"[8] i.e., maintain the supremacy of the United States, contain the Soviet Union, and subjugate Germany—as General Hastings Lionel Ismay, 1st Lord

---

[3]Noam Chomsky & Edward S. Herman, 1979, pp. 252–253.

[4]"Política Externa Norte-americana—Análise de Alguns Aspectos", Annex to letter no. 516/900.1 (22), secret, Embassy in Washington to the Ministry of Foreign Affairs, Washington, 13.06.1963, Archive of the Ministry of Foreign Relations-Brasília, 900.1 (00), International Politics, (10) (98), 1951/66.

[5]*Ibidem*, pp. 252–253.

[6]Jan K. Black, 1986, pp. 13–14.

[7]The German Democratic Republic (East Germany), Bulgaria, Hungary, Poland, Czechoslovakia, Romania, and Albania were the countries making up the Warsaw Pact.

[8]Michael Lind, *The American Way of Strategy—U.S. Foreign Policy and the American Way of Life.*

Ismay (1887–1965), then secretary-general of the Alliance (1952–1957), stated explicitly.

When the Western European countries were establishing the European Economic Community (EEC), they also joined NATO: a military, although seemingly defensive organization. This necessarily implied some loss of sovereignty. And so the United States subordinated them militarily and divided the world into opposing camps—the "Free World" versus "totalitarian communism." The United States promoted the expansion of financial capital—with a boom for such American banks as the National City Bank and others—linked international contradictions with the Soviet Union, and identified the ideals of freedom and democracy with free enterprise, free trade, and the multilateralization of commerce, allowing the dollar to take its position of international preeminence. Above all, the Cold War really broke out because of the economic needs and policies of the United States: the need to expand the consumer society, the substrate of the capitalist system, and its "way of life" and the need to feed the war industry and the security complex, which had become fundamental to its prosperity and dominance. The conflict with the Soviet Union was therefore fought through an arms race, interventions and military coups, civil and/or proxy wars between third countries, trade wars, covert operations, and acts of terror and assassinations, led by *Gladio* operations and a network of secret paramilitary organizations—stay-behind structures formed in Western Europe (1951) by NATO, the CIA, and the intelligence services from Italy and other countries under the central command of the Pentagon, including fascists, Nazi officials, and Gestapo agents. The pretext was resisting any invasion by the Soviet Union.[9] So when the Republican Party got General Dwight Eisenhower elected as President of the United States, Oswaldo Aranha (1894–1960), then Ambassador of Brazil in Washington, wrote a letter to his President Getúlio Vargas (1894–1954), warning that:

> This will be a republican and a military government. And my heart wavers as to which is worse. Wall Street will be chief of staff. The world will feel the reaction of the combination of these two forces in the greatest power ever built by a people and in the most uncertain and unsafe time for the lives of all people. Capitalism in power knows no bounds, especially those of an international nature. The efforts to return to world order will be the spectacle we'll have to behold. The new order which was underway with the liberation of the people under colonial rule will suffer further shocks. But it will eventually win, even because this people, it seems to me, is not united in support of this violent return to an international past that will inevitably lead the country to war with almost all other people.[10]

---

[9]Daniele Ganser, 2014, pp. 42–55, 96–97, 102–110; Gunther Latsch, "Die dunkle Seite des Westens". *Der Spiegel*, April 11, 2005.

[10]"Carta de Osvaldo Aranha, embaixador dos Estados Unidos em Washington, ao presidente Getúlio Vargas", Wash., 2, 12, 1952, folder of 1952—Getúlio Vargas' archives. This codex is from the time the archive was under the custody of his daughter, Alzira Vargas do Amaral Peixoto.

3.3   McCarthyism and the Denunciation of the Military-Industrial Complex by Eisenhower

At the time, the United States was flirting with protofascist totalitarianism. Under the cloak of anticommunism, Senator Joseph "Joe" McCarthy (1908–1957) of the Republican Party triggered a violent domestic repression campaign, through accusations of subversion, disloyalty and treason, without evidence, and investigations against several personalities, including artists and writers, to inhibit and restrict the rights of criticism and dissent. And since 1953, the United States expanded its *regime change* policy, with the CIA promoting covert operations and encouraging coups d'état directly or indirectly, as what happened in Iran (Operation Ajax—1953),[11] Guatemala (Operation PBSUCCESS—1954), Paraguay (1954), Thailand (1957), Laos (1958–1960), Congo (1960), and Turkey (1960) and with preparations being made for the invasion of Cuba (1959–1960). But when he handed over the administration to President John F. Kennedy (1961–1963) of the Democratic Party, President Eisenhower himself warned about the enormous military establishment and large arms industry the United States had built through a remarkable technological revolution. His successors should caution "against the acquisition of unwarranted influence, whether sought or unsought, by the military-industrial complex. The potential for the disastrous rise of misplaced power exists and will persist."[12]

President Eisenhower also stressed that "we must never let the weight of this combination endanger our liberties or democratic process," and he pointed out the danger of public policy becoming captive of a "scientific technological elite."[13] "We want democracy to survive for all generations to come, not to become the insolvent phantom of tomorrow."[14] The warning came late.

---

[11] Saeed Kamali Dehghan & Richard Norton-Taylor, "CIA admits role in 1953 Iranian coup—Declassified documents describe in detail how USA—with British help—engineered coup against Mohammad Mosaddeq". *The Guardian*, August 19, 2013.

[12] "*Now this conjunction of an immense military establishment and a large arms industry is new in the American experience. The total influence—economic, political, even spiritual—is felt in every city, every Statehouse, every office of the Federal government. We recognize the imperative need for this development. Yet, we must not fail to comprehend its grave implications. Our toil, resources, and livelihood are all involved. So is the very structure of our society. In the councils of government, we must guard against the acquisition of unwarranted influence, whether sought or unsought, by the military-industrial complex. The potential for the disastrous rise of misplaced power exists and will persist. We must never let the weight of this combination endanger our liberties or democratic processes.*"; "Military-Industrial Complex Speech," Dwight D. Eisenhower, 1961. *Public Papers of the Presidents, Dwight D. Eisenhower, 1960*, pp. 1035–1040.

[13] *Ibidem.*

[14] *Ibidem.*

3.4 Military Democracy and the Growth of Social Inequality in the United States

Democracy in the United States had already begun transforming into the "insolvent phantom of tomorrow." It had virtually degenerated into what Edmund Burke (1729–1797) had foreseen, i.e., into a "military democracy," in which the revolutionary Americans claimed the rights of men, but when African Americans (slaves) stood up against them, they employed "troops again—massacre, torture, hanging."[15] And in the first half of the nineteenth century, Alexis de Tocqueville (1805–1859) in turn realized that the government of the American Republic seemed to him "more centralized and more energetic than those of the monarchies of Europe."[16] Indeed, in 213 years of war from independence until the interventions in Iraq and Libya, the presidents of the United States have only requested Congress' authorization five times, as the constitution demands.[17] They almost always ignore Congress and public opinion.

This characteristic of a "military democracy" governed by a president of the republic with more powers than an absolute monarch has become more pronounced over time with the structural mutation of capitalism, increasing inequality in the appropriation of national income and reaching unprecedented levels in the 1970s and 1980s.[18] After 1982, the gulf widened even further. That year, the highest-earning 1% of families received 10.8% of all pretax income, while the bottom 90% received 64.7%. By 2012, they were receiving 22.5%, while the bottom 90%'s share fell to 49%.[19] According to the survey by the Organization for Economic Cooperation and Development (OECD), the United States occupies tenth place on the pretax income inequality scale based on "market incomes" among the 31 countries belonging to this organization and second place, behind Chile, after taxes, etc.[20] In 2013, income inequality has reached its highest level since 1928: 1645 men and women controlled a massive part of global finance, a staggering amount of US$6.5 trillion.[21] 492 of these 1645 billionaires lived in the United States, whose GDP was in the order of US

---

[15]Edmund Burke, 1986, pp. 332–333, e 345.

[16]"*aussi centralisé et plus énergique que celui des monarchies absolues de l'Europe.*" Alexis Tocqueville, 1968.

[17]Tyler Surdem, "American—'War, Or Peace?'" Available at: <http://www.zerohedge.com/news/2013-03-15/which-more-american-war-or-peace>.

[18]Thomas Piketty, 2013, pp. 463–465.

[19]Drew Desilver, "5 facts about economic inequality". *Fact Tank—Pew Research Center,* January 7, 2014. Available at: <http://www.pewresearch.org/fact-tank/2014/01/07/5-facts-about-economic-inequality/>.

[20]*Ibidem.* "OECD Income Distribution Database: Gini, poverty, income, Methods and Concepts. Social policies and data". Available at: <http://www.oecd.org/els/soc/income-distribution-database.htm>.

[21]Kerry A. Dolan & Luisa Kroll, "Inside the 2014 Forbes Billionaires List: Facts And Figures". *Forbes*, March 3, 2014. Available at: <http://www.forbes.com/sites/luisakroll/2014/03/03/inside-the-2014-forbes-billionaires-list-facts-and-figures/>.

$16.72 trillion (2013 est.),[22] of which they controlled more than US$2 trillion.[23] Inevitably, holy-declared *free enterprise* led to the accumulation of wealth and the structural asymmetry of power, as did the *free market*, which the presidents of the United States had tried so hard to impose on other countries, especially those with lower wage levels and rich in raw materials. The agreements and treaties always served the interests of large US corporations, which established industrial plants in other countries in search of cheaper production factors, including labor. Now they could export their offshore production to the American market and thus increase corporate profits, shareholder gains, and the multimillion-dollar bonuses paid to their executives.[24] Capital obtained huge rewards, but the cost fell upon American workers and came as taxes collected by cities and states—noted the economist Paul Craig Roberts.[25]

The international poverty research organization Oxfam International, headquartered in Great Britain, revealed on January 19, 2015, that the share in global wealth of the richest 1% in the world grew from 44% in 2009 to 48% in 2014, and only 80 billionaires detained more resources than 50% (3.5 billion) of the world's population. The trend was for the richest 1% to dominate more than 50% in 2016.[26] The wealth of those 80 richest billionaires doubled, in terms of liquidity, between 2009 and 2014 and could be used to lobby in favor of their interests. Winnie Byanyima, director of Oxfam International and one of the six coordinators of the World Economic Forum (WEF), warned that the increasing concentration of wealth since the severe recession of 2008–2009 was dangerous for development and governance, since it was leaving the poor voiceless.[27] These billionaires, with investments in various sectors, including finance and pharmaceuticals/healthcare, spent millions of dollars each year on lobbying to create an environment protective of their riches and future interests. The most prolific activities in the United States were in matters of budget and taxation.[28]

Furthermore, professor Nouriel Roubini of the Stern School of Business at New York University remarked during the meeting in Davos (Switzerland) in January 2015, in an interview with the journalist Tom Leene of *Bloomberg News*, that it would be very difficult for the United States to overcome the enormous social

---

[22]*CIA Fact Books*. Available at: <https://www.cia.gov/library/publications/the-world-factbook/geos/us.html>.

[23]Darrel M. West, 2014, p. 4.

[24]Paul Craig Roberts, "The Next Presidential Election Will Move the World Closer to War", November 16, 2014. *Institute for Political Economy*. Available at: <http://www.paulcraigroberts.org/2014/11/16/next-presidential-election-will-move-world-closer-war-paul-craig-roberts/>.

[25]*Ibidem.*

[26]"Wealth: Having it all and wanting more". *Oxfam Issue Briefing January 2015*—WWW.Oxfam.Org. Available at: <http://policy-practice.oxfam.org.uk/publications/wealth-having-it-all-and-wanting-more-338125>; Larry Elliott (economics editor) & Pilkington (editor). "New Oxfam report says half of global wealth held by the 1%". *The Guardian*, Monday, January 19, 2015.

[27]*Ibidem.*

[28]*Ibidem.*

inequality because its political system was based on "legalized corruption." This meant the billionaires, with more resources, could bribe politicians, and this is what they usually did.[29] According to Roubini, the lobbying firms concentrated in K Street in Washington could always influence legislation with the money they gave politicians, and those with financial resources therefore have a greater impact on the political system than those without. "So it's not a true democracy, it's a plutocracy," concluded Professor Nouriel Roubini.[30]

The economist Thomas Piketty, author of *Le Capital aux XXIe*, noted that "the professed equality of rights of all citizens contrasts sharply with the very real inequality of living conditions [...]."[31] Those living on interests, on capital gains, were the *"ennemi de la démocratie"*, he wrote.[32] This income inequality started to increase in the 1980s, and in the United States it grew wider than in any other country of the West.[33] According to data released by the American Federation of Labor and Congress of Industrial Organizations (AFL-CIO), the chief executive officers of 350 corporations earned, on average, US$11.7 million in 2013, while the yearly income of the average worker was only US$35,293.[34] The average income of corporate executives was 774 times higher than that of the workers earning only the hourly minimum wage of US$7.25, i.e., a total of US$15,000 per year.[35] And as a matter of fact, starting in the 1980s, the inequality in wages and property started increasing in the countries of the West[36] as a result of the policies of the neoconservative President Ronald Reagan (Reaganomics), who wiped out the middle class in the United States,[37] and of Margaret Thatcher, whose most important long-term legacy as head of the British government (1979–1990), according to *The Guardian*, was the immense growth in social and economic inequality, with the fastest ever-

---

[29]"Davos 2015: Nouriel Roubini says Income Inequality Creates U.S. Plutocracy". *Bloomberg Business*. Available at: <https://www.youtube.com/watch?v=t1Vv13XZ5Us>; "Obama Pledges to Push Trans-Pacific Partnership In State Of The Union The Roundup for January 21st, 2015", "Taken For Granted At Davos That US Government Run On 'Legalized Corruption'". *DSWright*, January 21, 2015. Available at: <http://news.firedoglake.com/2015/01/21/taken-for-granted-at-davos-that-us-government-run-on-legalized-corruption/>.

[30]*Ibidem.*

[31]Thomas Piketty, 2013, p. 672.

[32]*Ibidem*, p. 671.

[33]Thomas Piketty, 2015, pp. 20–21.

[34]Jim Lobe, "CEOs at Big U.S. Companies Paid 331 Times Average Worker". *Inter Press Service (IPS), April 16*, 2014. Available at: <http://www.ipsnews.net/2014/04/ceos-big-u-s-companies-paid-331-times-average-worker/>.

[35]*Ibidem.*

[36]Thomas Piketty, 2015, pp. 20–21.

[37]Thom Hartmann, "Reaganomics killed America's middle class. This country's fate was sealed when our government slashed taxes on the rich back in 1980". *Salon*, April 19, 2014. Available at: <http://www.salon.com/2014/04/19/reaganomics_killed_americas_middle_class_partner/>.

recorded widening of the gulf between rich and poor during the 1980s, especially after 1985.[38]

This phenomenon was not exclusive to the United States and Britain. It happened in all countries, reflecting the exploitation of the working class by direct and indirect means, taxes, outsourcing, etc. By increasing the productivity of labor and further boosting the internationalization/globalization of the economy, scientific and technological developments and advances in media and digital tools determined a deep mutation in the global capitalist system, in the social structure of the industrial powers, and in the nature of the working class itself, which no longer resembled the one existing in the nineteenth century and even in the early decades of the twentieth century.

After the Second World War (1939–1945), capital in the United States and the industrial powers of Europe migrated, *en masse*, to the countries of Asia and Latin America in search of cheaper production factors, such as labor and raw materials. After the collapse of the Soviet Union and the socialist bloc, this capital migration also occurred to Eastern Europe and to China and India, where it found more secure, stable, and profitable conditions for investment. There, the big corporations set up their industrial plants and began exporting to the markets of the economic powers they had left. In almost all developed countries, the decline of the share of industry in job creation was sped up through outsourcing and the displacement of the production of manufactured goods to the countries in the periphery of the system (*offshoring*), with lower wage levels and different social and political conditions. This had serious consequences for the labor market and contributed significantly to the increase in inequality. These processes contributed to sap the strength of the working class, and, as a result, the bargaining power and leverage of the unions and political parties— Socialists, Social Democrats, Labor Parties, Communists, etc.—who in one way or another defended their interests. At the same time, the global process of capitalist production accumulated and concentrated wealth on an international scale, and inequality grew.

Political and ideological contradictions between the political parties of the great powers of the West, such as Germany, France, and Great Britain, virtually vanished, and once in government, their measures barely differed. The great historian Eric Hobsbawm was right when he claimed in an interview to the news agency Télam in Argentina that "there is no longer a left as there once was," be it social democrat or communist. It was either fragmented or it had disappeared.[39] There was no contrast; opposition was virtually gone. The differences remained only in the colors of the parties. And so democracy stalled. In fact, it atrophied and began converging with totalitarian regimes in several countries, to the extent that the rule of law became the

---

[38]Richard Wilkinson & Kate Pickett, "Margaret Thatcher made Britain a less, not more, desirable place to do business". *The Guardian*, Wednesday, April 10, 2013. Available at: <http://www. theguardian.com/commentisfree/2013/apr/10/inequality-margaret-thatcher-britain-desirable-business>; Thomas Piketty, 2015, pp. 20–21.

[39]"Entrevista de Eric Hobsbawm a Martin Granovsky", president of the Télam news agency, published in the newspaper *Página 12*, Buenos Aires, March 29, 2009.

exception in a state that was increasingly outsourced, handing over its functions, including those of the police and military, to large corporations who only sought profit in the midst of the increasing social and economic inequality.

Under the title *Croissance et inégalités*, the OECD (Organization for Economic Cooperation and Development) revealed in 2008 that the distance between rich and poor had grown in most countries. Three years later, in 2011, the OECD came out with another study—*Toujours plus d'inégalité: Pourquoi les écarts de revenus se creusent*—showing that the economic and social gulf had widened even further in most countries. The Gini coefficient had gone from 0.29 to 0.32 between the mid-1980s and the end of the year 2000. At the same time, unemployment, aggravated by the automation of industry with the growing use of microchips (industrial robots), had reached 200 million workers across the globe.[40] They formed a powerful industrial reserve army that further drained the bargaining power of unions, whose political organization, restricted to their national states, could not keep up with the transnational scope of the capitalist system. Even in such countries as Germany, Sweden, and Denmark, which traditionally had more egalitarian economic and social conditions, the disparity between rich and poor—in the range of 5 to 1—grew to 6 to 1 after the 1980s.[41]

A study published by *The New York Times* revealed that the average income of the executives of the top 100 corporations in the United States was more than US$13 million in 2013.[42] And Wall Street executives earned even more, although the executives of financial companies didn't always show up among those receiving the highest wages. During the financial crisis of 2008, the president of the investment bank Goldman Sachs, Lloyd Blankfein, got a bonus of approximately US$20 million and in 2007, a total of US$68 million, in addition to possessing about US$500 million in shares.[43] He represented a mere fraction of some of his peers in the so-called "shadow-banking sector." These were the "corporate Caesars," as the American professor and journalist Henry Demarest Lloyd called them at the end of the nineteenth century, when they made their fortune by preying upon and appropriating other industries in the midst of the banking collapse and financial panic caused by the speculation with the construction of railroads in the United States.[44] "Liberty produces wealth, and wealth destroys liberty," Henry D. Lloyd wrote, pointing out that free competition would generate a monopoly with the appropriation by some of the property of others and the expropriation of the middle

---

[40]"L'Évolution des inégalités de revenus dans les pays riches". *Inequality Watch*, February 6, 2012. Available at: <http://inequalitywatch.eu/spip.php?article58&lang=fr>; *An Overview of Growing Income Inequalities in OECD Countries: Main Findings—Divided We Stand—Why Inequality Keeps Rising* © *OECD 2011*. Available at: <http://www.oecd.org/els/soc/49499779.pdf>.

[41]*Toujours plus d'inégalité: pourquoi les écarts de revenus se creusent. OECD*. Available at: <http://www.oecd.org/fr/els/soc/49205213.pdf>. Access on May 24, 2015.

[42]Peter Eavis, "Executive Pay: Invasion of the supersalaries". *The New York Times*, April 12, 2014.

[43]Norbert Kuls & Carsten Knop, "Goldman-Sachs-Chef Blankfein: Ich bin ein Banker, der Gottes Werk verrichtet". *Frankfurter Allgemeine Zeitung*, November 9, 2009.

[44]Henry Demarest Lloyd, 1965, pp. 5, 10 e 163.

class.[45] At the end of the depression in 1897, the large capitalists J.P. Morgan, John D. Rockefeller, and Andrew Carnegie took advantage and acquired the more debilitated and broken businesses in order to consolidate and concentrate their control over the banking, oil, and steel sectors.

Financial speculation through the most varied instruments provided another path for banks to accumulate more and more wealth. The financial market and the economy had become the biggest threat to the United States, and President Obama had to involve them directly in a war in order to avoid a recession, even more so than in the asymmetrical proxy wars, supplying third parties and countries with financial resources and armaments to defend their economic and/or geopolitical interests.

In the second half of the twentieth century, financial speculation started expanding again. This expansion really took flight after the 1990s, when Alan Greenspan, chairman of the Federal Reserve Bank (1987–2006), authorized commercial banks to issue financial securities. And it continued to grow after 1996, with the permission given to the subsidiaries of commercial banks to participate in investment banks, up to the limit of 25% of their capital. These measures sought to serve the interests of the companies Travelers Group and Citicorp, who wished to remove all regulatory barriers against their merger and the creation of the gargantuan banking and financial services conglomerate Citigroup. And on November 12, 1999, President Bill Clinton signed the Financial Services Modernization Act, also known as the Gramm-Leach-Bliley Act, repealing the Glass-Steagall Act (The Banking Act) approved by Congress in 1933 during the Great Depression to prevent the bank abuses and frauds that inflated the bubble and produced the crash of 1929. This law, the Glass-Steagall Act, considered "obsolete and outdated" by Alan Greenspan, had prevented the merger of commercial banks and investment banks for seven decades.

The objective of the Gramm-Leach-Bliley Act was to limit or eliminate government power over industry and banking through deregulation, and therefore increase the competition of private enterprises in the market. This act established a new classification for financial corporations, as *holdings*, with the power to underwrite and sell insurance and obligations (securities) and simultaneously participate in commercial and investment banks.

After the scandal caused by the bankruptcy of the Texan energy trading giant Enron in December 2001, President George W. Bush signed a new regulatory law, the Sarbanes-Oxley Act or Corporate and Auditing Accountability Act, which raised and established new public accountability standards for the boards, councils, and senior management of companies in order to protect investors. This energy trading company had been one of the major financial contributors to his presidential campaign and had always been involved in election campaigns, with enormous influence over the White House and Congress.

Since at least 1989, Enron had exercised extraordinary political influence in Washington, involving house representatives, senators, and the president of the United States himself, with large donations of thousands of dollars—about US\$5.9

---

[45]*Ibidem*, pp. 9–11.

million between 1990 and 2002—assigning 73% to the Republican Party and 27% to the Democratic Party, according to the Center for Responsive Politics.[46] More than 250 members of Congress were receiving contributions from Enron. President George W. Bush was their biggest recipient, starting with his campaign for governor of Texas in 1993, until 2000, when he ran for president.[47] He was an intimate friend of Kenneth L. Lay, Enron's CEO.[48] And among Enron's shareholders, we find Donald Rumsfeld, Secretary of Defense; Karl Rove, George W. Bush's senior adviser; Peter Fisher, Deputy Secretary of the Treasury; Robert Zoellick, US Trade Representative; and several other White House personalities.[49]

Despite the scandal and the implementation of the Sarbanes-Oxley Act, President George W. Bush, whose administration was guided by the interests of the major financial corporations, intertwined with the interests of the oil companies, continued Bill Clinton's initiative and expanded the deregulation to other sectors of the economy, ending the oversight from agencies of the federal government. And so the speculative activity of real estate brokers, facilitated by the deregulation, increased between 2002 and 2007. The speculation with mortgages based on subprime loans, insurance derivatives, and rotten securities, such as ABSs (asset-backed securities), MBSs (mortgage-backed securities), CDOs (collateralized debt obligations), SIVs (structured investment vehicles), and CDSs (credit default swaps), reached a total value of around 80% of GDP in the fourth quarter of 2008, about US$14.58 trillion.[50]

The floodgates for a frantic flow of money in the free market had been opened, enabling the formation of super banks and financial holding companies and the financialization of the entire US economy, with the creation of the most diverse and new forms of financing based on futures, options, swaps, and derivatives. These institutions took trillions of dollars in loans each day, from each other and from central banks, rebuying credits, collateral mortgage obligations, and rotten securities

---

[46]"The politics of Enron. Four committees in search of a scandal. As Congress cranks into action, there's not much sign of the dirt from Enron reaching the president." *The Economist*, January 17, 2002. Available at: <http://www.economist.com/node/940913>; CBSNews.com staff CBSNews.com staff. "Follow The Enron Money". *CBS,* January 12, 2002. Available at: <http://www.cbsnews.com/news/follow-the-enron-money/>.

[47]*Ibidem.*

[48]Richard A. Oppel Jr. & Don Van Natta Jr. "Enron's Collapse: The Relationship; Bush and Democrats Disputing Ties to Enron." *The New York Times*, Saturday, January 12, 2002.

[49]"The politics of Enron. Four committees in search of a scandal. As Congress cranks into action, there's not much sign of the dirt from Enron reaching the president." *The Economist*, January 17, 2002. Available at: <http://www.economist.com/node/940913.CBSNews.com/staff>; "Follow the Enron Money". *CBS,* January 12, 2002. Available at: <http://www.cbsnews.com/news/follow-the-enron-money/>.

[50]"Gross Domestic Product: Fourth Quarter 2008 (Final) Corporate Profits: Fourth Quarter 2008 (Final)". *US Bureau of Economic Analysis.* Available at: <http://www.bea.gov/newsreleases/national/gdp/2009/pdf/gdp408f.pdf>; "Gross Domestic Product & Corporate Profits: Second Quarter 2008 (Preliminary)." *US Bureau of Economic Analysis.* Available at: <http://bea.gov/newsreleases/national/gdp/2008/gdp208p.htm>.

and passing on what they internally knew as *junk,* so that another could securitize the transaction, i.e., provide certain guarantees in case of total default.

The explosion of the financial bubble had been predicted for a long time. The high oil prices and the appreciation of the Euro laid bare the profound crisis afflicting the US economy. And when it finally burst in the first half of 2007, major brokerage firms, such as Merrill Lynch and Lehman Brothers, suspended the sale of collaterals. In July of that same year, European banks registered losses on contracts based on subprime mortgages. The default on the mortgages triggered a financial debacle, affecting loans to companies, credit cards, etc. And after October 2007, a substantial part of the resources entering the United States came as help from sovereign wealth funds in Asia and the Middle East, who purchased securities convertible into shares of American banks, such as Citigroup, whose ordinary shares were purchased by the sovereign fund of Abu Dhabi for $7.5 billion. The rescue operations by the central banks were also stepped up to prevent the banks from putting their rotten assets on sale, which would have led to a complete collapse.

With the bankruptcy of Lehman Brothers and Bear Stearns, two of the largest investment banks, and others, such as Merrill Lynch and AIG Financial Products, between 2007 and 2008, threatening also Goldman Sachs, Citigroup, and Wachovia,[51] an intervention of the state in the economy had become inevitable, despite the liberal aversion against this measure in the United States. The Wall Street banks, the financial holding companies, were in such deep trouble in 2008 that the government of President George W. Bush had to resort to the money of American taxpayers to bail them out and prevent the country from diving into a deep recession. He used billions of dollars, in some cases without informing Congress. In a single day, December 5, 2008, certain banks requested a combined bailout of US$1.2 trillion, but the Federal Reserve Bank of the United States did not disclose who the beneficiaries were.[52] The bankers also evaded revealing the amount they had received. All we know is that the Treasury Department granted a bailout of US$700 billion through the Troubled Asset Relief Program (TARP), the emergency fund, according to Treasury Secretary Henry Paulson, the former CEO of Goldman Sachs.[53] In September 2008, the same Henry Paulson estimated about US$1 trillion would be needed to stabilize the financial market.

The financial research company CreditSights, however, stated that the US government employed a lot more resources, about US$5 trillion, to prevent the collapse

---

[51] *Ibidem*, p. xvi.

[52] Bob Ivry & Bradley Keoun & Phil Kuntz, "Secret Fed Loans Gave Banks $13 Billion Undisclosed to Congress". *Bloomberg*, November 28, 2011. Available at: <http://www. bloomberg.com/news/2011-11-28/secret-fed-loans-undisclosed-to-congress-gave-banks-13-billion-in-income.html>.

[53] Elizabeth Moyer, "Washington's $5 Trillion Tab". *Forbes,* November 12, 2008. Available at: <http://www.forbes.com/2008/11/12/paulson-bernanke-fed-biz-wall-cx_lm_1112bailout.html>.

of the financial system.[54] But this value has been exceeded. The FED injected approximately US$236 billion (then £117 billion; now £152 billion following the pound's collapse) to rescue several banks,[55] and it increased guarantees and credit limits, compromising US$7.7 trillion by March 2009, more than half the GDP of the United States in that year.[56]

During the crisis, dozens of banks in the United States and in other countries disappeared, absorbed by the more powerful ones. JPMorgan Chase acquired Bear Stearns, a deal brokered by the George W. Bush administration, while Bank of America agreed to buy Merrill Lynch for US$50 billion. Just as in the nineteenth century—1837, 1857, 1873, 1893, 1907, and 1933—the concentration of capital increased with the crash of 2007–2008. In 2009, financial holding companies, such as JPMorgan Chase, Bank of America, Citigroup, and Wells Fargo, had already become even larger and more powerful. They possessed 46% of assets and 42% of deposits, in addition to US$194 trillion in bets on derivatives.[57] Goldman Sachs and Morgan Stanley, which turned into financial holding companies during the crisis in order to receive the FED bailout, possessed a total of US$88 trillion in derivatives.[58] These two investment banks—Goldman Sachs and Morgan Stanley—had always dominated the most profitable industrial businesses, consulting companies, and governments on mergers and acquisitions, etc.[59] These six largest banks—JPMorgan Chase, Bank of America, Citigroup, Wells Fargo, Goldman Sachs, and Morgan Stanley—controlled almost half of the US economy, functioning as one vast casino headquartered in Wall Street. But according to the IMF, the United States was and is the only country where *shadow banking* (with banks that operate outside any regulation) far outweighs conventional banking.[60] And this was really the epicenter of the systemic shock of 2007–2008.

---

[54]Steve Watson, "Total Bailout Cost Heads Towards $5 Trillion. Numbers becoming meaningless as Paulson defends government intervention" Infowars.net, October 15, 2008. Available at: <http://infowars.net/articles/october2008/151008Bailout_figures.htm>.

[55]Nick Mathiason & Heather Stewart, "Three weeks that changed the world. It started in a mood of eerie calm, but then 2008 exploded into a global financial earthquake". *The Guardian—The Observer*, December 28, 2008. Available at: <http://www.theguardian.com/business/2008/dec/28/markets-credit-crunch-banking-2008>.

[56]Nomi Prins, 2014, p. xvi.

[57]John Hoefle, "LaRouche: Return to FDR's Glass-Steagall Standard Now!" *Executive Intelligence Review,* October 16, 2009. Available at: <http://www.larouchepub.com/other/2009/3640return_glass-steagall.html>.

[58]*Ibidem*; John Melloy, (Investing Editor of CNBC.com). "Goldman, Morgan Stanley May Shed 'Bank' Status: Analyst". *CNBC*, October 12, 2011. Available at: <http://www.cnbc.com/id/44875711>.

[59]Andrew Ross Sorkin & Vikas Bajaj, "Shift for Goldman and Morgan Marks the End of an Era". *The New York Times*, Sunday, September 21, 2008. Available at: <http://www.nytimes.com/2008/09/22/business/22bank.html?_r=0>.

[60]"Shadow banking system a growing risk to financial stability—IMF Fund report says tightening of bank regulations may be driving shift to lending by hedge funds and private equity". *The Guardian*, October 1, 2014.

The concentration of capital with the mergers of banks and industries could have no other outcome than the concentration of the political power of corporations, i.e., of Wall Street, which has always helped shape American foreign policy and driven economic and military expansion since Black Friday, the crash of 1929. And the debacle of the Soviet Union and the entire Socialist Bloc between 1989 and 1991, strongly inflated the ideology of "American exceptionalism" as "the necessary nation", "the anchor of global security", the lonely power, brief: the myth that it had always played a role in favor of humanity, with a foreign policy that "makes America different." This was the mantra many of its leaders kept repeating, including President Barack Obama, when he invoked it to invade Syria in 2013.[61]

---

[61]"Remarks by the President in Address to the Nation on Syria East Room". *The White House Office of the Press Secretary For Immediate Release,* September 10, 2013. Available at: <http://www.whitehouse.gov/the-press-office/2013/09/10/remarks-president-address-nation-syria>.

Chapter 4
9/11 and the Accelerated Mutation of the American Republic

4.1   September 11: The Decay of Democracy and *Mutazione dello Stato* in the United States

The financial collapse of 2007–2008 destabilized the entire international capitalist order. It reached the sovereign debts of countries in the European Union and further undermined confidence in the United States, whose influence as single world power had been declining since the war against Iraq due to the violation of international law, the lies about the existence of weapons of mass destruction to justify the military intervention against Saddam Hussein's regime, and the abuses and violations of human rights practiced by American soldiers.[1]

After the terrorist attacks against the Twin Towers on September 11, 2001, Democracy in the United States withered. The American scientist Francis Fukuyama, who himself had proclaimed "the end of History"[2] when the Soviet Union disintegrated, acknowledged in his work *Political Order and Political Decay* that the decline of democracy in the United States was more advanced than in other wealthy countries of the West. The United States was unable to adapt to changing circumstances, and its democratic traditions of governance were "gradually being replaced with feudal fiefdom ruling methods." According to Fukuyama, its weakening, inefficiency, and corruption increasingly corroded the American state, and one of the causes was the growing inequality and concentration of wealth, allowing the elites to buy immense political power and manipulate the system in line with their own interests. Fukuyama also warned that being a rich and stable liberal democracy didn't mean the system would remain that way forever.[3] "Indeed, democracy itself

---

[1] Luiz Carlos Bresser-Pereira, "A crise financeira de 2008." *Revista de Economia Política,* vol. 29 no 1. São Paulo, January/March 2009. ISSN 0101–3157. Available at: <http://www.scielo.br/scielo.php?pid=S0101-31572009000100008&script=sci_arttext>.

[2] Francis Fukuyama, 1992, pp. 463–464.

[3] *Ibidem*, pp. 463–467, 524.

© Springer Nature Switzerland AG 2019
L. A. Moniz Bandeira, *The World Disorder*,
https://doi.org/10.1007/978-3-030-03204-3_4

can be the source of decay," he wrote. And further on he reached the diagnosis that the United States, where the first and most advanced liberal democracy had been established, was suffering "from the problem of political decay in a more acute form than other democratic political system."[4]

The American state had been "*repatrimonalized*" in the second half of the twentieth century and the interest groups, the lobbies, had more success in corrupting its government. The number of lobbies registered in Washington in 1971 grew from 171 to 2500 a decade later and to more than 12,000 in 2013, when they spent around US$3.2 million to influence authorities and congressmen, i.e., corrupt them in favor of their interests.[5] There never has been absolute transparency about the actions of the lobbying industry, the identity of its clients, and on what and what for it employed these millions of dollars in resources. Cronyism and corruption also established themselves in Washington through the "*revolving door*," especially in recent decades: a form of institutional corruption through the continuous exchange of functions between executives of large corporations, who went on to occupy senior positions in the administrations and government officials, who became executives of large corporations once they left their positions with influence and strategic information, e.g., Dick Cheney (CEO of the contractor Halliburton, client of the Pentagon), the vice-president of George W. Bush. This is how the Pentagon war industry consortium was built, employing public relations and advertising specialists to convince the public that the United States needed more and more weapons to confront the Soviet Union and Communism.[6]

La mutazione dello Stato was underway in the United States, as Francis Fukuyama admitted but differently from what happened in Germany. There, Hitler got his *Ermächtigungsgesetz*[7] after the Reichstag fire on February 27, 1933, a provocation perpetrated by Marinus van der Lubbe, an alleged Dutch Communist, which was exploited by Heinrich Himmler, Reinhard Heydrich, and other Nazi officials. As the American writer Naomi Wolf observed, the United States certainly were not and are not vulnerable to a violent and "total closing-down of the system," as happened in Italy after Benito Mussolini's march on Rome or in Germany, where Adolf Hitler soon ordered the imprisonment of all his opponents based on the *Ermächtigungsgesetz*. Democratic values in the United States were resilient and the culture of freedom, opposed to the totalitarian regime in the Soviet Union, served as *ratio summa* for the political and moral condemnation of communism and, consequently, of an openly totalitarian regime. But Naomi Wolf also said, "our experiment in democracy could be closed down by a process of erosion."[8]

With the shutting of factories and the exporting of jobs, the strength of the workers' unions and the middle class virtually disappeared in the actual power

---

[4]Francis Fukuyama, 2014, pp. 461–462, 487.

[5]*Ibidem*, pp. 464–465, 478–481.

[6]Fred J. Cook, 1964, pp. 84–85, 88–89.

[7]The *Ermächtigungsgesetz* was approved by the Reichstag on March 23, 1933.

[8]Naomi Wolf, "Fascist America, in 10 easy steps." *The Guardian*, April 24, 2007.

relations (*realen tatsächlichen Machtverhältnisse*)[9] sustaining democracy in the United States. The resources of the Democratic Party for electoral campaigns dwindled, and they had to rely on the same sources of financing as the Republican Party. And so the democratic regime virtually became a one-party system. The two parties now represented practically the same interests, the interests of the most powerful economic and political forces of the country: the financial sector, i.e., Wall Street, the military-industrial security complex, the Israel lobby, the oil and other mining companies, and agribusiness.[10] In his classic work *Du Contrat Social ou Principes du Droit Politique*, published in 1762, Jean-Jacques Rousseau (1712–1778) already warned that "Nothing is more dangerous than the influence of private interests in public affairs, and the abuse of the laws by the government is a lesser evil than the corruption of the legislator, which is the inevitable sequel to a particular standpoint." And he added that "In such a case, the State being altered in substance, all reformation becomes impossible," and in these circumstances, "there never has been a real democracy."[11]

This phenomenon changed the substance of the American State. The system for funding electoral campaigns in the United States inevitably made and makes politicians beholden to big business, financial corporations, and the industries providing them with the most resources. And the erosion of democracy, latent in the presidential republic, followed the process of concentration of capital and became even more pronounced after the disintegration of the socialist bloc and the Soviet Union in 1991. The meaning of freedom was identified more and more with free market ideology and private enterprise, becoming disassociated from the concepts of public freedoms and civil rights.[12] And the attacks of September 11 in the United States worsened and accelerated the phenomenon Cicero called *commutatio rei publicae* (*De re publica*, 2–63).[13] Seven days after the strikes, on September 18, 2001, President George W. Bush signed the Authorization for Use of Military Force, which was quickly approved by Congress. "We're at war," he declared. And he pointed out that "we will not only deal with those who dare attack America, we will deal with those who harbor them and feed them and house them."[14] It would be a "permanent war."[15] But James Madison, the fourth president of the United States,

---

[9]Ferdinand Lassalle, 1991, pp. 94–97.

[10]Paul Craig Roberts, "The Next Presidential Election Will Move The World Closer To War." *Institute for Political Economy*. November 16, 2014. Available at: <http://www.paulcraigroberts.org/2014/11/16/next-presidential-election-will-move-world-closer-war-paul-craig-roberts/>.

[11]Jean-Jacques Rousseau, 1992, p. 95.

[12]Eric Foner, 1998, pp. 327–332.

[13]Marcus Tullius Cicero, 1979, p. 230.

[14]Mark Hosenball, "Bush: 'We're At War'." *Newsweek*, September 24, 2001.

[15]"President Signs Authorization for Use of Military Force bill. Resolution 23, Statement by the President. 'Today I am signing Senate Joint Resolution 23, the "Authorization for Use of Military Force."' *George W. Bush—The White House*, September 18, 2001. Available at: <http://georgewbush-whitehouse.archives.gov/news/releases/2001/09/20010918-10.html.>. Accessed on November 26, 2018.

had already warned "no nation could preserve its freedom in the midst of continual warfare."[16]

4.2   The War on Terror, the Patriot Act, and the Military Commission Act

On October 7, 2001, the United States began bombing Afghanistan with the support of the United Kingdom, starting a war that had been planned long before the September 11 attacks against the Twin Towers and the Pentagon. And on October 25, 2001, a large majority in Congress adopted the US Patriot Act almost unchanged.[17] President George W. Bush then signed it into law, dealing a blow to the domestic legal structure by openly violating the US Constitution. The Patriot Act not only expanded federal powers for the electronic surveillance of citizens by the National Security Agency (NSA), it also established the new crime of "*domestic terrorism*" in such broad terms that it could be used against any act of civil disobedience, whatever the political motivation. Through the curtailing of civil rights, individual guarantees, and public freedoms and the violation of human rights, the US Patriot Act therefore expedited the conditions for *la mutazione dello stato*, the establishment of a police state with similar traces to Fascist Italy and Nazi Germany, strengthened by the belief in American "exceptionality"[18] and the invincibility of its armed forces. And the Pentagon turned to internal political activities, called "*civilian bipolar conditions*" (CIDICON), violating the Posse Comitatus Act of 1878, which forbids the Armed Forces from engaging in internal political activities without the authorization of the Congress.

About a year later, on September 17, 2002, President George W. Bush announced the National Security Strategy of the United States,[19] declaring that the battle against terrorism could not be won on the defensive and that the United States reserved the right to wage preventive wars, unilaterally, including with the use of nuclear

---

[16]James Madison, 1865, p. 491.

[17]The Patriot Act was passed by 98 votes to 1 in the Senate, and by 357 to 66 in the House of Representatives.

[18]"Existe um mito fundamental para a autoestima dos norte-americanos: Sua crença na 'excepcionalidade' dos 102 puritanos que saíram da Inglaterra, no início do Século XVII, atravessaram o Atlântico no navio *Mayflower*, e desembarcaram em Massachusetts, no dia 21 de dezembro de 1620, com a decisão de criar uma nova sociedade no continente americano. Do ponto de vista dos mortais, eles eram apenas um grupo de ingleses pobres e puritanos que começaram a cultivar as terras da Nova Inglaterra, depois de fundar a cidade de Plymouth. Do ponto de vista da mitologia norte-americana, entretanto, estes senhores atravessaram o Atlântico para plantar a semente moral e ética de um povo escolhido para redimir os pecados da Europa"; Jose Luís Fiori, "A lenda dos peregrinos." *Valor Econômico*, São Paulo, September 13, 2006.

[19]*The National Security Strategy*. White House, September 2002. Available at: <http://www.state.gov/documents/organization/63562.pdf>.

weapons against nonnuclear countries. His intention, he said, was "fighting terrorists and tyrants" and extend "peace by encouraging free and open societies on every continent," which meant establishing "freedom, democracy, and free enterprise"[20] from Africa to Latin America and across the Islamic world. This could clearly only be achieved through war. And on March 19, 2003, the United States began unilaterally implementing its new strategy. It started bombing Baghdad with the sole support of Great Britain, after demanding Saddam Hussein and his sons Uday and Qusay surrender and leave Iraq within 48 hours. The United States did so without the approval of the UN Security Council and the backing of many countries, including its NATO allies Germany and France.

With good reason, the German Minister of Justice, Herta Dauber-Gmelin, of the Social Democratic Party (SPD), compared President George W. Bush's strategy to invade Iraq with Hitler's methods before starting the Second World War.[21] In the United States, the evolution toward this special, fascist-style regime, justified by 9/11, took place during the first decade of the twenty-first century, moving toward the "New American Century" and full-spectrum dominance, i.e., a global dictatorship representing the large corporations of Wall Street. With this perspective, President George W. Bush, signed three laws on October 17, 2006, which instantly transformed the republic into a police para-state, *simili modo* to what the lawyer Alberto da Rocha Barros called "white fascism in power, disguised in apparently democratic forms, but armed with special security and police laws."[22]

On September 29, 2006, after the approval by the House of Representatives, the Senate ratified the Military Commissions Act (MCA) by 65 votes (12 from the Democratic Party) to 35 as part of the War on Terror, investing President George W. Bush with exceptional and unprecedented powers in the history of the United States:

1. The right to *habeas corpus* was suspended for any American citizen detained as "unlawful enemy combatant" (a nonexistent qualification in any legislation), not just for those involved in combat but also for those who "purposefully and materially supported hostilities against the United States."

---

[20]George W. Bush. *The National Security Strategy of the United States of* America—White House, Washington, September 17, 2002. Available at: <http://www.informationclearinghouse.info/article2320.htm>; "President Bush Addresses the Nation: Following is the full text of President Bush's address to a joint session of Congress and the nation," September 20, 2001. *EMediaMillWorks— The Washington Post.* Available at: <http://www.washingtonpost.com/wp-srv/nation/specials/attacked/transcripts/bushaddress_092001.html>.

[21]"Angeblicher Bush-Hitler-Vergleich." *Der Spiegel*, September 20, 2002. Available at: <http://www.spiegel.de/politik/deutschland/angeblicher-bush-hitler-vergleich-daeubler-gmelin-fuehlt-sich-voellig-falsch-verstanden-a-215061-druck.html>; "Nach dem Bush-Hitler-Vergleich— Ministerin Däubler-Gmelin tritt ab." *Der Spiegel*, September 23, 2002. Available at: <http://www.spiegel.de/politik/deutschland/nach-dem-bush-hitler-vergleich-ministerin-daeubler-gmelin-tritt-ab-a-215291-druck.htm>. "Angeblicher Hitler-Vergleich Schröder schreibt an Bush/ Ministerin spricht von Verleumdung"—*Frankfurter Allgemeine Zeitung*, September 20, 2002.

[22]Alberto da Rocha Barros, 1969, p. 12.

2. Those accused of being "unlawful enemy combatants," imprisoned in Afghanistan and taken to the concentration camp in Guantanamo (Cuba), could not appeal to the courts of justice in the United States based on the Geneva Convention.
3. The president was granted the power to detain *indefinitely* any American or foreign citizen—in the United States and abroad—in the possession of material supporting anti-American hostilities, and the act even authorized the use of torture in secret prisons.
4. All legal actions were blocked that could be undertaken by someone arrested as *enemy combatant* due to damages and abuses suffered during his detention.
5. American military personnel and CIA agents were allowed to engage in torture, and it authorized the use of testimonies obtained through coercion in the trials carried out by the military commissions.
6. American military personnel and CIA agents were granted immunity against lawsuits for the torture of prisoners who were captured before the end of 2005.

4.3   The Implementation of "White Fascism," Without Black or Brown Shirts

President George W. Bush signed the Military Commissions Act on October 17, 2006. The Center for Constitutional Rights deemed it "a massive legislative assault on fundamental rights, including the right to *habeas corpus*—the right to challenge one's detention in a court of law."[23] And with the approval by congress on September 30, 2006, of the National Defense Authorization Act (NDAA), the establishment of this "white fascism, the white of hypocrisy and cowardice,"[24] without black or brown shirts, continued under the Star-Spangled Banner. The act was drafted by Senator John Warner (Republican Party—Virginia)[25] and was

---

[23]Anup Shah, "US Military Commissions Act 2006—Unchecked Powers?." *Global Issues*, September 30, 2006. Available at: <http://www.globalissues.org/article/684/us-military-commis sions-act-2006-unchecked-powers>; "FAQs: The Military Commissions Act." *Center for Constitutional Rights*. Available at: <http://ccrjustice.org/learn-more/faqs/faqs%3A-military-commisions-act>.

[24]Alberto da Rocha Barros, 1969, p. 12.

[25]"Text of the John Warner National Defense Authorization Act for Fiscal Year 2007. The John Warner National Defense Authorization Act for Fiscal Year 2007. This bill was enacted after being signed by the President on October 17, 2006. The text of the bill below is as of *Sep 30, 2006* (Passed Congress/Enrolled Bill). H.R. 5122 (enr)—An Act To authorize appropriations for fiscal year 2007 for military activities of the Department of Defense, for military construction, and for defence activities of the Department of Energy, to prescribe military personnel strengths for such fiscal year, and for other purposes." *U.S. Government Printing Office (GPO)*. Available at: <http://www.gpo. gov/fdsys/search/pagedetails.action?packageId=BILLS-109hr5122enr>; "One Hundred Ninth Congress of the United States of America at the Second Session Begun and held at the City of Washington on Tuesday, the third day of January, 2006 H. R. 5122." Available at: <https://www. govtrack.us/congress/bills/109/hr5122/text>; Scott Shane & Adam Liptak, "Detainee Bill Shifts Power to President." *The New York Times*, September 30, 2006.

enacted by President George W. Bush, on October 17, 2006, the same day the Military Commissions Act entered into effect. It effectively hollowed out the Posse Comitatus Act of 1878, which prohibits military operations directed against the American people,[26] by allowing the president to employ the armed forces to restore public order and enforce compliance with the laws of the United States in circumstances where domestic violence could reach such an extent that government authorities were unable, refused, or failed to maintain public order and suppress any uprising or conspiracy.[27]

In addition, the NDAA authorized President George W. Bush to impose martial law, dispatch units of the National Guard anywhere in the country, and employ Special Weapons and Tactics teams against the civilian population. These SWAT were first used by the Philadelphia police department (1964), pushing the United States further down the road of the militarization of the police, started by Daryl Francis Gates (1926–2010), head of the Los Angeles Police Department (1978–1992), during the Reagan administration (1981–1989), who expanded and intensified it under the pretext of the war on drugs.

4.4 Torture: The Concentration Camp in Guantánamo and the Secret CIA Prisons (Black Sites) in Eastern Europe

The purpose of the Military Commissions Act and National Defense Authorization Act, approved and sanctioned in 2006, consisted in legalizing war crimes and human rights violations, which the armed forces, the CIA, and other repression and intelligence agencies were practicing with the explicit consent of the Bush administration ever since Operation Enduring Freedom was unleashed against Afghanistan, on October 7, 2001.

Since the law did not allow for the detention, on American soil, of prisoners in complete isolation in secret prisons, more than 100 terrorist suspects captured after the invasion were taken by the CIA to Bagram Airbase, which British forces had

---

[26]"Domestic Operational Law: The Posse Comitatus Act and Homeland Security." COL (Ret) John R. Brinkerhoff. Reprinted with permission from the *Journal of Homeland Security*. Newsletter 10–16—December 2009. *Center for Army Lessons Learned*. Available at: <http://usacac.army.mil/cac2/call/docs/10-16/ch_12.asp>.

[27]*10 U.S.C. United States Code*, 2006 Edition—Title 10—ARMED FORCES Subtitle A—General Military Law—PART I—Organization and General Military Powers Chap. 15—Enforcement of the Laws to Restore Public Order from the U.S. Government Printing Office. Available at: <http://www.gpo.gov/fdsys/pkg/USCODE-2006-title10/html/USCODE-2006-title10-subtitleA-partI-chap15.htm>.

conquered in Afghanistan.[28] Only on January 11, 2002, did the first 20 *unlawful combatants* arrive at the concentration camp of the Guantanamo Bay Naval Base (G-Bay or GTMO), built especially to indefinitely imprison the Taliban and terrorist suspects captured in Afghanistan.[29] They were transported under sedation, hooded, and shackled.[30] "Unlawful combatants do not have any rights under the Geneva Convention," Secretary of Defense Donald Rumsfeld promptly declared.[31]

The prisoners weren't formally charged and enjoyed no rights. The White House's excuse consisted in the fact that Guantanamo wasn't a territory under the sovereignty of the United States, and therefore not subject to the jurisdiction of its courts of justice or international law. And the number of captives, of about 40 nationalities, increased to 779 during the year 2002, including children of 12/13 and 14/15 years of age.[32] The American Civil Liberties Union (ACLU) informed that the concentration camp at Guantanamo had received dozens of prisoners under the age of 18 between 2002 and 2004; and in 2008, 21 were still incarcerated there.[33] The Pakistani Mohammed Jawad, arrested in 2002 when he was 12, was only released in mid-2009, through a *habeas corpus* granted by the federal judge Ellen S. Huvelle, who overturned his confessions obtained through torture and death threats.[34] "Still I had to wonder about the wisdom of keeping kids so young in a place like Gitmo," wrote Sergeant Erik R. Saar, who served in Guantanamo Bay.[35]

---

[28]Dana Priest, (*Washington Post* Staff Writer). "CIA Holds Terror Suspects in Secret Prisons—Debate Is Growing Within Agency about Legality and Morality of Overseas System Set Up After 9/11." *The Washington Post*, November 2, 2005.

[29]Katharine Q. Seelye, "A Nation Challenged: The Prisoners; First 'Unlawful Combatants' Seized In Afghanistan Arrive At U.S. Base In Cuba." *The New York Times*, January 12, 2002. Available at: <http://www.nytimes.com/2002/01/12/world/nation-challenged-prisoners-first-unlawful-combat ants-seized-afghanistan-arrive.html?pagewanted=print>.

[30]Monica Whitlock, (BBC correspondent in Kabul). "Legal limbo of Guantanamo's prisoners." *BBC News*, May 16, 2003. Available at: <http://news.bbc.co.uk/2/hi/americas/3034697.stm>.

[31]Katharine Q. Seelye, "A Nation Challenged: The Prisoners; First 'Unlawful Combatants' Seized In Afghanistan Arrive At U.S. Base In Cuba." *The New York Times*, January 12, 2002. Available at: <http://www.nytimes.com/2002/01/12/world/nation-challenged-prisoners-first-unlawful-combat ants-seized-afghanistan-arrive.html?pagewanted=print>.

[32]Monica Whitlock, "Legal limbo of Guantanamo's prisoners." *BBC News*, May 16, 2003. Available at: <http://news.bbc.co.uk/2/hi/americas/3034697.stm>; Erik Saar & Viveca Novak, 2005, p. 114.

[33]Suzanne Ito, "Despite U.N. Objections, U.S. Continues to Detain Children at Guantánamo." *American Civil Liberties (ACLU)*, July 22, 2008. Available at: <https://www.aclu.org/print/blog/ human-rights-national-security/despite-un-objections-us-continues-detain-children-guantanamo>; Cori Crider, "Guantánamo children." *The Guardian*, Saturday, July 19, 2008. Available at: <http:// www.theguardian.com/world/2008/jul/19/humanrights.usa>.

[34]Jeremy Page, (Kabul), "Mohammed Jawad: 'I was 12 when I was arrested and sent to Guantanamo'." *The Economist*, August 27, 2009. Available at: <http://www.thetimes.co.uk/tto/ news/world/asia/afghanistan/article1843471.ece>; The Associated Press. "Guantánamo Detainee Released." *The New York Times*, August 24, 2009. Available at: <http://www.nytimes.com/2009/ 08/25/world/asia/25gitmo.html>; William Glaberson, "Obama Faces Court Test over Detainee." *The New York Times*, July 28, 2009; "Mohammed Jawad—Habeas Corpus." *American Civil Liberties (ACLU)*, August 24, 2009. Available at: <https://www.aclu.org/national-security/moham med-jawad-habeas-corpus>.

[35]*Ibidem.*

In addition to the concentration camp in Guantanamo, the CIA established a network of secret prisons, *detention black sites*, in Poland, Romania, Lithuania, and other Eastern European countries, as well as in the Middle East and Asia.[36] There, CIA, FBI, and other government agents could interrogate prisoners and subject them to all kinds of physical abuse without legal constraints. Through the *rendition program*, the CIA also extradited captured Islamists as alleged terrorists to such countries as Thailand, Pakistan, Morocco, and several others, so the local security services could interrogate and torture them (proxy torture). The offshore establishment of the concentration camp at the Naval Base in Guantanamo (Cuba) and the creation of the figure of the "*unlawful enemy combatant*" served the exact purpose of circumventing US law and international law, the Geneva Convention, and the UN Convention against Torture and Other Cruel, Inhuman, or Degrading Treatment or Punishment. It left the captives, hypocritically qualified as "*detainees*," at the mercy of the soldiers and inquisitors of the CIA and the security and intelligence services, who were allowed to commit arbitrary acts and abuses, all kinds of torture, listed as Enhanced Interrogation Techniques (EIT), and approved by President George W. Bush and his administration. Some of these acts included (1) sexual assault/humiliation; (2) sleep deprivation for several days; (3) sensory deprivation; (4) solitary confinement/isolation; (5) the threat of imminent execution/firing squad simulations[37]; (6) forced medication; (7) the use of dogs to intimidate prisoners; (8) leaving the prisoner naked and in handcuffs, subjected to continuous and extreme temperature changes, from 59 to 80 °F (10–26 °C); (9) sensory bombardment (noise); (10) seeing others being tortured; (11) submersion of the prisoner in a tray with ice; and (12) psychological techniques.[38]

---

[36]Dana Priest (*Washington Post* Staff Writer). "CIA Holds Terror Suspects in Secret Prisons—Debate Is Growing Within Agency about Legality and Morality of Overseas System Set Up After 9/11." *The Washington Post*, November 2, 2005.

[37]Julian Borger, (Diplomatic editor). "CIA mock executions alleged in secret report." *The Guardian*, August 23, 2009.

[38]*Report of the Senate Select Committee on Intelligence—Committee Study of the Central Intelligence Agency's Detention and Interrogation Program together with Foreword by Chairman Feinstein and Additional and Minority Views*. December 9, 2014—Ordered do be printed. Approved December 13, 2012—Updated for Release April 3, 2014, Desclassification Revisions December 3, 2014. United States Senate, 113th second Session, S. Report 113–288, pp. 96, 105–107, 429 *passim*. *Justice Campaign*. Available at: <http://thejusticecampaign.org/?page_id=273>. Accessed on November 17, 2014; in addition to the described techniques, the inquisitors also applied: "*(1) The Attention Grab: The interrogator forcefully grabs the shirt front of the prisoner and shakes him. (2) Attention Slap: An open-handed slap aimed at causing pain and triggering fear. (3) The Belly Slap: A hard open-handed slap to the stomach. The aim is to cause pain, but not internal injury. Doctors consulted advised against using a punch, which could cause lasting internal damage. (4) Long Time Standing: This technique is described as among the most effective. Prisoners are forced to stand, handcuffed and with their feet shackled to an eye bolt in the floor for more than 40 hours. Exhaustion and sleep deprivation are effective in yielding confessions. (5) The Cold Cell: The prisoner is left to stand naked in a cell kept near 50 degrees. Throughout the time in the cell the prisoner is doused with cold water. (6) Water Boarding: The prisoner is bound to an inclined board, feet raised and head slightly below the feet. Cellophane is wrapped over the*

"They have interrogated, tormented, and tortured me nearly every day for five years, but they never learned how to spell my name," Murat Kurnaz summed up his suffering during the 5 years he spent in Gitmo (Guantanamo Bay Naval Base) to this family.[39] He had a Turkish family but was born and raised in Germany (Bremen). And in a testimony given before US Congress, he described some of the torture he suffered, such as electrical shocks, water boarding, and solitary confinement, in addition to spending days hanging from his arms from the roof of a hangar.[40] Many of the prisoners subjected to sensory deprivation (*white noise*), listening repeatedly to the same music at more than 110 decibels for more than 8 hours, and also with sleep deprivation under constant light, ended up with hallucinations and without knowing their identity.[41]

The autopsies and reports declassified under the Freedom of Information Act (FOIA) at the request of the American Civil Liberties Union (ACLU) revealed that at least 44 prisoners in Guantanamo and Iraq died during the brutal interrogations conducted by the CIA, FBI, Navy Seals, and other US agencies. It was determined that 21 were intentionally assassinated. And all 44 who died during the torture were hooded, gagged, strangled, suffocated, beaten with blunt instruments, and subjected to sleep deprivation and extreme heat and cold. Until October 2005, more than 100 prisoners perished in Guantanamo and in Iraq. Most of these so-called natural deaths were attributed to "arteriosclerotic cardiovascular disease," heart attacks, possibly as a result of torture.[42]

---

prisoner's face and water is poured over him. Unavoidably, the gag reflex kicks in and a terrifying fear of drowning leads to almost instant pleas to bring the treatment to a halt." ROSS, Brian (*ABC News* Chief Investigative Correspondent); Richard Esposito, "CIA's Harsh Interrogation Techniques Described." *ABC News*. November 18, 2005. Available at: <http://abcnews.go.com/Blot ter/Investigation/story?id=1322866>.

[39]Murat Kurnaz, 2009, p. 224.

[40]Mariah Blake, (Correspondent of *The Christian Science Monitor*). "*Guantánamo ex-detainee tells Congress of abuse—Murat Kurnaz, who testified in a landmark hearing Tuesday, says he spent days chained to the ceiling of an airplane hangar. He was determined innocent in 2002, but held until 2006."*; *The Christian Science Monitor*. May 22, 2008. Available at: <http://www.csmonitor. com/World/Europe/2008/0522/p01s06-woeu.html>.

[41]*Report of the Senate Select Committee on Intelligence—Committee Study of the Central Intelligence Agency's Detention and Interrogation Program together with Foreword by Chairman Feinstein and Additional and Minority Views*. December 9, 2014—Ordered to be printed. Approved December 13, 2012—Updated for Release April 3, 2014, Declassification Revisions. December 3, 2014. United States Senate, 113th second Session, S. Report 113–288, p. 429.

[42]"U.S. Operatives Killed Detainees during Interrogations in Afghanistan and Iraq." *American Civil Liberties Union*, October 24, 2005. Available at: <https://www.aclu.org/news/us-operatives-killed-detainees-during-interrogations-afghanistan-and-iraq>. The documents are available at: <http:// action.aclu.org/torturefoia/released/102405/3164.pdf>; Lolita C. Baldor, (Associated Press). "ACLU reports 21 homicides in U.S. custody." Uruku.net. Last update 21/11/2014. Available at: <http://www.uruknet.info/?p=17119>.

On December 9, 2014, the Senate Intelligence Committee chaired by Senator Dianne Feinstein (Democratic Party—California) disclosed the report of the investigation on the methods used by the CIA agents and mercenaries (contractors) to interrogate the captives in Guantanamo and such prisons as Detention Site Cobalt, Detention Site Blue, Detention Site Green, and Detention Site Black—also called Dark Prison, or the Salt Pit—under the Detention and Interrogation Program. These report revealed that the torture was far more brutal—including "rectal feeding" or "rectal hydration," etc.[43]—and far less effective than purported, because they didn't lead to the thwarting of any terrorist plot or the capture of Osama bin Laden.[44]

Senator Dianne Feinstein stated that the CIA's "program of indefinite secret detention and the use of brutal interrogation techniques" was "a stain on our values and our history," and that "history will judge us by our commitment to a just society governed by law and the willingness to face an ugly truth and say 'never again'."[45]

This stain, however, had long been a blemish on the history of the United States. The torture techniques applied to prisoners in Guantanamo Bay and Abu Ghraib (Iraq)[46]—"an ugly truth"—were not new. They were similar to those described in the interrogation manual *KUBARK—Counterintelligence Interrogation—July 1963*, which the CIA had drafted for Vietnam, as well as those contained in the *Human Resource Exploitation Training Manual—1983*, whose purpose was to teach the techniques to the security services in Central America, Honduras, Nicaragua, El Salvador, in order to extract information from so-called subversives.[47] These manuals were used by the CIA to train and instruct the military and police forces of Latin American dictatorships between 1963 and 1987.

---

[43] *Report of the Senate Select Committee on Intelligence—Committee Study of the Central Intelligence Agency's Detention and Interrogation Program together with Foreword by Chairman Feinstein and Additional and Minority Views.* December 9, 2014—Ordered do be printed. Approved December 13, 2012—Updated for Release April 3, 2014, Declassification Revisions December 3, 2014. United States Senate, 113th second Session, S. Report 113–288, pp. xxii (13–19), 96, 104–105, 396–397, 464, 496–497.

[44] Mark Mazzetti, "Panel Faults C.I.A. Over Brutality and Deceit in Interrogations." *The New York Times*, Wednesday, December 10, 2014.

[45] *Report of the Senate Select Committee on Intelligence—Committee Study of the Central Intelligence Agency's Detention and Interrogation Program together with Foreword by Chairman Feinstein and Additional and Minority Views.* December 9, 2014—Ordered do be printed. Approved December 13, 2012—Updated for Release April 3, 2014, Declassification Revisions December 3, 2014. United States Senate, 113th second Session, S. Report 113–288, p. iv (Pages 2 of 6).

[46] For further details see Luiz Alberto Moniz Bandeira, 2014, p. -710.

[47] Gary Cohn & Ginger Thompson & Mark Matthews, "Torture was taught by CIA; Declassified manual details the methods used in Honduras; Agency denials refuted." The Baltimore Sun, January 27, 1997, final edition. Available at: <http://articles.baltimoresun.com/1997-01-27/news/1997027049_1_training-manual-torture-methods-counterintelligence-interrogation>. See also: <http://www.hartford-hwp.com/archives/40/055.html>.

Chapter 5
An Astonishing Continuity: From George W. Bush to Barack Obama

5.1 Support for Right-Wing Catholic and Evangelical Organizations

In addition to authorizing the torture carried out by the CIA, which played a similar role as the *Geheime Staatspolizei* (Gestapo) and other intelligence services, although in other historical circumstances, the administration of President George W. Bush also diverted billions of dollars from American taxpayers to fund the social services of extremely conservative, faith-based (Catholic and Evangelical) organizations. The political purpose of these organizations was to "dismantle American democracy and create a theocratic state."[1] In 2014, Bonnie Weinstein, married to Mickey Weinstein, founder of the Military Religious Freedom Foundation (MRFF), published the book *To the Far Right Christian Hater... You Can Be a Good Speller or a Hater, But You Cannot Be Both: Official Hate Mail, Threats, and Criticism from the Archives of the Military Religious Freedom Foundation*, in which she examines the "American fundamentalism" created by a segment of society that is white, more conservative, and angrier than the rest of America. "For some people the future of their faith and of the nation are in danger, threatened by secular forces controlled by Satan himself."[2]

Besides the dominionist and reconstructionist Christians who advocate Bible-based education—like Islamists take the Koran as foundation—traditional Evangelicals, with their intolerant, anti-democratic posture, want to establish a theocracy and amend the constitution with the statement that the United States is a

---

[1]Chris Hedges, 2006, pp. 22–25.

[2]Edwin Lyngar, "Christian right's rage problem: How white fundamentalists are roiling America. Far-right Christians like Todd Starnes think their nation's in danger. You won't believe what they want to do next." Salon, December 1, 2014. Available at <http://www.salon.com/2014/12/01/far_right_christian_haters_rage_and_cruelty_from_white_fundamentalist_america/?source=newsletter>.

© Springer Nature Switzerland AG 2019
L. A. Moniz Bandeira, *The World Disorder*,
https://doi.org/10.1007/978-3-030-03204-3_5

Christian nation.[3] In the first decade of the twenty-first century, they represented about 12% of the population and controlled more than 60 faith-based organizations, in reality right-wing organizations, which received US$2 billion in donations from the George W. Bush administration in just one year (2004), the equivalent of 10.3% of the federal competitive grants.

Conservative Evangelicals had been gaining influence since the 1960s, especially within the Republican Party, getting involved in social issues, such as the perceived discrimination of religious schools, abortion rights, the role of men and women in society, homosexuality, marriage, and divorce.[4] Such was the ideological profile of the far evangelical right that Patrick J. Buchanan defended the candidacy of George HW Bush (senior) by stating very clearly at the GOP convention in Houston that a "cultural war" could be as critical as the Cold War itself, "for this war is for the soul of America."[5] This was the trend that came to predominate the Republican Party, especially in the southern states, where it had grown since the 1960s to the detriment of the Democratic Party because of President Lyndon Johnson's (1963–1965) act determining the end of racial segregation.

5.2   Racism and Police Repression in the United States

Racism never disappeared from a vast demographic segment of the United States. A study conducted in 2011 by the Associated Press with researchers from Stanford University, the University of Michigan, and NORC at the University of Chicago revealed that 51% of Americans expressed prejudice against blacks, which was an increase in relation to 2008, when Barack Obama was elected president.[6] According to the report on human rights in the United States published by the Chinese government as a response to the State Department report, "racial discrimination has been a chronic problem in the U.S. human rights record," and ethnic minorities, which made up the poorest segments of the population, suffered discrimination in jobs, wages, etc.[7] In 2014, multiple cases of arbitrary killings of African Americans

---

[3]Chris Hedges, 2006, pp. 18–19.

[4]Jean Hardisty and Chip Berlet, Exporting Right-Wing Christianity. Jean Hardisty. Available at <http://www.jeanhardisty.com/writing/articles-chapters-and-reports/exporting-right-wing-chris tianity/>.

[5]Patrick J. Buchanan, "Address to the Republican National Convention." Houston, Texas: delivered 17 August 1992. American Rhetoric. Online Speech Bank. Available at <http://www. americanrhetoric.com/speeches/patrickbuchanan1992rnc.htm>; Adam Nagourney, "'Cultural War' of 1992 Moves In From the Fringe." The New York Times, August 29, 2012.

[6]Sonya Ross and Jennifer Agiesta, "AP poll: Majority harbor prejudice against blacks." AP Big Story, October 27, 2012. Available at <http://bigstory.ap.org/article/ap-poll-majority-harbor-preju dice-against-blacks>.

[7]"Full Text of Human Rights Record of the United States in 2014." Web Editor: Yangyang Xinhua, June 26, 2015. Available at <China.org.cn. http://www.china.org.cn/china/Off_the_Wire/2015-06/

by police triggered huge waves of protest in several cities across the country, including Ferguson (Missouri), Phoenix (Arizona), Detroit (Illinois), and others, casting doubt on the equality of the United States and kindling racial hatred.[8]

Discrimination was not only heavy against African Americans, who accounted for 13% of the population, 14% of monthly drug users, and 27.2% of those living below the poverty line in 2012, more than double the rate among whites (12.7%).[9] It also affected Hispanics, of whom 25.6% equally lived below the poverty line.[10] Deep America has always harbored a "profound hatred of the weak and the poor," according to the journalist Matt Taibbi.[11] And this mentality, coupled with racism, permeated the small towns and communities of the Sun Belt states—from Texas, Arizona, and New Mexico to California—whose population increased by more 15 million—twice as much as in the Northeast and Midwest. Together, these states already accounted for more than 60% of the American population in 2000, since the sunnier climate and lower taxes were attracting people.[12] And it was here that George W. Bush enjoyed his largest support during his presidential campaign. In the 2000 election, he received 68% of the white evangelical vote (which accounted for 23% of the total), a percentage that rose to 78% in 2004. Karl Rove, the marketing architect of George W. Bush's reelection in 2004, believed success depended on this vote, which formed a powerful bloc with Christian Zionists. And the religious, evangelical right saw Bush as one of their own.[13]

President George W. Bush in fact knew nothing. He ignored all countries and confused Switzerland with Sweden, and during the White House meetings, he seemed like "a blind man in a room full of deaf people," according to his former

---

26/content_35915205.htm>; CRIENGLISH News, June 26, 2015. Available at <http://english.cri.cn/12394/2015/06/26/2982s884702_5.htm>.

[8]Ibidem.

[9]Drew Desilver, "Who's poor in America? 50 years into the 'War on Poverty,' a data portrait." Pew Research Center, January 13, 2014. Available at <http://www.pewresearch.org/fact-tank/2014/01/13/whos-poor-in-america-50-years-into-the-war-on-poverty-a-data-portrait/>.

[10]Sonya Ross & Jennifer Agiesta, "AP poll: Majority harbor prejudice against blacks." AP Big Story, October 27, 2012. Available at <http://bigstory.ap.org/article/ap-poll-majority-harbor-prejudice-against-blacks>.

[11]Emily Tess katz, "Matt Taibbi: America Has A 'Profound Hatred Of The Weak And The Poor.'" HuffPost Live, HuffPost Businnes, December 1, 2014. Available at <http://www.huffingtonpost.com/2014/04/16/matt-taibbi-the-divide_n_5159626.html>.

[12]"The Rise of the Sun Belt (p. 197)". Access to Social Studies. Available at <http://access-socialstudies.cappelendamm.no/c316289/artikkel/vis.html?tid=357420>.

[13]Geoffrey C. Layman and Laura S. Hussey, "George W. Bush and the Evangelicals: Religious Commitment and Partisan Change among Evangelical Protestants, 1960–2004." University of Maryland. This paper originally was prepared for presentation at the University of Notre Dame conference on "A Matter of Faith? Religion in the 2004 Election," Notre Dame, In, December 2–3, 2005.—Department of Government and Politics, 3140 Tydings Hall, College Park, MD 20742. Ron Faith Suskind, "Certainty and the Presidency of George W. Bush." The New York Times—Magazine, October 17, 2004. Available at <http://www.nytimes.com/2004/10/17/magazine/17BUSH.html?_r=0>.

Secretary of the Treasury, Paul O'Neill.[14] And his messianic sentiment bordered so closely on insanity that he actually believed he was an emissary of God. Nabil Ali Muhammad (Abu Rashid) Shaath, the former Foreign Minister of the Palestinian Authority (2003–2005), revealed in an interview to the BBC that when George W. Bush was at the Israel-Palestine summit in Sharm el-Sheikh (2003), 4 months after the American invasion of Iraq, he told the entire delegation that "I am driven with a mission from God," who apparently told him "George go and fight these terrorists in Afghanistan" and then "George, go and end the tyranny in Iraq." And he added—"I did"—and he claimed he was listening to the words of God: "Go get the Palestinians their state and get the Israelis their security, and get peace in the Middle East." And he promised: "I'm gonna do it."[15]

5.3   The Weakening of George W. Bush's Administration

Nothing he said he had done to obey God's commands resulted in success: terrorism persisted, with the war in Afghanistan and elsewhere; the fall of Saddam Hussein produced chaos and a humanitarian disaster worse than the tyranny; and the bloodshed continued in Palestine, where the Arabs couldn't establish their state and the Israelis couldn't maintain their security. And in May 2008, an opinion poll by CNN/Opinion Research Corp. revealed that 71% of the US population disapproved of the way George W. Bush was governing the country and that he was the most "unpopular president in modern American history." "No president has ever had a higher disapproval rating in any CNN or Gallup Poll," said Keating Holland, CNN's polling director.[16] President George W. Bush's popularity, which peaked at 86–90% after the terrorist attacks of September 11, 2001, had plummeted to 25% between October 31 and November 2, 2008.[17] A larger percentage of the American population was already saying that the best way to reduce the threat of terrorism was to reduce the American presence abroad and not increase it. It was war fatigue, and

---

[14]Ron Suskind, "Faith, Certainty and the Presidency of George W. Bush." The New York Times—Magazine, October 17, 2004. Available at <http://www.nytimes.com/2004/10/17/magazine/17BUSH.html?_r=0>.

[15]Ewen Macaskill, "Bush: 'God told me to end the tyranny in Iraq'—President told Palestinians God also talked to him about Middle East peace." The Guardian, October 7, 2005. Available at <http://www.theguardian.com/world/2005/oct/07/iraq.usa>.

[16]Paul Steinhauser (CNN Deputy Political Director). "Poll: More disapprove of Bush than any other president." CNN Politics.com, May 1, 2008. Available at <http://edition.cnn.com/2008/POLITICS/05/01/bush.poll/Updated 0117 GMT (0917 HKT)>.

[17]Governance—Presidential Approval Ratings—George W. Bush. Gallup Poll. Available at <http://www.gallup.com/poll/116500/presidential-approval-ratings-george-bush.aspx>; "Overview: Bush and Public Opinion. Reviewing the Bush Years and the Public's Final Verdict." Pew Research Center, December 18, 2008. Available at <http://www.people-press.org/2008/12/18/bush-and-public-opinion/#>.

49% against 43% believed the decision to invade Iraq had been a mistake.[18] Another survey, conducted in 2008 by Project Pew Global Attitudes, revealed that the majority of the population in 19 countries, among the 24 polled, including strong allies of the United States, had little confidence in President George W. Bush, while a 2007 survey had already shown that anti-American sentiment in 45 nations was on the rise, just as the disapproval of central tenets of American foreign policy.[19]

5.4   Banks Electing Presidents in the United States

The withering of George W. Bush's administration in these circumstances, hastened by an equal or worse economic and financial crisis than the one of 1929, made the Wall Street corporations realize—particularly its most powerful exponent, Goldman Sachs—that they would be better off placing their bets on the candidate of the Democratic party, Senator Barack Obama, an African American, than on the Republican nominee, the ultraconservative John McCain. And Barack Obama, cultivating the image of the candidate who would change the country, was tremendously successful in raising substantial resources from the start of this campaign in 2007. In addition to the University of California, which gave him US$1,799,460, Barack Obama received US$1,034,615 from Goldman Sachs, US$900,909 from Harvard University, US$854,717 from Microsoft Co., US$847,895 from JPMorgan Chase & Co., US$755,057 from Citigroup Inc., US$817,855 from Google Inc., and many other donations from various entities and corporations, totaling US$745 million, of which he spent $730 million.[20]

On the other side, Goldman Sachs contributed only US$234,595 to the candidacy of John McCain, the inveterate warmonger, much less than the US$1,034,615 it donated to Barack Obama's run. The other banks gave McCain little more: Merrill Lynch donated US$354,570; JPMorgan Chase & Co., US$336,605; Citigroup Inc., US$330,502; Morgan Stanley, US$264,501; Credit Suisse Group, US$184,603; Bank of America, US$163,726; Lehman Brothers, US$121,932; and Bank of New York Mellon, US$121,701; in addition to other entities and corporations, totaling only US$368 million, of which he spent US$333 million.[21] Barack Obama raised more than three times as much money from bankers and financial corporations than John McCain.[22]

---

[18]"Public Attitudes toward the War in Iraq: 2003–2008." Pew Research Center, March 19, 2008. Available at <http://www.pewresearch.org/2008/03/19/public-attitudes-toward-the-war-in-iraq-20032008/>.

[19]Ibidem.

[20]2008 Presidential Election. Center for Responsive Politics—OpenSecrets.org. Available at <https://www.opensecrets.org/pres08/>.

[21]Ibidem.

[22]Nomi Prins, 2014, pp. 411–413.

Senator Barack Obama's victory in 2008 was not so much due to promises made during his campaign as to the amount of resources he raised, as is generally the case in the American elections. He kept very few promises. His 2009 Nobel Peace Prize notwithstanding, President Obama continued the disastrous work to convert the United States into a "rogue superpower," even if sometimes wavering, with the help of his Secretary of State Hillary Clinton. He further exacerbated the crises and multiple wars besetting the various regions of the world since, especially, the Bill Clinton administration.[23] The United States continued as the "necessary and indispensable nation" only to trigger a process of military coups, killings, devastation, ruins, exodus, chaos, and humanitarian catastrophes wherever it tried to employ its regime change and nation building policy.

5.5   The "Perpetual Wartime Footing" of the Nobel Peace Prize Winner

At the summit of the South and Southeast Asian Nations (SASEAN) Defense Chiefs' Dialogue—2014, held in Colombo (Sri Lanka), Russia's Deputy Minister of Defense Anatoly Antonov rightly accused the United States of being responsible for two-thirds of the military conflicts that flared up in the last decades, including those in Yugoslavia, Iraq, Afghanistan, and Syria, by taking advantage of economic and social difficulties, in addition to various ethnic and religious conflicts, intervening under the pretext of expanding democracy.[24] President Barack Obama's interference, just as that of his predecessors, in the internal affairs of countries around the world did not lead to peace and democracy, Anatoly Antonov added, pointing out that the result of overthrowing legal governments has always been chaos, massacres, lawlessness, and, in many cases, the establishment of a regime favorable to the West, and the terrorists certainly felt comfortable in such circumstances.

Speaking to the cadets at the West Point Military Academy on May 28, 2014, President Barack Obama stated that anyone who suggested America was declining and saw its global leadership fading had misinterpreted history or was engaging in

---

[23]Rodrigue Tremblay, "Bill Clinton's 'Neocon-inspired Decisions' Triggered Three Major Crises in our Times." Global Research, August 13, 2014. Available at <http://www.globalresearch.ca/bill-clintons-neocon-inspired-decisions-triggered-three-major-crises-in-our-times/5395715?print=1>.

[24]"US responsible for two-thirds of all military conflicts—Russia's top brass." RT, November 28, 2014. Available at <http://rt.com/news/209379-us-military-conflicts-antonov/>; Esther Tanquintic-Misa, "2/3 of Global Military Conflicts Instigated by the United States—Russian Minister; Willing To Share with Asian Countries Army Modernization Experience." International Business Times, November 28, 2014. Available at <http://au.ibtimes.com/articles/574282/20141128/military-conflicts-u-s-russia-asia-army.htm#.VHiV8LR3ucw>.

partisan politics. "Our military has no peer,"[25] he said. And with hubris and arrogance he added: "The United States is and remains the one indispensable nation," which "has been true for the century passed and will be true for the century to come."[26] And so he reaffirmed the sense of omnipotence, inflating the fervor, the "myth and rationale" of exceptionalism, in the West Point cadets so the country could remain permanently engaged in wars or proxy wars, whose background was a new Cold War against Russia and also against China. George Friedman remarked, "the United States has spent the past century [twentieth century] pursuing a single objective: avoiding the rise of any single hegemon that might be able to exploit Western European technology and capital and Russian resources and manpower."[27] President Barack Obama pursued the same goal and implicitly endorsed the Project for the New American Century, which President George W. Bush (2001–2009) had sought to implement. The goal was to establish the full-spectrum dominance of the United States, i.e., a global dictatorship, with the consolidation and expansion of its hegemony over the planet as the only truly sovereign power. And while he sometimes hesitated, President Obama kept the United States on a perpetual wartime footing, the forever war, the war on terror formalized by Congress in 2001, to fight an unseen, nameless unidentified enemy without parameters, giving continuity to it and unconstitutionally escalating the attacks and extrajudicial killings of terrorists or alleged terrorists through the tactic of targeted killings. Barack Obama took charge of the selection process, picking targets[28] from a top secret "kill list" drafted by the intelligence services (NSA, CIA, etc.), including the names of terrorists or suspected terrorists (capture was only theoretical), using unmanned aerial vehicles (UAVs), drones, or Navy SEAL Team 6 (ST6).[29]

5.6   The War on Terror as Overseas Contingency Operations

The War on Terror had merely changed its name. Now it was called Overseas Contingency Operations (OCO), for which President Obama requested US$65.8 billion from Congress in the budget proposal of the financial year 2015 submitted in

---

[25]"Remarks by the President at the United States Military Academy Commencement Ceremony." US Military Academy-West Point, New York. The White House—Office of the Press Secretary, May 28, 2014. Available at <http://www.whitehouse.gov/the-press-office/2014/05/28/remarks-president-west-point-academy-commencement-ceremony>.

[26]Ibidem.

[27]"George Friedman Viewing Russia from the Inside Stratfor—Global Intelligence." Geopolitical Weekly, December 16, 2014. Available at <https://www.stratfor.com/weekly/viewing-russia-inside#>.

[28]Jo Becker and Scott Shane, "Secret 'Kill List' Proves a Test of Obama's Principles and Will." The New York Times, May 29, 2012.

[29]Secret military commandos.

June 2014. These funds would be allocated to the Department of Defense (DOD), the State Department, and Other International Programs (State/OIP).[30] He also asked US \$4 billion for the Department of Defense and US\$1 billion for the State Department with three purposes:

1. To support counterterrorism capacity-building efforts for partner nations
2. To provide support to the moderate Syrian opposition and Syria's neighbors through a Regional Stabilization Initiative
3. To help the Department of Defence respond to unexpected crises

The United States budget, presented to Congress by the 2009 Nobel Peace Prize, also made financial room to:

1. Expand military presence in Europe, especially in Central and Eastern Europe
2. Increase bilateral and multilateral exercises and training with allies and partners
3. Improve infrastructure to allow for greater responsiveness
4. Enhance prepositioning of U.S. equipment in Europe
5. Intensify efforts to build partner capacity for newer NATO members and other partners[31]

5.7 Selective Assassinations Through Drones

The Overseas Contingency Operations grew after President Barack Obama's inauguration. In 2009, the year he was awarded the Nobel Peace Prize, the Pentagon and the CIA launched 291 drone strikes and eliminated between 1299 and 2264 militants or suspected terrorist militants by January 2013, while the Navy SEAL Team 6 commandos executed 675 in 2009 and 2200 in 2011.[32] According to the Bureau of Investigative Journalism, 362 of the 413 drone strikes carried out by the CIA against the Taliban and al-Qa'ida militants or suspected militants from 2004 to January 31, 2015, occurred during the Obama administration, which started on January 20, 2009, killing between 2342 and 3789 people, of whom 416–957 were civilians.[33] This undeclared war spread from Afghanistan and Pakistan to Yemen and Somalia.

---

[30]"The Administration's Fiscal Year 2015 Overseas Contingency Operations (OCO) Request. The White House—President Barack Obama." Office of the Press Secretary, June 26, 2014. Available at <http://www.whitehouse.gov/the-press-office/2014/06/26/fact-sheet-administration-s-fiscal-year-2015-overseas-contingency-operat>.

[31]Ibidem.

[32]Jonathan Masters, (Deputy Editor). "Targeted Killings." Council of Foreign Relations, May 23, 2013. Available at <http://www.cfr.org/counterterrorism/targeted-killings/p9627>.

[33]Jack Serle and Alice K. Ross, "Monthly Updates on the Covert War—July 2014 Update: US covert actions in Pakistan, Yemen and Somalia." All Stories, Covert Drone War, Monthly Updates on the Covert War. The Bureau of Investigative Journalism, August 1, 2014. Available at <http://www.thebureauinvestigates.com/2014/08/01/july-2014-update-us-covert-actions-in-pakistan-yemen-and-somalia/>.

According to the New America Foundation, President George W. Bush ordered between 45 and 50 drone strikes during his administration, killing 477 people, while Barack Obama ordered 316 drone attacks that eliminated 2363.[34] These numbers are likely to be underestimated, as the New America Foundation itself admits, and the casualties may amount to more than 3404, including 307 civilians—men, women, and children in Pakistan, Yemen, Somalia, and other countries.[35] Republican Senator Lindsey Graham, in turn, who favors the drone strikes, said the total death toll could reach 4700.[36] President Barack Obama, however, made drone killings the centerpiece of his anti-terrorism strategy.[37] These serial crimes led General Brent Scowcroft, former head of the Foreign Intelligence Advisory Board, to remark: "There is something very troubling about how we have become policeman, judge, jury, and executioner, all rolled up together."

Throughout his first term (2009–2012), the Nobel Peace Prize implemented and fomented civil and conventional wars, beginning with the sending of an additional 30,000 troops to Afghanistan. None of the military interventions and all-out shadow wars carried out by the United States actually sought to defend its population from real external threats, however. The United States military conceivably had no peer, as President Obama proclaimed to the West Point cadets to reaffirm American exceptionalism, the myth that it had always played a role in favor of humanity, with a foreign policy that "makes America different," the mantra he used when he planned to invade Syria in 2013.[38] But it also had not won a war since defeating Japan in 1945.

As Leonam Guimarães, an expert on nuclear issues, wrote: "No state can have exact certainty about the capabilities of its competitors and must therefore prepare for the worst scenarios and think the unthinkable." Sun Tzu summed up this concept

---

[34]Michael Hirsh and James Oliphant, "Obama Will Never End the War on Terror—The president stands to leave an open-ended conflict to his successor." National Journal, February 27, 2014. Available at <http://www.nationaljournal.com/magazine/obama-will-never-end-the-war-on-terror-20140227>.

[35]Peter Bergen, "Drone Wars—The Constitutional and Counterterrorism Implications of Targeted Killing"—Testimony presented before the US Senate Committee on the Judiciary Subcommittee on the Constitution, Civil Rights and Human Rights. New America Foundation, April 24, 2013. Available at <http://www.newamerica.net/publications/resources/2013/drone_wars>. Daniel L. Byman, "Why Drones Work: The Case for Washington's Weapon of Choice." Brookings, July/August 2013. Available at <http://www.brookings.edu/research/articles/2013/06/17-drones-obama-weapon-choice-us-counterterrorism-byman>.

[36]Tim Stanley, "Obama has killed thousands with drones, so can the Nobel committee have their Peace Prize back?" The Telegraph, October 10, 2013.

[37]Daniel L. Byman, "Why Drones Work: The Case for Washington's Weapon of Choice." Brookings, July/August 2013. Available at <http://www.brookings.edu/research/articles/2013/06/17-drones-obama-weapon-choice-us-counterterrorism-byman>.

[38]"Remarks by the President in Address to the Nation on Syria East Room." The White House Office of the Press Secretary For Immediate Release, September 10, 2013. Available at <http://www.whitehouse.gov/the-press-office/2013/09/10/remarks-president-address-nation-syria>.

of suspicion as such: "Can you imagine what I would do if I could do all I can?"[39] By boasting that the United States military had no "peer," President Barack Obama seemed to ignore the fact that his nuclear potential was the equivalent of Russia's, the heir to the entire nuclear might of the Soviet Union, and that the strategic parity between the two powers had not vanished. He didn't know his adversary, contrary to what Sun Tzu taught in The Art of War.[40] In the 1980s, however, the Pentagon already knew that the Soviet Union had built a powerful nuclear arsenal, establishing equilibrium with the United States, equivalent to the situation of MAD (mutual assured destruction).[41]

Russia remained a nuclear superpower and by 2013 it had between 1512 and 1600 strategic missiles with nuclear warheads. Both President Vladimir Putin and President Obama were always accompanied by military officers carrying a "nuclear briefcase," which can issue the launch codes for the warheads in a matter of seconds.[42] With regard to nuclear weapons, the United States had no advantage over Russia. The engineer and nuclear scientist Siegfried S. Hecker, a professor at Stanford University, confirmed in an article in the New York Times that Moscow had secured the recovery of the entire nuclear stockpile previously installed in Ukraine, Belarus, and Kazakhstan and that on his 49 trips to Russia since 1992, he'd witnessed a vast improvement in the management of this stockpile compared to 30 years earlier.[43] He quoted President Putin as saying that Russia's defense system "has risen from the ashes like the proverbial Phoenix." And he warned that the isolation of Russia "can lead to catastrophes."[44]

According to the New Strategic Arms Reduction Treaty (New START), the United States had 1585 strategic nuclear warheads deployed in 778 ICBMs, SLBMs, and strategic bombers, while Russia had approximately 1512 nuclear warheads in 498 ICBMs, SLBMs, and strategic bombers. The numbers of the Federation of American Scientists are higher (Table 5.1).[45]

---

[39]Leonam dos Santos Guimarães, (Planning, Management and Environment Director—Eletrobrás Termonuclear SA—Eletronuclear). "O Retorno de Giges à Caverna Nuclear." DefesaNet, July 10, 2015. Available at <http://www.defesanet.com.br/nuclear/noticia/19703/O-Retorno-de-Giges-a-Caverna-Nuclear/>.

[40]Sun Tzu and Sun Pin, 1996, p. 39, e 70.

[41]Ibidem.

[42]Steven Starr, "The Lethality of Nuclear Weapons: Nuclear War has No Winner." Global Research—Centre for Research on Globalization, June 5, 2014. Available at <http://www.globalresearch.ca/the-lethality-of-nuclear-weapons-nuclear-war-has-no-winner/5385611>. See also: <http://www.paulcraigroberts.org/2014/05/30/lethality-nuclear-weapons/>. paulcraigroberts.org>. Accessed on May 30, 2014.

[43]Siegfried S. Hecker, "For U.S. and Russia, Isolation Can Lead to Nuclear Catastrophe." The New York Times, Tuesday, November 18, 2014.

[44]Ibidem.

[45]Status of World Nuclear Forces 2014—Federation of American Scientists. Available at <http://fas.org/issues/nuclear-weapons/status-world-nuclear-forces/>; all numbers are estimates, updated on April 30, 2014, and published in the Bulletin of the Atomic Scientists and the nuclear appendix in the SIPRI Yearbook. The numbers are higher than those compiled for the New START Treaty, signed by Russia and the United States on April 2010, since they include the warheads in bombers.

Table 5.1 Status of the world nuclear forces—2014

Country	Deployed strategic	Deployed nonstrategic	Reserve/ nondeployed	Military stockpile	Total inventory
Russia	1800	0	2.500c	4300	8000
United States	1920	184	2661	4765	7315

Status of World Nuclear Forces 2014—Federation of American Scientists. Available at <http://fas.org/issues/nuclear-weapons/status-world-nuclear-forces/>

President Barack Obama signed New START with Dmitri A. Medvedev, then President of Russia (2008–2012), on April 8, 2010, and took on the moral responsibility of "achieving a nuclear-free world," of pursuing the "security of a world without nuclear weapons," as he declared in Prague to the applause of the crowd.[46] During his election campaign, he had repeated that he wanted "a nuclear-free world" and that disarmament would be a goal of US defense policy. He delivered on none of it. And under the pretext of the Ukrainian crisis and the tensions with Russia provoked by his own administration, President Obama authorized the National Nuclear Security Administration (NNSA) to expand the production of nuclear armaments in the south of Kansas, in an area of 140,000 square meters, larger than the Pentagon, to be built by Centerpoint Zimmer (CPZ) over a vast soybean field at a cost of US$673 million.[47] The goal was to revitalize and modernize the nuclear weapons—ballistic missiles, bombers, and submarines. This project, which was likely developed before 2011,[48] would cost more than US$3 trillion over the next three decades.[49]

As Henry Kissinger noted, when Nagasaki and Hiroshima were leveled in the bombings of 1945, the monopoly on nuclear weapons fueled a sense of omnipotence in many Americans, but by the late 1950s, it had become clear that each nuclear

---

[46]William J. Broad and David E. Sanger, "U.S. Ramping Up Major Renewal in Nuclear Arms." The New York Times, September 21, 2014.

[47]Lise Reuter, (Staff Writer). "NNSA completes move to new $687 M manufacturing plant." Kansas City Business Journal, July 8, 2014. Available at <http://www.bizjournals.com/kansascity/news/2014/07/08/national-nuclear-security-administration.html?page=all>; Lawrence S. Wittner, "Despite protests Kansas City gets a new nuclear power plant". LA Progressive—Alex Jones' Infowars, September 6, 2011. Available at <http://www.infowars.com/despite-protests-kansas-city-gets-a-new-nuclear-power-plant/>.

[48]Adam Weinstein, "A Privately Owned Nuclear Weapons Plant in... Kansas City? In a last-ditch court hearing, activists seek to block a new Honeywell project," Mother Jones, 29 de agosto de 2011. Available at <http://www.motherjones.com/politics/2011/08/nuclear-weapons-plant-kansas-city>.

[49]William J. Broad and David E. Sanger, "U.S. Ramping Up Major Renewal in Nuclear Arms." The New York Times, September 21, 2014.

superpower had the capacity to inflict an unthinkable level of devastation on the other, threatening civilization itself.[50]

"With the end of the Cold War, the threat of nuclear war between the existing nuclear superpowers has essentially disappeared," Kissinger wrote in one of his works—World Order—published in 2014.[51] Zbigniew Brzezinski also thought the usefulness of nuclear weapons as instruments of policy or even threats had been dramatically reduced.[52] A nuclear war between the two powers—United States and Russia—would not be a zero-sum game. There would be no winner. If the United States unleashed the first preemptive strike with strategic missiles, there would be no guarantee that it would destroy the entire Russian defense system without its immediate retaliation. And Russian submarines, with nuclear weapons, would likely be close to the territorial waters of the United States.

President Ronald Reagan (1981–1989), who had planned to build the Strategy Defense Initiative (SDI) system known as "Star Wars" during his administration, acknowledged in his memoirs that "no one could 'win' nuclear war," and even if it did not lead to the extinction of humanity, it would certainly mean the end of civilization; once the first nuclear strike had been launched, who knew where it would end?[53] The Pentagon had shown him—and it had shocked him—that at least 150 million Americans (more than half the population, in the order of 229.47 million) would die in the event of a nuclear war, even if the United States "won" it, in addition to poisoning the atmosphere with radioactivity.[54]

President Barack Obama had not learned a thing. He recycled the neocons' Project for the New American Century (PNAC), whose blueprint had been drawn up in 1992 under the supervision of Paul D. Wolfowitz, undersecretary of Dick Cheney, and then Secretary of Defense of President George HW Bush (1989–1993), asserting that it was the political and military mission of the United States after the Cold War to ensure that no superpower emerged in Western Europe, Asia, or the territories of the defunct Soviet Union,[55] in addition to preserving and extending "an

---

[50]Henry Kissinger, 1995, p. 607.

[51]Henry Kissinger, 2014, p. 336.

[52]Zbigniew Brzezinski, 1997, p. 97.

[53]Ronald Reagan, 1991, p. 550.

[54]Ibidem, p. 550.

[55]Patrick E. Tyler, (Special to The New York Times). "U.S. Strategy Plan Calls for Insuring No Rivals Develop A One-Superpower World—Pentagon's Document Outlines Ways to Thwart Challenges to Primacy of America," The New York Times, March 8, 1992. Available at <http://work.colum.edu/~amiller/wolfowitz1992.htm>.

international order friendly to our security, our prosperity, and our principles."[56] It was this doctrine that General Colin Powell, chief of the Joint Chiefs of Staff of the Armed Forces, substantiated in the military strategy to maintain US hegemony.[57]

---

[56]The original project, titled—Rebuilding America's Defenses Strategy, Forces and Resources For a New Century—A Report of The Project for the New American Century (PNAC), September 2000, was based on the following principles: "1—We need to increase defense spending significantly if we are to carry out our global responsibilities today and modernize our armed forces for the future; 2—we need to strengthen our ties to democratic allies and to challenge regimes hostile to our interests and values; 3—we need to promote the cause of political and economic freedom abroad; 4—we need to accept responsibility for America's unique role in preserving and extending an international order friendly to our security, our prosperity, and our principles."

[57]Colin L. Powell, The Military Strategy of the United States—1991–1992. Washington: US Government, Printing Office, ISBN 0–16–036125-7, 1992, p. 7. Draft Resolution—12 Cooperation for Security in the Hemisphere, Regional Contribution to Global Security—The General Assembly, recalling: Resolutions AG/RES. 1121 (XXX-091 and AG/RES. 1123 (XXI-091) for strengthening of peace and security in the hemisphere, and AG/RES. 1062 (XX090) against clandestine arms traffic.

Chapter 6
A New US Strategy to Confront China's and Russia's Growing Military Power

6.1 Russia, Iran, North Korea, and China as the Major Threats to the United States

The American National Military Strategy (2015 NMS), approved in June 2015 by President Barack Obama, singled out Russia, North Korea, Iran, and China as the nations that were strategically challenging and threatening to destabilize US national security interests in various regions, even though it stressed "none of these nations are believed to be seeking direct military conflict with the United States or our allies."[1] Meanwhile, President Barack Obama had announced a normalization of diplomatic relations with Cuba on December 17, 2014, after 54 years of rupture[2] and conflict, and reached a deal with Iran on the nuclear issue in July 2015, 1 month after that year's edition of the NMS. This deal overcame the most serious clashes, which had started 35 years earlier (1979) and were littered with economic sanctions, assassinations of Iranian nuclear scientists, cyberattacks, and threats of yet another war with unpredictable consequences in the Middle East.

But despite these historically relevant achievements, US foreign policy continued to be based, with some variations, on the general lines of neocon doctrine. Not only did President Obama try to prevent Russia's resurgence, but with the development of the strategic plan of January 2012, he also confronted China, which had become a potential adversary of the United States. He went about surrounding it with a network of naval and air bases, in addition to ports, in the South Pacific. The Pentagon assigned between US$13 million and US$19 million to about six firms, hiring think tanks, defense consultants, and academics tasked with developing

---

[1]*The National Military Strategy of the United States of America 2015* (2015 NMS). Available at <http://www.jcs.mil/Portals/36/Documents/Publications/National_Military_Strategy_2015.pdf>.

[2]President Dwight Eisenhower broke off US relations with Cuba, under the revolutionary government of Fidel Castro, in January 1960, shortly before passing the presidency of the country to John F. Kennedy.

© Springer Nature Switzerland AG 2019
L. A. Moniz Bandeira, *The World Disorder*,
https://doi.org/10.1007/978-3-030-03204-3_6

contingency plans for an eventual Air-Sea Battle with China, focusing on destroying its sophisticated radar and missile system and culminating with a broad assault of the Marine Corps on its mainland in order to maintain US aerial and maritime domination and preserve its hegemony as solitary power. Many analysts, however, believed this "blinding campaign" with conventional weapons would not be effective against China's dense defense capabilities, such as the vast expanse of its territory, potentially leading to nuclear warfare, a "nuclear Armageddon."[3] China also had a population of about 1.4 billion in 2014, equivalent to 19.3% of the world's population, while the United States' population was five times smaller, estimated at 319 million inhabitants (4.43% of the world population).

In case of any war, the demographic difference was without a doubt a potentially decisive factor in China's favor, especially in an Air-Sea Battle. And the authorization to develop contingency plans for an attack on China, as reported, couldn't be otherwise construed than as a serious symptom of acute paranoia; and, as far we know, no US president had taken such a measure. In 1951, President Harry Truman even dismissed General Douglas MacArthur, a World War II hero and commander of the UN forces in the Korean War (1950–1953), for his insistence on extending the conflict and attacking China. MacArthur had even proposed to launch a nuclear bomb, a weapon China didn't even possess. All this because of the recent victory of the revolution, which hadn't been consolidated yet, and even though MacArthur knew the country was militarily weakened.[4]

China has not only restructured but also modernized its nuclear arsenal. In 2013, the People's Liberation Army could count on Dongfeng-41 (DF-41) intercontinental missiles (ICBMs) with a range of 12,000 km (7500 miles)[5]; it was testing the Dong Feng 31A (DF-31A/CSS-10) and Dong Feng 5A (DF-5A/CSS-4) systems, which could strike the mainland of the United States; and it was constructing submarines capable of firing missiles with multiple and independent targets (MIRVs).[6]

According to the Annual Report to Congress on the Military and Security Developments of the People's Republic of China (2013), sent to Congress by the United States Department of Defense, China's arsenal consists of a total of 50–75 intercontinental missiles (ICBMs), including silo-based, liquid-fueled DF-5 (CSS-4) ICBMs; solid-fueled, road-mobile DF-31 (CSS 10 Mod-1) and DF-31A (CSS-10 Mod 2) ICBMs; limited-range DF-4 (CSS-3) ICBMs; liquid-fueled DF-3 (CSS-2) intermediate-range ballistic missiles; and DF-21 (CSS-5) road-mobile, solid-fueled

---

[3]Greg Jaffe. "U.S. model for a future war fans tensions with China and inside Pentagon." *The Washington Post*, August 1, 2012. Available at <http://www.washingtonpost.com/world/national-security/us-model-for-a-future-war-fans-tensions-with-china-and-inside-pentagon/2012/08/01/gJQAC6F8PX_story.html>.

[4]Henry Kissinger, 1995, pp. 484–485; Harry Truman, 1956, pp. 436–450.

[5]"China confirms new generation long range missiles. China's ownership of a new intercontinental ballistic missile said to be capable of carrying multiple nuclear warheads as far as the United States is confirmed by state-run media." *AFP—The Telegraph*, August 1, 2014.

[6]Zachary Keck, "Is China Preparing MIRVed Ballistic Missiles?" *The Diplomat*, August 8, 2014. Available at <http://thediplomat.com/2014/08/is-china-preparing-mirved-ballistic-missiles>.

MRBMs.[7] According to Major General Yang Huan, former deputy commander of the Second Artillery Corps (strategic missile forces), China had developed strategic nuclear weapons because it believed the "hegemonic power" (United States) "would continue to use nuclear threats and blackmail," since the People's Republic of China had faced economic and technological blockades and threats from "hegemonism" from the day of its establishment.[8]

6.2   The Catastrophic Consequences of a Nuclear Conflict

At the start of 2006, several of the leading climatologists, from Rutgers University, the University of New Jersey, the University of California (UCLA), John Hopkins University, and the University of Colorado-Boulder, published studies on the consequences of a nuclear war, including scenarios in which only 1% of the existing and ready-to-shoot explosive power in the United States and Russia would be used.[9] One of the conclusions presented at the technical session of the annual meeting of the American Geophysical Union in San Francisco, California, was that even a small-scale regional nuclear war would produce as much death as all the battles of World War II and destroy the global climate for a decade or more, with environmental effects that could devastate everything on the face of the earth. A single thermonuclear warhead could cause severe radiation, damaging hundreds of miles beyond the area of detonation; and such weapons, employed in an all-out war, would ravage the entire planet or large parts of it, making it uninhabitable.[10]

So even if the United States could devastate all of Russia or China in a preemptive strike, the consequences, according to scientists, would be catastrophic for the environment and all of humanity by profoundly altering the global climate. An intense nuclear winter could completely eliminate the seasons and all crops, starving humans and animals, with radioactivity also spreading through the melting of

---

[7]"China"—*Nuclear Threat Initiative* (NTI). Available at <http://www.nti.org/country-profiles/china/nuclear/>.

[8]Major General Yang Huan (former deputy commander of the Second Artillery Corps—strategic missile forces). "China's Strategic Nuclear Weapons." *Institute for National Strategic Studies.* Available at <http://fas.org/nuke/guide/china/doctrine/huan.htm.China>; See also: <http://www.nti.org/country-profiles/china/nuclear/>.

[9]Steven Starr, "The Lethality of Nuclear Weapons: Nuclear War has No Winner." *Global Research—Centre for Research on Globalization*, June 5, 2014. Available at <http://www.globalresearch.ca/the-lethality-of-nuclear-weapons-nuclear-war-has-no-winner/5385611>.

[10]"Regional Nuclear War Could Devastate Global Climate". Rutgers, the State University of New Jersey. *ScienceDaily*, December 11, 2006. Available at <http://www.sciencedaily.com/releases/2006/12/061211090729.htm>; See also: <http://news.rutgers.edu/news-releases/2006/12/regional-nuclear-war-20061210#.VAx8DBaQSM8>; "Nuclear War's Impact on Global Climate". Available at <http://www.aasc.ucla.edu/cab/200706140013.html>; "Nuclear War". Available at <http://www.aasc.ucla.edu/cab/200706140015.html>.

nuclear reactors. Much of the United States and Europe would become uninhabitable, and those who survived would starve.[11]

In an interview in 1949 with Alfred Werner of Liberal Judaism, Albert Einstein (1879–1955) said: "I do not know how the Third World War will be fought, but I can tell you what they will use in the Fourth—rocks!"[12] Einstein was right. He probably knew the Soviet Union had been developing its nuclear program since 1942 under the supervision of the Russian physicist Igor V. Kurchatov (1903–1960) and that Joseph Stalin had accelerated this program after the United States bombed Hiroshima and Nagasaki, in Japan, in August 1945. Indeed, on August 29, 1949, the Soviet Union detonated its first atomic bomb. And by mid-2014, Russia and the United States had approximately 17,300 nuclear warheads, of which 4300 deployed, which could reach their targets within 45 minutes, producing the greatest disaster for humanity.[13] And despite being a veteran "cold warrior," President Ronald Reagan himself acknowledged that maintaining nuclear weapons was "totally irrational, totally inhumane, good for nothing but killing, possibly destructive of life on earth and civilization."[14]

6.3 Russia's Nuclear Might

Russian military doctrine provided for an immediate and equal response in case the enemy used tactical (TNW) and battlefield nuclear weapons. But the United States would also have a hard time fighting and winning a conventional war against Russia, even if it could count on its allies of the European Union. Since taking office in 2000, President Vladimir Putin has begun restructuring the armed forces and continued to

---

[11]Steven Starr, "Senator Corker's Path to Nuclear War," August 23, 2014. Available at <http://www.paulcraigroberts.org/2014/08/23/guest-article-steven-starr-senator-corkers-path-nuclear-war/print/>; Starr, Steven. "The Lethality of Nuclear Weapons," May 30, 2014. Available at <http://www.paulcraigroberts.org/2014/05/30/lethality-nuclear-weapons/>.

[12]"Albert Einstein—Interview with Alfred Werner," *Liberal Judaism* (April/May 1949). Available at <http://wist.info/einstein-albert/25402/>; Alfred Werner, (1911–1979), *Albert Einstein Archives* 30–1104. The Hebrew University of Jerusalem, Israel. Available at <http://alberteinstein.info/vufind1/Search/Results?lookfor=%22Albert+Einstein+Archives%2C+The+Hebrew+University+of+Jerusalem%2C+Israel%22&type=Series&filter[]=enddate%3A%221949-03-31%22&sort=enddate+asc>.

[13]"Academics and scientists on preventing war," May 15, 2014. *Scientists as Citizens*. Available at <http://scientistsascitizens.org/tag/public-health/#sthash.urQJHF51.KP101NB6.dpuf>. Directly in: <http://scientistsascitizens.org/2014/05/15/academics-and-scientists-on-preventing-war/>. Accessed on November 27, 2018.

[14]Michael Shermer, "Does deterrence prohibit the total abolishment of nuclear weapons?" *Scientific American*, Volume 310, Issue 6. June 1, 2014. Available at <http://www.scientificamerican.com/article/will-mutual-assured-destruction-continue-to-deter-nuclear-war/?print=true>.

enhance Russia's nuclear potential, and Russia's arms industry has gradually reemerged from the ruins in which President Yeltsin's harsh neoliberal program left it. To ensure Russia's security, its armed forces had to be reinvigorated and made more compact, efficient, and modern, supplied with the latest weaponry.[15] By early 2013, Russia had already modernized much of its arsenal and possessed about 4500 nuclear warheads, of which about 1800 strategic, carried by missiles or by bombers. According to the Stockholm International Peace Research Institute, by 2015 Russia already possessed approximately 7500 nuclear warheads, 1780 or which deployed in missiles, while the United States had 7300 warheads, of which 2080 remained active.[16]

While President George W. Bush unilaterally denounced the Anti-Ballistic Missile Treaty (ABM) as a relic of the past, President Putin, since taking office, had taken it upon himself to shore up Russia's strategic forces through the construction of intercontinental MIRV (multiple independently targetable reentry vehicle) R-36, R-36M, and SS-18 missiles (called Satan by NATO), capable of carrying multiple independent warheads, 10 to 15, and reaching the most diverse targets at 6200 miles. He counted on supersonic anti-ship missiles, known as P-800 Oniks (П-800 Оникс) or Yakhont (Яхонт), and he was also developing the Topol-M, RS-24 Yars, and RS-26 Rubezh ballistic missiles.[17] And faced with the American intent to expand NATO's military structure to Russia's borders, sending heavy equipment to Poland and the Baltic countries, President Putin announced that his armed forces would receive an additional 40 missiles (ICBMs) capable of penetrating even the most advanced defense systems.[18]

Russia also had strategic Tu-95MC Bear bombers, capable of carrying and firing six cruise missiles at land targets, and the fifth-generation Sukhoi PAK-FA fighter plane, known as the T-50, an aerial robot capable of performing multiple functions. In addition, its arsenal included the *super-panzer* Armata T-14, considered to be the most powerful tank in the world due to its armor, satellite navigation system, and

---

[15]*Ibidem.*

[16]"15 June 2016: Nuclear force reductions and modernizations continue; peace operations increase." *New Stockholm International Peace Research Institute 2015 (SPRI).* Yearbook out now. Available at <http://www.sipri.org/media/pressreleases/2015/yb-june-2015>; *SIPRI Yearbook 2015* (Oxford: Oxford University Press, 2015). Available at <http://www.sipri.org/research/armaments/nuclear-forces>.

[17]Military-Today—*R-36 (SS-18 Satan)*—Intercontinental ballistic missile. Available at <http://www.military-today.com/missiles/ss18_satan.htm>; Dennis Lynch, "Russian Next-Gen 100-Ton Nuclear Missile Could Be Test-Fired By 2017, Says Russian News Wire." *International Business Times,* January 29, 2015. Available at <http://www.ibtimes.com/russian-next-gen-100-ton-nuclear-missile-could-be-test-fired-2017-says-russian-news-1799970>.

[18]"Putin: 40+ ICBMs targeted for 2015 nuclear force boost." RT, June 16, 2015. Available at <http://rt.com/news/267514-putin-ballistic-missiles-army/>; "Moscow will respond to NATO approaching Russian borders 'accordingly'—Putin." RT, June 16, 2015. Available at <http://rt.com/news/267661-russia-nato-border-weapons/>; "Military cooperation with Russia important for Belarusian security—defense minister." *TASS,* June 17, 2015. Available at <http://tass.ru/en/world/801299>.

automatic cannons (and next-generation, self-propelled Koalitsiya-CB cannons), capable of reaching targets at 70 km and equipped with a satellite navigation system.

Russia's nuclear arsenal was in nothing inferior to NATO's. And the most efficient defense systems had been deployed along its territory, including the S-300PMU anti-missile system, based on which the state-owned Almaz-Antey Corporation developed two more sophisticated systems: the S-400, against short and medium-range missiles, and the S-500 Prometheus, with the 7N6-N and 77N6-N1 radars and a range of 500 to 600 km, to intercept and destroy intercontinental ballistic missiles (ICBMs), supersonic aircraft, low-orbit satellites, and cruise missiles. The Buk-M2E, an effective medium-range air defense system, could shoot down tactical and strategic airplanes, helicopters, cruise missiles, tactical ballistic missiles, and so on. Its defense system also included a radar station capable of detecting aerial targets beyond the horizon long before they hit Russia.[19] And Russia was also deploying S-500 Prometheus ground-to-air defense missiles, capable of flying 15,400 miles and stopping any air strike over its entire territory, the center, Moscow, and its vicinity.

While President Putin modernized his arsenal of intercontinental and other ballistic missiles, he also determined the reconstruction of strategic bases, including those of Wrangel Island in Chukchi, in the Arctic Ocean Sea near Alaska, and of Mys Shmidta (Cape Schmidt, so named by James Cook, who discovered it in 1778) in the village of Ryrkaypiy.[20] From there they would supply the ships of the Northern Fleet, almost all equipped with antiaircraft systems, ready for use, with missile towers and cannons on deck.[21] The Northern Fleet is based in Murmansk in northwestern Russia, and the Arctic Circle has always been of extreme strategic importance, not only because of security but also because of its vast and unexplored reserves of natural resources, including gas, oil, and rare metals.

Moscow's decision to militarize the Arctic Circle and protect it with a radar system arose from Washington's threats, which were latent in its insistence to expand NATO to the small Baltic republics (Estonia, Lithuania, and Latvia). President Vladimir Putin himself, in an interview to the journalist Hubert Seipel of the German TV channel ARD on November 17, 2014, accused NATO of already having implemented two expansion waves in Eastern Europe since 2001 to co-opt seven countries, including Slovenia, Slovakia, Bulgaria, Romania, and three Baltic states—Estonia, Lithuania, and Latvia, allowed entry in 2004, representing significant changes in the geopolitical game.[22] President Putin also added that the number

---

[19]"Moscow will respond to NATO approaching Russian borders 'accordingly'—Putin." *RT*, June 16, 2015. Available at <http://rt.com/news/267661-russia-nato-border-weapons/>.

[20]Matthew Bodner and Alexey Eremenko, "Russia Starts Building Military Bases in the Arctic." *The Moscow Times*, September 8, 2014. Available at <http://www.themoscowtimes.com/business/article/russia-starts-building-military-bases-in-the-arctic/506650.html>.

[21]"Frigid fighting: Russian Arctic war games top off new base voyage." *RT*, September 29, 2014. Available at <http://rt.com/news/191536-arctic-mission-drills-missile/>.

[22]"Interview to German TV channel ARD." Vladivostok, November 17, 2014. *President of Russia*. Available at <http://eng.kremlin.ru/news/23253>.

of American military bases didn't stop growing. "Does Russia have military bases around the world?" He asked, noting that NATO and the United States, on the other hand, had scattered them all over the globe, including in regions close to Russia's borders, and the number was growing.[23] In these circumstances, Russia decided to establish an air base for the Sukhoi Su-27 aircraft and missiles in the province of Babruysk, in eastern Belarus, near the city of Lida and the border[24] with Poland and Lithuania in Europe.[25] Belarus, whose President Alexander Lukashenko also recognized the threat of NATO's advance, would also receive Mi-8/Mi-17 and Mil Mi-8 (Ми-8МТВ-5; Hip) helicopters and was negotiating the purchase of Russia's most advanced air defense system, the S-400, capable of destroying targets at 400 km with more than 72 missiles at once.[26]

Russia's military facilities abroad were located only in neighboring Armenia, Tajikistan, and Kyrgyzstan, and it sought to expand the Novorossiysk naval base in the Crimea to station eight K-535 Yuriy Dolgorukiy-Borei-class nuclear submarines, capable of carrying 12 cruise missiles with a range of more than 1500 km. This decision was taken due to the frequent excursion of NATO ships in the Black Sea and because it was a crucial point for the shipment of arms to Syria. Russia also had seven nuclear submarines (project 667BRDM Dolphin Delta-4), of which the Tula, Novomoskovsk, and SSBN Yekaterinburg were propelled with liquid ballistic fuel and equipped with RSM-54 Sineva intercontinental missiles. Moscow didn't plan to abandon the Intermediate-Range Nuclear Forces (INF) Treaty unless it had to face "serious threats" to the country's security, as Sergey Ivanov, President Vladimir Putin's Chief of Staff, declared.[27] In January 2014, however, the estimate was that Russia's strategic missile forces held 311 missile systems of five different types on standby, including intercontinental ballistic missiles, capable of carrying 1078 nuclear warheads.[28] And it possessed X-55 long-range missiles capable of carrying a 200 kilogram nuclear or conventional warhead to a target located at a distance of 3000 km, as well as strategic missiles, which could strike at a distance of 5000 km (3100 miles), launched from submarines or from Tupolev Tu-95, Tupolev Tu-160,

---

[23] *Ibidem.*

[24] "Russian Su-27 Airbase to Be Set Up in Belarus in 2016: Air Force Chief." *Sputnik*, October 15, 2014. Available at <http://sputniknews.com/military/20141015/194098896.html>.

[25] "Russia to Open Military Base in Belarus." *The Moscow Times*, Wednesday, June 26, 2013. Available at <http://www.themoscowtimes.com/news/article/russia-to-open-military-base-in-belarus/482355.html>.

[26] "Factbox: Russia's S-400 Air-Defense Missile System." *The Moscow Times*, Wednesday, November 26, 2014. Available at <http://www.themoscowtimes.com/business/article/factbox-russia-s-s-400-air-defense-missile-system/511884.html>; KECK, Zachary. "The Buzz—Russia's Massive Military Buildup Abroad: Should NATO Worry?" *The National Interest*, June 17, 2015. Available at <http://www.nationalinterest.org/blog/the-buzz/russias-massive-military-buildup-abroad-should-nato-worry-13132>.

[27] "Russia won't quit nuclear forces treaty unless it faces 'serious threat'—Kremlin." *RT*, September 23, 2014. Available at <http://rt.com/politics/189904-russia-inf-treaty-ivanov/>.

[28] "Strategic missile forces"—*Ministry of Defense of the Russian Federation—strategic missile forces*. Available at <http://eng.mil.ru/en/structure/forces/strategic_rocket.htm>.

and the strategic Tupolev-95MS bombers. These are high-precision ballistic missiles capable of hitting ground targets with rapid subsonic speeds.

For several years, the Strategic Rocket Forces (Raketnyye Voyska Strategicheskogo Naznacheniya-RVSN) had been testing various missiles, such as the R-36M, at Baikonur Cosmodrome, Russia's space launch base in the desert steppes of Kazakhstan, as well as the nuclear submarine.[29] And Russia also accelerated the construction of an adequate aerospace defense and missile intercept systems in space, such as the S-500, at an altitude of 200 km above the Earth's surface and at speeds of 8 km per second. These systems were similar to those of the US Conventional Prompt Global Strike (CPGS) doctrine, capable of striking within the hour anywhere in the world with conventional weapons, just as the nuclear ICBMs. The installation of MK 41 Vertical Missile Launch Systems (VLS) in Romania and Poland constituted a breach by the United States of the Intermediate-Range Nuclear Forces (INF) treaty. And soon after the Verkhovna Rada (Parliament) in Kiev approved the abolition of Ukraine's policy of political and military neutrality as non-aligned state,[30] President Putin sanctioned a new Russian military doctrine, now considering NATO's expansion the gravest threat to its security. And while he confirmed the dissuasive character of its nuclear power, i.e., deterring a potential enemy, he admitted to be willing to use it in case of any attack on its territory, even if carried out by conventional forces that actually threatened its existence.[31] This was a harsh warning to the United States and the government in Kiev.

Russia had also developed an electronic warfare system. And on April 12, 2014, it demonstrated this system 2 days after the destroyer USS Donald Cook entered the Black Sea in international waters, but near its border, equipped with Tomahawk cruise missiles with a range of 2500 km and, among others, the Aegis Combat System, an integrated naval weapon system with computer and radar technology that marks the trajectory and guides missiles against enemy targets. She was accompanied by another destroyer, the USS Arleigh Burke (DDG-51). It was meant as a show of strength by the United States/NATO. But a Sukhoi-24 (Su-24) fighter-bomber of the Russian Air Force, carrying no weapons, missiles, or bombs, simulated an attack by flying near the USS Donald Cook and activating the Jibiny (L-265) electronic system,[32] blocking all its radars, control and transmission devices, and entire air

---

[29]*Ibidem.*

[30]"No. 1014–3—On Amendments to Certain Laws of Ukraine Concerning Ukraine's Abolishment of the Policy of Neutrality. Verkhovna Rada abolished Ukraine's neutral status Denys Kolesnyk." *Info-News*, December 23, 2014. Available at <http://info-news.eu/verkhovna-rada-abolished-ukraines-neutral-status/#sthash.O9KFKoxv.i4tIzVYC.dpuf>.

[31]"Russia's new military doctrine lists NATO, US as major foreign threats." *RT*, December 26, 2014. Available at <http://rt.com/news/217823-putin-russian-military-doctrine/>.

[32]Russia has 5th-generation T-50 fighter jets, equipped with the most advanced electronic warfare system, Himalayas. Russian Military Forum—Russian Armed Forces-Russian Air Force. Available at <http://www.russiadefence.net/t2803p615-pak-fa-t-50-news>; "El PAK-FA tendrá un sistema que dejará indefenso cualquier objetivo." *RT*, April 25, 2014. Available at <http://actualidad.rt.com/actualidad/view/126348-pak-fa-sistema-guerra-radioelectronica-guimalai?print=1>.

defense system, the Aegis Combat System. Nothing worked on the mighty USS Donald Cook.[33] The sailors were stunned and felt demoralized. The Su-24 flew over the destroyer 12 times in "numerous close-range low-altitude passes" at 500 feet (150 m) above sea level, according to Army Col. Steve Warren, a spokesman of the Pentagon, who issued a protest.[34] "This provocative and unprofessional Russian action is inconsistent with international protocols and previous agreements on the professional interaction between our militaries," said Colonel Steve Warren.[35] The truth of the matter was that the USS Donald Cook promptly left the Black Sea toward Constanta, Romania, where she docked and was visited by President Traian Basescu.[36]

6.4   NATO's Expansion to Russia's Borders

When President Harry Truman (1945–1953) was pressed in 1947, at the start of the cold war, to roll back the Red Army inside the Soviet Union, which then occupied Eastern European countries, he considered that peace would not be achieved with the outbreak of new wars and that there were two immense land masses that no modern army in the West had ever been able to conquer: Russia and China.[37] "It would have

---

[33]"The PAK-FA will have a system that will leave any target helpless. Why so much importance is given to this event?" *Royal Moroccan Armed Forces: Armement et matériel militaire*, March 14, 2014. Available at <http://far-maroc.forumpro.fr/t1685p345-pak-fa>; "El PAK-FA tendrá un sistema que dejará indefenso cualquier objetivo." *RT*, April 25, 2014. Available at <http://actualidad.rt.com/actualidad/view/126348-pak-fa-sistema-guerra-radioelectronica-guimalai?print=1>.

[34]Maggie Ybarra, "Russian fighter jet buzzes U.S. Navy destroyer in Black Sea amid Ukraine crisis." *The Washington Times*, April 14, 2014. Available at <http://www.washingtontimes.com/news/2014/apr/14/russian-fighter-jet-buzzes-us-navy-destroyer-black/>.

[35]Jim Garamone, "Russian Aircraft Flies Near U.S. Navy Ship in Black Sea." *American Forces Press Service—US Department of Defense*, Washington, April 14, 2014. Available at <http://www.defense.gov/news/newsarticle.aspx?id=122052>; Lolita C. Baldor, (Associated Press). "Russian jet passes near US warship." *Boston Globe*, April 14, 2014. Available at <http://www.bostonglobe.com/news/world/2014/04/14/russian-jet-passes-near-warship/FK75kdLyhVJfOpC5eWdFRL/story.html>; "Russian fighter jet ignored warnings and 'provocatively' passed U.S. Navy destroyer in Black Sea for 90 minutes, getting as close as 1000 yards." *Daily Mail Online*, April 15, 2014. Available at <http://www.dailymail.co.uk/news/article-2604590/Russian-fighter-jet-ignored-warnings-provocatively-passed-U-S-Navy-destroyer-Black-Sea-90-minutes-getting-close-1-000-yards.html>.

[36]"USS Donald Cook Leaves Black Sea." *Naval Today*, April 25, 2014. Available at <http://navaltoday.com/2014/04/25/uss-donald-cook-leaves-black-sea/>; "Romanian President Traian Basescu (R) speaks with Cmdr. Scott Jones (L) and Cmdr. Charles Hampton during his visit to the ship on April 14 in Constanta, Romania. Stratfor," *Global Intelligence*, May 8, 2014. Available at <http://www.stratfor.com/image/romanian-president-traian-basescu-r-speaks-cmdr-scott-jones-l-and-cmdr-charles-hampton-during>.

[37]Harry Truman, 1956, p. 91.

been folly, and would be folly today, to attempt to impose our way of life on these huge areas by force."[38] Russia, whose territory stretched over all of northern Eurasia, i.e., 1/6 of the planet, had already demonstrated this twice: in 1812, during the reign of Tsar Alexander I (1777–1825), when Marshal Mikhail Kutuzov (1745–1813) destroyed the Grand Armée of emperor Napoleon Bonaparte, made up of about 564,000 soldiers[39], and in the twentieth century, when the Nazi troops of the Third Reich, with German, Italian, Romanian, Croatian, and other soldiers—over 1.5 million troops—were crushed by the Red Army in Stalingrad, the bloodiest battle of World War II, fought between August 23, 1942, and February 2, 1943. It was the turning point of World War II. There began the defeat of Nazi Germany, more than a year before the invasion of Normandy by the United States, Great Britain, and France on June 6, 1944. And by destroying the Wehrmacht, the Red Army advanced to Berlin and proved to be the most powerful war machine in Europe.

According to the Military Balance 2014 from Sweden's International Institute for Strategic Studies, in 2013 Russia had a powerful army and a stockpile with the most advanced armaments, with enormous firepower, capable of causing significant casualties to American forces, in addition to 171 warships, 25 of which in the Black Sea, off the coast of Ukraine.[40] The attempt to revitalize the NATO Response Force (NRF) with high-visibility exercises as part of the deployment of the Connected Forces Initiative Task Force (CFI TF), promoted by the Supreme Allied Commander Transformation (SACT), never intimidated Moscow. Since the Korean War (1953–1954), however, Washington had continued to increase its defense spending, as Henry Kissinger noted, transforming the Atlantic Alliance—established as a political coalition—into an integrated military organization under the Supreme Command of the Pentagon.[41] Its eastward expansion, designed in detail from the top-down by the Clinton administration, with the strong support of his National Security Adviser, Anthony Lake, and Secretary of State Warren Christopher, sought to occupy the vacuum left by the disappearance of the Soviet Union and deepen the hegemony of the United States in Europe, as the historian Perry Anderson emphasized.[42]

---

[38] *Ibidem.*

[39] Werner Scheck, 1980, p. lag, 2. Auflage, p. 287.

[40] Military Balance 2014—*The International Institute for Strategic Studies (IISS)*. Available at <https://www.iiss.org/en/publications/military%20balance/issues/the-military-balance-2014-7e2c>.

[41] Henry Kissinger, 1995, p. 491.

[42] Perry Anderson, "American Foreign Policy and its Thinkers." London: *New Left Review*, 83 September/October 2013, p. 152.

6.5   The Warning of George Kennan and Others Against the Expansion

In 1995, when the White House pressed Congress to accelerate NATO's expansion project to the countries of Central and Eastern Europe, i.e., to the borders of Russia, Theodore C. Sorensen, a former aide and friend of President John F. Kennedy (1961–1963), published an assertive article against President Bill Clinton's foreign policy in *The Washington Post*, noting that it was "hard to imagine a more provocative decision taken with less consultation and consideration for the consequences."[43] This initiative to allow Eastern European countries into NATO violated the commitments made by President George HW Bush to President Mikhail S. Gorbachev during the reunification of Germany. And on February 2, 1997, Ambassador George F. Kennan, the architect of the containment strategy of the Soviet Union, wisely warned that "expanding NATO would be the most fateful error of American policy in the entire post-cold-war era."[44] Such a decision could be expected to inflame nationalist, anti-Western, and militaristic tendencies in Russian public opinion, he added, with an adverse effect on the development of democracy in Russia, risking to restore the Cold War atmosphere in East-West relations and decisively pushing its foreign policy in the opposite direction of what the United States would like.[45]

On June 26, 1996, more than 40 public figures in the United States, from both sides of the aisle, senators, ambassadors, professors, military officers, and others, including Robert McNamara, former Secretary of Defense in the Kennedy and Johnson administrations, published an open letter to President Bill Clinton warning him, along the same lines as Ambassador George F. Kennan, that the effort to expand NATO discussed at the Helsinki and Paris summits was "a policy error of historic proportions."[46] The signatories of the letter predicted NATO's expansion would reduce the security of the allies and disrupt European stability for a number of reasons, such as drawing a "new line of division between the 'ins' and the 'outs',"[47] and they concluded:

---

[43]Theodore C. Sorensen, "The star spangled shrug." *The Washington Post*, July 2, 1995.

[44]George F. Kennan, "'A Fateful Error.' *The New York Times*, February 5 1997" in: *Wargaming italia*. Available at <http://www.netwargamingitalia.net/forum/resources/george-f-kennan-a-fateful-error.35/>; Thomas L. Friedman "Foreign Affairs: Now a Word From X." *The New York Times*, May 2, 1998. Available at <http://www.nytimes.com/1998/05/02/opinion/foreign-affairs-now-a-word-from-x.html>; Carl Conetta, "America's New Deal With Europe: NATO Primacy and Double Expansion, Project on Defense Alternatives Commentary." *Cambridge, MA: Commonwealth Institute*, October 1997. Available at <http://www.comw.org/pda/eurcom.htm>.

[45]George F. Kennan, "A Fateful Error." *The New York Times*, February 5, 1997. *Wargaming italia*. Available at <http://www.netwargamingitalia.net/forum/resources/george-f-kennan-a-fateful-error.35/>. Accessed on November 27, 2018.

[46]"Former Policy-Makers Voice Concern over NATO Expansion." *Open Letter to President Clinton*, June 26, 1997. Available at <http://www.bu.edu/globalbeat/nato/postpone062697>.

[47]*Ibidem.*

Russia does not now pose a threat to its western neighbors and the nations of Central and Eastern Europe are not in danger. For this reason, and the others cited above, we believe that NATO expansion is neither necessary nor desirable and that this ill-conceived policy can and should be put on hold.[48]

The signatories included Senators Sam Nunn, Gary Hart, Bennett Johnston, Mark Hatfield, and Gordon Humphrey; three former US ambassadors in Moscow, Jack F. Matlock Jr., Arthur Hart, and Arthur Hartman; the ambassadors George Bunn, Paul Nitze, Raymond Garthoff, David Fischer, Jonathan Dean, Herbert S. Okun, and Susan Eisenhower, President of the Center for Political and Strategic Studies, and others. A few days later, however, in July 1997, NATO leaders formally sent the invitation to Poland, Hungary, and the Czech Republic to become NATO members. As President Clinton himself said in Detroit, he took office "[...] convinced that NATO can do for Europe's East what it did for Europe's West: prevent a return to local rivalries, strengthen democracy against future threats, and create the conditions for prosperity to flourish."[49]

There have always been many bright men in the United States, regardless of the political attitudes and positions they eventually took, and many warned President Bill Clinton of the consequences a NATO expansion sooner or later would produce. In any case, despite the clairvoyance of Ambassador George Kennan and so many others from the American political and diplomatic elite, President Clinton persisted in his irresponsible and adventurous plan to push the NATO expansion process; and in 1998 the Senate ratified it by 80 votes against 19. And so, at the age of 94 and with a frail voice,[50] Ambassador George F. Kennan told *New York Times* columnist Thomas L. Friedman in a phone interview that:

I think it is the beginning of a new cold war. I think the Russians will gradually react quite adversely and it will affect their policies. I think it is a tragic mistake. There was no reason for this whatsoever. No one was threatening anybody else. This expansion would make the Founding Fathers of this country turn over in their grave.

Several other leading personalities also warned that NATO's expansion, planned by the Clinton administration and ratified by the Senate, would be imprudent and mean "perpetuating the cold war" and that "the best hope for long-term peace and stability in Europe requires including Russia politically, economically and militarily

---

[48] *Ibidem.*

[49] "In His Own"—Bill Clinton—Speaking yesterday in Detroit. *The New York Times*, October 23, 1996. Available at <http://www.nytimes.com/1996/10/23/us/in-his-own-words-939471. html>; "Top Ten Questions on NATO." *Sheet released by the NATO Enlargement Ratification Office—U.S. Department of State—Archive*, February 1998. Available at <http://1997-2001.state. gov/www/regions/eur/fs_980219_natoqanda.html>.

[50]Thomas L. Friedman, "Foreign Affairs; Now a Word from X." *The New York Times*, May 2, 1998. Available at <http://www.nytimes.com/1998/05/02/opinion/foreign-affairs-now-a-word-from-x.html?pagewanted=print>.

within the European community."[51] But the interests of the industrial-military complex and the chain of corruption (profits and commissions) that always sustained and still sustains it, in addition to the financial system, ended up prevailing in Capitol Hill and the White House. NATO was in fact becoming an economic and political instrument to align and subordinate the countries of Europe to the interests of Washington and its major banks (Chase Manhattan Bank, JP Morgan, Morgan Stanley, National City Bank of New York, Bank of America, Wells Fargo). It was a way to expand the market for the war industry and increase bank financing, selling weapons to the new members of the Atlantic Alliance while securing the economic and geopolitical interests of the United States outside the original scope of the 1949 treaty. From the start, the strategy of the military-industrial complex had been to capitalize on or even provoke conflicts to turn NATO seemingly indispensable and justify the bloated military budgets of the United States and its vassals. This is why President Bill Clinton decided, unilaterally and without an explicit mandate of the UN Security Council, to lead NATO's intervention in the Kosovo War (February 28, 1998, June 11, 1999) in favor of the so-called (Muslim) Kosovo Liberation Army, bombing the Republic of Yugoslavia (Montenegro and Serbia) governed by Slobodan Milošević (1986–1990) and creating a precedent for the declaration of war on the pretext of humanitarian reasons.

But hypocrisy—Hannah Arendt wrote—is the vice through which corruption manifests itself.[52] Hidden behind the decision to defend the human rights of the Albanian Islamists against Serbia were, among others, the economic interests of the billionaire George Soros, Eliot Engel, Frank Wisner, and the American-Albanian Sahit Muja, owner of the Bytyci Company and its partner in arms trafficking and money laundering, with businesses worth around US$1 trillion. They wanted the separation of Kosovo and, eventually, the occupation of all of Yugoslavia, so they could seize its immense natural wealth.[53] Kosovo alone harbored the most abundant and richest natural resources.

The Trepča Mines complex, to the north of the city of Mitrovice in Kosovo, had reserves of 425,000 tonnes in lead, 415,000 tonnes in zinc, 800 tonnes in silver, 185,000 tonnes in nickel, and 6500 tonnes in cobalt, in addition to huge reserves of gold, cadmium, and other minerals. The Grebnik mine, south of Galina, had proven reserves of 1.7 million tonnes of bauxite, while the ferronickel reserves in Metohija were estimated at 15 million tonnes, but could be even higher. And the lignite reserves, high-carbon coal, in the Kosovo and Metohija region were valued at more than US$300 billion, in addition to the iron, zinc, copper, silver, bauxite, magnesium, and other reserves, which were soon controlled by NATO troops, along

---

[51]Eugene J. Carroll Jr., *Deputy Director Center for Defense Information*. Washington, 1° de maio de 1998, To the Editor; "On NATO, How Will Russia React? Kennan's Warning." *The New York Times*, May 4, 1998.

[52]Hannah Arendt, 1993, p. 104.

[53]Milla Johanevich, "Serbia: Clinton, billionaire Muja and Soros to get $1 trillion dollars deal in Kosovo." *Digital Journal*, December 5, 2011. Available at <http://digitaljournal.com/blog/14219>.

with the Trepča mine. All these reserves represented more than US$1 trillion and were privatized.

The United States and its partners in the European Union planned to seize the wealth of 15% of Serbia's territory.[54] And the US-NATO bombardments killed more than 6000 people, compared to only 2000 during the civil war 1 year before the foreign humanitarian intervention.[55] The NATO-led Operation Allied Force lasted 78 days, from March 24 to June 10, 1999, and the aircraft from the United States and other NATO members fired 2300 missiles against 990 targets and 14,000 bombs, including depleted uranium and cluster munitions, killing more than 2000 civilians, including 88 children, and injuring thousands of others. The war displaced more than 200,000 ethnic Serbs, who had to leave their homes in Kosovo, and destroyed 300 community services buildings, including schools, libraries, hospitals, and 90 historic monuments.

At the end of the war in 2008, Kosovo was separated from Serbia, occupied by the Kosovo Force (KFOR) and placed under the management of the United Nations Interim Administration Mission in Kosovo (UNMIK). Its territory of 10,908 km^2 and with about 2.2 million inhabitants was divided into sectors under the control of NATO powers; and Trepča, under France's jurisdiction, was privatized. As a NATO protectorate, Kosovo then proclaimed its independence on February 17, 2008. The United States, Germany, France, and other European nations promptly recognized the new republic, but Russia vehemently objected and didn't recognize the country, just as China, Brazil, Spain, and other countries. The ultra-imperialist conglomerate (the United States and other NATO partners) had started the project to redraw the post-World War II borders in Europe and around the world. Yugoslavia was split in four. And as the Hungarian-American geopolitical scholar George Friedman noted, with the independence of Kosovo, the United States, Great Britain, France, and Germany crossed a river and put themselves in a position to challenge a space Russia had defined as crucial to its national interests.[56]

---

[54]"NATO countries are trying to take away 15% of the Serbian territory. Why?!" *Live Leak.* Available at <http://www.liveleak.com/view?i=861_1365352907>.

[55]Cliff Kincaid, "Clinton's Kosovo Whopper." *Free Republic*, September 28, 2006. Available at <http://www.freerepublic.com/focus/f-news/1709979/posts>.

[56]George Friedman, "Kosovar Independence and the Russian Reaction." *Stratfor—Geopolitical Weekly*, February 20, 2008. Available at <http://www.stratfor.com/weekly/kosovar_indepen dence_and_russian_reaction#axzz3DOb-NowiM>.

6.6   George HW Bush's Broken Promise to Mikhail S. Gorbachev During Germany's Reunification

Russia had long-standing ties with Serbia. In 1998, however, when it was led by President Boris Yeltsin, Russia was still weak and degraded, and the United States—as former Secretary of Defense and CIA director Robert Gates acknowledged—greatly underestimated the magnitude of the humiliation it had suffered with the debacle of the Soviet regime and the dissolution of the Socialist bloc.[57] The arrogance and hubris of the American authorities, academics, businessmen, and politicians, telling the Russians how to conduct their domestic and international affairs, Robert Gates remarked, provoked a deep and bitter resentment against the United States. But Washington continued to harass Russia, betraying its promise that NATO would not expand toward its borders, a key condition for Moscow to agree to the reunification of Germany and its permanence within the Atlantic Alliance. This commitment had been formally made by George HW Bush's Secretary of State, James A. Baker, in a private meeting with Mikhail S. Gorbachev, Secretary General of the Communist Party and leader of the Soviet Union, on February 8, 1990.[58] "There would be no extension of NATO's current jurisdiction eastward," the Secretary of State assured explicitly. And Mikhail S. Gorbachev stressed: "Any extension of the NATO zone is unacceptable." James A. Baker then reaffirmed: "I agree."[59]

Two days later, on February 10, the West German Foreign Minister Hans-Dietrich Genscher explicitly assured his colleague Eduard Shevardnadze of the Soviet Union: "NATO will not expand to the east."[60] This commitment was confirmed by declassified documents published by the magazine *Der Spiegel* in 2010, as well as by Hans-Dietrich Genscher himself and Jack Matlock, then US ambassador in Moscow, confirming that there was a "clear commitment" to Moscow that NATO would not extend its jurisdiction to the borders of Russia if Germany remained a member of the Alliance after reunification.[61] Eight years later, however, in March 1999, NATO incorporated three more countries of the former Socialist

---

[57]Robert Gates, 2014, pp. 156–157.

[58]Michael R. Gordon, "Anatomy of a Misunderstanding." *The New York Times*, May 25, 1997.

[59]*Ibidem.*

[60]Klaus Wiegrefe, "Germany's Unlikely Diplomatic Triumph an Inside Look at the Reunification Negotiations." *Spiegel Online*, September 29, 2010. Available at <http://ml.spiegel.de/article.do?id=719848&p=6>; Uwe Klußmann & Matthias Schepp Schepp & Klaus Wiegrefe, "NATO's Eastward Expansion—Did the West Break Its Promise to Moscow?" *Spiegel Online*, November 26, 2009. Available at <http://www.spiegel.de/international/world/nato-s-eastward-expansion-did-the-west-break-its-promise-to-moscow-a-663315-2.html>.

[61]*Ibidem.*

Block—Poland, Hungary, and the Czech Republic—expressly violating the commitments made by the governments of the United States and Germany.[62] And Mikhail S. Gorbachev, who had been extremely naive and deceived, later commented that "no one could trust American politicians."[63]

---

[62]Jane Perlez, "Expanding Alliance: THE OVERVIEW; Poland, Hungary and the Czechs Join NATO." *The New York Times*, March 13, 1999.

[63]Klaus Wiegrefe, "Germany's Unlikely Diplomatic Triumph An Inside Look at the Reunification Negotiations." *Spiegel Online*, September 29, 2010. Available at <http://ml.spiegel.de/article.do?id=719848&p=6>; Uwe Klußmann & Matthias Schepp &, Klaus Wiegrefe "NATO's Eastward Expansion—Did the West Break Its Promise to Moscow?" *Spiegel Online*, November 26, 2009. Available at <http://www.spiegel.de/iMargaretanternational/world/nato-s-eastward-expansion-did-the-west-break-its-promise-to-moscow-a-663315-2.html>.

Chapter 7
From Soviet Union to Russian Oligarchic Power System and to Putin

7.1 NATO's Different Purposes, the Soviet Union's Collapse, and the United States as Global Cop

NATO's different purposes—"to keep the Americans in, the Russians out and the Germans down,"[1] as defined by general Hastings Lionel Ismay, 1st Lord Ismay (1887–1965)—never went away, despite the disintegration of the Soviet Union in 1991. Soon after starting the Gulf War (August 2, 1990–February 28, 1991), President George H. W. Bush announced in a speech before a joint session of Congress on September 11, 1990, that "a new world order can emerge [...] freer from the threat of terror, stronger in the pursuit of justice, and more secure in the quest for peace." "An era in which the nations of the world, East and West, North and South, can prosper and live in harmony."[2] This new world aborted. What actually emerged was "quite different from the one we've known," but not the world predicted by President George H. W. Bush. It was worse, "thrown in an asymmetrical global conflict, pulverized in a constellation of conflicts" in which drones and cyberwarfare constituted both new weapons and "new forms of state terrorism," as the Portuguese political scientist António de Sousa Lara correctly pointed out.[3]

The United States took on the role of global cop and, one way or another, President Bill Clinton let his foreign policy be guided by the doctrine of the neocons Paul D. Wolfowitz and Dick Cheney. He underestimated Russia's political and security interests, and not only did he go about stealthily besieging it, co-opting the former countries of the Soviet bloc to NATO, but also curtailing its resurgence as a superpower with its own geopolitical and security interests. This is why, as Robert

---

[1]Michael Lind, 2006, p. 134.

[2]"George Bush, Address Before a Joint Session of Congress (September 11, 1990)." *Miller Center—University of Virginia*. Available at <http://millercenter.org/president/bush/speeches/speech-3425>.

[3]António Sousa Lara, 2014, pp. 18 and 25.

© Springer Nature Switzerland AG 2019
L. A. Moniz Bandeira, *The World Disorder*,
https://doi.org/10.1007/978-3-030-03204-3_7

Gates admitted, American relations with Russia were very poorly managed after 1993 when George H. W. Bush the elder left the Presidency, intentionally and/or not. While President Bill Clinton was busy extending NATO's jurisdiction to its entire vicinity, Russia, governed by President Boris Yeltsin (1991–1999), got mired in a serious crisis—a crisis, that occurred in the midst of the economic and political turmoil resulting from the neoliberal policies dictated by Washington, and from the decentralization of power, which the Communist Party had monopolized since the foundation of the Soviet Union in 1922.

7.2   Boris Yeltsin's Russia: Privatization, Corruption, and International Buccaneer Capitalism

Boris Yeltsin, General Secretary of the Communist Party, visited the United States in 1989 and was dazzled by the abundance and variety of products in the supermarkets of Houston. And so, Lilia Shevtsova of the Carnegie Endowment for International Peace remarked, "he became a reformer"[4] and was co-opted by Washington. This is why after rising to power, inebriated with Jack Daniel's, which he drank extensively in the United States, he decided to implement neoliberal economic and political reforms in Russia, moving the country toward capitalism, while Mikhail S. Gorbachev, who hated him as political adversary and individual, planned to undertake a reform according to socialist terms.[5] But Boris Yeltsin helped break the Communist Party. He instituted the free market and promoted the rapid privatization of industry, creating a kind of *international buccaneer capitalism*, with the oligarchs emerging from the bureaucracy of the Soviet state and Communist Party seizing the state enterprises auctioned at sell-off rhythm and discount prices.[6] On top of that, he broke up the Soviet Union, which extended 22.4 million km^2 from the Dnieper, one of the largest rivers in Europe (2145 km), and the Ural Mountains to the Pacific, through Central Asia, causing Russia to lose 5 million km^2.

President Boris Yeltsin played an instrumental role in the disintegration of the Soviet Union by allowing its former republics to become independent states.[7] And to sustain its weak government, the United States had given more than US$20 billion to Russia since 1992, directly or through such multilateral institutions as the IMF and

---

[4]"Back in the USSR—How could the Kremlin keep them down, after they'd seen our farms?" *Boston College—Winter Magazine* 2004. Available at: <http://bcm.bc.edu/issues/winter_2004/ll_ussr.html>. Access on September 21, 2014.

[5]Michael Lind, 1999, p. 511.

[6]Margareta Mommsen, 2003, pp. 56–57, 63–70 *passim*; Darrel M. West, 2014, pp. 7, 103–104.

[7]Marilyn Berger, "Boris N. Yeltsin, Reformer Who Broke Up the U.S.S.R., Dies at 76." *The New York Times*, April 24, 2007.

the World Bank.[8] And a report of the US House of Representatives issued in 2002 and entitled *Russia's Road To Corruption—How the Clinton Administration Exported Government Instead of Free Enterprise and Failed the Russian People* pointed out that since 1993, the year Bill Clinton inaugurated his administration, the United States-Russia policy had been managed by Vice-President Al Gore through telephone calls with President Boris Yeltsin, whose erratic and grotesque policies quickly wore down his government through the implementation of the neoliberal principles of the Washington Consensus, which consisted of the liberalization of the economy, monetary stabilization, and the privatization of state enterprises. This program was guided by the American economists Jeffrey Sachs and Andrei Schleite, of Harvard University, as well as by the lawyer Jonathan Hay, who advised the Deputy Prime Minister and Finance Minister Anatoli Borissowitsch (Tschubais) and secretly served the CIA, as President Putin later accused in a TV show. The economic measures adopted at that time weakened Russia even further, almost transforming it into an underdeveloped and peripheral country, as happened with the other republics of the defunct Soviet Union, which were now part of its successor, the Commonwealth of Independent States (CIS), and whose capital emigrated to Western Europe.

7.3   The Emergence of the Oligarchs as New Bourgeoisie

In March 1996, President Yeltsin was so enfeebled and unpopular that President Clinton had to induce the IMF to approve a bulky loan to Russia, in the amount of US$10.2 billion, to demonstrate the West's political support to his candidacy against Gennadii Zyuganov, the candidate of the Communist Party, and the ultranationalist Vladimir Zhirinovsky, of the Liberal Party.[9] Boris Yeltsin's election campaign in 1996 was financed and organized by Boris Berezovsky, Roman Abramovich, Anatoly Tschubais, Oleg Deripaska, Alexander Mamut, Yegor Gaidar, etc., oligarchs with umbilical ties to the Kremlin. And so they tried to raise funds. Corruption grew during this time with the accelerated privatization of state enterprises through the *loans-for-shares* scheme, in which some bankers granted loans to the government and received a free book of *vouchers* in return, with which they could buy state company shares at low prices during the upcoming auctions.

---

[8]"The Fundamental Flaws of the Clinton Administration's Russia Policy. Russia's Road to Corruption—How the Clinton Administration Exported Government Instead of Free Enterprise and Failed the Russian People—Chap. 4. Speaker's Advisory Group on Russia. United States House of Representatives 106th Congress. U.S. House of Representatives, Washington, D.C. Report Date: September 2000." Available at <http://fas.org/news/russia/2000/russia/part04.htm>.

[9]Michael Dobbs (*Washington Post*), "In Bid to Support Yeltsin, IMF Lends Russia $10.2 Billion." *The Seattle Times*, March 27, 1996. Available at <http://community.seattletimes.nwsource.com/archive/?date=19960327&slug=2321108>.

Vladimir Potanin, Boris Nemtsov, leader of the Union of Right Forces (Soyuz Pravykh Sil), Mikhail Khodorkovsky, and Kakha Bendukidze, owner of the Uralmash-Izhora industrial group, among others, were some of the *buccaneers*, the "robber barons," who usurped power and plundered the wealth of the country. Approximately 90% of entrepreneurs registered themselves offshore, as did the fleet of Russian vessels, and around US$580 billion of the private sector moved to other countries.[10] And when in 1998 George Soros, the magnate and financial speculator, criticized the way the state enterprises had been privatized by the Yeltsin government, he noted that a form of "crony capitalism" had been established in Russia and that the enormous resources of the country had been redistributed in accordance with the corresponding political power of a the lucky few.[11] "The assets of the state were stolen, and then when the state itself became valuable as a source of legitimacy, it too was stolen," George Soros added.[12]

In 1991, Vladimir Potanin founded the Interros Holding Company and acquired the control of more than 20 state companies during Russia's transition to a market economy, including Norilsk Nickel, the largest producer of nickel, platinum, and palladium. In 2014, his fortune was estimated at about US$14.3 billion or more, much of it outside Russia, hidden in other countries.[13] It was this Vladimir Potanin who inspired the Kremlin to adopt the loans-for-shares scheme in 1995, which allowed the Russian government to sell the most profitable state companies to the oligarchs through auctions (mortgaging auctions). YUKOS, LUKoil, Sibneft, Surgutneftegas, Novolipetsk Steel, Mechel, Norilsk Nickel, and others were sold for a small fraction of their real value in exchange for loans taken from foreign banks. Vladimir Potanin was then Deputy of Prime Minister Viktor S. Chernomyrdin and a friend of President Boris Yeltsin.

Similarly, in 1996 the Kremlin also sold about 50% of its most productive petroleum operations in Siberia. They were managed by Sibneft (OAO Siberian Oil Company), which was acquired by Finansovaya Neftyanaya Kompaniya (Finance Oil Corp), from the oligarch Boris Berezovsky, for a mere US$100.3 million, a fraction of its real worth at the time of approximately US$2.7 billion and its annual oil output of around US$3 billion. He later turned over the company's

---

[10]Rusland Dzarasov, "Cómo Rusia volvió al capitalismo." *Nueva Sociedad*, 253, Buenos Aires: Friedrich Ebert Stiftung, Septiembre/Octubre 2014, pp. 120–135.

[11]Yasmine Ryan, "Russia's oligarchs guard political might—Under Putin, a new middle class has emerged, but socio-economic changes haven't yet translated into political clout." *Al Jazeera*, March 4, 2012. Available at: <http://www.aljazeera.com/indepth/features/2012/02/2012225212624758833.html>.

[12]*Ibidem;* Grigory Yavlinsky, "Russia's Phony Capitalism." *Foreign Affairs—Council of Foreign Relations*, May/June 1998. Available at: <http://www.foreignaffairs.com/articles/54018/grigory-yavlinsky/russias-phony-capitalism>.

[13]Darya Pushkova (RT correspondent), "Prominent Russians: Vladimir Potanin." *RT*, February 1, 2010. Available at: <http://russiapedia.rt.com/prominent-russians/business/vladimir-potanin/>; Anastasia Barchenko, "The price of divorce for Russian oligarchs." *Russia Beyond the Headlines*, March 23, 2014. Available at: <http://rbth.com/business/2014/03/23/the_price_of_divorce_for_russian_oligarchs_35297.html>.

control to the billionaire Roman Abramovich for US$1.3 billion. Sibneft became even richer and, in 2003, its profit reached £770 million, an increase of 190% over the previous year.[14] And in 2014, Roman Abramovich's assets amounted to US $10.2 billion (13th in Forbes' list).[15]

Another oligarch favored by the scheme was Mikhail Khodorkovsky, former leader of the Communist Youth League (Komsomol) in Moscow. In the 1990s, the bank Menatep, which he founded, acquired a huge volume of company shares at discount prices—only US$350 million—through auctions in the loans-for-shares scheme, and together with his partner Platon Lebedev, he took control of Apatit, a fertilizer company, and the Yukos Oil Company, which at the time could be worth up to US$5 billion. This company—Yukos—became the second largest oil company in Russia and Mikhail Khodorkovsky accumulated a fortune estimated by Forbes magazine in 2003 at more than US$15 billion (£9.1 billion), second only to the oligarch Alisher Usmanov, valued at US$17.6 billion.[16] In 2005, Khodorkovsky was arrested[17] under the accusation of massive tax evasion and fraud, and Yukos, whose shares had passed to the banker Jacob Rothschild shortly before,[18] went bankrupt a year later. A large part of its assets was no longer in Russia, but under the protection of foundations registered in the Netherlands.[19]

---

[14]Adrian Levy and Cathy Scott-Clark, "'He won, Russia lost'—Roman Abramovich, Britain's richest man, has lavished millions and millions upon Chelsea Football Club." *The Guardian,* May 8, 2004.

[15]Anastasia Barchenko, "The price of divorce for Russian oligarchs." *Russia Beyond the Headlines*, March 23, 2014. Available at: <http://rbth.com/business/2014/03/23/the_price_of_divorce_for_russian_oligarchs_35297.html>.

[16]"Q&A: Mikhail Khodorkovsky and Russia." *BBC News-Europe*, December 23, 2013. Available at: <http://www.bbc.com/news/world-europe-25467275>.

[17]"Arrested Oil Tycoon Passed Shares to Banker Rothschild." *The Washington Times*, November 2, 2003.

[18]Kathrin Hille (Moscow), "The pursuit of Yukos' wealth." *Financial Times*, January 12, 2014. Available   at: <http://www.ft.com/cms/s/0/d4658d96-7b7d-11e3-84af-00144feabdc0.html#axzz3EWrKjn6p>.

[19]Lenin tried to develop state capitalism, not as the ownership and operation of companies by the State, as Stalin did afterward, but as private capitalism permitted and controlled by the State, and he pursued foreign investments through concessions to companies from Germany, the United States, etc., with plenty of optimism that they would flow to Soviet Russia. According to the traditional parameters of Marxist theory, Lenin argued that planning would only be effective with a highly developed and concentrated economy and not in a country with approximately 20 million small and scattered farms, a disintegrated industry, and primitive and barbaric forms of trade. Stalin extinguished the NEP, in 1927–1928, with the 5-year plan, nationalizing the economy and turning the Soviet Union into an autarchy, without considering that it was inserted in the capitalist world market from which it could not escape nor isolate itself. See Luiz Alberto Moniz Bandeira, 2009, pp. 63–72 and 142–143.

7.4 Confirmation of Trotsky's Prediction

This situation had been foreseen by Leon Trotsky, companion of Lenin and commander of the Red Army, which defeated the counterrevolutionary forces in the Civil War in Russia between November 1917 and October 1922. In 1935, when analyzing the degeneration of the revolution of 1917 under the totalitarian regime of Joseph Stalin, after he put an end to the New Economic Policy (NEP Novaia Ekonomitcheskaia—POLITIKA) established by Lenin since 1922,[20] Trotsky stressed that the economic crises the Soviet Union was suffering represented "something infinitely more serious than infant diseases or growth pains." They were "severe warnings" from the international market to which the Soviet Union was umbilically tied and from which it could not separate itself because of its commercial necessities—export/import.[21] He anticipated that if a political revolution failed to occur in the Soviet Union and democracy was not established, with full freedom for the trade unions and political parties, then the restoration of capitalism and private ownership of the means of production would become inevitable. The bureaucrats, technicians, and managers of the Communist Party would generally become the new owner class, and the conditions for this had been established.[22]

The autarchic socialistic model, with a planned economy under a monocratic, authoritarian political regime, had stagnated since the beginning of the 1970s. Due to its limitations and relative isolation within a capitalist international environment, it had neither the means nor the internal and external conditions to capture financial resources through credits, which would allow it to sustain the arms race and, at the same time, meet its domestic demand for consumer goods. The surge in development it had enjoyed in the 1960s through the incorporation of the Eastern and Central European countries into its economic sphere, including a part of Germany, had already exhausted itself. And the Soviet Union could not compete with the economic dynamism of the West.[23]

The successors of Leonid Brezhnev (1964–1982), Yuri Andropov (1982–1984), and Konstantin Chernenko, as former leaders of the KGB, were very well aware of the serious situation of the country, and of the need for profound reforms in the economic system, which lacked technological innovation for the development of the consumption industry and financial resources because of the rising costs of manufactured goods and raw materials imported from the West.[24] But they simply didn't have time to execute these reforms in their short time in government. Both

---

[20]Leon Trotsky, 1936. pp. 119, 283–287, 306, 324–325.

[21]*Ibidem*, p. 12.

[22]Silvio Pons, 2014, pp., 318–320.

[23]See Luiz Alberto Moniz Bandeira, 2009, pp. 131–132.

[24]Martin Armstrong, "The US did not cause the fall of the Soviet Union—that is a False Belief on Both Sides." *Armstrong Economics,* March 18, 2014. Available at <http://armstrongeconomics. com/2014/03/18/the-us-did-not-cause-the-fall-of-the-soviet-union-that-is-a-false-belief-on-both-sides/>.

soon passed away. They were succeeded by Mikhail S. Gorbachev, with the support of the KGB, who implemented *glasnost* (openness) and *perestroika* (restructuring), opening up the regime politically, rehabilitating the market economy and pushing through monetary reform, turning the ruble into a convertible currency, and recognizing various forms of ownership as the foundation of economic efficiency. This way he tried to save the Soviet Union, but he lost political control and the government. Boris Yeltsin (1931–2007), General Secretary of the Communist Party in Moscow, who was conspiring with the rulers of Ukraine and Belarus and whose project was to turn the Soviet Union into a mere commonwealth, staged the so-called august coup (Августовский путч Avgustovsky putch), counting also on the support of communists opposed to *perestroika* and *glasnost*.[25]

Under the government of Boris Yeltsin (1991–1999), Trotsky's prophecy was fulfilled. The vice president himself, Alexander Rutskoy, denounced his radical economic reform program as an "economic genocide."[26] Boris Yeltsin executed it nonetheless. And in the midst of a primitive capital accumulation process with the wild looting of the state's corporate assets, especially between 1995 and 1996 with the loans-for-shares auctions, the oligarchs emerged from the decomposing bureaucracy as the new ruling and owning class, becoming real factors of economic and political power, the Russian government's pillar of support.[27]

7.5   The Rise of Vladimir Putin and Russia's Recovery

With the privatization of the economy according to neoliberal parameters, the situation in Russia, which had experienced negative growth since 1991 and had only started to recover from recession in 1997, became calamitous when the country was hit in 1998 by the severe financial crisis that afflicted Thailand and had spread to Indonesia, South Korea and other Asian countries. With its fixed exchange rate and fragile, apparently unsustainable fiscal position, Russia suffered devastating effects. Capital flight intensified and the stock exchange crashed with a dizzying drop in share prices, which lost more than 75% of their market value since the beginning of the year.[28] The losses reached approximately US$14 billion. And in 3 weeks, the ruble plummeted to lose two-thirds of its value. In mid-1998, Russia had more than

---

[25]Ronald Hatchett, "Yeltsin: Fighting To Stay On Top." JOC.com, August 18, 1992. Available at: <http://www.joc.com/yeltsin-fighting-stay-top_19920818.html>.

[26]Brian Whitmore, "Russia: The End of Loans-For-Shares—Nearly a decade ago in a move that reshaped Russia's political landscape, the ailing and embattled Kremlin leader Boris Yeltsin sold off the crown jewels of the country's economy to a select group of oligarchs. Russian President Vladimir Putin is now ready to buy them back." *Radio Free Europe/Radio Liberty*, September 29, 2005. Available at: <http://www.rferl.org/articleprintview/1061761.html>.

[27]"The Russian Crisis 1998". *Economic Report—Rabobank—Economic Research Department*.

[28]Available at <https://economics.rabobank.com/publications/2013/september/the-russian-crisis-1998/>. Access on September 21, 2014.

1500 banks and most were expected to go bankrupt. About 75% of their obligations were short term, maturing in less than 90 days. The public lost confidence in the banking system and a run to withdraw deposits escalated. And more and more investors were selling rubles to buy dollars. In August 1998, Russia's Central Bank spent billions of dollars to sustain the ruble and its monetary reserves fell from US$18 billion to US$17 billion. In addition, Russia used more than US$4.8 billion in funds provided by the IMF to shore up its currency.[29] The World Bank had also granted it US$3 billion, with the requirement of more economic reforms in line with the neoliberal Washington Consensus.

Faced with the panic, Russia's Central Bank, spending a large part of the monetary reserves to maintain the link with the dollar, decided to remove the exchange rate bands and let the ruble fluctuate freely and thus prevent its value from debasing even further. In the end, however, Russia had no alternative but to default on its domestic and external debts. And the devaluation of the ruble increased inflation, which jumped from 27.6% in 1998 to 85.7% in 1999. The budget deficit was so high that state officials were not even receiving their paychecks. The number of people living below the poverty line touched almost 40%, and by the end of 1998, approximately 13 million, i.e., 7.7% of the country's total population, were left without jobs.[30] The crisis in Russia was worse than the one that hit the United States after Black Friday in the Wall Street crash of 1929.

In August 1998, faced with the deepening economic and financial crisis and the prospect of the banks' bankruptcy, the Duma, i.e., the lower chamber of the Federal Assembly of the Russian Federation, accused Yeltsin of not taking the necessary measures to protect the constitutional rights of its citizens, generating a real threat to the territorial integrity, independence, and security of the country. And it adopted a resolution by 245 votes against 32 recommending he resign the Presidency of the Federation.[31] Boris Yeltsin didn't. In May 1999, therefore, the Duma started an impeachment process against him, pushed by the communist leaders Aleksandr Volkov, president of the Security Committee, and Viktor Ilyukhin. This attempt to overthrow him failed because the quorum was not reached. Only 300 of the 442 active members voted since, inexplicably, 100 did not attend the session. President Yeltsin then deposed Prime Minister Yevgeny Primakov and replaced him with Sergei Stepashin, who took office when NATO was bombing Belgrade in favor of the separatists in Kosovo. Yeltsin then perceived the threat and stated that this intervention would not only represent a blow against Yugoslavia but also against Russia and

---

[29]"Russia—an economy on the brink". *BBC News*, August 24, 1998. Available at: <http://news.bbc.co.uk/2/hi/business/150383.stm>.

[30]*Russia's Road to Corruption—How the Clinton Administration Exported Government Instead of Free Enterprise and Failed the Russian People.* "Chap. 8—1998: Years of Bad Advice Culminate in Russia's Total Economic Collapse." U.S. House of Representatives, Washington, D.C. Report Date: September 2000. Available at: <http://fas.org/news/russia/2000/russia/part08.htm>.

[31]Alan Little, "Business; Economy—Parliament calls on Yeltsin to resign." *BBC News,* August 21, 1998. Available at: <http://news.bbc.co.uk/2/hi/business/155494.stm>.

conclusions should be drawn from this.[32] The strains on Russia's relationship with the United States reached a breaking point, therefore, since Yugoslavia/Serbia was Russia's ally and the NATO attack was carried out unilaterally by Washington. But President Yeltsin was not prepared for confrontation, nor did he have any choice, as a result of the severe economic and political situation of his country.

Sergei Stepashin didn't stay in office more than 3 months. On the morning of August 9, President Yeltsin fired him and appointed his deputy, Vladimir Putin, a colonel of the former KGB, the Soviet Union's intelligence service, who become his fourth prime minister 17 months into his second term. In addition to the economic crisis, the escalation of the war in Chechnya and the advance of Jihadists in Dagestan, secretly supported by the Saudi intelligence service and the British MI6, were some of the other factors that precipitated the fall of Sergei Stepashin. Dagestan, in the Caucasus, had a very significant strategic dimension for Russia, since the oil and gas pipelines from the Caspian Sea passed through its territory and because it could maintain ties with Azerbaijan, which became an independent republic after the disintegration of the Soviet Union. This is why, faced with such contingencies, on top of his cardiac problems, the difficulties of a stagnant economy, the hostility of the Duma, under opposition control, and the military failure in the war against the separatists in Chechnya, Boris Yeltsin resigned on December 31, 1999, on New Year's Eve, temporarily handing over the government to Vladimir Putin, until he was elected president on March 26, 2000. Boris Yeltsin was 68 years old and would have finished his term in June 2000.

Vladimir Putin was born in Leningrad (St. Petersburg), the heroic city that resisted the siege of the Nazi troops for around 900 days—September 8, 1941, to January 27, 1944—and refused to surrender, despite the death of 700,000 to 800,000 civilians, including 400,000 children. Putin had a legal background, a degree in law from the University of Leningrad, and vast experience gained during his career in the KGB, where he served as colonel, and as director of the FSB, the Federal Security Service (Federal'naya sluzhba bezopasnosti Rossiyskoy Federatsii), the most efficient of its kind in Europe. He rose to power with the support of the intelligence services of the former Soviet Union, maimed by the reforms of the Boris Yeltsin era. Under his government, however, the three major agencies—SVR, for operations abroad; FSB, in charge of internal security and counterintelligence; and GRU, military intelligence—soon recovered their operational capabilities. During the 2000s, President Vladimir Putin promoted Russia's economic resurgence and reduced the number of people living below the poverty level to 11% (2013 est.), down from almost 40% in 1998,[33] which was a lower percentage than in the United States, where 15.1% (2010) of the population was estimated to live in poverty.[34]

---

[32]Sharon Lafraniere, "Stepashin Confirmed as Russian Premier." *Washington Post—Foreign Service,* May 20, 1999, p. A19. Available at: <http://www.washingtonpost.com/wp-srv/inatl/longterm/russiagov/stories/stepashin052099.html>.

[33]*CIA Fact Book.* Available at: <https://www.cia.gov/library/publications/the-world-factbook/geos/rs.html>.

[34]*Ibidem.*

During this period, Russia benefited from the high oil and gas prices in the international market. Its industrial growth was approximately 75%, with an emphasis on the high technology sectors—nuclear and defense. Domestic and foreign investment, particularly in the automobile industry, jumped by 125% and GDP grew by 70%, putting Russia among the ten largest economies of the world.[35] And although its foreign debt was still about US$714.2 billion in 2013,[36] its reserves in strong currencies and gold stood at around US$469 billion/US$472 billion (among the 5th largest in the world), and its public debt-to-GDP ratio was only 12%, much lower than in the countries of the European Union.[37]

President Vladimir Putin confirmed Russia's position as a vigorous superpower by letting the State take control of a substantial part of oil and gas production through the acquisition by Gazprom of 75% of Sibneft, owned by the oligarch Roman Abramovich, who received US$13 billion, as well as of other sources of minerals, leaving the energy companies completely open and transparent to investors. President Putin therefore implemented a policy of compromises through the intermediation of the State, stabilizing the political elite and promoting the construction of a hybrid economic system, in which the State controlled almost 50% of the economy, i.e., the strategic sectors—energy, telecommunications, metallurgy, military, and nuclear industries—and leaving the production of consumer goods and agriculture to private initiative. In 2012, the State also controlled 49% of the banking and 73% of the transport sector.[38]

Russia had been defeated and humiliated with the collapse of the Soviet Union and the corrupt privatization of state assets, squandered during the administration of President Yeltsin amidst a devastating global financial crisis that broke out in the second half of the 1990s.[39] And as Gorbachev himself said, Russian citizens should remember that Putin "saved Russia from the beginning of a collapse," since "a lot of the regions did not recognize our constitution"[40] from December 25, 1993, ratifying the dissolution of the Soviet Union after the serious institutional conflict between President Yeltsin and the Duma and the Supreme Soviet. In fact, like Peter the Great

---

[35]"Russia's economy under Vladimir Putin: achievements and failures." Analysis and Opinion—*RIA Novosti*, January 3, 2008. Available at <http://en.ria.ru/analysis/20080301/100381963.html>.

[36]*CIA Fact Book.* Available at: <https://www.cia.gov/library/publications/the-world-factbook/geos/rs.html>.

[37]Chris Vellacott and Lidia Kelly (London/Moscow), "Russia can run on empty for a year if sanctions block new bonds." *Reuters,* September, 2014. Available at <http://www.reuters.com/article/2014/09/02/ukraine-crisis-russia-bonds-idUSLN0R330720140902>.

[38]"Russian State takes bigger part in the economy, despite trumpeted privatization plans." *RT,* November 6, 2012. Available at: <http://rt.com/business/russia-state-economy-privatization-043/>.

[39]Vivian Oswald, 2011, p. 75.

[40]"Gorbachev: Putin saved Russia from disintegration." *RT,* December 27, 2014. Available at: <http://rt.com/news/217931-gorbachev-putin-saved-russia/>; Ilya Pitalev, "Serious meetings needed to settle situation around Ukraine—Gorbachev." *Itar–Tass,* Moscou, December 26, 2014. Available at: <http://itar-tass.com/en/russia/769544>.

(Pyotr Alexeyevich—1672–1725), who reformed and modernized the empire, President Putin embodied the "Russian soul" (Русская душа), a patriot, with a strong personality, willing to fight, raising the morale and pride as well as the spirits and sense of grandeur of his people. And in order to consolidate power, he strove to marginalize the oligarchs, the fund brokers of Boris Yeltsin's administration, who participated in and enriched during the privatization orgy of state-owned enterprises, especially through the "loans-for-shares" auctions of 1995–1996. This is the reason for the campaign against the Yukos oil company, whose CEO Mikhail Khodorkovsky was arrested and accused of tax evasion, money laundering, and other frauds. President Putin then sought to reverse the detrimental effects of the loans-for-shares auctions. He chased the oligarchs tied to former President Yeltsin away from government, including Boris Berezovsky, Roman Abramovich, and Vladimir Potanin, and formed his team out of former KGB comrades—*siloviki*. And then he vigorously pursued Russia's resurrection, making every effort to lift it from its economic, social, political, and moral quagmire.

Chapter 8
The US/NATO Push Toward the East After the Collapse of the Soviet Union

8.1 The Debacle of the Soviet Union, the "Greatest Geopolitical Catastrophe of the Twentieth Century"

During his State of the Union address before the Duma in 2005, President Vladimir Putin correctly described the debacle of the Soviet Union as the "greatest geopolitical catastrophe of the twentieth century."[1] The disintegration of the Soviet Union was in fact "a real tragedy," as he pointed out, leaving hundreds of millions of Russians outside the federation, dispersed over 12 different republics in Eurasia. More than 8 million ethnic Russians lived in Ukraine alone (17% of the population of the country), and they remained there without any identity or major rights, just as a large part of the USSR's military and nuclear industry, an integral part of Russia's productive chain. But the Soviet Union's *desmerengamiento* (meltdown), to use an expression from Fidel Castro, produced an even greater disaster by upsetting the international order.

8.2 US Dominance Through NATO and the Privilege of Printing Dollars as Reserve Currency

Despite being a totalitarian regime, the Soviet Union represented a pole of power, a hard bulwark against the equally totalitarian global dictatorship the United States wanted to implement in the name of democracy,[2] resting, military, and financially,

---

[1]"Russia's President Vladimir Putin has described the collapse of the Soviet Union as 'the greatest geopolitical catastrophe' of the twentieth century." *BBC News*, April 25, 2005.

[2]Rodrigue Tremblay, "Bill Clinton's 'Neocon-inspired Decisions' Triggered Three Major Crises in our Times." *Global Research*, August 13, 2014. Available at <http://www.globalresearch.ca/bill-clintons-neocon-inspired-decisions-triggered-three-major-crises-in-our-times/5395715?print=1>.

© Springer Nature Switzerland AG 2019
L. A. Moniz Bandeira, *The World Disorder*,
https://doi.org/10.1007/978-3-030-03204-3_8

on two fundamental pillars: NATO, consisting of the European countries subordinated to Washington's guidelines, and the privilege of printing the dollar as fiat
currency, the world's single reserve currency. Only the Federal Reserve (FED), the
central bank of the United States, could and can issue the dollar at will. But although
this central bank, a joint-stock company created by the Federal Reserve Act
(December 23, 1913), appeared to have a state structure, it had a broad private
component controlled by the largest American commercial banks, of which only
six—Merry Lynch, JPMorgan Chase, Bank of America, Wells Fargo, Citigroup and
Goldman Sachs—amassed US$9.5 trillion in 2012, equivalent to 65% of the
country's GDP.[3]

The Republican Congressman Charles A. Lindberg (1907–1917) of Minnesota
warned that by creating the Federal Reserve System, the Federal Reserve Act would
establish "the most gigantic trust on earth" and legalize "the invisible government of
the Monetary Power."[4] According to the investigative reporter Dean Henderson,
despite what most Americans thought, the FED was not a government-controlled
institution, but actually a cartel controlled by Bank of America, JPMorgan Chase,
Citigroup, and Wells Fargo, intertwined with the oil companies Exxon Mobil, Royal
Dutch/Shell (of which the two largest shareholders are the former Dutch Queen
Beatrix, of the House of Orange, and Lord Victor Rothschild), British Petroleum,
and Chevron Texaco, and with such European financial behemoths as Deutsche
Bank, BNP, and Barclays.[5] And the most powerful branch of the FED, the
New York Federal Reserve Bank, fell under the command of eight families, of
which only four came from the United States: Goldman Sachs, Rockefeller, Lehman
and Kuhn Loeb, from New York. The other families included the Rothschilds from
Paris and London, the Warburgs from Hamburg, the Lazards from Paris, and Israel
Moses Seif from Rome.[6] These were the families still privately controlling the
Federal Reserve Bank in the twenty-first century, shaping the international financial
system, getting even wealthier after the financial crash of 2007–2008, and playing a
decisive role in the oil futures market, either directly or through subsidiaries, both on
the New York Mercantile Exchange and the London Petroleum Exchange.[7]

According to the Republican Senator Barry Goldwater (1909–1998), the powerful European banker Anselm Rothschild (1773–1855) once said: "Give me the
power to issue the nation's money, then I do not care who makes the laws."[8] This
is why the United States has no regard for and flouts international law. It enjoys the

---

[3]Nomi Prins, 2014, pp. 395 and 421.

[4]Eustace Mullins, 2010, pp. 21–26.

[5]Dean Henderson, 2010, pp. 28–30; "Thread: 'The Eight Families'—Why should everyone else
except them be communists? The Federal Reserve Cartel: The Eight Families. So who then are the
stockholders in these money center banks?" *Mail Online*, September 6, 2011. Available at <http://
boards.dailymail.co.uk/news-board-moderated/10233373-eight-families-why-should-everyone-
else-except-them-communists.html>.

[6]*Ibidem.*

[7]Ibidem, p. 31.

[8]Barry M. Goldwater, 1979, p. 296.

privilege of manufacturing dollars, when and how it pleases, without any backing, and manipulating its value through the discount rate. But the private banks dominating the Federal Reserve System need military power and wars to maintain their permanent position as state creditors by funding the continuous rearmament and production of war material, more profitable than granting private credits to agriculture and consumer goods industries. In 2011, the United States had a GDP of about US$14.9 trillion and owed approximately US$14 trillion to the private banks, and the Department of the Treasury and Federal Reserve Board estimated that US$4.4 trillion of this debt was held by foreign governments, who bought Treasury bonds like investors would buy a stake in a company.[9]

Senator Barry Goldwater correctly noted that most Americans didn't understand the operations of international bankers, the obscure ways through which the Rothschilds and Warburgs in Europe and the houses of JPMorgan, Kuhn, Loeb & Company, Schiff, Lehman and Rockefeller owned and controlled vast amounts of wealth. "How they acquire this vast financial power and employ it is a mystery to most of us." But the fact is international bankers manufactured money, said Barry Goldwater, conceding credit to governments. Since "the greater the debt of the political state, the larger the interest returned to the lenders."[10] The national banks of Europe were actually owned and controlled by private interests and the Federal Reserve System operated outside Congress' control, with no audits of its accounts, and through the Board of Governors it manipulated the credit of the United States,[11] whose public debt had jumped from US$1 billion during the FED's creation to US $17.9 trillion in October 2014, growing at a rate of US$2.43 billion per day since September 30, 2012.[12]

Ever since the geopolitician Zbigniew Brzezinski suggested the creation of the Trilateral Commission to David Rockefeller in 1973, the objective of these illuminati has always been to internationally control and consolidate the commercial and financial oil interests of the United States, as a monetary, political, intellectual, and ecclesiastical superior power, capable of capturing, involving, and forcing its will on the governments of nation states, allowing it to exert a full-spectrum dominance, handing over the monopoly of violence to NATO as global cop. And so corruption forms the life blood nurturing and nourishing the chronic militarism of the United States, cloaked and broadly enabled by the ambiguous role played by public/ business men who exchange large corporations for government, and vice versa,

---

[9]Greg Bocquet, "Who Owns the U.S.?". *Yahoo Finance*, February 28, 2011. Available at <http://finance.yahoo.com/news/pf_article_112189.html>.

[10]Barry M. Goldwater, 1979, pp. 295–296.

[11]Ibidem, pp. 294–195.

[12]"The Outstanding Public Debt as of 28 Oct 2014 at 04:14:26 PM GMT." In: U.S. National Debt Clock. Available at <http://www.brillig.com/debt_clock/>; "Timeline of U.S. Federal Debt since Independence Day 1776." *Debt.org*. Available at <http://www.debt.org/blog/united-states-federal-debt-timeline/>; Also available at: <http://www.usgovernmentdebt.us/>; Dean Henderson, 2010, p. 32.

through the revolving door of the predominant military-industrial and financial complex in Washington.

When President George W. Bush succeeded Bill Clinton, he sought to extend NATO's jurisdiction even further, not for security reasons, but in order to expand the market for the war industry, including through the absorption of Ukraine and Georgia, two countries of fundamental importance to Russia's security. The provocation went on, despite a confidential warning memo (code 08CA265) from the American ambassador in Moscow, William J. Burns, dated February 1, 2008, to the Secretary of State, with copies to the Secretary of Defense, the Joint Chiefs of Staff, the National Security Council, and other bodies. The memo stated Russia would resist the attempt to pursue Ukraine and Georgia's (and Croatia and Albania's) adherence to the NATO Membership Action Plan (MAP) during the 20th NATO Summit, to be held in Bucharest (Romania) on April 2 and 4 of that year.[13]

8.3   Minister Sergei Lavrov's Warning on Ukraine, the Georgia Question and Russia's Intervention in Defense of South Ossetia

The Russian minister of Foreign Affairs Sergei Lavrov and other authorities had reiterated that Moscow would strongly oppose NATO's expansion in Eastern Europe, since it perceived it as a potential military threat.[14] Ukraine, in particular, remained "an emotional and neuralgic point," Minister Sergei Lavrov stressed, adding that underlying strategic considerations and policies further strengthened Russia's opposition, just as it opposed Georgia joining NATO. Especially with regard to Ukraine, this issue could potentially fracture the country in two, unleash violence or even a civil war, as some warned, which would force Moscow to decide whether it should intervene or not, besides the broader impact it would have on the Russian defense industry, Russian-Ukrainian family ties and bilateral relations. In

---

[13]Nyet Means Nyet: Russia's NATO Enlargement. Cable 08MOSCOW265 Reference ID—2008-02-01—Confidential—Moscow   000265—FM   Amembassy   Moscow—Ref: A.   Moscow 147 B. Moscow 182—Classified By: Ambassador William J. Burns. Reasons 1.4 (b) and (d). Available at <http://wikileaks.org/cable/2008/02/08MOSCOW265.html>; Felicity Arbuthnot, "Ukraine: US Ambassador to Moscow's 2008 Cable—'Nyet, Means Nyet: Russia's NATO Engagement's Red Line.'" Global Research, May 9, 2014. Available at <http://www.globalresearch.ca/ukraine-us-ambassador-to-moscows-2008-cable-nyet-means-nyet-russias-nato-engagements-red-line/5381475>.

[14]Nyet Means Nyet: Russia's NATO Enlargement. Cable 08MOSCOW265 Reference ID—2008-02-01-Confidential—Moscow   000265—FM   Amembassy   Moscow—Ref: A.   Moscow 147 B. Moscow 182—Classified By: Ambassador William J. Burns. Reasons 1.4 (b) and (d). Available at: <http://wikileaks.org/cable/2008/02/08MOSCOW265.html>. Access on May 12, 2014.

Georgia, on the other hand, the Kremlin feared continuing instability and "provocative actions" of the separatist regions.[15]

During the meeting in Bucharest, President George W. Bush's efforts to involve Ukraine and Georgia in the Membership Action Plan (MAP), through which these nations would be qualified to join NATO, could not count on the support of Germany and France, who didn't want to run the risk of provoking Russia, arguing that neither country was sufficiently stable and that their adherence to the MAP would be an "unnecessary offense."[16] Despite "lobbying hard," President George W. Bush failed to obtain a consensus among the NATO members, and the decision was postponed to December.[17]

At that time, mid-2008, Daniel Russell, the Chargé d'Affaires of the United States in Moscow, informed Washington that the Minister of Foreign Affairs Sergei Lavrov had declared that the government in Kiev was acting against the will of the majority of the Ukrainian people, which would have "destructive consequences" and that Russia would do everything to prevent Ukraine joining NATO. Other authorities made similar pronouncements. One of them was the chairman of the Committee on Foreign Affairs of the Commonwealth of Independent States (CIS) in the Duma (Parliament), Alexey Ostrovsky, who predicted, in April, that the Russian Federation could reclaim Crimea if Ukraine was admitted in NATO.[18]

A few months after the meeting in Bucharest, on August 8, 2008, Russia intervened in Georgia, through which the largest oil pipeline from Baku (Azerbaijan) to the port of Cayhan (Turkey) passed. It wanted to defend the secessionist regions, the enclaves of ethnic Russians—South Ossetia and Abkhazia—bombarded by the air force of President Mikhail Saakashvili, who was certainly receiving military assistance from the United States. The war lasted only 5 days and Georgia was defeated.[19] In an emergency meeting, President George W. Bush and his allies of the European Union put everything on the table, from suspending relations with Russia to boycotting the Winter Olympics, scheduled for 2014 in Sochi. But they could do nothing, nor did they have any moral standing to come to Georgia's aid. On February 17, 2008, the United States, Germany, and other allies in the European Union had recognized the independence of Kosovo, the former province of Serbia, which until then had fallen under the jurisdiction of the United Nations Interim Administration Mission (UNMIK). This precedent made the rhetoric of sanctions on the pretext of the inviolability of borders ridiculous. In

---

[15]*Ibidem.*

[16]Steven Erlanger & Steven Lee Myers, "NATO Allies Oppose Bush on Georgia and Ukraine." *The New York Times*, April 3, 2008.

[17]*Ibidem.*

[18]"'Black Sea Fleet Stirs Controversy Between Russia And Ukraine' From: Russia Moscow To: Central Intelligence Agency|Defense Intelligence Agency|National Security Council|Russia Moscow Political Collective|Secretary of Defense|Secretary of State Date: 2008 June 4, 03:47 (Wednesday) Canonical ID: 08MOSCOW1568_a Original Classification: Unclassified, for official use only." Available at <https://wikileaks.org/plusd/cables/08MOSCOW1568_a.html>.

[19]Vicken Cheterian, 2010, pp. 63–75; Paula Garb, 2010, pp. 140–149.

addition, half the people in the Caucasus, and also Ukraine, where President Viktor Yushchenko proved favorable to Georgia, saw Russia's intervention to defend South Ossetia and Abkhazia as laudable, proportional, and humanitarian.[20]

Since then the relationship between Russia and the United States kept getting worse. President Putin's objective was to restore Russia's traditional sphere of influence, including the Caucasus. But as General Colin Powell, chairman of the Joint Chiefs of Staff, had recommended to President George H. W. Bush (1989–1993) based on the doctrine of the neocons—Paul Wolfowitz and co.—the United States should preserve the "credible capability to forestall any potential adversary from competing militarily,"[21] preventing the European Union from becoming a military power outside of NATO as well as the remilitarization of Japan and Russia and discouraging any challenge to its dominance or attempt to reverse the internationally established economic and political order.[22]

8.4 Killings, Chaos, and Humanitarian Disasters Persist in Afghanistan, the Middle East, and Africa

President Barack Obama didn't move away from neocon policy and left its strategic objective unaltered, i.e., consolidating the supremacy of the United States as the single pole of world power. But he inherited an even more difficult situation: the economic and financial crisis and the asymmetric military conflicts ignited by President George W. Bush with the invasion of first Afghanistan and then Iraq, where until October 2013, approximately half a million soldiers of the United States had intervened to overthrow Saddam Hussein's regime, to remove the weapons of mass destruction (which didn't exist) and open the gates for Western oil companies in the name of democracy.[23] And, at the end of 2014, 13 years after the start of the war on terror, the United States was still stuck in Afghanistan, unable to establish peace and democracy. The damage it had caused there was immeasurable. The heroine trade in the country kept growing, with production expected to reach 800 tonnes by 2014 with the doubling of opium poppy plantations to 250,000

---

[20]Charles King, "The Five-Day War—Managing Moscow after the Georgia Crisis." *Foreign Affairs*, November/December 2008 Issue. Available at: <http://www.foreignaffairs.com/articles/64602/charles-king/the-five-day-war>.

[21]Colin L. Powell, 1992, p. 7. Draft Resolution—12 Cooperation for Security in the Hemisphere, Regional Contribution to Global Security—The General Assembly, recalling: Resolutions AG/RES. 1121 (XXX-091 and AG/RES. 1123 (XXI-091) for strengthening of peace and security in the hemisphere, and AG/RES. 1062 (XX090) against clandestine arms traffic.

[22]*Ibidem*, p. 7.

[23]Kerry Sheridan (Agence France Press), Iraq Death Toll Reaches 500,000 Since Start Of U.S. Led Invasion, New Study Says. *TheHuffingtonPost.com*, October 15, 2013. Available at <http://www.huffingtonpost.com/2013/10/15/iraq-death-toll_n_4102855.html>.

hectares.[24] And although the CIA and DEA were aware of the location of the main heroin laboratories and deposits, mainly in southeastern Afghanistan, nothing was done to stop business operations.[25] And according to the UN High Commissioner for Refugees, there were still 3,600,449 people in need in Afghanistan in 2014, and the number of displaced people was set to reach 631,286.[26]

The killings, the chaos, and the humanitarian disasters ripping through Afghanistan, Iraq, Yemen, Gaza, and countries of Africa became worse during the Obama administration. He continued to send arms to the rebel factions in Syria, Saudi Arabia, Qatar, and Turkey. And instigated particularly by his Secretary of State Hillary Clinton, who had surrounded herself with neocons, Obama ordered the bombing of Libya by NATO in conjunction with the French President François Sarkozy and the British Prime Minister David Cameron. In addition, he sought confrontation with China by determining the installation of more military bases in those Asia Pacific countries President Barack Obama considered to be a "key priority" for US security strategy, with Australia, Japan, and South Korea (ANZUS) making up the hub-and-spokes of his structural system.[27]

Ultimately, Barack Obama wanted the *petrification* of world order, as the writer Norman Pollack put it,[28] and to implement the totalitarian domination of the United States, its full-spectrum dominance so ardently desired since the fall of the Soviet Union. Indeed, almost all regime change operations by the United States sought to gain strategic positions, influence wars, or open up market access to natural resources.[29] And so it strove to surround Russia; block its access to the Black Sea, the Mediterranean, and the North Sea; and confine it to isolation as a vast stretch of land without any exit to the sea or any influence in the Middle East, North Africa, Southeast Asia, and the North Atlantic.[30]

In August 2013, however, when Barack Obama was preparing the order to invade Syria, President Bashar al-Assad himself noted in an interview to the Russian newspaper *Izvestia* that since the fiasco in Vietnam, the United States had started

---

[24]"Afghan heroin major factor for destabilization in Russia—official." *ITAR-TASS*, August 19, 2014. Available at: <http://en.itar-tass.com/russia/745640>.

[25]James Risen, 2006, pp. 157–159.

[26]"2014 UNHCR country operations profile—Afghanistan." United Nations High Commissioner for Refugees. Available at: <http://www.unhcr.org/pages/49e486eb6.html>.

[27]Leon Panetta & Jim Newton, 2014, p. 396.

[28]Norman Pollack, "Obama's Foreign Policy—Militarization of Globalism." *Counterpunch*, August 18, 2014. Available at: <http://www.counterpunch.org/2014/08/18/militarization-of-globalism/print>.

[29]Stephen Kinzer, 2006, p. 321.

[30]James Petras, 2014, pp. 228–229.

many wars, but not achieved its goals.[31] "Global powers can wage wars, but can they win them?", Assad asked, adding that the United States had learned nothing nor had it been able to achieve its political objectives in any of the wars it pursued. It merely destroyed countries, as it was doing in the Middle East. "There are currently many Western politicians, but very few statesmen," President Bashar al-Assad remarked.[32]

Since the defeat of Germany in the Second World War, the United States had not been effectively victorious in any other country, except for Granada, a small island with 344 km^2 and little more than 100,000 inhabitants, where it intervened (Operation Urgent Fury) in 1983, and Panama, a strip of land in Central America with 75,517 km^2 and 2.2 million inhabitants, with the invasion (Operation Just Cause) in 2000 to overthrow and capture the dictator Manuel Noriega for drug trafficking. In fact, these could hardly be called wars, but rather military aggressions against defenseless countries. In Afghanistan and Iraq, the United States achieved very little or almost nothing since 2001 and 2003, when President George W. Bush set off the war on terror, despite the US' unparalleled military force. With its intensively and continuously trained ground forces, including in deserts, equipped with last-generation night vision devices, the most modern communication systems, and surveillance and target acquisition radars (JSTARS), in addition to other technologically sophisticated war tools, the United States couldn't even win wars against non-state actors (NSA), either in Vietnam or in the Middle East and Africa. Despite NATO's efforts, the Special Operations Forces/Navy Seal Teams, the CIA, and the drone strikes, the asymmetric wars dragged on in Afghanistan, Syria, Libya, Iraq, Somalia, and Yemen without any prospect of victory. They transcended the levels of political, tactical, and strategical operations. Strobe Talbott, president of the Brookings Institution and former Deputy Secretary of State during the Bill Clinton administration, acknowledged that the current era was different due to the diffusion of power from states to non-state forces, the rapid spread of technology, and the rise of Islamic extremism.[33] And he noted that the diffusion of power made it much harder to advance regional and global governance.[34]

The global governance President Obama sought to establish and consolidate in the twenty-first century was in fact the Project for the New American Century drawn up by the neocons of the Republican Party in the 1990s after the disintegration of the

---

[31]"Full text of the interview of President Assad to Izvestia—President of the Syrian Arab Republic told about threat of US invasion, about his relationship with Putin and about common fate of Russian and Syrian people." All in exclusive interview in Izvestia, August 26, 2013. *The Saker's 2nd blog*. Monthly Archives: August 2013 Available at: <http://thesaker.wordpress.com/2013/08/page/2/>; Bashar Al-Assad, "All contracts signed with Russia are implemented." 26 августа 2013, |Политика|Izvestia|написать авторам—Читайте далее: Available at <http://izvestia.ru/news/556048#ixzz3FBxhnBKi>.

[32]*Ibidem.*

[33]Thomas L. Friedman, "President Obama Talks to Thomas L. Friedman about Iraq, Putin and Israel." *The New York Times*, August 8, 2014; Peter Baker, "The World Boils, Fingers Point Obama's Way." *The New York Times*, August 15, 2014.

[34]*Ibidem.*

Soviet Union. It was the same program President George W. Bush tried to implement after the terrorist attacks of September 11, 2001, of which the government had prior knowledge, keeping this information hidden in a classified section of the 9/11 commission, according to former Senator Ron Paul (Republican Party).[35] The Director of the Center on Congress at Indiana University, Lee H. Hamilton (Democratic Party—Indiana), in turn stressed that Americans have a very strong tendency to think that whatever the United State does is the most important thing happening everywhere and that it has so much power and so much clout that it can control events everywhere.[36] "Presidents can influence but not dictate events," Lee H. Hamilton emphasized, however.[37] According to Jeremy Shapiro of the Brookings Institution, since the Second World War, at least, US presidents have been unwilling to discuss deficiencies in capability because they're expected to do everything. They liked this sense of omnipotence, which has gone so far and become so difficult to revert.[38]

---

[35]"Ron Paul: Government Had Foreknowledge of 9/11 Terror Attacks. Paul argues U.S. gov't more destructive than Osama Bin Laden." *Washington Free Beacon*, August 30, 2014—ICH—Information Clearing House. Available at: <http://www.informationclearinghouse.info/article39542.htm. docx>; "Ron Paul CG #23 Opening the Secret 9/11 Records." Interview—Money and Markets: Podca. Available at: <http://www.moneyandmarkets.com/podcasts/ron-paul-cg-23-opening-the-secret-911-records>; the former senator Robert Graham, former chairman of the Intelligence Committee, revealed that the classified pages were meant to "cover up Saudi activity in 9/11." *Ibidem.*

[36]Peter Baker, "As World Boils, Fingers Point Obama's Way." *The New York Times*, August 15, 2014.

[37]*Ibidem.*

[38]*Ibidem.*

Chapter 9
The Real Reasons of Washington's Intervention in Libya

9.1 Washington's Ignorance About the Countries It Wanted to Invade

In his memoirs, Robert Gates, former CIA director as well as Secretary of Defense of Presidents George W. Bush and Barack Obama, wrote that when the decision was made to invade Afghanistan in 2001, after the terrorist attacks against the WTC in New York, no one in Washington—not even him—had any idea of the country's complexities: its tribes, ethnic groups, power brokers, and the rivalries between towns and provinces.[1] The same applied to Iraq. "We begin military engagements—wars—profoundly ignorant about our adversaries and about the situation on the ground," Robert Gates confessed, adding that the government in Washington had no idea how broken Iraq was when it started the war and took over of the country in 2003; it was unaware of the devastation to the country's economy, society, and infrastructure after 8 years of tough sanctions imposed after the Gulf War with the United States between August 2, 1990, and February 28, 1991.[2]

Washington was just as ignorant with respect to Libya when on March 3, 2011, President Barack Obama, as a global dictator, ordained that Muammar Gaddafi "must go," less than a month after the beginning of the protests against his regime.[3] The United States didn't understand the country very well, the former Libyan Arab Jamahiriya, inhabited by various ethnic and tribal groups, Berbers (Amazigh) and

---

[1]Robert Gates, 2014, pp. 589–590.
[2]*Ibidem*, p. 589.
[3]Leon Panetta, 2014, pp. 380–382.

© Springer Nature Switzerland AG 2019
L. A. Moniz Bandeira, *The World Disorder*,
https://doi.org/10.1007/978-3-030-03204-3_9

Arabs, and with regions that were virtually autonomous, such as Tripolitania and Cyrenaica, Zentania, and others, only weakly unified under a federal constitution promulgated in 1951.[4] Only Gaddafi—after taking power in September 1, 1969— had been able to maintain a certain weak national structure in a country with approximately 140 tribes (qabila), of which only 30 to 40 were estimated to have political influence, divided into sub-tribes (buyut) and family groups (lahma), which identified themselves through common ancestry, traditions, language, and culture.[5]

Furthermore, when the United States and its partners proposed a no-fly zone to the UN Security Council, it didn't present the slightest evidence Gaddafi was using aircraft against protesters. Nothing could justify such a non-fly measure. The intelligence gathered by the CIA showed that the opposition, which had risen up in Benghazi, wasn't strong enough to take Tripoli and overthrow the regime.[6] The rebels were disorganized, despite the efforts by American (and Egyptian) special forces to train them in camps in eastern Libya, and they lacked basic command and maneuvering capabilities.[7] President Obama hesitated getting involved in a war in the Middle East when he was trying to leave Iraq.[8] The dominant belief in Washington, however, was the same as that of the George W. Bush administration: only through extreme violence—war—could authoritarian governments be expelled and al-Qa'ida crippled. Secretary of State Hillary Clinton pressed Obama any way she could to order an intervention in Libya. And after the UN Security Council approved the establishment of a no-fly zone, based on the specious principle of "protecting civilians," Barack Obama finally ordered the bombing of Libya along with Britain and France, under NATO's guise and violating Resolution 1973 (2011). "[…] A Libyan war was a NATO campaign and (Admiral Jim) Stavridis (Supreme Allied Commander Europe—SACEUR) was responsible for it," wrote Leon Panetta, then Secretary of Defense (2011–2013) of the Obama administration.[9]

---

[4]Mohammed Bescir Fergiani, 1983, pp. 46–70, 102–109.

[5]*Ibidem*, pp. 111–112; Jon Mitchell, "Libya—War in Libya and Its Futures—Tribal Dynamics and Civil War (1)." *The Red (Team) Analysis Society*, April 13, 2015. Available at: <http://www. google.de/imgres?imgurl=https%3A%2F%2Fwww.redanalysis.org%2Fwp-content%2Fuploads% 2F2015%2F04%2FTribes-Map.jpg&imgrefurl=https%3A%2F%2Fwww.redanalysis.org% 2F2015%2F04%2F13%2Fwar-libya-futures-tribal-dynamics-civil-war%2F&h=477&w=550& tbnid=LZASOPFCv39wlM%3A&zoom=1&docid=MzM39PpnHvjhWM& ei=xqyjVeKhFarNygOGhIXoCQ&tbm=isch&iact=rc&uact=3&dur=1719&page=1&start=0& ndsp=42&ved=0CDAQrQMwBQ>.

[6]*Ibidem*, p. 381.

[7]*Ibidem*, p. 380. "Libyan rebels 'receive foreign training'. Rebel source tells Al Jazeera about training offered by US and Egyptian special forces in eastern Libya." *Al Jazeera*, April 3, 2011. Available at: <http://www.aljazeera.com/news/africa/2011/04/201142172443133798.html>.

[8]Leon Panetta, 2014, p. 381.

[9]*Ibidem*, p. 382.

9.2   The Disintegration of the State in Libya and the Spread of Terrorism with Weapons Supplied by NATO

With the destruction of Muammar Gaddafi's regime, Libya became a stateless country. It virtually disintegrated, and since then, no de facto or de jure government has existed. The state lost power and no authority was or is safe from attacks. In October 2013, Prime Minister Ali Zeidan was kidnapped by militants of the group Libya Revolutionaries Operations Room and subsequently released. His government failed, and the security situation continued to deteriorate in Tripoli and Benghazi, the two largest cities in the country. In a March 2014 report to the Security Council, Tarek Mitri, Special Representative and Head of the United Nations Support Mission in Libya (UNSMIL), stressed that the security situation had deteriorated to such a point that the existing militias "challenge the state's monopoly on the legitimate use of force."[10] Libya's situation was what democracy looked like when exported through civil war, under the command of foreign agents and the NATO bombing campaigns.

Power was up for grabs in the streets of Benghazi, Sirtes, Derna, Misrata, and other cities, where the Islamic brigades and tribes used weapons supplied by NATO to fight Gaddafi and each other, escalating the chaos and bloodshed in the political vacuum left after his fall. They were battling each other for control of the rich oil deposits, in the order of 48 billion barrels (January 2014), with low extraction costs and situated in the Sirte (approximately 80%), Murzuk, Ghadames, Cyrenaica, and Kufra basins as well as offshore.[11]

The civil war between the various Islamic militias and tribes started reflecting the regional contradictions between the Persian Gulf countries and the conflicts among themselves and with others, including Egypt, Israel, and western countries. On May 16, 2014, General Khalifa Haftar triggered Operation Dignity and rose up against the defenseless government of the General National Congress, presided by Nouri Abusahmain. He wanted to dissolve it on several pretexts, including the fact that it had introduced Shariah law in December 2013, suppressing women's rights. Joined by several military contingents, including the Air Force based in Tobruk, General Haftar threw his troops against the fundamentalist militias of Ansar al-Shariah and other groups, predominant in Benghazi.[12] It seems Haftar, who the Islamic fundamentalists called a "renegade," had been both a supporter and opponent of Gaddafi,

---

[10]*U.N. Security Council Report*. Monthly Forecast, March 2014. Available at: <http://www.securitycouncilreport.org/monthly-forecast/2014-03/libya_8.php>.

[11]"Libya—Overview—Libya is a member of the Organization of the Petroleum Exporting Countries, the holder of Africa's largest proved crude oil reserves, and an important contributor to the global supply of light, sweet crude oil." *Energy Information Administration (EIA)*, November 25, 2014. Available at: <http://www.eia.gov/countries/cab.cfm?fips=LY>.

[12]Barak Barfi, "Khalifa Haftar: Rebuilding Libya from the Top Down." *The Washington Institute*, August 2014. Available at: <http://www.washingtoninstitute.org/policy-analysis/view/khalifa-haftar-rebuilding-libya-from-the-top-down>.

in addition to supposedly serving the CIA, since he had lived in exile in Virginia (United States) for 21 years and received the backing of General Abdel Fattah el-Sisi, the president of Egypt, who was trying to crush the Muslim Brotherhood after ousting President Mohamed Morsi in July 2013, a year after his election.[13] The so-called Arab Spring to promote democracy had resulted in a military dictatorship to prevent Egypt from plunging into the same chaos as Libya.

By the end of July, meanwhile, the Parliament in Libya, presided by Abu Bakr Biira, had taken refuge in Tobruk (Operation Dawn)[14] backed by a coalition of forces and requested an UN intervention. According to sources in the United States, aircraft from the United Arab Emirates (UAE) taking off from airbases in Egypt secretly bombed the Islamic militias of Libya Dawn, which were sponsored by the emirate of Qatar.[15] But the bombings were unable to deter them or prevent their success. A few days later, the Libya Dawn militias, allied with militias from Misrata, conquered Tripoli airport, until then under the command of the Zintan militias, and now controlled the devastated capital, where they installed another government.[16] Until mid-2015, however, no government—neither in Tobruk nor in Tripoli—had been able to exert authority in Libya on a national level or to obtain international recognition and legitimacy.

Since 2011, the United Arab Emirates, where the exiled Mahmoud Jibril led the National Forces Alliance (backed by the West), and Qatar, where the equally exiled Ali Salabi guided the Muslim Brotherhood, played central yet opposite roles in Libya and in opposition to the influence of Saudi Arabia and Iran.[17] The air attacks

---

[13] *Ibidem*; Mohamed Madi, "Profile: Libyan ex-General Khalifa Haftar." *BBC News*, October 16, 2014. Available at: <http://www.bbc.com/news/world-africa-27492354>; "Libyan Army General Khalifa Haftar a CIA operative: Analyst." *Press TV*, September 6, 2014. Available at: <http://www.presstv.ir/detail/2014/06/09/366288/gen-khalifa-haftar-cia-man-in-libya/>; Michael Pizzi, "Libya's rogue general, an ex-CIA asset, vaunts his anti-extremism services. Khalifa Haftar wants to rid Libya of the Muslim Brotherhood—something many regional powers may rally behind." *Al Jazeera*, July 24, 2014.

[14] Amro Hassan (Cairo), "Libya's parliament ducks fighting to meet in eastern city of Tobruk." *Los Angeles Times*, August 2, 2014. Available at: <http://www.latimes.com/world/middleeast/la-fg-libya-parliament-tobruk-20140802-story.html>.

[15] "UAE 'behind air strikes in Libya'. Two US officials say United Arab Emirates carried out air raids against militias using bases in Egypt." *Al Jazeera*, August 26, 2014. Available at: <http://www.aljazeera.com/news/middleeast/2014/08/uae-behind-air-strikes-libya-201482523130569467.html>; Patrick Kingsley (Cairo) & Chris Stephen & Dan Roberts (Washington), "UAE and Egypt behind bombing raids against Libyan militias, say US officials—Strikes said to be from planes flying out of Egyptian airbases signal step towards direct action in conflict by other Arab states." *The Guardian*, August 26, 2014.

[16] Steve Fox, "Libya burns as politicians and militia groups vie for control." *Middle East Eye*, August 24, 2014. Access on Tuesday, December 2, 2014. Available at: <http://www.middleeasteye.net/news/politicians-and-militia-groups-vie-control-battle-torn-libya-99372368>.

[17] "UAE 'behind air strikes in Libya'. Two US officials say United Arab Emirates carried out air raids against militias using bases in Egypt." *Al Jazeera*, August 26, 2014. Available at: <http://www.aljazeera.com/news/middleeast/2014/08/uae-behind-air-strikes-libya-201482523130569467.html>; Samira Shackle, "UAE-Egypt attack on Libya aimed at Islamists." *Memo–Middle East*

didn't prevent the conquest of Tripoli, however, although fighting continued in the vicinity as well as in Benghazi, the domain of another radical Islamic organization, Ansar al-Shariah. This group had first appeared in Yemen, just as al-Qa'ida in the Arabian Peninsula (AQAP), and multiplied into other groups—Movement for Unity and Jihad in West Africa (MUJAO), El Moulethemine Battalion, and Ansar al-Din, of Tuareg and Malian origin. Ansar al-Shariah advanced in Mali, Tunisia, Mauritania and other countries of the Maghrib. Boko Haram, a movement affiliated to the Islamic state, arose in northeastern Nigeria (in the city of Maiduguri), but evolved and became capable of organizing attacks in the northwest; in the cities of Kano, Zária, and Kaduna; in the center, in the city of Jos; and even in the capital city of Abuja. In addition, Boko Haram terrorists infiltrated neighboring countries: the north of the Republic of Cameroon and the Republic of Niger and Chad. Other Islamic terrorist movements flourished in Africa: Al-Shabaab in Somalia, a member of al-Qa'ida; AQMI (al-Qa'ida in the Islamic Maghreb), originally from Algeria and linked to al-Qa'ida, with activities in Libya and Mali; and al-Murabitun, also in Mali, the product of the merger between groups originating from the MUJAO (Movement for Unity and Jihad in West Africa), but with no alliance with the Islamic state, which acquired a strong base in Sirte, hometown of Muammar Gaddafi, on the south coast of the Gulf of Sidra, between Tripoli and Benghazi.

9.3   Banks Profit with the Funds Confiscated from Gaddafi

The fight over the hydrocarbon reserves, sources of economic and political power that could be used as bargaining chips, inflamed conflicts between all religious and political factions in Africa. And just as in other countries where such groups intensified their attacks and massacres, the political and economic situation in Libya also deteriorated. Libya had the largest oil reserves in Africa and produced on average nearly 1.6 million barrels per day (b/d), but had become the smallest supplier within the Organization of the Petroleum Exporting Countries (OPEC), with a supply of only 300,000 b/d in June 2014.[18] Moreover, its sovereign fund, which held about US$65 billion—the 2nd largest in Africa and the 20th in the world—was exploited and largely appropriated by banks in Wall Street and Europe, which profited from the war and the fall of Muammar Gaddafi's government. Goldman Sachs managed a Libyan sovereign fund and lost nearly US$1 billion with derivative products. Nevertheless, it earned at least US$350 million in profits, revealing nothing about this until it was sued in 2014 by the Libyan Investment Authority

---

Monitor, August 27, 2014. Available at: <https://www.middleeastmonitor.com/blogs/politics/ 13771-uae-egypt-attack-on-libya-aimed-at-islamists>.

[18]Tarek El-Tablawy, "Tripoli Clashes Toll Rises by 22 as Libya Crisis Deepens." *Bloomberg News*, August 3, 2014. Available at: <http://www.businessweek.com/news/2014-08-03/tripoli-fighting-death-toll-rises-by-22-as-libya-crisis-deepens>.

(Case no. 14-310) in the High Court of Justice, Chancery Division, in Britain.[19] The French Société Générale SA (GLE) was also being sued to answer for the loss of about US\$1 billion from the Libyan sovereign fund it managed. And so the United States, controlling the other members of NATO, showed how they could build a nation and deploy democracy. By mid-2014, Libya had virtually fallen under the command of fundamentalist Islamic militias after the capture of the airport, previously occupied by the Zintan Brigades.

9.4   The Death of Ambassador J. Christopher Stevens in Benghazi and Pentagon Support to Jihadists (Terrorists) in Syria

The scenario in Libya was a kaleidoscope and behind the fighting factions were several international actors, which used them as proxies.[20] The country had fragmented, becoming more and more feudal, falling apart along the geographical and tribal lines dividing a large part of the territory. The army and police structures had virtually disappeared. And the most diverse Jihadist and Salafi groups were fighting among themselves with the weapons the United States, France, and Great Britain had so widely dispersed to overthrow the Gaddafi regime. The bloodshed increased. The number of dead in the course of 2014 rose every day.[21] In just 6 weeks from mid-October to November 30, 2014, about 400 people died in armed clashes between militias and government forces in the vicinity of Benghazi.[22]

---

[19]kit Chellel, "Libyan Investment Authority Sues Goldman Sachs in London." *Bloomberg News*, January 22, 2014. Available at: <http://www.bloomberg.com/news/2014-01-22/libyan-invest ment-authority-sues-goldman-sachs-in-london-court.html>; "High court judge orders Goldman Sachs to disclose Libya profits—Libyan sovereign wealth fund, which is suing Goldman, estimates the US investment bank made \$350 million in upfront profit on nine derivatives products." *The Guardian*, November 24, 2014; Jenny Anderson, "Goldman to Disclose Profit It Made on Libyan Trades." *The New York Times*, November 24, 2014. Available at: <http://dealbook.nytimes.com/2014/11/24/goldman-to-disclose-profit-it-made-on-libyan-trades/?_r=0>.

[20]Chris Stephen, "War in Libya—the Guardian briefing—In the three years since Muammar Gaddafi was toppled by Libyan rebels and NATO airstrikes, fighting between militia has plunged the country into civil war and seen Tripoli fall to Islamists. The involvement of Qatar, Egypt and the UAE risks a wider regional war." *The Guardian*, August 29, 2014. Available at: <http://www.theguardian.com/world/2014/aug/29/-sp-briefing-war-in-libya>.

[21]AL Arabiya News. "Libya death toll rises as clashes in Benghazi continue." *Al Arabya*, October 2, 2014. Available at: <http://english.alarabiya.net/en/News/africa/2014/10/02/Seven-Libyan-sol diers-killed-in-Benghazi-bombs-and-clashes-army-official-says.html2014>. Access on December 3, 2014.

[22]"Some 400 killed over last 6 weeks in Libya clashes." *Press TV Wednesday*, December 3, 2014. Available at: <http://www.presstv.ir/detail/2014/11/30/388096/libyas-6-week-death-toll-reaches-400/>.

The report of the UN Human Rights Council submitted on February 23, 2016, emphasized that "the impact of the armed conflicts and internal instability in Libya in 2014 and 2015 has been devastating."[23] In just 5 months, between April and August 2015, 1539 people suffered violent deaths. The hemorrhaging produced by the NATO bombing campaign had not staunched in 5 years. The violence reached 2.5 million people and displaced over 430,000. In 2015, more than 2880 drowned while trying to reach Italy from North Africa. The cities were not rebuilt. Access to hospitals, schools, and essential services, such as power, sanitation, and water, was still in a very precarious state.

Said Boumedouha, director of Amnesty International for the Middle East and North Africa, declared the NATO members should assume responsibility for the "horrors that have unfolded in Libya,"[24] and added:

Over the past 5 years Libya has descended deeper into the abyss of human rights chaos, amid lawlessness, rampant abuse and war crimes by rival armed groups and militias, and the rising threat posed by the armed group calling itself Islamic state.

Da'ish in fact projected its influence from Syria and Iraq to the Maghrib. Terrorism overpowered Libya. Authorized by President Obama, Hillary Clinton, then Secretary of State, granted a record number of licenses to American dealers to sell the most sophisticated weapons and military technology, according to the Citizens Commission on Benghazi.[25] These weapons were handed to the terrorists of al-Qa'ida and others in the war against Gaddafi and served to assault the American compound in Benghazi, resulting in the deaths of Ambassador J. Christopher Stevens[26] and three other American citizens—Sean Smith and the Navy Seals Ty

---

[23] A/HRC/31/CRP.3. Human Rights Council—31st session, February 23, 2016. Agenda items 2 and 10—*Annual report of the United Nations High Commissioner for Human Rights and reports of the Office of the High Commissioner and the Secretary-General Technical* assistance and capacity-building—Investigation by the Office of the United Nations High Commissioner for Human Rights on Libya: detailed findings. Available at: <http://www.ohchr.org/en/hrbodies/hrc/pages/hrcindex.aspx>.

[24] "World must help pull Libya out of human rights chaos five years since uprising that ousted al-Gaddafi." *Amnesty International*—Libya Armed Conflict, February 16, 2016. Available at: <https://www.amnesty.org/en/latest/news/2016/02/world-must-help-pull-libya-out-of-human-rights-chaos-five-years-since-uprising-that-ousted-al-gaddafi/>; Magda Mughrabi, "Libya since the 'Arab Spring': 7 ways human rights are under attack." *Amnesty International*—LibyaArmed Conflict, London, February 16, 2016. Available at: <https://www.amnesty.org/en/latest/campaigns/2016/02/libya-arab-spring-7-ways-human-rights-are-under-attack/>.

[25] Catherine Herridge & Pamela Browne (Fox Business), "Exclusive: The Arming of Benghazi—The United States supported the secret supply of weapons to Libyan rebels while Hillary Clinton was Secretary of State according to federal court documents obtained by Fox News. In a sworn declaration." *Benghazi Accountability Coalition*, June 29, 2015. Available at: <http://benghazicoalition.org/>.

[26] Ambassador Christopher Stevens was beaten, was sodomized, had his genitals cut off, and was burned after he was killed. His murder was similar to that of Muammar Gaddafi.

Woods and Glen Doherty—on September 11, 2012.[27] These four Americans—
Ambassador Stevens and the three agents (two of whom mercenaries)—were coordinating directly with the Salafi terrorist Abdel Hakim Belhadj, head of the Libyan
Islamic Fighting Group (LFIG),[28] and working on the mission of removing heavy
weaponry for the Jihadists linked to al-Qa'ida, Ansar al-Shariah, and other terrorist
groups that had penetrated Syria. These fighters came from such countries as Yemen,
Saudi Arabia, Kuwait, Iraq, Libya, Jordan, Belgium, Pakistan, Bangladesh, Chechnya, France, Great Britain, and the Netherlands.[29] The Pentagon considered the
jihadists (terrorists) to be the best fighters against the regime of Bashar al-Assad.[30]

According to a document of the DIA Memo (Memorandum from the Defense
Intelligence Agency), dated September 16, 2012, copied by the National Security
Council, the CIA and other agencies had concluded that the terrorist attack on the
American installations had been planned at least 10 months or more prior to its
execution. But they did nothing. Secretary of State Hillary Clinton and her direct
assistants were informed of what would occur with just two hours' notice.[31] Ambassador J. Christopher Stevens was, in fact, redirecting armaments to al-Qa'ida, Ansar
al-Shariah, and Jabhat al-Nusra militants and other groups linked to the Muslim
Brotherhood, opponents of the ruling Socialist Ba'ath Party in Damascus. The Salafi
Jihadists in Syria accounted for more than half of all Salafi fighters worldwide,
according to the RAND Corporation, and they executed two thirds of the attacks
orchestrated by al-Qa'ida in 2013 against the regime of Bashar al-Assad.[32] These
groups—Ansar al-Shariah, Jabhat al-Nusra, and others—joined forces with Ansar
al-Islam, which constituted the core of Da'ish (Islamic State of Iraq and Syria/
Levant), and expanded until the Sinai. They lost space in Egypt, however, where

---

[27]Jerome R. Corsi, "Generals conclude Obama backed al-Qaida, Probe of military experts finds
U.S. 'switched sides' in terror war." *WND*, January 19, 2015. Available at: <http://www.wnd.com/
files/2012/01/Jerome-R.-Corsi_avatar-96x96.jpg>; Catherine Herridge & Pamela Browne (Fox
Business), "Exclusive: The Arming of Benghazi—The United States supported the secret supply
of weapons to Libyan rebels while Hillary Clinton was Secretary of State according to federal court
documents obtained by Fox News. In a sworn declaration." *Benghazi Accountability Coalition*,
June 29, 2015. Available at: <http://benghazicoalition.org/>.

[28]On the terrorist Abdel Hakim Belhadj, see Luiz Alberto Moniz Bandeira, 2014, pp. 319, 342,
351, and 404.

[29]Michael B Kelley. "Al-Qaeda Jihadists Are The Best Fighters Among The Syria Rebels."
Business Insider—Military & Defense, July 31, 2012. Available at: <http://www.businessinsider.
com/al-qaeda-jihadists-are-among-the-best-fighters-among-the-syria-rebels-2012-7?IR=T>.

[30]*Ibidem*; Michael B. Kelley, "There's A Reason Why All of The Reports about Benghazi Are So
Confusing." *Business Insider—Military & Defense*, November 3, 2012. Available at: <http://www.
businessinsider.com/benghazi-stevens-cia-attack-libya-2012-11?GO=T>.

[31]Jeremy Diamond, "Rand Paul skips hearing on State funding, hits Clinton on Benghazi." *CNN*,
April 22, 2015. Available at: <http://www.nationalreview.com/corner/414500/hillary-clintons-top-
aides-knew-first-minutes-benghazi-was-terrorist-attack-e-mails>.

[32]Seth G. Jones, "A Persistent Threat—The Evolution of al Qa'ida and Other Salafi Jihadists
(Prepared for the Office of the Secretary of Defense)." *RAND National Research Institute. RAND
Corporation*, 2014, p. x. ISBN: 978-0-8330-8572-6. Available at: <http://www.rand.org/content/
dam/rand/pubs/research_reports/RR600/RR637/RAND_RR637.pdf>.

the situation could have evolved similarly as in Libya if on June 3, 2013, Marshal Abdel Fattah el-Sisi, heading the Armed Forces, hadn't deposed President Muhamad Morsi, democratically elected by the Muslim Brotherhood, and crushed the Salafi movement, condemning hundreds of activists to death and imposing an atmosphere of fear to prevent demonstrations and chaos.

With regard to Syria, President Barack Obama committed a similar folly as in Libya. In August 2011, while submitting the regime of Bashar al-Assad to harsh sanctions, he once again resorted to giving orders as a global dictator: "For the sake of the Syrian people, the time has come for President Assad to step aside."[33] An order President Bashar al-Assad ignored, just as Muammar Gaddafi had. This is why the US ambassador to the United Nations, Susan Rice, presented a resolution to the Security Council in October authorizing the establishment of new sanctions and a no-fly zone in Syria. Russia and China vetoed, backed by Brazil, India, and South Africa. They voted against the adoption arguing that, in the case of Libya, NATO had overstepped and abused the resolution, which had been presented in bad faith by the powers of the West, not to protect civilians, but to justify 6 months of attacks against the Gaddafi regime. In fact, Seumas Milne correctly noted in *The Guardian* that NATO did not protect civilians in Libya, but rather multiplied the— countless—number of dead without losing even one soldier on the ground.[34] In the 6 months of civil war supported by the NATO bombing campaign, at least 30,000 people died, another 50,000 were wounded, and 4000 went missing, according to the Minister of Health of the provisional government installed in Libya in September/ October 2011.[35] And so, 3 years after President Obama declared that Gaddafi had lost legitimacy and "must step down from power and leave,"[36] the Arab Spring continued as proxy wars and terrorist attacks in the midst of chaos and humanitarian disaster.

---

[33]Scott Wilson & Joby Warrick, "Assad must go, Obama says." *The Washington Post*, August 18, 2011. Available at: <http://www.washingtonpost.com/politics/assad-must-go-obama-says/2011/08/18/gIQAelheOJ_story.html>; Kilic Bugra kanat, 2015, pp. 11, 77 e 83–84.

[34]Seumas Milne, "If the Libyan war was about saving lives, it was a catastrophic failure NATO claimed it would protect civilians in Libya, but delivered far more killing. It's a warning to the Arab world and Africa." *The Guardian*, October 26, 2011.

[35]Karin Laub, "Libya: Estimated 30,000 Died in War; 4000 Still Missing." *Huffpost World Post— The Huffington Post*, September 8, 2011. Available at: <http://www.huffingtonpost.com/2011/09/08/libya-war-died_n_953456.html>.

[36]Aamer Madhani, "White House—Obama Says Libya's Qaddafi Must Go." *National Journal*, March 3, 2011. Available at: <http://www.nationaljournal.com/obama-says-libya-s-qaddafi-must-go-20110303>.

9.5   The Humanitarian Tragedy of the Refugees

In August 2014, the UNHCR (United Nations High Commissioner for Refugees) stated in Geneva that it had recorded approximately 37,000 refugees in Tripoli and Benghazi, living under the worst conditions, without any security.[37] At the same time, thousands of people—around 88,000, of which 77,000 from Libya—were being illegally smuggled in boats to Europe. In the first half of 2014, more than 1000 refugees (boat people) drowned in the Mediterranean.[38] On August 22, 2014, a boat carrying at least 270 people sank with only 19 survivors.[39] According to the UNHCR, around 300 refugees died in August 2014, and the total number of drowned in the Mediterranean since the beginning of the year had already reached 1889, including 1600 who perished since June when the inflow increased exponentially due to the ever-deteriorating and unstable situation in Libya.

Until mid-2014, approximately 100,000 migrants/refugees had landed in Italy, of which 42,000 in 2013.[40] In May 2015, Bernardino León, head of the United Nations Support Mission in Libya (UNSMIL), declared that the country was on the verge of total economic and political collapse and that more than 500,000 people across the Mediterranean were waiting for asylum in Europe.[41] Thousands failed to reach Europe and went down with their boats. In the first half of 2014, approximately 42,000 people tried to cross the Mediterranean and reach Italy. And between January and April 2015 alone, approximately 1700 migrants, twice the number of 2014, succumbed in the crossing.[42] The boats foundered.

---

[37]"Concern mounts for refugees and asylum-seekers in Libya." *UNHCR*, Briefing Notes, August 5, 2014. Available at: <http://www.unhcr.org/53e0c0a09.html>.

[38]*Ibidem*; Nicholas Farrel, "Libya's boat people and Italy's tragic folly. The 'mare nostrum' policy has acted as a magnet for boat people; the crisis is only growing." *The Spectator*, September 6, 2014. Available at: <http://www.spectator.co.uk/features/9303722/italys-decriminalising-of-ille gal-immigration-has-acted-as-a-green-light-to-boat-people/>.

[39]Nicole Winfield (Associated Press), "Italy recovers more bodies of would-be refugees from Libya. Migrants fleeing in boats from unrest in Libya face deadliest few days, as more than 300 have drowned since Friday." *The star.com World*, August 26, 2014. Available at: <http://www.thestar.com/news/world/2014/08/26/italy_recovers_more_bodies_of_wouldbe_refugees_from_libya.html>.

[40]*Ibidem*.

[41]Sean Nevins, "2011 NATO Destruction of Libya Has Increased Terrorism Across Region." "From Libya to Mali, Nigeria and Somalia, NATO's 2011 intervention against Moammar Gadhafi has had an undeniable domino effect—but when do the dominoes stop falling?" *MintPress News*, May 20, 2015. Available at: <http://www.mintpressnews.com/2011-nato-destruction-of-libya-has-increased-terrorism-across-region/205801/>.

[42]Raziye Akkoc & Jessica Winch & Nick Squires, "Mediterranean migrant death toll '30 times higher than last year': as it happened. More than 1750 migrants perished in the Mediterranean since the start of the year—more than 30 times higher than during the same period of 2014, says the International Organisation for Migration." *The Telegraph*, April 21, 2015. Available at: <http://www.telegraph.co.uk/news/worldnews/europe/italy/11548995/Mediterranean-migrant-crisis-hits-Italy-as-EU-ministers-meet-live.html>.

The number of refugees and displaced people seeking asylum in all countries, driven by wars and persecutions, was growing year after year, and in 2014 it hit a new record, according to the Global Trends Report of the UNHCR (United Nations High Commissioner for Refugees).[43] It jumped from 37.5 million in 2005 to 51.2 million in 2013 and soared to 59.5 million at the end of 2014.[44]

According to the International Organization for Migration (IOM), more than 1 million irregular migrants and refugees entered Europe in 2015, and about 3690 refugees, 400 more than in 2014, drowned in the excruciating crossing of the Mediterranean.[45] The avalanche continued in 2016. And the large number of refugees who managed to get to Italy, France, and other countries became a serious economic, social, and political problem for Europe as a whole, creating all sorts of trouble for their housing and integration.[46] The UN agency for refugees— UNHCR—considered the war refugees issue a "colossal humanitarian catastrophe."[47]

And who was at fault for this humanitarian disaster? Who actually bore the responsibility for the tragedy and problems the European Union was facing with the war survivors, refugees, and migrants from the most diverse countries? The greatest responsibility has always fallen on the United States and the European Union itself, with their open and covert interventions in the Middle East, as well as on Qatar, Saudi Arabia, and the Sunni tyrannies of the Persian Gulf. The bombing of Libya and destruction of Gaddafi's regime, and with it the state apparatus, opened the floodgates to all kinds of trafficking through the Mediterranean, especially of people fleeing the conflicts and poverty in the Middle East and Africa, the areas occupied by Da'ish and its franchises, such as Ansar Bayt al-Maqd in Sinai province and other organizations, whose militants publicly executed people and left the corpses exposed in the streets to intimidate the people.[48] Could Hillary Clinton,

---

[43]"Worldwide displacement hits all-time high as war and persecution increase." UNHCR—Geneva. *Annual Global Trends Report*, June 18, 2015. Available at: <http://www.unhcr.org/print/ 558193896.html>.

[44]Ibidem.

[45]"Irregular Migrant, Refugee Arrivals in Europe Top One Million in 2015: IOM." *International Organization for Migration*, December 22, 2015. Available at: <https://www.iom.int/news/irregu lar-migrant-refugee-arrivals-europe-top-one-million-2015-iom>.

[46]"Europe's boat people—The EU's policy on maritime refugees has gone disastrously wrong." *The Economist. Europe in Trouble*, April 11, 2015. Available at: <http://www.economist.com/ news/leaders/21649465-eus-policy-maritime-refugees-has-gone-disastrously-wrong-europes-boat- people>.

[47]Harriet Sherwood & Helena Smith (Athens) & Lizzy Davies (Rome) & Harriet Grant, "Europe faces 'colossal humanitarian catastrophe' of refugees dying at sea. UN considers Africa holding centres as 'boat season' is expected to bring sharp increase in migrants making treacherous crossing." *The Guardian*, June 2, 2014.

[48]Magda Mughrabi, "Five years ago, an initially peaceful uprising in Libya quickly developed into armed conflict involving Western military intervention and eventually ended when Colonel Mu'ammar al-Gaddafi was killed in October 2011. Successive governments then failed to prevent newly-formed militias of anti al-Gaddafi fighters from committing serious crimes for which they

who had put so much pressure on President Obama to order an attack on Libya when she was his Secretary of State, have repeated what she gleefully said to a TV reporter in Kabul when she learned of the lynching of Muammar Gaddafi, savagely beaten and sodomized with a bayonet: "We came, we saw, he died."[49]

As the journalists Jo Becker and Scott Shane stressed in a report in *The New York Times*, despite Hillary Clintons claims to the contrary, Libyans saw NATO's intervention not as a noble act to save lives, but in far darker terms, and CIA officers had voiced their concern that without Gaddafi, the situation in Libya could spin out of control.[50] And this is what actually happened. Five years after Gaddafi's lynching, Da'ish penetrated Libya and occupied more than 150 miles around Sirtes, on the Mediterranean coast, and at the doorsteps of Europe. The truth of the matter, therefore, is that all the difficulties faced by Italy, Spain, France, Britain, Germany, and Spain and other countries of the European Union as a result of the migration of millions of refugees and displaced persons, not to mention the threat of terror, were mainly a result of the wars the United States promoted and the European Union, subjected to NATO, supported, instigated, and/or sustained in Afghanistan, Iraq, Syria, Libya, and other countries of Central Asia and the Middle East to North Africa.

Refugees from Libya and the Maghrib were not the only ones smuggled by traffickers over the Mediterranean. There were also refugees from Syria, Iraq, and Yemen, who also drowned or were confined in concentration camps in Lampedusa (Italy), Marseille (France), the "jungle" of Calais (France), Hungary, Cyprus, and other countries, where about 600,000 of them were deprived of their freedom in the first half of 2014. Meanwhile, Africans from sub-Saharan Africa—Eritrea, Somalia, Sudan, and Mali—were taken as slaves by Islamic militia for the transport of weapons, ammunition, and supplies to the front lines of battle in Libya. Simultaneously, Islamic fundamentalists continued their fight to impose their own caliphate,

---

never faced justice. The country remains deeply divided and since May 2014 has been engulfed in renewed armed conflict." *Amnesty International*, London, February 16, 2016. Available at: <https://www.amnesty.org/en/latest/campaigns/2016/02/libya-arab-spring-7-ways-human-rights-are-under-attack/>.

[49]The Jihadists, supported by NATO, captured approximately 150 people along with Gaddafi, who were transported to Misrata. More than 60 were found dead after suffering all sorts of violence in the vicinity of the Mahari Hotel. Jo Becker & Scott Shane, "The Libya Gamble Part 2. A New Libya, With 'Very Little Time Left'." *International New York Times*, February 27, 2016. Available at: <http://www.nytimes.com/2016/02/28/us/politics/libya-isis-hillary-clinton.html?_r=1>.

[50]Jo Becker & Scott Shane, "The Libya Gamble Part 1. Hillary Clinton, 'Smart Power' and a Dictator's Fall." *International New York Times*, February 27, 2016. Available at: <http://www.nytimes.com/2016/02/28/us/politics/hillary-clinton-libya.html?mabReward=A6&action=click&pgtype=Homepage&region=CColumn&module=Recommendation&src=rechp&WT.nav=RecEngine>.

as in Syria and Iraq. And in addition to plundering Gaddafi's arsenals, the Jihadists in Libya received so many weapons from the United States, France, and Britain that the brigades and non-state groups began smuggling them by air, land, and sea, via Turkey, Qatar, and Lebanon, to Islamic organizations in Syria, the Sinai, Nigeria, Tunisia, Algeria, Mali, Chad, Somalia, the Central African Republic, and Gaza.[51]

---

[51]Jo Becker & Scott Shane, "The Libya Gamble Part 1. Hillary Clinton, 'Smart Power' and a Dictator's Fall." *International New York Times*, February 27, 2016. Available at: <http://www. nytimes.com/2016/02/28/us/politics/hillary-clinton-libya.html?mabReward=A6&action=click& pgtype=Homepage&region=CColumn&module=Recommendation&src=rechp&WT. nav=RecEngine>.

Chapter 10
Geopolitical Lessons Learnt and Not Learnt: The Case of Syria

10.1 The Plans for Intervention in Syria

Robert F. Kennedy Jr.—nephew of President John F. Kennedy and son of Robert Kennedy (1925–1968), who was assassinated by the Jordanian Palestinian Sirhan Sirhan—courageously wrote that the American people should look beyond the convenient explanations of religion and ideology for the rise of Da'ish and the savagery that took so many innocent lives in Paris and San Bernardino.[1] They should instead focus on the "more complex rationales of history and oil, which mostly point the finger of blame for terrorism back at the champions of militarism, imperialism and petroleum here on our own shores."[2]

Indeed, as Robert F. Kennedy Jr. pointed out, the CIA had been meddling in Syrian affairs since March 1949, 2 years after the country's foundation. Two CIA agents, Miles Copeland and Stephen Meade, advised and certainly bribed Colonel Husni al-Za'im (1897–1949), Chief of Staff of the Army, who overthrew the democratically elected President Shukri al-Quwatli because he had hesitated in approving the construction of the Trans-Arabian Pipeline (Tapline) connecting the oil fields of Saudi Arabia to the ports of Lebanon, which the United States wanted to build through Syria.[3] Colonel Husni al-Za'im didn't last in government, however. He was executed in August 1949 after being ousted with the help of the United States

---

[1]On December 2, 2015, a devout Muslim couple shot and killed 14 in the city of San Bernardino, California, after returning from the Middle East. The man and woman were of Pakistani origin, both born in the United States, and were killed by the police, who described the attack as terrorism. The attacks in Paris and Saint-Denis occurred on the evening of November 13, 2015. 137 people were killed, including 7 terrorists.

[2]Robert F. Kennedy Jr., "Syria: Another Pipeline War." *EcoWatch*, February 25, 2016 http://ecowatch.com/2016/02/25/robert-kennedy-jr-syria-pipeline-war.

[3]Robert B. Durham, 2014, p. 392; Tim Weiner, 2007, pp. 138–14.

© Springer Nature Switzerland AG 2019
L. A. Moniz Bandeira, *The World Disorder*,
https://doi.org/10.1007/978-3-030-03204-3_10

by Colonel Adib Bin Hassan Al-Shishakli (1909–1964), who was himself deposed in 1954.[4]

Syria then embarked on a period of instability and turbulence, until Shukri al-Quwatli (1891–1967) was once again elected president through the National Party in 1955. He was in favor of nonalignment, however, and this didn't sit well with the administration of President Dwight Eisenhower in the midst of the Cold War against the Soviet Union. At that time—Robert Kennedy Jr. recalled—the CIA director Allen Dulles and his brother, Secretary of State John Foster Dulles, mounted a clandestine war against Arab nationalism, which they equated to communism, particularly when it threatened oil concessions.[5] The strategy outlined by CIA Planning Director Frank Wisner consisted in doing "everything possible to stress the 'holy war' aspect," as he said and General Andrew J. Goodpaster registered in a memo.[6] And this is why—Robert Kennedy Jr. emphasized—American soldiers tried to inflate the "conservative Jihadist ideologies that they regarded as a reliable antidote to Soviet Marxism [and those that possess a lot of oil]."

In his articles, Robert Kennedy Jr. recalled that in September 1957, nearly 50 years before the invasion of Iraq, President Dwight Eisenhower and Harold Macmillan, Prime Minister of Great Britain, adopted a covert operation plan to be led by the CIA and MI6 and to promote regime change through the invasion of Syria and other Arab countries and the assassination of its leaders, under the false accusation that they were promoting terror and threatening oil supplies to the West.[7] Documents to that effect were uncovered by Matthew Jones, reader in international history at Royal Holloway, University of London.

The regime change conspiracy for Syria began actually taking shape in 1955.[8] Allen Dulles considered Syria "ripe for a coup" and started coordinating with the British Secret Intelligence Service (SIS) and the Turkish Millî İstihbarat Teşkilatı (MİT), in collusion with the conservatives of the Syrian Social Nationalist Party. In September 1956 and on the pretext of containing the communist threat and Egypt's influence, Secretary of State John Foster Dulles instructed the US ambassador in Damascus, James S. Moos, to continue "to seek means of assisting Western firms which are bidding for the contract for construction of the Syrian national oil refinery in competition with bids from the Soviet bloc."[9] The construction of the refinery was

---

[4]*Ibidem*, p. 138; Miles Copeland, 1989, pp. 92–194.

[5]Robert Kennedy Jr., "Middle Eastern Wars Have ALWAYS Been About Oil." *WashingtonsBlog*, February 26, 2016. Available at: <http://www.washingtonsblog.com/2016/02/middle-eastern-wars-always-oil.html>. Also <https://www.globalresearch.ca/middle-eastern-wars-have-always-been-about-oil/5510640>, accessed: November 27, 2018

[6]Ian Johnson, 2000, p. 127.

[7]Robert F. Kennedy Jr., "Syria: Another Pipeline War." *EcoWatch*, February 25, 2016. Available at: <http://ecowatch.com/2016/02/25/robert-kennedy-jr-syria-pipeline-war/>.

[8]Arthur M. Schlesinger Jr., 1978.

[9]"334. Instruction From the Department of State to the Embassy in Syria." *Foreign Relations of the United States*, 1955–1957. Volume XIII, Near East: Jordan-Yemen, Document 334. Office of the

not the only thing on the agenda but also the Trans-Arabian Pipeline (Tapline), which would cross Syrian land and transport the oil from ARAMCO, explored in Qaisumah in Saudi Arabia, to the port of Sidon in Lebanon.[10] And in October, Operation Straggle to overthrow the government of President Shukri al-Quwatli was greenlighted after the outbreak of violence at the borders, instigated by officers of the Turkish, British, and American intelligence services.[11] Colonel Abdel Hamid al-Sarraj (1925–2013), head of the Syrian military intelligence service, discovered the plot, however, and arrested the main Syrian conspirators. The CIA agents, including Walter Snowden and the military attaché Robert W. Molloy, had to flee the country in haste.[12]

Operation Straggle was aborted on October 29, 1956, coincidentally at the time of the crisis in the Suez Canal, nationalized by Egyptian president Gamal Abdel Nasser (1918–1970), and the invasion of Egypt by Israel. And in December 1956, after the fiasco of Operation Straggle, Ambassador David K. E. Bruce (1898–1977) and former Secretary of Defense Robert Lovett (1895–1986), with the collaboration of Joseph P. Kennedy (1888–1969), in their capacity of members of the Board of Consultants on Foreign Intelligence Activities, delivered a report to President Eisenhower on the CIA undercover operations, which absorbed approximately 80% of the agency's budget. They criticized the CIA's fascination with "kingmaking" in the Third World and stated that its horde was mounting political intrigue campaigns instead of gathering intelligence on the Soviet Union. The Bruce-Lovett report[13] was kept secret and presumably included among the Robert F. Kennedy documents deposited at the John F. Kennedy Library. Until 2015, it had not been declassified. And apparently only Arthur M. Schlesinger (1917–2007), professor and former adviser to President John F. Kennedy, had access to the report to write Robert F. Kennedy's biography.[14]

But the United States did not stop subverting and changing the regime in Syria. In 1957, the CIA sent two covert operation specialists to Damascus, Howard "Rocky" Stone (1925–2004) and Kermit "Kim" Roosevelt (1916–2000),[15] the same agents who organized the coups d'état in Iran (Operation Ajax 1953) against Prime Minister Mohammad Mosaddegh) and Guatemala (Operation Success 1954) against

---

Historian, Bureau of Public Affairs, United States Department of State. Available at: <https://history.state.gov/historicaldocuments/frus1955-57v13/d334>.

[10]Daniel Yergin, 1990, pp. 335–337.

[11]Arthur M. Schlesinger, 1978, pp. 455–458.

[12]Bonnie F. Saunders, 1996, pp. 48–50, 62, 70; Salim Yaqub, 2004, pp. 48–52, 149.

[13]"The Elusive 'Bruce-Lovett Report'." *Cryptome—Center for the Study of Intelligence Newsletter.* Spring 1995 Issue N. 3. August 3, 2009. Available at: <https://cryptome.org/0001/bruce-lovett.htm>.

[14]Arthur M. Schlesinger Jr., 1978, pp. 455–458.

[15]Robert Kennedy Jr., "Middle Eastern Wars Have ALWAYS Been About Oil." *WashingtonsBlog,* February 26, 2016. Available at: <http://www.washingtonsblog.com/2016/02/middle-eastern-wars-always-oil.html>. Also: ibidem

President Jacobo Arbenz.[16] So Operation Straggle was reborn under the codename Operation Wappen,[17] which would try to organize the right wing of the officer corps and former politicians exiled in Beirut. But once again the conspiracy failed. Colonel Abdel Hamid al-Sarraj, fervently anti-imperialist and pro-Arab unity, had put the US embassy under constant surveillance and the army under strict control. And after the plot was denounced by officers who weren't taking the bribes, CIA agent Howard "Rocky" Stone was arrested and confessed, and ambassador James S. Moos was expelled from Syria.[18] President Dwight Eisenhower and Allen Dulles had no alternative but to accept the defeat. An invasion in Syria could lead to a Soviet intervention in Turkey. And in 1958, Syria joined Egypt, governed by President Gamal A. Nasser, to found the United Arab Republic (al-Jumhūriyyah al-'Arabīyah al-Muttaḥidah), which didn't last more than 3 years, however. On September 28, 1961, the unification with Egypt was undone by the section of the Syrian military opposing subordination to President Nasser.

In 1970, Air Force General Hafez al-Assad/Ḥāfiẓ al-'Asad (1930–2000), tied to the Arab Socialist Ba'ath party (Ḥizb Al-Ba'ath Al-'Arabī Al-Ishtirākī), took power. After the Yom Kippur War (1973), in which Israel defeated Syria and Egypt, he ruthlessly crushed various revolts of the Sunni-Salafi Muslim Brotherhood, including the one in Hama (1982), which the intelligence services of the United States and Turkey possibly encouraged, and stabilized the country. The continuing efforts by the United States to erode the regime in Syria pushed President Hafez al-Assad more and more toward an alliance with the Soviet Union.[19] And in October 1980, the two countries formalized the Treaty of Friendship and Cooperation. Hafez al-Assad died of a heart attack in 2000, and his son Bashar al-Assad took over the government.

After 2000, intervention in Syria returned once again to the agenda of the United States and its partners in the Middle East. Secret diplomatic cables published by WikiLeaks revealed that the Department of State had earmarked at least US$6 million to opposition groups in Syria, since at least 2005, to finance the operations of the satellite TV channel Barada River, linked to the Movement for Justice and Development, a network of Syrian exiles based in London, in addition to sponsoring other subversive activities and courses in Damascus.[20] In April 2009, TVA Barada

---

[16]Robert F. Kennedy Jr., "Syria: Another Pipeline War." *EcoWatch*, February 25, 2016. Available at: <http://ecowatch.com/2016/02/25/robert-kennedy-jr-syria-pipeline-war/>.

[17]William Blum, 2000, pp. 84–89; John Prados, 2006, 163–164.

[18]Caroline Attié, 2004, pp. 140–144.

[19]Jörg Michael Dostal. (Associate Professor, Graduate School of Public Administration, Seoul National University). "Post-independence Syria and the Great Powers (1946–1958): How Western Power Politics Pushed the Country Toward the Soviet Union." Paper Prepared for the 2014 Annual Meeting of the Academic Council on the United Nations System, June 19–21, 2014, Kadir Has University, Istanbul, Panel 14: Understanding and Responding to Crisis, Resistance and Extremism. Available at: <http://acuns.org/wp-content/uploads/2013/01/Syria-Paper-1946-1958-for-ACUNS-Conference-Website-12-June-2014.pdf>.

[20]Syria: Political Conditions and Relations with the United States After the Iraq War. Alfred B. Prados and Jeremy M. Sharp, Foreign Affairs, Defense, and Trade Division. Congressional

began instigating protests to overthrow Bashar al-Assad's regime. But according to another cable of the US embassy in Damascus, opposition funding in Syria between 2005 and 2010 had reached a much higher level—around US$12 million or more.[21] And one of the reasons the fall of Bashar al-Assad's regime was seen as crucial was the construction of the South Pars/North Dome pipeline through Syria.

Qatar possessed with Iran one of the largest natural gas fields in the world, second only to Russia, and it wanted to build the South Pars/North Dome pipeline, which would cost an estimated US$10 billion and extend 1500 km. It would pass through Saudi Arabia, Jordan, Syria, and Turkey, which would profit from the toll rates, to supply the markets of the European Union. In 2009, President Bashar al-Assad refused to sign the agreement, however, obstructing the construction of the pipeline on Syrian soil, certainly defending the interests of Russia, which had always been his ally. The contradictions with the Sunni tyrannies of the Persian Gulf further increased when he accepted the construction of an "Islamic pipeline" from Iran to Lebanon. This pipeline would turn Shiite Iran, and not Sunni Qatar, into the main energy supplier of the European markets and dramatically increase Tehran's influence in the Middle East and Europe. Its negotiation was announced in 2011, and the documents of the agreement were signed in 2012, foreseeing a construction that never materialized due to the war and chaos in Syria.[22] This was the real reason why Qatar tried to overthrow Bashar al-Assad's regime and channeled an estimated amount of at least US$3 billion to the rebel groups between 2011 and 2013, in addition to offering a reward of US$50,000 and shelter to the family of deserters from the Armed Forces, who began to be trained by the CIA.[23] Thus the Free Syrian Army was formed.

According to Robert Gates, former CIA director and Secretary of Defense of Presidents George W. Bush and Barack Obama, Syria had never ceased to be a problem for the United States after the end of the Cold War. It remained a "high priority intelligence target," given the possibility it could develop weapons of mass destruction, especially nuclear missiles, and because of its support to Ḥamās (the

---

Research Service Report RL32727—February 28, 2005. *WikiLeaks Document Release*, February 2, 2009. Available at: <http://wikileaks.org/wiki/CRS-RL32727>; Craig Whitlock, "U.S. secretly backed Syrian opposition groups, cables released by WikiLeaks show." *The Washington Post*, April 17, 2011. Available at: <https://www.washingtonpost.com/world/us-secretly-backed-syrian-oppo sition-groups-cables-released-by-wikileaks-show/2011/04/14/AF1p9hwD_story.html>.

[21]Craig Whitlock, "U.S. secretly backed Syrian opposition groups, cables released by WikiLeaks show." *The Washington Post*, April 18, 2011; "USA finanzieren offenbar syrische Opposition", *Focus Nachrichten*, 18 de abril de 2011; "U.S. secretly backed Syrian opposition groups, WikiLeaks reveals—$6 million for Syrian exiles to help." *Daily Mail*, April 18, 2011. *The Wiki Leaks Files*—Ther World to Accordin U.U. Empire—With an Introduction by Julian Assange. London: Verso, 2015, pp. 314–315. For further details see Luiz Alberto Moniz Bandeira, 2014, p. 371–390.

[22]Mitchell A. Orenstein & Romer, "George Putin's Gas Attack—Is Russia Just in Syria for the Pipelines?" *Foreign Affairs*, October 14, 2015. Available at: <https://www.foreignaffairs.com/articles/syria/2015-10-14/putins-gas-attack>.

[23]*Ibidem*.

acronym for Harakat al-Muqáwama al-Islamiya) and Hizballah, in conflict with Israel.[24] After the fall of Saddam Hussein and occupation of Baghdad in 2003, the US Secretary of Defense Donald Rumsfeld determined the development of contingency plans to extend the war to Syria and shape the strategic environment. President George W. Bush ended up vetoing this initiative, however.[25] He was warned that triggering another war would cause problems for the coalition with Great Britain,[26] and UN Secretary General Kofi Annan also expressed the fear that a military intervention in Syria would destabilize the entire Middle East. This is why General Colin Powell, then Secretary of State, declared to the press that the United States did not intend to attack another country "right now," even though it was concerned with Syria (because of Israel).[27] But the plan went even further and provided for the invasion of seven countries in 5 years. Apart from Iraq and Syria, the United States would bring war to Libya, Iran, Yemen, Somalia, and Sudan, as General (r) Wesley K. Clark revealed, who had been the Supreme Allied Commander Europe (SACEUR) and ran in several primaries of the Democratic Party for president of the United States in 2004.[28]

In 2008, the attack on Syria was back on the agenda because of Israel, not only on the pretext of preventing the trafficking of weapons to Hizballah and the training of militants within its territory but also due to the construction of the al-Albany nuclear reactor in the region of Deir ez-Zor. For various reasons, however, Robert Gates, then Secretary of State, didn't think the United States should undertake such an initiative. These reasons included the shaken US credibility after the invasion of Iraq, where the alleged weapons of mass destruction were never found, and the storm a preemptive attack against Syria would cause in the Middle East, Europe, and the United States, in addition to undermining the war effort in Afghanistan and Iraq.[29] President George W. Bush gave up on the idea despite the pressures from Vice-President Dick Cheney, the warmonger who had similarly manipulated the invasion of Iraq to deliver profits to Halliburton, the corporation he had presided and with which he maintained close ties, just as with other military-industrial contractors of the Pentagon and the Big Oil Companies.[30] The bombing of the reactor in Syria was left to Israel, which secretly carried out Operation Orchard on September 6, 2007,

---

[24]Robert Gates, 2014, p. 171.

[25]Julian Borger (Washington) & Michael White & Ewen Macaskill (Kuwait City) & Nicholas Watt, "Bush vetoes Syria war plan." *The Guardian*, April 15, 2003.

[26]Wesley K. Clarck, 2004, pp. 83–84.

[27]"No war plans for Syria: U.S." CNN, April 16, 2003. Available at: <http://edition.cnn.com/2003/WORLD/meast/04/15/sprj.irq.int.war.main/index.html>.

[28]Wesley K. Clark, 2004, p. 167.

[29]Robert Gates, 2014, pp. 169, 588.

[30]David Corn, "WATCH: Rand Paul Says Dick Cheney Pushed for the Iraq War So Halliburton Would Profit. As the ex-veep blasts Paul for being an isolationist, old video shows the Kentucky senator charging that Cheney used 9/11 as an excuse to invade Iraq and benefit his former company." *Mother Jones/Foundation for National Progress*, April 7, 2014. Available at: <http://www.motherjones.com/politics/2014/04/rand-paul-dick-cheney-exploited-911-iraq-halliburton>.

employing 17 tons of explosives and a total of 4 F-15I Strike Eagle jets, 4 F-16 Fighting Falcon jets, and 1 intelligence plane.[31]

On October 4, 2011, when the demonstrations against the Bashar al-Assad regime intensified, the United States, France, and Britain, with the support of Germany and Portugal, tried to repeat the same subterfuge in the UN Security Council they had used on Gaddafi, but this time against Syria. They presented a proposal for a resolution based on the R2P (Responsibility to Protect) principle, which provided for sanctions against the Bashar al-Assad regime on the grounds that the repression of the protests had already caused 2900 deaths and could not continue. The scenario set up for Syria was the same as for Libya. And this is why Russia and China vetoed the resolution, with the support of Brazil, India, and South Africa.[32] The Russian Ambassador in the Security Council, Vitaly Churkin, argued that the situation in Syria could not be seen separately from the experience in Libya and that the community had been warned about how NATO would interpret the UN resolution.[33] The pretext of the Responsibility to Protect resolution, as it was used in the bombing of Libya, had become the template to justify NATO interventions as the military instrument of the ultra-imperialist cartel led by the United States, Great Britain, and France.

10.2 Foreign Jihadists in the War Against Bashar al-Assad

President Barack Obama did not act as President George W. Bush, who invaded Iraq in 2003 without the approval of the Security Council. But together with his Pro-consuls in France and Great Britain, François Hollande and David Cameron, he set out to stealthily instigate the war against Bashar al-Assad, now no longer a civil war because of the increasing participation of thousands of foreign Jihadists, including

---

[31]"Report: U.S. officials say Israel would need at least 100." *Ha'aretz, Israel*, February 20, 2012. Available at: <http://www.haaretz.com/news/diplomacy-defense/report-u-s-officials-say-israel-would-need-at-least-100-planes-to-strike-iran-1.413741>; Aaron Kalman, "Israel used 17 tons of explosives to destroy Syrian reactor in 2007, magazine says, Mossad agents stole key information on Assad's nuclear project from Vienna home of Syrian atomic agency head, New Yorker claims." *The Times of Israel*, September 10, 2012. Available at: <http://www.timesofisrael.com/israel-uses-17-tons-of-explosives-to-destroy-syrian-reactor/>.

[32]"Russia and China veto UN resolution against Syrian regime." *Associated Press/The Guardian*, October 5, 2011.

[33]Carla Stea, "Manipulation of the UN Security Council in support of the US-NATO Military Agenda—Coercion, Intimidation & Bribery used to Extort Approval from Reluctant Members." *Global Research—Global Research Center on Globalization*, January 10, 2012. Available at: <http://www.globalresearch.ca/manipulation-of-the-un-security-council-in-support-of-the-us-nato-military-agenda/28586>. "Council Fails to Uphold its Responsibility to Protect in Syria." International Coalition for the Responsibility to Protect (ICRtoP)—*The Canadian Centre for the Responsibility to Protect*, October 7, 2011. Available at: <http://icrtopblog.org/2011/10/07/un-security-council-fails-to-uphold-its-responsibility-to-protect-in-syria/>.

approximately 1239 prisoners of various nationalities, sentenced to death for rape and smuggling, who Saudi Arabia had sent into combat in Syria in exchange for a pardon.[34] President Obama and other authorities knew "from classified assessments"[35] that most weapons sent through Saudi Arabia and Qatar fell into the hands of Islamic extremists and fundamentalists, who wanted to restore the Great Caliphate in Greater Syria—Bilad al-Sham—between the Euphrates river and the Mediterranean Sea. In collaboration with the CIA, the countries of the Persian Gulf and Turkey kept increasing the military aid to the Jihadists in Syria, sending them weapons by air.[36] In August 2013, *DEBKAfile*, an information agency headed by two investigative journalists and dedicated to the gathering of intelligence and security, stated that "the U.S., Jordan and Israel are quietly backing the mixed bag of some 30 Syrian rebel factions," some of which "seized control of the Syrian side of the Quneitra crossing, the only transit point between Israeli and Syrian Golan."[37] According to the same source, Turkey was allowing passage to Jihadist groups, including Jabhat al-Nusra and Ahrar al-Sham, affiliated to al-Qa'ida, so they could attack the northeast of Syria along the coast and the port of Latakia.[38]

Until September 2013, the Islamic brigades had reportedly received approximately 400 tons of weapons in 2 years from the Gulf countries, an extraordinary amount, consisting mainly in ammunition, machine guns, automatic antiaircraft weapons, and other equipment unloaded in the province of Hatay in Turkey.[39] And agents of the DGSE (Direction Générale de la Sécurité Extérieure) and DRM (Direction du Renseignement Militaire), the French intelligence services, as well as of the CIA and MI6, were already operating inside Syria.

---

[34]"Saudi Arabia Sent Death Row Inmates to Fight in Syria in Lieu of Execution." *Assyrian International News Agency—AINA News*, January 20, 2013. Available at: <http://www.aina.org/news/20130120160624.htm>; Michael Winter, "Report: Saudis sent death-row inmates to fight Syria. Secret memo says more than 1200 prisoners fought Assad regime to avoid beheading." *USA TODAY*, January 21, 2013. Available at: <http://www.usatoday.com/story/news/world/2013/01/21/saudi-inmates-fight-syria-commute-death-sentences/1852629/?siteID=je6NUbpObpQ-LvY5MH6LGuR644xcPiwBWQ>.

[35]David E. Sanger, "Rebel Arms Flow Is Said to Benefit Jihadists in Syria." *The New York Times*, October 14, 2012.

[36]C. J. Chivers & Eric Schmitt, "Arms Airlift to Syria Rebels Expands, With Aid From C.I.A." *The New York Times*, March 24, 2013.

[37]Nafeez Ahmed, "How the West Created the Islamic State." Part 1—Our Terrorists. Counterpunch. *Weekend Edition*, September 12–14, 2014. Available at: <http://www.counterpunch.org/2014/09/12/how-the-west-created-the-islamic-state/print>; "Erdogan usa a al-Qaeda para encobrir sua invasão à Síria." *Pravda*, May 30, 2014. (Portuguese edition). Available at: <http://port.pravda.ru/busines/30-03-2014/36510-erdogan-0/>.

[38]*Ibidem.*

[39]"Intervention en Syrie: derniers développements." *Agora Dialogue*, September 1, 2013. Available at: <http://agora-dialogue.com/intervention-en-syrie-derniers-developpements/>.

10.3 Joe Biden's Accusation: Turkey and the Gulf Countries Supporting the Islamic State

In a speech to students of the Institute of Politics at Harvard University on October 2, 2014, Vice-President Joe Biden publicly singled out Turkey, Saudi Arabia, and the United Arab Emirates as the "biggest problem" in the Middle East, accusing them of supporting with money and weapons the Sunni Salafis and Wahhabis who established the Islamic State.[40] These Gulf States and Turkey—Vice-President Joe Biden said—were so determined to overthrow President Bashar al-Assad that they initiated the "proxy Sunni-Shia war," pouring hundreds of millions of dollars and tens of thousands of tons in weapons.[41] Joe Biden, however, tried to disassociate the United States from the responsibility of fostering a civil war in Syria, including by training the Jihadists of the al-Nusra Front (an al-Qa'ida franchise) and providing the armaments that Saudi Arabia, Qatar, and the United Arab Emirates were handing over. But Biden did reveal that President Recep Tayyip Erdogan—"an old friend"— had admitted to him that he let many Jihadists penetrate Syria through the borders of Turkey and stressed that "the outcome of such a policy now is more visible": the radical fundamentalists of Da'ish were advancing on northern Syria and Iraq.[42]

Two days later, on October 4, Vice-President Joe Biden was forced to call President Erdogan, the king of Saudi Arabia and the emirs of Qatar and the United Arab Emirates, to apologize for implicating them intentionally in the supply of weapons and funding of Da'ish, enabling the rise of the Islamic State—his spokes-woman Kendra Barkoff informed the press.[43] The journalist Carol Giacomo then published an article in *The New York Times* entitled "Joe Biden Apologizes for Telling the Truth."[44] Yes, Joe Biden apologized for telling the truth, but not all of it. He didn't mention President Obama's decision to destroy the Assad regime and push the Middle East toward a regional war, which could lead to a confrontation between Russia and the United States.[45]

President Assad, however, was always very well informed about the relevant efforts by Turkey, Saudi Arabia, Qatar, and the United Arab Emirates, as well as the United States, to supply weapons and prepare the Jihadists infiltrated in Syria and waging war against his government. On August 26, 2013, in an interview to the

---

[40]"Biden blames US allies in Middle East for rise of ISIS." *RT*, October 3, 2014. Available at: <http://rt.com/news/192880-biden-isis-us-allies/>.

[41]*Ibidem.*

[42]*Ibidem.*

[43]Sebnem Arsuoct, "Biden Apologizes to Turkish President." *The New York Times*, October 4, 2014.

[44]Carol Giacomo, "Joe Biden Apologizes for Telling the Truth." *The New York Times—The Opinion Pages*, October 6, 2014.

[45]Mike Whitney, "The University of Al-Qaeda? America's—'Terrorist Academy' in Iraq Produced ISIS Leaders." *Counterpunch*, October 6, 2014. Available at <http://www.counterpunch.org/2014/10/06/americas-terrorist-academy-in-iraq-produced-isis-leaders/print>.

Moscow newspaper *Izvestia*, he had already pointed to Qatar and Turkey as the countries who were directly mobilizing and promoting terrorism in Syria.[46] According to Assad, in the first 2 years (2011 and 2012), Qatar mostly funded the terrorists, while Turkey provided logistical support and training before they entered Syria.[47] Saudi Arabia then replaced Qatar as the primary funder of the Jihad—Assad said—and Turkey, a large country with a strategic position and a liberal society, was regrettably being manipulated by a meager amount of dollars from the Gulf monarchies, home to one of the most regressive mentalities; the Turkish people were not responsible for this situation, but rather Prime Minister (and later president) Recep Tayyip Erdoğan.[48]

Turkey played a crucial role in promoting the war against the regime of Bashar al-Assad, perhaps more so than Qatar and Saudi Arabia. After the almost insurmountable resistance against Turkey's entry into the European Union had become clear, President Erdogan and his Prime Minister (and former Minister of Foreign Affairs) Ahmet Davutoğlu always cherished the desire to restore the Ottoman Empire, even if informally. And to accomplish this Syria would have to be subjugated. But President Erdoğan didn't act without the backing of Barack Obama.

10.4   Prince Bandar al Sultan's Mission in Moscow and President Vladimir Putin's No

The king of Saudi Arabia, Abdullah bin Abdul Aziz, was also involved in the operation against Bashar al-Assad's regime. Coordinating with the governments of the United States, France, and Britain, he had instructed Prince Bandar bin Sultan bin Abdulaziz Al-Saud, General Secretary of the National Security Council, head of the Saudi Intelligence Agency (Al-Mukhābarāt al-ʿĀmma) and former ambassador in Washington, to go to Moscow and negotiate the withdrawal of Russia's support to Bashar al-Assad in exchange for the protection of its interests in Syria.

Prince Bandar bin Sultan, who once considered sending Syria back to the stone age,[49] had arrived at the conclusion that the region as a whole, from the Maghrib to

---

[46]Bashar al-Assad: "All contracts signed with Russia are implemented." *Izvestia*, 26 августа 2013 (26 de agosto de 2013), |Политика|Izvestia|написать авторам—Читайте далее: <http://izvestia.ru/news/556048#ixzz3FBxhnBKi>.

[47]*Ibidem.*

[48]*Ibidem.*

[49]"Schmutzige Deals: Worum es im Syrien-Krieg wirklich geht." *Deutsche Wirtschafts Nachrichten*, August 31, 2013. Available at: <http://deutsche-wirtschafts-nachrichten.de/2013/08/31/schmutzige-deals-worum-es-im-syrien-krieg-wirklich-geht/>; Ambrose Evans-Pritchard, "Saudis offer Russia secret oil deal if it drops Syria Saudi Arabia has secretly offered Russia a sweeping deal to control the global oil market and safeguard Russia's gas contracts, if the Kremlin backs away from the Assad regime in Syria. *The Telegraph*, 27 de agosto de 2013; F. Michael Mallof, "Saudis Pressure Russians to Drop Syria—Effort coordinated with U.S., Europe." *WND*, August 26, 2013. Available at: <http://www.wnd.com/2013/08/saudis-pressure-russians-to-drop-syria/>.

Iran—the entire Middle East and Central Asia—was under the influence of a confrontation between the United States and Russia, which could become dramatic in Lebanon. His first meeting in Moscow, on August 2, 2013, was with General Igor Sergon, director of Glavnoye razvedyvatel'noye upravleniye (GRU), the Russian military intelligence service. He was then received by President Vladimir Putin, whom he offered, among other things, the purchase of US$15 billion in weapons, a package of economic resources and the assurance that Russia's interests in Syria, including the port of Tartus, would be guaranteed. In return, Moscow would no longer back the Assad regime nor block the resolution authorizing an intervention in the country, which would be presented at the UN Security Council.[50] "We understand Russia's great interest in the oil and gas in the Mediterranean from Israel to Cyprus. And we understand the importance of the Russian gas pipeline to Europe. We are not interested in competing with that," Prince Bandar bin Sultan declared.[51] But President Putin rejected the proposal and reiterated that he would continue to support the Assad regime as the one most suited to the Middle East, since it was secular.[52] Saudi Arabia, which supported the Salafi opposition, had tried to bribe him with the offer of buying a large volume of Russian weapons and promoting Moscow's influence among the Arab countries. The backdrop of this initiative were the preparations by the United States and its NATO allies to attack Syria.

---

[50]"Russia rebuffs Saudi offer to drop Syria support for arms deal: Report." *PressTV*, August 8, 2013. Available at: <http://www.presstv.ir/detail/2013/08/08/317827/russia-snubs-saudi-bid-for-shift-on-syria/>.

[51]Ambrose Evans-Pritchard, "Saudis offer Russia secret oil deal if it drops Syria—Saudi Arabia has secretly offered Russia a sweeping deal to control the global oil market and safeguard Russia's gas contracts, if the Kremlin backs away from the Assad regime in Syria." *The Telegraph*, August 27, 2013; Aryn Baker, "The Failed Saudi-Russian Talks: Desperate Diplomacy as Syria Implodes, Saudi Arabia's intelligence chief reportedly offered Russian President Vladimir Putin a multibillion-dollar arms deal to curb Moscow's support for the Syrian regime." *Time*, August 9, 2013.

[52]Rani Geha, "Russian President, Saudi Spy Chief Discussed Syria, Egypt." *Al-Monitor*, August 22, 2013. Available at: <http://www.al-monitor.com/pulse/politics/2013/08/saudi-russia-putin-bandar-meeting-syria-egypt.html#>; Patrick Henningsen, "Saudi Prince Bandar's second attempt at bribing Russia to drop support of Syria." *21st Century Wire*, August 27, 2013. Available at: <http://21stcenturywire.com/2013/08/27/saudi-prince-bandars-second-attempt-at-bribing-russia-to-drop-support-of-syria/>. *The real SyrianFreePress Network War Press Info*, August 13, 2013. Available at: <https://syrianfreepress.wordpress.com/2013/08/09/russia-rebuffs-saudi-offer-to-drop-syria-support-for-arms-deal-report/>.

10.5   Gas Attack in Ghouta as Pretext for Intervention in Syria

No understanding was reached. And on August 21, 2013, a sarin gas attack was carried out in Ghouta, near Damascus, killing several hundreds of civilians,[53] an act violating the "red line"[54] President Barack Obama had carelessly imposed to justify intervention in Syria. Without any proof or evidence, the United States, France, and Great Britain, as well as the Arab League, accused the forces of President Bashar al-Assad of using chemical weapons against the Jihadists; killing hundreds of civilians, about 1300; and leaving thousands injured.[55] This would be the pretext for the armed intervention of the United States and the European Union. The sources of the news were the Jihadists and terrorists themselves, unidentified NGOs.[56] The Syrian Minister of Foreign Affairs, Walid Muallem, rejected the accusation "utterly and completely." "There is no country in the world that uses a weapon of ultimate destruction against its own people," Muallem said.[57] But President Barack Obama continued the deception without any qualms:

---

[53]"Moscow rejects Saudi offer to drop Assad for arms deal." *Agence France-Presse—Global Post* August 8, 2013. Available at: <http://www.globalpost.com/dispatch/news/afp/130808/moscow-rejects-saudi-offer-drop-assad-arms-deal>; Ambrose "Saudis offer Russia secret oil deal if it drops Syria." *The Telegraph*, 27 2013. "Schmutzige Deals: Worum es im Syrien-Krieg wirklich geht." *Deutsche Wirtschafts Nachrichten* August 31, 2013. Available at: <http://deutsche-wirtschafts-nachrichten.de/2013/08/31/schmutzige-deals-worum-es-im-syrien-krieg-wirklich-geht/>; "Saudi Arabia tries to tempt Russia over Syria." *Al-Alam News Network*, August 7, 2013. Available at: <http://en.alalam.ir/print/1502972>.

[54]"Remarks by the President to the White House Press Corps." The White House—Office of the Press Secretary, 20 de agosto de 2012; James S. Brady Press Briefing Room. *White House President Obama.* Available at: <http://www.whitehouse.gov/the-press-office/2012/08/20/remarks-president-white-house-press-corps>.

[55]"Moscow rejects Saudi offer to drop Assad for arms deal." *Agence France-Presse—Global Post*, August 8, 2013. Available at: <http://www.globalpost.com/dispatch/news/afp/130808/moscow-rejects-saudi-offer-drop-assad-arms-deal>; Ambrose Evans-Pritchard, "Saudis offer Russia secret oil deal if it drops Syria." *The Telegraph*, August 27, 2013. "Schmutzige Deals: Worum es im Syrien-Krieg wirklich geht." *Deutsche Wirtschafts Nachrichten*/Veröffentlicht: August 31, 2013 Available at: <http://deutsche-wirtschafts-nachrichten.de/2013/08/31/schmutzige-deals-worum-es-im-syrien-krieg-wirklich-geht/>.

[56]"L'Armée syrienne accusée d'avoir utilisé du gaz toxique, l'ONU sommée de réagir." *Le Figaro*, August 21, 2013.

[57]"Syria crisis: Foreign minister denies chemical attacks." *BBC News Middle East*, August 27, 2013. Available at: <http://www.bbc.com/news/world-middle-east-23850274>.

We know the Assad regime was responsible ... And that is why, after careful deliberation, I determined that it is in the national security interests of the United States to respond to the Assad regime's use of chemical weapons through a targeted military strike. [. . .] I believe we should act. That's what makes America different. That's what makes us exceptional. With humility, but with resolve, let us never lose sight of that essential truth.[58]

[58]"Remarks by the President in Address to the Nation on Syria." *The White House*—Office of the Press Secretary. *White House President Obama*. Available at: <http://www.whitehouse.gov/the-press-office/2013/09/10/remarks-president-address-nation-syria>.

Chapter 11
Chemical Weapons Attack in Ghouta as a Pretext for US Intervention

11.1 Corporate Media, the News Produced by NGOs, and the Farce of the Chemical Weapons in Ghouta

Contrary to what President Obama said, what made "America different... exceptional" was neither its *humility* nor the fact it never lost "sight of that essential *truth*." What made "America different... exceptional" was the hypocrisy, the cynicism and the ability to lie of its rulers. The truth of the matter was that both President Barack Obama and Secretary of State John Kerry were simply deceiving public opinion when they said—"strongly and with *high confidence*"—that the report of the UN inspectors presented "crucial details that confirm that the Assad regime is guilty of carrying out that attack" in Ghouta.[1] The "Report on the Alleged Use of Chemical Weapons in the Ghouta Area of Damascus on 21 August 2013," released on September 15, 2013, and the final report published on December 12 corroborate the use of chemical weapons in Ghouta and other places in Syria. The inspectors who carried out the investigations *in loco*, however, never reached any conclusion about the perpetrators of the attack; they didn't point out the responsibility, much less were they able to blame it, unequivocally, on the regime of President Bashar al-Assad, contrary to what Obama said while corrupting the truth.[2]

---

[1]Jake Miller, "Kerry: 'Definitive' U.N. report confirms Assad behind chemical attack." *CBS News*, September 2013. Available at: <http://www.cbsnews.com/news/kerry-definitive-un-report-confirms-assad-behind-chemical-attack/>.

[2]"UN Report on Chemical Weapons Use in Syria." *Council on Foreign Relations*, December 12, 2013. Available at: <http://www.cfr.org/syria/un-report-chemical-weapons-use-syria/p31404>; "Full text of "U.N. report on the alleged use of chemical weapons in Syria." United Nations Mission to Investigate Allegations of the Use of Chemical Weapons the Syrian Arab Republic Report on the Alleged Use of Chemical Weapons in the Ghouta Area of Damascus on 21 August 2013. *Internet Archive*. Available at: <https://archive.org/stream/787426-u-n-report-on-the-alleged-use-of-chemical/787426-u-n-report-on-the-alleged-use-of-chemical_djvu.txt>; "Syria profile." *BBC News—Middle East,* March 19, 2014. Available at: <http://www.bbc.com/news/

© Springer Nature Switzerland AG 2019
L. A. Moniz Bandeira, *The World Disorder*,
https://doi.org/10.1007/978-3-030-03204-3_11

President Obama and his Secretary of State John Kerry must have known of the provocation coordinated by Prince Bandar bin Sultan as a consequence of Saudi Arabia's support to the rebels in Syria. It was no secret to anyone. Nevertheless they readily accused President Assad, attributing their information to the US intelligence services, just as George W. Bush and Colin Powell had done when they showed films to the UN—with great pomp and circumstance—to justify the invasion of Iraq in 2003. And as (r) General Wesley Clark noted, the corporate media, owned by *big business*, the great American consortia with their commercial and financial interests, was once again an integral part of the campaign against Syria, just as in other modern wars.[3] It manipulated the news most of the time by spreading—intensively and extensively— especially those statements by American, French, and British representatives and the news produced by NGOs, without checking it, to misinform and deceive the public.

The French minister of Foreign Affairs during the administration of Prime Minister Laurent Fabius, Roland Dumas (1984–1986), revealed in an interview to *La Chaine Parlementaire TV network* (LCP) that the British had been planning and organizing the war against Syria 2 years before the protests against the Assad regime broke out in the beginning of 2011. He had heard the information directly from British officers when he was in London in 2009, and "the reason given for this war is the anti-Israeli position of the Syrian government, which has made Syria a target for a regime change supported by the West."[4] This was no doubt one important reason, but as pointed out by Nafeez Ahmed, executive director of the Institute for Policy Research & Development, oil interests, entwined with the geopolitical competition for control of the Middle East and the pipeline routes, were the real factors driving the intervention plan in Syria.[5]

What we know for sure about the chemical weapons attacks in Syria is that President Obama and Secretary of State Kerry were simply misleading public

---

world-middle-east-14703995>; "AI—HRW im Solde der Giftgas Terroristen: Barak Obama: UN Bericht, der Gift Gas Angriff in Syrien, durch die Terroristen." *Geopolitiker's Blog,* December 26, 2013. Available at: <http://geopolitiker.wordpress.com/?s=chemical+attacks+syria>; Robert Parry, "UN Investigator Undercuts New York Times on Syria. Assad Government not Responsible for August 21 Chemical Attack." Available at: https://www.globalresearch.ca/un-investigator-undercuts-new-york-times-on-syria-assad-government-not-responsible-for-august-21-chemical-attack/5362559, accessed: November 28, 2018. Guy Taylor, "Obama lied about Syrian chemical attack, 'cherry-picked' intelligence: report." *The Washington Times*, December 9, 2013. Available at: <http://www.washingtontimes.com/news/2013/dec/9/obama-lied-about-syrian-chemical%2D%2Dattack-cherry-pic/>.

[3]Wesley K. Clark, 2004, pp. 64 and 187–188.

[4]*"La raison invoquée pour cette guerre est la position anti-israélienne du gouvernement syrien qui a fait de la Syrie une cible pour un changement de régime soutenu par l'Occident."* "UK planned war on Syria before unrest began: French ex-foreign minister." *Press TV*, June 16, 2013. Available at: <http://www.presstv.ir/detail/2013/06/16/309276/uk-planned-war-on-syria-before-unrest/>; "Roland Dumas: deux ans avant le début de la guerre, l'Angleterre préparait l'invasion des rebelles en Syrie." *Wikileaks Actu Francophone*. Available at: <https://wikileaksactu.wordpress.com/category/syrie/>.

[5]Nafeez Ahmed, "Syria intervention plan fueled by oil interests, not chemical weapon concern." *The Guardian*, August 30, 2013.

opinion. They suppressed those passages from the intelligence reports which suggested a group linked to al-Qa'ida had been responsible for the Sarin gas attack in Ghouta, on August 21, 2013.[6] Indeed, the outstanding journalist Seymour Hersh revealed in the *London Review of Books* that, one month before the sarin gas attack, US intelligence services had already produced a series of highly secret and confidential reports culminating in a formal Operations Order—the document preceding a major invasion. These reports pointed to evidence that the Jihadist group al-Nusra Front, affiliated to al-Qa'ida, possessed equipment capable of producing sarin gas in large quantities. When the attack occurred, suspicion could have fallen on this group, but according to Seymour M. Hersh, "Barack Obama did not tell the whole story this autumn when he tried to make the case that Bashar al-Assad was responsible for the chemical weapons attack near Damascus on 21 August."[7] He, Barack Obama, omitted *important intelligence—picked intelligence to justify the strike against Assad*—and in other occasions, presented assumptions as facts.[8]

The physicians who cared for the civilian victims were told that the chemical weapons used in Ghouta and other places had been delivered to the Jihadists by Saudi Arabia through Prince Bandar bin Sultan, who'd been responsible for the transport and trade in preparation of the attack.[9] This had been a *false flag operation* executed by agents of al-Mukhābarāt al-ʿĀmma, the Saudi intelligence service.

There is also another version dealing with the alleged sarin attack: the testimony of a Catholic nun, mother Agnès-Mariam de la Croix, head of the St. James Monastery, the Melkite Greek Catholic Church in Qara, Syria. Before a hearing of the UN High Commissioner for Refugees attended by Professor Paulo Sérgio Pinheiro, the representative of Brazil, she denounced that the incident near Damascus—with many videos surfacing of alleged victims of a chemical weapons attack on August 21—had in fact been staged and manufactured so as to serve as evidence for certain foreign governments that the Syrian government had used sarin gas against its own people and therefore crossed the *red line* drawn by President Barack Obama.[10]

---

[6]Guy Taylor, "Obama lied about Syrian chemical attack, 'cherry-picked' intelligence: report." *The Washington Times*, December 9, 2013. Available at: <http://www.washingtontimes.com/news/2013/dec/9/obama-lied-about-syrian-chemical%2D%2Dattack-cherry-pic/>.

[7]Seymour M. Hersh, "Whose sarin?" *London Review of Books*, December 19, 2013, Vol. 35, No. 24, pp. 9–12.

[8]*Ibidem.*

[9]Dale Gavlak & Yahya Ababneh, "Exclusive: Syrians in Ghouta Claim Saudi-Supplied Rebels behind Chemical Attack. Rebels and local residents in Ghouta accuse Saudi Prince Bandar bin Sultan of providing chemical weapons to an al-Qaida linked rebel group." *MintPress News,* August 29, 2013. Available at: <http://www.mintpressnews.com/witnesses-of-gas-attack-say-saudis-supplied-rebels-with-chemical-weapons/168135/>.

[10]M. Klostermayr, "Syria: Mother Agnes on the Chronology of Chemical Attack near Damascus—Mother Agnes speaks about the fabricated videos of the chemical attack near Syria's capital, Damascus." *SyriaNews*, September 26, 2013. Available at: <http://www.syrianews.cc/syria-mother-agnes-chemical-attack-damascus/>; "Mother Superior presents a 50 pages report to the Human Rights Commision regarding the gas attacks." Available at: <http://www.abovetopsecret.

In her speech before the UN High Commissioner for Refugees, Mother Agnès-Mariam de la Croix said there was no truth to the way the wars between the state and opposition forces in the heartland of Syria were being portrayed. And she accused:

> The war—which affects my country today—is a war between Syrian civil society on the one hand and Islamic terrorist groups on the other. These terrorists are supported by foreigners from various countries, and funded by various foreign countries, especially Saudi Arabia. Saudi Arabia has acknowledged that these groups belong to terrorist organizations; yet at the same time, Saudi Arabia is training the terrorists and funding them in order to destroy Syria.[11]

11.2 Obama's "Red Line" and the "Rat Line" to Introduce Weapons and Ammunition from Libya in Syria

It was no secret to the White House, the Palais d' Élysée, or 10 Downing Street that Saudi Arabia was funding and transferring armaments and ammunition from Libya, where NATO had dumped huge amounts for the Muslim rebels fighting against the Gaddafi regime. CIA officers, who collaborated with the smuggling of war material, knew Saudi Arabia was thoroughly committed to destroying President Bashar al-Assad's regime, so much so that King Abdullah had appointed Prince Bandar, *the veteran of the diplomatic intrigues of Washington*, where he had been ambassador, and veteran of the Arab world, to coordinate operations in Syria. He was able to deliver what the CIA couldn't, i.e., weapons and money to Jihadists in Syria and under-the-table clout (*wasta* in Arabic), as an American diplomat remarked.[12]

At the beginning of 2012, Obama himself had ordered the establishment of what the CIA called the *rat line*, a channel to bring weapons and ammunition originating from Libya to Syria, through the southern border of Turkey, in order to supply the *moderate rebels*, many of which—if not most—Jihadists and even al-Qa'ida

---

com/forum/thread972253/pg1>; "UN Commission of Inquiry on Syria 'is acting to incite further Massacres'—Hands Off Syria—Australia, Press Release." *Global Research News,* September 15, 2013. Available at: <http://www.globalresearch.ca/hands-off-syria-un-commission-of-inquiry-on-syria-is-acting-to-incite-further-massacres/5349937>.

[11]"Syria: Destruction and Murder Funded by Foreign Forces: Mother Agnes Mariam Challenges the UNHRC—Address by Mother Agnes Mariam of the Mussalaha Initiative given at the UNHCR in Geneva by Mother Agnes Mariam." *Global Research,* March 16, 2014. Available at: <http://www.globalresearch.ca/syria-destruction-and-murder-funded-by-foreign-forces-mother-agnes-mariam/5373684>; "Syrie: Destruction et assassinats financés par des puissances étrangères. Discours de Mère Agnès pour "l'Initiative Moussalaha" [Réconciliation] en réponse aux déclarations du Haut commissariat aux réfugiés [UNHCR]." *Mondialisation.ca, Centre de Recherche sür la Mondialisation,* March 24, 2014. Available at: <http://www.mondialisation.ca/syrie-destruction-et-assassinats-finances-par-des-puissances-etrangeres/5375060>.

[12]Adam Entous & Nour Malas & Margaret Coker, "A Veteran Saudi Power Player Works To Build Support to Topple Assad." *Wall Street Journal—Middle East News,* August 25, 2013. Available at: <http://online.wsj.com/news/articles/SB10001424127887323423804579024452583045962>.

militants.[13] And after February 2013, the United States stepped up its support to such *moderate* Jihadists, as if it there is such a thing, giving them US$60 million under the pretext of improving the basic services (health and education) of the anti-Assad coalition, while France openly advocated for the shipment of war material in spite of the embargo imposed by the UN.[14]

11.3   The Training of Jihadists by Blackwater, the CIA, and Navy Seals

Meanwhile, the Department of State had been developing a program to provide military training to Jihadists in camps in Jordan since 2012 or even before, at a cost of US$60 million and using Blackwater mercenaries (Academi) and CIA agents. A large part of the Jihadists from Da'ish, perhaps even most of them, received combat and terrorism instructions there.[15] CNN revealed that US assistance went much further and also included training in the use of sophisticated weapons—antitank and antiaircraft—and military organization.[16] In early March 2013, approximately 300 Jihadists had already completed the course and crossed the border to Syria.[17] Those receiving training from Blackwater contractors, Navy Seals, SOF officers, and agents of the CIA paramilitary force clearly weren't "Syrian rebels" or "moderates" but Sunni Jihadists and foreign terrorists from various countries, including from Europe.

At that time, June 2013, Abdullah Ensour, prime minister of Jordan, revealed that about 900 American soldiers were already stationed in the country on the border with Syria, 200 of them providing training on chemical weapons, if case they were used, and 700 in charge of managing the Patriot missile defense system and F-16 fighter jets.[18] On April 17, 2013, Chuck Hagel, the US Secretary of Defense, admitted in his testimony before the Senate Armed Forces Committee that "the best outcome for Syria—and the region—[…] is a negotiated political transition," but he asserted that "military intervention is always an option. It should be an option,

---

[13]Seymour M. Hersh, "The Red Line and the Rat Line." *London Review of Books*, April 6, 2014. Available at: <http://www.lrb.co.uk/2014/04/06/seymour-m%2D%2Dhersh/the-red-line-and-the-rat-line>.

[14]Michael R. Gordon, "U.S. Steps Up Aid to Syrian Opposition, Pledging $60 Million." *The New York Times*, February 28, 2013.

[15]*Ibidem.*

[16]Nick Paton Walsh, "Opposition source: Syrian rebels get U.S.-organized training in Jordan." *CNN*, March 15, 2013. Available at: <http://edition.cnn.com/2013/03/15/world/meast/syria-civil-war/index.html?hpt=hp_bn2>.

[17]*Ibidem.*

[18]"Jordan hosts 900 U.S. troops to shield against Syria." *Daily Star* (Lebanon)—*Associated Press,* June 22, 2013. Available at: <http://www.dailystar.com.lb/News/Middle-East/2013/Jun-22/221243-us-military-presence-in-jordan-expands-to-1000-soldiers.ashx#axzz3CMsQVR3F>.

but an option of last resort."[19] He said that the Syrian Opposition Coalition (SOC) would be recognized as the legitimate representative of the Syrian people and that President Obama had promised to provide US$17 million in nonlethal aid and medical equipment. He confirmed that the State Department and USAID would also provide assistance to the *moderate opposition*, which involved the training of 1500 *Syrian leaders and activists* and more than 100 local advisors.[20] If the United States opted for direct military intervention, however, it would necessarily have to employ special forces and regular units to lay the groundwork within Syria through *black ops* and *covert actions*, in addition to antiaircraft defense units to protect against retaliatory attacks in Jordan, where 200 soldiers of the 1st Armored Division were already stationed on the border with Syria. The plan, according to Hagel, provided for a rapid increase to 20,000 or more soldiers, awaiting orders from the White House to proceed with the invasion.[21]

In fact, al-Mukhābarāt al-Ammah from Saudi Arabia and Dairat al-Mukhābarāt al-Ammah (General Intelligence Department—GID), the Jordanian secret service, along with the CIA, selected and trained Jihadists in Jordan to fight and perpetrate attacks against the Bashar al-Assad regime and its allies of Hizballah,[22] while Adel al-Jubeir, the Saudi ambassador in Washington, was lobbying US Congress and President Obama for an expansion of the American efforts against Bashar al-Assad. Meanwhile, American, British, and French warships were already in the Mediterranean, equipped with Tomahawks missiles to attack Syria and support the Jihadists.[23] This fleet included five Destroyers, an amphibious assault ship—*the USS San Antonio (LPD-17)*—with a hundred *marines* on board and equipped with a helicopter platform, in addition to the aircraft carriers *USS Harry Truman* and *USS Nimitz* in the Persian Gulf region.[24] The bombing would focus on 50 targets, including air bases where Russian-made helicopters were parked, command places, arsenals, and military barracks, but it would not target the chemical weapons deposits due to the

---

[19]"Secretary of Defense Testimony—Statement on Syria before the Senate Armed Services Committee as Delivered by Secretary of Defense Chuck Hagel, Washington, D.C., April 17, 2013." *U.S. Department of Defense.* Available at: <http://www.defense.gov/Speeches/Speech.aspx? SpeechID=1771>.

[20]*Ibidem.*

[21]*Ibidem.*

[22]Bob Dreyfuss, "The CIA Is Training Syria's Rebels: Uh-Oh, Says a Top Iraqi Leader." *The Nation.* March 01, 2013. Available at: <http://www.thenation.com/blog/173149/cia-training-syrias-rebels-uh-oh-says-top-iraqi-leader#>.

[23]Ambrose Evans-Pritchard, "Saudis offer Russia secret oil deal if it drops Syria Saudi Arabia has secretly offered Russia a sweeping deal to control the global oil market and safeguard Russia's gas contracts, if the Kremlin backs away from the Assad regime in Syria." *The Telegraph*, August 27, 2013.

[24]"Un navire de débarquement de la marine américaine est arrivé en Méditerranée." *Le Voix de Russe.* Available at: <http://french.ruvr.ru/news/2013_08_31/Un-navire-de-debarquement-de-la-marine-americaine-est-arrive-en-Mediterranee-2627/>.

risk of causing an environmental and humanitarian catastrophe and opening the gates for *raids* by militant Muslims.[25]

11.4 Putin's Diplomatic Victories in Syria and Ukraine

The American military intervention, as announced by President François Hollande and his allies, was set to begin on September 4,[26] the day President Obama reaffirmed, as global emperor: "I didn't set a red line. The world set a red line."[27] In a fit of paranoia/schizophrenia, he now spoke as if the world had established a *red line*. President François Hollande was also willing to push the military intervention in Syria, together with the United States. But more than two-thirds of the French population (64%) opposed the idea of a French coalition with the United States for yet another war in the Middle East, according to the public opinion poll performed by the *Institut d'Études de Marché & d'Opinion BVA* and the information channel *i-Télé-CQFD*, published by the newspaper *Le Parisien*.[28] In addition, a survey conducted by *The Washington Post-ABC News* revealed that the vast majority of people in the United States—nearly six in ten Americans (60%), democrats and republicans—was against missile strikes and an intervention in Syria on the pretext of the alleged use of chemical weapons in a suburb of Damascus.[29]

Despite Washington's drums of war, the survey revealed people had *little appetite* for war operations in Syria and a similar result emerged from the survey conducted by *NBC News*.[30] Another study, conducted by CNN a couple of days later, showed

---

[25]Thom Shanker & C. J. Chivers & Michael R. Gordon, "Obama Weighs 'Limited' Strikes against Syrian Forces." *The New York Times,* August 27, 2013; Shiv Malik & Tom Mccarthy, "Syria: US sees 'no avenue forward' to 'meaningful action' by UN—as it happened." *The Guardian,* Wednesday, August 28, 2013.

[26]"Syrie: l'intervention militaire pourrait débuter le 4 septembre." *La Voix de la Russie,* October 30, 2013. Available at: <http://french.ruvr.ru/news/2013_08_30/Syrie-lintervention-militaire-pourrait-debuter-le-4-septembre-7767/>.

[27]Peter Baker, "Obama Says 'World Set a Red Line' on Chemical Arms." *The New York Times,* September 04, 2013; *Glenn* Kessler, "President Obama and the 'red line' on Syria's chemical weapon." *The Washington Post,* September 6, 2013.

[28]"Intervention en Syrie: Hollande sous la pression de l'opposition." *Le Parisien,* August 31, 2013; "Syrie: Obama veut un vote du Congrès, Hollande sous pression." *Le Parisien,* September 1, 2013. Available at: <http://www.leparisien.fr/recherche/recherche.php?q=sur+trois+%2864+%25%29+sont+oppos%C3%A9s+%C3%A0+une+intervention+militaire+en+Syrie+&ok=ok>.

[29]Scott Clement, "Most in U.S. oppose Syria strike, Post-ABC poll finds." *The Washington Post,* September 3, 2013; Gary Langer, "Six in 10 Oppose U.S.-Only Strike on Syria; A Closer Division if Allies are Involved." *ABC News,* September 3, 2013. Available at: <http://abcnews.go.com/blogs/politics/2013/09/six-in-10-oppose-u-s-only-strike-on-syria-a-closer-division-if-allies-are-involved/>.

[30]*Ibidem.*

that the opposition to the attacks had grown to 70% (seven in ten Americans).[31] In such conditions, without authorization from the UN, without support from domestic and international public opinion, the Nobel Peace Prize Barack Obama was forced to retreat from his objective of "punishing" President Bashar al-Assad, as a god on earth, for a crime with no evidence or proof that he had committed it. Neither Obama nor François Hollande were able to accomplish their war designs and thus serve the interests of the oil companies and Israel.

They had no allies. Twelve NATO countries refused to participate in the military initiative against Syria without authorization from the UN Security Council. Even Prime Minister David Cameron, the faithful vassal of President Obama, wasn't able to lead the United Kingdom into the adventure. The British Parliament rejected the government's proposal to intervene in Syria by 285 votes against 272.[32] The report of the Joint Intelligence Committee confirmed nothing, it merely assumed that it was *highly likely* that the Assad regime was responsible for the chemical weapons used in the attack of August 21.[33] No proof existed. It was mere supposition, a hypothesis, but the members of the Labor Party demanded sufficient evidence. Prime Minister David Cameron had to recognize, before Parliament, that he could not provide this and that, indeed, he was not 100% sure whether Bashar al-Assad had been responsible for the use of chemical weapons in Ghouta, a suburb of Damascus.[34] The German minister of Foreign Affairs Guido Westerwelle, in turn, manifested himself against an intervention in Syria; and the president of Iran, Hassan Rouhani, threatened to intervene in the conflict in favor of Assad.

---

[31]Paul Steinhauser & John Helton, "CNN poll: Public against Syria strike resolution." *CNN*, September 9, 2013. Updated 1649 GMT (0049 HKT). Available at: <http://edition.cnn.com/2013/09/09/politics/syria-poll-main/>.

[32]*Ibidem.*

[33]"Syria: reported chemical weapons use—Joint Intelligence Committee letter. From: Cabinet Office—History: Published 29 August 2013. Part of: Working for peace and long-term stability in the Middle East and North Africa and Syria. Letter from Jon Day, the Chairman of the Joint Intelligence Committee (JIC), about reported chemical weapons use in Syria." *Gov. UK*. Available at: <https://www.gov.uk/government/publications/syria-reported-chemical-weapons-use-joint-intelligence-committee-letter>.

[34]"Syria crisis: David Cameron makes case for military action." *BBC News UK Politics*, August 29, 2013. Available at: <http://www.bbc.com/news/uk-politics-23883427>; Andrew Sparrow, "MPs vote down military intervention in Syria: Politics live blog. Government intelligence on Syria. Government legal advice on attacking Syria. MPs vote down plan for military intervention in Syria. Government defeat—What it means." *The Guardian*, August 30, 2013; "Syrie: David Cameron contraint par l'opposition d'attendre le rapport des inspecteurs de l'ONU." *Slate Afrique*, August 30, 2013. Available at: <http://www.slateafrique.com/367024/syrie-david-cameron-contraint-par-l%E2%80%99opposition-d%E2%80%99attendre-le-rapport-des-inspecteurs-de-l%E2%80%99onu>; Haroon Siddique & Tom Mccarthy, "Syria crisis: US isolated as British MPs vote against air strikes—as it happened. Trouble for White House after UK parliamentary revolt. Doubts circulate about case tying Assad to chemical weapons." *The Guardian*, August 30, 2013; "Syrie/attaque chimique: 'pas 100% de certitude' (Cameron)—Dossier: Situation politique en Syrie." *RIA Novosti,* August 29, 2015. Available at: <http://fr.ria.ru/world/20130829/199146661.html>.

Forewarned by his Secretary of Defense Leon Panetta, President Obama understood that Syria was not Libya. It was more heavily armed and possessed a vast
stockpile of military ammunition, including chemical weapons and a modern air
defense system provided by Russia, and its territory was less accessible to a land
assault.[35] 75,000 to 90,000 soldiers would be needed, as much or more as the United
States had in Afghanistan.[36] The bombings could destroy, but not modify the
strategic situation, because without boots on the ground, there were no conditions
for an effective and permanent occupation of the territory.[37] And the rebels, actually
Jihadists, appeared to be more problematic than in Libya. The conclusion, therefore,
was that the war would have a huge cost in American soldiers' lives.[38]

Faced with Leon Panetta's considerations, with whom the military commanders
agreed, President Obama, hesitant as always about what to do, forgot about the *red
line* he had so lightly traced to order an intervention in Syria. And Secretary of State
John Kerry had no other alternative but to broker a deal with the Russian Minister of
Foreign Affairs Sergey Lavrov, on September 14, 2013, through which Syria
allowed for the inspection, control, and elimination of all chemical weapons stored
on its territory. President Assad was promptly prepared to point out their location to
the Organisation for the Prohibition of Chemical Weapons (OPCW), and the UN
Security Council approved the agreement, frustrating the plan for an invasion of
Syria. Barack Obama, the *Kriegspräsident*[39] (war president), so named in Germany
and in other countries of Europe, could no longer contest that his intention was
merely to "punish" President Assad under the pretext that the Syrian army had used
sarin gas against the opposition.[40]

The deal preventing the bombing of Syria was a great diplomatic victory for
President Vladimir Putin. He preserved Russia's influence and advanced its interests
in the Mediterranean. Three months later, SoyuzNefteGaz negotiated and closed an
agreement with the General Petroleum Corporation to exploit the oil and gas reserves
along the coast of Syria.[41] Meanwhile, President Putin persuaded the Ukrainian
President Viktor Yanukovych not to sign an association agreement with the
European Union, despite the relentless protests from a layer of the population,
which NGOs funded by the United States, Germany, and other countries of the
West promoted in Maidan Square in Kiev. Putin invited the Ukrainian president in
December to come to Moscow and offered a *bailout* to the Government of Ukraine

---

[35]Leon Panetta, 2014, p. 448.

[36]*Ibidem*, p. 448.

[37]António Sousa Lara, 2011, p. 134.

[38]Leon Panetta, 2014, p. 449–451.

[39]Andreas Ross (Nova York), "Kampf gegen IS—Amerikas nächster Kriegspräsident." *Frankfurter
Allgemeine Zeitung*, Septembe 24, 2014; Beat schmid, "Obama, der Kriegspräsident." *Schweiz am
Sonntag*, September 27, 2014. Available at: <http://www.schweizamsonntag.ch/ressort/meinung/
obama_der_kriegspraesident/>.

[40]The removal and destruction of chemical weapons in Syria was completed in June 2014.

[41]Nicholas Blanford (Beirut), "The Next Big Lebanon-Israel Flare-Up: Gas." *Time*, April 6, 2011.
Available at: <http://content.time.com/time/world/article/0,8599,2061187,00.html>.

of US$15 billion, of which he advanced US$3 billion in January with the purchase of *Eurobonds* and he promised to reduce the price of the gas supplied by Gazprom by one-third, which would drop from about US$400.00 to $268.50 per 1000 m^3. This substantial discount would allow Ukraine to save US$7 billion in one year.[42] President Putin, who was also giving asylum to Edward Snowden, the National Security Agency (NSA) agent who had revealed the vastness of the electronic espionage carried out by the United States, had won another diplomatic victory, thwarting the agreement between the Ukraine and the European Union.

---

[42] Andrew Mckillop, "Did Natural Gas Debt Trigger the Ukraine Crisis? The Market Oracle." Politics/Eastern Europe, February 28, 2014. Available at: <http://www.marketoracle.co.uk/Arti cle44628.html>; "Putin throws Ukraine $15 bn lifeline, slashes gas price—Russian President Vladimir Putin on Tuesday gave Ukraine precious backing by agreeing to buy $15 billion of its debt and slash its gas bill by a third as it battles mass protests over the rejection of a historic EU pact." Bangkok Post, December 17, 2013. Available at: <http://www.bangkokpost.com/lite/local/385256/pressure-mounts-on-ukraine-leader-ahead-of-russia-visit>.

Chapter 12
A New Piece in the Geopolitical Game: The Invention of Ukraine

12.1 The Kievan Rus': Varangian (Viking) Conquest Along the Dnieper River and Mixing with the East Slavs

Between the ninth and twelfth centuries, the Kievan Rus' was a confederation of East Slavic tribes mixed with Vikings (Rus'),[1] who occupied the regions of the Volga and Dnieper Rivers since at least the year 852. It was virtually the greatest power in Europe, stretching over Belarus and parts of Russia, from the Baltic to the Black Sea. The conquest of the region began with the Viking Rurik (862–879), a Varangian (sveas væringjar) from Svealand (Egentliga Sverige—Sweden). He occupied Ladoga in 862. His successor, Oleg, conquered Kiev[2] in 880 and expanded his rule from Novgorod along the Dnieper River to protect the trade routes between northern Europe and southwest Asia,[3] where a khanate was located to the south of Russia. According to several authors, the Ashkenazim Jews descended from these Khazaria tribes.[4]

---

[1]The Varangians were called *Rus'*, the word probably originating from the Nordic *roðs* or *roths*, referring to the Swedes/Scandinavians. The word can be found in the writings of the Franks in the year 839—*Annales Bertiniani*—and is no doubt the root of the word Russian. In Finnish and Estonian, the words *Ruotsi* and *Rootsi* still remain to designate the Swedes. By the end of the twentieth century, however, the issue of its origin had been resolved. Bertil Albegrin (Uppsala University) et al., 1975, pp. 132–133; Johannes Brøndsted, 1986, pp. 67–68.

[2]Kiev was under the domain of two Viking princes, Askold and Dir, between 860 and 862. Franklin D. Scott, 1983, p. 22.

[3]*Ibidem*, pp. 20–25; Bertil Albegrin (Uppsala University) et al., 1975, pp. 134–138.

[4]The Ashkenazim Jews, according to Arthur Koestler and several scholars, are ethnically not of Jewish-Semitic origin, but descendants of the Khazars, people of Turkish ethnicity, who adopted Judaism as the official religion presumably around 740, during the reign of Bulč'an "Sabriel" al-khazari. Arthur Koestler concluded that these Jews are more related to the Hungarian, Magyar, and Uighur tribes than to the 12 tribes of Israel, with the descendants of Abraham, Isak, and Jacob. The khanate of Khazar was located between the Black Sea and the Caspian Sea and was destroyed during the invasion of the Arabs and Mongols between the twelfth and thirteenth centuries. Its

© Springer Nature Switzerland AG 2019
L. A. Moniz Bandeira, *The World Disorder*,
https://doi.org/10.1007/978-3-030-03204-3_12

The Kievan Rus' then prospered, for it controlled the trade from the Baltic to the Black Sea and Byzantium, exporting large quantities of fur and beeswax.[5] Later, the Rurik dynasty split and the kingdom divided into two principalities. But in 980, the prince of Novgorod, Valdamarr (Vladimir I, the Great), restored the dominion over all of Kievan Rus' after he recaptured Kiev, then ruled by his brother Iaropolk (976). In so doing, he completed the unification of the East Slavs, establishing a legal and administrative framework and converting to Christianity. He was baptized as an apostle in the Orthodox Church and canonized in the mid-thirteenth century.[6]

12.2   Decomposition into Principalities

The Scandinavian hordes flocking to Kievan Rus' mingled with the East Slavs and became known as "Rus." Starting in the eleventh century, however, the Kievan Rus' gradually disintegrated into several principalities—the Principality of Kiev, which occupied the two banks of the Dnieper River; Galicia-Volhynia or the Kingdom of Ruthenia (Regnum Galiciæ et Lodomeriæ); the Principality of Chernigov, on the left bank of the Dnieper; the Principality of Pinsk Marshes, later called Belarus (Byelorussiya or White Russia); and, among others, the Principality of Moscow, ruled since 1478 by the Grand Prince Ivan III, or Ivan the Great. He reconquered Novgorod and consolidated its independence by defeating the Golden Horde (Mongols), who had invaded the Kievan Rus' in 1240 and expanded their khanate from Ukraine, Romania, the European part of Russia, Belarus, Kazakhstan, and Uzbekistan until northwestern Siberia.

The region of the Kievan Rus' remained in dispute through constant wars between Tatars, Poles, Cossacks, and Lithuanians, and in the seventeenth century, it fragmented. The Polish-Lithuanian Commonwealth annexed the predominantly rural right bank of the Dnieper River; the Austro-Hungarian Empire incorporated Galicia (Halychyna); but the Russian Empire (Rossiyskaya Imperiya), whose foundations had been laid by Ivan IV or Ivan the Terrible (1530–1584), absorbed the entire east, until the north of the Black Sea, where rich deposits of coal and a certain industrial development existed.

---

people dispersed; a huge part of the Jews of Khazaria emigrated to Poland, while another went to the region of the Rhine (Germany and France); Kevin Alan Brook, 2010; Arthur Koestler, 1976, pp. 13–19, 154–166, 223–226; Isaac Deutscher, 1970, p. 30.

[5]Johannes Brøndsted, 1986, pp. 64–67.

[6]Paulo R. Magocsi, 2010, pp. 64–67.

12.3 Ivan the Terrible and the Foundation of Rossiyskaya Imperiya

Ivan IV Vasilyevich was the son of Grand Prince Vasily III of the Ryurikovich dynasty, founded by the Viking Rurik, and he took over the Grand Principality of Moscow (1533–1547) at the age of three under the regency of his mother, Yelena Glinskaya. In 1547, he was crowned Emperor of All Russia, with the title of czar (derived from the Latin *Caesar*), and recognized by the Russian Orthodox Church. The effective reign of Ivan the Terrible began only in 1552, however. He reinvigorated the army and expanded the empire's territory with the conquest of the Khanate of Kazan (1552), inhabited by the Tatars on the bank of the Volga, and the Astrakhan Khanate near the mouth of the river on the Caspian Sea, making it easier to penetrate Central Asia and Siberia. And by expanding to the east, ensuring its own security through the expansion of its territory, the Russian Empire, which had adopted the Byzantine traditions, became multiethnic, multicultural, and multifaith. It was established not as a national state but as a "state of nationalities," as Leon Trotsky put it.[7]

12.4 Mikhail F. Romanov as Tsar of All Russia and the Creation of the Imperial Black Sea Fleet by Peter the Great

After a period of turbulence and chaos, representatives of the cities and rural areas met in a national assembly on February 21, 1613. They unanimously elected Mikhail Fedorovich Romanov (1596–1645) Tsar of all Russia. Mikhail I took the Romanov dynasty to the throne, and his third grandson, Tsar Pyotr I (Peter the Great), was the one to effectively modernize the empire, expanding its borders even further. Between the end of the seventeenth and beginning of the eighteenth century, he conquered the Sea of Azov (Azovskoye) to the north of the Black Sea in campaigns against Turkey (1695–1696—1686–1700). During the Great Northern War against Sweden (1700–1721), he ordered the construction of the Imperial fleet of the Baltic Sea, which he saw to after defeating the troops of the king of Sweden, Carl XII/Charles XII (1682–1718), on the eastern bank of the Dnieper River, at Poltava (Poltavs'ka Oblast) in Ukraine. The Swedes had invaded Russia under the command of Field Marshal Carl Gustaf Rehnskiöld (1651–1722) with the support of the hetman[8] of Ukraine,[9] Ivan S. Mazeppa (1639–1709).

---

[7]Leon Trotsky, 1977, pp. 736–737.

[8]Hetman (commander, Cossack military leader)—a Polish/Ukrainian word originating from the German "Hauptmann." In Spanish, Galician, and Portuguese, it is translated as atamán.

[9]Werner Scheck, 1980, pp. 217–218; Leon Trotsky, 1975, p. 30.

12.5   The Story of Ivan Mazeppa

Ivan Mazeppa was a popular personality and the subject of a long poem written by Lord Byron between 1817 and 1818 and published in 1819. In the poem, Byron tells that Mazeppa, who he calls a Cossack prince, had a love affair with countess Tereza when he was a young page for Jan II Kazimierz Waza (1609–1672), king of Poland. When her husband found out about the prevarication, he commanded his men to tie the page naked to the dorsum of a wild horse, letting it loose to gallop across the Ukrainian steppes. Half-dead, starving, and exhausted, he was allegedly saved by peasants.[10]

Ivan S. Mazeppa was the hetman of the Cossacks of the left margin of the Ukraine, i.e., the margin of the Dnieper River, which stretched across the central (Poltava and Cherkashchyna), northern (Chernihivshchyna and Sumshchyna), and eastern parts of Kiev. His plan was to bring together these territories as a unitary state, maintaining the traditional order of the Cossacks. At first he believed he could coexist with Russia according to the terms of the treaty of Pereiaslav, which was signed between the Cossack councils of Zaporozhian and Vasiliy Buturlin, the envoy of Tsar Alexander I of Russia, in 1654, during the uprising against the rule of Poland, which occurred between 1648 and 1657, under the leadership of Bohdan Khmelnytsky (c. 1595–1657), the hetman of Zaporozhian, allied to the Crimean Tatars. This is why Ivan Mazeppa supported Peter the Great with troops, ammunition, money, and other resources in the first stage of the war against Sweden, until 1708. But he was unable to unify the regions of Ukraine—controlled by Poland on the right margin (the west) and on the left margin by three semi-independent hetmanates (of which Zaporozhian Sich was the most powerful) falling under the formal sovereignty of Russia. And when Peter the Great went about abolishing the relative autonomy of the Cossacks to centralize his authority, sending Russian and German officers to command them, Mazeppa revolted and joined the king of Sweden, Carl XII, who promised him the independence of Ukraine. They were defeated, however, in the decisive Battle of Poltava between June 27/28 and July 8, 1709, by the troops of Peter the Great, with the support of another Cossack faction under the command of hetman Ivan Skoropadsky (1646–1722). Sweden lost 7000 men.[11] Mazeppa and Carl XII, along with 15,000 veterans, crossed the Dnieper with the aid of the Cossacks of Zaporozhian Sich and took refuge in the fortress of Bender/Bendery, then on Turkey's territory (Moldova/Transnistria).[12] Mazeppa died soon after, on September 21 (October 2 in the Gregorian calendar) of the same year.[13] The survivors of the battle, Cossacks and 2500 Swedish soldiers, were imprisoned and executed by order of Peter the Great, who then extinguished the

---

[10]George Gordon Byron (Lord), 1948, pp. 397–457; Victor Hugo also wrote a poem about Mazeppa's love affair, which served as theme to other artists, such as Franz Liszt and Pyotr Piotr Ilitch Tchaikovski.

[11]Franklin D. Scott, 1983, pp. 233–235.

[12]Currently Bender/Bendery, also known as Tighina, is a city in Moldavia.

[13]Paul Kubicec, 2008, pp. 48–51.

semi-independence of the Zaporozhian Sich hetmanate and continued to expand Russia toward the west of the Dnieper and the coast of the Black Sea, controlled by the Ottoman Empire.

12.6   Catherine the Great and the Conquest of the Donbass (Novorossiya)

In addition to the Great Northern War against Sweden between 1700 and 1721 and the fighting against the Turkish, Tatar and Nogai tribes in the Crimean peninsula and the surroundings of the Sea of Azov, other conflicts with Poland and Lithuania drove the Russian Empire to strengthen its army in the Middle Ages in order to provide the military resources necessary for the consolidation of its permanent existence as a state, especially since the reign of Peter the Great.[14] And Czarina Catherine II the Great (Yekaterina II Velikaya—1729–1796) continued his work. The victories of generals Alexander Suvorov and Mikhail Kamensky against the Ottoman Empire in the battles of Chesma and Kagul, in 1770, and Kozludzha, in 1774, paved the way for the Treaty of Kuchuk-Kainarji, through which the Russian Empire completed its conquest of the east and southeast of the former Kyïvska Rus, the north and the access to the Black Sea, annexing the greater part of the region known as Novorossiysk (Novorossiya), which covered Kharkov, Donetsk, Luhansk, Zaporizhia, Nikolayev, Kherson, Dnepropetrovsk, Mykolaiv, Yeakaterinoslav, and Odessa, where a port and naval base were built.

Until then, the Crimean Khanate (1441–1783), populated by Tatars and Nogais (tribes of Turkish origin)[15] and also by the Khazars, had been a vassal of the Ottoman Empire. Its conquest by Russia began in 1771. It wasn't until 1782, however, that Prince Grigory Aleksandrovich Potemkin (1739–1791), the greatest love of the then-ruling Czarina Catherine II (1762–1796),[16] officially annexed the peninsula to the Russian Empire. On April 8, 1783, Shaghin-Ghirei, the last khan of the Crimea (1777–1783), abdicated sovereignty over the khanate in favor of Catherine II, together with all its rights and privileges, including the suzerainty over the Nogais. The incorporation into Russian territory was recognized by the Ottoman Empire on June 20 of the same year.[17] Prince Grigory Aleksandrovich Potemkin was then tasked with the construction of a modern naval base in Sevastopol Bay, to the

---

[14]*Ibidem*, p. 30.

[15]The Tatars of the Crimea were an ethnic group related to the Turks and their language was of the same family. In the Middle Ages, when the Tartar tribes (Törk-Tatarlari) in Russia were subjugated by the "Golden Horde" (Zolotaya Orda), the Mongols, and integrated into the empire, the Christians started calling both the Tartars and Mongols "Tartarus," a term that in Greek mythology meant hell, the underworld from where the demons came. The demons were the Mongols mounted on their horses. This context explains the confusion between "Tartar" and "Tartarus"; Brian G. William, 2001, pp. 10–13; Greta Lynn Uehling, 2004, pp. 30–34.

[16]Werner Scheck, 1980, p. 259.

[17]*Ibidem*, pp. 258–262; John F. Baddeley, 1969, pp. 42–43; Shreen T. Hunter, 2004, p. 9.

southwest of the Crimea, from where the Black Sea Fleet could control the communications of important energy zones (oil and gas) through the Bosporus and Dardanelles straits and project its power across the Mediterranean.

The Sevastopol naval base was bombed several times between 1853 and 1856, when Russia, with a population of around 67 million, fought a war in the Crimea against the Ottoman Empire and two economically more powerful European countries, England and France (1854–1855), which prevented Russia from conquering Constantinople and controlling the Balkans and the straits of the Black Sea. The war ended with the Treaty of Paris of 1856 and the victory of Britain, France, and Sardinia, allied to the Ottoman Empire. The treaty established the neutrality of the Black Sea, but returned the occupied cities and ports to Russia, including Sevastopol and Balaklava. The Ottoman Empire was given the protectorates of Moldavia, Wallachia, and Serbia, while the Austro-Hungarian Empire would rule over the region of the ancient kingdoms of Galicia (Halychyna) and Lodomeria (Regnum Galiciæ et Lodomeriæ), conquered with the partition of Poland in 1772.

12.7   The Invention of Ukraine

Ukraine has always been a heterogeneous territory, penetrated through the centuries by different cultures, religions, and political currents.[18] Throughout its history, it never knew ethnic unity and cultural homogeneity or defined borders. It was often fragmented and crucified between four states, as Trotsky put it.[19] Its borders changed several times, just as the ethnic groups occupying its lands. And during the civil war (1917–1922) following the Bolshevik Revolution (1917), Leon Trotsky, commander of the Red Army, recognized it as a country (1919) when he proclaimed to the soldiers, according to the principle of self-determination of people defended by Lenin: "The Ukraine is the land of the Ukrainian workers and working peasants. They alone have the right to rule in the Ukraine, to govern it and to build a new life in it."[20]

---

[18]Grzegorz Rossoliński-Liebe, 2014, p. 90.

[19]Leon Trotsky, "Problem of the Ukraine" (April 1939)." *Written*: April 2, 1939. *Originally published*: *Socialist Appeal*, May 9, 1939. *Source*: *Arsenal of Marxism, Fourth International*, Vol. 10, n. 10, November 1949, pp. 317–319. *Transcription/HTML Markup*: Einde O'Callaghan for the *Trotsky Internet Archive*. Available at <http://www.marxists.org/archive/trotsky/1939/04/ukraine.html>.

[20]"Order N.174 By the Chairman of the Revolutionary War Council of the Republic and People's Commissar for Military and Naval Affairs to the Red forces entering the Ukraine," November 30, 1919, Moscow. "*Comrade soldiers, commanders, commissars! You are entering the Ukraine. By defeating Denikin's bands you are freeing a fraternal country from its oppressors. The Ukraine is the land of the Ukrainian workers and working peasants. They alone have the right to rule in the Ukraine, to govern it and to build a new life in it. While striking merciless blows at the Denikinites you must at the same time show fraternal care and love for the working masses of the Ukraine. Woe to anyone who uses armed force to coerce the working people of the Ukraine's towns or villages!*

In essence, Ukraine wasn't an actual country until the First World War. In the Middle Ages and the old maps, it was called Small Russia (Малая Русь or Rus' Minor), especially the left bank of the Dnieper. It was then under the dominion of the Polish-Lithuanian Commonwealth, from which it seceded with the Treaty of Pereyaslav (1654) when the Cossack Bohdan Khmelnytsky (1595–1657), hetman of Zaporizhian Sich, recognized the sovereignty of the Czar and Duke of Muscovy, Aleksey I (1629–1676), over the entire Rus' territory in return for support against Poland. But Ukraine was only established as a National Republic (Ukrayins'ka Narodnia Respublika—UNR) after the revolution in Russia and the fall of Tsar Nicholas II in February of 1917 (March in the Gregorian calendar), through the universal act issued by the Central Rada (Tsentralna Rada) in Kiev and adopted by the All-Ukrainian National Congress on June 11, 1917, before the uprising that led the Bolsheviks to power. The provisional government in Petrograd, headed initially by Prince Georgy Y. Lvov (1861–1925) and after July 21, 1917, by the revolution-ary socialist Alexander F. Kerensky (1881–1970), rejected Ukraine's claim of relative autonomy, arguing that such a concession would lead Russia to chaos and anarchy.

The Central Rada, under the leadership of the historian Mykhailo S. Hrushevsky (1866–1934) and other intellectuals, such as Volodymyr Naumenko (pedagogue), Dmytro Doroshenko (publicist), and Dmytro Antonovy (art historian and politician), was a body formed by Ukrainian landowners, small farmers, and businessmen, but Lenin recognized its legitimate aspiration of autonomy, also because they didn't seek the secession of Ukraine. And in a note published in Pravda No. 82, on June 28, 1917, Lenin wrote:

> These are perfectly clear words. They state very specifically that the Ukrainian people do not wish to secede from Russia at present. They demand autonomy without denying the need for the supreme authority of the "All-Russia Parliament". No democrat, let alone a socialist, will venture to deny the complete legitimacy of the Ukraine's demands. And no democrat can deny the Ukraine's right to freely secede from Russia. Only unqualified recognition of this right makes it possible to advocate a free union of the Ukrainians and the Great Russians, a voluntary association of the two peoples in one state.[21]

The workers and peasants of the Ukraine must feel secure under the defence of your bayonets! Keep this firmly in mind: your task is not to conquer the Ukraine but to liberate it. When Denikin's bands have finally been smashed, the working people of the liberated Ukraine will themselves decide on what terms they are to live with Soviet Russia. We are all sure, and we know, that the working people of the Ukraine will declare for the closest fraternal union with us. Do your duty, Red soldiers, commanders, commissars. Death to the aggressors and oppressors—the Denikinites, the landlords, the capitalists and kulaks! 'Long live the Red Army! Long live the free and independent Soviet Ukraine!'" The Military Writings of Leon Trotsky. How the Revolution Armed, Volume 2, 1919. The Southern Front III. *The Red Army's Second Offensive in the Ukraine. (August–December 1919).* Available at <https://www.marxists.org/archive/trotsky/1919/military/ch108.htm> and also in <https://www.marxists.org/archive/trotsky/index.htm>.

[21]Lenin, v. I. "The Ukraine," in Collected Works. London: Lawrence and Wishart, 1964, Volume 25 (June–September 1917), pp. 91–92.

In another article, published in Pravda No. 84, on June 30, 1917, he returned to the topic, stating:

> There is absolutely nothing terrible, not the shadow of anarchy or chaos, either in the resolutions or in the demands of the Ukrainians. Accede to their most legitimate and most modest demands and authority will be just as effective in the Ukraine as it is everywhere in Russia, where the Soviets (which have no "guarantees of regularity"!!) are the sole authority.[22]

When Lenin emphasized that the 1897 estimates pointed to the existence of 17% of Ukrainians in Russia, against 43% of Great Russians, he recognized that the largest part of the Donbass, including the industrial towns and other Russian-speaking villages, belonged to Ukraine.[23] The Bolsheviks, however, who enjoyed strong support in this region (Donbass) did not accept the idea of a separate Ukraine.[24] And on April 29, 1918, in the midst of the civil war following the rise to power by the Bolsheviks (October/November 1917), General Pavel Petrovyč Skoropads'kyi (1873–1945), an aristocrat of Cossack origin, overthrew the Central Council of the National Republic in Kiev, and the All-Ukrainian Union of Land-owners proclaimed him hetman (head of the Executive Council of the State Affairs) of Ukraine, the Central Rada (Tsentralna Rada). Hetman Skoropads'kyi proceeded to install an anti-Soviet government, backed by the German and Austro-Hungarian occupation forces, but he didn't remain in power for long. In November 1918, with the defeat and capitulation of the Central Powers—the alliance of the German Austro-Hungarian and Ottoman Empires in the First World War—the isolated Skoropads'kyi was overthrown by the nationalist politician Symon Petlyura (1879–1926), who founded the Ukrainian People's Republic (Ukrayins'ka Narodnia Respublika). And class war erupted in the Donbass. In December 1918, by order of General Sviatoslav V. Denisov (1978–1957), commander of the Don Cossack Army, one of each ten workers captured in Iuzivka, the industrial city of Donetsk, was hanged by his counterrevolutionary forces.[25]

The Bolsheviks, in turn, founded the Donets-Krivoy Rog Soviet Republic on January 12, 1918, with its capital in Kharkov and Luhansk, between the lower Donets (a tributary of the Don) and the Sea of Azov. And almost at the same time, on January 17, Vladimir Yudovsky, chair of the Bolshevik military revolutionary committee and the Red Guards, proclaimed Odessa a free city and established a Council of the People's Commissars there—Bolsheviks, anarchists, and representatives of the Socialist Revolutionary Party (narodniki, populist)—in solidarity with the Soviet government in Petrograd.[26] The sailors of the Russian fleet in Sevastopol,

---

[22]Lenin, v. I. "The Ukraine and the Defeat of the Ruling Parties," *Ibidem*, pp. 99–101.

[23]Hiroaki Kuromiya, 1998, p. 99.

[24]Paul Kubicek, 2008, p. 83.

[25]Hiroaki Kuromiya, 1998, p. 103.

[26]Maxim Edwards, "Symbolism of the Donetsk People's Republic." *OpenDemocracy*, June 9, 2014. Available at <https://www.opendemocracy.net/od-russia/maxim-edwards/symbolism-of-donetsk-people%E2%80%99s-republic-flag-novorossiya>.

in the Crimea, had already joined the Bolsheviks on March 19, 1918, and expelled the "Tatars and bourgeois nationalists," Islamic clerics and rich landowners from the city. They proclaimed the Taurida Soviet Socialist Republic, restoring the old name of the peninsula—Tauris or Tauric Chersonese. In his Phaedra, Seneca (6 B.C.–4 A. D.) already calls this region *inhospitalis Taurus*,[27] inhabited by nomadic tribes—the Indic-speaking Scythes/Scythians and Kimmerioi/Cimmerians)—and where the Greeks had established colonies around the fifth century (B.C.).[28] The German troops, with the support of the Tatars, invaded Crimea 1941 and put an end to the Soviet Republic, however.

Meanwhile, Nestor Makhno (1889–1935) was heading an anarchist-communist peasant uprising, known as the Makhnovshchina, from Huliaipole (Guliaipole or Gulai-Pole), a village in the oblast (province) of Zaporizhia. He formed the Revolutionary Insurrectionary Army of Ukraine (Revolyutsionnaya Povstancheskaya Armiya Ukrainy), the Black Army. Fyodor Shuss (1893–1921), another famous anarchist, joined him and lost his life in the battle against the 8th Cavalry Division of Red Cossacks, commanded by Vitaly M. Primakov (1897–1937).[29]

The communist-anarchists led by Nestor Makhno fought against both the revolutionary troops of the White Army of General Anton Iwanowistch Denikin (1872–1947) and the forces of the Red Army. His project consisted in leaving the Soviets free and installing libertarian, anarchic communities without institutions and authorities, i.e., without government and without state. This movement extended to the regions of Alexandrovski, Melitopal, Mariupol, Yekaterinoslav, and Pavlograd.[30] But at the end of 1920, the major Red Army commander General Mikhail V. Frunze (1885–1925) crushed not only the nationalist forces led by Symon Petlyura (1879–1926) but also the anarchist movement in battles fought in the peninsula of Chongar, the cove of Syvash, the coast of the Sea of Azov, and the Isthmus of Perekop, a narrow strip of land between the Crimea and Ukraine. General Frunze then proceeded to occupy northern Taurida and defeat the counterrevolutionary army of General Pyotr N. Wrangel (1878–1928). Thousands of anarchists died in combat, and the survivors were executed by the Bolsheviks. Nestor Makhno escaped to Bessarabia with a small group of companions and then to Romania and Poland, until arriving in Paris, where he died of tuberculosis in 1934.[31]

The Donbass (the acronym for Donetskii Bassein, the Donets Basin), to the southeast and east of Ukraine, was a sparsely populated land between the Carpathians and the Volhynian-Podolian plateau, which the Russian Empire had won from Turkey in the war of 1768–1774 and incorporated into its territory after

---

[27]Sénèque (L. Annaei Senecae), 1965, verses 165–170 and 906, pp. 51 and 132.

[28]Paulo R. Magocsi, 2010, p. 201.

[29]Vitaly M. Primakov was one of the many officers of the Red Army arrested and executed by Stalin between 1936 and 1939.

[30]Nestor Makhno, 1988, pp. 70–71 and 261–262.

[31]"Prominent Russians: Nestor Makhno (October 26, 1888-July 6, 1934)." *Russiapedia*. Available at <http://russiapedia.rt.com/prominent-russians/history-and-mythology/nestor-makhno/>.

liquidating the Cossack Hetmanate[32] (kozaki, kazaki)—Zaporizhian Sich (1873–1875)—a fortified and very powerful martial-peasant community in the south and southeast of the region.[33] Known as Novorossiisk/Novorossiya since then, this was the zone of the Russian Empire that went through the most rapid development.[34] And the fundamental factor driving the economy of the Donbass, increasing the production of the coal and steel industries, was the Crimean War (1853–1856) where the Russian Empire had lost to Britain and France, which were better armed and allied to the Ottoman Empire.[35]

In 1866, the government of Tsar Alexander II (1818–1881) commissioned the manufacture of steel platforms from the Millwall Iron Works & Shipbuilding Company, in England, for Fort Konstantin, next to the Kronstadt naval base, built during the reign of Tsar Peter the Great and inaugurated in 1704, on the island of Kotlin in the Baltic Sea. In return, he gave the company the concession to exploit the coal and iron deposits in the desolate steppes of the Donbass. The Welsh engineer and entrepreneur John James Hughes (1814–1889), director of the Millwall Iron Works & Shipbuilding Company, accepted the challenge and bought a concession from Prince Sergey Kochubey on the shores of the Sea of Azov to explore coal and iron as well as establish a steel plant and metallurgy industry in the Donbass.[36]

The formal agreement was signed by Tsar Alexander II in 1868, and John James Hughes registered the company New Russia Company Ltd. (Novorossiskoe-Rog) in London with a capital of £300,000. The place chosen for the project was located approximately 75 km from Taganrog and the Mariupol docks on the Sea of Azov.[37] John James Hughes imported machinery, furnaces, and other equipment from England and then began exploring the mines of Krivoy Rog, with hundreds of iron and coal (bituminous coal) mining specialists brought from England, along with 300,000 Welsh workers.[38] He then founded a community called Iuzovka/Iuzovskii zavod, renamed Staline (Сталіне) in 1924 and, lastly, Donetsk, where the Jews came to occupy administrative, accounting, and other activities or worked as merchants and artisans.[39] The number of Jews in Iuzovka jumped from 2476 in 1869 to 9469 in 1897.[40] And in the deployment of his venture, John James Hughes took on

---

[32]Cossack, word originating from the Turkish *Qasaq*.

[33]Hiroaki Kuromiya, *Freedom and Terror in the Donbas: A Ukrainian-Russian Borderland, 1870s–1990s*. New York/Cambridge: Cambridge University Press, 1998, pp. 35–37. In 2005, President Vladimir Putin introduced a law, approved by the Duma, recognizing the Cossacks not only as a distinct ethno-cultural entity but also as a powerful military and security force. *Of Russian origin: Cossacks—Russiapedia*. Available at <http://russiapedia.rt.com/of-russian-origin/cossacks/>.

[34]Orest Subtelny, 2000, pp. 266–271; Hiroaki Kuromiya, 1998, pp. 14–18.

[35]Theodore H. Friedgut/1989, p. 12.

[36]*Coalland—Faces of Donetsk*—Zoï Environment Network and UNEP/GRID-Arendal, ISBN: 978-82-7701-090-8. France: Global Publishing Services, 2011, p. 12.

[37]Richard Davenport-Hines (Editor), 1990, pp. 145–146.

[38]Theodore H. Friedgut, 1989, pp. 15–20.

[39]*Ibidem*, pp. 199–207.

[40]*Ibidem*, p. 203.

the construction of the Kursk-Kharkov-Azov railroad, for which he subcontracted the Russian entrepreneur Samuel Polyakov. The steel and metallurgical industry then flourished based on the intensive employment of the relatively inexpensive and large labor force, rather than the investment of more—scarce and expensive—capital for the exploitation of the abundant ore, coal, and iron deposits.[41]

The Donbass, the "wild steppe" (dyke pole, dikoe pole), was an open-bordered, semi-pastoral space with no administrative unit or integrated social structure, and thousands of Russian peasants, workers of various nationalities, and refugees from various corners and other countries had flocked to this region, historically situated between Cossack areas. It also received French, Belgian, and German capital, attracted by the rich mineral deposits, especially coal and iron, but also manganese, in the basin of Nikopol, more to the south, in Dnipropetrovsk.[42] Several languages were spoken there, although Russian was predominant in the cities,[43] and the population of the Donbass became mostly working class and multiethnic, extremely heterogeneous, unlike the peasants of the west, in the more agricultural zone around Kiev, with whom they were never on good terms.[44] The ethnic Ukrainians of Iuzovka/Donetsk and the Donbass contributed little to the growing industrial development of the area covering Luhansk, Dnipropetrovsk, Zaporizhia, Mykolaiv, Yekaterinoslav, Kherson, Odessa, and to the other oblasts of the Russian Empire.[45] The "Donbass was essentially Russian," noted historian Theodore H. Friedgut, emphasizing that "Russians populated it and gave the region its working muscles."[46]

---

[41] *Ibidem*, pp. 87–88.

[42] Hiroaki Kuromiya, 1998, pp. 14–18.

[43] *Ibidem*, p. 42.

[44] *Ibidem*, p. 207.

[45] Theodore H. Friedgut, 1989, pp. xii and 3.

[46] *Ibidem*, pp. 229–232.

Chapter 13
Lenin's Incentive to Self-Determination and Ukrainian Nationalism

13.1 Rosa Luxemburg's Criticism of Lenin's Nationalities Policy: An Independent Ukraine as Lenin's "Pet Project"

Rosa Luxemburg (1871–1919) made some of the most important contributions to Marx and Engels' economic theory and hailed the Russian Revolution as *das gewaltigste Faktum* (the most powerful deed) of the great war of 1914–1918.[1] But she expressed serious misgivings about Lenin and Trotsky's methods and initiatives in a text written between August and September 1918, while she was still imprisoned in Breslau (then Germany), from which she was released on November 18, on the eve of Kaiser Wilhelm II's abdication. One of her disagreements concerned the right to self-determination of the nationalities that had made up Russia's population for centuries. She referred particularly to the "silly Ukrainian nationalism" (*die Narretein des Ukraininschen Nationalismus*), stressing that Ukraine had been the center, the fortress, of the revolutionary movement in Russia before an "independent Ukraine" (*selbständige Ukraine*) was invented as "Lenin's pet project" (*Steckenpferd Lenins*).[2] Rosa Luxemburg recalled that it was from here—from Rostov, from Odessa, from the region of Donetz—that the torrents of lava flowed that set Southern Russia ablaze, already in 1902–1904, setting the stage for the insurrection of 1905.[3] The same happened during the revolution of 1917, since it was the proletariat of Southern Russia that provided the elite troops of the proletarian phalanxes (*die Elitentruppen der proletarischen Phalanx stellte*).[4]

---

[1] Rosa Luxemburg, 1990, Band 4, p. 355; Hiroaki Kuromiya, 1998, p. 42.

[2] Rosa Luxemburg, 1990, Band 4, p. 350.

[3] *Ibidem*, p. 350.

[4] *Ibidem*, p. 350.

© Springer Nature Switzerland AG 2019
L. A. Moniz Bandeira, *The World Disorder*,
https://doi.org/10.1007/978-3-030-03204-3_13

Rosa Luxemburg claimed that the Bolsheviks had furthered an ideology that masked the counterrevolution with the principle of self-determination of nationalities, strengthening the position of the petty bourgeoisie and weakening the proletariat. And she predicted that Ukraine would play a "fatal role" (*fatale Rolle*) in the fate of the Russian revolution. Ukrainian nationalism, she argued, was quite different from Czech, Polish, or Finnish nationalism, for example, since it was nothing more than extravagance, the vain pride of a dozen petty-bourgeois intelligentsia with no roots whatsoever in the economic, political, or spiritual situation of the land and no historical tradition, since Ukraine, populated by seven million people,[5] never constituted a nation or a state and was devoid of a national culture, except for the romantic-reactionary poetry of Schewtschenko.[6]

Rosa Luxemburg accused Lenin and his comrades of artificially inflating this "burlesque farce" (*diese lächerliche Posse*) of a couple of university professors and students, turning it into a political factor by stirring the doctrine of self-determination to the point it turned into dangerous bluster, a flag under which to rally the counterrevolutionaries.[7] Rosa Luxemburg repeated this idea in another text—*Fragment über Krieg, Nationale Frage und Revolution*—in which she noted that nationalism in the Russian Ukraine hadn't represented anything until the Bolshevik revolution in October 1917. It was a soap bubble, the vanity of a dozen professors and lawyers, the majority of which couldn't even read Ukrainian.[8] She believed Lenin should maintain the territorial integrity of the Russian Empire under the aegis of the socialist revolution.

Lenin upheld the decision to grant self-determination to the nationalities, however. And on March 10, 1919, the Third All-Ukrainian Congress of Soviets changed the name of the Ukrainian People's Republic of Soviets (1917–1918), with its capital in Kharkov (*Khirkiv*), to Ukrainian Soviet Socialist Republic, which technically became an independent state with its own government.[9] Meanwhile, the West Ukrainian People's Republic, which existed in Galicia between the end of 1918 and the beginning of 1919, merged with the Ukrainian National Republic under the name Ukrainian People's Republic (*Zapadnoukrajinska Narodna Republika*), with only four million inhabitants and governed by the nationalist Symon Petlyura (1879–1926), who continued the war against the Red Army, backed by the forces of the Polish dictator Marshal Józef Klemens Piłsudski (1867–1935).

---

[5] Paul Kubicek, 2008, p. 91. S. overview about demogaphic aspects in Ukraine in: Informationen zur politischen Bildung, 2015, Nr. 28.

[6] Rosa Luxemburg, 1990, Band 4, p. 351. Taras Hryhorowytsch Schewtschenko (1814–1861) was a poet whose work was written in the Ukrainian language.

[7] *Ibidem.*

[8] Rosa Luxemburg, "Fragment über Krieg, nationale Frage und Revolution." *Ibidem*, p. 369.

[9] Paul Kubicec, 2008, p. 90.

13.2 Pogroms and Peasant Uprisings

As Rosa Luxemburg had predicted, the prospect of self-determination of nationalities shattered Ukraine into pretentious small republics with different political directions in the midst of peasant uprisings—Cossacks led by the Hetman Alexei M. Kaledin (1861–1918)[10], worker revolts and bloody pogroms in every city. On February 15, 1919, 1700 Jewish men, women, and children were exterminated, and 600 more died the next day.[11] The Cossack atamans (Hetmen/warlords) of the Don, Angell, Kazakov, Kozyr-Zyrko, Struk, Volynets, Zeleny, Tutunik, Shepel, and Grigoryev pillaged the country with their cavalry, torturing, raping, and massacring 6000 Jews in mid-1919. The slogan of the counterrevolution was: "Beat up the Yids and save Russia!"[12] It is estimated that the atamans, the nationalist forces under the command of Simon Petlyura,[13] at the helm of the Central Rada established in Kiev, as well as the counterrevolutionary White Army of General Anton I. Denikin, whose backbone was formed by the Kuban Cossacks (*Kubanskiye Kazaki*), carried out 1236 pogroms between 1917 and 1921 in more than 524 locations in Ukraine, especially in the east, killing between 30,000 and 60,000 Jews.[14] Other sources say approximately 150,000 Jews (125,000 in Ukraine, 25,000 in Belarus) were annihilated between 1918 and 1922.[15] The massacres perpetrated by the counterrevolutionary forces extended from Belarus to the North Caucasus, Siberia, and Mongolia. And the Jews sought protection from the Red Army.[16]

13.3 The Victory of the Red Army

Between June 1920 and March 1921, the Red Army, with about 3.5 million highly organized and disciplined troops under the command of General Mikhail N. Tukhachevsky (1893–1937), surrounded and captured Kiev, then ruled by the forces of Józef Klemens Piłsudski (1867–1935), dictator of Poland. Piłsudski recognized the sovereignty of Russia over all Ukraine until the Donbass and Belarus

---

[10]Peter Kenez, 1977, pp. 162–163.

[11]Paulo R. Magocsi, 2010, pp. 506–507.

[12]Louis Rapoport, 1999, pp. 14–15; Hanoch Teller, 1990, p. 314.

[13]In 1926, Simon Petlyura, the head of the government of the People's Republic of Ukraine in exile in Paris, considered to be the main responsible for the large-scale massacres, was executed by the Jewish anarchist Sholem Schwartzbard (1886–1938). Schwartzbard was arrested, tried, and acquitted by a popular jury. He died 12 years later in Kapstatd, South Africa; Paul Kubicek, 2008, p. 89.

[14]*Ibidem*, pp. 506–507. *Modern Jewish History: Pogroms. Jewish Virtual Library.* 2a ed., pp. 71–73. Available at: <http://www.jewishvirtuallibrary.org/jsource/History/pogroms.html>.

[15]Nicolas Werth, "Crimes and Mass Violence of the Russian Civil Wars (1918–1921)." *Online Encyclopedia of Mass Violence*®—ISSN 1961-9898. April 3, 2008. Available at: <http://www.massviolence.org/crimes-and-mass-violence-of-the-russian-civil-wars-1918?artpage=3>.

[16]Louis Rapoport, 1999, p. 15.

by signing the Treaty of Riga (1921), ending the war. And on December 30, 1922, the Soviet Union was formed when Ukraine, still suffering from the devastation and famine caused by the Civil War, joined the Soviet Republics of Russia, Belarus, and Transcaucasia as the Ukrainian Soviet Socialist Republic. The Bolshevik government then granted Ukraine the Novorossiysk region, which stretched over Kharkov, Donetsk, Luhansk, Zaporizhia, Kherson, Dnepropetrovsk, Mykolaiv, and Odessa and where a large part of the inhabitants were Russian or of Russian origin. By transferring the more industrialized zone of Novorossiya to Ukraine, it seems the Bolsheviks hoped to balance power in the New Soviet Republic by increasing the number of workers. Because in the predominantly rural west of Ukraine, on the right bank of the Dnieper, peasants and petty-bourgeois nationalist sectors prevailed.

The borders of the Ukrainian Soviet Socialist Republic did not extend to the Crimean peninsula, whose population at that time was 623,000, including 150,000 Tatars, who considered themselves to be its first inhabitants (*korenni narod*). In 1921–1922, the peninsula was heavily affected by the famine and the population declined by around 21%.[17] About 100,000 people, including 60,000 Tatars, starved to death and more than 50,000 fled to Romania. Many later returned and established two dozen settlements and towns on the peninsula between 1925 and 1927. And according to the 1939 census of the Soviet Union, 218,179 Tatars lived in the Crimea. This number fell to 165,259 in 1953; however, after the mass forced migration to Kazakhstan, Central Asia, the Urals, and Siberia ordered by Stalin between 1943 and 1945,[18] despite the cultural autonomy (*korenzatsiia*) which presumably followed from the policy of respect for nationalities, established since Lenin and the Bolsheviks took power in 1917.[19] After the Molotov-Ribbentrop Pact (August 23, 1939), through which the Soviet Union and Germany invaded, divided, and annexed parts of Poland, Ukraine received from Romania the region of Bessarabia, the northeast of Bukovina, and the region of Hertza, in addition to reincorporating Galicia and Volhnia (Lodomeria-Volodymyr-Volynsky/Vo-Lodymer) to its territory.

---

[17] Alan W. Fisher, 1978, pp. 37–38.

[18] *Ibidem*, p. 151.

[19] Otto Pohl, J. "The Deportation and Fate of the Crimean Tatars." International Committee for Crimea. Washington, DC, 2003. This paper was presented at the Fifth Annual World Convention of the Association for the Study of Nationalities: "Identity and the State: Nationalism and Sovereignty in a Changing World." New York: Columbia University, April 13–15, 2000. It was part of the panel "A Nation Exiled: The Crimean Tatars in the Russian Empire, Central Asia, and Turkey." Available at: <http://www.iccrimea.org/scholarly/jopohl.html>.

13.4   The Wehrmacht's Invasion of the Soviet Union

In 1941, after the start of Operation Barbarossa—the invasion of the Soviet Union by the Wehrmacht—the troops of the 11. Armee and the 22. Panzer Division commanded by Field Marshal Erich von Manstein reached and occupied the Crimea, but they only managed to conquer the naval base of Sevastopol after a siege of 250 days and heavy fighting between July and October of 1942. During the occupation of the Crimea, the Nazis exterminated more than half of the 65,000 Jews living there, both Ashkenazi and mountain Jews—juhuro/quba—and the karaites/qarays, karaism/kærə.aɪt/kærə.ɪzəm/. And in Ukraine, with an estimated population of 30 million people, approximately 3 million Jewish men, women, and children were exterminated, in addition to the slaughter of 850,000–900,000 to 1.5 million or more non-Jews.[20]

While the vast majority of Ukrainians joined the Red Army, and the cruelty of the Wehrmacht troops increased the resistance, the oppression of the Stalinist regime—the Great Terror of the 1930s, among other historical factors—had generated a strong and deep-seated nationalist, anti-Soviet, and therefore anti-Russian sentiment, which was picked up by the NKVD (Narodnyy Komissariat Vnutrennikh Del/ *People's Commissariat for Internal Affairs of the Soviet Union*).[21] Pavel Y. Meshik (1910–1953) himself, head of the NKVD station in the Ukraine,[22] told Moscow he feared the Ukrainian nationalists would form a fifth column in the case of an invasion by the forces of the Third Reich, and rumors were already swirling about this possibility.[23] He also warned about the rumors that 200 Ukrainian nationalist activists had gone to Berlin to take special courses on how to run an "independent Ukraine" and that more than 1000 groups formed by criminal and heavily armed elements under the leadership of Stepan Andriyovych Bandera (1909–1959) were already preparing to engage in activities against the Soviet Union.[24] On February 27, 1941, before Operation Barbarossa was unleashed, Pavel Y. Meshik also informed Stalin that teachers were encouraging and teaching pupils in schools to write about the history and geography of an "independent Ukraine," and maps with this configuration were hanging in Cracow establishments.[25] In such circumstances, part of the population not only welcomed the Wehrmacht troops as liberators but fought alongside them against the Soviet Union. More than 100,000 Ukrainians

---

[20]William L. Shirer, 1960, Book Five—Beginning of the End, pp. 1257–1258; Paul Kubicec, 2008, p. 109.

[21]Katrin Boeckh, 2007, pp. 190–191.

[22]Pavel Y. Meshik was expurgated and shot along with Marshal Lawrenty P. Beria (1889–1953), head of the MVD and the NKVD, and seven other generals and ministers on December 23, 1953, when Nikita Khrushchev took power in the Soviet Union. "Russia: Death of a Policeman." *Times*, January 4, 1954. Available at: <http://content.time.com/time/magazine/article/0,9171,860194,00. html>; Beria was in favor of Germany's reunification and neutralization. See Luiz Alberto Moniz Bandeira, 2009, pp. 107–113.

[23]Gabriel Gorodetsky, 1999, pp. 299–300.

[24]*Ibidem*, p. 300.

[25]*Ibidem*, p. 299.

collaborated with the Nazis, joining the ideologically motivated local police (*Schutzmannschaften*)[26] and forming several units within the Waffen-SS and Wehrmacht, including the SS-Galichina Division, the 14th SS Volunteer Division (*Galizien Division*), and the Nachtigal and Roland battalions.

These military units were made up of the proto-Nazis of the Organization of Ukrainian Nationalists-B (*OUN-B/Banderivtsi*) commanded by Stepan A. Bandera, a direct agent of the Abwher, the Wehrmacht's intelligence service,[27] and head of the Ukrainian Insurgent Army (*Ukrayins'ka Povstans'ka Armiya-UPA*), whose militias were trained by the Waffen-SS. The OUN-B/Banderivtsi was a radical splinter group of the Organization of Ukrainian Nationalists (*OUN/Melnykivtsi*), founded in 1929 under the leadership of General Andriy Melnyk (1890–1964).[28] It not only received support from the Abwher led by Admiral Wilhelm F. Canaris (1987–1945) but also counted since the mid-1930s on the backing of Admiral Sir Hugh Sinclair and then head of the MI6 in Britain, in its struggle against Bolshevism.[29] All three organizations were racist, anti-Semitic, and anti-communist and collaborated intensively with the forces of the III Reich—Waffen-SS, Gestapo, Einsatzgruppen, etc.—in the promotion of pogroms since the beginning of the invasion of Ukraine.[30] And in collusion with the Nazis, they tried to implicate the Jews in the crimes of Joseph Stalin, who many accused of having deliberately caused the deaths of millions of people during the famine of 1931–1932 that crippled Ukraine, with the Donbass being one of the most affected areas.[31]

13.5   Dekulakization and the Famine of 1931–1932

Controversies exist about the causes of the famine.[32] But it did happen. In his memoirs, Nikita Khrushchev wrote that he could not imagine that the famine would hit Ukraine when he left Iuzovka/Stalino (Donetsk)[33] in 1929, because food

---

[26]Ray Brandon and Wendy Lower (Editors), *The Shoa in Ukraine—History, Testimony, Memoralization*. Bloomington, Indianapolis: Indiana University Press, 2008, pp. 54–55; Anatoly Podols, "Collaboration in Ukraine during the Holocaust: Aspects of Historiography and Research." *The Holocaust in Ukraine—New Sources and Perspectives—Conference Presentations*, pp. 187–195; Center for Advanced Holocaust Studies United States Holocaust Memorial Museum, 2013. Available at: <http://www.ushmm.org/m/pdfs/20130500-holocaust-in-ukraine.pdf>.

[27]Nikita Krushchev, *Memoirs of Nikita Khruschev*, vol. I, todo por Comissar (1918–1945), Edited by Sergey Khruschev. Pennsylvania: Pennsylvania State University Press, 2004, p. 240; Stephen Dorril, 2000, pp. 197–198, 225–226.

[28]Ray Brandon and Wendy Lower (Editors), 2008, pp. 126 and 143.

[29]Stephen Dorril, 2000, pp. 224–225.

[30]Grzegorz Rossoliñke-Liebe, 2014, pp. 196–198.

[31]Iroaki Kuromiya, 1998, p. 2.

[32]David R. Marples, 2012, pp. 40–45.

[33]In 1938, the *oblast* of Donetsk was divided in Stalino (Donetsk) and Voroshylovhrad (Luhansk).

production had reached pre-civil war levels (1917–1922) and returned to the standard of 1913.[34] He recalled what he was told by Anastas I. Mikoyan (1895–1978), then a member of the Politburo of the CPSU: in 1936, Nikolai N. Demchenko,[35] secretary of the communist party in Kiev, had told Mikoyan that in those days, trains from Kharkov would arrive overflowing with corpses; he presumed Stalin knew nothing and was afraid to pass on the information. He only dared speak to Mikoyan.[36]

The truth of the matter is Stalin no doubt knew of the disastrous situation. When he met in Moscow (August 12, 1942) with Winston Churchill, then Prime Minister of Great Britain, and was asked whether the stresses of the war against Nazi Germany were as bad to him as carrying through the policy of the collective farms, Stalin replied "Oh no, the Collective Farm policy was a terrible struggle." "Ten millions [. . .] it was fearful."[37] In fact, a large part of the ten million kulaks was extirpated and displaced in the Soviet Union.[38] And it is estimated that between six and eight million people starved between 1931 and 1933 alone, most of them in Ukraine—with even cannibalism being reported—as a consequence of the very serious agricultural crisis and the extreme drop in the grain harvest. The disaster was caused, among other things, by the requisition of grain for exports and the forced collectivization amid the bloody repression and expropriation of lands from the more affluent peasants (kulaks) but also from poorer peasants.

Stalin's goal was to destroy the kulaks as a social class by carrying out the dekulakization (raskulachivanie) and establishing the *kolkhozy* (agricultural cooperatives/collective farms).[39] Thousands were deported to Siberia or executed. In addition to those who died during the famine in the early 1930s, about 4.2 million people perished until 1950, victims of the purges ordered by Stalin, as Wladimir Krjutschkow (1924–2007), director of the KGB, later revealed.[40] The historian Roy Medvedev, in turn, estimated around 12 million people died and another 38 million suffered through the most varied types of repression (imprisonment, labor camps, etc.).[41]

---

[34]Nikita Krushchev, 2004, pp. 631–632.

[35]N. Demchenko (1896–1937), first secretary of the Communist Party of Kiev Oblas, disappeared in 1937. He was probably executed during the purges Stalin carried out in the 1930s.

[36]Nikita Krushchev, 2004, p. 631.

[37]Winston S. Churchill, 1995, pp. 722–724.

[38]*Ibidem*, pp. 723; William Taubman, 2003, p. 73.

[39]Leon Trotsky, 1936. pp. 51–59.

[40]*Correio Braziliense*, June 16, 1991.

[41]Stephen White et al., *Developments in Soviet Politics*. London: MacMillan, 1990, p. 22. *Correio Braziliense*, June 16, 1991.

13.6   Stepan Bandera, the Nazi Fifth Column, and the Shoah in Ukraine

Dekulakization certainly wasn't the only factor in the famine. But during the occupation by the forces of the Third Reich, the famine of the 1930s nevertheless served as propaganda against the Jews/Bolsheviks, by blaming them for the event. And the Ukrainian nationalists, intimately associated with the Nazis, participated in the terrible successive massacres carried out by the Einsatzgruppen A, C, and D[42] in the most diverse oblasts of Ukraine.[43] In the regions of Galicia, Volhynia, Bukovina, and many others, the Organization of Ukrainian Nationalists-B (*OUN-B, Banderivtsi*) and the Ukrainian Insurgent Army (*Ukrayins'ka Povstans'ka Armiya-UPA*) proceeded with ethnic cleansing, massacring about 100,000 or more people in 1943. According to some sources, the nationalists/proto-Nazis exterminated between 40,000 and 60,000 Polish civilians in the territory of Volhynia and between 25,000 and 30,000 in the region of Galicia.[44] And in 2 days—September 29 and 30, 1941—more than 33,000 Jews, in addition to Communists, priests of the Orthodox Church,[45] Gypsies (Romas), and Russian prisoners of war,[46] were forced to dig their own collective grave in the ravine of Babyn Yar (Бабий Яр), north of the city of Kiev. Most were executed and their corpses thrown on top of others, who were buried alive. The number of victims is estimated to have reached 100,000.[47]

Stepan A. Bandera and his companions proclaimed the independence of Ukraine with the support of the Ukrainian proto-Nazi unit Nachtigall, on June 30, 1941, shortly after the conquest of the town of L'viv, where thousands of Jewish men, women, and children were summarily exterminated.[48] His ideal was a Nazi, but

---

[42]The Einsatzgruppen der Sicherheitspolizei (Sipo) were mobile special operations squads, created by the Reichsführer-SS (SS commander Heinrich Himmler). They were made up of members of the Security Police (Sicherheitspolizei—Sipo) and the Security Service (Sicherheitsdienst—SD).

[43]William L. Shirer, 1960, Book Five—Beginning of the End.

[44]*Кајгана—Пресвртница за Украина.* Available at: <http://forum.kajgana.com/threads/%D0% 9F%D1%80%D0%B5%D1%81%D0%B2%D1%80%D1%82%D0%BD%D0%B8%D1%86% D0%B0-%D0%B7%D0%B0-%D0%A3%D0%BA%D1%80%D0%B0%D0%B8%D0%BD% D0%B0.71107/page-204>; HILL, Henryk. *Second Polish Republic-The Book.* Chapter 20: War crimes and atrocities. Available at: <https://sites.google.com/a/secondpolishrepublic.net.pe/se-cond-polish-republic-the-book/chapter-20>.

[45]"Orthodox public concerned for threat of neo-nazism in Ukraine." *Interfax*, October 27, 2006. Available at: <http://www.interfax-religion.com/?act=news&div=2192>.

[46]Ray Brandon and Wendy Lower (Editors), 2008, pp. 55–56, 274–275, 291–310. Of the 5.8 million Russian prisoners of war, about 3.3 million were executed by the Nazis, of which 1.3 million in Ukraine; Orest Subtelny, 2000, p. 468.

[47]"Kiev and Babi Yar." *Holocaust Encyclopedia.* Available at: <http://www.ushmm.org/wlc/en/article.php?ModuleId=10005421>.

[48]Anatoly Podols, "Collaboration in Ukraine during the Holocaust: Aspects of Historiography and Research." *The Holocaust in Ukraine—New Sources and Perspectives—Conference Presentations*, p. 191. Center for Advanced Holocaust Studies United States Holocaust Memorial Museum, 2013. Available at: <http://www.ushmm.org/m/pdfs/20130500-holocaust-in-ukraine.pdf>.

"independent" Ukraine. Its government would be aligned with Hitler to consolidate the "new ethnic order in Europe" and destroy "the seditious influence of the Bolshevik Jews."[49] He believed that after the war, the victorious Third Reich would withdraw its troops from the ethnically clean and independent Ukraine, liberated from both Poland and the Soviet Union.[50] Volodymyr Stakhiv, elected foreign minister, wrote Hitler to seek support for "our ethnic struggle."[51]

After some hesitation, however, the authorities in Berlin ordered the arrest of Stepan Bandera and other heads of the OUN-B/Banderivtsi and OUN/Melnykivtsi, despite their cooperation in the execution of the Shoah (Holocaust), not only in Ukraine but also in Poland, with the massacres, ethnic cleansing of the Warsaw ghetto, and the sending of thousands of Jews to the extermination camps in Auschwitz-Birkenau. Many of Bandera's companions and followers were persecuted, some arrested and even killed. They may have been allied to Germany and the Axis powers against the Jews/Bolsheviks and the Soviet Union, but they also sought the complete independence of Ukraine. Stepan Bandera was taken to Berlin, interned in the Sachsenhausen concentration camp and then transferred to Zellenbau Bunker.

Establishing an independent Slav state was not in Hitler's interests. He wanted to expand the Lebensraum (vital space) of Germany, i.e., clear the steppes of Ukraine for the colonization and settlement by German peasants, who the Slavs would have to serve as slaves, since he considered them *Untermenschen* (subhumans).[52] Since the beginning of the occupation, the Wehrmacht command in L'viv had used Ukraine as the main source of agricultural supplies for its troops, but also as a source of slave labor.[53] In September 1944, faced with the advancing Red Army, the Nazis released Stepan Bandera and others and transported them to Ukraine so they could collaborate in the fight against the Soviet Union.

One faction, led by Mykola Lebed (1909–1998), established close ties with the OSS (Office of Strategic Services), the American intelligence service and predecessor of the CIA. And Stepan Bandera managed to escape to the British Occupied Zone in Germany. From there he guided the reform of OUN-B/Banderivtsi and once again made his services available to the MI6.[54] He then continued coordinating guerrilla and terrorist activities against the Soviet Union in Ukraine, assassinating Red Army conscripts and their entire families, burning down houses and forests, devastating

[49]Stephen Dorril, 2000, pp. 227–228; Wolfgang Benz, 2013, pp. 468–471.

[50]Nikita Krushchev, 2004, p. 391.

[51]Stephen Dorril, 2000, pp. 227.

[52]Anatoly Podols, "Collaboration in Ukraine during the Holocaust: Aspects of Historiography and Research." *The Holocaust in Ukraine—New Sources and Perspectives—Conference Presentations*, p. 191. Center for Advanced Holocaust Studies United States Holocaust Memorial Museum, 2013. Available at: <http://www.ushmm.org/m/pdfs/20130500-holocaust-in-ukraine.pdf>; Orest Subtelny, 2000, pp. 468–471.

[53]*Ibidem*, p. 69.

[54]Stephen Dorril, 2002, pp. 231–232 and 236.

villages, and blowing up bridges.[55] About 35,000 members of the Polish and Soviet secret services, soldiers, and Communist Party members were murdered by the guerrillas of the OUN-B/Banderivtsi and Ukrainian Insurgent Army in the 2 years following the end of the Second World War.[56] At that time, Ukraine once again suffered through a severe drought that severely affected agriculture, drastically reducing grain production. Famine became imminent and cannibalism occurred in some regions, where corpses were used as food.[57] When Aleksei I. Kirichenko (1908–1975), general secretary of the CP in Odessa, arrived at a collective farm, he witnessed a peasant woman slicing the corpse of her own child on the table to share the pieces with others.[58] And in his memoirs, Khrushchev recalled that it was difficult to convince Stalin that the terrible harvest had not resulted from sabotage,[59] even though the OUN-B guerrillas could have contributed significantly. Which in fact they did. The terrorist campaign guided by Bandera and other OUN-B leaders devastated plantations and depopulated vast areas of the steppes. The climax of this terrorist campaign occurred on September 28, 1948, with the murder of the Carpathian-Russian theologian and priest Gabriel Kostelnik (1866–1948) of the Orthodox Church. Kostelnik was killed as he climbed the stairs of the Church of the Transfiguration in L'viv by Vasily Pankiv, a militant of the Ukrainian Insurgent Army, commanded in exile by Stepan Bandera. Vasily Pankiv took his own life immediately after the crime. The attacks continued, however.

The strategy of the Western intelligence services was to expand the armed resistance from Ukraine to Belarus, Moldova, Poland, the Baltic countries, and other republics of the Soviet Bloc.[60] And in order to carry out paramilitary operations and covert operations, the OSS, headed by Allen Dulles, recruited General Reinhard Gehlen (1902–1979), former head of Fremde Heere Ost (FHO), the Abwehr department in charge of collecting intelligence in Eastern European countries, who had surrendered to the Counterintelligence Corps (CIC) of the United States in 1944 and negotiated his services and files in exchange for his release and that of his companions, members of the spy and secret operations network in Ukraine and throughout the Soviet Union.[61] Hundreds of Abwehr and SS officers were freed and sent to the mountains of Spessart in the region of Lower Franconia, between Bavaria and Hesse, where they joined General Reinhard Gehlen, already in the service of the US Forces European Theater (USFET) since he returned from the United States, where he had become a good friend of Allen Dulles.[62] Many agents of

---

[55]Pavel Sudoplatov and Anatoli Sudoplatov (With collaboration of Jerrol L.; Leona P. Schecter), 1995, pp. 235–237 and 250–252.

[56]Stephen Dorril, 2000, pp. 237, 245–248.

[57]Nikita Krushchev, 2004, pp. 3–6.

[58]*Ibidem*, p. 7.

[59]*Ibidem*.

[60]*Ibidem*, p. 248.

[61]Harry Rostizke, 1977, pp. 168–169; Reinhard Gehlen, 1971, pp. 134–139.

[62]*Ibidem*, pp. 141–142, 242.

Organization Gehlen, of whom Bandera would become a protégée,[63] were then infiltrated in southwest Ukraine, and several were captured by the NKVD (НКВД— Narodnyy Komissariat Vnutrennikh Del), the security service of the Soviet Union, renamed KGB since 1954.[64] But while General Gehlen claimed that Bandera "was one of our men," US advisers warned the CIA that his organization in Ukraine— OUN-B/Banderivtsi—had been infiltrated by NKVD agents.[65] General Gehlen was later tasked with organizing the Bundesnachrichtendienst (BND), the West German intelligence service. The paramilitary operations in Ukraine decreased after the death of Gen. Roman Shukhevych (1907–1950), commander of the Independent Ukrainian Army, killed by General Viktor Drozdov of the NKVD,[66] but they persisted until November 1953.[67]

In 1959, the KGB (Komitet gosudarstvennoy bezopasnosti), the State Security Committee of the Soviet Union, under the leadership of Alexander Shelepin and with the approval of Khruschev, decided to eliminate the Nazi leaders who had fled from Ukraine to Germany. On October 15, 1959, agent Bohdan Stashinsky, who had previously killed Lev Rebet (1912–1957), another OUN-B leader, executed Stepan Bandera at the entrance to his apartment in Munich with a shot of cyanide ampoules to the guerrilla's face.[68] Yaroslav Stétsko, also condemned by the KGB, had more luck and managed to evade the attacks plotted against him. Stétsko was the author of a book that served as the ideological foundation for the establishment of the Pan-Ukrainian Union/Union of All Ukrainians in 1991, registered in 1995 as the Social-National Party of Ukraine (SNPU), known as Svoboda, a nationalist, extreme right, anti-Semitic party with a symbol that evoked the Nazi swastika.

Viktor Yushchenko, one of the leaders of the Orange Revolution (November 2004–January 2005) funded and encouraged by NGOs from the United States and the European Union, posthumously awarded the title of "Hero of Ukraine" to Stepan Bandera on January 22, 2010, shortly before leaving the presidency. And a statue was also erected in L'viv.[69] Several Nazi collaborators, companions of Stepan Bandera, were equally rehabilitated and honored. These facts shocked much of the country's population, mainly in the east and southeast. Viktor F. Yanukovych,

---

[63]Grzegorz Rossolińke-Liebe, 2014, p. 335.

[64]*Ibidem*, pp. 246–247.

[65]Stephen Dorril, 2000, p. 246.

[66]Pavel Sudoplatov and Anatoli Sudoplatov and Jerrol L. Schecter and Leona P. Schecter, 1995, p. 250.

[67]Harry Rostizke, 1977, p. 169.

[68]Christopher Andrew and Oleg Gordvietsky, 1991, pp. 464–465; Grzegorz Rossolińke-Liebe, 2014, p. 348.

[69]Michael Bernhard and Jan Kubik (Ed.), 2014, pp. 157–158, 166; "President confers posthumous title Hero of Ukraine to Stepan Bandera—President Victor Yushchenko awarded Ukrainian politician and one of the leaders of Ukrainian national movement Stepan Bandera a posthumous title Hero of Ukraine and the Order of the State." *Official Website of President of Ukraine—Press office of President Victor Yushchenko*, January 22, 2010. Available at: <http://www.president.gov.ua/en/news/16473.html>.

former governor of the Donetsk Oblast for the Party of Regions, predominant in the Donbass, east and southeast, announced when he was still a presidential candidate that he would rescind the title of "Hero of Ukraine" and other tributes paid to Bandera, a Nazi collaborator during the Second World War, which he did shortly after taking office.[70] The journalist Clifford J. Levy of *The New York Times* noted that the controversy over the honoring of Stepan Bandera "reflects the longstanding geographic schism in Ukraine and its impact on the nation's politics."[71] The contradiction was perfectly perceptible, and the latent fracture revealed the existence of two Ukraines, as Eleonora Narvselius of the Center for European Studies at the University of Lund in Sweden pointed out.[72]

---

[70]Clifford J. Levy, 2011.

[71]*Ibidem.*

[72]Timothy Snyder, "A Fascist Hero in Democratic Kiev." *The New York Review of Books*, February 24, 2010. Available at: <http://www.nybooks.com/blogs/nyrblog/2010/feb/24/a-fascist-hero-in-democratic-kiev/>; Eleonora Narvselius, s./d. pp. 343–344; Timothy Snyder, "Who's Afraid of Ukrainian History?" *The New York Review of Books*, September 21, 2010. Available at: <http://www.nybooks.com/blogs/nyrblog/2010/sep/21/whos-afraid-ukrainian-history/?printpage=true>.

Chapter 14
Ukraine as Soviet Republic and After: Focus on Donbass

14.1 The Economic and Geopolitical Relevance of the Donbass: Coal and Iron Mines in the Novorossiysk Region

Ukraine grew to be of vital economic and geopolitical importance to the Russian Empire, and therefore to the Soviet Union, ever since Catherine the Great incorporated Novorossiysk (Novorossiya, in the Donets Basin) into the empire and the Welsh businessman John James Hughes transformed the region into an important industrial center in the second half of the nineteenth century, when he founded the New Russia Company Ltd. (Novorossiskoe-Rog) to explore the vast coal and iron reserves that existed there. During the Seventh Moscow Gubernia (Province)[1] Conference of the Communist Party in October 1921, Lenin singled out the Donets Basin (the Donbass) as "one the main industrial centers" in Russia, where some of its oldest companies operated, in nothing inferior to the capitalist enterprises of Western Europe. Lenin noted that the first task of Soviet Power was to restore the large industrial enterprises, and it was easier to start with the Donets industry because of its relatively small amount of workers.[2]

Deeply acquainted with Marx and Engels' doctrine, Lenin clearly understood that socialism was not a path to economic development. It could only be established if the productive forces of capitalism had reached a level in Russia where the increase in the supply of goods and services, in both quantity and quality, would allow for class differences to be liquidated consistently, for socialism would only mean real progress if it didn't bring with it the stagnation or even the decadence of society's mode

---

[1]Administrative region of the former Russian Empire.

[2]W. I. Lenin, "VII Moskauer Gouvernement-Parteikonferenz," Oktober 1921, pp. 29–31, in: W. I. Lenin, *Werke*, August, 1921—March 1923. Berlin: Dietz Verlag, 1962, Band 33, pp. 75–76.

© Springer Nature Switzerland AG 2019
L. A. Moniz Bandeira, *The World Disorder*,
https://doi.org/10.1007/978-3-030-03204-3_14

of production.[3] This is why he retreated in 1921 from the "military communism" of the civil war and implemented the NEP (Novaya Ekonomicheskaya Politika), state capitalism, i.e., private capitalism under state control. As a success case in the unleashing of private enterprise and free trade (buying and selling), Lenin pointed particularly to the increased production of the small mines leased to the peasants. These small mines were working well and sent about 30% of the extracted coal revenues to the state. Lenin argued that the increase in production in the Donets basin, especially of the small mines, revealed a "considerable general improvement" over the "catastrophic" situation of the previous year.[4]

As chairman of the Council of People's Commissars of the Soviet Union, Lenin referred to the Donbass as "our fortress"[5] in a letter to Wjatscheslaw V. Molotov (1890–1986) and other comrades, dated November 21, 1921. A few months later, on March 27, 1922, at the opening of the 11th Congress of the Russian Communist Party, he declared that while Ukraine was an independent republic, the Central Committee had to interfere due to the divergences occurring among some of its leaders. The Donets Basin—Lenin explained—was the "center, the real basis of our entire economy," and left without it, it would be "utterly impossible to restore large-scale industry in Russia, to really build socialism—for it can only be built on the basis of large scale industry." This is why the industry in the Donbass had to be repaired and developed to an appropriate level.[6] Further on, he emphasized that the Donbass was "not an ordinary district, but a vital one, without which socialist construction would simply remain a pious wish."[7]

After Lenin's death (1923), Stalin consolidated himself as General Secretary of the CPSU and took control of all power. He ended the NEP in 1928 and promoted the total nationalization of the economy as part of the First Five-year Plan. But to sustain and accelerate economic development so as to build socialism in the Soviet Union in isolation, Moscow continued in one way or another to develop and modernize the exploitation of the coal and iron ore reserves, metallurgy, and all industrial sectors in Donetsk, Luhansk, and the other oblasts of Ukraine. And in 1938, when Nikita Khrushchev rose to the position of first secretary of the Communist Party of Ukraine, Stalin advised him to pay attention to other sectors of the

---

[3]"Erst auf einem gewissen, für unsere Zeitverhältnisse sogar sehr hohen Entwicklungsgrad der gesellschaftlichen Produktivkräfte wird es möglich, die Produktion so hoch zu steigern, daß die Abschaffung der Klassenunterschiede ein wirklicher Fortschritt, daß sie von Dauer sein kann, ohne einen Stillstand oder gar Rückgang in der gesellschaftlichen Produktionsweise herbeizuführen." Engels, F. "Soziales aus Rußland," in: K. Marx; F. Engels, *Werke*. Band 18, Berlin: Dietz Verlag, 1976, pp. 556–559. This same article can also be found in K. Marx and F. Engels, *Ausgewählte Schriften*, Band II, Berlin: Dietz Verlag, 1976, p. 39.

[4]W. I. Lenin, "VII Moskauer Gouvernement-Parteikonferenz," Oktober 1921, pp. 29–31, in: W. I. Lenin, *Werke*, August, de 1921—March 1923. Berlin: Dietz Verlag, 1962, Band 33, pp. 75–76.

[5]"An W. M. Molotow et al.," November 21, 1921, in: W. I. Lenin, *Briefe—Band IX*, November 1921–March 1923. Institut für Marxismus-Leninismus bei der SED. Berlin: Dietz Verlag, 1974, p. 32.

[6]W. I. Lenin, "Rede bei der Öffnung des Parteitags 27 März 1922," in: W. I. Lenin, *Werke*. August 1921–March 1923 Berlin: Dietz Verlag, 1962, Band 33, pp. 285–287.

[7]*Ibidem*, p. 287.

economy despite his passion for the coal, metalworking, and chemical industry of the Donbass where he was born. One of these other sectors was agriculture, the organization of collective and state farms, from which the Soviet Union obtained its wheat and other grains, potatoes and various other vegetables, milk, and meat.[8] "Of course you must pay attention to the industrial sectors," Stalin remarked, noting that Ukraine represented "a huge industrial complex." But its production was already well organized, with good managerial cadres, while agriculture was still "fragmented and loosely dispersed."[9]

14.2 The Wehrmacht's Defeat in Stalingrad

Adolf Hitler, meanwhile, also considered the Donbass indispensable for Germany's war efforts because of its agricultural and mineral resources and enormous industrial park.[10] And so the Wehrmacht's high command refocused its strategy in the end of the 1940s to the east. On June 22, 1941, it launched Operation Barbarossa, invading Russia from the Baltic Sea in the north, Belarus in the center, and the Black Sea in the south, with three million soldiers divided over three armies, commanded by Marshal Wilhelm Ritter von Leeb, Fedor von Bock, and Gerd von Runstedt, in addition to 650,000 fighters from Finland and Romania and reinforcement units from Italy, Hungary, Slovakia, and Croatia.[11] The strategic objective was to attack and occupy Leningrad, Moscow, and Kiev, as well as the industrial center of the Donets Basin and Crimea and the oil fields of the Caucasus.[12]

Bloody battles were fought in the Donbass. The forces of the Third Reich defeated the Red Army and captured thousands of soldiers during the battles of Uman, Kiev, Odessa, and Dnipropetrovsk (formerly called Novorossiysk and also Yekaterinoslav). In the battle of Kiev alone, the Wehrmacht made more than 665,000 prisoners after laying siege to the city and its vicinity for over a month, from August 7 to September 26, 1941.[13] And by seizing the territory of Ukraine, it isolated the fertile farmlands, the iron, the coal, and other mineral deposits from the rest of the Soviet Union and began exploiting them with the slave labor of millions of Ukrainians. Stalin himself wrote to Winston Churchill on September 4, 1941, that he had already lost more than half of Ukraine, the iron mines of Krivoi Rog, and that he had been forced to evacuate the metal workers over the Dnieper River, as well as

---

[8]Nikita Krushchev, 2004, p. 255.

[9]*Ibidem*, p. 255.

[10]Reinhard Gehlen, 1971, pp. 29–32; Iroaki Kuromiya, 1998, pp. 351–352; P. Zhilin, et al., 1985, pp. 25–26; Winston Churchill, 1985, p. 251.

[11]Autorenkollektiv, 1985, pp. 147–155, 163–174.

[12]Winston Churchill, 1985, p. 347.

[13]Joachim C. Fest, 1974, p. 653.

aluminum workers in Tikhvin,[14] in the Leningrad oblast. "This has weakened our power of defence and faced the Soviet Union with a mortal menace," Stalin wrote.[15] These words dramatically underscored the Donbass's importance to Russia and, consequently, to the entire Soviet Union.

Churchill wrote in his memoirs that German troops had already penetrated 500 thousand miles (804,672 km) into the Soviet Union, overrunning the industrial area of the Donbass and the rich wheat lands of Ukraine, but it had not yet managed to conquer Crimea, from where Stalin deported most of the Tatar population due to their ostensive collaboration with the Nazis.[16] But the Red Army was far from defeated. It started fighting better than before and its strength would surely grow. After winning the Battle of Smolensk between July 10 and September 10, 1941, 360 km from Moscow, the Wehrmacht arrived in the vicinity of Russia's capital in December. But it was incapable of invading or occupying Leningrad, despite surrounding the city for more than 2 years, i.e., 872 days, from September 8, 1941 to January 27, 1943. The Germans were unable to achieve their three main objectives: occupy Moscow, Leningrad, and the lower Don. The resistance of the Red Army became increasingly fierce, and the coming winter put the Wehrmacht even further in disadvantage, as Churchill had foreseen.[17] The temperature abruptly plummeted to $-20°$ (sometimes $-60°$), and the Nazi troops were not properly equipped for a long campaign in such weather conditions.[18] The victory of the blitzkrieg, on which Hitler so relied, was not consummated. The 1.1 million troops of the 6. Armée and the Panzer Division, commanded by marshals Erich von Manstein and Friedrich von Paulus, didn't reach the oil fields of Baku in the Caucasus. Between August 23, 1942 and February 2, 1943, the Red Army commanded by General Georgy Zhukov, with about 1.1 million troops, stopped the advance of the forces of the Third Reich and crushed them at the Battle of Stalingrad.

The exact number of dead in Stalingrad was not and will never be known. Around 750,000 and 850,000 German and axis soldiers are estimated to have perished in battle, and the Red Army also took 91,000 prisoners of war, including 2500 officers, 24 generals, and Marshal Friedrich von Paulus.[19] The Chilean poet Pablo Neruda wrote: "Today, under your mountains of punishment, not only is your people buried: the dead's flesh is trembling, dead that touched your front, Stalingrad."[20]

An enormous part of Germany's military potential in human and military material was wasted with the loss of about 800,000 troops and the complete destruction of the

---

[14]"Premier Stalin to Prime Minister—4 Sept. 41," in: Winston Churchill, 1985, pp. 405–406.

[15]*Ibidem*, p. 405.

[16]Uehling Greta Lynn, 2004, pp. 3–4.

[17]Winston Churchill, 1985, pp. 476–477.

[18]*Ibidem*, p. 477; Joachim C. Fest, 1974, p. 653.

[19]Autorenkollektiv, 1985, p. 358; Antony Beevor, 1999, p. 396; Zhilin et al., 1985, p. 198.

[20]"Hoy bajo tus montañas de escarmiento no sólo están los tuyos enterrados: tremblando está la carne de los muertos que tocaron tu frente, -Stalingrado." Pablo Neruda, 1951, pp. 83–87.

6. Armée and the *4. and 16. Panzer Divisionen*—2000 assault tanks and cannons, 10,000 artillery pieces, and 3000 combat and transport aircraft. The Wehrmacht now lacked the fortitude and conditions to stop the advance of the Red Army to Berlin.

14.3   The Transfer of Crimea to Ukraine by Khrushchev

After the end of World War II, the Ukrainian Soviet Republic was one of the founding countries of the United Nations. Stalin wanted to make it a permanent member of the Security Council, but Britain objected. It did not want the Soviet Union to have one more vote with veto power on the Security Council.[21] The borders of Ukraine, as then established by Stalin, contained parts of Rus' Minor (left bank of the Dnieper River), vast areas with a Russophone population, such as the east and southeast regions (Novorossiisk), Galicia, the north of Bucovina, the south of Bessarabia, and Carpathian Ruthenia (Subcarpathian Rus'). Many Ukrainians in the east, in the Donbass region, could only read and speak Russian or a mixture of Russian and Ukrainian, and they were considered the most developed.[22]

After 1918, Crimea became an autonomous republic within the Russian Soviet Federative Socialist Republic. It only became part of Ukraine after February 19, 1954, when Nikita S. Khrushchev (1894–1971), as president of the Presidium of the Supreme Soviet, signed a decree transferring Crimean oblast, surrounded by the Black Sea and the Sea of Azov, from the structure of the Russian Soviet Federative Socialist Republic (RSSR) to the Ukrainian Socialist Soviet Republic.

According to Article 18 of the Soviet Union' constitution,[23] however, the borders of any republic within the Soviet Union could not be redrawn without the consent of that republic, in this case the **Russian** Soviet Federative Socialist Republic to which Crimea belonged. So even though the Presidium of the Supreme Soviet of the **Soviet Union** approved the transfer of Crimea, it wasn't allowed to do so according to the Constitution. Hence the transfer had no legitimacy. This is why days later, on February 27, the Supreme Soviet announced a decree modifying Articles 22 and 23 of the Soviet Constitution in order to legalize the transfer.[24] The population of

---

[21]This is why the Soviet Union and Britain didn't accept the inclusion of Brazil in the council, as President Franklin D. Roosevelt had promised to Getúlio Vargas, since he was then closely allied with the United States.

[22]Grzegorz Rossoliński-Liebe, 2014, pp. 243–244.

[23]"Article 18. The territory of a Union Republic may not be altered without its consent." *1936 Constitution of the USSR*. Bucknell University, Lewisburg, PA 17837. Available at: <http://www.departments.bucknell.edu/russian/const/1936toc.html>.

[24]"Article 22. The Russian Soviet Federated Socialist Republic consists of the Altai, Krasnodar, Krasnoyarsk, Ordjonikidze, Maritime and Khabarovsk Territories; the Archangel, Vologda, Voronezh, Gorky, Ivanovo, Irkutsk, Kalinin, Kirov, Kuibyshev, Kursk, Leningrad, Molotov, Moscow, Murmansk, Novosibirsk, Omsk, Orel, Penza, Rostov, Ryazan, Saratov, Sverdlovsk, Smolensk, Stalingrad, Tambov, Tula, Chelyabinsk, Chita, Chkalov and Yaroslavl Regions; The Tatar, Bashkir,

Crimea was 1.1 million at the time, of which approximately 75% were Russians and 25% Ukrainians.[25] And on June 27, 1954, the Presidium of the Supreme Soviet of the Ukrainian Socialist Soviet Republic accepted the transfer.

There are several opinions about why Khrushchev took the decision to transfer Crimea to Ukraine. He explains nothing in his memoirs. It is said that he did so in order to celebrate the 300th anniversary of its unification with the Russian Empire, but the documents in Moscow's *Istoricheskii arkhiv* also fail to shed more light on this issue.[26] What is known is that the Presidium of the Supreme Council of the Communist Party of the Soviet Union approved a preliminary resolution on January 25 in which it authorized the Presidium of the Supreme Soviet of the Russian Soviet Federative Socialist Republic to approve the transfer, which took place on February 19, 1954—with the presence of only 13 of the 27 members, under the chairmanship of General Kliment Y. Voroshilov (1881–1969).[27] The decision was said to have been taken unanimously, even though there was no quorum. And this is why in 1992, the Supreme Council of Russia reviewed the case and considered the transfer of the peninsula to be illegitimate, which it now called the Autonomous Republic of Crimea.[28]

Nikita S. Khrushchev, Stalin's successor at the head of the Soviet Union, was born in the town of Kalinovka on the Russian border with Ukraine, where he worked in the iron and coal mines. And he loved Crimea, where he spent his holidays. In 1962, he decided to place missile platforms in Cuba after the United States put bases in Turkey, on the other side of the Black Sea. Between 1938 and 1947, he served as first secretary of the Ukrainian Communist Party and collaborated in the bloody purges of the 1930s. And during World War II, when the troops of Nazi Germany set Operation Barbarossa in motion and invaded the Soviet Union across the borders of Ukraine and Belarus on June 22, 1941, he actively participated in the dismantling

---

Daghestan, Buryat-Mongolian, Kabardino-Balkarian, Kalmyk, Komi, Crimean, Mari, Mordovian, Volga German, North Ossetian, Udmurt, Checheno-Ingush, Chuvash and Yakut Autonomous Soviet Socialist Republics; and the Adygei, Jewish, Karachai, Oirot, Khakass and Cherkess Autonomous Regions." "Article 23. The Ukrainian Soviet Socialist Republic consists of the Vinnitsa, Volynsk, Voroshilovgrad, Dnepropetrovsk, Drogobych, Zhitomir, Zaporozhe, Izmail, Kamenets-Podolsk, Kiev, Kirovograd, Lvov, Nikolaev, Odessa, Poltava, Rovno, Stalino, Stanislav, Sumy, Tarnopol, Kharkov, Chernigov and Chernovitsy Regions. Chapter II—The Organization of the Soviet State." *1936 Constitution of the USSR.* Adopted December 1936. Available at: <http://www.departments.bucknell.edu/russian/const/36cons01.html#article14>.

[25]Mark Kramer, "Why Did Russia Give Away Crimea Sixty Years Ago?". *Cold War International History Project.* Available at: <http://www.wilsoncenter.org/publication/why-did-russia-give-away-crimea-sixty-years-ago>.

[26]*Ibidem*; Dmitri Volkogonov, 1999, pp. 196–200.

[27]Mark Kramer, "Why Did Russia Give Away Crimea Sixty Years Ago?". *Cold War International History Project.* Available at: <http://www.wilsoncenter.org/publication/why-did-russia-give-away-crimea-sixty-years-ago>.

[28]"USSR's Nikita Khrushchev gave Russia's Crimea away to Ukraine in only 15 minutes." *Pravda*, February 19, 2009. Available at: <http://english.pravda.ru/history/19-02-2009/107129-ussr_cri mea_ukraine-0/>.

and removal of the industries located in the southeast and east of Ukraine until the Urals.

14.4 The Disintegration of the Soviet Union and the Economic Decline of Ukraine

After World War II, the development of Ukraine's industrial park, located mainly in the Donbass, took off, especially in the first half of the 1960s. Growth slowed down after 1965, however, and virtually stagnated in the 1970s. And when Ukraine separated from the Soviet Union and became an independent republic in 1991, its national fragility was both populational and economic in nature. Of its 44.6 million inhabitants, 77% were Ukrainians, 17% were ethnic Russians, and 6% were of several other nationalities: Belarusians, Tatars, Poles, Lithuanians, Jews, and Romanians.[29] And there was no economic unity. Agriculture was still relatively prevalent in the poorer west, where only television sets and buses were manufactured, while the Novorossiysk region (east and southeast) had not only rich coal reserves but a vast industrial park—steel mills, metallurgy, and heavy machinery plants—umbilically tied to the Russian economy since the times of the Soviet Union, with its production chain for rockets and other military artifacts, in addition to medicines. From this region came a large part of the exports that sustained Ukraine, a multiethnic and multilinguistic country whose connections with Russia had been carved out historically by economic relations, the integration with the Russian industrial chain and market, and the cultural and family ties arising from interethnic marriages.[30]

Ukraine, however, was one of the poorer republics of the defunct Soviet Union.[31] And just as the other dismembered republics, Ukraine suffered through a big decline in production and hyperinflation due to several factors, such as the fact it didn't have domestic financial institutions or sufficient access to the foreign market and because

---

[29]John Kozy, "Mother Russia." *Nueva Sociedad*—253, Buenos Aires: Friedrich Ebert Stiftung, September–October 2014, pp. 131–137.

[30]Yakov Feygin, "Ukraine is stuck in a post-Soviet condition." *OpenDemocracy*, March 12, 2014. Available at: <https://www.opendemocracy.net/od-russia/yakov-feygin/ukraine-is-stuck-in-post-soviet-condition-east-vs-west-ukrainian-economy>.

[31]Pekka Sutela, "Ukraine after Independence—The Underachiever—Ukraine's economy since 1991." *Paper*, March 9, 2012. *Carnegie Endowment for International Peace*. Available at: <http://carnegieendowment.org/files/ukraine_economy.pdf>; Yernar Zharkesho (Director of Research Institute). "Comparative analysis of trends and challenges to maintain adequate institutional and human resource capacities of public administrations in post-Soviet countries." Background discussion paper. *Academy of public Administration under the President of Kazakhstan*. Available at: <http://workspace.unpan.org/sites/Internet/Documents/UNPAN93486.pdf>.

it had to cover its budget deficits with bonds and loans from the Central Bank.[32] Between 1991 and 1996, its economy contracted even further, between 9.7% and 22.7% annually, amid hyperinflation and a large decline in industrial production, concentrated in the manufacture of military equipment in the Donbass region.[33]

According to the available data—although the statistics of the time are questionable—Ukraine's per capita GDP fell from an estimated US$1748 in 1990 to US $1337 in 1993, declining even further until the year 2000.[34] Its inhabitants nurtured the expectation that a greater integration with the Euro-Atlantic countries, the establishment of a democracy, and the free-market economy would improve their standard of living. But despite such hopes, the promotion of democracy and free enterprise did not provide stability or wealth to Ukraine. The impetuous process of privatizations, deregulations, and trade liberalizations under the Washington Consensus further ruined the economy and favored corruption and the emergence of a new ruling class, a circle of billionaire oligarchs, who constituted a small political elite.[35]

Ukraine had depended—and continued to depend—on Russia, which virtually sustained its economy by supplying it with 70% of the oil and gas it imported at a subsidized price. Thirty percent of the Soviet Union's industrial defense complex, on the other hand, was located in Ukraine's territory. Around 750 factories and 140 technical institutions—with 1 million workers—remained linked with the production chain in Russia, which was its most significant market and the source of most of the components for the armaments it produced,[36] components such as gears for warships, satellite-based attack warning systems, and the designs for the heaviest international ballistic missiles, the SS-18 Satan, and other nuclear weapons.[37] After Ukraine broke off from the Soviet Union, however, Russia withdrew two-thirds of the defense industry installed there, and its imports of machinery and armaments dropped to 40%,[38] about US$15.8 billion, or 5% of all its imports in 2013, which represented about 53% of Ukraine's exports to Russia in iron and steel (14%);

---

[32]Vadym Lepetyuk, "Hyperinflation in Ukraine"—Econ1102—Guest Lecture. *University of Minnesota*. Available at: <http://www.econ.umn.edu/~dmiller/GLhyperinflation>.

[33]Pekka Sutela, "The Underachiever—Ukraine's Economy Since 1991." Ukraine March 2012. *Carnegie Papers. Carnegie Endowment for International Peace*. Available at: <http://carnegieendowment.org/files/ukraine_economy.pdf>.

[34]"Gross Domestic Product (GDP) in Ukraine—GDP of Ukraine, 1990–2013." *World macroeconomic research*. Available at: <http://kushnirs.org/macroeconomics/gdp/gdp_ukraine.html>.

[35]Nathaniel Copsey, 2010, pp. 32–33.

[36]"Analysis: Ukraine's and Russia's aerospace industries will be hit hard by deteriorating relations." London. *Flightglobal*, September 23, 2014.

[37]Pekka Sutela, "The Underachiever—Ukraine's Economy Since 1991"—Ukraine March 2012. *Carnegie Papers. Carnegie Endowment for International Peace*. Available at: <http://carnegieendowment.org/files/ukraine_economy.pdf>.

[38]Jan Cienski, (Warsaw). "Russia's reliance on Ukraine for military hardware raises fears." *The Financial Times*, April 20, 2014. Available at: <http://www.ft.com/cms/s/0/9cc89022-c87b-11e3-a7a1-00144feabdc0.html#axzz3QtFrdlkm>.

machinery and mechanical equipment, nuclear reactors (14%); railways and loco-
motives, wagons (12%); equipment and electrical machinery (7%); and iron or steel
products (6%).[39]

After 1991–1992, therefore, Ukraine's defense industry was reduced to approximately 300 companies and institutions—75 of which were registered and licensed
to produce military equipment, including rockets and missiles—employing 250,000
workers. In 2010, the government created the holding company Ukroboronprom,
which came to control 134 state defense industries with 120,000 workers. In 2012,
its sales reached US$1.44 billion and US$1.79 billion in 2013.[40] Ukroboronprom is
ranked among the world's 100 largest arms manufacturers in the list of the Stockholm International Peace Research Institute (SIPRI) of 2011 and 2012. This conglomerate located in Donetsk, which in 2014 included Ukrspetsexport, has always
been integrated into the industrial complex in Russia, supplying it with electronic
radio components, vision and electronic radio devices, guidance systems for robots
and airplanes, TV3-117/VK-2500 aircraft engines for combat and transport helicopters, and digital communication and navigation systems. Motor Sich, located in
Zaporizhia, 230 km west of Donetsk, produced most military helicopters for the
Russian Armed Forces, including the Mi-24. Factories producing medium-range air-
to-air R-27 missiles and other sensitive components were also located in the Donbass. Ukraine's domestic market or armed forces weren't large enough to consume
the substantial output of its armaments industry, and without the technological
collaboration of Russia, which absorbed most of this output, it lost its competitiveness in the international market. But it survived thanks to the continued demand from
Moscow, since its close involvement with Russia's industry could not evaporate so
quickly.

Ukraine's agriculture, which once represented a quarter of the agricultural production of the Soviet Union, also embarked on a prolonged crisis with the end of
economic planning; in 1990, the government closed about 12,000 kolkhozy (collective farms) and sovkhozy (state farms), which employed more than 40% of the rural
population of Ukraine, in order to privatize the rich and fertile black lands. A new
and small class of entrepreneurs then emerged with the large private agricultural
companies, while the majority of the rural population impoverished and social

---

[39]Alexander Dembitski, (CEIC Analyst). "The Economic Implications of Ukraine-Russia Trade
Relations." *CEIC Russia Data Talk*, July 8, 2014. Available at: <http://www.ceicdata.com/en/blog/
economic-implications-ukraine-russia-trade-relations.> And also in: <http://www.ceicdata.com/
en/blog/economic-implications-ukraine-russia-trade-relations#sthash.bdvfLVlj.dpuf>.

[40]Alexandra Mclees and Eugene Rumer, "Saving Ukraine's Defense Industry," July 30, 2014.
Carnegie Endowment for International Peace. Available at: <http://carnegieendowment.org/2014/
07/30/saving-ukraine-s-defense-industry>; "Sales by largest arms companies fell again in 2012 but
Russian firms' sales increased sharply." *Stockholm International Peace Research Institute (SIPRI).
2014*. Munich, January 31, 2014. Available at: <http://www.sipri.org/media/pressreleases/2014/
top100_january2014>.

inequality rose.[41] This reform was extremely difficult since the emerging entrepreneurs in Ukraine lacked experience in markets and capital. The fall in agricultural prices, after 1991, made the crisis in the sector worse and quality of life in rural areas fell, the social structure rapidly deteriorated, and the rural population decreased by 15.9% (2.7 million people) between 1991 and 2013, causing a serious demographic imbalance.[42]

Separated from Russia, Ukraine improved neither its economic nor its political situation. It did not diversify its exports and was only able to balance its budget in one single year, 2002.[43] GDP collapsed between 1990 and 1994 and declined throughout the decade. Meanwhile the shadow economy continued to swell, accounting for a staggering 68% of official GDP at its peak in 1997.[44] And with the Parliament's approval of the resolution "On Perfection of the Privatization Mechanism in Ukraine and Intensifying the Control of Its Conduct," the privatization of state-owned enterprises began to take effect. It really took off during the administration of Leonid Kučma (1994–2005), successor of Leonid Kravchuk (1992–1993), both closely linked to the financial speculator George Soros.[45] And this privatization process was significantly helped along by the World Bank, USAID, and EC TACIS (European Commission Technical Assistance to the Commonwealth of Independent States), whose consultants monitored the transition of the Soviet Republics to the market economy. On September 2, 1996, the government of President Leonid Kučma replaced the old currency—the karbovanets—with the new sovereign currency, the hrywnja (Гривня—grivnia), which was little used[46] because of the prevalence of rubles and dollars. Largely due to the capital flight in 1988,[47] Ukraine's economy contracted by around 15% in 1999, with its production output

---

[41]Arkadiusz Sarna, "The transformation of agriculture in Ukraine: from collective farms to agroholdings." *OSW Commentary—Centre for Eastern Studies*. Number 127, June 2, 2014. Available at: <www.osw.waw.pl. Also in: http://aei.pitt.edu/57943/1/commentary_127.pdf>.

[42]*Ibidem.*

[43]Pekka Sutela, "The Underachiever—Ukraine's Economy Since 1991"—Ukraine March 2012. *Carnegie Papers. Carnegie Endowment for International Peace.* Available at: <http://carnegieendowment.org/files/ukraine_economy.pdf>.

[44]Lucio Vinhas Souza and Phillippe Lombarde, 2006, pp. 276–278.

[45]David Snelbecker, "The Political Economy of Privatization in Ukraine." *Center for Social & Economic Research: CASE Research Foundation*, Warsaw 1995: Paper was prepared for the project: "Economic Reforms in the former USSR." Reformy gospodarcze na terenie dawnego ZSRR, financed by the Comittee of Scientific Research (Komitet Badań—Naukowych); Bohdan Hawrylyshyn. *Ten years of work on behalf of Ukraine: notable highlights.* Part II. A Washington dinner. Available at: <http://www.ukrweekly.com/old/archive/1999/099921.shtml>.

[46]Pekka Sutela, "Ukraine after Independence—The Underachiever—Ukraine's economy Since 1991." Paper—March 9, 2012. *Carnegie Endowment for International Peace.* Available at: <http://carnegieendowment.org/files/ukraine_economy.pdf>.

[47]CIA Fact Book. Available at: <https://www.cia.gov/library/publications/the-world-factbook/fields/print_2116.html>.

declining to below 40% of 1991 levels. To a certain extent, Ukraine had become unproductive.[48]

14.5 Appropriation of Assets by the Oligarchs and the Emergence of Yulia Tymoshenko Through Money Laundering and Tax Evasion

Even in the midst of the severe economic crisis, however, the managers of the state-owned enterprises became rich and powerful captains of industry—oligarchs—appropriating state-owned enterprises at low costs during the privatization process. They started financing political parties, as political leaders, to vie for the control of the state and turn it into their own business, guiding the decisions of the government at all levels. Political instability, cultivated by endemic corruption, has since marked the history of Ukraine. And these were the fertile grounds where Yulia (née Telehina) Tymoshenko, owner of a video rental store, was able to accumulate billions of dollars. After the collapse of the Soviet Union, she became the director of a small company—Ukrainian Oil Company (UOC)—and developed it as a trading company, United Energy Systems of Ukraine, to import natural gas from Russia. As it turned out, however, Yulia Tymoshenko enriched herself as a "poacher-turned-gamekeeper" through lucrative money laundering operations, tax evasion, and the diversion of huge amounts of gas, paying kickbacks to Prime Minister Pavlo Lazarenko[49] (1996–1997) for the access to classified information and special concessions, enabling her to consolidate one-third of the gas sector and one-fifth of Ukraine's GDP.[50]

---

[48]"Ukraine and Russia. Why is Ukraine's economy in such a mess?". *The Economist*, March 5, 2014.

[49]During his tenure as Prime Minister, Pavlo Lazarenko illegally appropriated US$250 million, and in August 2006, he was arrested in the United States, tried, and sentenced to 9 years in prison for money laundering, fraud, and extortion. He was released from the US Federal Correctional Institution (FCI) Terminal Island in California, in 2012. The US government has located funds deposited in several banks in various places, including Guernsey, Antigua, Switzerland, Liechtenstein, and Lithuania; Daryna Kaleniuk and Halyna Senyk, "Who will get stolen Lazarenko money?" *Kyiv Post*, September 12, 2013. Available at: <http://www.kyivpost.com/opinion/op-ed/who-will-get-stolen-lazarenko-money-329296.html>.

[50]Chrystia Freeland, "Lunch with the FT—Tea with the FT: Yulia Tymoshenko." *The Financial Times*, August 16, 2008. Available at: <http://www.ft.com/cms/s/0/f4b1341a-6a58-11dd-83e8-0000779fd18c.html>; John Daly, "Ukraine's Yulia Timoshenko—Victim or Crook?". *OilPrice. com*, October 12, 2011. Available at: <http://oilprice.com/Energy/Energy-General/Ukraines-Yulia-Timoshenko-Victim-Or-Crook.html>; "Julia Tymoshenko: The iron princess." *The Independent*, October 28, 2007. Available at: <http://www.independent.co.uk/news/people/profiles/julia-tymoshenko-the-iron-princess-397875.html>; Christopher Dickey, "Yulia Tymoshenko: She's No Angel." *The Daily Beast*, February 23, 2014. Available at: <http://www.thedailybeast.com/articles/2014/02/23/yulia-tymoshenko-she-s-no-angel.html>; Julia Ioffe, "Kiev Chameleon." *New Republic*, January 5, 2010. Available at: <http://www.newrepublic.com/article/world/kiev-chameleon>.

Born in Dnipropetrovsk, in the Russian-speaking region of the Dnieper Basin, Yulia Tymoshenko was arrested in 2001 (as was her husband Oleksandr Tymoshenko) for illegally transferring US$1 billion from Ukraine and paying millions of dollars in bribes to Pavlo Lazarenko.[51] She was detained for 42 days, but then the accusation was dropped and she was released. And although she didn't appear on the list of Ukrainian billionaires,[52] she was able to heap together a personal fortune valued at US$11 billion through her shadowy gas trading business,[53] making her entrance in the political scene during the Orange Revolution of 2004/2005.[54] She then became Prime Minister in the government of Viktor A. Yushchenko, governor of the Bank of Ukraine, who assumed the presidency of the country after an election replete with fraud, promoting the privatization of the state-owned companies and defending the adherence to NATO. And the United States gave him massive economic and political support.

---

[51]Julia Ioffe, "Kiev Chameleon." *New Republic*, January 5, 2010. Available at: <http://www.newrepublic.com/article/world/kiev-chameleon>.

[52]Mark Rachkevych, "50 Richest Ukrainians." *Kyiv Post*, June 11, 2009. Available at: <http://www.kyivpost.com/content/ukraine/50-richest-ukrainians-43241.html>.

[53]James Meek, "The millionaire revolutionary". *The Guardian*, November 26, 2004. Available at: <http://www.theguardian.com/world/2004/nov/26/ukraine.gender>; "Julia Tymoshenko: The iron princess". *The Independent*, October 28, 2007. Available at: <http://www.independent.co.uk/news/people/profiles/julia-tymoshenko-the-iron-princess-397875.html>.

[54]On the subject of the Orange Revolution, see Luiz Alberto Moniz Bandeira, 2014, pp. 98–100.

Chapter 15
US Efforts to Drive a Wedge Between Ukraine and Russia

15.1 Economic Decline of Ukraine, the 2008 Crisis, and the Threatening Collapse of Ukraine

Yulia Tymoshenko returned to the post of prime minister from 2007 until 2010, when she ran for the presidency of Ukraine against the Viktor F. Yanukovych. Yanukovych also spoke Russian and was born in Yenakiieve in the Donetsk Oblast district, an important coal, metallurgy, chemical, and manufacturing center where the Party of Regions supporting him enjoyed a large majority. Yulia Tymoshenko lost the election, however, and in 2011 she was put on trial for abuse of power during her time as prime minister in Viktor A. Yushchenko's administration and sentenced to 7 years in prison, just as the former Interior Minister Yuriy Lutsenko (2007–2010). Ukraine, meanwhile, had fallen on very hard times after the Orange Revolution. In 2009, the economic and financial crisis that exploded in the United States in 2007–2008 spreads to the European Union and shook Greece, threatening Ireland, Portugal, Spain, and the entire Eurozone (16 of the 27 EU Member States and the 9 nonmembers who adopted the Euro). Ukraine, which on average received 35% of its economic resources from Russia each year, also took a hard hit.

Ukraine's public debt had jumped from US$550.8 million in 1992 to US$13.9 billion in 1999 and to more than US$30 billion in 2007.[1] Per capita debt rose from US$10.6 in 1992 to US$282.1 in 1999, US$498 in 2005, and US$827 in 2010.[2] And with the financial crisis of 2007–2008, funds dried up. In 2010, the IMF agreed to grant Ukraine a loan of US$15 billion, but in 2011 it suspended credit because President Viktor F. Yanukovych failed to meet the drastic conditions linked to the aid, such as cutting off gas subsidies and reducing the public deficit to 2.8% of GDP, which would only be possible by cutting capital expenditures, wages, pensions, etc.

---

[1]Ararat L. Osipian, 2009, pp. 123–124.

[2]*Ibidem*, p. 123.

© Springer Nature Switzerland AG 2019
L. A. Moniz Bandeira, *The World Disorder*,
https://doi.org/10.1007/978-3-030-03204-3_15

Ukraine's foreign debt of around US$137.07 million in 2013 inflated to US $142.5 million in January 2014.[3] The exchange rate of the hryvnia in relation to the dollar fell to 10:1 (previously set at 8:1).[4] The depreciation of the currency increased the burden of public debt, half of which denominated in foreign currency, and made it harder to acquire new debts. The deficit of the balance-of-payments current account jumped from US$14.3 billion in 2012, or 8.1% of GDP,[5] to US$16.4 billion in 2013,[6] equivalent to 9% of GDP. Gold reserves plummeted from US$41.7 billion to US$20.2 billion in 2013 and continued their fall to US$13.40 billion in 2014, barely enough to cover 2 months of imports.[7] "The default in Ukraine is in de facto status, and its theoretical possibility is 100%," said Olexandr Sugonyako, president of the Ukrainian Banking Association.[8] And this default predicted by Sugonyako only failed to occur because of the complacency of creditors.

The Ukrainian state-owned company Naftogaz owed between US$2.2 billion and $2.4 billion to Gazprom—which shipped Russia's gas to the European Union—and it was virtually bankrupt in 2009. There was no cash to pay the 500 million in outstanding Eurobonds. Its creditors—Deutsche Bank, Credit Suisse, and Depfa— had filed suits against Ukraine in the London court, and in order to persuade them to accept debt restructuring and avoid the bankruptcy of the company, whose budget deficit had reached the sum of 33 billion hryvnia[9] (US$3.9 billion), the Ukrainian government was forced to grant a US$2 billion sovereign guarantee to the credi-

---

[3]Ukraine External Debt 2003–2015. *Trading Economics*. Available at: <http://www. tradingeconomics.com/ukraine/external-debt>. Also in: <http://www.bank.gov.ua/doccatalog/doc ument?id=8388817>; Sujata Rao, "Big debts and dwindling cash—Ukraine tests creditors' nerves." *Reuters*, 17 de outubro de 2013—Available at: <http://uk.reuters.com/article/2013/10/ 17/uk-emerging-ukraine-debt-idUKBRE99G06P20131017> *Trading Economics*. Available at: <http://www.tradingeconomics.com/ukraine/external-debt>.

[4]"Ukraine and Russia. Why is Ukraine's economy in such a mess?". *The Economist*, March 5, 2014. Available at: <http://www.economist.com/blogs/freeexchange/2014/03/ukraine-and-russia>.

[5]National Bank of Ukraine. Balance of Payments and External Debt of Ukraine in the First Quarter of 2014, p. 82. Available at: <http://www.bank.gov.ua/doccatalog/document; jsessionid=D3E06465B2108ABB86DD04A0A4677539?id=10132249>.

[6]National Bank of Ukraine. Balance of Payments and External Debt of Ukraine in 2013, p. 5. Available at: <http://www.bank.gov.ua/doccatalog/document?id=8388817>.

[7]National Bank of Ukraine. Balance of Payments and External Debt of Ukraine in the First Quarter of 2014, p. 82. Available at: <http://www.bank.gov.ua/doccatalog/document; jsessionid=D3E06465B2108ABB86DD04A0A4677539?id=10132249>. Ukraine External Debt 2003–2015. *Trading Economics*. Available at: <http://www.tradingeconomics.com/ukraine/exter nal-debt>.

[8]"Sugonyako: Since 2005, we have accumulated the external debt from $14 to $74 billion. Our economy is unprofitable, and our government is inefficient." *Gordon.com*, January 12, 2015. Available at: <http://english.gordonua.com/news/exclusiveenglish/Sugonyako-60898.html>.

[9]Ukrainian currency.

tors.[10] Nonetheless, the rating agencies Standard & Poor's, Moody's, and Fitch Ratings downgraded Ukraine's long-term sovereign debt rating at the end of January 2014, with a negative outlook and a high risk of default aggravated by the turbulence and instability in the country.[11]

Mired in a deep economic and financial crisis, Ukraine's prospects were dire. Its economy contracted by 15% in 2009. After 1992, when Ukraine's economy was larger than that of Latvia and Romania, GDP dropped continuously, only registering a tiny growth in 2010, still well below the level it had enjoyed before separating from Russia in 1991. GDP per capita was comparable to Kosovo or Namibia, behind Poland, Slovakia, and Hungary.[12]

About a hundred oligarchs—0.00003% of the population—controlled between 80 and 85% of the wealth in this country with the lowest income level in Europe.[13] A significant share of the population lived below the poverty line—about 25% according to the official statistics. And 45 million Ukrainians, i.e., about 99.9999% of the population, were left with only 15–20% of the wealth.[14] According to the government, unemployment was around 8%, rising to 9.3% in the first 4 months of 2014. The malnutrition index was estimated to range from 2% to as high as 16%. The average salary was around US$332, one of the lowest in Europe. And the rural areas in the west were even poorer. The emergence of rural entrepreneurs, with the rapid dissolution of the kolkhozy, resulted in the progressive impoverishment of the majority of the rural population and exacerbated wealth inequality.[15] Young Ukrainians imagined that the European Union could improve their standard of living and increase the country's prosperity. Ukrainians—the youth first and foremost—dreamt of the European Union, of the freedom to travel, of comfort, of good wages, of prosperity, etc.

---

[10]Roman Olearchyk (in Kiev), "Ukraine offers to guarantee Naftogaz debt." *Financial Times*, September 21, 2009. Available at: <http://www.ft.com/intl/cms/s/0/f04c0740-a6b8-11de-bd14-00144feabdc0.html#axzz37w0928mV>; Roman Olearchyk, "Ukraine's Naftogaz battles to avert default." Financial Times, September 30, 2009. Available at: <http://www.ft.com/intl/cms/s/0/6efad0e2-add7-11de-87e7-00144feabdc0.html#axzz37w0928mV>.

[11]*EcoFinanças*. Available at: <http://www.ecofinancas.com/noticias/moody-s-rebaixa-rating-soberano-ucrania-para-caa2/relacionadas>.

[12]USAID—Ukraine Country Development Cooperation Strategy 2012–2016, p. 8. Available at: <https://www.usaid.gov/sites/default/files/documents/1863/USAID_Ukraine_CDCS_2012-2016.pdf>; *CIA—Country Comparison: GDP—Per Capita* (PPP). Available at: <https://www.usaid.gov/sites/default/files/documents/1863/USAID_Ukraine_CDCS_2012-2016.pdf>. Also: <https://www.cia.gov/library/publications/resources/the-world-factbook/geos/up.html>.

[13]"Ukrainian Oligarchs and the—"Family", a New Generation of Czars—or Hope for the Middle Class?". *International Research and Exchange Board (IREX)*—Department of State—August 2013. Available at: <https://www.irex.org/sites/default/files/Holoyda%20EPS%20Research%20Brief.pdf>.

[14]*Ibidem.*

[15]"The transformation of agriculture in Ukraine: From collective farms to agroholdings." *OSW—Ośrodek waschodnich, in Marka Kapia*, July 2, 2014. Available at: <http://www.osw.waw.pl/en/publikacje/osw-commentary/2014-02-07/transformation-agriculture-ukraine-collective-farms-to>.

15.2   Ukraine as a Geopolitical Pivot Country and Zbigniew Brzezinski's Theory

Because of its location between Russia and the European Union and centrifugal tendencies, Ukraine was and is a geopolitical pivot country. Zbigniew Brzezinski, former National Security Advisor to President Jimmy Carter, once wrote that Russia would no longer be an Eurasian empire on the world's chessboard without Ukraine. It could still fight for imperial status, but it would only be prevalent in Asia, in conflict with the other states that became independent from the Soviet Union.[16] Ukraine could be in Europe without Russia—so he understood—but Russia could not be in (Western) Europe without Ukraine. Without Ukraine, Russia's borders were pushed 500,000 miles (804,672 km) to the east, losing a powerful industrial zone and fertile agricultural lands, in addition to 52 million inhabitants (1997), many of which Russian-speaking and ethnically linked to the Russian population. This is why—Zbigniew Brzezinski argued—the United States should prevent Russia from restoring its imperial status by regaining control of Ukraine, a country with vast resources and access to the Black Sea through the naval base of Sevastopol.[17]

Due to this geographic, demographic, and strategic dimension—and because Ukraine still possessed a large nuclear arsenal—President Bill Clinton gave priority to that country within the framework of the project to extend NATO's jurisdiction to the former republics of the Soviet Union when he assumed the presidency of the United States in 1993. He feared that if Ukraine was left in isolation to the southeast of Russia, it would once again fall into the orbit of its sphere of influence.[18] So when he visited President Leonid Kravchuk (1991–1994) in Kiev in January 1994,[19] he proposed the integration of Ukraine (and the other Warsaw Pact Republics) into NATO's architecture by joining the Partnership for Peace (PfP) program, developed by his Secretary of State Warren Christopher and Secretary of Defense Les Aspin.

---

[16]Zbigniew Brzezinski, 1997, pp. 46–47.

[17]*Ibidem*, pp. 46–47.

[18]Taylor Branch, 2009, p. 168; William J. Clinton: "The President's News Conference with President Kučma of Ukraine," November 22, 1994. Online by Gerhard Peters and John T. Woolley. *The American Presidency Project*. Available at: <http://www.presidency.ucsb.edu/ws/?pid=49507>.

[19]"President's New Conference with President Leonid Kravchuck of Kiev, January 12, 1994," in: William J. Clinton, Public Papers of the Presidents of the United States: William J. Clinton, 1994, pp. 43–46. Available at: <https://books.google.de/books?id=NCThAwAAQBAJ&pg=PA46&lpg=PA46&dq=Clinton+Partnership+For+peace+Ukraine&source=bl&ots=xAVnTwVIs-&sig=rnoNdxUxlugp_6qfOJFYzP0D97Q&hl=de&sa=X&ei=gd_pVLiHOsb9UOGRgtAN&ved=0CFMQ6AEwBQ#v=onepage&q=Clinton%20Partnership%20For%20peace%20Ukraine&f=false>.

15.3   The Entangled Issues of Crimea, Oil and Gas, and Nuclear Weapons

Ukraine has always been an extremely contradictory country. With its varying ethnic, economic, social, political, and cultural differences, not all regions accepted NATO or European Union membership.[20] And the offer to associate Ukraine to the US Armed Forces through NATO, strongly favored by nationalist sectors in Kiev and Galicia, produced sufficient oxygen to fan the flames in the relations with Russia regarding the control of the Sevastopol naval base and, consequently, the entire Crimean peninsula.[21] This control was also intertwined with the supply of natural gas, for which Ukraine depended on Gazprom for at least 40%. In addition, in 2013 approximately 3.0 trillion cubic feet (tcf) of natural gas from Russia, i.e., 86 billion cubic meters (bcm), passed through Ukraine's territory to supply Austria, Bosnia and Herzegovina, Bulgaria, Croatia, the Czech Republic, Germany, Greece, Hungary, Moldavia, Poland, Romania, Slovakia, and Turkey.[22]

In 2011, Russia supplied about 35% of Western Europe's crude oil demand through the southern branch of the Druzhba oil pipeline,[23] which went through Ukraine. In addition, it exported approximately 7.4 million barrels per day (BPD) of total liquid fuels in 2012, including 5 million BPD in crude oil and 2.4 million BPD in petroleum products.[24] In 2013, the countries of Europe, especially Germany, Poland, and the Netherlands, and the countries in Eastern Europe imported 79% of crude oil from Russia, about 300,000–400,000 BPD—most of the fuel consumed by Hungary, Slovakia, the Czech Republic, and Bosnia.[25]

The controversies involving the Sevastopol naval base begun in 1992 amid negotiations over the withdrawal of the Soviet Union's nuclear arsenal, which finally occurred after a trilateral agreement reached in January 1994 with President Bill

---

[20]Ian Mcallister and Stephen Whithe, "Rethinking the Orange Revolution," 2010, pp. 138–139.

[21]Taras Kuzio, "The Crimea: Europe's Next Flashpoint?—November 2010." Washington. *The Jamestown Foundation*, p. 4. Available at: <http://www.peacepalacelibrary.nl/ebooks/files/372451918.pdf>.

[22]"Ukraine—Country Analysis Note." *US Energy Information Administration*. Available at: <http://www.eia.gov/countries/country-data.cfm?fips=up>; Frank Umbach (Associate Director at the European Centre for Energy and Resource Security (EUCERS). "Russian-Ukrainian-EU gas conflict: who stands to lose most?" *NATO/OTAN*. Available at: <http://www.nato.int/docu/review/2014/NATO-Energy-security-running-on-empty/Ukrainian-conflict-Russia-annexation-of-Crimea/EN/index.htm>; Karolina Chorvath (Special to *CNBC.com*), "Why Ukraine needs Russia—for now, anyway." Wednesday, June 4, 2014. CNBC.com. Available at: <http://www.cnbc.com/id/101727421>.

[23]"Facet Sheet—Russia Europe liquid relationship often overlooked." *Clingendael International Energy Programme (CIEP)*. Available at: <http://www.clingendaelenergy.com/files.cfm?event=files.download&ui=9C1E06F0-5254-00CF-FD03A39927F34043>.

[24]"Russia—Overview, November 26, 2013 (Notes)." *US Energy Information Administration*. Available at: <http://www.eia.gov/countries/country-data.cfm?fips=up>.

[25]"Ukraine—Country Analysis Note." *US Energy Information Administration*. Available at: <http://www.eia.gov/countries/country-data.cfm?fips=up>.

Clinton's visit to Kiev, after strenuous talks involving Russia, the United States, and Britain. Through this agreement, Ukraine would receive security guarantees, economic compensation for the highly enriched uranium (HEU) of the 1500 warheads, and assistance in dismantling the 176 intercontinental ballistic missiles (ICBMs), silos, bombers, and nuclear infrastructure on its territory.[26] The United States and Britain were able to involve themselves and apply pressure in the issue of the removal of atomic artifacts from Ukraine because it was part of the denuclearization effort undertaken by the great powers under the framework of the Strategic Arms Reduction Treaty I (START) and the Treaty on the Non-Proliferation of Nuclear Weapons (NPT). But the controversy of the naval base in Sevastopol was a bilateral issue, although in reality the efforts by the United States (and political sectors in Kiev) to extend NATO's military structure to Ukraine were powerful obstacles.

Sevastopol had been the port of the fifth squadron of the defunct Soviet Union and was always considered a Russian city. The nationalist sectors in Moscow were pushing Russia to regain jurisdiction over both the naval base and the entire territory of Crimea, which was predominantly Russian and a favorite holiday resort for Russian tourists.[27] The mayor of Moscow, Yuri Luzhkov (1992–2010), publicly suggested Nikita Khrushchev was intoxicated when he took the decision to donate the peninsula to Ukraine.[28] More than 80% of the Crimean people who spoke Russian had always considered themselves Russians and advocated for the secession from Ukraine and the reintegration of the peninsula to Russia.[29] Many of Sevastopol's inhabitants were former Soviet sailors, with anchors tattooed on their hands and arms. They were pro-Russia and fiercely opposed NATO, which they considered the enemy.[30] Kiev, however, wanted to take over 50% of the Soviet Black Sea Fleet stationed in Sevastopol, giving it the status of Ukraine's main naval base, something neither Russia nor the Crimean people accepted. In addition, one-third of the Soviet Union's vast nuclear arsenal was installed in Ukraine.

Crimea proclaimed itself independent in May, 6 1992, separating itself from Ukraine as a republic, establishing its own constitution, which the Rada in Kiev revoked in 1995. In May of the same year, 1992, the Russian parliament voted to annul the decision that had transferred the peninsula to the jurisdiction of Ukraine.[31]

---

[26]Bill Clinton, 2004, p. 570; Steven Pifer, "The Trilateral Process: The United States, Ukraine, Russia and Nuclear Weapons." Paper l May 2011. *Brooking*. Available at: <http://www.brookings.edu/research/papers/2011/05/trilateral-process-pifer>.

[27]Thomas Gerlach and Gert Schmidt, 2009, pp. 448–449.

[28]"The new Crimean war: how Ukraine squared up to Moscow." *The Independent*, January 9, 2006. Available at: <http://www.independent.co.uk/news/world/europe/the-new-crimean-war-how-ukraine-squared-up-to-moscow-522213.html>.

[29]Tyler Felgenhauer, "Ukraine, Russia, and the Black Sea Fleet Accords." *WWS Case Study 2/99*. Available at: <http://www.dtic.mil/dtic/tr/fulltext/u2/a360381.pdf>; Stephen White and Ian McAllister, 2010, p. 180.

[30]"The new Crimean war: how Ukraine squared up to Moscow." *The Independent*, January 9, 2006. Available at: <http://www.independent.co.uk/news/world/europe/the-new-crimean-war-how-ukraine-squared-up-to-moscow-522213.html>.

[31]Karen Dawisha and Bruce Parrot, 1995, pp. 210–211.

In December of 1992, the Congress of People's Deputies of Russia decided to investigate the legality of Ukraine's claim to Sevastopol. And the Duma in Moscow adopted a resolution on June 9, 1993, reaffirming the status of Sevastopol as a Russian federal city and the indivisibility of the Black Sea Fleet. In a survey conducted in May 1994, more than 90% of Sevastopol's inhabitants also expressed their support for the naval base remaining with Russia[32], and public demonstrations were organized to the same effect. In that same year (1994), Leonid Kučma (1994–2005) assumed the presidency of Ukraine and took on a more conciliatory tone with respect to Crimea and Russia. And when President Bill Clinton suggested Ukraine should join NATO during their meeting in Kiev on November 22, 1994, he dodged the issue. Ukraine, whose GDP had fallen by about 25% during Leonid Kravchuk's government in the first half of the 1990s, was in no position to confront either Russia or the United States.

Russia's gas supply, which met about 70% of Ukraine's consumption demand, the naval base at Sevastopol, the Black Sea Fleet with about 800 warships, and the alignment with NATO were entangled, conflicting, and incompatible issues. When Vice-Admiral Eduard Baltin took command of the Black Sea Fleet in 1993, he noted that Ukraine had become an autonomous country, with its own vision on domestic and foreign policy, different from Russia, but that it would be difficult for the people to see Russian ships sailing east and Ukrainian ships west, subordinate to NATO.[33]

15.4   The Strategic Interdependence Between Ukraine and Russia

President Leonid Kučma (1994–2005) finally realized that for Ukraine, economic relations with Russia were a matter of survival, and not just of prosperity, and that Kiev would be unable to negotiate with Moscow from a position of strength.[34] At that time, Russia exported about 156.1 bcm of gas (US$35 billion) to Western Europe through the Bratstvo (Urengoy-Pomary-Uzhhorod) and Soyuz pipelines.[35] It also supplied 37.6 bcm (US$3.4 billion) directly to Ukraine, whose debt with Gazprom had already reached US$1.52 billion, a debt Ukraine was in no condition to pay,[36] which led Russia to cut off supply.

---

[32]Edward Ozhiganov, "The Crimean Republic: rivalries concepts," 1997, p. 123.

[33]Dale B. Stewart, "The Russian-Ukrainian Friendship Treaty and the Search for Regional Stability in Eastern Europe." December 1997. Thesis S714366. N PS Archive 1997, 12. Naval Postgraduate School—Monterey, California. Available at: <https://archive.org/stream/russianukrainian00stew/russianukrainian00stew_djvu.txt>; Jane Shapiro Zacec and I. Ilpyong Kim (Editores), 1997, pp. 110–112.

[34]Paul J. D'anieri, 1999, p. 17, 20–205.

[35]*Gazprom Export*—Transportation. Available at: <http://www.gazpromexport.ru/en/projects/transportation/>.

[36]Jeffrey Ringhausen, "Refuting the Media: Punishment and the 2005–2006 Gas Dispute," pp. 3–33. University of North Carolina at Chapel Hill—Department of Slavic, Eurasian, and East European Studies. 2007- UMI Number: 1445454. Available at: <http://media.proquest.com/media/pq/classic/doc/1372035111/fmt/ai/rep/NPDF?_s=E21sZ9Yq1ee87kdZ1Xdh24phC7U%3D>.

A strategic interdependence existed between both countries, and Ukraine needed to accept the asymmetry and maintain normal relations with Russia.[37] The divergences regarding the demarcation and recognition of borders were smoothed out with the signing of the Russian-Ukrainian Friendship Treaty pursuing security and stability in Eastern Europe, signed on May 28, 1997, by the Prime Ministers Pavlo Lazarenko of Ukraine and Viktor S. Chernomyrdin of Russia. Russia would keep the bulk of the Black Sea Fleet, along with ownership of the name, while Ukraine would get only 18.3% and financial compensation, in addition to ownership of Sevastopol, with the obligation to lease it to Russia for US$97.7 million during a 20-year period,[38] extendable for the amount of US$100 million and with a possibility of review for an increase.[39]

The lease of the naval base for 20 years, with an option to extend, was implicitly linked to the supply of subsidized gas to Ukraine.[40] In these circumstances—and at the same time (1997) he signed the Friendship Treaty with Russia on the Sevastopol naval base and the Black Sea Fleet—President Leonid Kučma settled the relationship with NATO under the terms of the Charter on a Distinctive Partnership, reinforced by another instrument in 2009, creating the NATO-Ukraine Commission (NUC) for political dialogue and an annual program of practical cooperation. Various factors and pressures—both domestic and foreign—compelled President Leonid Kučma to attempt to establish Ukraine's double and difficult understanding with both Russia and NATO at the same time. The United States, meanwhile, did not abandon its efforts to encircle, confine, and separate Russia from Western Europe by occupying Ukraine economically and militarily.

---

[37]Dale B. Stewart, "The Russian-Ukrainian Friendship Treaty and the Search for Regional Stability in Eastern Europe." December 1997. Thesis S714366. N PS Archive 1997, 12. *Naval Postgraduate School*—Monterey, California. Available at: <https://archive.org/stream/russianukrainian00stew/russianukrainian00stew_djvu.txt>.

[38]Daniel W. Drezner, 1999, pp. 203–205.

[39]*Ibidem*; Francisco J. Ruiz González, "La Arquitectura de Seguridad Europea: Un Sistema Imperfecto e Inacabado"—De la Caída del Muro de Berlín (1989) a la Guerra De Georgia (2008). Tesis Doctoral—Tutora: Fanny Castro-Rial Garrone, Profesora Titular de Derecho Internacional Público y RRII. UNED. Universidad Nacional de Educación a Distancia. Instituto Universitario General Gutiérrez Mellado, 2012 pp. 168–160. Available at: <http://e-spacio.uned.es/fez/eserv/tesisuned:IUGM-Fjruiz/Documento.pdf>.

[40]Tyler Felgenhauer, "Ukraine, Russia, and the Black Sea Fleet Accords." *WWS Case Study 2/99*. Available at: <http://www.dtic.mil/dtic/tr/fulltext/u2/a360381.pdf>; Stephen White and Ian McAllister, 2010.

Chapter 16
Russia Opposes a New Orange Revolution in Ukraine

16.1 Washington's Expansionist Policy in Eurasia and the Attempt to Prevent Russia's Resurgence

The conciliation efforts by President Leonid Kučma masked, but failed to resolve the throbbing domestic and international contradictions in the geopolitical pivot country that was Ukraine. At the core of these conflicts were not only Ukraine's adherence to NATO's Partnership for Peace program, but the omnipresence of the United States, which sought to turn Ukraine into a bridgehead to conquer the rest of Eurasia and hamper Russia's presence in the Mediterranean, where it had begun construction of another military base in Novorossiysk for the silent diesel-electric submarines Varshavyanka (Project 636 class), capable of navigating through deep waters undetected by USA and NATO sonars. In one way or another, the underlying sources of combustion remained latent, and they would once again ignite to set Ukraine ablaze.

The United States wanted to block Russia's resurgence as great power, preventing it from re-establishing hegemony in the Eurasian space. And since it could not defeat Russia, Washington's strategy would be to create chaos to keep it from gaining strength, as the American geopolitical scholar George Friedman remarked.[1] At the heart of the problem, therefore, lay the United States' blatant ambition to build a bridge from Ukraine for its strategic expansion through Eurasia, a pivotal area of global equilibrium, and prevent Russia from regaining its dominant

---

[1] "In Ukraine, US interests are incompatible with the interests of the Russian Federation." Stratfor chief George Friedman on the roots of the Ukraine crisis Interview by Elena Chernenko & Alexander Gabuev—*us-russia.org*, January 17, 2015. Available at: <http://us-russia.org/2902-in-ukraine-us-interests-are-incompatible-with-the-interests-of-the-russian-federation-stratfor-chief-george-friedman-on-the-roots-of-the-ukraine-crisis.html>; Elena Chernenko & Alexander Gabuev (Kommersant—Russian daily), "Stratfor Chief's "Most Blatant Coup in History." Interview Translated in Full. *Insider Russia*, 20.01.2015. Available at: <http://russia-insider.com/en/2015/01/20/256>.

© Springer Nature Switzerland AG 2019
L. A. Moniz Bandeira, *The World Disorder*,
https://doi.org/10.1007/978-3-030-03204-3_16

position in the Black Sea, where Odessa served as its main trading port with the Mediterranean and other regions around the Atlantic. The Commonwealth of Independent States (CIS), established in Viskuli (Belarus) on December 8, 1991, to bring together the former republics of the Soviet Union (except for the Baltic republics), never really took off. And so the crisis throughout the region deepened when President Vladimir Putin signed the treaty for the establishment of the Single Economic Space of Eurasia with the presidents of Belarus and Kazakhstan on September 19, 2003, in Yalta.

NGOs such as Freedom House, the American Enterprise Institute (AEI), the National Democratic Institute (NDI), and many others, funded by USAID, NED, the CIA, and agencies of the United States and European Union and/or private groups,[2] went on to encourage the so-called color revolutions in the countries of the Caucasus.[3] The Orange Revolution in Ukraine sought to nullify the election of Viktor Yanukovych, governor of the province of Donetsk (1997–2002), and bring his opponent to power, opposition leader Viktor A. Yushchenko, who was pro-West, contrary to the agreement with Russia regarding the Sevastopol base and the gas supply by the company RosUkrEnergo, a Swiss-based joint venture owned for 50% by Gazprom. Yushchenko even admitted to the press that he was also voicing the concerns of political and economic groups and NGOs in Kiev,[4] which were being instigated from abroad to keep on the agenda the plans to integrate Ukraine into the European Union, NATO, and other Western institutions.[5] Indeed, according to a report by the Associated Press, the George W. Bush administration spent more than US$65 million in 2 years—2003 and 2004—on organizations in Ukraine, even paying for Yushchenko's trip to meet authorities in the United States so he could signal that he would win the decisive election against Viktor Yanukovych,[6] which came about and led him to the presidency of Ukraine on January 23, 2005.

[2]Gerald Sussman, *Branding Democracy: U.S. Regime Change in Post-Soviet Eastern Europe*. New York: Peter Lang Publishing, 2010, pp. 108–109; Luiz Alberto Moniz Bandeira, 2014, pp. 92–102.

[3]Anders Åslund & Michael Mfaul (Editors), 2006, pp. 184–188.

[4]"Yushchenko said he wants clarity on gas sector." *The Ukrainian Weekly,* February 19, 2006, p. 8. Available at: <http://ukrweekly.com/archive/pdf3/2006/The_Ukrainian_Weekly_2006-08.pdf>.

[5]Taras Kuzio, "Comments on Black Sea Fleet talks" *The Ukrainian Weekly,* February 19, 2006, p. 8. Available at: <http://ukrweekly.com/archive/pdf3/2006/The_Ukrainian_Weekly_2006-08.pdf>.

[6]"U.S. Spent $65M to Aid Ukrainian Groups." *Associated Press—Fox News.com,* February 10, 2004. Available at: <http://www.foxnews.com/story/2004/12/10/us-spent-65m-to-aid-ukrainian-groups/print>.

16.2   Kissinger's Warning that Ukraine Would Never Be "a Foreign Country" to Russia

In many ways, however, it was very difficult to disassociate Ukraine from Russia. Although the 2001 census recorded that only 17% of Ukrainians considered themselves ethnically Russian, several other surveys indicated that 80% of the population in 2012 spoke Russian as their first language and that the culture was predominantly Russian: more than 60% of newspapers, 83% of journals, 87% of books, and 72% of television programs were edited and transmitted in Russian.[7]

Always astute, the learned former Secretary of State Henry Kissinger (1973–1977) wrote: "the West must understand that, to Russia, Ukraine can never be just a foreign country."[8] He explained that at first Russia had been Kievan Rus'; that Ukraine had been a part of its territory for centuries; that the histories of both countries were closely intertwined; and that "Ukraine has been independent for only 23 years; it had previously been under some kind of foreign rule since the fourteenth century. Not surprisingly, its leaders have not learned the art of compromise, even less of historical perspective."[9] Henry Kissinger considered this to be the cause of the crisis, since each faction, representing different regional and cultural interests, tried to impose its will on the other recalcitrant part of the country. But Ukraine, traditionally called "little Russia," was divided between the ethnic Ukrainians in the West and the Russophones in the east and south, in the Donbass, resulting in profound political contradictions.

16.3   Gas Treaty of Kharkov and the Leasing of Sevastopol

In these circumstances, Viktor Yanukovych of the Party of Regions, the largest party in the Donbass, defeated Yulia Tymoshenko, leader of the Orange Revolution, on February 7, 2010, in a clean and transparent election, held shortly after Russia, Belarus and Kazakhstan approved (November 2009) the plan for the creation of the Eurasian Economic Community (EurAsEC). Ukraine's adherence to this union was therefore foreseeable. Since 1991, its relations with Russia had been very unstable, but Viktor Yanukovych had always favored an understanding between both countries. And on April 21, 2010, little more than a month after taking office, he signed an agreement in Kharkov (Kharkiv) on the supply of gas with Russia's then President Dmitry Medvedev. He obtained a discount of US$30–US$100 per 1000 cubic meters on the current price of US$330 in exchange for the extension to 2042 of

---

[7]Richard Sakwa, 2015, pp. 58–59.

[8]Henry A. Kissinger, "How the Ukraine crisis ends." *The Washington Post*, Wednesday, March 5, 2014.

[9]*Ibidem.*

the Sevastopol naval base lease in the Black Sea.[10] His predecessor, Viktor Yushchenko (2005–2010), had promised and tried to end this lease on the grounds that it
violated Ukraine's sovereignty and represented a destabilizing factor in Crimea,
whose population was mostly Russian and felt a strong sympathy for the Soviet
model.[11] Some groups protested against the renewal of the Sevastopol lease because
it would mean the Orange Revolution was well and truly over.[12]

The lease of the Sevastopol naval base in the Black Sea—set to expire in 2017—
was extended for another 25 years until 2042, with a possible extension for another
5 years.[13] Russia, on the other hand, would invest in the economic and social
development of Sevastopol and ensure the supply of natural gas to Ukraine 30%
below market prices, impacting an estimated US$40 billion in imports. The Kharkov
deal provided for industrial cooperation and joint projects in such strategic sectors as
nuclear energy and aviation, as well as modernization and integration of technologies, just as occurred in Soviet times in aeronautics, satellite production, armaments,
shipbuilding, and other fields. This would allow President Yanukovych to pull
Ukraine out of the severe recession and put its economy back on a path to sustainable
growth. The agreement would favor the integration of both countries and also
prevent Ukraine from joining NATO, whose charter prevented the establishment
of bases on Ukraine's territory until the end of the lease by Russia.

After the agreement between Presidents Yanukovych and Medvedev, the IMF
approved a bailout of US$15.2 billion in December 2013 for two and a half years.[14]
But the imposed conditions were very harsh. They implied a cut in the fiscal deficit
through a severe reduction of about 50% in energy subsidies, social programs and
pensions, the immediate dismissal of state employees, the strengthening of banks, a
free floating exchange rate for the hryvnia-currency, which would consequently
devalue, and the privatization of state-owned enterprises, i.e., their delivery at
discount prices to foreign corporations. These were the same terms of the US$15
billion bailout offered in 2010, whose conditions President Yanukovych was unable
to meet and the IMF canceled in 2011.[15]

---

[10]Luke Harding (Moscow), "Ukraine extends lease for Russia's Black Sea Fleet—Deal with new
President Viktor Yanukovych to cut Russian gas prices sees Ukraine tilt backs towards Moscow."
The Guardian, Wednesday, April 21, 2010.

[11]*Ibidem.*

[12]"Ukraine's Orange Revolution Well and Truly Over." *Kiev Ukraine News Blog,* April 30, 2010.

[13]Luke Harding, "Ukraine extends lease for Russia's Black Sea Fleet. Deal with new President
Viktor Yanukovych to cut Russian gas prices sees Ukraine tilt backs towards Moscow." *The
Guardian*, Wednesday, April 21, 2010.

[14]"IMF Board Approves $15.2 Billion Loan to Ukraine." *Bloomberg News*, Thursday, July
29, 2010. Available at: <http://www.bloomberg.com/news/articles/2010-07-28/imf-approves-15-
2-billion-loan-to-ukraine-on-fiscal-adjustment-pledge>.

[15]Jack Rasmus, 2014, pp. 120–121; David M. Rasmus, "I.M.F. Criticizes Ukraine Plan for
Economy." *The New York Times*, December 19, 2013.

16.4   Ukraine's Flirt with the EU and the Inevitable Conflict with Russia

Under the administration of President Yushchenko, Ukraine had renewed negotiations on the European Union Association Agreement, which would be signed in the city of Vilnius, Lithuania, together with the presidents of Armenia, Azerbaijan, Belarus, Georgia, and Moldova on November 21, 2013.[16] It was a dubious position to take, arising from domestic disputes and foreign pressures. And in October 2013, President Vladimir Putin imposed customs controls, quotas, and duties on Ukrainian products bound for Russia, causing its exports to drop more than 25%, charged Kiev for the payment of US$1 billion for gas supplies, and also threatened to increase the price of fuel and restrict the entry of Ukrainians to work in the country.[17] If Ukraine entered the free trade zone of the European Union, it would suffer a loss of about US$500 billion in business with Russia, which would necessarily withdraw its preferential treatment for free access to a market of US$2.5 trillion and 146 million consumers.[18] Already in the summary of the Brussels proposal for entry into the European Union, it was anticipated that Ukraine's exports to Russia would decline by 17% or US$3 billion a year.[19]

In 2013, Ukraine sold US$16 billion worth of goods to Russia, about 25% of its total exports, and about US$17 billion to the European Union, a US$17 trillion-market with about 500 million consumers.[20] The difference in trade was small and would not compensate for any losses, such as the gas price discount. The European Union was not the solution to Ukraine's economic problems. It was already exhausted by the financial crisis that hit Greece, Spain, and Portugal and also threatened France and the very survival of the Eurozone. Even Germany, which accounted for most of the resources to bailout these countries, had accumulated a public debt of about 76% of its GDP,[21] although still much lower than the 101.53%

---

[16]David R. Cameron, "Putin's Gas-Fueled Bailout of Ukraine—Europe may have given up too quickly on bailout and potential trade agreement for Ukraine." *YaleGlobal Online,* January 2, 2014. Available at: <http://yaleglobal.yale.edu/content/putin%E2%80%99s-gas-fueled-bailout-ukraine>.

[17]*Ibidem*; Robert Coalson, "Ukraine's Choice: East or West?" *Israel Military.net,* November 15, 2013. Available at: <http://www.rferl.org/content/ukraine.../25169110.html>.

[18]*Ibidem.* "5 facts you need to know about Ukraine-EU trade deal." *RT,* June 27, 2014. Available at: <http://rt.com/business/168856-ukraine-europe-trade/>.

[19]Spiegel Staff, "Summit of Failure—How the EU Lost Russia over Ukraine." *Spiegel Online,* November 24, 2014. Available at: <http://www.spiegel.de/international/europe/war-in-ukraine-a-result-of-misunderstandings-between-europe-and-russia-a-1004706-druck.html>.

[20]"5 facts you need to know about Ukraine-EU trade deal." *RT,* June 27, 2014. Available at: <http://rt.com/business/168856-ukraine-europe-trade/>.

[21]Germany Government Debt to GDP 1995–2015. *Trading Economics.* Available at: <http://www.tradingeconomics.com/germany/government-debt-to-gdp>.

Table 16.1 Ranking of war
material exporting countries

Ranking	Country	%
1	United States	31
2	Russia	27
3	China	5
4	Germany	5
5	France	5
6	United Kingdom	4
7	Spain	3
8	Italy	3
9	Ukraine	3
10	Israel	2

Source: SIPRI Arms Transfers Database (*Ibidem*)

of the United States.[22] Germany's war industry had been hit hard by the protracted financial crisis, which forced all eurozone governments to take hard measures, including cuts in defense spending, because of the ballooning public debts and the prospect of economic stagnation. On the other hand, numerous state-owned weapon companies were privatized and faced intense competition not only in the foreign market but also within the European Union itself.[23]

Ukraine was one of the world's major largest exporters of war material. Between 2010 and 2014, it ranked 9th, according to data from the SIPRI Arms Transfers Database, and its main markets were in China (22%), Russia (10%), and Thailand (9%) (Table 16.1).[24]

In the ranking for conventional weapons, Ukraine ranked fourth among exporters in 2012.[25] Ukrinmash, together with Ukroboronservice and Prohres, which merged under the name Ukrespetexport, sold armaments to Russia and the countries of Eurasia, in addition to Angola, Cuba, Croatia, Pakistan, Mongolia, China, Sri Lanka, South Yemen, etc.[26] And the state corporation Ukroboronprom produced war material, high-tech devices, electronic-nuclear, metallurgical, and other heavy

---

[22]United States Government Debt to GDP 1940–2015. *Trading Economics.* Available at: <http://www.tradingeconomics.com/united-states/government-debt-to-gdp>.

[23]Marko Savković (Belgrade Centre for Security Policy (BCSP). "Europe's Defence in Times of Austerity: Spending Cuts as a One-Way Street?" *International Relations and Security Network (ISN)* ETH Zurich, October 9, 2012. Available at: <http://www.isn.ethz.ch/Digital-Library/Articles/Detail/?id=154133>; *"Capitalist crisis and European defense industry."* Stop Wapenhandel. Available at: <http://www.stopwapenhandel.org/node/751>.

[24]Pieter D. Wezeman & Siemon T. Wezeman, "Trends in International Arms Transfers, 2014." *SIPRI Fact Sheet,* March 25. Stockholm International Peace Research Institute (SIPRI). Available at: <http://books.sipri.org/files/FS/SIPRIFS1503.pdf>.

[25]"Ukraine world's 4th largest arms exporter in 2012, according to SIPRI." *Interfax--Ukraine Kiev Post,* March 18, 2013. Available at: <http://www.kyivpost.com/content/ukraine/ukraine-worlds-4th-largest-arms-exporter-in-2012-according-to-sipri-321878.html?flavour=full>.

[26]Gary K. Bertsch & Suzette Grillo Grillot (Editores), *Arms on the Market—Reducing the Risk of Proliferation in the Former Soviet Union.* New York: Routledge, 1998, p. 73; Gary K. Bertsch & William C. Potter (Editores), 1999, p. 65.

equipment, including for hydroelectric plants. Its headquarters and most of its facilities and factories operated in the east and southeast of Ukraine, in the Donetsk Oblast with 4.5 million inhabitants, most of which of Russian origin or ethnically linked through family ties. This corporation—Ukroboronprom—controlled 134 defense industries and in 2013 it signed a cooperation deal with Russia's Aviaexport to develop helicopters and aircraft for new markets. It produces radar equipment, air defense missiles, artillery cannons, armored tank production systems, and a modern acoustic system to locate the source of shots and the position of snipers and artillery. More than 45% of its total exports went to the markets of the Commonwealth of Independent States, made up of the former Soviet republics, including Russia, Belarus, Kazakhstan, Kyrgyzstan, and Tajikistan, which signed the treaty creating the Eurasian Economic Union.

The 25,900 km^2 of the Donetsk Basin (the Donbass) covered Kharkov, Dnipropetrovsk, Donetsk, Zaporizhzhya, Makiyivka, Mariupol, and Luhansk and harbored the largest industrial production park in Ukraine, one of the largest industrial concentrations in the world, in addition to considerable titanium, nickel, zinc, mercury, petroleum, natural gas, bauxite, coal (anthracite), and ferrous mineral deposits. The basin stretches across the Russian border and is identified with the Rostov Oblast, an area with 100,800 km^2 and a population of 4.3 million (2010 est.). The steel mills and coal mines of Ukraine were concentrated in Donetsk and Luhansk, and even after the dissolution of the Soviet Union in 1991, Russia continued to be its largest market by a considerable margin. In 2012 and 2013, 25% and 27% of its exports, respectively, were shipped to Russia, from which 32% of its imports came, mainly gas.[27]

If Ukraine were to join the European Union's free trade zone, its iron and steel industry, mostly in the Donbass, would lose competitiveness due to the IMF's demand for higher energy prices and the stiff competition in both the domestic and foreign markets.[28] Many factories would close and/or be sold to European corporations, while the large agribusiness enterprises of the West would ruin small farmers.

All this economic potential would fall under the control of the European Union, which had little to offer to Ukraine, however, except for the lifting of customs barriers, the massive export of Western products and investments through the purchase of domestic companies. The EU wasn't willing at the time to assume new commitments to resolve the serious financial situation in Ukraine. It had offered Kiev a loan of 600 million € (equivalent to US$827 million at the time), along with a

---

[27]*Bloomberg Visual Data*. Available at: <http://www.bloomberg.com/visual-data/best-and-worst/ukraines-biggest-trading-partners-countries>. *Ukraine: Economy—Infoplease.com*. Available at: <http://www.infoplease.com/encyclopedia/world/ukraine-economy.html#ixzz387gacUF3>; *CIA—The World Fact Book*—Fact Available at: <https://www.cia.gov/library/publications/the-world-factbook/geos/up.html>.

[28]Michael Emerson et al., 2006, pp. 150, 154 and 206.

vague prospect of 1 billion € from the International Monetary Fund.[29] A laughable amount compared to Ukraine's high debt, insufficient to even cover what it owed Gazprom.

Ukraine, on the other hand, would have to bear a cost of US$104 billion[30] to implement the profound changes in its institutions, laws, and policies required to adjust to the standards and dimensions of the *Acquis Communautaire*, the institutional and administrative framework of the European Union, systematically modeled and built over more than 40 years.[31] And in November 2013, president Yanukovych learned from a study of the Institute for Economics and Prognostics of the Ukrainian National Academy of Sciences that the country would actually have to pay US$160 billion if it entered the EU, 50 times the amount listed in Brussels' proposal summary and informed by the German advisor of the negotiating group.[32] Ukraine's financial costs would therefore be daunting, not to mention the other uncomfortable and high-risk reforms demanded by the IMF and the European Union, including budget cuts, tax increases, and a 40% hike in gas prices. Ukraine would not be able to bear these costs without escalating social tensions and further exacerbating the recession. The situation in Ukraine would look like Greece, where 4 years had passed since the first EU-IMF bailout program, unemployment had reached 27% of the workforce, and the risk of impoverishment continued to grow.

On September 22, 2013, 2 months before the summit in Vilnius to sign the European Union Association Agreement together with the presidents of Armenia, Azerbaijan, Belarus, Georgia, and Moldova, Sergey Glazyev, born in Zaporizhia, Ukraine, a member of the Russian Academy of Sciences and an advisor to President Putin, warned the oligarch Petro Poroshenko, former Ukrainian Minister of Trade and Economic Development (2012), that Ukraine's entry into the European Union would be catastrophic.[33] He argued that Ukraine could only stabilize its balance of payments through a customs union with Russia, its main creditor, and he emphasized the economic costs his country would have to bear if the agreement with the European Union came to fruition. For Moscow would certainly adopt sanctions

---

[29]"Putin's Gambit: How the EU Lost Ukraine." *Der Spiegel,* November 25, 2013. Available at: <http://www.spiegel.de/international/europe/how-the-eu-lost-to-russia-in-negotiations-over-ukraine-trade-deal-a-935476.html>.

[30]Robin Emmott (Brussels), "Q&A-What is Ukraine's association agreement with the EU?" *Reuters,* June 26, 2014. Available at: <http://www.reuters.com/article/2014/06/26/eu-ukraine-idUSL6N0P61N720140626>.

[31]Igor Burakovsky et al., "Costs and Benefits of FTA between Ukraine and the European Union." *Institute for Economic Research and Policy Consulting*—Kyiv 2010, pp. 32–35. УДК 339.54: 339.56: 339.924 ББК 65,58Б91—Recommended for publication by the Academic Board's Decision of Diplomatic Academy of Ukraine under the Ministry of foreign affairs of Ukraine (Protocol No. 1 as of October 13, 2010). Available at: <http://www.ier.com.ua/files/Books/Ocinka_vytrat/ocinka_vitrat_eng.pdf>; Michael Emerson et al., 2006, p. 20–21.

[32]Spiegel Staff, "Summit of Failure—How the EU Lost Russia over Ukraine." *Spiegel Online,* November 24, 2014. Available at: <http://www.spiegel.de/international/europe/war-in-ukraine-a-result-of-misunderstandings-between-europe-and%2D%2Drussia-a-1004706-druck.html>.

[33]*Ibidem.*

and withdraw from the bilateral treaty, which delimited the borders between the two countries. He also foresaw the high risk of separatist movements in the Russian-speaking regions of the east and south of the country, in the Donbass.[34]

Neither the authorities in Brussels nor the government in Berlin under Angela Merkel, however, were considering the realities of power and Russia's concerns about its encirclement by NATO during the year-long negotiations for entry into the European Union, as the German magazine Der Spiegel reported.[35] Although they had been warned, they still failed to consider what Ukraine's membership of the European Union would mean to Russia. The Ukrainian oligarch Victor Pinchuk, owner of EastOne Group LLC, admonished European Union commissioners that business with Ukraine would be considered a provocation by Russia. And so everyone knew what might happen, as in Sophocles' Oedipus Rex and other tragedies. They certainly did not want a conflict with Russia to occur, yet all the actors did everything to make it inevitable.

The terms of the agreement offered to Ukraine by the European Union would not offset the domestic consequences it would suffer through the increase in gas prices and taxes, etc. The country was dramatically impoverished, its reserves were almost exhausted, and it would likely not manage to meet the tough debt repayment program it would have to accept.[36] Against this background, President Yanukovych signed Legal Ordinance 905-r on November 21, 2013, in Boryspil, Kiev's International Airport, instructing the suspension of negotiations with the European Union with the support of Prime Minister Mykola Azarov and despite the pressures of some oligarchs and political sectors in Kiev. This decision certainly implied a clear geopolitical choice. Ukraine would turn to the Eurasian Economic Union with Russia, Belarus, and Kazakhstan, perceived by the United States as an attempt to resuscitate the Soviet Union, even if neither Russia nor any other state planned to do so or confront the West.

President Yanukovych's reasoning was mainly economic in nature. He went to Moscow less than a month after breaking off negotiations with the EU, on December 17, where President Vladimir Putin offered him a securities investment worth US$15 billion, of which he anticipated US$3 billion with the purchase of bonds from Ukraine, and he established a new gas price at around US$268.5 per 1000 m^3, which meant reducing the price by 1/3 from the level of US$400 per 1000 m^3 then in

---

[34]Shaun Walker (Yalta), "Ukraine's EU trade deal will be catastrophic, says Russia—Kremlin claims neighbouring state faces financial ruin and possible collapse if integration agreement goes ahead." *The Guardian*, Sunday, September 22, 2013.

[35]Spiegel Staff, "Summit of Failure—How the EU Lost Russia over Ukraine." *Spiegel Online*, November 24, 2014. Available at: <http://www.spiegel.de/international/europe/war-in-ukraine-a-result-of-misunderstandings-between-europe-and-russia-a-1004706-druck.html>.

[36]Kataryna Wolczuk & Roman Wolczuk, "What you need to know about the causes of the Ukrainian protests." *The Washington Post*, December 9, 2013.

force, allowing Ukraine to save US$3.5 billion per year with the current annual consumption rate of 26–27 billion cubic meters.[37]

The deal was much cheaper and more advantageous for Ukraine, which also avoided raising the price of gas and losing Russia's market, its main trading partner, importing 24% of Ukraine's production and exporting 31% of its consumption needs, on average.[38] Although it was a temporary solution, since a long-term understanding was still to be reached, the agreement nevertheless represented a "historic deal," according to Ukraine's Prime Minister Mykola Azarov, enough to balance payments for about 2 years and enable the country to return to economic growth[39] with Russia's industrial cooperation and the modernization and integration of technologies in aeronautics, satellite production, armaments, shipbuilding, and other fields.

16.5 Washington's US$5 Billion Investment in Regime Change and George Soros and the Subversive NGOs

The protests against President Yanukovych intensified, however. They had started in November after the suspension of negotiations with the European Union, when the parliamentarian Oleg Tsariov of the Party of Regions denounced in the Verkhovna Rada (Parliament) that the United States Embassy, then headed by Ambassador Geoffrey R. Pyatt, was training experts in information warfare and the discrediting of state institutions, under the umbrella of the TechCamp project,[40] using the

---

[37]Darina Marchak & Katya Gorchinskaya, "Russia gives Ukraine cheap gas, $15 billion in loans." Gazprom will cut the price that Ukraine must pay for Russian gas deliveries to $268 per 1000 cubic metres from the current level of about $400 per 1000 cubic metres. *KyivPost*, December 17, 2013. Available at: <http://www.kyivpost.com/content/ukraine/russia-gives-ukraine-cheap-gas-15-billion-in-loans-333852.html>; Carol Matlack. "Ukraine Cuts a Deal It Could Soon Regret" & Shaun Walker (Moscow) & agencies. "Vladimir Putin offers Ukraine financial incentives to stick with Russia—Moscow to buy $15bn of Ukrainian government bonds and cut gas price after Kiev resists signing EU deal amid mass protests." *The Guardian*. Available at: <http://www.theguardian.com/world/2013/dec/17/ukraine-russia-leaders-talks-kremlin-loan-deal>; David Stern, "Russia offers Ukraine major economic assistance." *BBC Europe*, December 17, 2013. Available at: <http://www.bbc.com/news/world-europe-25411118>. *Bloomberg*, Tuesday, December 17, 2013. Available at: <http://www.bloomberg.com/bw/articles/2013-12-17/ukraine-cuts-a-deal-it-could-soon-regret>.

[38]*Observatory of Economic Complexity*. Available at: <http://atlas.media.mit.edu/profile/country/ukr/>. See also: http://atlas.media.mit.edu/profile/country/ukr/>.

[39]Shaun Walker (Moscow) & agencies. "Vladimir Putin offers Ukraine financial incentives to stick with Russia—Moscow to buy $15bn of Ukrainian government bonds and cut gas price after Kiev resists signing EU deal amid mass protests." *The Guardian*, December 18, 2013.

[40]"TechCamp Ukraine—TechCamp is a workshop where civil society organizations share current challenges they are facing with peers and technologists and brainstorm how technology can play a role in addressing these challenges. This interactive event brings together American and Ukrainian technology experts working with educators, NGO staff, and social media enthusiasts to find

revolutionary potential of modern media to manipulate public opinion and organize protests to subvert the established order in the country.[41] These were the same techniques that were used in Tunisia, Egypt, Libya, and Syria during the so-called Arab Spring. As Oleg Tsariov revealed, the last TechCamp conference was held on November 14 and 15, 2013, in the heart of Kiev, on the terrain of the United States embassy.[42] And the trainings had been taking place at least since 2012.[43]

The activists trained by TechCamp and other protestors driving the mass demonstrations against President Yanukovych's decision came from NGOs, organized by the CIA and funded mainly by the US Agency for International Development (USAID), the National Endowment for Democracy (NED), the Open Society

---

effective, low-cost ways to address real social problems by using technology. This is not a typical technology camp. Participants will work in small groups and directly with international and local technology experts in sessions designed to show how to apply new, online technologies to fundraise for their missions, build organizational capacity, plan for project implementation and management, increase public relations skills, and much more." Available at: <https://www.flickr.com/photos/usembassykyiv/collections/72157633190416346/>.

[41]"Party of Regions MP Tsariov accuses US Embassy in Ukraine of training revolutionaries for street protests." *KyivPost,* November 20, 2013. | Politics–*Interfax-Ukraine* Available at: <http://www.kyivpost.com/content/politics/party-of-regions-mp-tsariov-accuses-us-embassy-in-ukraine-of-training-revolutionaries-for-street-protests-332162.html>. Also in: <http://en.interfax.com.ua/news/general/175839.html>.

[42]"Must watch: Ukrainian Deputy: US to stage a civil war in Ukraine! This was 20.11.2013!! Before Maidan." *The Vineyard of the Saker,* January 28, 2015. Available at: <http://vineyardsaker.blogspot.de/2015/01/must-watch-ukrainian-deputy-us-to-stage.html>; "Must Watch: 20.11.2013!! (pre-Maidan!): Ukraine Deputy has proof of USA staging civil war in Ukraine." Transcript—*Investment Watch.* Tuesday, January 27, 2015 Available at: <http://investmentwatchblog.com/proof-of-us-sponsored-coup-in-ukraine-ukrainian-politician-before-the-violent-demonstrations-on-maidan-us-embassy-in-kiev-ran-a-project-called-techcamp-to-train-activists-in-organizing-pro tests/>.

[43]"TechCamp Kyiv 2012—July 29, 2012—U.S. Embassy Kyiv is happy to announce the open call for applications to attend TechCamp Kyiv September 12 and 13 at Master Klass," *in:* Kyiv, Ukraine. TechCamp is a program under Secretary of State Hillary Clinton's Civil Society 2.0 initiative—an effort to galvanize the technology community to assist civil society organizations across the globe by providing capabilities, resources, and assistance to harness the latest information and communications technology advances to build their digital capacity. TechCamp Kyiv is a two days conference where civil society organizations share current challenges they are facing with peers and technologists and brainstorm how technology can play a role in addressing these challenges. Over 100 highly motivated participants will attend from throughout Ukraine and Belarus. This interactive event will bring together American, Ukrainian, and Belarusian technology experts working with educators, NGO staff, and social media enthusiasts to find effective, low-cost ways to address real social problems by using technology. Please visit this link to learn more and apply for the chance to attend. *Embassy of the United States—Kiyv—Ukraine.* Available at: <http://ukraine.usembassy.gov/events/tech-camp.html>; "The U.S. Embassy in Kyiv in partnership with Microsoft Ukraine hosted TechCamp Kyiv 2.0 on March 1, 2013, at the Microsoft Ukraine Headquarters. TechCamp support the U.S. State Department's Civil Society 2.0 initiative that builds the technological and digital capacity of civil society organizations around the world." US Embassy Hosted TechCamp Kyiv 2.0 to Build Technological Capacity of Civil Society—Events 2013. *Embassy of the United States—Kyiv-Ukraine.* Available at: <http://ukraine.usembassy.gov/events/techcamp-2013-kyiv.html>.

Foundations, under the name Renaissance Foundation (Міжнароднийфонд—Відродження), from the billionaire George Soros, Freedom House, Poland-America-Ukraine Cooperation Initiative, etc.

"Ukraine or the western part of the country is full of NGOs maintained by Washington," warned the economist Paul Craig Roberts, former Assistant Secretary of the Treasury under Ronald Reagan (1981–1989), adding that their goal was "to make Ukraine available for looting by USA banks and corporations and to bring Ukraine into NATO so that Washington can gain more military bases on Russia's frontier."[44] He explained:

> The protests in the western Ukraine are organized by the CIA, the US State Department, and by Washington—and EU—financed Non-Governmental Organizations (NGOs) that work in conjunction with the CIA and State Department. The purpose of the protests is to overturn the decision by the independent government of Ukraine not to join the EU.[45]

These NGOs have operated since the 1990s as a front to promote regime change without the need for a military coup. And the Assistant Secretary of State for European and Eurasian Affairs herself, Victoria Nuland, wife of the neocon Robert D. Kagan[46] of the far right of the Republican Party, admitted in an interview with the National Press Club in Washington on December 13, 2013, that the United States had "invested" US$5 billion in Ukraine:

> Since the declaration of Ukrainian independence in 1991, the United States supported the Ukrainians in the development of democratic institutions and skills in promoting civil society and a good form of government—all that is necessary to achieve the objectives of Ukraine's European [sic]. We have invested more than 5 billion dollars to help Ukraine to achieve these and other goals.[47]

In just 2 years, 2003 and 2004, the George W. Bush administration spent more than US$65 million in support of political organizations in Ukraine, including on a

---

[44]Paul Craig Roberts, "Washington Orchestrated Protests Are Destabilizing Ukraine," February 12, 2014. Institute for Political Economy. Available at: <http://www.paulcraigroberts.org/2014/02/12/washington-orchestrated-protests-destabilizing-ukraine/>.

[45]*Ibidem.*

[46]"Ukraine: Nuland feeds hungry Maidan protesters and police." Video Id: 20131211-054. Ukraine: Nuland feeds hungry Maidan protesters and police. *RT—Ruptly*, December 11, 2013. Available at: <http://ruptly.tv/site/vod/view/6876/ukraine-nuland-feeds-hungry-maidan-protesters-and-police>.

[47]"Regime Change in Kiev—Victoria Nuland Admits: US Has Invested $5 Billion In The Development of Ukrainian, 'Democratic Institutions.'" Video—International Business Conference at Ukraine in Washington—National Press Club—December 13, 2013—Victoria Nuland—Assistant Secretary of State for Europe and Eurasian Affairs. Posted on February 9, 2014; Finian Cunningham, "Washington's Cloned Female Warmongers," *in: Information Clearing House,* February 9, 2014. Available at: <http://www.informationclearinghouse.info/article37599.htm>; Alice Bota & Kerstin Kohlenberg, "Ukraine: Haben die Amis den Maidan gekauft? Die USA gaben in der Ukraine über Jahrzehnte Milliarden aus. Wohin floss das Geld?" *Die Zeit*, No. 20/2015, May 17, 2015. Available at: <http://www.zeit.de/2015/20/ukraine-usa-maidan-finanzierung/komplettansicht>.

group tour led by Viktor Yushchenko[48] to meet authorities in the United States to signal that he would win the final round of the presidential election in Ukraine.[49] The International Republican Institute (IRI), headed by Senator John McCain, also sponsored Yushchenko's campaign and arranged meetings in Washington with Vice President Dick Cheney, Deputy Secretary of State Richard Armitage and Republican Senators.

Several NGOs were funded by the billionaire George Soros,[50] who has been ostensibly pouring tens of millions of dollars into Ukraine and other Eastern European countries for over two decades, using his own International Renaissance Foundation (IRF) and various other institutes and foundations, labeled Open Society foundations, under the pretext of helping them become an "open" and "democratic society."[51] The International Renaissance Foundation's Annual Report for 2012 assigned a spending of 63 million in UAH (hryvnia), equivalent at the time to US $6.7 million, for the engagement of NGOs, using anti-corruption initiatives and democratic reforms as catalysts. This meant co-opting politicians and media support (newspapers, TV, and the Internet) in opposition to the government of President Yanukovych, which was stepped up after his election in 2010.[52] In the 20 years from 1991 to 2011, George Soros' Open Society Foundations sprinkled about US$976 million in Eastern European countries, the former allies of the Warsaw Pact, and in the republics that broke away from the Soviet Union.[53] And the NGOs and other entities in Ukraine—publishers, academic and cultural groups—were the largest recipients of donations, more than US$100 million.[54]

---

[48]Viktor Yushchenko had worked in a far-right think tank, the Heritage Foundation. And his wife, Katherine Chumachenko Yushenko, an American citizen, served in the White House Public Liaison Office during the administration of President Ronald Reagan as a recruiter, and in that capacity she set up a number of far-right and anti-communist groups. She was also director of the neoconservative think tank New Atlantic Initiative.

[49]Matt Kelley (*Associated Press*), "Bush Administration Spent $65 Million to Help Opposition in Ukraine,"—*Associated Press—Fox News*, December 10, 2004. Available at: <http://www.foxnews.com/story/2004/12/10/us-spent-65m-to-aid%2D%2Dukrainian-groups/>.

[50]Katerina Tsetsura & Anastasia Grynko & Anna Klyueva, "The Media Map Project—Ukraine— Case Study on Donor Support to Independent Media, 1990–2010," p. 14. Available at: <http://www.academia.edu/3295647/Media_Map_Project._Ukraine_Case_study_on_donor_support_to_independent_media_1990-2010>.

[51]William F. Jasper, "George Soros' Giant Globalist Footprint in Ukraine's Turmoil." *The New American*. Available at: <http://www.thenewamerican.com/world-news/europe/item/17843-george-soros-s-giant-globalist-footprint-in-ukraine-s-turmoil>.

[52]*Ibidem*; Wayne Madsen, "Nuland attempts Kiev Version 2.0 in Skopje." *Strategic Culture Foundation*, February 16, 2015. Available at: <http://m.strategic-culture.org/news/2015/02/16/nuland-attempts-kiev-version-2-skopje.html>.

[53]Katerina Tsetsura & Anastasia Grynko & Anna Klyueva, "The Media Map Project—UkraineCase Study on Donor Support to Independent Media, 1990–2010." Available at: <http://www.academia.edu/3295647/Media_Map_Project._Ukraine_Case_study_on_donor_support_to_independent_media_1990-2010>.

[54]William F. Jasper, "George Soros' Giant Globalist Footprint in Ukraine's Turmoil." *The New American*, March 14, 2014. Available at: <http://www.thenewamerican.com/world-news/europe/item/17843-george-soros-s-giant-globalist-footprint-in-ukraine-s-turmoil>.

When George Soros was interviewed by the journalist Fareed Zakaria on the CNN show *On GPS: Will Ukraine detach from Russia?*, he admitted that in 1989 he funded dissidents in Eastern European countries, such as Poland and the Czech Republic, and he revealed that before Ukraine separated from the Soviet Union he had established a foundation there that was not only fully operational, but also played an important role in the protests that erupted in Maidan Nezalezhnosti (Independence Square) after November 2013 and prompted the overthrow of President Yanukovych.[55]

Orysia Lutsevych, who worked for Freedom House and was executive-director of the Open Ukraine Foundation,[56] wrote that in a number of countries, such as Ukraine, NGOs had become synonymous with civil society and monopolized its discourse, superseding institutions and eroding democracy.[57] The NGOs—she stressed—had turned into a "NGO-cracy, where professional leaders use access to domestic policy-makers and Western donors to influence public policies, yet they are disconnected from the public at large."[58] And in three countries in Eurasia— Ukraine, Georgia, and Moldavia—this NGO-cracy undermined what really could be considered democracy.[59]

In November 2014, the Russian and Chinese Defense Ministers, Anatoly Antonov and Chang Wanquan, spoke in Beijing about the new forms of foreign aggression because of the intensive "pro-democracy" protests occurring in Hong Kong, where even the Union Jack was displayed.[60] They decided to join forces to counter the threat of the so-called "color revolutions," which happened in Ukraine and to which no country was immune.[61] According to the director of the Chinese

---

[55]"Fareed Zakaria: During the revolutions of 1989, you funded a lot of dissident activities, civil society groups in eastern Europe; Poland, the Czech Republic. Are you doing similar things in Ukraine? Soros: I set up a foundation in Ukraine before Ukraine became independent of Russia. And the foundation has been functioning ever since and played an important part in events now," "Soros on Russian ethnic nationalism." *CNN*, May 25, 2014. Available at: <http://cnnpressroom. blogs.cnn.com/2014/05/25/soros-on-russian-ethnic-nationalism/>.

[56]Orysia Lutsevych worked in the United States for Freedom House and Project Harmony International. She was also executive director of the Open Ukraine Foundation and, after 2005, she implemented the strategy for the creation of the Polish-Ukraine Cooperation Foundation (PAUCI), the resource allocation vehicle of the USAID program, of which she became the director in Ukraine.

[57]Orysia Lutsevych, "How to Finish a Revolution: Civil Society and Democracy in Georgia, Moldova and Ukraine," pp. 4–7. Briefing paper Russia and Eurasia | January 2013 | REP BP 2013/01. *Chatham House*. Available at: <http://www.chathamhouse.org/sites/files/chathamhouse/ public/Research/Russia%20and%20Eurasia/0113bp_lutsevych.pdf>.

[58]*Ibidem.*

[59]*Ibidem.*

[60]Keith Bradsher, "Some Chinese Leaders Claim U.S. and Britain Are Behind Hong Kong Protests." *The New York Times*, Friday, October 10, 2014.

[61]"Russia, China should jointly counter color revolutions—Russian Defense Ministry. The Russian and Chinese defense ministers focused on the recent Hong Kong protests and acknowledged that no country is immune from 'color revolutions'." *ITAR-TASS*, Beijing, November 18, 2014. Available at: <http://tass.ru/en/russia/760349>.

Department of Strategic Studies, Chen Xulong, the campaign labeled "Occupy Central" in Hong Kong failed because the central government in Beijing and the authorities of the Hong Kong Special Administrative Region quickly recognized the similarities and perceived that it was a version of the "color revolutions" carried out in another part of the world, with street protests, blocking of public buildings and demands for the resignation of authorities.[62]

The Russian Foreign Minister Sergey Lavrov stated that the conflict in Ukraine had been triggered through outside pressure in order to force Kiev to make a decision in favor of the West. He referred to the turmoil in the Middle East and North Africa, where the threat of terrorism grew, including through the sharp amplification and transformation of the Islamic State (ISIS/ISIL) into an actual terrorist army.[63] And he pointed out that "a very serious destabilizing factor" was being employed in various regions of the world with the attempts to "export democracy, change [political] regimes with the aim of staging 'color revolutions'"[64] President Yanukovych's fall, on the night of February 21–22, 2014, actually meant a replay of the so-called Orange Revolution that brought down the government of President Leonid Kučma between November 2004 and January 2005, sponsored by the West, i.e., the United States and the European Union.[65]

The circumstances were no longer the same as a decade ago, however. And on December 26, 2014, after the Verkhovna Rada approved Ukraine's withdrawal from the neutrality status, President Putin approved a review of Russia's military doctrine of 2010, identifying not only the expansion of NATO to its borders as a fundamental threat to Russia's national security but also adding the use of political forces and public movements financed and steered from abroad and the utilization of nonmilitary means along with military strength, including the population's willingness for protests, as typical features of modern military conflicts.[66] Even though Russia admitted the use of nuclear weapons, if necessary, its military doctrine remained primarily defensive in nature, reserving military action only for those case where all non-violent options were exhausted.[67]

---

[62]Zhang Dan (Editor), "Failure of Hong Kong version of 'Color Revolution' would be a bliss." *CCTV.com*, October 22, 2014. Available at: <http://english.cntv.cn/2014/10/22/ARTI1413962823597930.shtml>.

[63]Artyom Geodakyan, "Lavrov: trends of color revolutions and democracy export can be changed. The Russian foreign minister said the Ukrainian conflict also erupted under outside pressure on Kiev." *ITAR-TASS*, December 12, 2014. Available at: <http://tass.ru/en/world/766611>.

[64]*Ibidem*.

[65]Nathaniel Copsey, 2010, pp. 30–31, 37–40.

[66]Valery Sharifulin, "Russia's new military doctrine says use of protest moods typical for conflicts nowadays. The doctrine also stresses amassed combat employment of high-precision weaponry, drones and robots." *ITAR-TASS*, Friday, December 26, 2014. Available at: <http://tass.ru/en/russia/769513>.

[67]Dr.Alexander Yakovenko, Russian Ambassador to the United Kingdom of Great Britain and Northern Ireland, Deputy foreign minister (2005–2011). "The truth about Russia's new military doctrine." RT Op-Edge, February 27, 2015. Available at: <http://rt.com/op-edge/236175-president-putin-military-doctrine-document/>.

Chapter 17
The Ukrainian Shift Away from Russia and Putin's Reaction

17.1 The United States' Geostrategic Interests in Ukraine Behind the Negotiations with the European Union and NATO Expansion

The background of both the conflict in Ukraine and the war in Syria was shaped by the geostrategic objectives of the United States/NATO, manifested among other things by the desire to take complete control of the oil and gas reserves and corridors not only in Eurasia but also in the Middle East and North Africa. The George W. Bush administration had been shoring up the opposition financially since at least 2005, and in 2007 it approved the release of funds and logistical support to the National Salvation Front in Syria and the Muslim Brotherhood, through Saudi Arabia. By way of a finding,[1] President George W. Bush also authorized the CIA to carry out covert actions to weaken and overthrow the Bashar al-Assad regime.[2] One of the reasons for this was the fact that Syria rejected the United States' proposal for the construction of a gas pipeline through its territory that would link up with the projected Nabucco pipeline, transporting gas from the Caspian Sea (Azerbaijan, Turkmenistan, and Kazakhstan) to the Middle East and Europe, diverting the supply of 160 bcm per year from Russia.[3]

---

[1]A finding is an authorization given by the president of the United States, almost always in writing, in which he states (finds) that a covert action is important for national security.

[2]Seymour M. Hersh, "Annals of National Security—The Redirection. Is the Administration's new policy benefitting our enemies in the war on terrorism?" *The New Yorker*, March 5, 2007 Issue. Available at: <http://www.newyorker.com/magazine/2007/03/05/the-redirection?currentPage=all>; Nafeez Ahmed, "Syria intervention plan fueled by oil interests, not chemical weapon concern." *The Guardian*, August 30, 2013. Available at: <http://www.theguardian.com/environment/earth-insight/2013/aug/30/syria-chemical-attack-war-intervention-oil%2D%2Dgas-energy-pipelines>.

[3]Tamsin Carlisle, "Qatar seeks gas pipeline to Turkey." The National—Business. August 26, 2009. Available at: <http://www.thenational.ae/business/energy/qatar-seeks-gas-pipeline-to-turkey>;

© Springer Nature Switzerland AG 2019
L. A. Moniz Bandeira, *The World Disorder*,
https://doi.org/10.1007/978-3-030-03204-3_17

Likewise, strong economic interests linked with the geostrategic targets of the United States nurtured the movement against President Yanukovych in Ukraine. The prospect of high profits in agriculture and the technically exploitable shale gas reserves dawned. According to estimates from the US Energy Information Administration in 2013,[4] Ukraine had 128 trillion cubic feet of shale gas, the fourth largest reserve in Europe behind only Russia (285 tcf), Poland (148 tcf), and France (137 tcf).[5] It also possessed 0.2 billion barrels of oil in the shale gas fields located in the oil shale of Deniep, in the Donets Basin to the east of the country.[6] Most reserves could be found in Oleska in western Ukraine, between Lviv and the Lublin basin, with an estimated 1.47 trillion cubic meters; and in Yuzivska, to the east in Deniepr, between Kharkov and the regions of the Donetsk basin, with estimated shale gas reserves in the order of 2.15 trillion cubic meters,[7] or more than 4 trillion cubic feet.[8]

Political sectors in Kiev viewed the exploitation of shale gas as an alternative to free the country from its economic dependence on Russia, Iran, and Qatar, the countries with half of the world's largest natural gas reserves.[9] And oil companies

---

Judy Dempsey, "Victory for Russia as the EU's Nabucco Gas Project Collapses." *Carnegie Europe*, July 1, 2013. Available at: <http://carnegieeurope.eu/strategiceurope/?fa=52246>; Erkan Erdoğdu. "Bypassing Russia: Nabucco project and its implications for the European gas security." MPRA Paper from University Library of Munich, Germany. Published in *Renewable and Sustainable Energy Reviews*, 9.14(2010): pp. 2936–2945. Available at: <http://econpapers.repec.org/paper/pramprapa/26793.htm>; Ralf Dickel et al., "Reducing European Dependence on Russian Gas: distinguishing natural gas security from geopolitics." *Oxford Institute for Energy Studies*. October 2014 OIES PAPER: NG 92. ISBN 978-78467-014-6. Available at: <http://www.oxfordenergy.org/wpcms/wp-content/uploads/2014/10/NG-92.pdf>.

[4]"Ukraine crisis sharpens focus on European shale gas." *Reuters*, London, March 4, 2014. Available at: <http://www.reuters.com/article/2014/03/14/europe%2D%2Dshale-ukraine-idUSL6N0MB1WI20140314>.

[5]"Countries outside the United States—June 2013." Executive—Summary, Table 5. *U.S. Energy Information Administration*, June 13, 2013. Available at: <http://www.eia.gov/analysis/studies/worldshalegas/pdf/fullreport.pdf?zscb=84859470>.

[6]"Ukraine's Oil and Natural Gas Reserves—A Pawn in Geopolitical Chess Game?" *Viable Opposition*. Sunday, March 16, 2014. Available at: <http://viableopposition.blogspot.fr/2014/03/ukraines-oil-and-natural-gas-reserves.html>.

[7]"Shale gas reserves and major fields of Ukraine"—Projects in Ukraine, 14.6.2013. *Unconventional Gas in Ukraine*. Available at: <http://shalegas.in.ua/en/shale-gas-resources-in-ukraine/>.

[8]"Kiev fights in Ukraine's southeast for shale gas deposits to be controlled by US—Pushkov-Russia." *Itar-TASS*, August 16, 2014. Available at: <http://tass.ru/en/russia/745305>. "Corporate Interests behind Ukraine Putsch." *Consortiumnews.com*, March 16, 2014. Available at: <https://consortiumnews.com/2014/03/16/corporate-interests-behind-ukraine-putsch/>.

[9]Stanley Reed & Andrew E. Kramernov, "Chevron and Ukraine Set Shale Gas Deal." *The New York Times*, November 5, 2013; Roman Olearchyk (Kiev) & Gregory Meyer (Nova York), "Cargill acquires stake in Ukraine agribusiness." *Information Clearing House*, March 13, 2014. Available at: <http://www.informationclearinghouse.info/article37931.htm>; *JP Sottile for Buzzflash at Truthout*. "The Business of America Is Giving Countries Like Ukraine the Business," March 12, 2014. Available at: <http://www.truth-out.org/buzzflash/commentary/the-business-of-america-is-giving-countries-like-ukraine-the-business>.

of the United States and the European Union had since long shown interest in exploiting these reserves so that they could conquer the markets of Ukraine, occupied by Russia, as well as Poland, Bulgaria, France, the Czech Republic, Hungary, and other countries in Europe.[10]

In May 2012, the Anglo-Dutch company Royal Dutch Shell won the bid to exploit the Yuzivske reserves. On January 24, 2013, despite the protests of the population of the Donbass, Shell signed an agreement with the Ukrainian company Nadra Yuzivska to exploit an area of approximately 8000 km^2 with over 1.5 trillion cubic meters of shale gas between the cities of Kharkov and Donetsk in eastern Ukraine.[11] Through another contract, signed in September 2013, the company received the broadest of permissions to make investments and extract the shale gas reserves of Dnepropetrovsk-Donetsk, in the Burisma region of Ukraine.[12]

The Ukrainian company Nadra Yuzivska also signed a US$10 billion deal with Chevron on November 5, 2013, for the development of the oil and gas production in the western region of Oleska for 50 years,[13] and it was close to reaching another agreement with Exxon Mobil (XOM) and Royal Dutch Shell (RDS.B), which would invest US$735 million in the production of shale gas in the southwest of Crimea, in the region of Skifska.[14] In addition to these contracts, the Ukrainian government closed a deal on November 27 with a consortium of investors led by the Italian company ENI for the development of the nonconventional production of hydrocarbons in the Black Sea.

In Washington, the election of Viktor Yanukovych to the Presidency of Ukraine in 2010 was seen as the defeat of the Orange Revolution, and it seems clear

---

[10]Nat Parry, "Beneath the Ukraine Crisis: Shale Gas." *Consortiumnet.com*, April 24, 2014. Available at: <https://consortiumnews.com/2014/04/24/beneath-the-ukraine-crisis-shale-gas/>.

[11]"Milieudefensie/FoE Netherlands: Harmful shale gas deal between Shell and Yanukovych must be halted." *Friends of the Earth International*. Available at: <http://www.foei.org/news/milieudefensie-foe-netherlands-harmful-shale-gas-deal%2D%2Dbetween-shell-and-yanukovych-must-be-halted-2/>; "Ukraine Shale Gas: Shell Moves Forward While Chevron Stalled." *Natural Gas—Europe*, January 20, 2013. Available at: <http://www.naturalgaseurope.com/regional-ukraine-governments-approve-shell-shale-gas-production-sharing-agreement>; "Ukraine's Nadra Yuzivska and Shell Entered into Shale Gas Production PSA." *Oil Market Magazine*, January 24, 2013. Available at: <http://oilmarket-magazine.com/eng/shownews.phtml?id=221>.

[12]"Ukraine's government and Shell sign operation agreement to develop shale deposit." Projects in Ukraine. *Unconventional Gas in Ukraine*, September 12, 2013. Available at: <http://shalegas.in.ua/en/uryad-ukrajiny-i-shell-pidpysaly-uhodu-pro-operatsijnu-diyalnist-z-vydobutku-vuhlevodniv/>; Mike Orcutt (Technology Review), "Shale gas has become the geopolitical energy that can change ruling power globally. Kiev fights in Ukraine's southeast for shale gas deposits to be controlled by US." *Gunnars tankar och funderingar*. Available at: <http://gunnarlittmarck.blogspot.de/2014/08/shale-gas-has-become-geopolitical.html>.

[13]Stanley Reed & Andrew E. Kramer, "Chevron and Ukraine Set Shale Gas Deal." *The New York Times*, November 5, 2013.

[14]Carol Matlack, "Losing Crimea Could Sink Ukraine's Offshore Oil and Gas Hopes." *Bloomberg*, March 11, 2014. Available at: <http://www.bloomberg.com/bw/articles/2014-03-11/losing-crimea-could-sink-ukraines-offshore-oil-and%2D%2Dgas-hopesatlack>.

preparations to destabilize his government had begun well before Yanukovych suspended negotiations for a free trade agreement with the European Union.[15] Despite the contracts signed with Royal Dutch Shell, Chevron, and Exxon Mobil, some in Washington feared that Yanukovych would lead Ukraine to join the Eurasian Economic Union, which President Putin was shaping with Belarus and Kazakhstan, and that the shale gas and other natural gas and oil deposits in Ukraine, Crimea, and on the coast of the Black Sea would ultimately fall into the hands of Russia, where the company Gazprom controlled approximately 1/5 of the existing gas reserves in the world. And it should be no surprise that Chevron and Royal Dutch Shell were directly or indirectly funding the NGOs active in Maidan Square. In Nigeria, both companies have already been accused by the Center for Constitutional Rights (CCR), EarthRights International (ERI), and other human rights entities of recruiting soldiers and supplying resources to armed forces involved in human rights abuses and massacres in the Ogoni region, to the south of the country, where they wanted to build a pipeline.[16]

The fall of Viktor Yanukovych's government became crucial for the United States' strategic objectives, especially the goal of preventing Russia from regaining influence in Ukraine and restoring its imperial status in Eurasia, according to Zbigniew Brzezinski's view.[17] Ukraine's agreement with the European Union, therefore, covered multiple and complex objectives, not only economic and commercial ones. *Sub omni lapide scorpio dormit.* Indeed, under the cover of free trade, the agreement obliged Ukraine to gradually converge with the Defence Policy and European Defence Agency (CSDP).[18] This meant Ukraine would fall indirectly under NATO's military structure[19] and open its doors for the establishment of military bases and the stationing of troops on its territory, on the border with Russia. This initiative could be compared to the deployment of missile platforms in Cuba by the Soviet Union in 1962, which provoked a reaction from the United States and brought the Cold War to a head. The United States had already incorporated Lithuania, Latvia, and Estonia into NATO and extended its war and submission

---

[15]USAID—Ukraine Country Development Cooperation Strategy 2012–2016. Available at: <https://www.usaid.gov/sites/default/files/documents/1863/USAID_Ukraine_CDCS_2012-2016. pdf>.

[16]"Factsheet: The Case against Shell." *Consortiumnews.com.* Available at: <https://ccrjustice.org/ learn-more/faqs/factsheet%3A-case-against-shell-0>; Nat Parry, "Beneath the Ukraine Crisis: Shale Gas." *Consortiumnews.com.* April 24, 2014 Available at: <https://consortiumnews.com/ 2014/04/24/beneath-the-ukraine-crisis-shale-gas/>.

[17]Zbigniew Brzezinski, *The Grand Chess Board—American Primacy and its Geostrategic Imperatives.* New York: Basic Books—Perseus Books Group, 1997, p. 46.

[18]EU-Ukraine Association Agreement—the complete texts. Available at: <http://eeas.europa.eu/ ukraine/assoagreement/assoagreement-2013_en.htm>.

[19]The North Atlantic Treaty Organization (NATO) was created on April 4, 1949, at the initiative of the United States and joined by over 11 countries—Belgium, Canada, Denmark, France, Iceland, Italy, Luxembourg, the Netherlands, Norway, Portugal, and Great Britain.

machine from Europe to the Baltic states. And if the alliance were to expand to Ukraine, its military forces would arrive at 1600 km from St. Petersburg and only 480 km from Moscow.

17.2   Ukraine and Syria: Russia's Keys to the Mediterranean

The adherence to the European Union would make NATO's advance to Ukraine possible and therefore disrupt the geopolitical balance in Eurasia, a vast terrestrial and pluvial region stretching to the Middle East, covering the truly important Bosporus and Dardanelles straits, which allowed for the communication of the Black Sea and important energy (oil and gas) areas with the Mediterranean, which the United States aspired to control and dominate completely.

President Vladimir Putin has always made clear he would tolerate neither the extension of NATO's war machine to Russia's borders, threatening Russia's strategic position, nor the establishment of a missile defense system in Poland and the Czech Republic. Putin perceived the implied risk of the military initiatives of the United States and other western powers, pursuing the full control of the Mediterranean, the elimination of Russia and China's influence in the Middle East and the Maghrib, and the political isolation of Iran. He restored the Russian Atlantic fleet, expanded the Sevastopol fleet, and established a constant presence in the eastern part of the Mediterranean Sea since December 2012, which could count on 11 war vessels by 2012: the Aleksandr Shabalin, the Admiral Nevelskoy, the Peresvet, the Novocherkassk, the Minsk, the Nikolay Filchenkov, the large anti-submarine ship Admiral Panteleyev, the escort ship Neustrashimy, the patrol vessel Smetlivy, the large landing ship Yamal, and the missile cruiser Moskva. This is why the Latakia port and Tartus naval base in Syria were expanded to strengthen Russia in the Mediterranean, which didn't sit well with the United States, NATO, and especially Israel and Turkey, since it significantly restricted their margin of maneuver in the region. And President Barack Obama also persevered in his support of the Islamic jihadists against the Bashar al-Assad regime because of the US$90 million deal Syria signed with Russia on December 25, 2013, giving the company Soyuzneftegaz the right to explore and produce oil for 25 years in 2190 km^2 (845 square miles) of Block 2, in the Exclusive Economic Zone of Syria, between the cities of Tartus and Banias.[20]

---

[20]For Russian ships in the Mediterranean Sea: http://www.transasianaxis.com/showthread.php?8100-Syria/page82. Jonathan Saul (London), "Russia steps up military lifeline to Syria's Assad—sources." *Reuters*, Fri Jan 17, 2014. "Syrian energy deal puts Russia in gas-rich Med." *UPI*. Beirut, Lebanon. Business News/Energy Resources, 16 January 2014.

17.3   Senators John McCain and Christopher Murphy as Agitators in Kiev and Victoria Nuland's "Fuck the E.U."

The geostrategic objectives of the United States included, therefore, the establishment of submissive governments in Damascus and Kiev to remove the Russian bases in Syria and Sevastopol, on the Black Sea, which were interconnected and assured Russia's access to the warm waters of the Mediterranean and the Atlantic Ocean. And on December 5, 2013, less than 15 days after the start of the protests against the suspension of the agreement with the European Union, two US senators, John McCain (Republican Party) and Christopher Murphy (Democratic Party), were already in front of the demonstrations on Maidan Nezalezhnosti. As vulgar agitators, they shouted: "America will stand with Ukraine" and "Ukraine will make Europe better and Europe will make Ukraine better."[21]

The open involvement of Senators John McCain and Christopher Murphy[22] in the Maidan Square protests was not only an outrageous interference in the internal affairs of Ukraine, it also laid bare the geostrategic objectives of the United States behind the free trade negotiations with the European Union. John McCain, a notorious warmonger and lobbyist,[23] has always defended the interests of the "international arms dealers, oil sheikhs and angry Ukrainians," with whom he appeared during the 50th Security Conference in Munich, Germany (31/1/2014–2/2/2014).[24] He has always provided his services to the war industry and the oil companies, including Chevron, from whose executives and employees he received the net amount of US$700,000 in donations from 1989 to 2006, the year he also raised at least US$305,277,[25] in addition to the US$1.7 million he collected in 2008

---

[21]"John McCain tells Ukraine protesters: 'We are here to support your just cause'." *The Guardian*, December 15, 2013. Available at: <http://www.theguardian.com/world/2013/dec/15/john-mccain-ukraine-protests-support-just-cause>; "Ukraine—manifestation monstre des pro-européens à Kiev." *Le Monde*.fr avec AFP, December 15. 2013. Available at: <http://www.lemonde.fr/europe/article/2013/12/15/ukraine-200-000-pro-europeens-rassembles-a-kiev_4334662_3214.
html>: Nick Paton Walsh & Susanna Capelouto, "Ukrainian protesters get visit from Sen. John McCain—McCain: America stands with Ukrainians." *CNN*, December 15, 2013. Available at: <http://edition.cnn.com/2013/12/14/world/europe/ukraine-protests/> (Acessed on March 10, 2015).

[22]"John McCain tells Ukraine protesters: 'We are here to support your just cause'." *The Guardian*, December 15, 2013. Available at: <http://www.theguardian.com/world/2013/dec/15/john-mccain-ukraine-protests-support-just-cause>.

[23]Seth Colter Walls, "New Questions over McCain Campaign Chief's Ties to Ukraine." *The Huffington Post*, 6/27/2008. Available at: <http://www.huffingtonpost.com/2008/06/20/new-questions-over-mccain_n_108204.html>. Accessed on June 1, 2015.

[24]Jeffrey Goldberg, "How Much Does It Cost to Be Ambassador to Hungary?" *Bloomberg*, Tuesday, February 11, 2014. Available at: <http://www.bloombergview.com/articles/2014-02-11/how-much-does-it-cost-to-be-ambassador-to-hungary->.

[25]Josh Dorner John & David Willett, "McCain's Million Dollar Big Oil *Quid Pro Quo* Campaign Cash from Big Oil Flows In After Offshore Drilling Flip-Flop." *Sierra Club*. Available at: <http://

for his presidential campaign.[26] And he had been active in Ukraine since 1989 under the mantle of the International Republican Institute (IRI), the NGO he led internationally.

Senators John McCain and Christopher Murphy on Maidan Square were certainly in contact with the State Department, where Assistant Secretary of State Victoria Nuland was helping stage the protests to bring down the regime in Ukraine. On February 4, 2014, 2 days before going to Ukraine, she had already chosen who should lead the country after President Yanukovych's fall, as revealed by her conversation with the American ambassador in Kiev, Geoffrey Pyatt, probably intercepted by some hacker of the SVR RF or another Russian intelligence service and uploaded to YouTube under the title "Maidan's puppets."[27]

In evaluating the strategy and the best opposition figure to take over the Ukraine's government after the ousting of President Yanukovych, Victoria Nuland dismissed the names of Oleh Tyahnybok, the extremist leader of Svoboda, and the boxing champion Vitali V. Klitschko, founder of the Ukrainian Democratic Alliance (UDAR/УДАР) and the candidate supported by German chancellor Angela Merkel. She claimed neither had the skills or experience for the function.[28] She pointed to the banker Arseniy Yatsenyuk, affectionately using his nickname: "I think Yats is the guy who's got the economic experience, the governing experience. He's the... what he needs is Klitsch and Tyahnybok on the outside."[29] Annoyed, she then revealed her dissatisfaction with the European Union's hesitation vis-à-vis Ukraine because of its relations with Russia, and exclaimed: "Fuck the E.U."[30] The European Union didn't matter. The United States would act unilaterally.

The State Department spokesman Jen Psaki acknowledged the leaked recording of the conversation on YouTube was authentic and said Victoria Nuland had apologized to the authorities of the European Union. But the obscene and aggressive

---

action.sierraclub.org/site/MessageViewer;jsessionid=9C3A870C38955027BEF958DFC1084DC5. app207a?em_id=65021.0>.

[26]Matthew Mosk (Washington Post Staff Writer), "Industry Gushed Money after Reversal on Drillin." *The Washington Post*, July 27, 2008. Available at: <http://www.washingtonpost.com/wp-dyn/content/article/2008/7/26/AR2008072601891.html>.

[27]Anne Gearan Gearan, "In recording of U.S. diplomat, blunt talk on Ukraine." *The Washington Post*, February 6, 2014; Anne Gearan, "In recording of U.S. diplomat, blunt talk on Ukraine." *The Washington Post*, February 6, 2014.

[28]"Ukraine crisis: Transcript of leaked Nuland-Pyatt call." *BBC News* (From the section Europe)— A transcript, with analysis by *BBC* diplomatic correspondent Jonathan Marcus)—February 7, 2014. Available at: <http://www.bbc.com/news/world-europe-26079957>; Noah Rayman, "Leaked Audio Depicts U.S. Diplomat Cursing E.U. Diplomacy. Americans pointed the finger at Russia for the leak." *Time*, February 6, 2014. Available at: <http://world.time.com/2014/02/06/victoria-nuland-leaked-audio-european-union/>. Марионетки Майдан. www.youtube.com/watch?v=MSxaa-67yGM04.02.2014. Hochgeladen von Re Post. "Victoria Nuland gaffe: Angela Merkel condemns EU insult." *BBC Europe*, February 7, 2014. Available at: <http://www.bbc.com/news/world-europe-26080715>.

[29]*Ibidem.*

[30]*Ibidem.*

language she used should not have come as a surprise to anyone. Victoria Nuland was simply expressing what authorities in Washington had always thought, the contempt they felt for not only the European Union but also the rest of the world.

Five weeks after the suspension of the agreement with the European Union, therefore, Victoria Nuland traveled at least twice to Kiev. While she was there, between December 6 and 12, she was received by President Yanukovych and she actually issued orders as if Ukraine was a colony of the United States, telling him to fold immediately to overcome the crisis and to take "immediate steps to deescalate the security situation and immediate political steps to end the crisis and get Ukraine back into a conversation with Europe and the International Monetary Fund."[31]

During her stay in Kiev, accompanied by Catherine Ashton, High Representative of the European Union for Foreign Affairs and Security Policy, Victoria Nuland also met with protest leaders, including Oleh Tyahnybok, leader of Svoboda (Freedom Party), the extreme right nationalist party, and Arseniy Yatsenyuk, of the Fatherland Party,[32] and walked on Maidan Square alongside Ambassador Geoffrey Pyatt, distributing sandwiches to the demonstrators as a "symbol of sympathy" for the "horrible situation" she claimed Yanukovych had placed them in, "putting them against each other."[33] Meanwhile, US Secretary of State John Kerry declared in Washington that the United States

> expresses disgust with the decision of the Ukrainian authorities to meet the peaceful protest in (Kiev's) Maidan Square with riot police, bulldozers and batons, rather than respect for democratic rights and human dignity. This response is neither acceptable nor does it benefit democracy.[34]

John Kerry conveniently forgot President Yanukovych had been democratically elected and that if Ukraine's government was indeed using its police forces to suppress the demonstrations, then it was merely behaving like the government of the United States or any other country would in the same situation. For even though thousands of people joined the demonstrations, outraged by economic stagnation, poverty, and a corrupt regime, its leaders were not better, more honest, and more capable than President Yanukovych; and the protesters on Maidan Square were neither unarmed nor protesting peacefully. They were Svoboda activists with a clear

---

[31]"Remarks—Victoria Nuland, Assistant Secretary, Bureau of European and Eurasian Affairs. Washington, DC, December 13, 2013." *U.S. Department of State.* Available at: <http://www. state.gov/p/eur/rls/rm/2013/dec/218804.htm>; Richard Sakwa, *Frontline Ukraine—Crisis in the Boarderlands.* London: I.B. Tauris, 2015, pp. 86–88.

[32]"Top U.S. official visits protesters in Kiev as Obama admin. ups pressure on Ukraine president Yanukovych." *CBS/Wire Services,* December 11, 2013. Available at: <http://www.cbsnews.com/ news/us-victoria-nuland-wades-into-ukraine-turmoil-over-yanukovich/>.

[33]"Sandwiches Are Symbol of Sympathy to Ukrainians at Maidan: Nuland"- *Sputnik News— International,* December 18, 2014. Available at: <http://sputnik-news.com/politics>.

[34]Paul D. Shinkman, "U.S., John Kerry Disgusted With Ukrainian Response to Protests. Response to protests not acceptable for democracy, Secretary of State John Kerry says." *U.S. News,* December 11, 2013. Available at: <http://www.usnews.com/news/articles/2013/12/11/us-john-kerry-dis gusted-with-ukrainian-response-to-protests>.

xenophobic, racist, anti-Semitic, and anti-Russian inclination, taken from Lviv (Lwow, Lemberg) in the east of Galicia (Halychyna) to Kiev. In front of them were 500 heavily armed paramilitaries of the Right Sector (Pravyi sektor/Правий сектор), patrolling the streets in organized militias in groups of ten. Some wore helmets and the uniforms of the Galicia SS division (14. Waffen-Grenadier-Division der SS, which fought alongside Nazi Germany against the Soviets in 1943–1945), carrying an emblem resembling the Nazi Swastika,[35] under the command of Dmytro Yarosh.[36] The ranks of the militias were also swollen by football hooligans, further escalating the hostilities. And on December 1, 2013, in the midst of the uninterrupted and violent demonstrations, the Svoboda and Right Sector militias carrying neo-Nazi insignia[37] led the way for other activists—trained since 2004 within the IREX-USAID program for the so-called Orange Revolution[38]—and attacked and occupied administration buildings and the entire government district. They also erected barricades with burning tires, destroyed old monuments for communists and workers who participated in the 1918 uprisings, assaulted journalists, and destroyed their cameras. These militias also raided the headquarters of the Communist Party of Ukraine and raised neo-Nazi flags. An atmosphere of terror was created.

In a private message, a witness residing in Kiev reported what was actually occurring in Maidan Square, stressing how the media manipulated the information on Ukraine:

> Yes, it is actually very hot in the streets (the temperature reached 35 degrees last week). I went to see the barricades last night, on the first row just before the members of the military police. It is quite impressive. The protestors in the streets occupying that area are armed, very well organized in military companies. They carry out patrols in combat groups of ten people, with helmets and weapons. I crossed two men wearing uniforms of the SS Galizien division (which fought alongside the Germans against the Soviets in 1943–1945). I think it's very

---

[35]"A l'Est, les Nazis de hier sont réhabilités. En Ukraine et ailleurs dans l'ex-URSS: honneur aux anciens SS." Available at: <http://www.resistances.be/ukraine.html>.

[36]"Profile: Ukraine's ultra-nationalist Right Sector." *BBC Europe*, April 28, 2014. Available at: <http://www.bbc.com/news/world-europe-27173857>; see also: "Administration on December 1, 2013, and on the parliament in the end of January and on February 18, 2014. Shortly after midnight on February 20, Dmytro Yarosh. Available at: <https://newcoldwar.org/wp-content/uploads/2015/02/The-%E2%80%9CSnipers%E2%80%99-Massacre%E2%80%9D-on-the-Maidan-in-Ukraine-revised-and-updated-version-Feb-20-2015.pdf>.

[37]Svoboda, led by Oleg Tiagnibog, had its greatest influence in eastern Galicia, which had belonged to Poland and where many inhabitants collaborated with the Wehrmacht troops and formed the 14. Waffen-Grenadier-Division der SS (galizische SS-Division Nr. 1) der Waffen-SS. It has always been a stronghold of the extreme right and the so-called activists instigating and leading the pro-Western demonstrations belonged to the leadership of Svoboda, the Right Sector (*Pravyy Sektor*) and the paramilitary forces of the Ukrainian National Assembly—Ukrainian People's Self-Defence, and other groups with neo-Nazi tendencies and clear xenophobic, racist, anti-Semitic and anti-Russian ideas.

[38]Sreeram Chaulia. "Democratisation, Colour Revolutions and the Role of the NGOs: Catalysts or Saboteurs?" *Global Research*, December 25, 2005. Available at: <http://www.globalresearch.ca/democratisation-colour-revolutions-and-the-role%2D%2Dof-the-ngos-catalysts-or-saboteurs/1638>.

funny to see European politicians make grandiose statements about "Maidan" and democracy when virtually all these types facing the police in the streets are fascists. It is one big hypocrisy. The Euro-Atlantics are willing to work with anyone (such as the islamists in Syria) as long as this contributes to weakening Russia.[39]

17.4   The Fall of President Yanukovych, and the Rise of Arseniy Yatsenyuk and the Right Sector

On February 20, 2014, Laurent Fabius, Radoslaw Sikorski, and Frank-Walter Steinmeier, the Ministers of Foreign Affairs from France, Poland, and Germany, arrived in Kiev and tried to broker a deal between President Yanukovych and the representatives of the opposition, Vitali Klitschko and Arseniy Yatsenyuk.[40] The agreement provided for the formation of a "national unity" government, the calling of elections for the presidency and the Verkhovna Rada in November, and the restoration of the 2004 Constitution, removing some of the president's powers. The negotiations had hardly finished on midnight of February 20, however, when Dmytro Yarosh, leader of the neo-Nazis of the Right Sector, announced that he would not accept any understanding with President Yanukovych and that he would undertake decisive actions to overthrow the government.

The violence reached its peak. Bloody confrontations followed in the center of Kiev with the police forces of Berkut, Alpha, Omega, Falke and Titan, special units of the Ukrainian Security Service (Sluzhba Bezpeky Ukrayiny—SBU). And although no possibility can be entirely dismissed, everything pointed to the fact that others were responsible for the massacre of both protestors and police officers on February 20, 2014. Snipers posted at the windows of the Music Conservatory shot into the crowd and some shooters probably came from a Baltic country and/or the Dnipro battalion, formed by paramilitaries of the Right Sector. After thoroughly investigating the events in Maidan Square, Ivan Katchanovski, a professor at the

---

[39]Original in French: *"Oui effectivement ici c'est très 'chaud' dans la rue! (Même si on a eu –35 degrés la semaine dernière). Je suis justement alle voir les barricades hier soir, en 1ère ligne juste devant les rangées de la police militaire. C'est assez impressionant. Les opposants dans la rue qui occupent la zone sont sur-armes, très bien organisés militairement en compagnies, on les voit patrouiller en groupe de combat de 10 personnes, avec des casques, des boucliers et des armes. J'ai croisé hier soir 2 types en uniforme de la division SS 'Galicie' (qui se battait avec les allemands contre les soviétiques en 1943–45). Ça m'amuse beaucoup de voir les politiciens europeens fairent de grandes declarations sur le 'Maidan' et la democratie alors que pratiquement tous ces types dans la rue qui se battent contre la police sont fascistes. Bref une grande hypocrisie. Les Euro-atlantistes sont prêt à s'allier à n'importe qui (comme les Islamistes en Syrie) du moment que cela affaiblisse la Russie [. . .]."* Private message by e-mail, February 13, 2014. (Author's archive).

[40]"Diplomatische Bewegung in der Ukraine-Krise." *Tagsspiegel*, February 20, 2014. Available at: <http://www.tagesspiegel.de/politik/eu-aussenminister-in-kiew-diplomatische-bewegung-in-der-ukraine-krise/9513942.html>; "Klitschko erzählt von der Todes-Nacht auf dem Maidan." *Focus Online*. Available at: <http://www.focus.de/politik/ausland/news-ticker-zur-eskalation-in-der-ukraine-25-tote-busse%2D%2Dkarren-demonstranten-vom-land-nach-kiew_id_3625618.html>.

School of Political Studies & Department of Communication of the University of Ottawa, wrote that "this violent overthrow constituted an undemocratic change of government"[41] and revealed the alliance of the Maidan square activists with the extreme right, involved in the massacre of demonstrators, while nothing could be proven regarding the participation of the police and other units of the Ukrainian government. The new government of Ukraine—Professor Ivan Katchanovski affirmed—emerged broadly as a result of the deception around the massacre, and the Ukrainian media contributed by misrepresenting the mass killing of demonstrators and police officers.[42] The research conducted by Professor Ivan Katchanovski concluded that "the far right played a key role in the violent overthrow of the government in Ukraine."[43]

It was a provocation designed to blame the President amid the bloody conflicts, stirring up national and international public opinion and setting the stage for the coup d'état. In such circumstances, the agreement brokered by the French, Polish, and German Ministers for Foreign Affairs was aborted. It was of no interest to the opposition. And the mob became even more unruly. After occupying the Central Post Office and the State Committee for Television and Radio, in addition to other public bodies, the storm-trooper groups in their former SS Galicia division uniforms, the ultranationalists of Svoboda, and the neo-Nazis of the Right Sector, as well as the Azov Battalion, the Patriots of Ukraine, and other fascist groups, joined forces and invaded the Verkhovna Rada under the command of Dmytro Yarosh during the night of February 21–22. To avoid being assassinated, President Yanukovych fled from Kiev to Kharkov (Kharkiv), one of his electoral strongholds,[44] after denouncing what was occurring in Kiev as "vandalism, banditism and a coup d'Etat."[45] Democratically elected in 2010, Yanukovych had been ousted with the collaboration and support of the oligarchs,[46] including the Party of Regions, bribed and pressured to join the coup.[47] "The extreme right, although a minority, was a highly effective minority. These can play out-of-proportion roles precisely in revolutions or similar

---

[41]Ivan Katchanovski, "The 'Snipers' Massacre" on the Maidan in Ukraine." Available at: <http://www.scribd.com/doc/244801508/Snipers-Massacre-on-the-Maidan%2D%2Din-Ukraine-Paper-libre>.

[42]*Ibidem.*

[43]*Ibidem.*

[44]"Ukraine crisis: Viktor Yanukovych leaves Kiev for support base. US warns deal remains 'very, very fragile; as president visits eastern stronghold of Kharkiv." *The Telegraph.* London, February 22, 2014.

[45]Andrew Higgins & Andrew E. Kramerfeb, "Archrival Is Freed as Ukraine Leader Flees." *The New York Times,* February 22, 2014.

[46]Christian Neef (Kiev), "Yanukovych's Fall: The Power of Ukraine's Billionaires." *Spiegel Online International,* February 25, 2014. Available at: <http://www.spiegel.de/international/europe/how-oligarchs-in-ukraine-prepared-for-the-fall-of%2D%2Dyanukovych-a-955328.html>.

[47]"Ukraine president Viktor Yanukovych denounces 'coup d'État' after protesters take control in Kiev." *ABC News.* Available at: <http://www.abc.net.au/news/2014-02-22/ukraine-president-viktor-yanukovych-leaves-kiev-reports/5277588>.

situations," remarked Professor Tarik Cyril Amar of Columbia University, special-
ized in the study of Ukraine.[48]

Another Kiev resident, who asked to remain anonymous, told in a private
correspondence what he had witnessed:

> Yes, here was armed coup d'État made by local Nazi terrorists that was made under total
> false slogans for "integration in EU", "democracy" and 'freedom'. Actually, now is a total
> bedlam here and Nazi terror against Russians and Russian-speaking people, and against
> Russian Orthodox Church. The authority here was catched by hard criminals and bandits,
> and they are started with a dirty company against former authorities. The former authorities
> was not angels in real life, of course, but compared with the current—the former authorities
> was Angels from Heaven... [...] Situation here is very and very dangerous now... Kiev
> teeming with thousands of armed gangs of local Nazi of different independent movements
> and absolutely mad and stupid armed lumpens... The rampant terror and banditry in Kiev
> and in almost all regions of Ukraine, except Crimea.[49]

Meanwhile, the Hungarian American geopolitical scholar George Friedman,
linked to the Washington establishment, wrote in the magazine *Stratfor Geopolitical—Weekly* that "it is not clear what happened in Kiev. There were of course many
organizations funded by American and European money that were committed to a
reform government."[50] But in an interview to the Russian publication *Kommersant*,
he later confirmed that Russia was right to consider the events that occurred in Kiev
in the early hours of February 22 as a coup d'état organized by the United States.[51]
And he added: "it truly was the most blatant coup in history."[52]

Indeed, as George Friedman acknowledged, the ousting of the Ukrainian President was truly a conspicuous coup d'état and allowed for the establishment of an
"openly pro-Western Ukrainian government,"[53] formed by notorious supporters of

---

[48]David Stern (Kiev), "Ukraine's revolution and the far right." *BBC News Europe*, March 7, 2014.
Available at: <http://www.bbc.com/news/world-europe-26468720?print=true>.

[49][Sic]. Private message by e-mail, March 23, 2014. Original with errors in English. (Author's
archive).

[50]George Friedman, "Russia Examines Its Options for Responding to Ukraine." *Stratfor—Geopolitical Weekly*, March 18, 2014. Available at: <http://www.stratfor.com/weekly/russia-examines-
its-options-responding-ukraine#axzz38IEGZtks>.

[51]"In Ukraine, U.S interests are incompatible with the interests of the Russian Federation` Stratfor
chief George Friedman on the roots of the Ukraine crisis Interview by Elena Chernenko &
Alexander Gabuev (Translation: Paul R. Grenier)—*us-russia.org*, January 17, 2015. Available at:
<http://us-russia.org/2902-in-ukraine-us-interests-are-incompatible-with-the-interests-of-the-rus
sian-federation-stratfor-chief-george-friedman-on-the-roots-of-the-ukraine-crisis.html>;   Elena
Chernenko & Alexander Gabuev (*Kommersant*—Russian daily)>; "Stratfor Chief's "Most Blatant
Coup in History" Interview Translated in Full. *Insider Russia*, January 20, 2015. Available at:
<http://russia-insider.com/en/2015/01/20/256>; "Интересы РФ и США в отношении Украины
несовместимы друг с другом." Глава Stratfor Джордж Фридман о первопричинах
украинского кризиса- *Коммерсантъ от* December 19, 2014. Available at: <http://www.
kommersant.ru/doc/2636177>.

[52]*Ibidem.*

[53]George Friedman, "Russia Examines Its Options for Responding to Ukraine." Stratfor—*Geopolitical Weekly*, March 18, 2014. Available at: <http://www.stratfor.com/weekly/russia-examines-
its-options-responding-ukraine#axzz3HYiHNE4r>.

Nazi-fascism. Yulia Tymoshenko, sentenced and imprisoned for fraud and other criminal offenses, was released. Stepan A. Bandera (1909–1959), the anti-Semite and anti-Russian ally of Hitler in the Second World War, was hailed as a national hero. Assistant Secretary of State for European Affairs Victoria Nuland, Senator John McCain and National Endowment for Democracy President Carl Gershman had effectively crafted a coup following the instructions formulated by professor Gene Sharp in *From Dictatorship to Democracy*[54] in order to expel the fleet Russia had maintained in the Black Sea for over 230 years and to seize the naval base of Sevastopol for NATO. Because of the ever increasing economic and political permeability of national borders, the NGOs constituted the tactical tool for the penetration and informal intervention of the United States, using such programs as the International Research & Exchange Board (IREX-USAID) and the Global Undergraduate Exchange Program (Global UGRAD) in Eurasia and Central Asia, with as *raison d'être* the consolidation of American hegemony on all continents.

Victoria Nuland's puppet, Arseniy "Yats" Yatsenyuk, president of the Open Ukraine Foundation linked to the Chatham House, NATO's Center for Information, and Documentation, and to the Swiss bank Horizon Capital,[55] proclaimed himself Prime Minister and put ultranationalists and neo-Nazis in key positions of government. The position of interim president fell to Olexandr Turchynov, an intimate ally of the oligarch Yulia Tymoshenko. Admiral Ihor Tenyukh Yosypovych, a senior leader of Svoboda, temporarily assumed the Ministry of Defence in Ukraine. Dmytro Yarosh, founder of the Right Sector, began exercising the vice-presidency of the National Security and Defense Council of Ukraine. And Oleh Yaroslavovych Tyahnybok, the neo-Nazi leader of Svoboda in the Verkhovna Rada, sworn enemy of what he called "the Jewish-Russian mafia," became one of the pillars of power. This illegal and illegitimate government headed by the banker Arseniy Yatsenyuk, arising from a putsch and promptly recognized by President Barack Obama, then signed the Association Agreement with the European Union on March 21, 2014.[56] And on

---

[54]The strategy for coups developed by Professor Gene Sharp consisted in a non-violent, but complex struggle waged by various means, such as protests, strikes, noncooperation, disloyalty, boycotts, marches, car parades, processions, etc., in the midst of psychological, social, economic, and political warfare, aiming at the subversion of order. It was the pattern of the so-called color revolutions in Eurasia and the Arab Spring in North Africa and the Middle East. And NGOs, funded by the National Endowment for Democracy (NED), USAID, the CIA, and other public and private institutions, were manipulated for the *shadow wars* promoted by Washington. Gene Sharp is a professor at the University of Massachusetts Dartmouth and director of the Albert Einstein Institution in Boston. After the cold war, with the support of Colonel Robert Helvey, the Albert Einstein Institution held the Conference on Non Violent Sanctions at the Center for International Affairs of Harvard University, with the participation of 185 specialists from 16 countries. Reuben Gal, an Israeli psychologist and author of several works, among which *Service Without Guns*, was one of them. The translation and distribution of the book *From Dictatorship to Democracy* from professor Gene Sharp was sponsored by entities of the United States and the European Union. See Luiz Alberto Moniz Bandeira, 2014, pp. 25–26, 100, 107–109.

[55]Arseniy Yatsenyuk. Available at: <http://openukraine.org/en/about/partners>.

[56]"Adrian Croft European Union signs landmark association agreement with Ukraine." *Reuter—World*. Brussels, March 21, 2014. Available at: <http://www.reuters.com/article/2014/03/21/us-ukraine-crisis-eu-agreement-idUSBREA2K0JY20140321>.

February 23, the Verkhovna Rada banned Russian as the second official language of Ukraine, causing indignation and revolt in the Russian-speaking population of the country. Such a decision would inevitably fracture Ukraine, where more than two-thirds of the population spoke Russian as their native language, especially in Crimea and in the region of the Donbass—Donetsk, Luhansk, and other oblasts to the south and to the east. Russia would be forced to support them.

Chapter 18
Crimea Back to Russia and Economic Sanctions Against Russia

18.1 President Putin's Countercoup: Crimea's Reintegration into Russia with Popular Support

President Putin had considered an immediate solution to the economic crisis in Ukraine by granting it a bailout of US$15 billion on December 17, 2013, reducing the price of gas and providing other benefits. But he realized the unrest in Kiev would evolve toward the overthrow of President Yanukovych, representing a grave threat to Russia's interests—such as the withdrawal from the Kharkov pact (gas-for-fleet) on the Sevastopol naval base. This is why he prepared to deploy a decisive countercoup.

He had certainly already contemplated the possibility of Russia reinstating its jurisdiction over Crimea. The authorities of the West and Kiev had even been warned several times, especially by Minister Sergey Lavrov, about the consequences that could ensue, including the risk of Ukraine breaking into two pieces. As a result of a secretly held survey during the protests against President Yanukovych, President Putin knew that 80% of the peninsula's population favored the reincorporation into Russia, and he told his colleagues in office that "...the situation in Ukraine has turned such a way that we are forced to begin efforts to reunify with Crimea, because we cannot leave this territory and people living there to the mercy of fate, we cannot throw them under a steamroller of nationalists."[1]

The Sevastopol naval base, which gave Russia substantial operational and defensive capabilities, harbored well-equipped war ships with the most advanced supersonic cruise missiles, air defense systems, and the BSF's 11th Independent Coastal Missile-Artillery Brigade, armed with the K-300P missile defense system and

---

[1] "Putin explained why he decided to return Crimea to Russia." *Itar-TASS*. Available at <http://tass.ru/en/russia/781790>; "Putin reveals secrets of Russia's Crimea takeover plot." *BBC News—Europe*, March 9, 2015. Available at <http://www.bbc.com/news/world-europe-31796226?print=true>.

© Springer Nature Switzerland AG 2019
L. A. Moniz Bandeira, *The World Disorder*,
https://doi.org/10.1007/978-3-030-03204-3_18

Yakhont anti-ship missiles. Russia was also building another naval base in Novorossiysk, on its continental territory in the province Krasnodar Krai on the Black Sea, to the east of Crimea, for the eventuality it couldn't reach an agreement with Kiev and had to abandon Sevastopol one day. If Ukraine were to adhere to the Common Security and Defense Policy of the European Union, this possibility was real.

The largest Russian commercial port on the Black Sea could also be found in Novorossiysk, hailed a heroic city because of its resistance to the Nazis in the Second World War. This zone was of great geopolitical and strategic importance because of its location at the crossing of major oil and gas pipelines transported by OAO Gazprom from the Caspian Sea. Russia wanted to strengthen its presence in the Mediterranean with the expansion of the Tartus naval base and the port of Latakia in Syria. The naval base in Novorossiysk would serve as harbor for submarines carrying missiles with a range exceeding 1500 miles, and it acquired greater relevance after the reincorporation of Crimea into Russia because of the frequent incursion of NATO ships into the Black Sea, as Commander Aleksandr Vitko stressed.[2] And it was through this Black Sea, and then through the Mediterranean, that the Sevastopol fleet could reach the Atlantic and Indian Ocean. President Putin considered the presence of the Russian Black Sea Fleet a pillar of regional security. Russia feared its encirclement by the West and the threat to its southeastern border. The region had fallen in its sphere of influence since the earliest of times, and it was part of its national security axis.

So Russia could not lose its strategic position in Crimea. Most of the oil and natural gas from the Caucasus passed through the ports of this peninsula—Sevastopol, Varna, Sohum, Trabzon, Konstanz, Poti, and Batumi. And the Black Sea Fleet controlled the communications of important energy-supply areas with the West through the Bosporus and Dardanelles straits. The energy corridors increased the geopolitical dimension of the Black Sea and of its entire expanse.

Crimea, which had been part of Russia since 1783, had in 1991 become an autonomous republic (Avtonomnaya Respublika) within Ukraine, to which it was connected only by the isthmus of Perekop. Its population consisted of 60% Russians, 25% Russian-speaking Ukrainians, and 15% Tatars and small minorities. President Putin's initiative to reintegrate Crimea with the Russian Federation was a reaction to the putsch perpetrated in Kiev by the storm troopers of the Right Sector (Pravyi sektor) and Svoboda (Freedom Party). There was no invasion. 15,000 Russian soldiers and sailors were already stationed at the Sevastopol naval base, in accordance with the Kharkov pact, which allowed for the presence of up to 25,000 soldiers in the region. Others soon joined them to ensure the defense of the peninsula against a possible attack from Kiev.[3] There was no proper annexation, but a de facto

---

[2]"Russia's Black Sea port of Novorossiysk to house subs carrying long-range cruise missiles." *Itar-TASS—Russia*, September 23, 2014. Available at <http://tass.ru/en/russia/750841>.

[3]Kathrin Hille (Moscou), "Ukrainian port is key to Russia's naval power." *The Financial Times*, February 27, 2014. Available at <http://www.ft.com/cms/s/0/1f749b24-9f8c-11e3-b6c7-00144feab7de.html#axzz3X7DJLGGh>.

and de jure reintegration of the Autonomous Republic in the Russian Federation. This Republic of Crimea (Respublika Krym) was approved by 96.77% of the voters in the referendum called by the regional parliament and held on March 16, 2014, with massive participation (83.10%).

18.2 The Escalation of the Second Cold War and Russia's Reclaimed Influence in the Black Sea

The Cold War had been intensifying since the George W. Bush administration. And it escalated further after unhinged provocations by NATO Secretary General Anders Fogh Rasmussen and General Phillip Breedlove, Supreme Allied Commander Europe (SACEUR)—provocations with unpredictable consequences. The United States and its allies of the European Union were in no political and military condition to oppose the Russian initiative, nor did they have any moral authority to condemn the reintegration of Crimea into its territory. The Western powers had promoted and sustained the unilateral declaration of independence of Kosovo on February 17, 2008, at the International Court of Justice, which ruled in 2010 that there was no violation of international law and of resolution no. 1244.[4] And with the separation of Kosovo, the borders of Serbia had been changed not by peaceful means, but by force of arms. NATO carried out a brutal military intervention (Operation Allied Force), bombing the country without authorization from the UN Security Council for 75 days,[5] and destroying its entire infrastructure, as it would subsequently do in Iraq and Libya. A frontal violation of international law, of the principle of national sovereignty, enshrined in the Helsinki Accords (Finland) of 1975, which were signed by 35 nations as a result of the Conference on Security and Co-operation in Europe.

Unlike Serbia, there was no violence in Crimea. Russia didn't bomb Ukraine to separate the peninsula. With the fall of Yanukovych, the people were demanding the secession from Ukraine. Thousands were already in the streets of Sevastopol carrying the Russian flag and shouting "Russia, Russia, Russia" and "we won't surrender to these fascists," referring to those that took power in Kiev. And the great Portuguese poet Fernando Pessoa already wrote: "language is the foundation of the

---

[4]"Sumary 2010/2—22 July 2010—Accordance with international law of the unilateral declaration of independence in respect of Kosovo. Summary of the Advisory Opinion, On July 22, 2010. The International Court of Justice gave its Advisory Opinion on the question of the Accordance with international law of the unilateral declaration of independence in respect of Kosovo." Available at <http://www.icj-cij.org/docket/files/141/16010.pdf>.

[5]Conference on Security and Co-operation in Europe—Final Act—Helsinki 1975, p. 4. Available at <https://www.osce.org/mc/39501?download=true>.

nation."[6] The 2.3 million or so inhabitants of Crimea—most ethnically Russian (58/60% Russian, 24% Ukrainian, and 12% Tartar, according to the 2001 Census[7])—would not submit to the government of Svoboda and the Right Sector. To resist any military force from Kiev, self-defense militias were promptly organized in Simferopol, Crimea's capital city with a population of 337,285, mostly Russians with a small tartar minority. The Kremlin could not abandon this population.

Crimea, a peninsula that has arid and mountainous areas, had effectively remained under Russian sovereignty since the Treaty of Küçük Kaynarca, signed with the Ottoman Empire in 1774 during the reign of Tsarina Catherine II the Great (1729–1796). As President Vladimir Putin recalled, it had been the Bolsheviks who ceded Russian territories to Kiev without any ethnic considerations after the revolution of 1917, forming the South and South-East of Ukraine. Nikita Khrushchev, General Secretary of the USSR's Communist Party, transferred Crimea to Ukraine in 1954, along with Sevastopol and its fleet guarding the Black Sea, which was 60% wider than the Persian Gulf, transported 60% of Russia's total exports, and had a coastline stretching from Ukraine to Bulgaria, Romania, Georgia, and Turkey. After the reintegration of Crimea and its ports shipping Russia's agricultural, metal, and energy output, Moscow reclaimed domain over the Kerch Strait, the key route between the Sea of Azov and the Black Sea, and the complete control of the Kerch-Yenikalskiy canal, which allowed both the passage of larger vessels between the two seas and entrance to the Volga, the largest river in Europe with unhindered access to the Caspian Sea. Ukraine under its neo-Nazi government was left quite vulnerable. If it tried for war, it could be attacked by Russia on three fronts, the Northeast, Southeast, and South, and find itself occupied within a week.

One of the main goals of Arseniy "Yats" Yatsenyuk, Victoria Nuland's puppet operating in the shadows of the Association Agreement with the European Union, was for Ukraine to join NATO. The Kharkov deal negotiated with President Yanukovych was based on Russia's military doctrine of 2010, which identified the Atlantic Alliance (NATO) as one of its main external threats. The West (the United States and its partners) had delegated global functions to NATO in order to violate international laws and rules and expand the block's military structure close to Russia's borders.[8] And the extension of the lease of Sevastopol implied that Ukraine

---

[6] *"A base da pátria é o idioma."* Fernando Pessoa, *Sobre Portugal—Introdução ao Problema Nacional.* (Recolha de textos de Maria Isabel Rocheta e Maria Paula Morão. Introdução organizada por Joel Serrão.). Lisbon: Ática, 1979, p. 19. Available at <http://multipessoa.net/labirinto/portugal/12>.

[7] "Everything you need to know about Crimea. Why is the Crimean peninsula part of Ukraine? Why does Russia have military presence there? Here is a short guide for the perplexed." *Há'aretz*, March 11, 2014. Available at <http://www.haaretz.com/world-news/1.577286>.

[8] "Text of newly approved Russian military doctrine. Text of report by Russian presidential website on 5 February" ("The Military Doctrine of the Russian Federation" approved by Russian Federation presidential edict on February 5, 2010). Available at <http://carnegieendowment.org/files/2010russia_military_doctrine.pdf>.

could not join NATO until 2042, because with the exception of the Baltic states, Russia would oppose adherence to the alliance by any defunct Soviet republic.

18.3 Kiev's Lost Assets

With the reintegration of Crimea into Russia, President Putin retaliated against the impudent offensive of the United States and its allies in the European Union. And the government in Kiev lost physical access to its virtual sources of energy through the Black Sea and approximately 127 billion hryvna (US$10.8 billion) in assets, according to Denis Khramov, Ukraine's Deputy Minister of Ecology and Natural Resources. Ukraine also lost significant infrastructure, such as Simferopol International Airport, the third largest in the country, through which 1.2 million people traveled in 2013, airline routes, the port of Yalta, and the tourism and trade potential offered by the peninsula.[9]

Likewise, no less than 93,000 km^2 of the surface of the Black Sea, Sea of Azov and surroundings, a huge area of approximately 27,000 square nautical miles, passed to Russia's domain, according to the Convention on the Law of the Sea of 1982,[10] with the right to explore the rich oil and natural gas reserves of the Black Sea and the Sea of Azov, which could produce 70 million barrels of crude oil per year and reduce the dependence of Ukraine on energy imports. After the referendum ratifying the secession on March 17, 2014, and the Duma's confirmation in Moscow, the Parliament of Crimea nationalized the Ukrainian companies existing there— Chornomornaftogaz and Ukrtransgaz—as well as the pipelines and the fields of Skifska and Foroska, 80 km southwest of the peninsula, which would be exploited in a consortium with the oil companies Royal Dutch Shell Plc (RDSA), Exxon Mobil Corp. (XOM) Shell and Chevron Corp, and Eni Span (ENI). As a result, these companies canceled their contracts with the government in Kiev.[11] The energy

---

[9]Natalia Zinets and Elizabeth Piper (Kiev), "Crimea cost Ukraine over $10 billion in lost natural resources." *Reuters*, April 7, 2014; Maksym Bugriy, "The Cost to Ukraine of Crimea's Annexation." *Eurasia Daily Monitor*, Volume: 11, Issue: 70. April 14, 2014. *Jamestown Foundation.* Available at <http://www.jamestown.org/regions/europe/single/?tx_ttnews[tt_news]=42227&tx_ttnews[backPid]=51&cHash=5bd3d36f8fd90bb8c050304f4aff136a#.VS0P0JM-7_A>; "Росія захопила в Криму майна на 127 мільярдів—Мохник." Українська правда, Понеділок, 07 квітня 2014. Available at <http://www.pravda.com.ua/news/2014/04/7/7021631/view_print/>.

[10]"Section 2. Limits of the Territorial Sea Article 4—Outer limit of the territorial sea—The outer limit of the territorial sea is the line every point of which is at a distance from the nearest point of the baseline equal to the breadth of the territorial sea." United Nations Convention on the Law of the Sea." Available at <http://www.un.org/depts/los/convention_agreements/texts/unclos/unclos_e.pdf>.

[11]Roland Flamini, "Crimea: Putin's War for Oil and Gas?" *World Affairs—Corridors of Power*, May 20, 2014. Available at <http://www.worldaffairsjournal.org/blog/roland-flamini/crimea-putins-war-oil-and-gas>; "Ukraine Crisis Endangers Exxon's Black Sea Gas Drilling: Energy." *Bloomberg*, March 11, 2014. Available at <http://www.bloomberg.com/news/articles/2014-03-10/ukraine-crisis-endangers-exxon-s-black-sea-gas-drilling-energy>.

reserves off the coast of the Black Sea were estimated at 1.5 trillion cubic meters, including the newly discovered methane hydrate[12] and natural gas deposits, calculated between 200 billion and 250 billion cubic meters.[13] One of the largest gas deposits, capable of producing 1.5 billion cubic meters per year, could be found in the Kerch strait. This way Russia formally assumed jurisdiction over the largest stretch of the Black Sea, along the entire eastern coast of Crimea, involving the iron ore mining and processing plants of the Kerch strait and, to the southwest, the Russian cities and the port of Novorossiysk and Sochi, the Krasnodar region. All gas and oil reserves of the Black Sea and Sea of Azov now fell under the control of Gazprom.

18.4   The Shortsighted Sanctions Against Russia, Devaluation of the Ruble, and the Drop in Oil Price

The countercoup struck by President Putin had been decisive. Washington felt its blow, and President Barack Obama got ahead of himself. He promptly recognized the government installed in Kiev by neo-Nazis and received the self-proclaimed Prime Minister of Ukraine, the banker Arseniy "Yats" Yatsenyuk, at the White House, further demonstrating his incompetence as head of state and government. As almost always, the diplomacy of the State Department had proven inept with its partisan foreign policy. And it could hardly have been any different, managed as it was by business men, amateurs, ignorant men, and women intoxicated by the ideology of America's "exceptionalism."

According to data from the American Foreign Service Association, slightly more than 40% of the American ambassadors appointed by President Barack Obama were not career diplomats, but business men who had contributed financially to his campaign.[14] The qualifications of Colleen Bradley Bell, producer of the CBS show *The Bold and the Beautiful* and nominated as ambassador in Hungary, were touted by saying she had exported a product to "more than 100 countries, for daily consumption with more than 40 million viewers."[15] In reality, Colleen Bradley Bell

---

[12]*Ibidem.*

[13]Nick Cunningham, "Russia Eyes Crimea's Oil and Gas Reserves." *Oil Price*, March 16, 2014. Available   at   <http://oilprice.com/Energy/Energy-General/Russia-Eyes-Crimeas-Oil-and-Gas-Reserves.html>.

[14]"President Obama's Second-Term Ambassadorial Nominations. Updated April 17, 2015." *American Foreign Service Association.* Available at <http://www.afsa.org/secondterm.aspx>; Cathal J. Nolan (Editor), *Notable U.S. Ambassadors since 1775: A Biographical. Dictionary.* Westport, Connecticut: Greenwood Press, 1997, p. 90. Tamara Keith. "When Big Money Leads To Diplomatic Posts." *NPR*, December 3, 2014. Available at <http://www.npr.org/2014/12/03/368143632/obama-appoints-too-many-big-donors-to-ambassadorships-critics-say>.

[15]*Ibidem*; Leslie Larson, "Senate sneers as soap opera exec is confirmed Ambassador to Hungary." *Daily News*, New York, December 3, 2014. Available at <http://www.nydailynews.com/news/politics/soap-opera-producer-confirmed-ambassador-hungary-article-1.2031496>.

had donated US\$500,000 to the Obama campaign and raised US\$2.1 million during 2011 and 2012.[16] In Norway, President Obama appointed George Tsunis, CEO of the Chartwell Hotels in Long Island (New York) because he donated US\$1.5 million to this campaign in 2012. This led to harsh criticisms from Oslo, because when questioned in the Senate, Mr. Tusnis revealed he didn't even know that the country was a monarchy.[17] Noah Bryson Mamet, appointed to lead the United States embassy in Buenos Aires, also showed his almost complete ignorance about Argentina. During the Senate hearing he confessed he had never set foot in the country. He knew nothing about it. His qualifications for the post were the no less than US \$500,000 he had collected, as notified by OpenSecrets.[18]

The appointment of business men and donors to presidential campaigns is not a unique practice of President Obama. It has been happening since the nineteenth century. By giving generous businessmen, Hollywood superstars and other billionaires the leadership of embassies, they could close big business deals and receive commissions to compensate, with profits, the resources they had donated to the campaign. Corruption has always been endemic in the presidential republic, the lifeblood of its elections. The Israeli-American journalist Jeffrey Goldberg remarked on Bloomberg's site that:

> [. . .] there is the corruption of governance and diplomacy, in which ambassadorships are sold to the highest bidder. And then there is a more subtle form of corruption, in which the people's representatives are made to feel as if they must provide cover for the corrupt practices of the executive branch.[19]

---

[16]*Ibidem*; "Obama's Top Fund-Raisers." *The New York Times*, September 13, 2012. Available at <http://www.nytimes.com/interactive/2012/09/13/us/politics/obamas-top-fund-raisers.html?_r=0. Access on April 18, 2014. "Ambassador to Hungary: Who Is Colleen Bell." *AlllGov*. Monday, 2 de junho de 2014. Available at <http://www.allgov.com/news/appointments-and-resignations/ambassador-to-hungary-who-is-colleen-bell-140602?news=853292>.

[17]Alex Lazar, "Oslo Mayor Unhappy With Obama's Norway Ambassador Nominee." *The Huffington Post*, August 7, 2014. Available at <http://www.huffingtonpost.com/2014/07/08/george-tsunis-norway_n_5567351.html>; Michael A. Memoli and Lisa Mascaro (Washington), "Obama donor George Tsunis ends his nomination as Norway ambassador." *Los Angeles Times*, December 13, 2014. Available at <http://www.latimes.com/world/europe/la-fg-norway-ambassador-nominee-withdraws-20141213-story.html>.

[18]"Argentina ambassador pick, and Obama bundler, has never been to Argentina." *FoxNews.com*, February 7, 2014. Available at <http://www.foxnews.com/politics/2014/02/07/nominee-for-argentina-ambassador-and-obama-bundler-has-never-been-to-argentina/>; "Barack Obama's Bundlers. Bundlers are people with friends in high places who, after bumping against personal contribution limits, turn to those friends, associates, and, well, anyone who's willing to give, and deliver the checks to the candidate in one big bundle." *OpenSecrets—The Center for Responsive Politics*. Available at <http://www.opensecrets.org/pres12/bundlers.php?id=N00009638>.

[19]Jeffrey Goldberg, "How Much Does It Cost to Be Ambassador to Hungary?" *Bloomberg*, February 11, 2014. Available at <http://www.bloombergview.com/articles/2014-02-11/how-much-does-it-cost-to-be-ambassador-to-hungary->.

Despite the existence of an outstanding academic and intellectual elite in the United States, clear-sighted men and women, journalists, and others, with a profound and clear understanding of other countries, deep America has always ignored the rest of the world. And this deep America has always elected the majority of Congress, the president and, therefore, influenced the more and more militarized foreign policy of the republic, based on the belief of the invincibility of its military might, even though the United States has not won any war since 1945, as former President Bill Clinton himself has recognized.

This same ignorance led authorities in Washington to believe that the "color revolutions" model, initially successful in Georgia (Rose Revolution, 2003), Ukraine (Orange Revolution, 2004), and Kyrgyzstan (Tulip Revolution, 2005), could be exported to other countries as a special form of subversive war to achieve its geostrategic and economic objectives.[20] The outcome was negative, however. After the overthrow of President Yanukovych, the situation in Ukraine turned extremely unstable. The United States protested against the reintegration of Crimea, accusing Russia of violating the principle of territorial integrity, but they couldn't do anything except trigger an economic war, starting by decreeing successive sanctions against Russia, such as the freezing of financial assets and visa bans, in order to cause economic damage to the businesses and personalities linked to the Kremlin. The ruble took a nosedive in the international market. And according to some hypotheses, the precipitous drop in the price of oil, falling from US$110 per barrel to less than US$50 since June 2014, was the result of a concerted maneuver by the United States and Saudi Arabia to further bleed the economy of Russia—as well as Iran and Venezuela—not only because of Crimea but also because of Syria, where President Putin refused to abandon the Bashar al-Assad government.[21] The sanctions, the devaluation of the ruble and the drop in oil prices are estimated to have caused around US$140 billion per year in losses and a decline of almost 5% in Russia's GDP in 2015.[22]

The European Union followed the United States subserviently. But American exports to Russia didn't reach 1% of its foreign trade, and President Obama could afford sanctions with his country hardly suffering. The European Union couldn't. Although the leaders of the European Commission in Brussels calculated that the

---

[20]Lincoln A. Mitchell, 2012, pp. 86, 94, 141–146.

[21]Tim Bowler (Business reporter), "Falling oil prices: Who are the winners and losers?" *BBC News*, January 19, 2015. Available at <http://www.bbc.com/news/business-29643612>; TOPF, Andrew. "Did the Saudis and the US Collude in Dropping Oil Prices?" *OilPrice.com*, December 23, 2014. Available at <http://oilprice.com/Energy/Oil-Prices/Did-The-Saudis-And-The-US-Collude-In-Dropping-Oil-Prices.html>.

[22]"Russia losing $140 billion from sanctions and low oil prices." *CNN Money*. Available at <http://money.cnn.com/2014/11/24/news/economy/russia-losing-140%2D%2Dbillion-oil-sanctions/>; "Northwestern Mutual Voice Team, Northwestern Mutual. Who Wins And Who Loses As Oil Prices Fall?" *Forbes—Investing*, December 16, 2014. Available at <http://www.forbes.com/sites/northwesternmutual/2014/12/16/who-wins-and-who-loses-as-oil-prices-fall/>.

sanctions would cause a loss in Russia of 23 billion € in 2014 (1.5% of GDP) and 75 billion € (4.8% of GDP) in 2015,[23] all countries of the block would have to withstand the severe consequences of such a measure.[24] In 2013, Russia had become the main destination of agricultural exports from the European Union (19%), leaving Turkey in second place (15%),[25] and the second largest market for its exports of foodstuffs, beverages, and raw materials, growing each year to reach the value of 12.2 billion € (£9.7 billion) in 2013.[26] And all the members of the European Union were forced to swallow heavy losses when President Putin signed Edict no. 560 on August 6, 2014, suspending the imports of various products from the countries of the European Union for 1 year, including fruits, vegetables, meat and derivatives, fish, milk, and all its derivatives. The embargo also included products from Australia, Canada, Norway, and Japan. The losses hit the perishable products hardest, exceeding the losses in foreign trade and industrial sectors.[27] The European Union's trade and economy felt the impact of the sanctions against Russia much more than the United States.[28]

For various economic and political reasons, President Putin ruled out cutting off oil and gas supply as part of the sanctions adopted against the European Union. Even so, the losses resulting from the ban on the imports of agricultural products and derivatives would be much larger than Brussels imagined. According to a study conducted by the Austrian Institute of Economic Research (WIFO), the sanctions imposed on Russia and Moscow's retaliations would cost the European Union 100 billion € in economic development and affect 2.5 million jobs.[29] Germany alone would lose approximately 500,000 jobs.

---

[23]Valentina Pop, "Multi-billion losses expected from Russia sanctions." *EuObserver*, Brussels, July 28, 2014. Available at <https://euobserver.com/economic/125118>.

[24]William Mauldin, "Europeans Face Export Losses as Sanctions Bite Russian Ruble." *The Wall Street Journal*, December 19, 2014. Available at <http://blogs.wsj.com/economics/2014/12/19/europeans-face-export-losses-as-sanctions-bite%2D%2Drussian-ruble/>.

[25]*European Commission*—Monitoring Agri-trade Policy—Agricultural trade in 2013: EU gains in commodity exports. Available at <http://ec.europa.eu/agriculture/trade-analysis/map/2014-1_en.pdf>. *European Commission*—Monitoring Agri-trade Policy (MAP—2014)—Agricultural trade in 2013: EU gains in commodity exports. Available at <http://ec.europa.eu/agriculture/trade-analysis/map/2014-1_en.pdf>.

[26]Jennifer Ranking and agencies, "Russia responds to sanctions by banning western food imports." *The Guardian*, August 7, 2014.

[27]Alan Matthews, "Russian food sanctions against the EU." *CAP Reform.I*, August 15, 2014. Available at <http://capreform.eu/russian-food-sanctions-against-the-eu/>.

[28]Simond de Galbert, *A Year of Sanctions against Russia—Now What?: A European Assessment of the Outcome and Future of Russia Sanctions*. Washington: Center for Strategic and International Studies, 2015, pp. 8–9.

[29]"Anti-Russian sanctions hurt Europe harder than expected, threaten 2.5mn jobs—study." *RT*, June 19, 2015. Available at <http://rt.com/news/268336-russian-sanctions-hurt-europe/>; "Russia crisis will cost EU up to 100 billion in value—Press." *Start your bag*, June 19, 2015. Available at <http://startyourbag.com/germany/russia-crisis-will-cost-eu-up-to-100-billion-in-value-press/>.

Germany had initially tried to resist. It hesitated in adopting sanctions due to the internal opposition from public opinion, strong economic sectors and such social democrat leaders as Helmut Schmidt and Gerhard Schröder.[30] More than 6200 companies maintained business ties with Russia, involving about 76 billion € and more than 300,000 jobs in Germany, according to Anton Boerner, director of the export firm BGA.[31] The chemical industry BASF had to cancel lucrative business deals with Gazprom for the extraction and distribution of natural gas. Opel and Volkswagen also had to call off their operations in Russia. According to Tassilo Zywietz, director of the Chamber of Commerce and Industry in Stuttgart, a total of 6500 companies (at least one in every three companies) had operations in Russia, whose market had always been very important for Germany.[32]

Former *Kanzler* Helmut Schmidt warned that the sanctions against Russia in response to the reintegration of Crimea constituted a *dummes Zeug*, a stupid instrument of the United States and the European Union.[33] He emphasized the similarities with the climate of 1914 preceding the First World War, and said that Germany should neither encourage another conflict nor require more financial resources or armaments from NATO.[34] *Kanzlerin* Angela Merkel supported and adopted the sanctions against Russia, however, sparingly assisted by the social democrats of her Grand Coalition government, the Minister of Foreign Affairs Frank-Walter Steinmeier and *Vizekanzler* Sigmar Gabriel. She bowed to the pressure from Washington and NATO and went against Germany's economic and political interests. This was hardly a surprise. In 2003, when then *Kanzler* Gerhard Schröder (social democrat) opposed the invasion of Iraq with the President of France, Jacques Chirac (Union of French Democracy—Center-right), Angela

---

[30]"Krim-Krise—Altkanzler Schmidt verteidigt Putins Ukraine-Kurs." *Spiegl Online*, March 26, 2014. Available at <http://www.spiegel.de/politik/ausland/helmut-schmidt-verteidigt-in-krim-krise-putins-ukraine-kurs-a-960834-druck.html>; "Ukraine-Konflikt—Schröder macht EU für Krim-Krise mitverantwortlich." *Spiegel Online*, March 9, 2014. Available at <http://www.spiegel.de/politik/deutschland/krim-krise-ex-kanzler-gerhard-schroeder-kritisiert-eu-a-957728.html>; 'It's a dead end': German FM joins chorus of discontent over Russia sanctions rhetoric." *RT*, May 18, 2014. Available at <http://rt.com/news/159716-germany-sanctions-russia-criticism/>.

[31]"German trade group BGA warns sanctions 'life-threatening' to Russia, hurting Germany." *DW (Deutsche Welle)*, March 12, 2014). Available at <http://www.dw.de/german-trade-group-bga-warns-sanctions-life-threatening-to-russia%2D%2Dhurting-germany/a-17492056>; "Above 6000 German companies to be hit by sanctions on Russia-export body." *RT*, March 21, 2014. Available at <http://rt.com/business/germany-russia-sanctions-businesses-365/>.

[32]Sergey Guneev, "German Businesses Suffer Losses Due to EU Anti-Russia Sanctions: Official." *Sputnik*, January 14, 2015. Available at <http://sputniknews.com/business/20150114/1016894488.html>.

[33]"Sanktionen dummes Zeug Schmidt verteidigt Putins Krim-Politik." *Frankfurter Allgemeine Zeitung*, March 26, 2014. Available at <http://www.faz.net/aktuell/politik/inland/schmidt-verteidigt-putins-krim-politik-12864852.html>.

[34]Leon Mangasarian, "Ukraine Crisis Echoes 1914, German Ex-Leader Schmidt Says." *Bloomberg*, May 16, 2014. Available at <http://www.bloomberg.com/news/articles/2014-05-16/ukraine-crisis-resembles-europe-1914-says-helmut%2D%2Dschmidt>.

Merkel published an article in *The Washington Post* as leader of the Christian-Democrats saying that he (Schröder) did not speak for all of Germany. She defended the armed intervention against Saddam Hussein and sympathized with President George W. Bush, who received her with open arms in the Oval Office of the White House.[35]

---

[35]Max Cohen, "Angela Merkel schreibt in der *Washington Post*: 'Schroeder Doesn't Speak for All Germans' By Angela Merkel." *The Washington Post*, February 20, 2003. Available at <http:// www.ariva.de/forum/Angela-Merkel-schreibt-in-der-Washington-Post-153840>; "Merkel und der Irak-Krieg—Ein Golfkriegssyndrom ganz eigener Art." *Süddeutsche Zeitung*, May 17, 2010. Available   at   <http://www.sueddeutsche.de/politik/merkel-und-der-irak-krieg%2D%2Dein-golfkriegssyndrom-ganz-eigener-art-1.747506>; Markus Becker, "Beitrag in US-Zeitung—Merkels Bückling vor Bush—Angela Merkel hat für einen handfesten Eklat gesorgt: In einem Beitrag für die *Washington Post* stimmte die CDU-Chefin in den Kriegsgesang der US-Regierung ein, wetterte gegen die Bundesregierung—und brach damit nach Ansicht der SPD eine Tradition deutscher Politik." *Spiegel Online*, February 20, 2003. Available at <http://www.spiegel.de/politik/ ausland/beitrag-in-us-zeitung-merkels-bueckling-vor-bush-a-237040-druck.html>;   Norman M. Spreng, 2015, pp. 285–286.

Chapter 19
Ukrainian Regime Change, Civil War, and the USA-Russia Proxy War

19.1 Warnings About the Sanctions Against Russia and Escalation of the Conflict in Ukraine

The sanctions decreed by the United States and the European Union would never turn around Crimea's reintegration into Russia, approved in the referendum of March 17 by more than 90% of the voters and celebrated with Russian flags in Lenin square in Simferopol.[1] They would never bend the knee of President Vladimir Putin, who recognized the sovereignty of Crimea as an independent state by decree soon after the referendum. Gregor Gysi, leader of the party *Die Linke* (the Left) in Germany, warned that the punitive economic measures against Russia and NATO's meddling would only serve to further escalate the crisis in Ukraine.[2] A crisis that had not been provoked by Russia. As the former German *Kanzler* Gerhard Schröder (social democrat) pointed out, the United States, assisted by the European Union, had been to blame. It had tried to force Kiev to sign a treaty of association, ignoring

---

[1] Mark Kramer, "Why Did Russia Give Away Crimea Sixty Years Ago?" CWIHP (Cold War International History Project) e-Dossier No. 47. *Wilson Center*. Available at: <http://www.wilsoncenter.org/publication/why-did-russia-give-away-crimea-sixty-years-ago>; "95.7% of Crimeans in referendum voted to join Russia—preliminary results." *RT*—March 17, 2014. Available at: <http://www.rt.com/news/crimea-vote-join-russia-210/>.

[2] Bernd Ulrich, "Die Deutschen und Russland: Wie Putin spaltet." *Die Zeit*, N°. 16/2014, April 10, 2014. Available at: <http://www.zeit.de/politik/ausland/2014-04/germans-russia-media-putin/komplettansicht>; Christian Unger, "Krim-Krise Gregor Gysi: "Sanktionen gegen Russland verschärfen die Krise," March 26, 2014; *Hamburger Abendblatt*. Available at: <http://www.abendblatt.de/politik/article126202086/Gregor-Gysi%2D%2DSanktionen-gegen-Russland-verschaerfen-die-Krise.html>; Christopher Alessi & Monica Raymunt (Reuters), "Germans wary of Merkel's tough line on Russia." *Chicago Tribune*, 25 April 2014. Available at: <http://articles.chicagotribune.com/2014-04-25/news/sns-rt-us-germany-russia-20140424_1_germans-economic-sanctions-gregor-gysi>; "Democratic vote, govt. without fascists needed in Ukraine before any talks." *RT*, March 25, 2014. Available at: <http://rt.com/news/ukraine-government-fascists-gysi-997/>.

© Springer Nature Switzerland AG 2019
L. A. Moniz Bandeira, *The World Disorder*,
https://doi.org/10.1007/978-3-030-03204-3_19

the deep cultural divide in Ukraine, the fact that the people in the south and east had always been more engaged with Russia than the West,[3] and the opposition of the Party of Regions to NATO membership.[4] Washington also ignored the repeated warnings from Moscow. And it failed to calculate the consequences that would arise from the overthrow of Viktor Yanukovych's legitimate government, the inevitable shattering of the fragile domestic political balance in Ukraine and instability in Europe. "The White House rudely interfered in the inter-Ukrainian affairs by orchestrating and supporting an anti-constitutional *coup d'état* in Kiev relying on the ultranationalist and neo-Nazi forces," declared Russian minister of Foreign Affairs Sergei Lavrov.[5] This accusation was backed up by President Vladimir Putin personally when he opened the plenary session of the St. Petersburg International Economic Forum in 2015. While taking questions from participants, he pointed out that the West's support to the anti-constitutional coup against President Yanukovych had been the prime mover of the crisis in Ukraine.[6]

19.2   Fiasco of the Regime Change Policy

The political scientist Albert Alexander Stahel, professor of Strategic Studies at the ETH Zürich (Federal Institute of Technology) and the University of Zurich, noted that the Parliament's violent overthrow of Viktor Yanukovych had destabilized and fractured Ukraine, with the separatists in the Donbass fighting the army and the militias from Kiev. Based on this case and others, Prof. Stahel wrote, one could conclude that the United States' regime change policy hadn't ushered in democracy anywhere.[7] On the contrary, civil wars and chaos had been the result wherever the

---

[3]"Ukraine-Konflikt—Schröder macht EU für Krim-Krise mitverantwortlich." *Der Spiegel Online*, March 9, 2014. Available at: <http://www.spiegel.de/politik/deutschland/krim-krise-ex-kanzler-gerhard-schroeder-kritisiert-eu-a-957728.html>; "Es war ein Fehler, die Ukraine vor die Wahl zwischen der EU und Russland zu stellen, sagte Schröder. Die EU habe ignoriert, dass die Ukraine ein kulturell tief gespaltenes Land sei."; "Alt-Kanzler Schröder macht EU für Ukraine-Krise verantwortlich." Welt am Sonntag. Available at: <http://deutsche-wirtschafts-nachrichten.de/2014/05/11/alt-kanzler-schroeder-macht-eu-fuer-ukraine-krise-verantwortlich>; "Ex-PM da Alemanha. Culpa do que se passa na Ucrânia é da EU—diz Schroeder." *Diário de Notícias/Globo*, May 11, 2014. Available at: <http://www.dn.pt/inicio/globo/interior.aspx?content_id=3856448&seccao=Europa&page=-1>.

[4]Lincoln A. Mitchell, 2012, pp. 86, 94.

[5]"Russia says US rudely interfered, The US leadership ignored Moscow's repeated warning that shattering the fragile inter-political balance in Ukraine would result in the emergence of a serious hotbed of instability in Europe in Ukraine's affairs by backing coup." TASS-World, May 7, 2015. Available at: <http://tass.ru/en/world/793425>.

[6]Mikhail Metzel (TASS), "West's support for state coup in Ukraine prime cause of crisis in Ukraine—Putin." *TASS*, June 19, 2015. Available at: <http://tass.ru/en/world/802418>.

[7]Albert A. Stahel, "Regime-change—fortwährende Fehlschläge der USA." *Strategische Studien*, January 17, 2015. Available at: <http://strategische-studien.com/2015/01/17/regime-change-fortwaehrende-fehlschlaege-der-usa-2/>.

United States tried to promote regime change on the pretext of strengthening democracy—stressed Stahel. Among other examples, he cited: Afghanistan, where an endless war linked with the drug business was raging since 2001; Iraq, where events since 2003 have led to the rise of the Islamic State; Tunisia, which became unstable after the fall of dictator Zine al-Abidine Ben Ali and saw the strengthening of radical Islam; Egypt, where the overthrow of Hosni Mubarak was followed by the election by the Muslim Brotherhood of Mohammed Morsi to the presidency, from which he was soon ousted through the coup by Marshal Abdel Fattah el-Sisi, whose army went on to fight radical Islamists in the Sinai Peninsula; Syria, where the United States, Turkey, and Saudi Arabia fomented protests against the Bashar al-Assad regime and provided material support to the Salafist organizations Jabhat al-Nusra and the Islamic State in a war that left more than 279,000 dead until the beginning of 2016, in addition to more than 4.5 million refugees between March 2011 and February 2016; and Libya, which transformed into a failed state and mired in a brutal civil war after the destruction of Muammar Gaddafi's regime by NATO's (the United States, Britain, and France) air war in support of the Islamist militias. According to Stahel, the United States would be better served by investing the money of these regime change operations in the solution of such internal problems as the restoration of its infrastructure, which had practically broken down, and its bad educational, health-care, and social welfare systems.[8]

In a conversation with Ambassador Geoffrey Pyatt, the American Assistant Secretary of State Victoria Nuland had already declared that the United States spent US$5 billion on the "development of democratic institutions" in Ukraine.[9] That is, it had funded the Orange Revolution (2004–2005) and paid for the protests that erupted in late November 2013 in Maidan Nezalezhnosti to bring down President Viktor Yanukovych after he blocked the association agreement with the European Union. In the 50th Munich Security Conference (January 31 to February 2, 2014), Secretary of State John Kerry said that the objective of the demonstrations against President Yanukovych in Kiev was to implement democracy. What democracy? Yanukovych had been democratically elected in 2010, including by more than 90% of the voters of the Donbass. And the nationalism the West (the United States

---

[8]"Aufgrund dieser verschiedenen Beispiele kann der Schluss gezogen werden, dass die amerikanische Politik des Regime-Change nirgends zur Demokratie geführt hat. Im Gegenteil—beinahe in allen diesen Staaten herrschen heute Bürgerkriege und Chaos. Die USA hätten sinnvoller das dafür verwendete Geld zur Lösung ihrer eigenen Probleme eingesetzt und damit ihre beinahe nicht mehr funktionierende Infrastruktur, ihr schlechtes Bildungs-und Gesundheitswesen und ihr darniederliegendes Rentenwesen saniert"; *Ibidem.*

[9]"Regime Change in Kiev—Victoria Nuland Admits: 'US Has Invested $5 Billion In The Development of Ukrainian, 'Democratic Institution'." Victoria Nuland—Assistant Secretary of State for Europe and Eurasian Affairs—International Business Conference at Ukraine in Washington—National Press Club—December 13, 2013, Full Speech—Video in: *Information Clearing House.* Available at: <http://www.informationclearinghouse.info/article37599.htm>; Peter Scholl-Latour, *Die Flucht der bösen Tat. Das Scheitern des Westens im Orient.* Berlin: Propyläen, 2014, pp. 16–17; Finian Cunningham, "Washington's Cloned Female Warmongers." *Information Clearing House.* Available at: <http://www.informationclearinghouse.info/article37599.htm>.

and its vassals of the European Union) had inflated in Ukraine was actually the resurgence of Nazism. The crowds of the "Euromaidan" in Kiev shouting in favor of the association agreement with the European Union did not represent the entire Ukraine. The movement was supported by no more that 2 million Ukrainians,[10] while the rebelling provinces of Donetsk and Luhansk were inhabited by more than 7 million people (4.5 million in Donetsk alone) and accounted for about 20–30% of Ukraine's GDP.[11]

19.3   The Uprising in the Industrial Center, South, Southeast, and East of Ukraine: The Popular Republics of Novorossiya

Washington's regime change policy had failed again. The attempt to reproduce the Orange Revolution of 2004–2005, which then started to sour relations between the United States and Russia,[12] turned Ukraine into an economically and politically bankrupt state. It was ruled by Prime Minister Arseniy Yatsenyuk of the Fatherland party (Batkivshchyna) and Oleksandr Turchynov,[13] elected president of the Verkhovna Rada and interim president of Ukraine, with the participation of the neo-Nazis of Svoboda and the support of the paramilitary militias of the Ukrainian National Assembly—Ukrainian People's Self-Defence and the Right Sector (*Pravyi sektor*). But the people of the east, southeast, and south of the country, the industrial heart of Ukraine, didn't recognize the legitimacy of the junta headed by Arseniy Yatsenyuk and revolted against the putsch perpetrated in Kiev. The insurrection soon spread to other provinces of Novorossiya, in the Donbass, especially Donetsk, Kharkov (Kharkiv), and Luhansk, where the population rose up in Slavyansk, Mariupol, Yenakiyevo, Kramatorsk, Zaporizhzhya, Makiyivka, and other cities, around 32 of them. They demanded referendums on the autonomy status of the

---

[10]John Haines, "Ukraine—Still Here After Autumn?" *The Foreign Policy Research Institute* (FPRI), May 2014. Available at: <http://www.fpri.org/articles/2014/05/ukraine-still-here-after-autumn>.

[11]Jeanette Seiffert, "The significance of the Donbas. The Donbas is Ukraine's industrial heartland. But its coal-based economy is a heavily-subsidized millstone for Ukraine, not a powerhouse, no matter how important its arms exports might be to the Russian military." *Deutsche Welle (DW)*, April 15, 2014. Available at: <http://www.dw.com/en/the-significance-of-the-donbas/a-17567049>; Acessado em 1° de agosto de 2014; "Ukraine's war-torn east home to third of country's GDP—minister." *TASS*, March 31, 2015. Available at: <http://www.rt.com/business/245597-ukraine-donbass-third-of-gdp/>; RAY, Lada. "7 Million People, 30% of GDP Say Goodbye to Ukraine: Donetsk and Lugansk Vote to Secede," May 11, 2014. *Futurist TrendCast*. Available at: <https://futuristrendcast.wordpress.com/2014/05/11/live-voting-now-donetsk-peoples-republic-independence-referendum/>. Accessed on August 1, 2015.

[12]Lincoln A. Mitchell, 2012, pp. 86, 92–99.

[13]Olexandr Turchynov was Yulia Tymoshenko's right-hand man.

region, the federalization of Ukraine, greater integration with Russia and the resignation of the authorities in Kiev, the same demands put forth in the general strike of 1993 by the workers of 250 mining regions and over 400 companies.[14]

The provinces of Donetsk and Luhansk, home to steel mills and an estimated 10 billion ton in coal reserves, were widely populated by miners and Cossacks and strongly inclined toward the Russian Federation, sharing not only ethnic ties but economic interests: Russia was their biggest trade partner, far ahead of all the others, absorbing 25% and 27% of their exports in 2012 and 2013, respectively and providing 32% of their imports, especially gas.[15] The defense and space industries of the Donbass, in Dnipropetrovsk, Belmar, and other cities, depended on the demand from Russia's armed forces, for which its systems and equipment—12 kinds of ballistic missiles, tanks, combat helicopters, and other war material—had been specifically designed.[16] The uprising of the population in this region, representing approximately one-third of Ukraine's economy, brought the country to the brink of a complete collapse in the money markets and threatened the political survival of the junta in Kiev. It would not be easy to find other countries to sell Ukraine's weapon production, manufactured in accordance with Russian standards.

Indeed, the conflict meant the secession from Ukraine. The insurgents occupied the headquarters of the Security Service and the National Guard barracks, where they took control of war material and convened a meeting of the Regional Council of the Donbass, held on April 7, 2014. This council voted unanimously on the formal declaration of independence as the People's Republic of Donetsk (*Donetskaya Narodnaya Respublika*) and asked Russia for support.[17] The same took place days later in the province of Luhansk, which was established as the People's Republic of Luhansk (*Luganskaya Narodnaya Respublika*). The independence of the republics of Luhansk and Donetsk was approved through referenda held on May 11, 2014.

---

[14]Yuri M. Zhukov, "Rust Belt Rising. The Economics behind Eastern Ukraine's Upheaval." *Foreign Affairs*—Council of Foreign Relations, June 11, 2014. Available at: <http://www.foreignaffairs.com/articles/141561/yuri-m-zhukov/rust-belt-rising>.

[15]*Bloomberg Visual Data*. Available at: <http://www.bloomberg.com/visual-data/best-and-worst/ukraines-biggest-trading-partners-countries>; *Ukraine: Economy- Infoplease.com*. Available at: <http://www.infoplease.com/encyclopedia/world/ukraine-economy.html#ixzz387gacUF3>; *CIA—The World Fact Book*—Fact. Available at: <https://www.cia.gov/library/publications/the-world-factbook/geos/up.html>.

[16]Jeanette Seiffert, "The significance of the Donbas. The Donbas is Ukraine's industrial heartland. But its coal-based economy is a heavily-subsidized millstone for Ukraine, not a powerhouse, no matter how important its arms exports might be to the Russian military." *Deutsche Welle (DW)*, April 15, 2014. Available at: <http://www.dw.com/en/the-significance-of-the-donbas/a-17567049>. Accessed on August 1, 2014.

[17]"RT—Donetsk activists proclaim region's independence from Ukraine." *RT*, April 7, 2014. Available at: <http://on.rt.com/peotvghttp://www.rt.com/news/donetsk-republic-protestukraine-841/>.

89.07% and 96.2% voted for the self-determination and independence of Donetsk and Luhansk, respectively.[18]

When Denis Pushilin assumed the presidency of the Council and proclaimed the People's Republic of Donetsk, "following the expression of the will of the people" and "in order to restore historical justice," he requested the integration in the Russian Federation. Valery Bolotova proceeded similarly when he proclaimed the People's Republic of Luhansk as a sovereign state in a big rally, declaring that "in accordance with international law, its territory and its borders are indivisible and inviolable."[19] The goal was to form the Federal State of Novorossiya (*Federativnoye Gosudarstvo Novorossiya*) or the Union of Republics of Novorossiya (*Soyuz Narodnykh Respublik*) in the Donbass, which would include Kharkov, Dnepropetrovsk, Zaporizhia, Kherson, Mykolaiv, and Odessa. There was certain nostalgia of the Soviet Union.

19.4   Beginning of the Civil War and Russia's Assistance to the Rebels

The events in the Donbass didn't surprise Moscow. They had been predicted since 2008, when Minister Sergei Lavrov warned Washington of the consequences of expanding NATO's military machine to Ukraine. And the rebels, labeled as separatists, could no doubt count on the assistance of officers from the Federal Security Service (*Federal'naya sluzhba bezopasnosti Rossiyskoy Federatsii—* FSB), the special forces (*spetsnaz*) of the Military Intelligence Service (*Glavnoye razvedyvatel'noye upravleniye—*GRU), airborne troops (*Vozdushno-desantnye voyska—*VDV), and the naval infantry (*Морская пехота, Morskaya Pekhota—* VDV '90), who were training and providing weapons and equipment to the self-defense militias organized by the rebels and joined by dozens of Russians.[20] Armed conflict was inevitable. The porosity of the border permitted such support and Russia focused 12,000–20,000 soldiers on Ukraine's borders. As far we know, however, President Putin was not planning to intervene. And he didn't officially recognize the

---

[18]Ben Piven & Ben Willers, "Infographic: Ukraine's 2014 presidential election." *Al Jazeera*, May 23, 2014. Available at: <http://america.aljazeera.com/multimedia/2014/5/ukraine-presidenti alelectioninfographic.html>. Accessed on August 5, 2014.

[19]"Protesters Declare Independent People's Republic in Ukraine's Luhansk," *Sputnik* (RIA Novosti), April 28, 2014. Available at: <http://sputniknews.com/world/20140428/189420422. html#ixzz3h677L7fE>.

[20]Igor Sutyagin, "Russian Forces in Ukraine." *Briefing Paper—Royal United Services Institute for Defence and Security Studies*. March 2015. Available at: <https://www.rusi.org/downloads/assets/ 201503_BP_Russian_Forces_in_Ukraine_FINAL.pdf –>; Sean Crowley, "(Not) Behind Enemy Lines I: Recruiting for Russia's War in Ukraine." *LEKSIKA*, June 25, 2015. Available at: <http:// www.leksika.org/tacticalanalysis/2015/6/24/not-behind-enemy-lines-i-recruiting-for-russias-war-in-ukraine>.

republics of Donetsk and Luhansk so as not to deepen the contradiction with the European Union, especially with Germany, one of Washington's apparent objectives. Putin acted firmly but with caution, without aggression. He did not cut off gas exports to the European Union or Ukraine, despite the failure of the Kiev junta to pay the US$2.2 billion owed to Gazprom on time,[21] in order to preserve this special source of foreign currency. He didn't shut down the space for negotiations, but neither did he abandon the insurgents against the repression in Kiev. Putin always defended the federalization and the autonomy of the provinces of the Donbass, both in principle and as a fundamental condition for the solution of the crisis.

19.5 NATO Mobilization, IMF Funding, and Mercenaries of American Military Companies Mixed with Kiev Troops

The junta headed by Arseniy Yatsenyuk and Oleksandr Turchynov called the rebels "terrorists," Washington's preferred label, and launched the military operation to crush the uprising. The troops of the Ukrainian Army—the National Guard—including the paramilitary militias of the Right Sector under the command of the neo-Nazi Dmitry Yarosh,[22] a militant of the paramilitary organization Tryzub, which brought together all the Stepan Bandera Ukrainian Organizations (named after the well-known Nazi collaborator), were sent to the provinces of the Donbass. They were joined by members of the Security Service of Ukraine (Sluzhba Bezpeky Ukrayiny—SBU), foreign mercenaries (Poles, Croatians, Georgians, Chechen Islamists, and several other nationalities[23]), and 300 mercenaries from western Ukraine returning from Syria, where they had fought against the Bashar al-Assad regime.[24] According to the *Bild am Sonntag*, one of the largest-circulation newspapers in Germany, around 400 mercenaries of the military company Academi (formerly Blackwater) and Greystones were active in Ukraine as elite troops, and

---

[21]"Ukraine misses Gazprom's deadline to pay gas debt." *BBC News*, April 8, 2014. Available at: <http://www.bbc.com/news/business-26930998>.

[22]Ralf Schulten, "Experte warnt vor Folgen einer Aufrüstung der UA!". *Focus Online*, April 6, 2015. Available at: <http://www.focus.de/politik/ausland/ukraine-krise/experte-warnt-vor-folgen-einer-aufruestung-der-ua-ukraine-krise-kommentar_id_6343836.html>.

[23]Jacques Frère, "Ukraine/Donbass: Debaltsevo est libérée!" *NationsPresse*, February 17, 2015. Available at: <www.nationspresse.info/.../ukraine-donbass-debaltsevo>; DanleMiel Guimond, "UKRAINE—Crimes de guerre de l'OTAN à Debaltsevo? Joe Biden redessine la carte de Lvov à Kahrkiv." ESC_Niouze, February 9, 2015. Available at: <https://entretiensentresoi.wordpress.com/2015/02/09/ukraine-que-peut-bien-cacher-lotan-a-debaltsevo/>.

[24]"About 300 Ukrainian mercenaries from Syria fighting in south-eastern Ukraine—source—Most of the mercenaries are from western regions of Ukraine, a source in the General Staff of the Russian Armed Forces says." *TASS*, May 29, 2014. Available at: <http://tass.ru/en/world/733865>.

although it was unclear who hired them,[25] it was later revealed that they were recruited with funding from NATO and several Ukrainian oligarchs, including Interim President Oleksandr Turchynov, former President Viktor Yanukovych, Rinat Akhmetov, and the powerful Jewish multi-billionaire Ihor Kolomojski, governor of the province of Dnepropetrovsk, home of Ukraine's aerospace industry, and the companies Aerosvit Airlines, Dniproavia, and Donbassaero, which he controlled through PrivatBank.[26] These mercenary troops participated in the campaigns against the pro-federalization rebels in the surroundings of Slowjansk, Mariupol, and other small towns in eastern Ukraine.[27] On March 10, the website *Infowars.com* already reported the presence of mercenaries from American military corporations in Donetsk and other industrial towns on the banks of the river Kalmius.[28] Academi and Greystone,[29] which allegedly recruited between 100 and 150 American mercenaries, denied the news and information from Moscow. The German intelligence

---

[25]"Einsatz gegen Separatisten: Ukrainische Armee bekommt offenbar Unterstützung von US-Söldnern." *Spiegel Online*, May 11, 2014. Available at: <http://www.spiegel.de/politik/ausland/ukraine-krise-400-us-soeldner-von-academi-kaempfen-gegen-separatisten-a-968745. html>; "Laut Zeitungsbericht: amerikanische Söldner sollen in Ostukraine kämpfen." *Frankfurter Allgemeine Zeitung*, May 11, 2014. Available at: <http://www.faz.net/aktuell/politik/ausland/laut-zeitungsbericht-amerikanische-soeldner-sollen-in-ostukraine-kaempfen-12933968.html>; "Blackwater lässt grüßen. Kämpfen US-Söldner in der Ukraine?," *N—TV*, Sonntag, May 11, 2014. Available at: <http://www.n-tv.de/politik/Kaempfen-US-Soeldner-in-der-Ukraine-article12808976. html>; "EIL—Kiew entsendet Blackwater-Söldner zur Unterdrückung der Proteste im Osten der Ukraine." *Sputnik* (RiaNovosti), April 7, 2014. Available at: <http://de.sputniknews.com/politik/20140407/268223480.html>.

[26]Konrad Schuller (Warschau), "Ukraine Der gestürzte Oligarch und der Rechte Sektor." *Franfurter Allgemeine Zeitung*, March 26, 2015. Available at: <http://www.faz.net/aktuell/politik/ausland/europa/ihor-kolomojskijs-entmachtung-inszenierte-abschiedszeremonie-13505871. html>.

[27]"Einsatz gegen Separatisten: Ukrainische Armee bekommt offenbar Unterstützung von US-Söldnern." *Spiegel Online* Sonntag, May 11, 2014. Available at: <http://www.spiegel.de/politik/ausland/ukraine-krise-400-us-soeldner-von-academi-kaempfen-gegen-separatisten-a-968745.html>; "Laut Zeitungsbericht: Amerikanische Söldner sollen in Ostukraine kämpfen." *Frankfurter Allgemeine Zeitung*, May 11, 2014. Available at: <http://www.faz.net/aktuell/politik/ausland/laut-zeitungsbericht-amerikanische-soeldner-sollen-in-ostukraine-kaempfen-12933968. html>; Sam Sokol, "Diaspora. Election results buoy Ukrainian Jews." *Jerusalem Post*, October 27, 2014. Available at: <http://www.jpost.com/Diaspora/Election-results-buoy-Ukrainian-Jews-379969>; "Ukraine-Krise NATO sichert Ukraine Hilfe gegen Russland zu—Das westliche Militärbündnis will die Regierung in Kiew im Konflikt mit Russland unterstützen. NATO-Generalsekretär Rasmussen hat Berater und andere Mittel zugesichert." *Die Zeit Online* (Ausland), August 7, 2014.

[28]Kurt Nimmo, "Russia Says U.S. Mercenaries in Eastern Ukraine—Coup government in Kyiv moves to quell separatism as civil war brews." *Infowars.com*, March 10, 2014. Available at: <http://www.infowars.com/russia-claims-greystone-mercenaries-team-up-with-right-sector-in-eastern-ukraine/>.

[29]Kirit Radia & James Gordon Meek & Lee Ferran & Ali Weinberg, "US Contractor Greystone Denies Its 'Mercenaries' in Ukraine." *ABC News*, April 8, 2014. Available at: <http://abcnews.go.com/Blotter/greystone-firm-accused-disguising-mercenaries-ukrainians/story?id=23243761>.

service BND (*Bundesnachrichtendienst*), however, apparently confirmed this fact—the participation of mercenaries in the Kiev troops—to the federal government in Berlin on April 29, 2014.

NATO Secretary General Anders Fogh Rasmussen publicly reiterated the full support to the government in Kiev.[30] As a show of strength and to justify the Alliance's survival, NATO sent more than 4000 soldiers from 13 nations, including from such nonmembers as Georgia and Lithuania, and tons of training equipment to the Joint Multinational Training Centers of the US Army Garrison Bavaria in Grafenwöhr, Germany, and carried out the Combined Resolve II exercises.[31] The Pentagon no doubt wished President Putin would order a military intervention in favor of the Novorossiya republics—Donetsk and Luhansk. It would justify Europe's submission to its strategic objectives and maintain the discord with Russia. But NATO was unlikely to embark in a direct military confrontation with Russia to defend the forces of Kiev. The conflict in the Donbass was clearly a proxy war between the United States and Russia.

The backing of the Kiev junta by the United States and the European Union was not limited to NATO's show of strength and the hiring of mercenaries from such military companies as Academi. Despite the depleted monetary reserves and full-blown civil war in the virtually bankrupt Ukraine, the International Monetary Fund (IMF) disregarded its own risk standards and granted a stand-by credit line of US $17.01 billion (SDR 10.976 billion[32]), of which the junta in Kiev could dispense SDR 2.058 billion immediately (approximately US$3.19 billion) after the commitment to carry out "structural adjustment" programs that would ensure the macro-economic and financial stability of the country.[33] As IMF President Christine Lagarde herself acknowledged, the deep vulnerabilities of Ukraine and the political shocks would produce the gravest of crises in Ukraine, which already found itself in a recession with a terrible fiscal balance and a financial sector under significant stress. She knew the US$17.01 billion credit would not be enough and had been extended, predicting that Ukraine would sink in a protracted recession and that the tensions in the east of the country would escalate.[34] But the reforms required by the

---

[30]"Ukraine-Krise NATO sichert Ukraine Hilfe gegen Russland zu—Das westliche Militärbündnis will die Regierung in Kiew im Konflikt mit Russland unterstützen. NATO-Generalsekretär Rasmussen hat Berater und andere Mittel zugesichert." *Die Zeit Online* (Ausland), August 7, 2014.

[31]Matthew Schofield (McClatchy Foreign Staff), "Rumors of American mercenaries in Ukraine spread to Germany—NATO flexes muscles as Combined Resolve II unfolds in Hohenfels." *Stars and Stripes*, May 12, 2014. Available at: <http://www.stripes.com/news/europe/nato-flexes-muscles-as-combined-resolve-ii-unfolds-in-hohenfels-1.282650>.

[32]SDR is the "currency" of the IMF.

[33]Interview With Reza Moghadam—Ukraine Unveils Reform Program with IMF Support. *IMF Survey*, April 30, 2014. Available at: <http://www.imf.org/external/pubs/ft/survey/so/2014/new043014a.htm>.

[34]Angela Monaghan, "Ukraine bailout of $17bn approved by IMF who warns reforms are at risk. Kiev agrees to a sweeping economic programme but may need to extend bailout if the unrest in east of country escalates." *The Guardian*, May 1, 2014.

IMF consisted in a series of austerity measures, starting with tax hikes, privatizations, pension freezes and also the increase of the natural gas price, among other neo-liberal measures that further impoverished the population.

19.6   Petro Poroshenko Elected President of Ukraine

Ukraine's presidential election, convened since the government of Viktor Yanukovych for February 26, 2015, occurred earlier on May 25, 2014, funded by Washington with US$11.4 million.[35] The billionaire oligarch Petro Poroshenko, supported by the Popular Front block, won with 54.7% of the votes against a pack of 21 candidates led by Yulia Tymoshenko of the Fatherland party, who obtained no more than 12.81% of the vote. The election was practically limited to the oblasts of the west and the center of Ukraine. Virtually no votes were cast in the rebelling regions of the south, southeast, and east, especially Donetsk and Luhansk.[36] The Popular Front Block won 214 seats and controlled the absolute majority (248 seats) of the Verkhovna Rada through a coalition with another party, Samopomich (Self-Reliance). Poroshenko then allied himself with Yulia Timoshenko's Fatherland. Arseniy Yatsenyuk was confirmed as prime minister and led the government under the guidance of American Ambassador Geoffrey Pyatt and Assistant Secretary of State Victoria Nuland.

Petro Poroshenko owned five TV stations, two shipyards (one of which the Sevastopol Marine Plant [Sevmorzavod] on the shores of the Sea of Azov-Black Sea, southwest of Crimea),[37] an international investment bank, the agrarian conglomerate Ukrprominvest and Roshen Confectionery Corp., 1 of the 20 largest chocolate industries in the world with 19 factories that served mainly the Russian market (7% of its sales) and had a net profit of US$1.021 billion in 2013. It suffered huge losses with the embargo on imports from Ukraine decreed by President Vladimir Putin. Its production, amounting to 400,000 tons in 2012, fell 25% in the two following years, and the assets of the plant in Lipetsk, southwest of Moscow—the Likonf Confectionery Factory (Likonf OAO)—were judicially dispossessed for

---

[35] Ben Piven & Ben Willers, "Infographic: Ukraine's 2014 presidential election." *Al Jazeera*, May 23, 2014. Available at: <http://america.aljazeera.com/multimedia/2014/5/ukraine-presidenti alelectioninfographic.html>. Accessed on August 5, 2015.

[36] Sergiy Kudelia, "Ukraine's 2014 presidential election result is unlikely to be repeated." *The Washington Post*, June 2, 2014; Shaun Walker (Donetsk) & Alec Luhn (Kiev), "Petro Poroshenko wins Ukraine presidency, according to exit polls—'Chocolate king' expected to secure 56% of vote and vows to restore peace following election billed as most important since independence." *The Guardian*, May 25, 2014.

[37] This shipyard was 1 of 12 private companies nationalized by the government of the city of Sevastopol in 2014.

US$40 million under the accusation of massive tax fraud.[38] President Petro Poroshenko lost 30% of his fortune, which according to Forbes amounted to somewhere between US$1.3 billion and US$1.60 billion in 2013,[39] and fell to around US$720 million in 2014, according to the Bloomberg Billionaires Index.[40]

President Poroshenko was not the only one to lose much of his fortune. All other oligarchs in Ukraine suffered immeasurable losses. As a result of the closing off of the Russian market for Ukrainian exports and the civil war in the region of Novorossiya, the value of their assets dropped by approximately 54% from US$29 billion in 2012 to US$13.5 billion in the first half of 2015. Rinat Akhmetov, one of the financiers of the mercenaries fighting the rebels, lost more than half his wealth, concentrated in the production of coal and iron in Donetsk and Luhansk, and he continued to hemorrhage money with the blows resulting from the civil war and the destruction of Ukraine's economy.[41]

---

[38]Kateryna Choursina & Alexander Sazonov, "Russia Seizes Candy Factory Owned by Ukraine Leader Poroshenko." *Bloomberg*, April 29, 2015. Available at: <http://www.bloomberg.com/news/articles/2015-04-29/russia-seizes-candy-factory-owed-by-ukraine-president-poroshenko>; "Media: Poroshenko sold ROSHEN to Yanukovy—Poroshenko's chocolate empire Poroshenko sells his chocolate empire to Yanukovych—via the Rothschilds." *Seemorerocks*, September 2, 2014. Available at: <http://robinwestenra.blogspot.de/2014/09/poroshenkos-chocolate-empire.html>.

[39]Tatyana Zenkovich Pa, "Poroshenko's fortune estimated at $750 million—Forbes.-Ukraine—Ukrainian president ranks eighth in the ranking, which is topped by Rinat Akhmetov ($6.9 billion), Viktor Pinchuk ($1.5 billion) and ex-Dnipropetrovsk region governor Igor Kolomoysky ($1.4 billion)." *TASS*, March 27, 2015. Available at: <http://tass.ru/en/world/785423>.

[40]Kateryna Choursina & Volodymyr Verbyany & Alexander Sazono, *Billionaire No More: Ukraine President's Fortune Fades With War.* Bloomberg, May 8, 2015; Anders Aslund, "How oligarchs are losing out." *KyivPost*, May 29, 2015. Available at: <http://www.kyivpost.com/opinion/op-ed/how-oligarchs-are-losing%2D%2Dout-390953.html>; See also: http://www.bloomberg.com/news/articles/2015-05%2D%2D08/billionaire-no-more-ukraine-president-s-for tune-fades-with-war; Iryna Yakovenko & Oleksandra Poloskova & Yevhen Solonina & Daisy Sindelar, "A Sticky Situation for Poroshenko As Russians Seize Candy Assets." *Radio Free Europe—Radio Liberty*, April 29, 2015. Available at: <http://www.rferl.org/content/ukraine-poroshenko-roshen-russia-seizes-candy-lipetsk/26985196.html>.

[41]"Forbes Billionaires 2015: Which Billionaires Lost The Most Money—Rinat Akhmetov on Forbes Lists." Available at: <http://www.forbes.com/profile/rinat-akhmetov/>; Anders Aslund, "How oligarchs are losing out." *KyivPost*, May 29, 2015. Available at: <http://www.kyivpost.com/opinion/op-ed/how-oligarchs-are-losing-out-390953.html>.

Chapter 20
Ukrainian Separatists and the War in Donbass

20.1 Petro Poroshenko's Government and Ukraine's National Guard Dominated by Neo-Nazis

Petro Poroshenko took over the government on June 7, 2014. This, in a way, legitimized the junta, i.e., the neo-Nazi dictatorship established in Kiev, since even President Putin declared he would recognize him as president of Ukraine and respect the outcome of the election, monitored by the Organization for Security and Cooperation in Europe (OSCE).[1] Poroshenko was committed to start a dialog with President Putin and negotiate a new treaty to replace the Budapest Memorandum[2] signed in December 1994. In this treaty, Russia, the United Kingdom, and the United States pledged not to threaten the use of force against Ukraine's territorial integrity or political independence or to use economic coercion to subordinate this nonnuclear power to their interests.[3] The peace plan Poroshenko presented included five points for negotiation. It provided for the end of special operations in the Donbass, amnesty to all those who laid down their weapons and hadn't committed serious crimes, the

---

[1]"Russia will recognise outcome of Ukraine poll, says Vladimir Putin—Putin says Russia will 'respect the choice of Ukrainian people', but separatist authorities vow to disrupt weekend's presidential election." Shaun Walker (Donetsk), *The Guardian*, May 23, 2014; Michael Birnbaum and Fredrik Kunkle and Abigail Hauslohner, "Vladimir Putin says Russia will respect result of Ukraine's presidential election." *The Washington Post*, May 23, 2014.

[2]Shaun Walker (Donetsk) and Alec Luhn (Kiev), "Petro Poroshenko wins Ukraine presidency, according to exit polls—'Chocolate king' expected to secure 56% of vote and vows to restore peace following election billed as most important since independence." *The Guardian*, May 25, 2014. Michael Birnbaum et al., "Vladimir Putin says Russia will respect result of Ukraine's presidential election." *The Washington Post*, May 23, 2014.

[3]"Budapest Memorandums on Security Assurances, 1994," in *Council of the Foreign Relations*, December 5, 1994. Available at <http://www.cfr.org/nonproliferation-arms-control-and-disarma ment/budapest-memorandums-security%2D%2Dassurances-1994/p32484>.

© Springer Nature Switzerland AG 2019
L. A. Moniz Bandeira, *The World Disorder*,
https://doi.org/10.1007/978-3-030-03204-3_20

release of prisoners, and moving toward government decentralization, protection of the Russian language, and reform of the constitution.

President Poroshenko was not fully in control of the National Guard, however. From the beginning of the insurrection, the Kiev junta had lost control of Eastern Ukraine. Thousands of National Guard soldiers (more than 17,000) and part of the police forces, demoralized by lack of training and faced with the inhabitants' anger, had defected to the rebels with all their weapons and other military equipment. Such defections continued.[4] Even in August 2014, approximately 311 soldiers and border guards ran toward Russia under an intense barrage of fire at the Gukovo checkpoint.[5] The many defections didn't inspire a lot of confidence in those regular troops, which is possibly why Viktor Muzhenko, head of the Ukrainian Armed Forces, made a deal with Dmytro Yarosh, the leader of the Right Sector, incorporating the battalions of neo-Nazi volunteers, ideologically motivated to fight the rebels of the Donbass, into the National Guard. These battalions would keep an independent status although they had to obey the orders of the chiefs of staff of the armed forces in the war against the "external enemy," meaning the insurgents of the Donbass.[6] And even though the oligarch Ihor Kolomoyskyi was fired from his post as governor of Dnipropetrovsk by President Poroshenko, he maintained his armed units on the front line.

20.2 Proclamation of the Popular Republics of Donetsk and Luhansk and Putin's Moderate Position

President Putin, in turn, had urged the rebels to abstain from the referendum to declare the independence of the popular republics of Donetsk and Luhansk.[7] He needed room to negotiate the crisis with President Poroshenko within the framework of the federalization and self-determination of the oblasts, without tearing Ukraine

---

[4]Luke Harding (Luhansk), "Ukraine's government has lost control of east, says acting president—Oleksandr Turchynov says security forces are unable to control situation in Donetsk and Luhansk regions." *The Guardian*, April 30, 2014. Available at <http://www.theguardian.com/world/2014/apr/30/ukraine-government-lost-control-east-acting-president—Alec Luhn>; "Ukrainian troops 'demoralised' as civilians face down anti-terror drive. General Vasily Krutov says main force is security service with army as back-up, but analysts criticise lack of plan from Kiev." *The Guardian*, April 16, 2014. Available at <http://www.theguardian.com/world/2014/apr/16/ukrainian-troops-civilians-kiev-anti-terrorist-krutov>.

[5]"Many Ukraine soldiers cross into Russia amid shelling." *BBC News*, August 4, 2014. Available at <http://www.bbc.com/news/world-europe-28637569>.

[6]*German-Foreign-Policy.com*. April 10, 2014. Available at <http://www.german-foreign-policy.com/en/fulltext/58837/print>.

[7]Ian Traynor (Editor) and Shaun Walker (Donetsk) and Harriet Salem (Slavyansk) and Paul Lewis (Washington), "Russian president also calls for halt to Ukrainian military operations against pro-Russia activists in eastern towns." *The Guardian*, May 8, 2014. Available at <http://www.theguardian.com/world/2014/may/07/ukraine-crisis-putin-referendum-autonomy-postponed>.

apart and formally maintaining its territorial integrity. His calls went unanswered. Putin had no control and could not contain the insurgency with deep roots in the population of the Donbass, incensed by the regime in Kiev, where the Verkhovna Rada had banned Russian as a second official language in Odessa (94% Russian-speaking), Kharkov (74%), Zaporizhzhya (81%), Dnipropetrovsk (72%), Luhansk (89%), Donetsk (93%), Mykolaiv (66%), and many other regions soon after the coup of February 22.[8] Russian films and television shows were banned in the midst of the campaign by the neo-Nazis and radical nationalists, who officially called for "ethnic purification," set fire to two Russian bookstores in Kiev on April 24 and 25, and intensified the anti-Russian and anti-Semitic rhetoric. Around 90% of the combatants of the popular republics in Donetsk and Luhansk were locals, therefore. Russian soldiers would only join the fight later, in mid-August 2014,[9] according to the testimony of Igor Vsevolodovich Girkin, also known as Igor Strelkov,[10] a retired colonel from the Federal Security Service (FSB) and one of the main leaders of the uprising in the Donbass.[11] The Russians participating in the fighting in Donbass (estimated between 3500 and 6000–6500)[12] possibly came from the Spetsnaz brigades, special forces of the GRU (*Glavnoje Razvedyvatel'noje Upravlenije*), retired so as not to compromise Russia. Igor Girkin also said that the rebels were very disappointed by the lack of further assistance from Moscow, which refused to expand the supply of heavy weaponry—mortars, cannons, machine guns, missiles, etc.—and always recommended talks with Kiev when the integration into the Russian Federation was brought up.[13] The United States and the subservient European Union, however, insisted on accusing Moscow of fostering the breakup of Ukraine and imposed new sanctions against Russian citizens, politicians, business people, and companies.

---

[8]Stanislav Byshok and Alexey Kochetkov, *Neonazis and Euromaidan—From democracy to dictatorship*. (North Charleston United States): CreateSpace Independent Publishing Platform (www.kmbook.ru), 2nd ed., 2014, p. 74.

[9]Igor Sutyagin, "Russian Forces in Ukraine." *Royal United Service Institute for Defence and Security Studies*, March 3, 2015. Available at <https://www.rusi.org/downloads/assets/201503_BP_Russian_Forces_in_Ukraine_FINAL.pdf>. Accessed on August 12, 2014.

[10]Florian Hassel (Donezk), "Igor Strelkow, Kommandeur in der Ostukraine, der Mann hinter der Schreckensherrschaft." *Süddeutsche Zeitung*, May 12, 2014. Available at <http://www.sueddeutsche.de/politik/igor-strelkow-kommandeur-in-der-ostukraine-der-mann-hinter-der-schreckensherrschaft-1.1958675>. Accessed on February 14, 2016; Igor Vsevolodovich Girkin was a Russian national and worked from 1976 to 2013 for the FSB, the internal anti-terrorism department. He fought in Chechnya, Transnistria, and Serbia.

[11]Anna Dolgov, "Russia's Igor Strelkov: I Am Responsible for War in Eastern Ukraine." *The Moscow Times*, November 21, 2014. Available at <http://www.themoscowtimes.com/news/article/russias-igor-strelkov-i-am-responsible-for-war-in-eastern-ukraine/511584.html>.

[12]Igor Sutyagin, "Russian Forces in Ukraine." *Royal United Service Institute for Defence and Security Studies*, March 3, 2015. Available at <https://www.rusi.org/downloads/assets/201503_BP_Russian_Forces_in_Ukraine_FINAL.pdf>. Accessed on August 12, 2014.

[13]*Ibidem.*

20.3   Humanitarian Disaster: Massacre of Odessa, Devastation of Luhansk and the Donbass, Flow of Refugees, and Blockade of the Cities of the Donbass

The violence that erupted during the demonstrations on Maidan Nezalezhnosti didn't die down. Instead, it escalated with the massacres perpetrated by the neo-Nazi paramilitary militias of Svoboda, the Right Sector, and other organizations[14] incorporated into the National Guard with the indiscriminate bombing of insurgent-controlled cities, destroying mainly homes, schools, and hospitals, and the apparent plan to exterminate the Russian-speaking civilian population of the Donbass. On May 2, these militias carrying their Nazi-swastika-like insignia,[15] joined by "autonomous nationalist" groups and football hooligans, under the command of Mykola Volkov, attacked the port city of Odessa on the Black Sea coast, where they exterminated dozens of people—according to conflicting reports, the number could vary between 48 and more than 116 people—using Molotov cocktails and grenades to set fire to the House of Trade Unions, where 39 workers, trade union leaders, and other pro-federalization militants choked, burned, or fell to their deaths by jumping out the windows to escape the flames.[16] Approximately 200 were wounded, according to the numbers made public.[17] The instructions had come from the neo-Nazi leader of the Kiev junta Andriy Parubiy, secretary of the National Security and Defense Council and co-founder of the Social-National Party of

---

[14]Sergey Kirichuck, "Ukraine: far-right extremists at core of 'democracy' protest—As violent scenes play out on the streets of Kiev, we look at the major role extremist right-wing movements have played in Ukraine's 'pro-democracy' movement." *Channel 4 News (Ukraina)*, January 24, 2014. Available at <http://www.channel4.com/news/kiev-svoboda-far-right-protests-right-sec tor-riot-police>; Max Blumenthal, "Is the US backing neo-Nazis in Ukraine?—John McCain and other State Department members have troubling ties to the ultra-nationalist Svoboda party." (VIDEO)—*Salon*, February 25, 2014. Available at <http://www.salon.com/2014/02/25/is_the_ us_backing_neo_nazis_in_ukraine_partner/>.

[15]"Ukraine's 'Romantic' Nazi Storm Troopers." *Consortiumnews.com*, September 15, 2014. Available at <https://consortiumnews.com/2014/09/15/ukraines%2D%2Dromantic-nazi-storm-troopers/>.

[16]Roland Oliphant (Odessa), "Ukraine crisis: death by fire in Odessa as country suffers bloodiest day since the revolution." *The Telegraph*, May 3, 2014. Available at <http://www.telegraph.co.uk/ news/worldnews/europe/ukraine/10806656/Ukraine-crisis-death-by-fire-in-Odessa-as-country-suf fers-bloodiest-day-since-the-revolution.html>; Stanislav Byshok and Alexey Kochetkov, *Neonazis, and Euromaidan—From democracy to dictatorship*. (North Charleston United States): CreateSpace Independent Publishing Platform (www.kmbook.ru), 2a ed., 2014, pp. 129–132. "39 people die after radicals set Trade Unions House on fire in Ukraine's Odessa." "Ukraine clashes: dozens dead after Odessa building fire—Trade union building set alight after day of street battles in Black Sea resort city." *The Guardian*, May 2, 2014. Available at <http://www.theguardian.com/ world/2014/may/02/ukraine-dead-odessa-building-fire>; *RT*, 2 de maio de 2014. Available at <http://www.rt.com/news/156480-odessa-fire-protesters-dead/>. Accessed on August 2, 2014. "Radicals stage disorder at May Odessa massacre trial in southern Ukraine." *TASS*, January 22, 2015. Available at <http://tass.ru/en/world/772769>. Accessed on August 2, 2015.

[17]*Ibidem.*

Ukraine (subsequently renamed Svoboda).[18] And in the offensive to recapture the city of Slavyansk, several other atrocities and war crimes were committed by the Kiev forces. Accusations have been made about the torture and execution of prisoners and the murder of hundreds of civilians through the indiscriminate bombing of homes, schools, hospitals, and other nonmilitary buildings. The artillery of the National Guard launched missiles from old multiple rocket launchers (BM-21—Grad)[19] against the city of Slavyansk. The Aidar battalion, made up of volunteers and paid for by the oligarch Ihor Kolomoyskyi, who supported Nazi forces despite being Jewish, operated alongside the Kiev troops and committed all kinds of crimes, including kidnappings, thefts, bank robberies, extortions, and executions, much like the cruelties practiced by the Islamic State (ISIS/ISIL).[20]

On June 27, President Poroshenko signed a trade agreement with the European Union, and the truce he decreed with the insurgents of the Donbass didn't last more than 10 days. In late June and early July, the troops of the National Guard led by the State Security Service (*Sluzhba Bezpeky Ukrayiny*—SBU) intensified the offensive "anti-terrorist operation" against the oblasts of the southeast and east. The heavy artillery bombardment continued, along with the air strikes by the Su-25 aircraft of the 299th Tactical Aviation Brigade and the MiG-29, Mi-24, and Mi-8 of the 40th Aviation Brigade from Vasilkovo. They deliberately sought out the densely populated areas, civilian targets, killing a growing number and dispersing thousands of inhabitants with the devastation of towns and cities. At the same time, they attacked coal mines and destroyed public utility services—water, electricity, sewage, railroads, and the entire infrastructure of Donetsk and Luhansk, which had been under blockades to force the insurgents to surrender.[21] "The rule of law no longer existed and was replaced by the rule of violence," as declared by the United Nations High Commissioner for Human Rights (UNHCHR). Along with the World Health Organization (WHO), this body estimated that at least 1000 people, including military

---

[18]Stanislav Byshok and Alexey Kochetkov, *Neonazis and Euromaidan—From democracy to dictatorship.* (North Charleston United States): CreateSpace Independent Publishing Platform (www.kmbook.ru), 2ª ed., 2014, pp. 13–132; Michel Chossudovsky, "The U.S. has installed a Neo-Nazi Government in Ukraine." *Global Research*, February 26, 2015. Available at <http://www.globalresearch.ca/the-u-s-has-installed-a-neo-nazi-government-in-kraine/5371554?print=1>.

[19]These rockets dated from the time of the Soviet Union.

[20]"Ukraine must stop ongoing abuses and war crimes by pro-Ukrainian volunteer forces." *Amnesty International*, September 8, 2014. Available at <https://www.amnesty.ie/news/ukraine-must-stop-ongoing-abuses-and-war-crimes-pro%2D%2Dukrainian-volunteer-forces>; Damien Sharkov, "Ukrainian Nationalist Volunteers Committing 'ISIS-Style' War Crimes." *Newsweek*, October 9, 2014. Available at <http://europe.newsweek.com/evidence-war-crimes-committed-ukrainian-nationalist-volunteers-grows-269604>.

[21]"Office of the United Nations High Commissioner for Human Rights Report on the human rights situation in Ukraine." July 15, 2014 Available at <http://www.ohchr.org/Documents/Countries/UA/Ukraine_Report_15July2014.pdf>. Accessed on 8 August 2014; Valeriy Melnikov and Novosti Ria, "Kiev official: Military op death toll is 478 civilians, outnumbers army losses." *RT*, July 10, 2014. Available at <http://www.rt.com/news/171808-eastern-ukraine-civilians-killed/s>.

personnel and civilians, had already perished between mid-April and July 15 in the eastern part of Ukraine.[22]

On June 4, the Kiev security forces supported by the neo-Nazi and ultranationalist militias reconquered several rebelling cities, including Slavyansk, Kramatorsk, Artyomovsk, and Druzhkovka, in addition to the nearby airports of Slavyansk/ Kramatorsk and Donetsk. However, they were unable to break the resistance of the Novorossiya Defense Forces in Donetsk, Luhansk, Gorlovka, Snezhnoye, and other regions. There, the climate of hatred, terror, and intimidation imposed on the populations by the neo-Nazis in Kiev's forces reached such intolerable levels that approximately 110,000 or more people had already fled to Russia by June 2014, while 54,400 dispersed within Ukraine, according to the United Nations High Commissioner for Refugees (UNHCR).[23] And the flow of refugees crossing the border into Russia did not slow down, it increased. Until the beginning of August, approximately 730,000 inhabitants of Eastern Ukraine sought asylum in Russia.[24] But according to the Russian Minister of Foreign Affairs Sergey Lavrov, the number of inhabitants of the Donbass who had crossed the Russian border to flee from civil war had already reached 1 million by June 2014.[25] In any case, the UNHCR confirmed in September that at least 814,000 inhabitants of the Donbass took refuge in Russia, while 260,000 migrated to other regions of Ukraine.

In mid-July, Kiev troops surrounded the territory controlled by the self-defense militias of the popular republics—Donetsk, Luhansk, Gorlovka, and Makeyevka— separating them from the Russian border with a corridor only 8–10 km deep.[26] The blockade was complete, and even banking transactions were paralyzed. The situation of the population in Luhansk, a city with more than 400,000 inhabitants, was becoming increasingly dire. Homes, hospitals, clinics, schools, and other buildings had been destroyed with the indiscriminate bombing by the Kiev forces. There was a shortage of shelter, medicines, essential supplies, and money, since no pensions and salaries were being paid in the midst of massive unemployment. Power was out for over a month, cut off by the Kiev forces. And Luhansk was not the only city to suffer

---

[22]"Office of the United Nations High Commissioner for Human Rights Report on the human rights situation in Ukraine." July 15, 2014 Available at <http://www.ohchr.org/Documents/Countries/ UA/Ukraine_Report_15July2014.pdf>.

[23]"UN refugee agency warns of 'sharp rise' in people fleeing eastern Ukraine." United Nation High Commissioner for Refugees (UNHCR). *UN Centre*, June 27, 2014. Available at <http://www.un. org/apps/news/story.asp?NewsID=48159#.VcYWd_k-7_A>.

[24]"Gefechte im Osten: 730.000 Ukrainer wandern nach Russland aus. Seit Jahresbeginn sind rund 730.000 Menschen aus der Ukraine nach Russland ausgewandert. Das Uno-Flüchtlingswerk hält die Zahlen aus Moskau für glaubwürdig." *Spiegel Online*, August 5, 2014. Available at <http:// www.spiegel.de/politik/ausland/kaempfe-im-osten-730-000-ukrainer-fliehen-nach-russland%2D% 2Da-984567.html>.

[25]Alexei Malgavko, "Lawrow: Eine Million Flüchtlinge aus Ukraine 2014 in Russland eingetroffen." *Sputnik*, June 1, 2014. Available at <http://de.sputniknews.com/panorama/ 20150601/302576655.html>. Accessed on June 7, 2014.

[26]Sergey Averin, "One Year of Civil War in Ukraine: Timeline and Facts." *Sputnik*, March 7, 2015. Available at <http://sputniknews.com/europe/20150407/1020582134.html>.

such degradation. The situation in the other besieged cities also took the tragic contours of a humanitarian catastrophe.[27] More than half of the population fled, mostly to refugee camps in Russia.[28]

Several units of the National Guard confronted fierce resistance and were surrounded by the insurgents, however. Suffering heavy casualties, and without ammunition, food, or water, they began to desert, including 438 Ukrainian soldiers who asked the border patrol of the Russian Federation for asylum on August 3, 2014.[29] Many others subsequently defected under intense artillery fire near the Gukovo checkpoint.[30] The self-defense militias of the popular republics regained some control of parts of the border with Russia.

20.4   The Tragedy of Flight MH17 and More Sanctions Against Russia

While the fighting in the Donbass intensified, a Boeing 777-2H6ER (flight MH17) from Malaysian Airlines flying from Amsterdam to Kuala Lumpur crashed in the Donetsk region on July 17, 2014. All 298 passengers and 15 crew members aboard were killed. Without any evidence, the authorities in Kiev, the governments of the United States and the European Union, and the entire corporate media promptly accused the self-defense militias of the People's Republic of Donetsk and/or Russia of having brought down the airplane with a missile. Until mid-August 2014, the controversies surrounding the responsibility for the tragedy continued. But why would the self-defense militias in Donetsk want to bring down a civilian airplane over its territory? What interest would this serve? No interest, actually. Who would benefit from committing such a crime? Everything indicates that only the government in Kiev would gain from this tragedy, perhaps concocted in collaboration with the CIA. Hypocrisy has always been the essential characteristic of Washington's foreign policy: carrying out black ops and covert operations, illegal, criminals acts, but always in such a way so as to allow for *plausible deniability* and not seriously affect diplomatic relations and the image of the United States as the "indispensable nation." And shooting down civilian aircraft appears on the United States' rap sheet. On July 3, 1988, it brought down the Airbus of Iran Air Flight 655 (IR655) flying

---

[27]Stéphane Dujarric, "Daily Press Briefing by the Office of the Spokesperson for the Secretary-General," April 21, 2015. Available at <http://www.un.org/press/en/2015/db150421.doc.htm>.

[28]Shaun Walker (Luhansk), "Despair in Luhansk as residents count the dead—The worst-hit city in eastern Ukraine is struggling with the aftermath of violence as a semblance of normality return." *The Guardian*, September 11, 2014. Available at <http://www.theguardian.com/world/2014/sep/11/despair-luhansk-residents%2D%2Dcount-dead>.

[29]"The Ukrainian soldiers taking refuge in Russia." *BBC News*, August 5, 2014. Available at <http://www.bbc.com/news/world-europe-28652096>. Accessed on August 6, 2014.

[30]"Many Ukraine soldiers cross into Russia amid shelling." *BBC Europe*, August 4, 2014. Available at <http://www.bbc.com/news/world-europe-28637569>. Accessed on August 6, 2014.

from Bandar Abbas to Dubai with a SM-2MR missile launched from the cruise ship USS Vincennes, killing 290 passengers, including 66 people from six different nations.[31]

Everything points to a false flag operation in the Boeing 777—MH17 disaster, a psychological operations (PSYOP), and psychological warfare (PSYWAR) tool used against the insurgents of Donetsk and Luhansk and Russia. And there is a precedent. In 1962, Gen. Lyman l. Lemnitzer (1899–1988), Chairman of the Joint Chiefs of Staff of the United States' armed forces, delivered a series of suggestions, one more criminal than the other, to President John F. Kennedy in the context of Operation Mongoose. They were meant to serve as pretext for the military intervention in Cuba planned by Task Force W. One proposal included blaming Fidel Castro in case of any failure in the launch of the first manned spacecraft Mercury, carrying the Astronaut John Glenn, by planting evidence of electronic interference. Another suggested shooting down a civilian airplane over Havana, which the CIA would explode over the radio.[32] The hypothesis that something similar happened with flight MH17 cannot be effectively dismissed. Declassified CIA documents under the Freedom of Information Act (FOIA—1946, in force in 1967)[33] widely support the existence of similar proposals and warrant the suspicion that flight MH17 may have been shot down in Ukraine by a missile fired from another plane or by a land-based platform of the Ukrainian military forces to incriminate the militias of Donetsk and Russia.

The former republican senator and former presidential candidate Ron Paul contradicted the version spread by Washington, which blamed the rebels of Donetsk and Russia for the tragedy. In his column "Texas Straight Talk" on the Ron Paul Institute website, he wrote that "just days after the tragic crash of a Malaysian Airlines flight over eastern Ukraine, Western politicians and media joined together to gain the maximum propaganda" against President Putin and the insurgents of

---

[31]"Unfassbare Unglücke. 290 Menschen sterben beim Abschuss eines iranischen Jet." *Focus*, July 18, 2014. Available at <http://www.focus.de/politik/ausland/flugzeugabschuesse-der-historie-nach-mh17-diese-fluege-wurden-ziele-von-flugzeugabschuessen_id_4001088.html>.

[32]"Operation Mongoose Priority Operations Schedule-21 May, 30 June 1962, Washington, May 17, 1962." *Foreign Relations of the United States* (FRUS), vol. X, 1961–1962, Cuba, pp. 810–820; Program Review by the Chief of Operations, Operation Mongoose (Lansdale)—The Cuba Project, Washington, January 18, 1962. *Ibid.* pp., 710–718. See photocopies of the original documents in: Luiz Alberto Moniz Bandeira, 2009, pp. 769–784; "How to Start a War: The Bizarre Tale of Operation Mongoose," report presented in the TV show *Nightline* of the ABC network in the United States, by Aaron Brown, on January 29, 1998. General (r) Alexander Haig, who participated in Operation Mongoose and served as secretary of state in the Reagan Administration, said in that ABC show: "I'm sorry to say. But we were a democracy and I believe that when presidents delude themselves, thinking that they can risk lives and conduct such arrogant operations with no say from the American people, hiding the facts from the population, then this is crazy behavior." Ferreira, Argemiro—"Documentos secretos revelam mais truques sujos planejados nos EUA para derrubar Fidel," in: *Tribuna da Imprensa*, Rio de Janeiro, January 5, 1998.

[33]Declassified at the request of the National Security University, George Washington University, Washington, D.C.

Donetsk, given the impact of the disaster.[34] Ron Paul further stressed that the crisis in Ukraine had started in 2014 when the European Union and the United States supported the protests in the conspiracy for the "overthrow of the elected Ukrainian president, Viktor Yanukovych" and that without "the US-sponsored 'regime change', it is unlikely that hundreds would have been killed in the unrest that followed. Nor would the Malaysian Airlines crash have happened."[35]

According to the research report of an expert group on aviation safety, leaked by the LiveJournal of Albert Naryshkin (aka albert_lex), fight MH17 was hit by a Python air-to-air missile manufactured by Rafael Advanced Defense Systems of Russian origin, fired from a MiG-29 or SU-25 fighter jet and detected gaining height by the Russian military intelligence service at 3–5 km from the Malaysian Air Boeing on the day of the disaster. This fact was revealed by Lieutenant General Andrey Kartapolov, chief of staff of operations of the Russian armed forces (*GRU Generalnovo Shtaba*).[36] And even if researchers from the Netherlands had found fragments of a Russian air-to-ground missile,[37] which they denied,[38] this fact alone would only confirm that it had been fired by one of the two or three Kiev battalions, since they were equipped with Buk-M1 SAM (ground-to-air missiles) in the vicinity of Donetsk.[39]

Yan Novikov, executive director of the Russian state company Almaz-Antey (ОАО Концерн ВКО Алмаз-Антей) producing anti-aircraft systems, stated to the press that his analysts examined the wreck of the missile that brought down flight MH17 and concluded that it had been a BUK 9M38M1 land-air missile armed with a 9H314M warhead, out of production since 1999 and no longer used by the Russian armed forces, which had migrated to the BUK system with 9M317M warheads.[40]

---

[34]Alexandra Le Tellier, "After MH17, questions of trust from Ron Paul and others." *Los Angeles Times*, July 21, 2014. Available at <http://www.latimes.com/opinion/opinion-la/la-ol-malaysia-airlines-flight-17-mh17-ron-paul-mainstream%2D%2Dmedia-20140721-story.html>.   Accessed on August 11, 2015.

[35]*Ibidem.*

[36]"Ukrainian Su-25 fighter detected in close approach to MH17 before crash—Moscow." *RT*, July 21, 2014. Available at <http://www.rt.com/news/174412-malaysia-plane-russia-ukraine/>. Accessed on July 22, 2014.

[37]Jason Hanna and Claudia Rebaza, "MH17 investigators: Possible missile parts found." *CNN*, August 11, 2015. Available at <http://edition.cnn.com/2015/08/11/europe/mh17-investigation/index.html>. Accessed on August 12, 2015; Lizzie Dearden, "MH17 crash: Fragments of Russian missile BUK launcher found at crash site." *The Independent*, August 11, 2015. Available at   <http://www.independent.co.uk/news/world/europe/mh17-crash-investigators-find-parts-of-buk-missile-possibly-used-to-shoot-plane-down-10450053.html>. Accessed on August 12, 2015.

[38]"MH17 investigators to RT: No proof east Ukraine fragments from 'Russian' Buk missile." *RT*, August 11, 2015. Available at <http://www.rt.com/news/>.

[39]"10 more questions Russian military pose to Ukraine." US over MH17 crash. *RT*, July 21, 2014. Available at <http://www.rt.com/news/174496-malaysia-crash-russia-questions/>. Accessed on July 22, 2014.

[40]Gabriela Baczynska (Moscou), "Missile maker says Russia did not shoot down Malaysian plane over Ukraine." *Reuters*, June 2, 2015. Available at <http://www.reuters.com/article/2015/06/02/us-

The holes in the airplane fragments were consistent with the type of missile that hit flight MH17.[41] Novikov concluded that the evidence suggested that the plane had been shot down by a 9M38M1 self-propelled ground-to-air missile from Ukraine, launched from a BUK-M1 (SA-11) system located on Zaroschenskoe, in the Donetsk region.[42] The Russian Union of Engineers, however, examined all the hypotheses, and based on the analysis of the airplane's fuselage, they concluded that the typology and location of holes suggested that an air-to-air missile had most likely been fired, presumably by a Su-25 or MiG-29 jet with a GSh-2-30 or SPPU-22 cannon, hitting the cockpit of the Boeing 777, suddenly depressurizing the plane, destroying its control system, and disabling the automatic pilot, followed by a high-altitude explosion, which is why the wreckage dispersed over 15 km.[43] The self-defense militias of Donetsk had shot down 16 or 17 combat aircraft that attacked them at low altitude, including military transport aircraft. They also brought down six helicopters and destroyed planes in airports. But they lacked both the air force and the artillery capable of reaching a plane flying at an altitude of 10,100 m (approximately 33,000 ft high) at a speed of 905 km/h. They also didn't have a radar to locate it. On July 17, however, the day the Boeing 777 was shot down, the newspaper *Kyiv Post* reported that the National Security and Defense Council of Ukraine (NSDC) had logged the incursion of a Russian military aircraft in its airspace, which fired against an SU-25 jet of the Ukrainian Armed Forces.[44] Interestingly, the Russian military plane missed the target and therefore failed to shoot down the Ukrainian SU-25. On the other hand, according to information from the authorities in Kiev, the Boeing 777 was being escorted by two SU-27 Flankers of the Ukrainian Air Force minutes before being hit. The hypothesis that it was shot down because of a mistake of an operator on the ground in a BUK (SA-11) SAM (ground-to-air missile) TELAR system doesn't seem plausible, however. The

---

ukraine-crisis-mh17-russia-idUSKBN0OI1S620150602>. Accessed on August 14, 2015; "Informational Briefing from the Russian Union of Engineers, 08/15/2014—Analysis of the causes of the crash of Flight MH17 (Malaysian Boeing 777). Ivan A. Andrievskii, First Vice-President of the All-Russian Public Organization Russian Union of Engineers—Chairman of the Board of Directors of the Engineering Company 2K." Available at <http://www.globalresearch.ca/wp-content/uploads/2014/09/MH17_Report_Russian_Union_of_Engineers140818.pdf>.

[41] *Ibidem.*

[42] Nikolai Novichkov (Moscow), "Country Risk—MH17 'shot down by Ukrainian SAM', claims Almaz-Antey." *IHS Jane's Defence Weekly*, June 4, 2015. Available at <http://www.janes.com/article/52019/mh17-shot-down-by-ukrainian-sam-claims-almaz-antey>. Accessed on August 14, 2014.

[43] Informational Briefing from the Russian Union of Engineers, 15/08/2014—Analysis of the causes of the crash of Flight MH17 (Malaysian Boeing 777). Ivan A. Andrievskii, First Vice-President of the All-Russian Public Organization Russian Union of Engineers—Chairman of the Board of Directors of the Engineering Company 2K." Available at <http://www.globalresearch.ca/wp-content/uploads/2014/09/MH17_Report_Russian_Union_of_Engineers140818.pdf>.

[44] "Russian military plane shot down Ukrainian Su-25 aircraft in Ukraine." *Kyiv Post—Interfax-Ukraine*, July 17, 2014. Available at <http://www.kyivpost.com/content/ukraine/russian-military-plane-shot-down-ukrainian-su-25-aircraft%2D%2Din-ukraine-356422.html>.

operator inside the BUK would have seen it was a Boeing 777, and the transponder—the electronic communication device transmitting all data on the plane—would perfectly identify that it was a civil airplane en route from Amsterdam to Kuala Lumpur.[45] In any event, until mid-August 2015, neither the Netherlands nor Belgium and Australia had published the results of their investigations. And the spokesman of Prosecutor General Yuri Boychenko stated that this would only be announced after the consent of all parties.[46]

Without any evidence, proof, or consensus, President Barack Obama—as some kind of supreme judge—and his vassals of the European Union nevertheless promptly enacted extensive sanctions against Russia, including broader restrictions on access to capital markets, defense, dual use goods, and sensitive technologies and bans targeting President Putin's inner circle.[47] As a false flag operation, the goal of bringing down the airplane would certainly have been to intensify the psychological operations (PSYOP), the propaganda through the media, and the economic warfare to destabilize Russia and the Putin government.

When Ukraine separated from the Soviet Union, it had inherited dozens (approximately 40) of fighter jet regiments with Sukhoi SU-25 (Сухой Су-25) and other aircraft, including MiGs, and an enormous arsenal (about 1000) of air-to-air and ground-to-air missiles designed by the Yuzhnoye Design Office, with some parts manufactured in the A. M. Makarov plant in Dnipropetrovsk and others in Russia. Ukraine had a tradition in the space industry, therefore, and its factories were designing and building the Cyclone-4 missile as well as a platform for launch vehicles. This would even involve Brazil in accordance with the terms of the cooperation agreement signed in 2003 for the use of the premises of the Alcântara island base.[48] On July 24, 2015, however, Brazilian President Dilma Rousseff signed Decree No. 8494, withdrawing from the Treaty on Long-Term Cooperation in the use of the launch vehicle Cyclone-4, signed in 2005 with the government of

---

[45]David Cenciotti, "According to an authoritative source, two Su-27 Flankers escorted the Boeing 777 Malaysian minutes before it was hit by one or more missiles." *The Aviationist*, July 21, 2014. Available at <http://theaviationist.com/2014/07/21/su-27s-escorted-mh17/>.

[46]Eric Zuesse, "MH-17 'Investigation': Secret August 8th Agreement Seeps Out—Perpetrator of the downing in Ukraine, of the Malaysian airliner, will stay hidden." *Infowars.Com*, August 25, 2014. Available at <http://www.infowars.com/mh-17-investigation-secret-august-8th-agreement-seeps-out/>.

[47]Julian Borger (Brussels) and Alec Luhn (Moscow) and Richard Norton-Taylor, "EU announces further sanctions on Russia after downing of MH17." *The Guardian*, July 22, 2014. Available at <http://www.theguardian.com/world/2014/jul/22/eu-plans-further-sanctions-russia-putin-mh1>.

[48]"Ukraine: Space Deal With Brazil Uncertain, 2009 December 22, 14:22 (Tuesday) CONFIDENTIAL.BR—Brazil I ECON—Economic Affairs—Economic Conditions, Trends and Potential I ETRD—Economic Affairs—Foreign Trade I TSPA—Technology and Science—Space Activities I UP—Ukraine Office Origin:—N/A or Blank—From: Ukraine Kyiv To: Brazil Brasilia I Department of Commerce I Group Destinations Commonwealth of Independent States I NATO—European Union Cooperative I National Aeronautics and Space Administration. Public Library of U.S. Diplomacy I Secretary of State." Available at <https://wikileaks.org/plusd/cables/09KYIV2182_a.html>.

President Leonid D. Kuchma (1994–2005). This decision was prompted, among other reasons, by the crisis in Ukraine triggered by the putsch of February 22, 2014, since the Alcântara site would also serve to launch the Russian Angara vehicle,[49] designed and manufactured by the Khrunichev Research and Production Space Center in Moscow.[50]

20.5 Humanitarian Aid from Russia

At the same time the Boeing 777 (MH17) was brought down, the suffering with extreme food, clothing, and medicine shortages in Luhansk and Donetsk reached such a point that Moscow decided to send a convoy of 280 trucks with humanitarian aid. In the evening of August 12, however, the convoy was forced to stop in the town of Yelets, approximately 220 miles (354.05 km) from Ukraine's border.[51] Kiev's forces were there to prevent food and medicines from reaching the population. As were the paramilitary battalions—Aidar, Azov[52]—carrying neo-Nazi flags and other similar symbols.[53] Those battalions were legalized after the putsch of February 22, 2014, after the great deterioration of the police forces and the National Guard.[54] Some raised the suspicion that the convoy of 280 trucks was a ploy and that the invasion of Ukraine by Russia was the actual objective. This idea of a Trojan

---

[49]"Russia to create Angara rocket launch pad." *Business Standard*. Moscou, July 28, 2015. Available at <http://www.business-standard.com/article/news-ians/russia-to-create-angara-rocket-launch-pad-115072801010_1.html>.

[50]"Russia to carry out 10 test launches of Angara heavy carrier rocket by 2020." *TASS*, July 28, 2015. Available at <http://tass.ru/en/non-political/811139>.

[51]Alec Luhn (Moscou) and Luke Harding, "Russian aid convoy heads for Ukraine amid doubts over lorries' contents—Kiev says it will turn back shipment which Moscow describes as humanitarian but which west says could be prelude to invasion." *The Guardian*, August 12, 2014; Alec Luhn (Moscou) and Luke Harding, "Ukraine refuses to permit Russian aid convoy to enter country—West fears 280-truck operation is a prelude to invasion while Moscow insists it wants to help residents trapped by conflict." *The Guardian*, August 13, 2014.

[52]The Azov Battalion, consisting of the Neo-Nazis of the Patriots of Ukraine, was under the command of the neo-Nazi Sandriy Biletsky, one of the founders of the Right Sector and leaders of manifestations in Maidan Square, the military arm of the National Assembly of Ukraine, a racist and neo-Nazi organization.

[53]Gabriela Baczynska (Urzuf, Ucrânia), "Ultra-nationalist Ukrainian battalion gears up for more fighting." *Reuters*, May 25, 2015. Available at <http://www.reuters.com/article/2015/03/25/us-ukraine-crisis-azov-idUSKBN0ML0XJ-20150325>; Tom Parfitt (Urzuf, Ukraine), "Ukraine crisis: the neo-Nazi brigade fighting pro-Russian separatists—Kiev throws paramilitaries—some openly neo-Nazi—into the front of the battle with rebels." *The Telegraph*, August 11, 2014. Available at <http://www.telegraph.co.uk/news/worldnews/europe/ukraine/11025137/Ukraine-crisis-the-neo-Nazi-brigade-fighting-pro-Russian-separatists.html>.

[54]"Starvation as warfare: Pro-Kiev forces "block food, medicine, aid from reaching east." *RT*, December 24, 2014. Available at <http://www.rt.com/news/217279-ukraine-aid-battalions-blockade/>.

horse was spread especially by the warmonger Anders Fogh Rasmussen, then NATO's secretary-general. However, under pressure from the International Committee of the Red Cross, which had traveled to Kiev, and from the German and French governments, President Poroshenko authorized the entry of the 280 trucks with 1,856,300 tons of medicines, cereals, sugar, and food stuffs, including milk for children, sleeping bags, winter clothing, and other supplies.[55] It was up to the Red Cross and the OSCE to monitor, support, and supervise the distribution. Since then, Russia has sent several other truck convoys with humanitarian aid to the popular republics of Donetsk and Luhansk.

---

[55]Neil MacFarquhar, "A Russian Convoy Carrying Aid to Ukraine Is Dogged by Suspicion." *The New York Times*, August 12, 2014. "Ukraine officially recognizes Russian aid convoy as humanitarian." *RT*, August 16, 2014. Available at <http://www.rt.com/news/180844-ukraine-recognizes-russia-humanitarian-aid/>. Accessed on August 17, 2014; Alec Luhn (Moscou) and Luke Harding, "Russian aid convoy heads for Ukraine amid doubts over lorries' contents—Kiev says it will turn back shipment which Moscow describes as humanitarian but which west says could be prelude to invasion." *The Guardian*, August 12, 2014.

Chapter 21
The Ukrainian Government, the Rise of the Extreme Right, the Minsk Agreements, and the Persistence of Conflict

21.1 Peace Plan in Ukraine and Cease-Fire Violations

On September 3, 2014, President Putin presented a plan to end the violence and resolve the conflict in the southeast and east of Ukraine. Direct talks would be started between the representative of the government in Kiev (Leonid Kuchma) and the representatives of the popular republics of Novorossiya—Donetsk and Luhansk (Alexander Zakharchenko and Igor Plotnitsky, respectively)—through the Trilateral Contact Group formed in May 2014 after the election of President Poroshenko. The summit took place in Minsk (Belarus) on September 5, 2014, and the Trilateral Contact Group generally accepted the clauses proposed by President Putin. Among other measures, the parties in the adopted protocol would undertake to ensure an immediate bilateral cease-fire monitored and inspected by the OSCE, withdraw mercenaries from the conflict, and remove heavy artillery to a distance of 15 km (9.3 miles) on each side of the front line, creating a buffer zone of 30 km (19 miles). The government in Kiev, in turn, would promote the decentralization of power, including constitutionally by enacting the Law of Ukraine "with respect to the temporary status of local self-government in certain areas of the Donetsk and the Lugansk regions," which meant establishing the right to self-determination.[1]

---

[1] "PROTOCOL on the results of consultations of the Trilateral Contact Group (Minsk, September 5, 2014)—PROTOCOL on the results of consultations of the Trilateral Contact Group with respect to the joint steps aimed at the implementation of the Peace Plan of the President of Ukraine, P. Poroshenko, and the initiatives of the President of Russia, V. Putin—Mission of Ukraine to the European Union—8 September 2014, Ministry of Foreign Affairs of Ukraine." Available at <http://mfa.gov.ua/en/news-feeds/foreign-offices-news/27596-protocolon-the-results-of%2D%2Dconsultations-of-the-trilateral-contact-group-minsk-05092014>; "О временном порядке местного самоуправления в отдельных районах Донецкой и Луганской областей" (Закон об особом статусе). Закон об особом порядке местного самоуправления в отдельных районах Донецкой и Луганской областей (Закон об особом статусе Донбасса), текст проекта № 5081 от 16.09.2014. *Закон и Бизнес*. Available at <http://zib.com.ua/ru/print/100900-zakon_ob_osobom_poryadke_mestnogo_samoupravleniya_v_otdelnih.html>.

© Springer Nature Switzerland AG 2019
L. A. Moniz Bandeira, *The World Disorder*,
https://doi.org/10.1007/978-3-030-03204-3_21

But the start of NATO exercises in Poland and the Baltic countries had raised tensions with the West to Cold War levels, as General Valery Gerasimov, Commander in Chief of the Russian Armed Forces, pointed out.[2] As an integral part of modern conflicts, the mainstream international media, owned by "big businesses, large American consortia," and for commercial reasons forced "to capture the attention of part of its audience,"[3] intensified its disinformation campaign against President Putin, demonizing him as the new Stalin or Hitler. The cease-fire in Ukraine, therefore, lasted no more than 10 days. The remaining provisions of the protocol weren't even met, either because President Poroshenko didn't want to or because he didn't control his Cabinet, led by Prime Minister Arseniy Yatsenyuk, and much less his National Guard, filled almost completely with neo-Nazi fanatics (Azov, Aidar, etc., receiving wages of 6000 hryvnia or US\$316); radicals and criminals; soldiers of fortune from various countries, including contractors (former Navy Seals and other American special forces) recruited by the corporation Academi (formerly Blackwater)[4]; and bandits and fugitives from Russia itself.[5] The Azov Battalion with its inverted symbol of the Wolfsangel of the second SS-Panzer-Division[6] was commanded by the neo-Nazi Andriy Biletsky, carried heavy artillery, and was 1000 men strong, men trained in the village of Urzuf, 40 km southwest of the city of Mariupol, on the shores of the Sea of Azov.[7] On December 5, 2014, one of

---

[2]Michael Birnbaum et al., "Vladimir Putin says Russia will respect result of Ukraine's presidential election." *The Washington Post*, May 23, 2014.

[3]Wesley Clarck, *L'Irak, le terrorisme et l'Empire Américain*. Paris: Éditions du Seuil, 2004, pp. 64, 187–188.

[4]Sergey Dolzhenko Epa, "According to the General Staff, there are also facts of participation of private military companies in the Ukrainian events." *TASS*, 23 de maio de 2014; Gabriela Baczynska (Urzuf, Ucrânia), "Ultra-Nationalist Ukrainian Battalion Gears Up For More Fighting." *Reuters*, March 25, 2015. Available at <http://www.reuters.com/article/2015/03/25/us-ukraine-crisis-azov-idUSKBN0ML0XJ20150325; Caleb Maupin, "Nazis to Enforce Neoliberalism: 'Operation Jade Helm' and the Ukrainian National Guard." *Neo Eastern Outlook (NEO)*, July 20, 2015. Available at <http://journal-neo.org/2015/07/20/nazis-to-enforce-neoliberalism-operation-jade-helm-and-the-ukrainian-national-guard/>.

[5]"Rota: de Maidan até a guerra no Donbass." [22/8/2015, Alexey Zotyev (ru. Cassad.net; esp. in slavyangrad), translated]. *Vila Vudu*—Samstag, 22. August 2015. Original in Russian: Закон об особом порядке местного ?????????????самоуправления в отдельных районах Донецкой и Луганской областей (Закон об особом статусе Донбасса), текст проекта № 5081 от 16.09.2014. Закон и Бизнес. Available at <http://zib.com.ua/ru/print/100900-zakon_ob_osobom_poryadke_mestnogo_samoupravleniya_v_otdelnih.html"; "Rota: de Maidan até a guerra no Donbass." *Pravda.ru*, August 23, 2015. Available at <http://port.pravda.ru/mundo/23-08-2015/39316-maidan_donbass-0/#sthash.l0BIcUeA.dpuf>.

[6]Division of the German Waffen-SS during the Second World War.

[7]Gabriela Baczynska (Urzuf, Ukraine), "Ultra-nationalist Ukrainian battalion gears up for more fighting." *Reuters*, March 25, 2015. Available at <http://www.reuters.com/article/2015/03/25/us-ukraine-crisis-azov-idUSKBN0ML0XJ20150325>; Shaun Walker (Mariupol), "Azov fighters are Ukraine's greatest weapon and may be its greatest threat—The battalion's far-right volunteers' desire to 'bring the fight to Kiev' is a danger to post-conflict stability." *The Guardian*, September 10, 2014. Available at <http://www.theguardian.com/world/2014/sep/10/azov-far-right-fighters-ukraine-neo-nazis>.

its commanders, the notorious neo-Nazi and terrorist Sergey Korotkykh (codename "Malyuta"), born in Belarus, received the Ukrainian citizenship and the medal of recognition of merit from President Poroshenko.[8] Groups like the Azov and Aidar battalions were committing the greatest atrocities, abusing and executing prisoners, just as the Islamic State (Da'ish) in Syria and Iraq, to such an extent that Amnesty International requested the government in Kiev to investigate this accusation on September 2014.[9]

21.2   NATO's Military Aid to Kiev

In September 2014, at the same time the heads of the German, French, Russian, and Ukrainian governments were discussing the cease-fire and other initiatives to move the Ukraine peace process forward, NATO Secretary-General Anders Fogh Rasmussen announced that the alliance's leaders had pledged in their summit in Wales to grant a "comprehensive and tailored package of measures," including treatment of the wounded, cyber defense, logistics, command and control, communications, and a donation of US\$15 million to Ukraine.[10] Some NATO countries (probably Poland, the Baltic countries, and others), however, were already sending lethal weapons illegally to the government in Kiev for its fight against the rebels in the Donbass, as the Ukrainian Minister of Defense Valeriy Heletey revealed.[11] And according to the political scientist Mateusz Piskorski, director of the European Center for Geopolitical Analysis in Warsaw, about 17 former elite soldiers of the JW GROM (*Grupa Reagowania Operacyjno-Manewrowego*), Polish special forces dedicated to covert

---

[8]Halya Coynash, "Poroshenko grants Belarusian Neo-Nazi Ukrainian citizenship." *Kyiv Post*, December 9, 2014. Available at <http://www.kyivpost.com/opinion/op-ed/halya-coynash-poroshenko-grants-belarusian-neo-nazi-ukrainian-citizenship-374562.html>.

[9]"Ukraine: Abuses and war crimes by the Aidar Volunteer Battalion in the north Luhansk region." *Amnesty International*, September 8, 2014, Index number: EUR 50/040/2014. Available at <http://www.amnesty.org/en/documents/EUR50/040/2014/en/>; Linda Wurster, "Das Bataillon Asow— Schmutziger Kampf in der Ukraine: Neonazis im Dienst der Regierung." *Focus-Online*, Aktualisiert am Donnerstag, August 14, 2014. Available at <http://www.focus.de/politik/ausland/das-bataillon-asow-schmutziger-kampf-in-der-ukraine-neonazis-im-dienst-der-regierung_id_4058717.html>.

[10]"NATO leaders pledge support to Ukraine at Wales Summit." *NATO/OTAN—North Atlantic Treaty Organization*, September 4, 2014. Available at <http://www.nato.int/cps/de/natohq/news_112459.htm>.

[11]"NATO countries have begun delivering weapons to Ukraine to help fight pro-Russian separatists, the country's defence minister claimed last night." *The Times*, September 15, 2014. Available at <http://www.thetimes.co.uk/tto/news/world/europe/article4206727.ece>; NATO countries have begun arms deliveries to Ukraine: defense minister." *Reuters*, September 14, 2014. Available at <http://www.reuters.com/article/2014/09/14/us-ukraine-crisis-heletey-idUSKBN0H90PP20140914>. Accessed on August 30, 2015; "NATO to give Ukraine 15mn Euros, lethal and non-lethal military supplies from members." *RT*, September 4, 2014. Available at <http://www.rt.com/news/185132-nato-ukraine-aid-support/>.

operations (*Cichociemni Spadochroniarze Armii Krajowej*), were fighting in Ukraine and earning up to US$500.[12] Since September 2013, as far as we know, approximately 86 militants of the Right Sector (Pravy Sektor) were attending trainings in crowd control and combat tactics in the Legionowo police center, 23 km from Warsaw, at the invitation of the Polish Foreign Minister T. Radosław Sikorski.[13] And according to information from Igor Strelkow, then Minister of the People's Republic of Donetsk, 139 mercenaries of the Polish military company ASBS (*Analizy Systemowe Bartlomiej Sienkiewicz*) Othago had been killed in the Donbass until July 2014, while the contractor Academi (formerly Blackwater) lost 125 mercenaries and American Greystone Ltd., a subsidiary of Vehicle Services Company LLC, lost 40 of its 150 men fighting in Ukraine. All this was denied, of course.[14]

21.3   The Battle in Debaltseve

The militias of the popular republics of Novorossiya commanded by Alexander Zakharchenko encircled the seething *cauldron* and fought a bloody battle between February 12 and 17, 2015, inflicting heavy casualties on the Kiev troops and conquering the strategically important rail and road center of Debaltseve, a connecting point between the Donetsk and Luhansk regions and a town near the border with Russia, where the shops no longer sold goods in hryvnia, the Ukrainian currency, but in rubles. Three thousand to 3500 of the 5000–8000 National Guard troops, including mercenaries, perished in Debaltseve. Others surrendered, leaving tanks, armored vehicles, and the other heavy weapons in the region for the insurgents. According to President Poroshenko, the column of 2000 troops that retreated from Debaltseve represented 80% of his forces, i.e., the National Guard

---

[12]Alexander Lüders, "Polnische Spezialisten." *Focus*, September 13, 2014. Available at <http://www.focus.de/politik/ausland/polnische-spezialisten%2D%2Dukraine-krise-kommentar_id_5967578.html>.

[13]Thierry Meyssan, "Ukraine: Poland trained putchists two months in advance." *Voltaire Network*. Damascus (Syria). April 19, 2014 Available at <http://www.voltairenet.org/article183373.html>. Accessed on August 25, 2015; Nikolai Malishevsk, "Polish Death Squads Fighting in Ukraine. CIA Covert Operation?" *Global Research*, May 28, 2014. Strategic Culture Foundation. Available at <http://www.globalresearch.ca/polish-death-squads-fighting-in%2D%2Dukraine-cia-covert-operation/5384210>.

[14]Fred Widmer, Forum: Politik Kämpfe in der Ostukraine: "Praktisch jedes Haus zerstört—Mär vom faschistischen Putsch." *Spiegel Online*, August 30, 2014. Available at <http://www.spiegel.de/forum/politik/kaempfe-der-ostukraine%2D%2Dpraktisch-jedes-haus-zerstoert-thread-141429-11.html>; Kirit Radia et al., "US Contractor Greystone Denies Its 'Mercenaries' in Ukraine." *ABC News*, April 8, 2014. Available at <http://abcnews.go.com/Blotter/greystone-firm-accused%2D%2Ddisguising-mercenaries-ukrainians/story?id=23243761>.

stationed there had been only 3000 men strong.[15] This wasn't true. Semyon Semyenchenko, commander of the Donbass battalion made up of mercenaries, declared that President Poroshenko had fallen victim to a small clique that was lying about the number of dead and wounded in order to conceal their own failures and preserve influence.[16] Ukraine's *Kyiv Post* estimated that approximately 4000–8000 soldiers of the National Guard were still stationed in Debaltseve on February 17.[17] The information and counterinformation make it hard to make a more or less exact assessment of the number of casualties. Corpses of soldiers filled the morgues in Artemivsk, a town about 50 km from Debaltseve and still under Kiev's control.[18] Civilians had also died, and hundreds of wounded crowded the hospitals in this city. Debaltseve was left in ruins. The retreat of Kiev's troops laid bare the ignominious defeat of Poroshenko's government. The debacle of the Anti-Terrorist Operation (ATO) was more severe than the military commanders would admit.[19]

Correspondents of *The New York Times* reported that "demoralized Ukrainian soldiers straggled into the town of Artemivsk, griping about incompetent leadership and recounting desperate conditions and gruesome killing as they beat a haphazard retreat from the strategic town of Debaltseve," while many others were drinking heavily and commandeering taxis after escaping the siege and weeks of shelling.[20] There was no ammunition and food. The soldiers were exhausted and hungry. It was unclear whether the survivors of the assault on Debaltseve had places to sleep. And according to Andrew E. Kramer and David M. Herszenhorn of *The New York Times*,

---

[15] Andrew E. Kramer and David M. Herszanhorn, "Ukrainian Soldiers' Retreat from Eastern Town Raises Doubt for Truce." *The New York Times*, February 18, 2015.

[16] Lucian Kim, "Debaltseve debacle puts Ukraine's leader in jeopardy. That suits Vladimir Putin just fine." *Reuters*, February 19, 2015. Available at <http://blogs.reuters.com/great-debate/2015/02/19/debaltseve-debacle-put-ukraines-leader%2D%2Din-jeopardy-and-that-suits-vladimir-putin-just-fine/>. Accessed on February 27, 2015.

[17] Anastasia Vlasova (*Kyiv Post*) and Oksana Grytsenko, "Thousands of Ukrainian soldiers trapped as Debaltseve pocket closes." *Kyiv Post*, Wednesday, February 18, 2015. Available at <http://www.kyivpost.com/content/kyiv-post-plus/thousands-of-soldiers-endangered-in-debaltseve-pocket-380978.html>.

[18] Sarah Rainsford (Artemivsk, Ukraine), "Ukraine civilians stranded as shells pound Debaltseve." *BBC News*, January 30, 2015. Available at <http://www.bbc.com/news/world-europe-31055060>. Accessed on August 27, 2015.

[19] Anastasia Vlasova (*Kyiv Post*) and Oksana Grytsenko, "Thousands of Ukrainian soldiers trapped as Debaltseve pocket closes." *Kyiv Post*, February 18, 2015. Available at <http://www.kyivpost.com/content/kyiv-post-plus/thousands-of-soldiers-endangered-in-debaltseve-pocket-380978.html>; Alec Luhn (Artemivsk) and Oksana Grytsenko (Luhansk), "Ukrainian soldiers share horrors of Debaltseve battle after stinging defeat—Thousands of Ukrainian soldiers retreat from strategic town taken by pro-Russia separatists, leaving their dead and wounded comrades behind." *The Guardian*, February 18, 2015. Available at <http://www.theguardian.com/world/2015/feb/18/ukrainian-soldiers-share-horrors-of-debaltseve-battle-after-stinging-defeat>.

[20] Andrew E. Kramer and David M. Herszenhorn (Artemivsk, Ukraine), "Retreating Soldiers Bring Echoes of War's Chaos to a Ukrainian Town." *The New York Times*, February 19, 2015. Available at <http://www.nytimes.com/2015/02/20/world/europe/leaders-speak-by-telephone-to-try-to-impose-ukraine-cease-fire.html>.

who were in Artemivsk, more than 5000 people had died in the conflict.[21] The troops of the National Guard, including 17 battalions of mercenaries, called volunteers,[22] also lost dozens of soldiers as prisoners to the militias of the People's Republic of Donetsk commanded by Alexander Zakharchenko.[23]

Kiev, Washington, and other NATO countries accused the rebels of breaking the truce, but Commander Alexander Zakharchenko had said before the assault that he would respect the cease-fire everywhere, except in Debaltseve, because this city belonged to the People's Republic of Donetsk. President Obama, however, took advantage of the situation as a pretext to enact a new series of sanctions against Russia, accompanied by the governments of the European Union, accusing it of having supported the rebel militias militarily.[24] Russia had certainly helped the militias of the People's Republic of Donetsk with artillery located at the border, the shipment of heavy weaponry, GRU instructors, and Spetsnaz special forces on leave, as volunteers.[25] Nor could Russia have done otherwise, for it knew the United States/NATO was secretly sending military instructors, armaments, and other war material to the Kiev forces and considering to intensify this assistance.[26] Canada was

---

[21]*Ibidem*. Lucian Kim, "Debaltseve debacle puts Ukraine's leader in jeopardy. That suits Vladimir Putin just fine." *Reuters*, February 19, 2015. Available at <http://blogs.reuters.com/great-debate/2015/02/19/debaltseve-debacle-put-ukraines-leader-in-jeopardy-and-that-suits-vladimir-putin-just-fine/>. Accessed on February 27, 2015.

[22]*Ibidem*.

[23]Associated Press—AP (Artemivsk, Ukraine), "Embattled Debaltseve falls to Ukraine rebels; troops retreat." *Mail Online*. Available at <http://www.dailymail.co.uk/wires/ap/article-2958163/Ukraine-says-rebels-continue-onslaught-Debaltseve.html>; Courtney Weaver (Artemivsk) and Roman Olearchyk (Kiev), "City of Debaltseve emerges as a tipping point in Ukraine's war." *Financial Times*, February 9, 2015. Available at <http://www.ft.com/intl/cms/s/0/7fe1d32e-b047-11e4-92b6-00144feab7de.html#axzz3jwzpgTib>; Lucian Kim, "Debaltseve debacle puts Ukraine's leader in jeopardy. That suits Vladimir Putin just fine." *Reuters*, February 19, 2015. Available at <http://blogs.reuters.com/great-debate/2015/02/19/debaltseve-debacle-put-ukraines-leader-in-jeopardy-and-that-suits-vladimir-putin-just-fine/>; Accessed on February 27, 2015.

[24]Andrew E. Kramer and Michael R. Gordon, "U.S. Faults Russia as Combat Spikes in East Ukraine." *The New York Times*, February 13, 2015.

[25]David Blair (Chief Foreign Correspondent), "Capture of Debaltseve shreds the latest Ukraine ceasefire deal—The pro-Russian rebels must now decide whether to press on with their advance—but Ukraine's president is out of options, writes David Blair." *The Telegraph*, February 18, 2015. Available at <http://www.telegraph.co.uk/news/worldnews/europe/ukraine/11421390/Capture-of-Debaltseve-shreds-the-latest-Ukraine-ceasefire-deal.html>; "US blames Russia for rebel ceasefire violations in Ukraine—Joe Biden warns Moscow it will face 'costs' if Russian forces and separatists fail to respect the Minsk agreement and continue to attack Debaltseve." *The Telegraph*, February 18, 2015. Available at <http://www.telegraph.co.uk/news/worldnews/europe/ukraine/11419309/US-condemns-rebel-ceasefire-violations-in-Ukraine.html>; Igor Sutyagin, "Russian Forces in Ukraine. Briefing Paper, March 2015." *Royal United Services Institute*. Available at <https://www.rusi.org/downloads/assets/201503_BP_Russian_Forces_in_Ukraine_FINAL.pdf>.

[26]Richard Norton-Taylor, "US weapons to Ukraine 'would be matched by Russian arms to rebels'—International Institute for Strategic Studies warns that Moscow could arm separatists more quickly than US could reinforce Ukraine's forces." <https://www.theguardian.com/world/2015/feb/11/us-weapons-to-ukraine-would-be-matched-by-russian-arms-to-rebels>. Accessed on December 03, 2018.

planning to send 200 troops to western Ukraine, which would join the 800 American and 80 British soldiers assigned there since 1 year to train the troops of the National Guard.[27]

21.4 The Minsk II Agreement

Germany's *Kanzlerin* Angela Merkel, meanwhile, had taken the lead in the talks with Russia. On February 12, 2015, just when war was boiling over in Debaltseve, Merkel and the French President François Hollande once again met in Minsk with President Poroshenko and President Putin, after various meetings and dozens of phone calls, where they ratified the commitments assumed in the Protocol of September 19, 2014, within the Normandy Format, i.e., in accordance with the understandings reached on June 6, 2014, at the Château de Bénouville, during the celebration of the 70th anniversary of Operation Overlord during the Second World War. And one of the clearly expressed items was the reform of the Constitution that was to come into effect at the end of 2015, establishing "decentralization as a key element (including a reference to the specificities of certain areas in the Donetsk and Luhansk regions)."[28] Prisoners were exchanged and heavy artillery was withdrawn, even if partially, by the Kiev forces. But the cease-fire imposed by the Minsk II protocol was never fully respected. Continuous violations, especially by the National Guard, were recorded in the reports of the Special Monitoring Mission to Ukraine (SMM) of the OSCE. The bombing continued in the surroundings of the airport of Donetsk and Mariupol, in the villages of Mayorsk, Sal Rei, and Sokilnyky, as well as in the area of Kominternove.[29]

---

[27]Pat Buchanan, "A U.S.-Russia War Over Ukraine?" *Creators.com*. April 17, 2015. Available at: <http://www.creators.com/opinion/pat-buchanan/a-us-russia-war-over-ukraine.html>. Accessed on September 2, 2015; Matthew Fisher, "Canadians take part in NATO war games aimed at sending message to Russia over Ukraine aggression." *National Post*, 25 de maio de 2015. Available at: <http://news.nationalpost.com/news/world/canadians%2D%2Dtake-part-in-nato-war-games-aimed-at-sending-message-to-russia-over-ukraine-aggression>. Accessed on September 2, 2015.

[28]"Package of Measures for the Implementation of the Minsk Agreements." *Présidence de la République française*—Élysée.fr. Available at <http://www.elysee.fr/declarations/article/package-of-measures-for-the-implementation-of-the-minsk-agreements/>; "Minsk agreement on Ukraine crisis: text in full." *The Telegraph*, February 12, 2015. Available at <http://www.telegraph.co.uk/news/worldnews/europe/ukraine/11408266/Minsk-agreement-on-Ukraine-crisis-text-in-full.html>.

[29]"Daily updates from the Special Monitoring Mission to Ukraine." *OSCE Special Monitoring Mission to Ukraine*. Available at <http://www.osce.org/ukraine-smm/daily-updates>; Andriy. "Ukrainian Armed Forces de-mine Kominternove." *Ukraine Crisis Media Center*. Kyiv, March 16, 2015. Available at <http://uacrisis.org/20074-andrijj-lisenko-59>.

21.5   American Influence in the Recovery of Nazism: Rehabilitation of Stepan Bandera and the Nazi Collaborators of the Second World War

The contradictions created and/or fomented by the United States and the European Union in Ukraine to encourage the coup against President Viktor Yanukovych proved difficult to manage. In the parliamentary elections held on October 25, 2014, the block led by President Poroshenko won 132 seats, but without Arseniy Yatsenyuk's People's Front, which won 82 seats, it could not hold the majority of 226 seats in the Verkhovna Rada. The People's Front was aligned with the extreme right, and Arseniy Yatsenyuk was the man Washington relied on, the man Assistant Secretary of State Victoria Nuland had picked for the job. And the American Vice-President Joe Biden had approved or induced a private gas company owned by the oligarch Nikolai Zlochevskyi (Burisma Holdings Ltd.) to hire Hunter Biden, his youngest son, as a member of the Board of Directors,[30] which exposed not only a lack of ethics but influence peddling and corruption, in an attempt to attract American investors to Ukraine, and influence the government in Kiev. And on December 2, 2014, the American banker Natalie Ann Jaresko, born in Elmhurst, Illinois, received the Ukrainian nationality from President Poroshenko and assumed the Ministry of Finance. She had worked in the Treasury Department and other bodies of the US government, acted as the CEO of the Western NIS Enterprise Fund (WNISEF), and was the founder and CEO of the investment bank Horizon Capital. This last organization sponsored the Open Ukraine Foundation of Prime Minister Arseniy Yatsenyuk together with NATO and the US State Department[31] and planned to manipulate business in Ukraine and Moldova in favor of the strategic interests in Washington together with the Emerging Europe Growth Fund, L.P. (EEGF).[32]

In these circumstances, the ultranationalist right maintained its predominance in the Verkhovna Rada, with the encouragement of the United States and the European Union, even if the neo-Nazi parties of Svoboda and Right Sector only conquered seven seats (six and one, respectively). And this Rada would certainly reject several clauses of the Minsk Protocol. So much so that on December 23, 2014, it promptly abolished Ukraine's nonaligned status in order to increase cooperation with NATO

---

[30]"Vice President Joe Biden's son joins Ukraine gas company." *BBC News*, May 14, 2014. Available at <http://www.bbc.com/news/blogs-echochambers-27403003>; BRAUN, Stephen (Associated Press). "Ukrainian energy firm hires Biden's son as lawyer." *The Washington Times*, Saturday, June 7, 2014. Available at <http://www.washingtontimes.com/news/2014/jun/7/ukrainian-energy-firm-hires-biden-son-as-lawyer/?page=all>.

[31]"Arseniy Yatsenyuk Foundation Open Ukraine." Available at <http://openukraine.org/en/about/partners>.

[32]"Plünderung der Welt—Ukraine: US-Investment-Bankerin ist neue Finanzministerin." *Deutsche Wirtschafts Nachrichten*, December 2, 2014. Available at <http://deutsche-wirtschafts-nachrichten.de/2014/12/02/ukraine-us-investment%2D%2Dbankerin-ist-neue-finanzministerin/>.

and fulfill the criteria required for its entry into the alliance. Subsequently, on May 9, 2015, it withdrew from all logistics and military cooperation agreements with Russia. A few months later, the Verkhovna Rada led by Prime Minister Arseniy Yatsenyuk approved a "decommunisation" package, banning the Communist party, abolishing any mention that could evoke the Soviet Union and communism, which was equated to Nazism, and rehabilitating the militants of the Organization of Ukrainian Nationalists (*Orhanizatsiya Ukrayins'kykh Natsionalistiv*—OUN) and the Ukrainian Insurgent Army (*Ukrayins'ka Povstans'ka Armiya*—UPA) as freedom fighters.[33]

During the Second World War, these freedom fighters of Ukraine, the "banderivets," had carried out the ethnic cleansing of Polish and Jewish populations, exterminating between 60,000 and 100,000 Poles in Volhynia in the east of Galicia, according to some estimates.[34] Later, during the Cold War, both organizations— Organization of Ukrainian Nationalists OUN and Ukrainian Insurgent Army UPA— continued their fight against the Soviet Union with the support of the British SIS (MI6), the CIA, and the German BND, which maintained contact with Stepan Bandera through Brigadier General Heinz Danko Herre, and the dictatorship of Francisco Franco of Spain.[35] The decommunisation laws passed by parliament and signed by President Poroshenko further divided Ukraine, therefore, and hindered any agreement to maintain its unity, since the vast majority of the population of the popular republics of Novorossiya in the Donbass not only didn't accept but also abhorred these laws.

---

[33]Lily Hyde (Kiev), "Ukraine to rewrite Soviet history with controversial 'decommunisation' laws—President set to sign measures that ban Communist symbols and offer public recognition and payouts for fighters in militias implicated in atrocities." *The Guardian*, April 20, 2015. Available at <http://www.theguardian.com/world/2015/apr/20/ukraine-decommunisation-law-soviet>; "Ukraine bans Communism & Nazism, celebrates UPA nationalists as 'freedom fighters'." *RT*, April 9, 2015. Available at <http://www.rt.com/news/248365-ukraine-bans-communism-nazism/>. Accessed on April 11, 2015; "Ukraine pushes to 'ban communism' by 70th anniversary of victory over Nazism." *RT*, April 6, 2015. Available at <http://www.rt.com/news/247009-ukraine-communism-ban-nazism/>. Accessed on April 6, 2015; "Ukraine's neo-Nazi leader becomes top military adviser, legalizes fighters." *RT*, April 6, 2015. Available at <http://www.rt.com/news/247001-ukraine-army-adviser-yarosh/>. Accessed on April 6, 2015.

[34]Josh Cohen (Reuters), "Putin says Ukraine being overrun by fascists—and he may be right—Kiev has now handed the Kremlin 'evidence' for Putin's claim that Russia is facing off against fascists." *The Jerusalem Post*, May 16, 2015. Available at <http://www.jpost.com/International/Putin-says-Ukraine-being-overrun-by-fascists-and-he-may-be-right-4032>.

[35]Grzegorz Rossoliński-Liebe, *Stepan Bandera: The Life and Afterlife of a Ukrainian Nationalist: Fascism, Genocide and Cult*. Stuttgart: *Ibidem* Verlag, 2014, pp. 332–334.

21.6   Shipment of Lethal Weapons and American Instructors to Ukraine While the Country Approaches a Financial Collapse

On March 24, soon after the ratification of the Minsk II Agreement by the heads of the German, French, Russian, and Ukrainian governments on February 12, 2015, the US House of Representatives adopted a resolution by 348 votes against 48 urging President Obama to send lethal weapons to the government in Kiev.[36] Heavy weapons were already being secretly shipped by the NATO countries, and based on the Global Security Contingency Fund, President Obama decided in April to send 300 soldiers of the 173rd Airborne Brigade, stationed at the US Army Garrison Vicenza (Caserma Carlo Ederle) in Italy, to train the troops of the National Guard[37] "as part of a joint DoD-State Department initiative to strengthen Ukraine's internal defense capabilities with a focus on internal security and territorial defense."[38] On March 25, the first shipments of Humvees (High Mobility Multipurpose Wheeled Vehicle—HMMWV), radios, counter-mortar radars, camouflage clothing, and other lethal and nonlethal equipment, valued at US\$75 million, started to arrive openly at Boryspil International Airport.[39]

But the reforms required by the IMF focusing on the correction of economic imbalances had lowered consumption levels even further and deepened the recession. When Moscow suspended the imports of agricultural products in retaliation to the imposed sanctions, it severely hurt Ukraine's economy, which had its main market in Russia. Ukraine's cattle herd shrank to less than 14% of the level at the time of the Soviet Union.[40] And this affected not only the export of meat but also of milk, in which Russia had a share of 71% since 2011.[41] On the other hand, poor

---

[36]"US House urges Obama to send arms to Ukraine." *RT*, March 24, 2015. Available at <http://www.rt.com/news/243417-us-house-weapons-ukraine>. Accessed on March 24, 2015.

[37]"US sends 300 troops to Ukraine to train forces fighting pro-Russian rebels—Russia criticized the arrival of US military personnel, saying the move could further destabilize Ukraine." *Al Jazeera*, April 17, 2015. Available at <http://america.aljazeera.com/articles/2015/4/17/us-sends-300-troops-to-ukraine.html>.

[38]Cheryl Pellerin, DoD News, Defense Media Activity. "DoD Moves Forward on Ukraine National Guard Training." *US Department of Defense. Washington*, March 20, 2015. Available at <http://www.defense.gov/News-Article-View/Article/604322>; DoD = U.S. Department of Defense.

[39]"Ukraine Receives First Batch of US Humvees." *Kiev Ukraine News*, March 27, 2015. Available at <http://news.kievukraine.info/2015/03/ukraine-receives-first-batch-of-us.html>; "Ukraine Receives First Batch of US Humvees." *Agence France-Presse*, March 25, 2015. "Defense News." Available at <http://www.defensenews.com/story/defense/international/europe/2015/03/25/ukraine-receives-first-batch-us-humvees/70445154/>. Accessed on March 26, 2015.

[40]"Dairy woes to shrink Ukraine cattle herd to 14% of Soviet levels." *Blackseagrain*, September 18, 2015. Available at <http://www.blackseagrain.net/novosti/dairy-woes-to-shrink-ukraine-cattle-herd-to-14-of-soviet-levels>. Accessed on September 21, 2015.

[41]*Ibidem.*

weather conditions—the drought and heat in the summer of 2015—undermined the sowing and harvest of rapeseed for biodiesel, which occupied 685,000 ha in 2015 against 865,000 in 2014.[42] The same was expected to occur in 2016. As a result, rapeseed exports were expected to fall 17.6% in 2015–2016 to 1.58 million tons, according to the estimate of UkrAgroConsult.[43] The harvest of grains, of which Ukraine was one of the largest exporters with a planted area of 5–7%, was equally expected to drop by more than 7% in 2015. Industrial production—minerals, machinery, and other manufactured goods—had been on the decline since June 2012, and the war in the Donbass further affected this sector located mainly in the east and southeast of Ukraine.[44] The fall in coal (−22%) and steel (−17%) production, which had a share of 25% in total exports in 2013, led to the collapse of Ukraine's exports.[45] Exports from the steel industry, which had once been the main source of revenue, plunged by 11 billion, i.e., from US$26.5 billion in 2008 to US $14.6 billion in 2014.[46]

The agreement President Poroshenko signed with NATO Secretary-General Jens Stoltenberg on September 21, 2015 did little to help the government in Kiev in the conflict in the Donbass. Apparently, Stoltenberg just promised greater cooperation with Ukraine, especially in the area of strategic communications, and the increase of NATO troops in Eastern Europe to 40,000, but no weapons,[47] although the alliance

---

[42]"2016 rapeseed harvest in Ukraine is imperiled." *World News Report—Ukrainian Biofuel Portal*—September 21, 2015. Available at <http://world.einnews.com/article/287393651/P1Iu7e-i9RjcBYu4>.

[43]Sandra Boga, "Ukraine 2015/16 rapeseed exports seen down 18%." *Informa—Public Ledger*, August 4, 2015. Available at <https://www.agra-net.net/agra/public-ledger/commodities/oils-oil seeds/rapeseed/ukraine-201516-rapeseed-exports-seen-down-18%2D%2D1.htm>. Accessed on September 21, 2015. Sabine Crook. "Slow sowing pace raises concern for Ukraine's rapeseed crop—Ongoing dryness during the current sowing window is likely to cut Ukraine's rapeseed harvest to between 1 and 1.5 million tonnes compared with 1.7 mln for this year's harvest, analyst UkrAgroConsult said today." *Informa—Public Ledger*, September 15, 2015. Available at <https://www.agra-net.net/agra/public-ledger/commodities/oils-oilseeds/rapeseed/slow-sowing-pace-raises-concern-for-ukraines-rapeseed-crop%2D%2D1.htm>. Accessed on September 21, 2015.

[44]"Collapse of Ukrainian exports to Russia and Europe in first six months of 2015." *Introduction by New Cold War.org—The New Cold War: Ukraine and beyond*, August 20, 2015. Available at <http://newcoldwar.org/collapse-of-ukrainian%2D%2Dexports-to-russia-and-europe-in-first-six-.months-of-2015/>.

[45]Tadeusz Iwański, "The collapse of Ukraine's foreign trade," March 18, 2015. Available at <http://www.osw.waw.pl/en/publikacje/analyses/2015-03-18/collapse-ukraines-foreign-trade>.

[46]Oleksandr Kramar, "Back on the Ground—Agribusiness becomes the biggest component of Ukraine's economy. What will it take for the growth to continue?." *Ukrainian Week*, August 25, 2015. Available at <http://ukrainianweek.com/Economics/144123>.

[47]Robin Emmott—Kiev (Reuters), "In symbolic visit, NATO offers Ukraine support but no arms— The head of NATO pledged to help Ukraine defend itself against pro-Russian separatists on Tuesday but disappointed some in Kiev who seek supplies of defensive weaponry that the West fears would threaten a fragile ceasefire with the rebels. In an opulent gilded state room in the presidential palace, Secretary-General Jens Stoltenberg told Ukraine...." *World News Report*. Available at <http://world.einnews.com/article_detail/287643883/3njHxBQ7N2T1sbWX?n=2& code=P21DsWBPJxF7hfqq>.

had provided them before.[48] President Poroshenko and Prime Minister Arseniy Yatsenyuk's plan to tell him that Ukraine was confronting a nuclear power was futile.[49] Even if Ukraine obtained more armaments from NATO, the government in Kiev would find it extremely hard to crush the popular republics of Donetsk and Luhansk, sustained by Russian special forces (*Spetsnaz*) and its foreign intelligence service (*Sluzhba vneshney razvedki—SVR RF (CBP PФ)*). Likewise, pointing to the supposed Russian threat was the manifestation of the old paranoia of the United States and certain sectors in Europe. A threat the government in Kiev tried to evoke to numb internal and external public opinion and obscure the economic and political fiasco to which the putsch of February 2014 had led.

Nevertheless, Vladislav Deinego and Denis Pushilin, the representatives of the People's Republic of Donetsk and Luhansk in the negotiations of the Contact Group with Kiev, advanced on the agreement for the removal of small arms from the front line (mortars and missiles with a diameter of less than 100 mm). And on October 2, 2015, the quartet—the heads of the French, Russian, German, and Ukrainian governments who had previously met in Normandy—once again convened in Paris and apparently reached an understanding regarding the implementation of the Minsk agreements.[50] As a result, the local elections in Donetsk and Luhansk scheduled for November were postponed to February after intermediation by President Putin, but in return the insurgents required that Kiev fully comply with the Minsk agreement, granting a special status to the provinces of the Donbass and declaring a general amnesty, in addition to other issues. President Petro Poroshenko said that even though the truce was maintained, the war would not end as long as the territory was occupied. It seemed, however, that the financially collapsing government in Kiev would be unable to sustain the conflict with the republics of Novorossiya, which was costing it between US$5.5 and US$8 million per day and had already reached a total cost of US$1.5 billion by January 2015, as President Poroshenko confirmed.[51] GDP was expected to contract by approximately 11% at the end of 2015, with the reduction in investments and consumption resulting from the ongoing

---

[48]"NATO to give Ukraine 15mn euros, lethal and non-lethal military supplies from members." *RT*, September 4, 2014. Available at <http://www.rt.com/news/185132-nato-ukraine-aid-support/>. Accessed on July 5, 2014; "NATO countries have begun arms deliveries to Ukraine: defense minister." *Reuters*, September 14, 2014. Available at <http://www.reuters.com/article/2014/09/14/us-ukraine-crisis-heletey-idUSKBN0H90PP20140914>. Accessed on August 30, 2015.

[49]"Ukraine wants help to build nuclear defence shield." *Ukraine Today Weekly Digest*, September 22, 2015. Available at <http://uatoday.tv/politics/ukraine-wants-help-to-build-nuclear-defence-shield-arseniy-yatsenyuk-498674.html>.

[50]Anne-Sylvaine Chassany, "Ukraine talks in Paris end on positive note," October 2, 2015. Available at <http://www.ft.com/intl/cms/s/0/0b24a898-693f-11e5-a57f-21b88f7d973f.html#axzz3ntbj5Ujy>.

[51]"Ukraine's Poroshenko Says War Costing $8 Million Per Day." *The Moscow Times*, February 5, 2015. Available at <http://www.themoscowtimes.com/business/article/ukraine-s-poroshenko-says-war-costing-8-million-per-day/515488.html>.

conflict, despite the declared truce.[52] And by the end of 2015, the drop in Ukraine's GDP was indeed of the order of 10%.

---

[52] *Focus Economics—Economic Forecasts from the World's Leading Economists*, October 6, 2015. Available at <http://www.focus-economics.com/countries/ukrain>.

Chapter 22
Ukraine: The Same Political Environment as in the Middle East and North Africa

22.1 Heightening International Contradictions: Assad's Overthrow as Washington's Central Objective Since 2006 and the Destruction of Libya's State

The war in Syria occurred in the same environment as the conflict in Ukraine. It reflected the heightening international contradictions, particularly between Russia and the United States, the first reemerging as world power and the latter trying to sustain its hegemony anchored on the dollar and NATO at any cost. This end—maintaining its position as the single pole of global power—justified the means, no matter how disgraceful. And the uncontestable fact was that Bashar al-Assad's removal had been on Washington's agenda since at least 2005–2006, 5 years before the Arab Spring broke out during the Obama administration. A cable entitled "Influencing the SARG (Syrian government) in the end of 2006"[1] and written in December of the same year by the diplomat William Roebuck, Chargé d'Affaires of the United States in Damascus, already pointed to a central motif of Washington's foreign policy: destabilization of the Bashar al-Assad regime.[2] President George W. Bush proved to be cautious, however, and in his time, he heeded the warning his predecessor John Quincy Adams had professed in 1821 and avoided going "abroad in search of monsters to destroy," as he had done in Afghanistan and Iraq. He continued to fund the Syrian opposition with millions of dollars, but he did not invade the country, confronted with the warning of the Israeli Prime Minister Ariel Sharon (2001–2006), who said the alternative to Bashar al-Assad, the "devil we know," would certainly be the rise to power of the Muslim Brotherhood.[3]

---

[1]"Influencing the SARG in the end of 2006," December 13, 2006. Available at: <https:/wikileaks.org/cable/2006/12/06DAMASCUS5399.html>. The Wikileak Files—The World According to U.S. Empire—With an Introduction by Julian Assange. London/New York, pp. 298–299.
[2]Ibidem.
[3]Itamar Rabinovich, 2012, p. 52; Luiz Alberto Moniz Bandeira, 2014, pp. 372–373.

© Springer Nature Switzerland AG 2019
L. A. Moniz Bandeira, *The World Disorder*,
https://doi.org/10.1007/978-3-030-03204-3_22

In March 2011, soon after the uprising in Benghazi had begun, President Barack Obama—backed by some European heads of governments—declared that the "world had an obligation to prevent any massacre of civilians" and that Muammar Gaddafi should "step down."[4] No sooner said than done. When his Secretary of State Hillary Clinton visited Tripoli on October 21, 2011, she mockingly remarked on the lynching of Gaddafi in an interview to the press: "We came, we saw, he died!"[5] We know, however, that the head of the Libyan intelligence service (Abdullah Senussi, Jamahiriya el-Mukhabarat) had already informed CIA Deputy Director Michael Morrel that Gaddafi hated and feared al-Qa'ida just as much as the United States and that several emissaries of bin Laden were assisting the protesters in Benghazi.[6] The White House nevertheless insisted on saying Gaddafi "had to go." Michael Morrel, meanwhile, acknowledged that "there was no doubt that mixed among various rebel factions were some extremists loyal to bin Laden's ideology" and that the military support—the lethal weapons—of the agitators "eventually" came from NATO and other allies.[7] The collapse of the State in Libya subsequently opened the floodgates for a massive spread of conventional weapons over the entire Maghrib and the expansion of al-Qa'ida to Egypt, Mali, and other African countries.[8]

22.2   The Warnings from Henry Kissinger and Senator Rand Paul and the Spread of Islamic Terror

When the rebellion in Syria escalated in August 2011, President Obama once more took on the mantle of universal dictator, issuing the edict that "for the sake of the Syrian people, the time has come for President Assad to step aside."[9] The so-called Arab Spring then flourished, with seeds planted by Washington and the field plowed for the budding and flowering of other groups with al-Qa'ida's ideology. Professor Henry Kissinger, however, with all his experience as former National Security Advisor and Secretary of State for presidents Richard Nixon (1969–1974) and Gerald Ford (1974–1977), warned that the Syrian State could collapse if President Bashar al-Assad fell, creating a vacuum of power. Syria could turn into a blank

---

[4]"Libya: US and EU say Muammar Gaddafi must go." BBC—Seccion Africa, March 11, 2011. Available at: <http://www.bbc.com/news/world-europe-12711162>.

[5]"Flashback 2011: Hillary Clinton Laughs About Killing Muammar Gaddafi: 'We Came, We Saw, He Died!'." Real Clear Politics (Video), June 19, 2015. Available at: <http://www.realclearpolitics.com/video/2015/06/19/flashback_2011_hillary_clinton_laughs_about_killing_moammar_gaddafi_we_came_we_saw_he_died.html>.

[6]Michael Morell & Bill Harlow, 2015, pp. 188–191.

[7]Ibidem, p. 181.

[8]Ibidem, p. 195.

[9]Scott Wilson & Joby Warrick, "Assad must go, Obama says." The Washington Post, August 18, 2011.

space, a base for terrorism, or the supply of weapons to neighboring countries, with lawlessness and no central authority, just as had happened in Yemen, Somalia, Northern Mali, Libya, and northwestern Pakistan.[10] Henry Kissinger's omen was virtually confirmed when Da'ish invaded Iraq 2 years later. In June 2014, Senator Rand Paul (Republican—Kentucky) stated in an interview with NBC News that Washington's neocon policies had created a safe haven for Islamic radicals in the Middle East. The United States—he pointed out—had entered Libya, overthrown the "terrible Gaddafi," and transformed the country into a wonderland for Jihadists who had spread everywhere.[11] And just as Kissinger, he warned that "if we were to get rid of Assad it would be a jihadist wonderland in Syria. It's now a jihadist wonderland in Iraq, precisely because we got over-involved."[12]

During the Jimmy Carter administration, National Security Advisor Zbigniew Brzezinski had formulated a strategy to foment and manipulate Islamic fundamentalism as an ideological weapon against communism. The United States would sponsor the training of Jihadists as freedom fighters, and it would employ agents, such as Osama bin Laden, to recruit mujahidin from the most diverse countries of the Middle East, Africa, and Central Asia to fight the Soviet troops in Afghanistan and destabilize the eastern republics of the Soviet Union,[13] inhabited largely by Muslims. President Carter hesitated in encouraging the terrorists. And to convince him, Brzezinski asked: "What is more important to the history of the world? The Taliban or the collapse of the Soviet empire? Some stirred-up Moslems or the liberation of Central Europe and the end of the cold war?"[14]

So the United States started constructing its "creature" with no "equal in deformity and wickedness,"[15] its own Frankenstein monster called al-Qa'ida. And just as in Mary Shelley's novel, Zbigniew Brzezinski strategy backfired. The "creature" escaped from its CIA lab, with the help of Saudi Arabia and Pakistan, and terrorists "propagated upon the earth who might make the very existence of the species of man a condition precarious and full of terror."[16] The creature multiplied from the

---

[10]Henry A. Kissinger, "Syrian intervention risks upsetting global order," The Washington Post, June 2, 2012.

[11]"We went into Libya and we got rid of that terrible Qaddafi, now it's a jihadist wonderland over there. [...] There's jihadists everywhere. If we were to get rid of Assad it would be a jihadist wonderland in Syria. It's now a jihadist wonderland in Iraq, precisely because we got over-involved."; Laura Basset, "Rand Paul: We Created 'Jihadist Wonderland' In Iraq." Huffpost Politics, June 23, 2014. Available at: <http://www.huffingtonpost.com/2014/06/22/rand-paul-iraq_n_5519287.html>; Kurt Nimmo, "Sen. Feinstein: 'There Will Be Plots to Kill Americans'." Infowars.com On June 23, 2014. In: Featured Stories, Infowars Exclusives, Tile. Available at: <http://www.infowars.com/sen-feinstein-there-will%2D%2Dbe-plots-to-kill-americans/print/>.

[12]Laura Bassett, "Rand Paul: We Created 'Jihadist Wonderland' In Iraq." The Huffington Post – Huff Post, June 23, 2014. Available at: <http://www.huffingtonpost.com/2014/06/22/rand-paul-iraq_n_5519287.html>.

[13]See Luiz Alberto Moniz Bandeira, 2014, pp. 395–402.

[14]Arnold Schuchter, 2004, p. 118; Peter Dale Scott, 2003, p. 35.

[15]Mary Shelley, 1818 Edition 2015, pp. 106–107.

[16]Ibidem.

Caucasus to the Middle East and Maghrib and spawned several terrorist organizations, such as al-Qa'ida in Iraq (AQI), al-Qa'ida in the Arabian Peninsula (al-Qā'idah fī Jazīrat al-'Arab—AQPA), Jabhat al-Nusra, and the Islamic Front, forming a terrorist franchise.[17] Saudi Arabia, Qatar, and Kuwait nourished it with money and American weapons and continued to nourish it with the cooperation of Turkey and Jordan to overthrow Bashar al-Assad in Syria. According to Assad, the Islamists had taken hold in Syria with the backing of the West and the Gulf emirates, especially Qatar and Saudi Arabia, and with the logistical support of Turkey's President (2014–) and then Prime Minister Recep Tayyip Erdogan (2003–2014), an intellectual supporter of the Muslim Brotherhood who imagined that the changes in regime in Iraq, Egypt, and Syria would let him create a new sultanate under his regency, a sultanate of the Muslim Brotherhood from the Atlantic to the Mediterranean.[18] This was the dream he shared with his Minister for Foreign Affairs, then prime minister, Ahmet Davutoğlu. And to make it come true, they would topple the Assad regime and destroy the Kurdish Workers' Party (*Partiya Karkerên Kurdistanê*, PKK) at any price.[19] In 2013, the Turkish intelligence service (*Millî İstihbarat Teşkilatı*, MİT) transferred about US$1.6 million in weapons and ammunition to the Islamist rebels in Syria.[20]

Meanwhile, Daish's *takfiris* advanced and occupied areas in the north of Mesopotamia, where Abu Bakr Al-Baghdadi established the Islamic State in 2013. He then commandeered 20 Russian T-55 tanks in Syria and crossed the border to Iraq, where he captured army bases and all the equipment supplied by the United States with little to no fight, with the exception of the area of the Kurdish government, where he faced relevant resistance. Dozens of foreign fighters, mostly former British and American soldiers, had voluntarily joined the Kurdish troops—the People's Protection Units stationed in northern Syria, better known in Iraq as the Peshmerga (those who face death),[21] commanded by Masoud Barzani, president of the Autonomous Kurdish Region.[22] They fought against Da'ish/ISIS/ISIL and other terrorist groups along 1050 km (642 miles) in alliance with the Dwekh Nawsha (self-sacrifice in Aramaic) militias, formed in 2014 to defend the ethnic-religious minorities in

---

[17]"Al-Qaida als Franchise-System—Lose verbunden, unabhängig finanziert, zu Ad–hoc-Kämpfern ausgebildet: Die neue Terroristen-Generation ist nicht kontrollierbar." Die Welt, July 8, 2014.

[18]"Cause of Syrian civil war, ISIS & Western propaganda: Assad interview highlights." RT, September 18, 2015. Available at: <http://www.rt.com/news/315848-assad-syria-isis-interview/>.

[19]Bruno Schirra, 2015, pp. 174–180.

[20]Ibidem, p. 184.

[21]Dieter Bednarz et al. (Spiegel Staff). "A Country Implodes: ISIS Pushes Iraq to the Brink." Spiegel Online, June 17, 2014. Available at: <http://www.spiegel.de/international/world/the-implosion-of-iraq-at-the-hands-of-the-isis-islamists%2D%2Da-975541.html>.

[22]John Hall (for MailOnline), "Meet the Peshmerga's International Brigade: From IT workers to ex-soldiers, the men from the West teaming up with Kurdish forces to fight ISIS." MailOnline, April 21, 2015. Available at: <http://www.dailymail.co.uk/news/article-3049019/Peshmerga-s-foreign-legion-fighting-alongside-defeat-ISIS-workers-ex-soldiers-brave-men-world-teaming-Kurdish-forces.html>.

Kurdistan's capital Erbil (former Irbilum) and entire Mesopotamia: about 700,000 Assyrian Christians, 900,000 Catholics, and 1 million followers of the Chaldean Catholic Church,[23] a group to which Tariq Aziz (Mikhail Yuhanna—1936–2015) belonged, the former Vice President of Saddam Hussein.

Da'ish flourished in the crisis President George W. Bush had provoked with his war on terror and preemptive attacks in Afghanistan (2001) and in Iraq (2003), where he brought down Saddam Hussein with the lie that he had weapons of mass destruction. The entire region became politically unstable. On January 18, 2007, General William E. Odom, former director of the National Security Agency (1985–1988) and professor at Yale University, told the Senate Foreign Relations Committee headed by then-Senator Joe Biden that the military intervention to overthrow Saddam Hussein had been a "strategic error of monumental proportions," for the war had not been confined to Iraq. It vastly exceeded its borders and not only unleashed an armed resistance against American occupation, with the sympathy and material support from other Arab countries, but also the open outburst of the previously shimmering conflict between Sunni and Shia, setting the stage for Iranian influence in Iraq.[24] "It presumed that establishing a liberal democracy in Iraq would lead to regional stability," recalled General William E. Odom. Instead— he stressed—"the policy of spreading democracy by force of arms has become the main source of regional instability."[25] Michael Morell, former deputy director of the CIA, also noted that not all countries were ready for democracy; democracy actually meant much more than free and fair elections.[26]

22.3   General el-Sisi's Coup in Egypt: The Crushing of the Muslim Brotherhood and Terrorists in the Sinai

Egypt would have been caught up in the chaos, just as Iraq, Libya, and Yemen, if not for the head of the armed forces, General Abdel Fattah el-Sisi, who deposed President Muḥammad Mursī/Mohamed Morsi (June 30, 2012–July 3, 2013), democratically elected by the Muslim Brotherhood, under the justification that the country was under threat from Salafist-Jihadist groups.[27] President Putin himself said that the "determination and wisdom" of Egypt's leadership saved the country

---

[23]Margo Kirtikar, Once Upon a Time in Baghdad: The Two Golden Decades The 1940s and 1950s. Crossways, Dartford (U.K.); Xlibris Corporation, 2011, pp. 270–271.

[24]"Strategic Errors of Monumental Proportions. What Can Be Done in Iraq?" Lt. Gen. William E. Odom (Ret.). Text of testimony before the Senate Foreign Relations Committee, 18 January 2007. AntiWar.com, January 26, 2007. Available at: <http://www.antiwar.com/orig/odom.php?articleid=10396>.

[25]Ibidem.

[26]Michael Morell & Bill Harlow, 2015, p. 196.

[27]Ibidem.

from the chaos and aggressiveness of the extremists.[28] The 270 terrorist attacks had occurred in 2013, during the government of the Muslim Brotherhood, about 79% against Egyptian military and police targets in the Sinai. Intelligence reports indicated that groups like Ansar al-Shariah, Tawhid wal-Jihad, and Takfir wal-Hijra wanted to proclaim the independence of this strategic peninsula, which bordered Gaza, Israel, and the Gulf of Aqaba to the east, the Suez Canal to the west, the Mediterranean to the north, and the Red Sea to the south.[29] And the attacks didn't stop after the fall of President Mursī. The Salafist-Jihadists mobilized Bedouin tribes, which accounted for about 70% of the Sinai's population, and continued to spread terror by kidnapping tourists, engaging in other criminal activities (drugs and arms trafficking) and setting off bombs in Cairo, Minya, and other cities of Egypt.

But General el-Sisi, elected president in 2014, somehow managed to control the situation through harsh repression and human rights abuses on an unprecedented scale. He did not allow Egypt to sink into chaos and fall apart, as had happened in Libya. More than 1000 militants of the Muslim Brotherhood perished in street battles with the security forces; and the courts condemned hundreds to death (many executed, some not), including its spiritual leader Muḥammad Badī and former President Muḥammad Mursī. In September 2015, approximately 40,000 Islamists still remained in prison. In Sinai, however, the terrorists joined Da'ish and killed 190 conscripts and officers of the Egyptian army in 2014 alone.[30] The terrorist attacks, although intermittent, didn't stop in Egypt.

22.4   The Arab Spring, Chaos, and Terror in Yemen

Yemen, a country strategically located between the Gulf of Aden and Saudi Arabia, hadn't achieved any sort of democracy, even after the collapse of the regime of President Alī 'Abdullāh Ṣāliḥ in 2012, in the midst of the Arab Spring. The government was taken over by Abdrabbuh Mansour Hadi, who was subsequently democratically elected. But with a population (26.7 million, July 2015 estimate) divided between 65% Sunni and 35% Shia,[31] Yemen's instability had become

---

[28]Vladimir Putin, "The World Order: New Rules or a Game without Rules." Meeting of the Valdai International Discussion Club. 24 October 2014, 19:00, Sochi. Official site of the President of Russia. Available at: <http://en.kremlin.ru/events/president/news/46860>. Accessed on October 12, 2015.

[29]Emily Dyer & Oren Kessler & Kit Waterman & Samuel James Abbott, Terror in the Sinai. London: The Henry Jackson Society, 2014, p. 4. Available at: <http://henryjacksonsociety.org/wp-content/uploads/2014/05/HJS-Terror-in-the-Sinai-Report-Colour-Web.pdf>.

[30]Steven A. Cook & Eni Enrico Mattei (Senior Fellow for Middle East and Africa Studies), "How to Get Egypt's Generals Back on Our Side." ForeignPolicy.com, January 5, 2015. Available at: <http://www.cfr.org/egypt/get-egypts-generals-back-our-side/p35922>.

[31]CIA—The World Fact Book. Available at: <https://www.cia.gov/library/publications/the-world-factbook/geos/ym.html>.

chronic after the reunification in 1990,[32] especially after al-Qa'ida in the Arabian Peninsula (AQPA) got a foothold and claimed the bombing of the destroyer USS Cole (DDG-67), anchored in the port of Aden, killing 17 sailors and injuring at least 40 in the year 2000. The country became one of the main targets of the CIA and the Joint Special Operations Command (JSOC). The situation deteriorated further in 2004, however, when the Shia insurgency erupted led by the cleric Hussein Badreddin al-Houthi. Violence spread in the midst of the assassinations of alleged terrorists by Special Operations Forces (SOF) and drone strikes from air bases in Ramstein (Germany) and Mogadishu (Somalia), where the CIA also installed secret prisons.[33]

According to the Bureau of Investigative Journalism, the Obama administration escalated the targeted killing strikes,[34] employing them as a central tactic in its strategy to combat terrorism. In Yemen, the United States carried out 103 attacks, including 88 drone strikes and land raids by the SOF, killing at least 580 people (424 of which hit by drones), including 131 civilians.[35] And the Shia insurgency led by the cleric Hussein al-Houthi intensified, spread, and transformed into an increasingly bloody civil, tribal, and sectarian war.

22.5 Indiscriminate Bombing by Saudi Arabia with Washington's Backing

The Houthis (as the Shia of the Zaidiyyah tribe in Yemen became known) conquered the capital Sanaa in January 2015 and toppled the regime of President Abdrabbuh Mansour Hadi. Saudi Arabia perceived this as a serious threat, especially after the escalating hostilities and the conquest of Mocha and the International Airport of Taiz, Yemen's third largest city. The Houthis, who the Saudis considered proxies of Iran, could now project themselves over the Horn of Africa. Soon after, therefore, the Saudis started an air campaign, Operation Decisive Storm ('Amaliyyat 'Āṣifat al-Ḥazm), leading a coalition of the United Arab Emirates, Jordan, Morocco,

---

[32]Until 1990, Yemen was divided into two states: The Yemen Arab Republic (North Yemen) and the People's Democratic Republic of Yemen (South Yemen).

[33]Jeremy Scahill, "The CIA's Secret Sites in Somalia Renditions, an underground prison and a new CIA base are elements of an intensifying US war, according to a Nation investigation in Mogadishu." The Nation, December 10, 2014. Available at: <http://www.thenation.com/article/cias-secret-sites-somalia/>.

[34]Siobhan Gorman & Adam Entous, "CIA Plans Yemen Drone Strikes—Covert Program Would Be a Major Expansion of U.S. Efforts to Kill Members of al Qaeda Branch." The Wall Street Journal, June 14, 2011.

[35]Jack Serle, "Drone strikes in Yemen—Analysis: What next for Yemen as death toll from confirmed US drone strikes hits 424, including 8 children." The Bureau of Investigative Journalism, January 30, 2015. Available at: <https://www.thebureauinvestigates.com/2015/01/30/analysis-death-toll-drone-strikes-yemen%2D%2Dcrisis-what-next/>.

Egypt, and Sudan to bomb Houthi positions with the logistical support of the United States. At the same time, the Salafist-Jihadists of al-Qa'ida in the Arabian Peninsula (AQPA) invested against the Houthis, whose militias represented the only force that actually opposed their advance in Yemen. With its backing of Saudi Arabia, the United States was strengthening Da'ish's offensive. In September 2015, the forces of President Hadi retook the city and the port of Aden, however. Until then, the beastly and indiscriminate bombings carried out by Saudi Arabia and its allies had already killed more than 2355 civilians.[36]

At the beginning of 2016, the humanitarian crisis in Yemen deteriorated and hit approximately 55.6% of the population (14.4 million), affecting the security of 7.6 million people, including in relation to food. At the same time, the entity Action on Armed Violence (AOAV) based in Great Britain had already recorded 6119–7514 civilian casualties as a result of explosives, i.e., the bombings carried out by Saudi Arabia since March 2015.[37]

At a meeting of the signatory countries of the Arms Trade Treaty (ATT), the organization control arms presented a report accusing France, Germany, Italy, Montenegro, the Netherlands, Spain, Sweden, Switzerland, Turkey, the United Kingdom, and the United States of providing US$25 billion worth in licenses for the sale of arms to Saudi Arabia—e.g., drones, bombs, torpedoes, rockets, and missiles—which were being used in major human rights violations and possible war crimes in Yemen.[38] And in an article published in London's *The Telegraph*, the Yemeni-British journalist Nawal al-Maghafi singled out the United Kingdom and the United States as the two primary causes of the problem in Yemen for giving assistance and allowing the richest country in the Middle East, Saudi Arabia, to gather forces and continue to bomb the poorest, Yemen, devastating the country and starving its population.[39]

---

[36]Kareem Fahim, "Saudis Face Mounting Pressure over Civilian Deaths in Yemen Conflict." The New York Times, September 29, 2015.

[37]"Yemen: Yemen—Conflict (ECHO, UN, EP, Media) (ECHO Daily Flash of 29 February 2016) February 29, 2016. UN Office for the Coordination of Humanitarian Affairs Country: Iraq, Jordan, Nepal, Nigeria, Ukraine, World, Yemen—European Commission Humanitarian Aid Office Country: Saudi Arabia, United Arab Emirates, Yemen." Available at: <http://www.unocha.org/aggregator/sources/80>; Khaled Abdullah, "UN 'conservative estimates' show 700 children among 6000 Yemen fatalities." RT, February 17, 2016. Available at: <https://www.rt.com/news/332710-yemen-humanitarian-catastrophe-fatalities/>.

[38]"Yemen needs peace, not more bombs February 29, 2016." Available at: <http://controlarms.org/en/>; "Campaigners urge States to stop selling billions of dollars in weapons to Saudi Arabia that are killing civilians in Yemen," February 26, 2016. Available at: <http://controlarms.org/en/news/campaigners-urge-states%2D%2Dto-stop-selling-billions-of-dollars-in-weapons-to-saudi-arabia-that-are-killing-civilians-in-yemen/>.

[39]Nawal al-Maghafi. "Yemen is becoming the new Syria—and Britain is directly to blame. Our support for the brutal Saudi Arabian intervention is creating a lawless wasteland where extremist groups like ISIL can thrive." The Telegraph, February 24, 2016. Available at: <http://www.telegraph.co.uk/news/worldnews/middleeast/yemen/12171785/Yemen-is-becoming-the-new-Syria-and-Britain-is%2D%2Ddirectly-to-blame.html>.

With Great Britain and the United States operating in the shadows, the war still endured in the early months of 2016, therefore. And a military solution certainly wouldn't be found, since the conflict involved profound tribal, regional, social, ideological, religious, and international contradictions, aggravated by the dismay in a locally and economically troubled environment.[40]

22.6 Chaos as the Predictable Result of US Foreign Policy

The chaos and conflict were nothing but predictable for those who knew the ethnic, tribal, and religious contradictions, in addition to the conflicting regional and international economic and geopolitical interests brewing in the Middle East and its surroundings. Countries such as Iraq, Syria, Libya, etc., created artificially by the Sykes-Picot Agreement,[41] would certainly implode without strong men like Saddam Hussein, Muammar al-Gaddafi, and Bashar al-Assad. As dictators, they managed in one way or another to maintain the unity of their countries as secular states, bringing together communities whose different beliefs—Sunnis, Salafi-Wahhabis, Shia, Kurds, etc.—superseded a national awareness, despite the fact that Arabs occupied a vast region and spoke the same Arabic language (with varying dialects). And faith, professed in absolute terms by various sects, fragmented Islam and excluded reason, doubt, and tolerance. Faith was the greatest passion, the leap into the absurd—as Søren Kierkegaard[42] taught us. It was absolutely faith that compelled Abraham to almost sacrifice Isaac on Mount Mōriyāh, obeying an order from God, who only sent an angel to stop the sacrifice of Abraham's only son after confirming this faith (Genesis 22). This is the seed that usually perverts monotheism, causing it to degenerate into terror. It's the syndrome of Islamic fundamentalism, whose main interpreter in the 1960s was the Egyptian intellectual Sayyid Qutb (1906–1966), the founder of the Muslim Brotherhood executed during the rule of President Gamal Abdel Nasser (1956–1970).[43]

---

[40]Barak A. Salmoni & Bryce Loidolt & Madeleine Wells, "Regime and Periphery in Northern Yemen—The Huthi Phenomenon." National Defense Research Institute—RAND, 2010. pp. 264–265. Prepared for the Defense Intelligence Agency. Available at: <http://www.rand.org/content/dam/rand/pubs/monographs/2010/RAND_MG962.pdf>.

[41]The Sykes-Picot agreement was negotiated in secret during the First World War (May 1916) by the diplomats François Georges-Picot, from France, and Sir Mark Sykes, from Great Britain, with the agreement of Russia, still under the reign of Tsar Nicholas II Romanov (1894–1917). The border line drawn by the Sykes and Picot ran from Acre (Akko), in Haifa Bay on the Mediterranean coast, to Kirkuk, in the vicinity of Persia, and the states that were then born were a tapestry of ethnicities, cultures, religions, sects and subsects, clans, and tribes, most of them nomads living in the deserts of Arabia.

[42]Søren Kierkegaard, 1993, pp. 58–59, 140–141.

[43]Emmanuel Sivan, 1985, pp. 117–118.

Profoundly ignorant about the deep Middle East, presidents George W. Bush and Barack Obama tried to implement their regime change and, consequently, nation-building policy. That is, they endeavored to overthrow the governments refusing to align with the economic and geopolitical interests of the United States and Israel. The neocons (neoconservatives), the majority of which were ethnically Jewish, many with dual citizenship, imagined that the disintegration of Syria, Iraq, and other Arab nations would promote Israel's hegemony in the Middle East, block Iran, and stop the traffic of weapons to Hizballah in Lebanon.[44]

President George W. Bush set the Middle East ablaze when he invaded Iraq based on "lies and fabrications," as the former American congressman and presidential candidate Ron Paul of the Republican Party (Texas) put it, based on later declassified CIA documents.[45] "From the sectarian violence unleashed by the USA invasion of Iraq emerged al-Qaeda and then its more radical spin-off, ISIS," Ron Paul said.[46] And he noted that it was hard to believe that in a society supposedly governed by the rule of law, "US leaders can escape any penalty for using blatantly false information—that they had to know at the time was false—to launch a pre-emptive attack on a country that posed no threat to the United States."[47] Indeed, former President George W. Bush, his Secretary of Defense Donald Rumsfeld, his National Security Advisor Condoleezza Rice, and his Secretary of State Colin Powell continued to go unpunished after rushing the country into a war without end. And this war grew and spread, inflicting enormous losses on the nation and costing thousands of lives, based on the falsehood that Saddam Hussein had chemical weapons and was rebuilding his nuclear program.[48] And according to Ron Paul, these same neocons who had defended the intervention in Libya and Syria were likely doing the same with the claims of a Russian "invasion" in Ukraine.[49]

President Obama stayed the same course as the neocons, irresponsibly ordering the bombing in Libya, an event that resulted in carnage and a humanitarian disaster. And he encouraged the war in Syria, training Jihadists, and arming those he called "moderate rebels" with weapons that mostly (70%) fell into the hands of the terrorists of the Islamic State, many sold at a good market price.[50] He had been

---

[44]Paulo Craig Roberts Interviewed by the Voice of Russia, 27 de junho de 2014-US war against Russia is already underway. PaulCraigRoberts.org. Available at: <http://www.paulcraigroberts. org/2014/07/01/us-war-russia-already-underway-pcr-interviewed-voice-russia/>.

[45]Ron Paul, "After a Twelve Year Mistake in Iraq, We Must Just March Home." The Ron Paul Institute for Peace & Prosperity, March 22, 2015. Available at: <http://www.ronpaulinstitute.org/ archives/featured-articles/2015/march/22/after%2D%2Da-twelve-year-mistake-in-iraq-we-must-just-march-home/>.

[46]Ibidem.

[47]Ibidem.

[48]Ibidem.

[49]Ibidem.

[50]Daniel Lazare, "Climbing into Bed with Al-Qaeda." Information Clearing House, May 2, 2015. Available at: <http://www.informationclearinghouse.info/article41742.htm>; "Media Blacks Out Pentagon Report Exposing U.S. Role In ISIS Creation." MintPress. Available at: <http://www.

told, however, that Sunni of the most radical ideological currents were the "major forces driving the insurgency in Syria" against Bashar al-Assad, who they considered *jibha ruwafdh* (a vanguard of the Shia). These forces included Salafists, the Muslim Brotherhood and AQI (al-Q'aida in Iraq), under the name of Jabhat al-Nusra (Victorious Army), Liwa al-Adiyat (Brigade of Great Punishments)—and were sustained by the countries of the Persian Gulf (Qatar and Saudi Arabia) and Turkey.[51] President Obama was also aware that since 2001, the terrorists had been shipping all types of armaments from Benghazi, Libya, where NATO had handed them out to oust Gaddafi, to the ports of Banias, and Borj Islam in Syria. Concerning this matter, on September 12, 2012, a Defense Intelligence Agency (DIA) report was sent to the White House, Secretary of State Hillary Clinton, Secretary of Defense Leon Panetta, the Chairman of the Joint Chiefs of Staff, and the National Security Council. And before his reelection in November 2012, Obama already knew that these rebels wanted to establish a caliphate throughout the Middle East, molded according to the one that existed in the seventh century and governed by Islamic law, the Shari'ah.[52] Their purpose was to *baqiya wa tatamadad*, i.e., endure and expand.[53]

22.7 The Rise of the Islamic State

As *The New York Times* clearly reported, Obama, the Pentagon, and the State Department knew from their intelligence that the majority of lethal weapons sent to Saudi Arabia and Qatar to supply the groups fighting against Bashar al-Assad was falling into the hands of radical Jihadists and not the supposedly "democratic-minded opposition,"[54] which existed only as fiction in order to justify the intervention in Syria. This is why the Russian Minister of Foreign Affairs Sergey Lavrov called the Free Syrian Army a "phantom group"; nobody knew where it operated or where its units could be found.[55] And when the journalist Robert Fisk was asked

---

mintpressnews.com/media-blacks-out-pentagon-report-exposing-u-s-role-in-isis-creation/206187>.

[51] Judicial Watch—Documents Archive.—pp. 1–3 (2–3) from JW v DOD and State 14–812. Available at: <http://www.judicialwatch.org/wp-content/uploads/2015/05/Pgs.-1-3-2-3-from-JW-v-DOD-and-State-14-812-DOD-Release-2015-04-10-final-version1.pdf>.

[52] Judicial Watch: Defense, State Department Documents Reveal Obama Administration Knew that al-Qaeda Terrorists Had Planned Benghazi Attack 10 Days in Advance. May 18, 2015 Available at: <http://www.judicialwatch.org/press-room/press-releases/judicial-watch-defense-state-department-documents-reveal-obama-administration-knew-that-al-qaeda-terrorists-had-planned-benghazi-attack-10-days-in-advance/>.

[53] Charles R. Lister, The Islamic State—A Brief Introduction. Washington, D.C., Brooking Institution Press, 2015, p. 5.

[54] David E. Sanger, "Rebel Arms Flow Is Said to Benefit Jihadists in Syria." The New York Times, October 14, 2012.

[55] "Russian Foreign Minister calls Free Syrian Army 'phantom' group', October 05." Available at: <http://tass.ru/en/politics/826244>. Accessed on October 5, 2015.

about the Free Syrian Army on the ABC network, he replied, "I think [it] drinks a lot of coffee in Istanbul," adding that it was a myth and that he had not seen any of its soldiers in Syria when he travelled the country as a correspondent for *The Independent* in London.[56]

On November 28, 2014, the German agency *Deutsche Welle* (DW) published a video clip of the journalist Anthony Cartalucci showing that Da'ish/ISIS/ISIL wasn't getting the resources for its weapons, clothes, and food from the "sale of oil on the black market," "ransoms from kidnappings," or private donations from Saudi Arabia and the United Arab Emirates alone. The NATO member countries were also providing billions of dollars in goods transported each day in trucks across the border of Turkey and Syria.[57] In another publication, Anthony Cartalucci wrote that by 2012, it was already clear that NATO was using the border with Turkey, north of Aleppo and Idlib, as the main route (Jordan, the second) to ship arms and terrorists from Libya to Syria.[58] Several reporters had "amply-documented the role of the NATO-Gulf-Zionist-Turkey alliance" in arming, training, and allowing passage to the terrorists of the so-called Free Syrian Army. On more than one occasion, NATO even used parachute drops to send weapons to the terrorists of Jabhat al-Nusra, the Islamic Front and Da'ish.[59]

President Putin was always very well aware that the United States and its allies were funding and directly arming the rebels, as they had done in the past, and providing mercenaries from various countries to fill their ranks. In a speech during the Valdai International Discussion Club on October 14, 2014 (near Veliky Novgorod), he said: "Let me ask where do these rebels get their money, arms and military specialists? Where does all this come from? How did the notorious ISIL manage to become such a powerful group, essentially a real armed force?"[60] The Free Syrian

---

[56]"Syrian soldiers are fighting for their lives as well as their country." Robert Fisk, Middle East correspondent for the Independent discusses the current situation in Syria. Transcript. Reporter: Emma Alberici. Lateline, Broadcast: November 10, 2014 Available at: <http://www.abc.net.au/lateline/content/2014/s4125600.htm>.

[57]Anthony Cartalucci, "Focus on Europe'IS' supply channels through Turkey." "Every day, trucks laden with food, clothing, and other supplies cross the border from Turkey to Syria. It is unclear who is picking up the goods. The haulers believe most of the cargo is going to the 'Islamic State' militia. Oil, weapons, and soldiers are also being smuggled over the border, and Kurdish volunteers are now patrolling the area in a bid to stem the supplies" (Video). Deutsche Welle (DW), November 28, 2014. Available at: <http://www.dw.com/en/is-supply-channels-through%2D%2Dturkey/av-18091048>.

[58]Tony Cartalucci, "US-Turkey 'Buffer Zone' to Save ISIS, Not Stop Them." NEO (New Eastern Outlook). Available at: <http://journal-neo.org/2015/10/24/us%2D%2Dturkey-buffer-zone-to-save-isis-not-stop-them/>.

[59]Eva Bartlett, "Distorting the story of Syria's Heritage destruction." Crescent International, February 2015. Available at: <http://www.crescent-online.net/2015/02/distorting-the-story-of-syrias-heritage-destruction-eva-bartlett-4815-articles.html>.

[60]Vladimir Putin, "The World Order: New Rules or a Game without Rules." Meeting of the Valdai International Discussion Club. 24 October 2014, 19:00, Sochi. Official site of the President of Russia. Available at: <http://en.kremlin.ru/events/president/news/46860>. Accessed on October 12, 2015.

Army had actually been set up by the United States and Western countries,[61] formed by officers who defected from Assad's army, and many, if not most, joined or were already members of Da'ish/ISIS/ISIL. On July 8, 2013, these "moderate rebels" President Obama had given weapons, ammunition, and other war material invaded the Christian Village of Oum Sharshouh, in the vicinity of the city of Homs, killing many Christians, torching buildings, and forcing around 250 families from their homes.[62] Most of these "moderate rebels" actually belonged to the Islamic Organization Dawlat al-'Iraq al-Islāmīyah, linked to al-Qa'ida in Iraq (AQI), which the neocon Senator John McCain, with his usual obtuseness, considered a "heroic organization."[63] Its commander was Abu Abdullah al-Rashid al-Baghdadi, later replaced by Abu Bakr al-Baghdadi, who established the Islamic State of Iraq and Syria—Da'ish—on April 8, 2013, and proclaimed himself Caliph Ibrahim, the successor of the Prophet.

In mid-2014, President Obama nevertheless requested, and Congress approved US$500 million—a higher amount than expected—to train and arm *moderate Syrian rebels* in camps in Turkey and Jordan, further expanding the oblique involvement of the United States in the war against the Bashar al-Assad regime.[64] And one of the reasons for this was to compensate for the lost profits of the war industry and the private military corporations, such as KBR (Kellogg Brown & Root, Inc.), a division of Halliburton, which had received around US$39.5 billion in contracts from the George W. Bush administration without competing bids to provide services in Iraq.[65]

---

[61]Peter Scholl-Latour, 2014, pp. 11–12.

[62]"Editors Christians Massacred by 'Free' Syrian Army Terrorists (Rebels)." OrtodoxNet.com. Blog. August 24, 2013 Available at: <http://www.orthodoxytoday.org/blog/2013/08/christians-massacred-by-free-syrian-army-terrorists-rebels/>; Robert Spencer, "U.S. training Free Syrian Army in Jordan—a group that violently targets Christians." Jihad Watch, February 7, 2014. Available at: <http://www.jihadwatch.org/2014/02/u-s-training-free-syrian-army-in-jordan-a-group-that-violently-targets-christians>; Tom Cohland & Norhan Keshik, "West bankrolls Free Syrian Army fightback." The Times—The Australian, February 8, 2014. Available at: <http://www.theaustralian.com.au/news/world/west%2D%2Dbankrolls-free-syrian-army-fightback/story-fnb64oi6-1226820979028?nk=7f805021fdbcc30f4ca8b9d3cd537c47#>.

[63]Alex Newman, "What is the Obama-backed Free Syrian Army?" New American, September 17, 2013. Available at: <http://www.thenewamerican.com/world%2D%2Dnews/asia/item/16550-what-is-the-obama-backed-free-syrian-army>.

[64]Julian E. Barnes & Adam Entous & Carol E. Lee, "Obama Proposes $500 Million to Aid Syrian Rebels—Program to Train and Equip Moderate Opposition Would Expand U.S. Role in Civil War." The Wall Street Journal, June 26, 2014.

[65]Angelo Young, "And The Winner For The Most Iraq War Contracts Is... KBR, With $39.5 Billion In A Decade." International Business Times, March 19, 2013. Available at: <http://www.ibtimes.com/winner-most-iraq-war-contracts-kbr-395-billion%2D%2Ddecade-1135905>;   RSN. Available   at: <http://readersupportednews.org/news-section2/308-12/16561-focus-cheneys-halliburton-made-395-billion-on-iraq-war>.

The program proposed by President Obama resulted in a completely ridiculous and utmost fiasco, however.[66] The press secretary of the Department of Defense, Peter Cook,[67] revealed that the first 54–70 graduates crossed the border from Turkey to Syria near Azaz and Bab al-Salama, north of Aleppo, on July 31, 2015, after 2 months of training and armed by the Army Special Forces and CIA at a cost of US $41.8 million. They were promptly attacked in the village of Mariameen by militias of Jabhat al-Nusra, however, and fled. Others died or were captured, including Lieutenant Farhan al-Jassem, with all their heavy weaponry, about 25% of the total supplied by the Pentagon.[68] These "moderate" rebels recruited by the US Central Command (CENTCOM) were mercenaries, many of Turkish ethnicity, others Arabs from the most diverse countries, and earned a monthly salary of US $225 as soldiers and US$350 as officers.[69]

This information could hardly have come as a surprise to the Pentagon's CENTCOM. The commander of the "moderate rebels," Abd al-Jabbar al-Okaidi, retreated from the battle front and criticized the lack of support from the United States and Britain,[70] but the truth is that he had "good" relationships with the

---

[66]Eric Schmitt & Ben Hubbard, "U.S. Revamping Rebel Force Fighting ISIS in Syria." The New York Times, September 6, 2015. Available at: <http://www.nytimes.com/2015/09/07/world/middleeast/us-to-revamp-training-program-to-fight-isis.html>. Accessed on September 7, 2015.

[67]Richard Sisk, "Syrian Rebel Training Program Costs Millions and Counting." DoD–Buzz—Military.com Network, September 9, 2015. Available at: <http://www.dodbuzz.com/2015/09/09/syrian-rebel-training-program-costs-millions-and-counting/>; Martin Matishak, "$42 Million for 54 Recruits: U.S. Program to Train Syrian Rebels Is a Disaster." The Fiscal Times, September 10, 2015. Available at: <http://www.thefiscaltimes.com/2015/09/10/42-Million-54-Recruits-US-Program-Train-Syrian-Rebels-Dud>.

[68]Ibidem; Karen Deyoung, "Commander of U.S.-backed rebels captured by al-Qaeda militants in Syria." The Washington Post, July 30, 2015. "West suffers new Syria setback as US-trained rebels arrested." The Times, September 21, 2015. Available at: <http://www.thetimes.co.uk/tto/news/world/middleeast/article4562713.ec>; "Capture of U.S.-Trained Fighters in Syria Sets Back Fight Against ISIS—Lieutenant Farhan al-Jassem spoke to the Center for Public Integrity before he was taken." Syrian Observatory for Human Rights, August 3, 2015. Available at: <http://www.syriahr.com/en/2015/08/capture-of-u-s-trained-fighters-in-syria-sets%2D%2Dback-fight-against-isis/>; "Syria's rebel fighters recruited to fight Isis, but captured and beaten by Jabhat al-Nusra for 'collaborating with crusaders'." The Independent, September 28, 2015. Available at: <http://www.independent.co.uk/news/world/middle-east/syrias-rebel-fighters-recruited-to-fight-isis-but-captured-and-beaten-by-jabhat-alnusra-for-collaborating-with-crusaders-10432686html>; "Syria conflict: 75US-trained rebels crossed into Syria from Turkey, monitoring group says." ABC News. Available at: <http://www.abc.net.au/news/2015-09-20/75-us-trained-rebels-enter-syria-monitoring-group-says/6790300>.

[69]Eric Schmitt & Ben Hubbard, "U.S. Revamping Rebel Force Fighting ISIS in Syria." The New York Times, September 6, 2015. Available at: <http://www.nytimes.com/2015/09/07/world/middleeast/us-to-revamp-training-program-to-fight-isis.html>. Accessed on September 7, 2015.

[70]Ruth Sherlock, "Syria rebel quits after battlefield defeat—Syria rebel commander lashes out at his western patrons as he quits in protest at losses to regime." The Telegraph, November 4, 2013.

"brothers" of Da'ish.[71] In September 2014, the Syrian Observatory for Human Rights reported that the Free Syrian Army, commanded by Colonel Riad al-Asaad, had signed a nonaggression pact with Da'ish, since the priority was to overthrow President Bashar al-Assad.[72] And in April 2015, between 9000 and 12,000 Jihadists of approximately 40 Wahhabi/Salafist terrorist groups, including Ahrar al-Sham, Jund al-Aqsa, Liwa al-Haqq, Jaysh al-Sunna, Ajnad al-Sham and Faylaq al-Sham, and members of the Jaysh Al Fateh (Army of Conquest) alliance, conquered the strategic city of Jisr al-Shughour between Aleppo and Latakia on the Mediterranean coast. They were led by Jabhat al-Nusra, a franchise of al-Qa'ida in Iraq (AQI), and counted with the support of the 13th Division of the Free Syrian Army, which attacked the forces of President Bashar al-Assad through the lines of Idilib.[73] The town of Jisr al-Shughour was freed days later by the forces of President Bashar al-Assad, however.

Da'ish expanded from Bab and Manbij in the east of Aleppo in Syria, conquering al-Raqqa, where it established its de facto capital and general headquarters to the province of Hasaka, spreading its terror over hundreds of miles. It crossed the border from Syria to Iraq, taking control of the Euphrates River and a population of around 8 million people, in addition to 11 oil fields with a production of 25,000–40,000 barrels per day with an estimated value of US$1.2 million, which it smuggled to Iran, Kurdistan, Syria, and Turkey.[74] With the marginal fields in northern Iraq alone, the Jihadists gained US$730 million per year in resources, enough to fund their operations beyond the borders of the country.[75] Indeed, Mehmet Ali Ediboğlu, a

---

Available at: <http://www.telegraph.co.uk/news/worldnews/middleeast/syria/10425001/Syria-rebel-quits-after-battlefield-defeat.html>.

[71]Eva Bartlett, "Distorting the story of Syria's Heritage destruction." Crescent International, February 2015. Available at: <http://www.crescent-online.net/2015/02/distorting-the-story-of-syrias-heritage-destruction-eva-bartlett-4815-articles.html>.

[72]Rebecca Shabad, "US-backed Rebels and Islamic State sign Ceasefire/Non-aggression Pact—ISIS, Syrian rebels reach ceasefire." Information Clearing House, Saturday, September 13, 2014. Available at: <http://www.informationclearinghouse.info/article39665.htm.MEEstaff>; "Free Syrian Army will not join US-led coalition against IS">; Nairaland, September 14, 2014. Available at: <http://www.nairaland.com/1902522/free-syrian-army-not-join>.

[73]Lizzie Dearden, "Jabhat al-Nusra seizes control of major Syrian government stronghold with rebel coalition—The city of Jisr al-Shughur lies on a strategic motorway from the capital to coast." The Independent, April 25, 2015. Available at: <http://www.independent.co.uk/news/world/middle-east/jabhat-al-nusra-seizes-control-of-major-syrian-government-stronghold-with-jihadist-coalition-10203764.html>.

[74]Chris Dalby, "Who Is Buying The Islamic State's Illegal Oil?" OilPrice.com, September 30, 2014. Available at: <http://oilprice.com/Energy/Crude-Oil/Who-Is%2D%2DBuying-The-Islamic-States-Illegal-Oil.html>; Claude Salhani, "Islamic State's Ultimate Goal: Saudi Arabia's Oil Wells." OilPrice.com, September 9, 2014. Availableat: <http://oilprice.com/Geopolitics/Middle-East/Islamic-States-Ultimate-Goal-Saudi-Arabias-Oil-Wells.html>.

[75]Luay Al-Khatteeb (Special to CNN), "How Iraq's black market in oil funds ISIS." CNN, August 22, 2014. Available at: <http://edition.cnn.com/2014/08/18/business/al-khatteeb-isis-oil-iraq/>. Accessed on October 2, 2015.

congressman of the Republican People's Party elected by the province of Hatay (Turkey, on the border with Syria), denounced in mid-2014 that Da'ish/ISIS/ISIL had earned US$800 million by selling the oil from the occupied regions (Rumeilan, northern Syria—and later Mosul, northern Iraq) in Turkey.[76] And Luay Al Khatteeb, director of the Iraq Energy Institute, reported that the crude and refined oil for trade in cash were being treated in refineries in Syria captured by Da'ish[77] and "transported by tankers to Jordan via Anbar province, to Iran via Kurdistan, to Turkey via Mosul, to Syria's local market and to the Kurdistan region of Iraq, where most of it gets refined locally."[78]

Despite the support from Saudi Arabia, Qatar, and other emirates, Da'ish probably cherished the dream of occupying Mecca and Medina, the holy cities of Islam, taking control of the oil and gas existing in the Persian Gulf and eliminating the borders throughout the Middle East and its surroundings in Africa.[79] Its resources were estimated to have exceeded US$2 billion at the end of 2014.[80] And in addition to oil smuggling, the Jihadists' war chest was filled through extortion, the taxation of the dominated populations, kidnappings, the confiscation of bank deposits, and the sale of small antiques intended for the London market.[81] A large part of the trafficking, which also included drugs, was done through the Sahara by Jihadists of al-Qa'ida in the Islamic Maghrib (AQMI) and other equally criminal but less ideological operators working only for money. The drugs stemmed mainly from South America and arrived by boat and plane at the coast of West Africa. From there they were transported (by plane and other means) to the edge of the desert, where the smugglers of the Sahara were tasked with delivering the resources to the various terrorist groups.

When the Jihadists of the Islamic State, Jabhat al-Nusra and other groups, entered Iraq in early 2014 counting with the support of the Sufi Naqschbandīya militias, they plundered many cities, including Fallujah, Ramad, Kirkuk, Tikrit where Saddam Hussein was born, and Mosul, all the while conquering bases and arsenals of the

---

[76]Guler Vilmaz, "Opposition MP says ISIS is selling oil in Turkey"—"The Islamic State of Iraq and al-Sham (ISIS) has been selling smuggled Syrian oil in Turkey worth $800 million, according to Ali Ediboglu, a lawmaker for the border province of Hatay from the main opposition Republican People's Party (CHP)." Al-Monitor, June 13, 2014. Available at: <http://www.al-monitor.com/pulse/business/2014/06/turkey-syria-isis-selling-smuggled-oil>.

[77]Ibidem. Chris Dalby, "Who Is Buying The Islamic State's Illegal Oil?" OilPrice.com, September 30, 2014. Available at: <http://oilprice.com/Energy/Crude-Oil/Who-Is-Buying-The-Islamic-States-Illegal-Oil.html>. Accessed on October 2, 2015.

[78]Ibidem.

[79]Claude Salhani, "Islamic State's Ultimate Goal: Saudi Arabia's Oil Wells." OilPrice.com, September 9, 2014. Available at: <http://oilprice.com/Geopolitics/Mid-dle-East/Islamic-States-Ultimate-Goal-Saudi-Arabias-Oil-Wells.html>.

[80]Catherine Shakdam, "Genesis: The real story behind the rise of ISIS." RT, July 25, 2015. Available at: <http://www.rt.com/op-edge/310731-isis-rise-sup-port-terror/>.

[81]Tarek Radwan, "Top News: Syrian Antiquities and the ISIS Billion-Dollar Economy." Atlantic Council, August 26, 2015. Available at: <http://www.atlanticcouncil.org/en/blogs/menasource/top-news-syrian-antiquities-and-the-isis-s%2D%2Dbillion-dollar-economy>.

Iraqi army, such as Atareb, Taftanaz, Jirah, and Tiyas, where they took possession of the arms supplied by the United States—F-16s, Apache helicopters, Humvees, M-1 tanks, antitank missiles, and armored BGM-71 TOW vehicles, manufactured by Eagle-Piche IND (Indiana) Inc.[82] The Iraqi army's divisions didn't put up any resistance. They routed, and many Sunni soldiers and police officers joined Da'ish, despite the approximately US$25 billion the United States had spent on the training of these troops for several years.[83] And so the Jihadists advanced, occupying Baquba, 60 km (37 miles) from Baghdad, and carrying out successive massacres with the dimension of a genocide. They took no prisoners, beheading those who were captured or surrendered. They engaged in sexual crimes, raping women of the religious minorities—Assyrian Christians, Catholics, and Yazidis[84]—whose villages to the south of Mount Sinjar, northeast of Iraq, they had attacked in August 2014. After executing between 2000 and 5000 men, women, and children, they raped and captured 3000 or more young women to use them as sex slaves. After her release, one of these women testified to the US Congress and revealed that she was brutally raped and enslaved by a Jihadist of Da'ish's high command, an American-born and very white 23-year-old called Abu Abdullah al-Amriki (the American).[85] Abdullah is one of the more than 250 American citizens, among the more than 4500 other westerners, recruited by Da'ish, where the community of foreign Jihadists—Al Muhajirun[86]—kept growing at an estimated pace of 1000 per month, on average, since 2011.[87] The number of foreigners among the Jihadists

---

[82]Dieter Bednarz et al. (Spiegel Staff), "A Country Implodes: ISIS Pushes Iraq to the Brink." Spiegel Online, June 17, 2014. Available at: <http://www.spiegel.de/international/world/the-implosion-of-iraq-at-the-hands-of-the-isis-islamists%2D%2Da-975541.html>.

[83]Ibidem.

[84]The Yazidis, a minority that professes a syncretic religion, which included elements from Christianity, Islam, and Zoroastrianism, are ethnically Kurdish, and their population was estimated to be 700, 000 people, mostly concentrated in the vicinity of Mount Sinjar.

[85]"ISIS told Yazidi sex slaves that rape is part of their twisted corruption of Islam." Mirror, August 14, 2015. Available at: <http://www.mirror.co.uk/news/world-news/isis-told-yazidi-sex-slaves-6251415>; "Yazidi Slave Reveals: American Jihadi is 'Top ISIS Commander'." AhlulBayt News Agency (BNA), September 29, 2015. Available at: <http://en.abna24.com/service/middle-east-west-asia/archive/2015/09/29/712912/story.html>; PARRY, Hannah (Dailymail.com). "Yazidi sex slave claims she was raped by 'white American ISIS jihadi' in Syria." Daily Mail, September 24, 2015. Available at: <http://www.dailymail.co.uk/news/article-3248173/Yazidi-sex-slave-claims-raped-American-teacher-turned-ISIS-jihadi%2D%2Dtestify-Congress.html>. Accessed on September 29, 2015.

[86]Thomas Joscelyn, "Jihadist front established to represent foreign fighters in Syria." The Long War Journal—Foundation for Defense of Democracies. Available at: <http://www.longwarjournal.org/archives/2015/07/jihadist-front-established-to%2D%2Drepresent-foreign-fighters-in-syria.php>.

[87]"Final Report of the Task Force on Combating Terrorist and Foreign Fighter Travel." Homeland Security Committee—U.S. House of Representatives, September 29, 2015. Available at: <https://homeland.house.gov/wp-content/uploads/2015/09/TaskForceFinalReport.pdf>, pp. 11–12. Accessed on September 28, 2015. "Number of foreign fighters in Syria has doubled in past year—report." RT, September 27, 2015. Available at: <https://www.rt.com/news/316644-jihadists-flow-double-syria/>. Accessed on September 28, 2015.

grew from 8500 in 2013 to more or less 15,000 in 2014[88] and exceeded 25,000, almost 30,000, more than triple, by September 2015, according to a report from the Homeland Security Committee of the House of Representatives.[89] The bombings carried out by the coalition led by the United States did not prevent Da'ish from swelling its ranks, filled to approximately 50% by foreigners. And Da'ish expanded its influence to Afghanistan, Egypt, Libya (with 5000 Jihadists at the beginning of 2015), Tunisia, and other countries in Africa, where it was joined by the Islamic terrorist groups Boko Haram, in Nigeria, and al-Shabaab, in Kenya.[90]

---

[88]Michael Weiss & Hassan Hassan, 2015, pp. 166–167.

[89]"Final Report of the Task Force on Combating Terrorist and Foreign Fighter Travel." Homeland Security Committee—U.S. House of Representatives, September 29, 2015. Available at: <https://homeland.house.gov/wp-content/uploads/2015/09/TaskForceFinalReport.pdf, pp. 11–12>.

[90]Ibidem, pp. 11–13.

Chapter 23
Israel Under Right-Wing Government

23.1 Gas Reserves in Gaza, Ḥamās' Victory, and the IDF's Massacre and Destruction of the Gaza Strip

Saudi Arabia, Qatar, and Turkey's interests in promoting civil war in Syria were intertwined with those of the United States and some European Union countries. These interests were economic, religious, geopolitical and strategic in nature, complex, and often contradictory and irreconcilable. Despite the Gulf nation's close economic and financial ties with the United States—ties resting on the corruption of the oil-for-weapons swap—they also cherished such political and religious objectives as regional dominance and the establishment of the Great Caliphate ruled by *Shariah* and the Prophet's hadith. Turkey's President Recep Tayyip Erdoğan had similar ambitions with the Muslim Brotherhood. And these goals didn't align with those of the United States and its puppet governments in France and Great Britain. Among other things, these western nations wanted to take control of the entire Mediterranean, close the naval bases of Tartus and Latakia operated by Russia there, and prevent the completion of the pipeline linking the estimated 14 trillion cubic meters in natural gas and 18 billion barrels in condensed gas of Southern Iran (Pars South) and Qatar in the Persian Gulf with the east of the Mediterranean and the coast of Syria.[1]

Extensive gas reserves were also discovered along the coast of the Gaza Strip in 2000, estimated at 1.4 trillion cubic meters and valued at approximately US$4 billion by British Gas (BG Group), which had signed a contract to exploit them with the Palestinian Authority. In 2007, the former chief of staff of the Israel Defense Forces

---

[1]"Iran to double gas production at South Pars largest Phase." PressTV, May 30, 2014. Available at: <http://www.presstv.ir/detail/2014/05/30/364764/iran-to%2D%2Dboost-south-pars-gas-out put/>; "Iran's South Pars phases to be completed by 2017: Official." PressTV, May 30, 2014. Available at: <http://www.press%2D%2Dtv.ir/detail/2014/05/30/364764/iran-to-boost-south-pars-gas-Ooutput/>.

© Springer Nature Switzerland AG 2019
L. A. Moniz Bandeira, *The World Disorder*,
https://doi.org/10.1007/978-3-030-03204-3_23

(IDF), Moshe Ya'alon, publicly accused the Security Council of Prime Minister Ehud Olmert's government. He said they had failed to order military action in Gaza so as not to undermine negotiations with British Gas regarding the purchase of the gas to be extracted from the region.[2] His argument, like the one made by Mossad's head Meir Dagan, was that the gas resources in Gaza would fund terror attacks against Israel. The following year, on December 27, 2008, Tel Aviv carried out Operation Cast Lead and invaded Gaza, where Ḥamās, the acronym for *Ḥarakat al-Mu-qāwamah al-'Islāmiyyah* (Islamic Resistance Movement), had won the elections and taken power after a brief armed conflict with the Palestinian National Authority presided by Mahmoud Abbas. The IDF suffered only 17 casualties but slaughtered 1385–1417 Palestinians, including more than 1000 civilians, mainly women and children, and left around 5000–7000 injured. It caused massive damage to the 12,000 people who had to disperse with the destruction of more than 4000 homes, buildings, and much of Gaza's infrastructure. The losses were estimated at almost US$2 billion.[3]

Conflicts never ceased in Palestine, especially in Gaza. And between November 14 and 21, 2012, 4 years after Operation Cast Lead, the IDF launched another operation—Operation Pillar of Cloud/Pillar of Defense.[4] It resulted in the deaths of Ahmed al-Jabari, commander of Ḥamās' Izz ad-Din al-Qassam Brigades,[5] and about 1168 Palestinians, 101 of whom presumably civilians, including 33 children and 13 women. Hundreds were wounded during the destruction of homes, health centers, banks, and mosques, while Gaza's agricultural sector suffered US$20 million in losses.[6] About 2300 Palestinian were displaced, and the entire population

---

[2]Avi Bar-Eli, "Ya'alon: British Gas natural gas deal in Gaza will finance terror. Former IDF Chief of Staff accuses Gov't of not Ordering Military action in Gaza so as not to Damage BG Deal." Haaretz.com, October 21, 2007. Available at: <http://www.haaretz.com/misc/article-print-page/ya-alon-british-gas-natural-gas%2D%2Ddeal-in-gaza-will-finance-terror-1.231576?trailingPath=2. 169%2C2.216%2C>; Raji Sourani, (Director of the Palestinian Centre for Human Rights, in Gaza). "History is repeated as the international community turns its back on Gaza—As was the case in Operation Cast Lead, the international community is once again turning its back on Gaza." Al Jazeera, November 17, 2012. Available at: <http://www.aljazeera.com/indepth/opinion/2012/11/20121117115136211403.html>.

[3]"Life in the Gaza Strip." BBC News, July 14, 2014. Available at: <http://www.bbc.com/news/world-middle-east-20415675?print=true>.

[4]For the Hebrews the operation took the name Pilar of Cloud (עמוד ענן), a reference to the presence of the God of Israel during the day, who guided the Jews in the crossing of the Jordan during the exodus from Egypt (Exodus 13: 21–22) as Pillar of Fire during the night.

[5]Sheikh Izz ad-Din al-Qassam (1882–1935) was born in Latakia (Syria) and led the first intifada in 1935 against the rule of Great Britain and increasing Zionist penetration in Palestine. He was shot by English soldiers on November 20, 1935.

[6]"Human Rights Council—20-Second Session—Agenda items 2 and 7 Annual report of the United Nations High Commissioner for Human Rights and reports of the Office of the High Commissioner and the Secretary-General Human rights situation in Palestine and other occupied Arab territories—Report of the United Nations High Commissioner for Human Rights on the implementation of Human Rights Council resolutions S 9/1 and S-12/1—Addendum Concerns related to adherence to international human rights and international humanitarian law in the context of the escalation

of Gaza suffered with the lack of shelter, food, and medical care.[7] It was the IDF's answer to the Ḥamās rockets fired against Israel, which had killed only 6 Israelis, including 4 civilians, injured 259 people, including 239 civilians, and destroyed 80 homes.[8] Israel's reprisal was brutal and asymmetrical, and the escalation of violence only served to feed the vicious cycle of terrorism and massacres.

23.2 Continuing Expansion of Settlements

Conflict in Palestine had been chronic and inevitable since before Israel's creation, and it escalated after the end of First World War. The prospect of a perpetual war was set on November 2, 1917, when the powerful banker Lord Lionel W. Rothschild induced the British Foreign Secretary, Lord James A. Balfour, to declare that Britain would favor "the establishment in Palestine of a national home for the Jewish people (Eretz Yisrael)." Colonel Thomas E. Lawrence, who had commanded the Arab insurgency against Ottoman rule in First World War, clearly saw what was on the horizon. He warned the director of Britain's military intelligence (MI6), Sir Gilbert Clayton, that the mass migration of Jews to Palestine, where only an estimated 58,000 of them lived against 74,000 Christians and an overwhelming Muslim majority of 568,000, would ignite permanent conflict in the region. The Arab peasants would not be willing to give up their land to Jewish settlers and "the Jewish influence in European finance might not be enough to deter the Arabs from refusing to quit—or worse!"[9] But as Voltaire already emphasized many years ago, the belief prevailed of what God had told Abraham: "to thy seed will I give this land, from the river of Egypt even to the great river Euphrates" (Genesis, 15:18).[10] Perhaps Prime Minister Benjamin Netanyahu thought he could expand the God-given Land of Israel from the waters of the Nile to the Euphrates. In any case, it was clear that he meant to occupy not only Judea, Samaria, and Galilee, the lands where David, Solomon, Isaiah, and Jeremiah had lived, but all of Palestine, resurrecting the cradle of the Jewish people, Eretz Israel (Land of Israel). The borders of Israel have continued expanding since al-Nakba, the humanitarian disaster of 1948 and the exodus of 700,000 Arabs with the depopulation of Haifa, Jaffa, Acre, Nazareth,

---

between the State of Israel, the de facto authorities in Gaza, and Palestinian armed groups in Gaza that occurred from 14 to 21 November 2012." Avance version Distr.: General 6 March 2013, pp. 6–11. Available at: <http://www.ohchr.org/Documents/HRBodies/HRCouncil/RegularSession/Session22/A.HRC.22.35.Add.1_AV.pdf>.

[7]Ibidem, p. 11.

[8]Ibidem, p. 12.

[9]Lawrence James, 1995, pp. 275–391. See also Luiz Alberto Moniz Bandeira, 2014, pp. 177–180.

[10]Voltaire (François Marie Arouet), 1964, p. 248.

Safed, and other towns and villages strangled by first the Jewish paramilitary forces Haganah (the Defense) and then the Israel Defense Forces.[11] At the end of the 1947–1948 war, Tel Aviv also tried to incorporate the Gaza Strip into its jurisdiction during the peace negotiations with the Arab countries (Egypt, Iraq, Lebanon, Saudi Arabia, Syria, Transjordan, and Yemen).[12] Egypt vetoed the attempt, however. But after winning successive armed conflicts (Six-Day War, 1967; Yom Kippur War, 1973; and other disputes), Israel incorporated most of Palestine's territory and occupied the West Bank through land confiscations and the settlement of Jewish colonists. More than 1 million Israelites, survivors of the Holocaust, emigrated to Israel between 1949 and 1960. And this flow did not stop. From 1970 to 1980, Israel dispossessed the lands owned by the Arab refugees, who were prevented from returning.[13] Between 1993 and 1998, it confiscated more than 117,000 dunums,[14] equivalent to about 28,000 acres, from Arab refugees or as war reparations.[15] The United States remained silent, as it had to. Although Jews didn't make up more than 2.2% of its population in 2014, their influence in Congress and the White House had reached the highest of levels because of their immense financial sway and the powerful Jewish lobby (Israel Public Affairs Committee, AIPAC), which poured millions of dollars into elections and heavily influenced Washington's foreign policy. The confiscation of Palestinian lands was a *fait accompli*.[16] And Tel Aviv authorized the construction of an additional 15,000 residential units' in the West Bank and the arrival of more than 55,000 settlers between 1993 and 1998.

Under Prime Minister Benjamin Netanyahu (1996–1999), who took over administration after the assassination of Yitzhak Rabin by a Jewish fundamentalist in 1996, the expansion of settlements advanced even further after the lifting of building restrictions in the West Bank and Gaza. The number of settlers jumped to 380,000 in 1999, and the West Bank was divided in Palestinian cantons, located to the north, center, and south, with no connections among themselves.[17] These settlements made any reversal of the situation more difficult, almost impossible even. For Catherine Ashton, High Representative of the European Union for Foreign and Security Affairs, these "settlements are illegal, constitute an obstacle to peace and threaten to make a two-state solution impossible."

---

[11]Benny Morris, 1987, pp. 89–96, 101–111.

[12]Ibidem, 268–275.

[13]Michael R. Fischbach, 2003, pp. 315–317.

[14]1 dunum (measure of Turkish origin) is equivalent to 0.247105 acres.

[15]Michael R. Fischbach, 2003, pp. 315–317.

[16]Ibidem, p. 363.

[17]Leila Farsakh (Research fellow at the Trans-Arab Research Institute, Boston), "The Palestinian Economy and the Oslo Peace Process." Trans-Arab Institute (TARI). Available at: <http://tari.org/index.php?option=com_content&view=article&id=9&Itemid=11>.

23.3   The Elimination of Yasser Arafat Planned by Ariel Sharon and George W. Bush

Tel Aviv had no motivation to resolve the conflict in Palestine, and neither did Washington since at least the Jimmy Carter administration. When King Abdullah II of Jordan was received in the Oval Office in 2002, he realized President George W. Bush didn't have the slightest interest in the peace process in Palestine.[18] Bush only attacked Yasser Arafat, accusing him of siding with the terrorists. He justified not only his house arrest ordered by Prime Minister Ariel Sharon (2001–2006) but also the destruction of the infrastructure of the Palestinian Authority in the West Bank.[19] During the photo opportunity with King Abdullah, Bush took a question about how "Prime Minister Sharon spoke yesterday about his sorrow not to eliminate President Arafat in Lebanon, as if it was a mistake he would like to correct now." President George W. Bush replied that the best way to peace was indeed to derail what was holding it back "and what derails peace is terror."[20] And he stressed that the "more quickly we eliminate terror, the more likely it is we'll have a peaceful resolution in the region."[21] Israel's Prime Minister Ariel Sharon was himself received by Bush in the Oval Office on February 8, 2002, where he said that he and his government considered Arafat "an obstacle to peace" and that Arafat had chosen "the strategy of terror."[22] In the equation of Sharon and Bush, Yasser Arafat meant terror. So eliminating terror implied the assassination of Yasser Arafat (1929–2004), the leader of the Palestine Liberation Organization and president of the Palestinian Authority (As-Sulṭah Al-Waṭaniyyah Al-Filasṭīniyyah) created by the Oslo Accords, through which he had recognized Israel's right to exist in return for the withdrawal of its forces from the West Bank and Gaza.

At the same time, 2002, Graham E. Fuller, former vice-president of the CIA's National Intelligence Council, wrote in *The Los Angeles Times* that "Sharon believes

---

[18]King Abdullah II of Jordan, 2011, pp. 201–202.

[19]"Remarks Prior Discussions with King Abdullah II of Jordan and an Exchange with Reporters—February 1 2002." Public Papers of the Presidents of the United States—George W. Bush, Book I, January 1 to June 30 2002. Washington: United States Printing Office, 2004, pp. 160–162. Available at: <https://books.google.de/books?id=f_vhrnvPUqwC&pg=PA191&lpg=PA191& dq=George+W.+Bush+on+Arafat&source=bl&ots=-dNb0FG8py&sig=VZFu2d1XF-CaQvIUoxjR-4zesV0&hl=de&sa=X&ved=0CEoQ6AEwCWoVChMI6N_ VyZzWyAIVxdssCh2G8A54#v=onepage&q=Jordan&f=false>.

[20]Ibidem, p. 161.

[21]Ibidem.

[22]"Remarks Following Discussions with Prime Minister Ariel Sharon—February 7." Public Papers of the Presidents of the United States—George W. Bush, Book I, January 1 to June 30 2002. Washington: United States Printing Office, 2004, pp. 190–192. Available at: <https://books. google.de/books?id=f_vhrnvPUqwC&pg=PA191&lpg=PA191&dq=George+W.+Bush +onArafat&source=bl&ots=-dNb0FG8py&sig=VZFu2d1XF-CaQvIUoxjR-4zesV0&hl=de& sa=X&ved=0CEoQ6AEwCWoVChMI6N_VyZzWyAIVxdssCh2G8A54#v=onepage& q=Jordan&f=false>.

that Arafat's elimination is desirable, and most of the Israeli Cabinet is ready to assassinate him."[23] He added that Washington acquiesced with Sharon's strategy. "If Israel is about to eliminate Arafat, fine, as long as Sharon and Bush are convinced that what succeeds him will be better, more malleable," Graham E. Fuller noted.[24] President George W. Bush had already told the press that the Palestinians needed new leaders and that only through change, i.e., the replacement of Arafat, would the United States support the creation of the Palestinian state, whose borders would remain provisional until a solution for the settlements.[25] Yasser Arafat's extrajudicial killing was in fact being discussed in the White House[26] and viciously defended by Vice-President Dick Cheney since August 2001, before the attacks of September 11 of that year and the eruption of the second intifada (September 2000–February 2005)[27] provoked by the visit of Likud leader Ariel Sharon to the Temple of the Mount, where the Al-Aqsa Mosque (Haram al-Sharif) was located.[28] The United States believed that Ariel Sharon should take on the task, however. Because when faced with international criticism, he could claim he had done so "in self-defence, necessitated by Arafat's failure to stop bombings by Palestinian militants."[29] Since 1989, Sharon had been proclaiming that the way to end the intifada was "to eliminate the heads of the terrorist organizations and first of all Arafat."[30]

But the truth was that Arafat didn't have the means to curtail the intifada. He had tried a few times and failed. The terror was fueled by the oppression and repression of the State of Israel, the terror of the IDF. Opinion polls showed that 80% of Palestinians supported Ḥamās' bombings and rocket attacks as a method of self-defense against the occupation and violence by Israel,[31] which had confiscated their

---

[23]Graham E. Fuller (ex-vice-president do National Intelligence Council at the CIA), "Bush Must See Past the Acts of Terror to the Root Causes." Los Angeles Times, January 29, 2002. Available at: <http://articles.latimes.com/2002/jan/29/opinion/oe-fuller29>.

[24]Ibidem; Uri Dan (Ariel Sharon's companion of combat), "Der Feind: Er ist ein Mörder—Im Todesbett ist Arafat dort, wo er hingehört." Die Weltwoche, Ausgabe 46/2004 Available at: http://www.weltwoche.ch/ausgaben/2004-46/artikel-2004-46-er-ist-ein-moerder.html. Accessed on: October 23, 2015.

[25]Julian Borger (Washington), "Bush says Arafat must go." The Guardian, June 25, 2002. Available at: <http://www.theguardian.com/world/2002/jun/25/usa.israel>.

[26]Tony Karon, "Israel Violence Means Big Trouble for Sharon, Arafat and Bush." Time, August 6, 2001. Available at: <http://content.time.com/time/world/article/0,8599,170235,00.html>.

[27]The first intifada, the Palestinian uprising against the dominion of Israel, occurred between 1987 and 1993. But an intifada had already occurred against the English in 1935.

[28]Tony Karon, "Israel Violence Means Big Trouble for Sharon, Arafat and Bush." Time, August 6, 2001. Available at: <http://content.time.com/time/world/article/0,8599,170235,00.html>.

[29]Ibidem.

[30]"Sharon Urges 'Elimination' of Arafat, Terrorist Leaders." Deseret News, July 17, 1989. Available at: <http://www.deseretnews.com/article/55557/SHARON-URGES-ELIMINATION-OF-ARAFAT-TERRORIST-LEADERS.html?pg=all>. Accessed on October 23, 2015.

[31]Howard Witt (Washington Bureau), "Arafat's power to stop terror attacks debated." Chicago Tribune, December 4, 2001. Available at: <http://www.chicagotribune.com/chi-0112040122dec04-story.html>.

lands, devastated their economy, and prevented their movement. They were disillusioned with Arafat's efforts to reach an understanding with Israel's Prime Minister Yitzhak Rabin and Foreign Minister Shimon Peres, which led them to share the Nobel Peace Prize in 1994. The intifada reflected Palestinian desperation, frustration, and impotence in the face of the harsh and bloody repression the IDF had unleashed in 2001 with extrajudicial killings and the detention of hundreds of people.[32] Violence escalated as the Palestinians saw their lands plundered and Israeli settlements expanding.

The first attempt to eliminate Arafat took place on June 6, 2002, after Prime Minister Ariel Sharon returned from Washington. Before dawn, IDF helicopters bombarded the headquarters of the Palestinian Authority in Ramallah surrounded by tanks. The pretext was an attack that killed 17 Israelis, including 13 soldiers.[33] The Israeli infantry advanced, killed several Palestinians, and then employed bulldozers to raise the entire building, Arafat's residence, and its surroundings to the ground. President George W. Bush told the press he had repeatedly received "a pledge from Prime Minister Sharon not to try to kill or harm Mr. Arafat."[34] This statement was not made in good faith. On the contrary, in his talks with Ariel Sharon, Bush had agreed on the need to eliminate Yasser Arafat and replace him with someone more docile and malleable. The United States could then collaborate in the construction of the Palestinian state. And he insisted with the Knesset (Israel's parliament) that a solution to the Israeli-Palestinian conflict would only be found with the emergence of a "more decent, responsible" Palestinian entity committed to "free and fair elections, liberty, tolerance, compromise, transparency, and the rule of law."[35] What President George W. Bush was advocating, in one way or another, was Arafat's elimination. On the eve of the destruction of the headquarters of the Palestinian Authority by IDF helicopters, White House Press Secretary Ari Fleischer declared that President George W. Bush considered Arafat irrelevant and that he "never played a role of someone who can be trusted or effective."[36] In a speech at the

---

[32]Yearbook of the United Nations 2001. Vol. 55. Department of Public Information. United Nations, New York, 2003, pp. 408 and 648. Available at: <https://books.google.de/books? id=Yt3o624miKQC&pg=PA407&lpg=PA407&dq=Palestine+more+than+14+months222 +Israelis+killed+compared+to+742+Palestinians&source=bl&ots=9vhs9RceFM& sig=KRN8BCZqK8FH6iwLi2cKyMsJHeE&hl=de&sa=X& ved=0CD8Q6AEwBWoVChMI1deIvdPYyAIVitYsCh1azAMq#v=onepage&q=Arafat& f=false>.

[33]James Bennet, "Israel Attacks Arafat's Compound in Swift Response After a Bombing Kills 17." The New York Times, June 6, 2002. Available at: <http://www.nytimes.com/2002/06/06/interna tional/middleeast/06MIDE.html>.

[34]Ibidem.

[35]Robert Maranto & Tom Lansford & Jeremy Johnson (Editors), 2009, p. 233.

[36]Toby Harnden (Washington), "Bush sees Arafat as irrelevant." The Telegraph, June 6, 2002. Available at: <http://www.telegraph.co.uk/news/worldnews/middleeast/israel/1396455/Bush-sees-Arafat-as-irrelevant.html>.

Rose Garden of the White House about 2 weeks later, on June 25, 2002, President George W. Bush virtually reiterated that he considered Arafat to be irrelevant and said that "peace requires a new and different Palestinian leadership, so that a Palestinian state can be born."[37] President George W. Bush, Ariel Sharon, and his entire cabinet considered Arafat irrelevant.[38]

Suddenly and mysteriously, Yasser Arafat fell ill in Ramallah, where he was confined. He was transported by air ambulance to the Hôpital d'Instruction des Armées Percy in Clamart, France,[39] where he died on November 11, 2004, at the age of 75. The most likely hypothesis was that the Mossad had poisoned him with polonium-210, an isotope that emits highly radioactive alpha particles and that was found in his bones by specialists at the University of Legal Medicine in Lausanne/ Geneva.[40] But how it was done was beside the point; Yasser Arafat had been eliminated. And the fact is that this elimination, i.e., the assassination of Yasser Arafat, had clearly been on the agenda of Prime Minister Ariel Sharon with the consent of President George W. Bush for about 2 years before he died. Sharon celebrated the event as a possible "historic change" in Palestine.[41] But no such change occurred. Ariel Sharon was never really interested in peace talks in Palestine.[42] Nor did he want the creation of a Palestinian state bordering Israel, much less so his successor, Benjamin Netanyahu.

23.4   The Dream of Eretz Yisrael

Tel Aviv's objective has always been to rebuild the Land of Israel (Eretz Israel), the land promised by Yahweh (יהוה—God) to Abraham, Jacob, and their descendants, which according to the Bible extended "from the river of Egypt[43] to the great river,

---

[37]"President Bush Calls for New Palestinian Leadership." The Rose Garden—Office of the Press Secretary for Immediate Release, June 24, 2002. White House—Presidente George W. Bush. Available at: <http://georgewbush-whitehouse.archives.gov/news/releases/2002/06/20020624-3. html>.

[38]David Singer & Lawrence Grossman, 2003, pp. 210–211.

[39]Thomas G. Mitchell, 2015, p. 179.

[40]David Poort & Ken Silverstein, "Swiss study: Polonium found in Arafat's bones—Scientists find at least 18 times the normal levels of radioactive element in late Palestinian leader." Al Jazeera, November 7, 2013. Available at: <http://www.aljazeera.com/investigations/killing-arafat/swiss-study-polonium-found-arafats-bones-201311522578803512.html>.

[41]"Friedensprozess: Scharon spricht von historischer Wende—Nach dem Tod von Palästinenserpräsident Arafat gibt es neue Hoffnung für einen Friedensprozess in Nahost. Israels Ministerpräsident Scharon sprach von einer möglichen 'historischen Wende'. Auch US-Präsident Bush hofft auf Fortschritte im Friedensprozess. Frankreichs Präsident Chirac rief zur Umsetzung der 'Road Map' auf." Spiegel Online, November 11, 2004. Available at: <http://www.spiegel.de/politik/ausland/friedensprozess-scharon-spricht-von-historischer-wende-a-327352.html>.

[42]King Abdullah Ii of Jordan, 2011, pp. 131, 196 and 200.

[43]The "river of Egypt" referred to in Genesis was probably the Nile, but several scholars identify it as Wadi al-Arish, a brook north of the Sinai Peninsula on the Mediterranean coast.

the river Euphrates."[44] This is a vast territory stretching from the Nile valley in North Africa to Mesopotamia on the Syrian-Turkish border, covering the entire Middle East, over 1560 km (972 miles). Since the nineteenth century, Theodor Herzl (1860–1904) and Isidore Bodenheimer (1865–1940), the pioneers and theorists of Zionism, advocated the idea of establishing Jewish settlements in Palestine and Syria, the space where the Hebrews had lived in ancient times.[45]

David ben Gurion (1886–1973), the Hebrew name David Grün had adopted after arriving in Jaffa in 1906,[46] hinted at this ambition to occupy the entire Promised Land on May 14, 1948, when he proclaimed "by virtue of our natural and historic right and on the strength of the resolution of the United Nations general assembly[47] [. . .] the establishment of a Jewish state in Eretz-Israel, to be known as the State of Israel."[48] For the Zionists, the State of Israel occupied only a small fraction of the Land of Israel (Eretz Yisrael), the land promised by Yahweh in the solemn covenant (b'rit) celebrated with Abraham. David ben Gurion's phrase reveals the rejection by the Zionists of any partition of Palestine through the creation of another state, an Arab State. They believed the entire territory belonged to the Jewish people as a "natural and historical right," even though the founders of the State of Israel were no ethnic descendants of the Hebrews. The Arab states, however, openly opposed the creation of a Jewish state and launched the first Arab-Israeli war—called the "Israeli War of Independence"—which was fought between November 29, 1947, and May 15, 1948.

The expulsion of the Palestinians then began under David ben Gurion, the first head of government of the State of Israel (1948–1954). Between 700,000 and 900,000 were forced to leave their homes and businesses. Or they were killed, as in Deir Yassin (April 9, 1948), where the paramilitary militias of Hā-'Irgun Ha-Tzva'ī Ha-Leūmī b-Ērētz Yiśā'el and Lohamei Herut Israel—Lehi, responsible for terrorist actions during the British Mandate, decimated thousands of Palestinians under the command of Menachem Begin and Yitzhak Shamir, both of whom would later

---

[44]"Minnəhar miṣrayim 'aḏ-hannāhār haggāḏōl nəhar-pərāṯ" (river: Nāhār). Genesis (Bərēšīṯ), 15:18. Biblia Hebraica Stuttgartensia, editio quinta emendata, Stuttgart: Deutsche Bibelgesellschaft, 1997, p. 21; Genesis—Kapitel 15:18–21—Die Heilige Schrift des Alten und Neuen Testaments. Aschaffenburg: Paul Pattloch Verlag, 17. Auflage, 1965, p. 15.

[45]Daniel Pipes, "Imperial Israel: The Nile-to-Euphrates Calumny." Middle East Quarterly, March 1994. Available at: <http://www.danielpipes.org/247/imperial-israel-the-nile-to-euphrates-calumny>.

[46]Born in Płońsk, in the Kingdom of Poland, David ben Gurion's original name was David Grün (David, Green or Grien).

[47]"UN General Assembly—Resolution 181 (Partition Plan), November 29, 1947." Israel Ministry of Foreign Affairs. Available at: <http://www.mfa.gov.il/mfa/foreignpolicy/peace/guide/pages/un%20general%20assembly%20resolution%20181.aspx>.

[48]"Declaration of Establishment of State of Israel—14 May 1948." Israel Ministry of Foreign Affairs. Available at: <http://www.mfa.gov.il/mfa/foreignpolicy/peace/guide/pages/declaration%20of%20establishment%20of%20state%20of%20israel.aspx>.

govern the State of Israel, in 1977–1983 and 1986–1992, respectively.[49] The Palmach militia commanded by Yitzhak Sadeh also committed the most ignominious massacres in the Arab villages of Balad al-Sheikh, Hawassa, and Ein al Zeitun (May 1, 1948). These Haganah militias, later formalized as the Israel Defense Forces (IDF), caused at least 55% of the Palestinian exodus. They displaced about 391,000 people between December 1, 1947, and June 1, 1948, and expropriated assets: 73,000 abandoned homes; 7800 stores, workshops, and warehouses; 5 million Palestinian pounds in bank accounts; and more than 300,000 ha of land.[50] Seventy-three percent of the total emigration was forced in various ways by the rulers of the State of Israel, according to Israeli historian Benny Morris, professor in the Ben-Gurion Department of Negev University in the city of Beersheba (Israel) and author of the book *The Birth of the Palestinian Refugee Problem*.[51]

No Zionist leader actually recognized the rights of the Palestinian people or their sovereignty over part of the territory, as determined by the partition plan (Resolution 181) approved by the UN General Assembly on November 29, 1947. In 1969, the important Zionist leader Golda Meir (1898–1978), then serving as the prime minister of Israel (1969–1974), told *The Sunday Times*: "There was no such thing as Palestinians… They did not exist."[52] According to her conception, the borders of Israel were not limited by lines drawn on a map. On another occasion she said: "this country exists as the fulfillment of a promise made by God Himself. It would be ridiculous to ask it to account for its legitimacy."[53] Faith was the law.

In 1974, after Golda Meir's renunciation because of a lymphoma, Menachem Begin from Likud took over as prime minister (1977–1983). After secret negotiations brokered by USA President Jimmy Carter, he signed the Camp David Accords (Framework for Peace in the Middle East) with Anwar El Sadat, president of Egypt, the first Arab country to recognize the State of Israel.[54] But just like Golda Meir, he declared in Oslo on December 12, 1978, that "this land has been promised to us and we have a right to it,"[55] and so Begin promoted the expansion of Israel's borders by

---

[49]Benny Morris Morris, "For the record." The Guardian, January 14, 2004. Available at: <http://www.theguardian.com/world/2004/jan/14/israel/print>.

[50]Dominique Vidal, "10 years of research into the 1947–1949—WAR. The expulsion of the Palestinians re-examined." Le Monde diplomatique (English Edition). December 1997. Available at: <http://mondediplo.com/1997/12/palestine>.

[51]Ibidem.

[52]Apud. Benny Morris, "Palestinian Identity: The Construction of Modern National Consciousness (review)." Israel Studies, Volume 3, Number 1, Spring 1998, pp. 266–272. Available at: <https://muse.jhu.edu/login?auth=0&type=summary&url=/journals/israel_studies/v003/3.1morris.html>. The Myths of the twentieth Century. 4—The myth of a "land without a people for a people without a land." Source Le Monde, 15 October 1971. Source: Mrs. Golda Meir. Statement to The Sunday Times, June 15, 1969. Available at: <http://www.biblebelievers.org.au/zionmyth6.htm>.

[53]Ibidem.

[54]The Peace Treaty between Egypt and Israel was signed in 1979.

[55]Roger Garaudy, "The Myth of a 'Land without People for a People without land." The Holocaust Historiography (Project). Available at: <http://www.historiography-project.com/jhrchives/v18/v18n5p38_Garaudy.html>.

establishing Jewish settlements in Judea and Samaria (West Bank). And committed to maintaining Israel's preeminence in the Middle East, he ordered Operation Opera/ Operation Babylon, the codename for the bombing of Iraq's nuclear plant Osirak in 1981, in addition to the 1982 invasion of Lebanon. With the complicity of President Ronald Reagan (1981–1989), Ariel Sharon, then Minister of Defense, ordered the destruction of the PLO camps and rekindled and deepened the civil war raging there (1975–1990). Israeli troops surrounded Sabra and Shatila, and, together with the Christian Phalanges, they massacred refugees, mostly Palestinians and Lebanese Shia, all of them civilians. The magnitude of the massacre is not known exactly: according to some sources between 762 and 3550 people were killed (of which about 2000 Palestinians)[56]; according to other estimates, the number of people killed ranges from 2000 to 3000.

23.5   Yitzhak Rabin's Assassination and the Push for Settlements Under Benjamin Netanyahu

The peace process was only effectively resumed when Yitzhak Rabin of the Labor Party took over Israel's government (1992–1995). He believed that the Arab-Israeli conflict would not be resolved militarily. And Yasser Arafat, leader of the Palestine Liberation Organization (PLO), also changed the strategy to fight the occupation of the West Bank and Gaza after the failure of the 1988 intifada. Both men reached an understanding and signed the Oslo I and II Accords in 1993 and 1995 with the blessing of President Bill Clinton (1993–2001). These agreements, based on UN Security Council Resolutions 242 (November 22, 1967) and 338 (October 22, 1973), enabled the creation of the Palestinian Authority, not as a state but as an interim government whose sovereignty was limited to Areas A and B, i.e., the West Bank and Gaza, isolated territories occupied by Israel since the 1967 war. Israel and the PLO formally and mutually recognized each other and took on the commitment to negotiate the territorial issue and conflict remaining since the 1967 war. The implication, although not explicit, would be the gradual creation of a Palestinian State, restricted to a small part of Palestine, but without exactly defining the limits of its jurisdiction and the recognition of the sovereignty of the State of Israel by the PLO over almost the entire historical territory of Palestine. But as Baruch de Spinoza (1632–1677) wrote to his friend Jarig Jelles in a letter dated June 2, 1674, "figure is nothing but determination, and determination is negation" (*quia ergo figura non aliud, quam determinatio, et determinatio negatio est*). And based on the Oslo

---

[56]"Sabra and Shatila massacre: General info." The WikiLeaks Supporters Forum, January 14, 2014. Available at: <http://www.wikileaks-forum.com/sabra-and%2D%2Dshatila-massacre/613/sabra-and-shatila-massacre-general-info/26766/>.

Accords, the State of Israel was in and of itself indefinite and indivisible, undetermined, while the Palestinian Authority was determined. There was no balance of powers and rights between the parties.[57] The asymmetry was enormous between the State of Israel, the highest instance, and the political and administrative command of a society, with economic, diplomatic, and military power, and the Palestinian Authority, which wasn't even a state, separated between the Gaza Strip and the West Bank, where Jewish settlements continued to grow overwhelmingly and almost uninterrupted.

Among the Arabs, Ḥamās, founded during the 1987 intifada, opposed the Oslo Accords, as did Likud, Israel's conservative party. And Yitzhak Rabin paid with his own life for having reached an understanding with Yasser Arafat and resuming the peace process in Palestine. On November 4, 1995, during a political rally in support of the peace process in Tel Aviv, the radical orthodox Jew Yigal Amir shot him dead.[58] And in 1996, with the election victory of the conservative Likud, Binjamin (Bibi) Netanyahu took over as prime minister and opposed Israel's withdrawal from the West Bank. No effort was made to conceal or disguise his opposition to the Oslo Accords, because he considered them incompatible with the historical rights of the State of Israel. And during the first 3 years of his mandate (1996–1999), he undertook to expand Jewish settlements in the West Bank.

In 2001, according to a video published by the newspapers *The Guardian* and *Ha'aretz*, Netanyahu, unaware that he was being recorded, told a group of victims of terrorism: "I know what America is. [...] America is a thing you can move very easily, move it in the right direction. They won't get in the way."[59] Arrogantly, he boasted how he had cheated and sabotaged the Oslo process when he became prime minister of Israel. Prior to his election, the Clinton administration had asked him if he would honor the Oslo Accords. "I said I would," Netanyahu replied. But he would interpret them in such a way as to authorize him to put an end to the "67 borders."[60] According to Netanyahu, no one had said where the zones were and as far he knew, the entire Jordan Valley was defined as a military zone.[61] Israeli journalist Gideon

[57] Hani A. Faris, 2013, p. 80.

[58] Serge Schmemann, "Assassination in Israel: The Overview—Assassination in Israel: The Overview; Rabin Slain After Peace Rally in Tel Aviv; Israeli Gunman Held; Says He Acted Alone." The New York Times, November 5, 1995. Available at: <http://www.nytimes.com/1995/11/05/world/assassination-israel-overview-rabin-slain-after-peace-rally-tel-aviv-israeli.html?pagewanted=all>.

[59] Avi Shalaim, "It's now clear: the Oslo peace accords were wrecked by Netanyahu's bad faith—I thought the peace accords 20 years ago could work, but Israel used them as cover for its colonial project in Palestine." The Guardian, September 12, 2013.

[60] Glenn Kessler, "Netanyahu: 'America is a thing you can move very easily.'" The Washington Post, July 16, 2010.

[61] Avi Shalaim, "It's now clear: the Oslo peace accords were wrecked by Netanyahu's bad faith—I thought the peace accords 20 years ago could work, but Israel used them as cover for its colonial project in Palestine." The Guardian, September 12, 2013.

Levy, admired for his independence, noted in an article in the newspaper *Ha'aretz* that Israel has had many right-wing leaders, "but there has never been one like Netanyahu, who wants to do it by deceit, to mock America, trick the Palestinians, and lead us all astray."[62]

---

[62]Gideon Levy, "Tricky Bibi—Israel has had many rightist leaders since Menachem Begin promised many Elon Morehs, but there has never been one like Netanyahu, who wants to do it by deceit." Há'aretz, Thursday, July 15, 2010. Available at: <http://www.haaretz.com/misc/article-print-page/tricky-bibi-1.302053?trailingPath=2.169%2C2.225%2C2.227%2C>; Glenn Kessler, "Netanyahu: 'America is a thing you can move very easily.'" The Washington Post, July 16, 2010.

Chapter 24
Netanyahu's Occupation Policy and the Israel–Palestine War

Netanyahu was heavily criticized by people like Jimmy Carter and Shimon Perez for this policy that could only lead to perpetual war and the misery and despair of the Palestinians. But his administration hardly seemed to care. His press officer even called Secretary of State John Kerry a mental 12-year-old and accused Obama of antisemitism. Obama shot back with some verbal digs, but on the other hand, he approved billions in military aid, maintaining the IDF as the most sophisticated military force in the Middle East.

24.1 Maḥmūd 'Abbās, the End of Sharon and the Rise of Ḥamās

After the elimination of Yasser Arafat, Maḥmūd 'Abbās (also known as 'ABŪ Māzin) was elected president of the PLO and the Palestinian Authority. President George W. Bush welcomed him in the White House in his speech at the Rose Garden as a leader capable of creating a "peaceful, democratic" Palestinian State and of rejecting violence.[1] He further said that Israel "must remove unauthorized outposts and stop settlement expansion" and that a viable two-state solution "must ensure

---

[1]"President Welcomes Palestinian President Abbas to the White House." The Rose Garden. *The White House—President George W. Bush.* Office of the Press Secretary, May 26, 2005. Available at: <http://georgewbush-whitehouse.archives.gov/news/releases/2005/05/print/text/20050526.html>; *Public Papers of the Presidents of the United States. George W. Bush (In Two Books) Book I: January 1 to June 30, 2005.* Washington: US Government Printing Office, p. 880. Available at: <https://books.google.de/books?id=5VVC1YI72DoC&pg=PA880&lpg=PA880&dq=George +W.+Bush+%E2%80%9Cmust+remove+unauthorized+outposts+and+stop+settlement+expansion. #v=onepage&q=George%20W.%20Bush%20%E2%80%9Cmust%20remove%20unauthorized% 20outposts%20and%20stop%20settlement%20expansion.&f=false>.

© Springer Nature Switzerland AG 2019
L. A. Moniz Bandeira, *The World Disorder*,
https://doi.org/10.1007/978-3-030-03204-3_24

contiguity of the West Bank, and a state of scattered territories will not work."[2] Shortly after, on June 24, 2002, Bush declared in the same Rose Garden that "it is untenable for Israeli citizens to live in terror," just as it was "untenable for Palestinians to live in squalor and occupation." This situation, he said, brought no prospect of improvement in life, since the Israelis would continue "to be victimized by terrorists" and Israel had to defend itself, while "the Palestinian people will grow more and more miserable." The only solution was the creation of "two states, living side by side in peace and security."[3]

President George W. Bush was turning the equation on its head, however. Certainly, the terror bombings and rocket attacks perpetrated by Ḥamās and the Islamic Jihad against Israel's civilian population could not be justified; but it was not Ḥamās' violence that was causing the occupation of Palestine's territory by the State of Israel. It was exactly this continuous occupation of its territory, and therefore the "more and more miserable" situation of the Palestinian people, that led to the violence and fed the terror of Ḥamās and the Islamic Jihad. The road map submitted by the so-called Middle East Quartet, made up of representatives of the UN, European Union, the United States, and Russia to salvage the peace process, was initially accepted by Maḥmūd 'Abbās, then prime minister of the Palestinian Authority, and Ariel Sharon, prime minister of Israel and whose cabinet approved the deal, but with numerous unfeasible caveats. The Israeli government started the removal of 21 settlements from the Gaza Strip in 2005, in the midst of extensive resistance from thousands of Israeli settlers, many of whom had to be evicted by IDF soldiers from the basements and synagogues where they were holding up.[4] Four settlements were equally removed.

On January 4, 2006, however, Ariel Sharon suffered a stroke with massive cerebral hemorrhage, leaving him in a vegetative state in the Sheba Medical Center. There he died 8 years later on January 11, 2014, at the age of 85. The State of Israel didn't hold up any part of the agreement. Maḥmūd 'Abbās, on the other hand, lacked Arafat's charisma, leadership skills, and strength, despite being one of the founders of the PLO (al-Fatah) and elected president of the Palestinian Authority. He could not contain the radical trends represented mainly by Ḥamās and the Islamic Jihad, organizations sustained by the Muslim Brotherhood.

And so the PLO (Fatah) lost the election of 2006 to Ḥamās. Tensions boiled over and armed conflicts broke out between the two factions in June 2007. The Palestinian National Authority presided by Maḥmūd 'Abbās, whose jurisdiction once covered the territories occupied by Israel (Gaza, East Jerusalem, and the West Bank/Gaza), was now restricted to the West Bank.

---

[2]*Ibidem.*

[3]"President Bush Calls for New Palestinian Leadership." *White House. Office of the Press.* The Rose Garden, June 24, 2002. For Immediate Release. Available at: <http://georgewbush-whitehouse.archives.gov/news/releases/2002/06/20020624-3.html>.

[4]Alon Ben-Meir (Senior Fellow, Center for Global Affairs, NYU), "The Fallacy of the Gaza Withdrawal," *in: HuffPost News,* November 13, 2014. Available at: <http://www.huffingtonpost.com/alon-benmeir/the-fallacy-of-the-gaza-w_b_6152350.html>. Accessed on October 25, 2015.

24.2 Netanyahu, Jewish Settlements, and Undermining of the Palestinian State

With Ariel Sharon's illness, Ehud Olmert of Kadima assumed as Prime Minister (2006–2009). And although President George W. Bush had defended the creation of two states in Palestine, the truth of the matter was that the United States would not or could not prevent Israel from expanding its borders. No international condemnation, no resolutions of the UN General Assembly, and no decisions of the International Court of Justice were able to stop the irrepressible expansion of Jewish settlements, whose population grew 5% per year, on average. The Middle East Quartet failed to resume the peace process.

Since 1996, when Benjamin Netanyahu rose to power for the first time with broad support from the ultraorthodox Jews and Russian Jewish immigrants, illegal settlements had grown rapidly in both the West Bank and East Jerusalem, despite his signing of the Hebron Protocol (1997) and the Wye River Memorandum (1998) with Yasser Arafat in the United States, both under the auspices of President Bill Clinton. Netanyahu's entire policy was geared to preventing the creation of a sovereign and contiguous Palestinian State neighboring the State of Israel.

Netanyahu had never concealed his opposition to the creation of a Palestinian State. He had been traumatized and certainly held a personal grudge against the Palestinians. His older brother, Lieutenant-Colonel Yonatan (Yoni) Netanyahu, commander of an IDF detachment, was killed in Operation Thunderbolt on July 4, 1976, when he was 30 years old. The operation's goal was the rescue of 105 Jews captured by terrorists of the Popular Front for the Liberation of Palestine and the German organization Baader-Meinhof, who had hijacked an Air France Airbus flying from Tel Aviv to Paris and forced it to divert to the airport in Entebbe, Uganda.[5] A year later in Boston, when Benjamin Netanyahu was 28 years old, he openly expressed his rejection of the idea of a Palestinian State alongside the State of Israel. Such a state, he said, already existed and it was called Jordan. And he added that "there is no right to establish a second one on my doorstep, which will threaten my existence, there is no right whatsoever."[6]

Shortly after becoming Prime Minister in 1996, Netanyahu visited Ariel, a large settlement in the West Bank (West Bank). "We will be here permanently forever," he said and promised to establish new Jewish communities there, in the lands belonging to a future Palestinian State.[7] During the 2009 election campaign, however, he

---

[5]The goal of the Popular Front for the Liberation of Palestine was to exchange the hijacked Israelis for Palestinian militants arrested in Israel.

[6]Tovah Lazaroff, "Has Netanyahu been boom or bust for Israel's West Bank settlement enterprise?." *The Jerusalem Post*, March 17, 2015. Available at: <http://www.jpost.com/Israel-Elec tions/Has-Netanyahu-been-boom-or-bust-for%2D%2DIsraels-West-Bank-settlement-enterprise-394135>.

[7]Jodi Rudoren and Jeremy Ashkenas, "Netanyahu and the Settlements—Israeli Prime Minister Benjamin Netanyahu's settlement policy resembles his predecessors' in many ways, but it is a

declared that if he had assurance of demilitarization and if the Palestinians recognized Israel as a Jewish State, he would be willing to agree to a real peace treaty, "a demilitarized Palestinian State alongside the Jewish State."[8] Netanyahu's words were no more than a smoke screen and actually meant he would not accept any Palestinian State. Demilitarization implied a lack of sovereignty. It meant the State of Israel could continue its incursions to occupy the entire West Bank, gradually reducing the area of 5640 km^2 left to a population of approximately 4.6 million Arabs,[9] already dispersed in isolated pockets, without even the right to vote.

Before being elected in 2009, Benjamin Netanyahu, in his capacity as Minister for Foreign Affairs, proclaimed that the immigration issue (aliyah) and the absorption of immigrants were high on his government's list of priorities, which would work vigorously so that Jews from all countries would come live in Israel.[10] Demographic pressure made the expansion of the borders of the State unstoppable, therefore, and Prime Minister Netanyahu promoted this expansion at an unprecedented pace through the illegal authorization of new settlements in the West Bank and East Jerusalem. From 1948 to 2014, 3,152,146[11] or more Jews emigrated to Israel, including 1,223,723 from the former Soviet Union and many others from countries like Ethiopia and France. And from the moment Netanyahu returned to power in 2009 until the beginning of 2014, the number of Jewish settlers in the West Bank jumped by 23% to 355,993. The total population of Israel, estimated at 8 million, increased by only 9%.[12] During a tree planting ceremony in the West

march toward permanence in a time when prospects for peace are few." *International New York Times*, March 12, 2015. Available at: <http://www.nytimes.com/interactive/2015/03/12/world/middleeast/netanyahu%2D%2Dwest-bank-settlements-israel-election.html?_r=0>;   Serge Schmemann, "Netanyahu, Scorning Critics, Visits West Bank Settlement." *The New York Times*, November 27, 1996. Available at: <http://www.nytimes.com/1996/11/27/world/netanyahu-scorning-critics-visits-west-bank-settlement.html>.

[8]"Full Text of Netanyahu's Foreign Policy Speech at Bar Ilan." *Há'aretz*, June 14, 2009. Available at: <http://www.haaretz.com/news/full-text-of-netanyahu-s-foreign-policy-speech-at-bar-ilan-1. 277922>.

[9]"Experts clash over Palestinian demographic statistics on eve of 2015, Israel's population hits 8.3 million—data predicted equal Jewish, Arab population in Israel and territories by 2016." *The Jerusalem Post*, October 22, 2015. 9 Heshvan, 5776. Available at: <http://www.jpost.com/Mid dle-East/Experts-clash-over-Palestinian-demographic-statistics-386443>.

[10]Ian S. Lustick, "Israel's Migration Balance—Demography, Politics, and Ideology," pp. 33–34. *Israel Studies Review*, Vol. 26, Issue 1, Summer 2011: 33–65 © Association for Israel Studies doi: 10.3167/isr.2011.260108. Available at: <https://www.sas.upenn.edu/polisci/sites/www.sas.upenn. edu.polisci/files/Lustick_Emigration_ISR_11.pdf>.

[11]Immigration to Israel: Total Immigration, by Year (1948—Present 2014). *Jewish Virtual Library*. Available at: <https://www.jewishvirtuallibrary.org/jsource/Immigration/Immigration_to_Israel. html>.

[12]Dan Perry and Josef Federman, "Netanyahu years continue surge in settlement." *Associated Press*, December 15, 2014. Available at: <http://news.yahoo.com/netanyahu-years-see-surge-west-bank-settlements-075922371.html>.

Bank, Netanyahu declared: "we are planting here, we will stay here, we will build here. This place will be an inseparable part of the State of Israel for eternity."[13]

And the aliyah kept going. More and more Jews arrived to establish settlements in the territories occupied by Israel, especially the West Bank and East Jerusalem. In just 3 months from January to March 2015, about 6499 Jews arrived in Israel, the vast majority from Europe, including 1971 from Ukraine, an increase of 215% in relation to the 625 who had migrated in the same period of 2014, while the number of Russians reached 1515, an increase of 50%.[14] At the same time, Prime Minister Benjamin Netanyahu called on the Jews to emigrate to Israel en masse, saying that they would be received "with open arms."[15] Around 310,000–500,000 Jews still lived in France,[16] one third or half of the 1 million who lived in Europe in 2010, while in the eastern countries of the defunct Soviet Bloc, the number has fallen dramatically since then.[17]

The growing demographic pressure resulting from the aliyah directly fed the expansion of settlements in the West Bank and East Jerusalem, preventing the creation of another state in Palestine. And this was Netanyahu's strategy: keep increasing Israel's Jewish population, which grew from 806,000 in 1949 to 6.3 million (74.9%) in 2015, when Arabs represented 20.7% of the population (1.7 million) and other ethnic groups and nationalities made up 4.4% (366,000).[18] The Palestinian Central Bureau of Statistics, however, estimated that of a total population of 12.1 million Palestinians, 2.9 million were living in the West Bank, 1.85 million in Gaza, 1.47 million in the state of Israel, another 5.49 million as refugees in Arab countries, and 675,000 in other parts of the world.[19] For 2016, the number of Palestinians in the West Bank and Gaza was predicted to be equal to the total number of Jews, in the order of 6.4 million. This number would reach 7.14 million by 2020, while the number of Jews would only increase to 6.87 million if the current

---

[13]Isabel Kershnerjan, "Netanyahu Says Some Settlements to Stay in Israel." *The New York Times*. 24, 2010. Available at: <http://www.nytimes.com/2010/01/25/world/middleeast/25mideast.html?_r=0>.

[14]Mairav Zonszein (Tel Aviv), "Jewish migration to Israel up 40% this year so far—Ukrainians and Russians account for surge as numbers leaving Western Europe in first three months remains steady despite Paris attacks in January, report shows." *The Guardian*, May 3, 2015.

[15]*Ibidem*.

[16]*Ibidem*.

[17]Michael Lipka, "The continuing decline of Europe's Jewish population." *Pew Research Center*. Available at: <http://www.pewresearch.org/fact-tank/2015/02/09/europes-jewish-population/>.

[18]Vital Statistics: Latest Population Statistics for Israel—(Updated September 2015). *Jewish Virtual Library*. Available at: <http://www.jewishvirtuallibrary.org/jsource/Society_&_Culture/newpop.html>.

[19]"Experts clash over Palestinian demographic statistics on eve of 2015, Israel's population hits 8.3 million—Data predicted equal Jewish, Arab population in Israel and territories by 2016." *The Jerusalem Post*, October 22, 2015 | 9 Heshvan, 5776. Available at: <http://www.jpost.com/Middle-East/Experts-clash-over-Palestinian-demographic-statistics-386443>.

rate of growth was maintained.[20] According to Professor Sergio Della Pergola of the University of Jerusalem, it was crucial for Israel to preserve a clear and indisputable Jewish majority in the total population.[21] In his opinion, this was the prerequisite for its "future existence as a Jewish and democratic state."[22] Indeed, a democracy exclusively for Jews. This is why Netanyahu didn't annex the territories occupied by Israel. He certainly didn't accept the creation of a Palestinian State, but he also didn't want to give the Palestinians the same rights as the Jews. Netanyahu never had nor manifested any democratic tendencies, and he never valued the life of Palestinians.

In March 2009, when the American Vice-President Joe Biden visited Israel, Netanyahu challenged President Barack Obama's policy by announcing the plan to build 1600 new residences in the eastern part of Jerusalem, where the capital of a future Palestinian State would be established.[23] This violated international human-itarian law (especially the Fourth Geneva Convention), according to the resolutions adopted by the Security Council and the General Assembly of the UN. "This is starting to get dangerous for us," Biden told Netanyahu, adding that "what you're doing here undermines the security of our troops who are fighting in Iraq, Afghan-istan and Pakistan. That endangers us, and it endangers regional peace."[24] But Netanyahu did not give in and Joe Biden could do nothing because of Israel's support through the multibillion-dollar Jewish lobby. The American-Israeli Public Affairs Committee (AIPAC) was one of the real power factors in the United States, without which no congressman was elected.

In February 2011, the Security Council adopted a resolution presented by two-thirds of the United Nations. Fifteen of the 14 members condemned the Israeli settlements in the West Bank as illegal and an obstacle to peace, but the United States vetoed the resolution, as usual. The Brazilian ambassador to the UN, Maria Luiza Viotti, then exercising the rotating presidency of the Security Council, reaffirmed in the press that "Israel's ongoing settlement activity had become the most important obstacle to a comprehensive solution." She emphasized that the text

---

[20] Ariel Ben Solomon, "On eve of 2015, Israel's population hits 8.3 million. Experts clash over Palestinian demographic statistics. Data predicted equal Jewish, Arab population in Israel and territories by 2016." *The Jerusalem Post*, January 1, 2015. Available at: <http://www.jpost.com/Middle-East/Experts-clash-over-Palestinian-demographic-statistics-386443>; Palestinian Central Bureau of Statistics (PCBS)—"Palestinians at the End of 2015," 30 de dezembro de 2015. Available at: <http://www.pcbs.gov.ps/site/512/default.aspx?tabID=512&lang=en&ItemID=1566&mid=3171&wversion=Staging>.

[21] Sergio Della Pergola, "Jewish Demographic Policy Population Trends and options in Israel and in the diaspora." The Hebrew University of Jerusalem Editors Barry Geltman, Rami Tal. *The Jewish People Policy Institute* (ppi) (established by the Jewish agency for Israel, Ltd). Available at: <http://jppi.org.il/uploads/Jewish_Demographic_Policies.pdf>.

[22] *Ibidem*.

[23] The west side would be the capital of the State of Israel.

[24] Hani A. Faris, 2013, pp. 77–78.

of the resolution declared all settlements "illegal and an obstacle to peace" and added that both parties should seek a resolution "in support of a two-state solution."[25]

Nothing could halt the occupation of the West Bank by Israel, however. Prime Minister Ehud Olmert (2006–2009) encouraged the construction of 5120 homes in 2 years there.[26] According to Israel's Central Bureau of Statistics (CBS), 350,010 people were living in West Bank settlements in 2013, excluding East Jerusalem. At that time, 2013, the UN Human Rights Council (HRC) sent a Fact-Finding Mission to Palestine. Based on its findings, the HRC considered that the growing settlements promoted by Israel constituted a "creeping form of annexation which compromised the right to self-determination of the people of the Occupied Palestinian Territories," and it urged the international community to put pressure on Israel to dismantle "all settlements which were in flagrant violation of international law."[27] But in January 2014, Netanyahu announced the construction of another 1400 homes and apartments in areas that would belong to a future Palestinian State in the West Bank and East Jerusalem, where 500,000 Israelis already lived.[28] And in the first half of 2015, the number of settlers there jumped to 547,000, living among 2.8 million Palestinians.[29] The continuing growth of these illegal settlements, forming towns and cities, increasingly harder or even impossible to remove, was indeed the greatest obstacle to peace and the creation of a sovereign Palestinian State in a contiguous territory.

Likewise, Israel annexed the eastern part of Jerusalem during the Six-Day War (1967), despite the fact that UN Resolution 181 (1947) had designated it as a *corpus separatum*, with Israel controlling the western part and Jordan the left. The plan was for the entire city to remain as the eternal and indivisible capital of the Jewish people.

---

[25]"Security Council Fails to Adopt Text Demanding That Israel Halt Settlement Activity as Permanent Member Casts Negative Vote." *United Nations—Security Council.* 6484th Meeting (PM) February 18, 2011. Available at: <http://www.un.org/press/en/2011/sc10178.doc.htm>. Shamir, "The UN is ripe for advancing the Palestinian Agenda—The settlements have been defined as the number-one problem impeding peace, and the Israeli attempt to blame the stalemate on the Palestinians will be accepted at the UN." *Há'aretz*, Tuesday, February 22, 2011. Available at: <http://www.haaretz.com/print-edition/opinion/the-un-is-ripe-for-advancing-the-palestinian-agenda-1.344905>; "Illegal Israeli Settlements" *Council for European Palestinian Relations.* Available at: <http://thecepr.org/index.php?option=com_content&view=article&id=115:illegal-israeli-settlements&catid=6:memos&Itemid=34>.

[26]Mitzpe Kramim (West Bank) & Maayan Lubell, "In Netanyahu's fourth term, what's next for Israeli settlements?." *Reuters*, April 6, 2015. Available at: <http://www.reuters.com/article/2015/04/06/us-israel-palestinians-settlements-in%2D%2Dsig-idUSKBN0MX0T220150406>. Accessed on November 1, 2015.

[27]"The United Nations—Human Rights Council holds interactive dialogue with Fact-finding Mission on Israeli Settlements Human Rights Council." March 18, 2013. Available at: <http://www.ohchr.org/EN/NewsEvents/Pages/DisplayNews.aspx?NewsID=13156&LangID=E>.

[28]William Booth, "Israel announces new settlement construction in occupied West Bank, East Jerusalem." *The Washington Post*, January 10, 2014. Available at: <https://www.washingtonpost.com/world/middle_east/israel-announces-new%2D%2Dsettlement-construction-in-occupied-west-bank-east-jerusalem/2014/01/10/1669db6-7a0b-11e3-a647-a19deaf575b3_story.html>.

[29]"The Israeli Information Center for Human Rights in the Occupied Territories." *B'Tselem*, May 11, 2015. Available at: <http://www.btselem.org/settlements/statistics>.

The Knesset legalized this plan in 1980 by proclaiming Jerusalem the "eternal and indivisible capital" of the State of Israel.[30] And this goal was indeed pursued over the years, robbing Palestinians from their homes and rights. From 1967 to 2006, a total of 8269 Palestinian residents in East Jerusalem lost their homes; in 2006 alone, 1363 Palestinians were deprived of their right to live in the city; and, between 2007 and 2009, 5585 Palestinians in East Jerusalem were stripped of everything by the Israeli government.[31]

24.3   Hamas/PLO Reconciliation and the Operation Protective Edge in Gaza

Since 2005, when Ariel Sharon dismantled 21 settlements, withdrew the IDF troops, and gave up Gaza to the Palestinian Authority, this small enclave of 225,000 square miles (582,747 km²) between Israel, Egypt, and the Mediterranean Sea continued under a strict naval and land blockade, assisted by Egypt, which closed the passage through its border to prevent the entry and exit of individuals and goods (except those it considered "humanitarian aid"). This had virtually paralyzed industry in Gaza, depriving it of raw materials and export markets. The pretext was preventing the smuggling of weapons to Ḥamās, but Netanyahu always justified the eradication of Palestinians in the West Bank with the argument that the withdrawal of IDF forces from Gaza in 2005 had led to Ḥamās' victory in the parliamentary elections there.

This perception was wrong. Ḥamās' candidate Ismaʻīl Haniyya almost certainly won the 2006 elections in Gaza because of the elimination of Yasser Arafat, whose leadership was far superior compared with Maḥmūd ʻAbbās. Yasser Arafat was more objective and pragmatic and understood that coexistence with the State of Israel was inevitable; Israel was an economic, social, political, and military reality, recognized as a legal entity through international law: an irreversible reality. And with the charisma he'd built along many struggles, he led the PLO (al-Fatah) to accept UN Security Council Resolutions 242 (November 1967) and 338 (October 1973), which implied recognizing the State of Israel and renouncing the strategy of terrorism, which had not produced any results. Arafat's objective was to facilitate the end of the conflicts and advance negotiations, so the creation of an independent Palestinian State, within the framework of the Oslo agreements, would be feasible in 22% of historic Palestine, parallel to the State of Israel, which already occupied the other 78%. But he was tougher in the negotiations with Sharon and refused to grant Israel the control over the Noble Sanctuary, i.e., the al-Aqsa Mosque and Dome of the Rock. After Arafat's elimination, Ḥamās gained strength and not only won the

---

[30]Charles M. Sennott, *The Body and the Blood: The Middle East's Vanishing Christians and the Possibility for Peace*. New York: Public Affairs—Perseus—Book Group, 2002, pp. 66–67; Hani A. Faris, 2013, p. 45.

[31]*Ibidem*, pp. 44–45.

elections but also defeated the PLO in armed clashes in 2007 and consolidated power in Gaza. Maḥmūd ʿAbbās could count on the support of MI6 to strengthen the Palestinian Authority he still presided, but its jurisdiction was now restricted to the West Bank, where more and more Jewish settlements were being established.

When Ḥamās and the PLO reconciled themselves in 2014 to form a coalition government, the terms of the understanding between the two organizations would implicitly lead to the recognition of the State of Israel according to the 1967 borders.[32] But Netanyahu suspended negotiations with the Palestinian Authority and stepped away from the peace process, which in fact had never been more than an illusion. Tensions rose and Ḥamās then persevered in rejecting Israel's existence as a Jewish state. It continued to fire Qassam rockets against Israeli cities. But the truth of the matter is that Prime Minister Netanyahu triggered Operation Protective Edge after the reconciliation agreement between Fatah and Ḥamās; the retaliation against the acts of terrorism was a pretext.

The difficulties in the negotiations with Israel led Maḥmūd ʿAbbās and Fatah to reconnect with Ḥamās. The two factions formed a unity government to combine the political strength of the West Bank with Gaza, provisionally recognized by the State Department, even if it still classified Ḥamās as a terrorist organization. Netanyahu, however, warned Maḥmūd ʿAbbās that he must choose between peace with Israel or Ḥamās.[33] The reconciliation of the governments of Gaza and Ramallah was a significant and historic event, but it did not align with Netanyahu's interests. It didn't suit him. Hostilities would therefore erupt sooner or later. It was inevitable. And on June 10, 2014, three young Israelis between 16 and 19 years of age—Naftali Frenkel, Gilad Shaar, and Eyal Yifrach—were abducted while hitchhiking back to their homes in the settlement Alon Shvut in Gush Etzion, in the West Bank occupied by Israel.[34]

Without any proof, Prime Minister Netanyahu immediately accused Ḥamās of the kidnapping. Ḥamās' main leader, Khālid Mashʿal, and the government of the Palestinian Authority denied responsibility for the incident,[35] even though members

---

[32]Munib Al-Masri, "United, the Palestinians Have Endorsed 1967 Borders for Peace. Will Israel? Now Ḥamās has indicated its recognition of the 1967 borders, the main Palestinian players all seek an historic agreement with Israel. But is Netanyahu's government strong enough to respond?." *Háʾaretz*, May 7, 2014. Available at: <http://www.haaretz.com/opinion/1.589343>.

[33]Rushdi Abu Alouf (Gaza City), "Ḥamās and Fatah unveil Palestinian reconciliation deal." *BBC News*, April 23, 2014. Available at: <http://www.bbc.com/news/world-middle-east-27128902>. Accessed on Thursday, October 29, 2015.

[34]Peter Beaumont (Jerusalém) and Orlando Crowcroft (El Ad), "Bodies of three missing Israeli teenagers found in West Bank—Naftali Frenkel, Gilad Shaar, and Eyal Yifrach were kidnapped while hitchhiking back from their religious schools." The *Guardian*, June 30, 2014.

[35]Adnan Abu Amer, "Ḥamās denies link to murders of Israeli students. Palestinians and Israelis have been living in uncertainty in the past three weeks following the murders of three Israeli settlers and Palestinian teenager Mohammed Abu Khdeir. The discovery of the bodies of the three Israeli boys has opened the door to further speculation as to what actually happened, for Israel insists Ḥamās was responsible, while Ḥamās continues to deny involvement." *Al Monitor*, July 3, 2014. Available at: <http://www.al-monitor.com/pulse/originals/2014/07/palestine-Ḥamās%2D% 2Dlinks-murder-israeli-teens-unclear.html>.

of the Izz ad-Din al-Qassam brigades could have acted alone and without their knowledge and kidnapped and murdered the three young men. Ḥamās had no interest in escalating the conflict, but Israel's purpose was not only to avenge the assassination of the young settlers but also to demolish everything what was left of Gaza's infrastructure after the bloody destruction wrought by Operation Cast Lead (2008) and Pillar of Cloud/Defense (2012). Netanyahu reacted as if Ḥamās was in fact to blame for the event. With the excuse of looking for the three young men, the IDF deployed in Operation Brother's Keeper, which lasted 11 days and arrested 419 Palestinians in the West Bank, including all Ḥamās leaders.[36] Three IDF soldiers were killed during the skirmishes, and dozens died on the side of the Palestinians.[37] The searches lasted 3 weeks, and the corpses of the three young men were discovered near the city of Hebron, semi-buried under rocks. On the same day, July 1, the Israeli Air Force executed three precision strikes against the structures of Ḥamās and the Islamic Jihad in response to 18 rockets fired from their bases in the Gaza Strip.[38] After the boys' funeral in Halhul, Israeli fundamentalists held protests shouting "death to the Arabs." As a retaliation, some of them kidnapped, beat up, and burned alive the 16-year-old Palestinian teenager Mohammed Abu Khdeir. A series of attacks on Arab children then occurred.

Salah al-Arouriri, the organizer of the Izz ad-Din al-Qassam brigades in 1991,[39] had told clerics in Turkey, where he was exiled, that his militants had kidnapped and killed the three young Israelis. But this could well have been propaganda, since the leader of Ḥamās, Khālid Mashʿal, continued to deny his organization had committed the atrocity against the young Israelis.[40] And with good reason. The Israeli

---

[36]Yifa Yaakov and Marissa Newman, "Israel's three murdered teens buried side-by-side amid national outpouring of grief. PM says Israel will expand action against Ḥamās if need be; missiles hit Eshkol region; tens of thousands mourn teens at joint burial service, separate funerals; Israel vows to apprehend killers 'dead or alive'; US warns Israel against 'heavy-handed' response." *The Times of Israel*, July 1, 2014. Available at: <http://www.timesofisrael.com/idf-hunts-for-two-suspects-in-teens%2D%2Dmurder/>.

[37]Gili Cohen, "Two Soldiers Killed by Gaza Militants Who Breached Border—Two more wounded; Palestinian militants launch anti-tank missile at IDF unit." *Háʾaretz*, July 19, 2014. Available at: <http://www.haaretz.com/israel-news/.premium-1.606012>.

[38]"Israeli jets strike 34 targets in Gaza Strip—Air force hits Ḥamās, Islamic Jihad structures; 4 reported wounded; 2 rockets explode in Israel causing damage, hours after discovery of kidnapped teens' bodies." *The Times of Israel*, July 1, 2014. Available at: <http://www.timesofisrael.com/palestinians-israeli-jets-strike-over-30-targets-in-gaza/>.

[39]"In first, Ḥamās official takes credit for kidnap and murder of Israeli teens." *The Jerusalem Post*, Wednesday, August 20, 2014. Available at: <http://www.jpost.com/Arab-Israeli-Conflict/In-first-Ḥamās-official-takes-credit-for-kidnap-and-murder-of-Israeli-teens-371703>.

[40]Adnan Abu Amer, "Ḥamās denies link to murders of Israeli students. Palestinians and Israelis have been living in uncertainty in the past three weeks following the murders of three Israeli settlers and Palestinian teenager Mohammed Abu Khdeir. The discovery of the bodies of the three Israeli boys has opened the door to further speculation as to what actually happened, for Israel insists Ḥamās was responsible, while Ḥamās continues to deny involvement." *Al Monitor*, July 3, 2014. Available at: <http://www.al-monitor.com/pulse/originals/2014/07/palestine-Ḥamās-links-murder%2D%2Disraeli-teens-unclear.html>.

government and the international media gave little importance to a pamphlet circulating in Gaza in which the first organization to claim responsibility for the murder of the young men was Da'ish, saying that it was a retaliation for the death of three of their militants in the West Bank.[41] And it is very well possible that militants of the al-Qassam brigades joined Da'ish, committed to establishing a foothold in the West Bank. Ḥamās, however, certainly wasn't interested in challenging Israel with so heinous a crime, a mere act of terror without any political purpose, just a few months after establishing a coalition government with the PLO. It was clear banditry and a cruel provocation.

Ḥamās knew it could not put an end to the State of Israel. It lacked the military conditions to defeat it. The asymmetry was immense. It was a non-state actor with limited weaponry. Israel's Iron Dome missile defense system intercepted approximately 90% of the Qassam rockets, which had a range of only 3–4.5 km. These were crude, locally manufactured, self-propelled rockets without guidance systems that could not penetrate military targets. The terror was more psychological than physical, even if the Qassam rockets sometimes reached densely populated areas and hurt Israeli civilians. In any case, even though Ḥamās didn't pose any real threat,[42] Netanyahu, in his obsessive hate of the Palestinians, could not endure a focus of resistance to a strategic objective of his government: the expansion of the State of Israel. The assault on Gaza was therefore a matter of timing, climate, and battleground conditions.

Netanyahu's government was waiting for the self-defense excuse, a reason to escalate the conflict. And in the course of a week, the radicals of the Qassam Brigades and/or the Islamic Jihad fired about 29 rockets and mortars against Hayfa, Jerusalem, and Asdod in Israel. At the request of the leader of Ḥamās, Khālid Mashʻal, the Egyptian Minister of Foreign Affairs, Sameh Shoukry, tried to calm affairs with Netanyahu. He failed. And on July 7 and 8, 2014, infantry troops, tanks, artillery, and military engineers of the IDF invaded Gaza, unleashing Operation Protective Edge with the participation of the air force and naval vessels. It also received the support of Shin Bet, one of the three intelligence services in Israel and known in Hebrew through its acronym Shabak (Sherut ha'Bitachon ha'Klali or General Security Service) and which went by the motto "Magen Velo Yera'e" (defender that shall not be seen).

---

[41]M.A. Hussein and R. Abraham, "ISIS, Not Ḥamās, Claimed Responsibility For Kidnapping Three Israeli Teens." *Counter Current News*, August 22, 2014. Available at: <http://countercurrentnews.com/2014/08/isis-in-the-west-bank-not-Ḥamās-first%2D%2Dclaimed-responsibility-for-kidnapping-those-israeli-teens/>. Accessed on October 31, 2014; BAR'EL, Zvi. "Has ISIS Infiltrated the West Bank?—The pamphlet claiming responsibility for the kidnappings doesn't seem to have come from the Salafi group now terrorizing Iraq and Syria. But maybe a local cell decided to claim affiliation with ISIS to inspire fear." *Há'aretz*, July 14, 2014. Available at: <http://www.haaretz.com/israel-news/.premium-1.598648>. Accessed on October 31, 2014.

[42]Nathan J. Brown, "Five myths about Ḥamās." *The Washington Post*, July 18, 2014.

The campaign lasted 50 days, from July 8 to August 26, 2014, and killed 2251 Palestinians, mostly civilians, including 539 children. Another 11,231[43] were maimed, injured, or permanently disfigured.[44] The IDF, on the other hand, suffered 66 casualties and seven Israeli civilians died as a result of the Ḥamās rockets.[45] Thousands of homes were destroyed by this land offensive that indiscriminately deployed artillery, other explosives, and air strikes against densely populated areas. Nearly 20,000 people lost their homes; more than 100,000 buildings were fully or partially ruined in an area of 360 km²;[46] and 148 schools, 15 hospitals, 45 medical centers, 247 factories, 300 commercial centers including a modern one in Rafah, fuel tanks, and power and water supply plants were razed to the ground.[47] The IDF destroyed the entire civilian infrastructure in Gaza and damaged its agriculture.[48] At the end of July 2014, the UN estimated that almost a quarter of the 1700 residents in Gaza had been displaced by the attacks and all were facing a shortage of basic supplies.[49] The fact was that about 300,000 Palestinians were homeless and many sought refuge in the units of UNRWA (United Nations Relief and Works Agency for Palestine Refugees in the Near East).[50]

Amnesty International accused the IDF of committing "war crimes" during the 50-day campaign, with the disproportionate and indiscriminate attack against densely populated areas, destroying schools and other buildings where civilians

---

[43] Gaza Emergency—UNRWA—United Nations Relief and Works Agency for Palestine Refugees in the Near East. October 15, 2015 Available at: <http://www.unrwa.org/gaza-emergency>; "Annual Report. Israel and Occupied Palestinian Territories." *Amnesty International Report 2014/15*. Available at: <https://www.amnesty.org/en/countries/middle-east-and-north-africa/israel-and-occupied%2D%2Dpalestinian-territories/report-israel-and-occupied-palestinian-territories/>.

[44] Dalia Gebrial, "Unrecovered and Unremembered: Gaza One Year After Operation Protective Edge." *Egyptian Streets*, July 31, 2015. Available at: <http://egyptianstreets.com/2015/07/31/unrecovered-and-unremembered-gaza-one-year%2D%2Dafter-operation-protective-edge/>.

[45] "Gaza crisis: Toll of operations in Gaza." *BBC News*, September 1, 2014. Available at: <http://www.bbc.com/news/world-middle-east-28439404>. Accessed on November 1, 2015.

[46] Dalia Gebrial, "Unrecovered and Unremembered: Gaza One Year After Operation Protective Edge." *Egyptian Streets*, July 31, 2015. Available at: <http://egyptianstreets.com/2015/07/31/unrecovered-and-unremembered-gaza-one-year%2D%2Dafter-operation-protective-edge/>.

[47] "UN: Gaza Could Become 'Uninhabitable' By 2020—Israeli military action and economic blockade have rendered the coastal strip unfit for civilian life, report says." *MiniPress News*, September 2, 2015. Available at: <http://www.mintpressnews.com/un-gaza-could-become-uninhabitable-by-2020/209180/>.

[48] "Annual Report. Israel and Occupied Palestinian Territories." *Amnesty International Report 2014/15*. Available at: <https://www.amnesty.org/en/countries/middle-east-and-north-africa/israel-and-occupied-palestinian-territories/report%2D%2Disrael-and-occupied-palestinian-territories/>.

[49] Lazaro Gamio and Richard Johnson and Adam Taylor, "The crisis in Gaza." *The Washington Post*, August 1, 2014. Available at: <http://www.washingtonpost.com/wp-srv/special/world/the-gaza-crisis/>. Accessed on November 3, 2012.

[50] *Ibidem.*

had taken shelter under the allegation that they were used to hide rockets.[51] And the United Nations Human Rights Council (HRC) subsequently adopted a resolution in which it not only expressed serious concern with "possible war crimes" committed by Israel but also condemned all human rights violations breaking international laws. The HRC stated it was "appalled at the widespread and unprecedented levels of destruction, death and human suffering caused" in Gaza.[52]

Indeed, during Operation Protective Edge, hundreds of people were arrested in the Palestinian territories occupied by Israel without charge or trial, based only on secret information and with no access to lawyers. And cut off from the outside world for several days, sometimes weeks, they were tortured and mistreated by agents of the Israeli security service Shin Bet/Shabak.[53] The methods were similar to those used by the CIA in Guantanamo Bay and Abu Ghraib (Iraq) and included several physical aggressions, beatings and strangulations, shackling, and prolonged stress situations, in addition to threats against their families.[54]

According to the World Bank, the blockade, wars, and poor governance strangled Gaza's economy and the unemployment rate became the highest in the world, reaching 43% of the population and more than 60% of young people at the end of 2014.[55] The population was suffering with the very precarious public services, with shortages in electricity and water, and approximately 80% depended for their survival on the assistance of the United Nations Relief and Works Agency for Palestine Refugees, while more than 40% lived below the poverty line. The city of Gaza had not been rebuilt after the wars of 2008 and 2012 because Israel would not allow it. According to the World Bank, "while shocking, these numbers fail to fully convey the difficult living conditions that nearly all Gaza's residents have been experiencing."[56]

Even more shocking—the World Bank report stressed—was the fact that more than 1.8 million residents were confined to an area of 160 km^2, one of the most densely populated areas in the world, and could not go beyond these limits without permission.[57] Ever since Gaza's blockade was established in 2007, Israel's purpose had been to keep the population in misery and the economy on the brink of collapse.

---

[51]*Ibidem.*

[52]"Times of Israel staff. Full text of UNHRC resolution on Gaza war probe—Motion passed on Friday by UN Human Rights Council welcomes findings of McGowan Davis commission." *The Times of Israel*, July 3, 2015. Available at: <http://www.timesofisrael.com/full-text-of-unhrc-resolution/>.

[53]"Annual Report. Israel and Occupied Palestinian Territories." *Amnesty International Report 2014/15*. Available at: <https://www.amnesty.org/en/countries/middle-east-and-north-africa/israel-and-occupied-palestinian-territories/report-israel-and-occupied-palestinian-territories/>.

[54]*Ibidem.*

[55]"Gaza Economy on the Verge of Collapse, Youth Unemployment Highest in the Region at 60 Percent." *World Bank*, May 21, 2015. Available at: <http://www.worldbank.org/en/news/press-release/2015/05/21/gaza-economy-on-the-verge-of-collapse>.

[56]*Ibidem.*

[57]*Ibidem.*

Israel's Defense Minister, Ehud Barak, maintained the most strict and severe of controls over the products that entered Gaza. He banned the most diverse food stuffs, including spaghetti and other pasta, coriander, herbs, spices, and even ketchup, because he considered them unnecessary.[58] And the children suffered the consequences even more. According to the Center for Mind-Body Medicine based in Washington, more than one third of the children in Gaza showed signs of "post-traumatic stress disorder," even before the armed conflict in 2014, and much more after it.[59] "The status quo in Gaza is unsustainable."[60] A status quo was further entrenched by the blockade and three brutal Israeli military operations in 2008, 2012, and 2014. Gaza *delenda est (= must be destroyed, as Marcus Porcius Cato claimed against Carthage, 2nd century BC)*. It lay ruins. In November 2015, the number of refugees had reached 7.1 million people in various countries of the world, and approximately 427,000 were internally displaced, with the destruction of their homes, according to the United Nations Refugee Agency (UNHCR).[61]

24.4   Jimmy Carter Against Netanyahu and Conflicts in the al-Aqsa Mosque

When the former American President Jimmy Carter visited the West Bank in May 2015, he said in an interview to the press that the situation in Gaza was "intolerable." He met with Maḥmūd 'Abbās in Ramallah, but not with Prime Minister Netanyahu because he considered it a "waste of time."[62] And although he condemned the criminal acts by Ḥamās, he also said that its leader Khālid Mash'al was not a terrorist and defended the conciliation with Fatah so that new elections could be held for the

---

[58]Zvi Bar'el and Barak Ravid, "Gaza Prohibitions Were 'Too Harsh,' Livni Tells TurkelLivni said the Defense Ministry was responsible for banning numerous food products from entering Gaza, such as pasta, coriander, spices and even ketchup." *Há'aretz*, Tuesday, October 26, 2010. Available at: <http://www.haaretz.com/print-edition/news/gaza-prohibitions-were-too-harsh-livni-tells-turkel-1.321157>. Accessed on November 3, 2015.

[59]"Gaza Economy on the Verge of Collapse, Youth Unemployment Highest in the Region at 60 Percent." *World Bank*, May 21, 2015. Available at: <http://www.worldbank.org/en/news/press-release/2015/05/21/gaza-economy-on-the-verge->.

[60]*Ibidem.*

[61]Middle East: Palestinian refugee numbers/whereabouts. *IRIN—Humanitarian news and analysis*. Available   at: <http://www.irinnews.org/report/89571/middle%2D%2Deast-palestinian-refugee-numbers-whereabouts>.

[62]"Times of Israel staff & AFP Carter says Ḥamās leader committed to peace, Netanyahu not—Ex-president doesn't meet PM, says it would be a 'waste of time'; claims Mashaal is 'not a terrorist' and 'strongly in favor of peace process.'" *The Times of Israel*, May 2, 2015. Available at: <http://www.timesofisrael.com/carter-says-Ḥamās-leader-committed-to-peace-netanyahu-not/>. "Ex-U.S. President Jimmy Carter Says Situation in Gaza Is 'Intolerable'. Speaking at a press conference in Ramallah, Carter lamented that 'not one destroyed house has been rebuilt' in Gaza since the war last summer." *Há'aretz* and The Associated Press, May 2, 2015. Available at: <http://www.haaretz.com/israel-news/1.654622>.

Palestinian National Authority.[63] Former President Jimmy Carter was right. Ḥamās was actually a nationalist and militant political faction committed to establishing a Palestinian State, and although it didn't recognize the legitimacy of the State of Israel and carried out terror actions that hurt civilians, its leader Khālid Mashʻal publicly rejected any comparison with ISIS,[64] made by Netanyahu in order to justify the war against Gaza. "At the moment, there is zero chance of the two-state solution," Jimmy Carter said in August 2015.[65] And emphasizing that the prospects for peace were the worst possible,[66] he stressed that Prime Minister Netanyahu didn't have "any intention" of making progress in this direction,[67] i.e., achieving peace, that he had never sincerely wanted the two-state solution, and that he had long ago decided on the "one-state solution," but without giving equal rights to Palestinians.[68]

This was indeed Netanyahu's intent, even if Israel could earn approximately US $120 billion in a decade with a two-state solution, while the Palestinians would only get US$50 billion according to the estimates of the Rand Corporation.[69] At a meeting of the Knesset's Foreign Affairs and Defense Committee in October 2015, Netanyahu revealed to other members that he was of no mind to hand control of the West Bank to the Palestinians as part of the peace process. And he said: "At this time, we need to control all of the territory for the foreseeable future."[70] He believed that "half

---

[63] *Ibidem.*

[64] Ari Soffer, "Ḥamās Leader Objects: Don't compare us to ISIS. Khaled Meshaal objects to Netanyahu's comparison between Ḥamās and Islamic State, says Ḥamās 'isn't a violent religious group.'" *Arutz Sheva 7—Israelnationalnews.com*, August 23, 2014. Available at: <http://www.israelnationalnews.com/News/News.aspx/184333#.VjoltCt0f_B>; Max Fisher, "Ḥamās is not ISIS. Here's why Netanyahu says it is anyway." *Vox—Israel-Palestine Conflict*, August 25, 2014. Available at: <http://www.vox.com/2014/8/25/6064467/no-netanyahu-Ḥamās%2D%2Dis-not-isis-isis-is-not-Ḥamās>.

[65] Bronwen Maddox, "Jimmy Carter: there is zero chance for the two-state solution. The US has withdrawn from tackling the Middle East's most intractable problem, says the former President." *Prospect*, August 13, 2015. Available at: <http://www.prospectmagazine.co.uk/world/jimmy-carter-there-is-zero-chance-for-the-two-state-solution>. "Carter: Zero Chance for Two-state Solution—Netanyahu decided 'early on to adopt a one-state solution, but without giving the Palestinians equal rights,' former U.S. president accuses in interview." *Háʼaretz*, August 13, 2015. Available at: <http://www.haaretz.com/israel-news/1.671056>.

[66] *Ibidem.*

[67] *Ibidem.*

[68] *Ibidem.*

[69] C. Ross Anthony et al., "The Costs of the Israeli-Palestinian Conflict: Executive Summary." *Rand Corporation*, June 18, 2015. Available at: <http://www.rand.org/pubs/research_reports/RR740-1.html>; "Israelis Stand to Gain $120 Billion, Palestinians $50 Billion in Two-State Solution Over Next Decade." *Rand Corporation*, Monday, June 8, 2015. Available at: <http://www.rand.org/news/press/2015/06/08.html>.

[70] Jessica Schulberg (Foreign Affairs Reporter, *The Huffington Post*), "Benjamin Netanyahu's Latest Rejection of a Palestinian state. 'You think there is a magic wand here, but I disagree,' he told his political opponents, who have been pushing for peace talks." *The World Post—The Huffington Post*, 27 de outubro de 2015. Available at: <http://www.huffingtonpost.com/entry/israel-benjamin-netanyahu-reject-palestinian-state_562e5f1be4b0c66bae58b878>.

of the Palestinians are ruled by extreme Islam that wants to destroy us; if there were elections tomorrow, Ḥamās would win."[71] And in those circumstances, Ḥamās was indeed expected to win. It wasn't involved in the fruitless negotiations with Israel, and, furthermore, it ran an assistance service for the Arab population that the Palestinian Authority did not. But the disastrous situation was not only unsustainable in Gaza. In East Jerusalem and the West Bank, trouble was also brewing. And between September 13 and 15, on the eve of Rosh Hashanah (the Jewish New Year), conflicts broke out on the Temple Mount, where the al-Aqsa Mosque stood next to the Dome of the Rock, the Noble Sanctuary (Haram al-Sharif), revered as the place where the Prophet Muhammad ascended to heaven to receive the al-Qur'ān directly from Allah.

The underlying tensions between Israelis and Palestinians were fermenting in all territories occupied by Israel. And they escalated further after the Israeli police invaded the al-Aqsa Mosque to tear down the barricades the Palestinians had erected inside it, using tear gas and stun grenades.[72] After that the clashes did not relent. The Palestinians resorted to the same methods used by the nationalist Jewish Zealots[73] who unleashed a terror campaign to ignite an uprising against Roman rule from 48 BC, during the reign of Herod the Great, until the fall of Jerusalem (70 AD) and Masada (73 AD). The Sicarii infiltrated cities and stabbed Roman legionaries and Jewish collaborators with the *sica* (curved dagger) hidden underneath their cloak. And so did the Palestinians about 2000 years later, after the invasion of the al-Aqsa Mosque. Several Israelis were killed this way in Jerusalem. The revolt grew, with Palestinians confronting Israeli soldiers with stones, many using slings as David had against Goliath in the valley of Elah (Emek HaElah).

The stabbings, shootings, stones, and fires became daily occurrences, and the IDF responded with aggressive and lethal repression against those suspected of terrorism. In October alone, hundreds of Palestinians, including 150 children, were arrested. Dozens of Palestinians, especially young people, were killed by the IDF,[74] whose troops also blocked the access of Palestinians to the olive tree plantations to prevent the harvest near the town of Nablus, where they demolished homes and confiscated lands. And in early November, the IDF invaded the Palestinian radio station Al Hurria in Hebron (West Bank) in the dead of night, destroying equipment and

---

[71] *Ibidem.*

[72] "Jerusalem's al-Aqsa mosque sees Israeli-Palestinian clashes." *BBC News*, September 13, 2015. Available at: <http://www.bbc.com/news/world-middle-east-34237219>.

[73] Reza Aslan, 2013, pp. 74–76.

[74] Kate Shuttleworth (Jerusalém), "Ultraorthodox Jews at the Damascus gate in Jerusalem after a Palestinian man was shot dead by police after allegedly stabbing and injuring a 15-year-old Jewish youth." *The Guardian*, Sunday, October 4, 2015. Available at: <http://www.theguardian.com/world/2015/oct/04/israel-second-stabbing%2D%2Djust-hours-after-two-jewish-men-fatally-stabbed>.

confiscating transmitters under the allegation that they were used to incite attacks on Israelis.[75]

Prime Minister Netanyahu accused Maḥmūd ʿAbbās of inciting a wave of violence by the Palestinians and warned that the Israelis accepted that there was no likelihood of peace and so they would continue to "live by the sword." But the chief of the Israeli Military Intelligence Directorate (*Agaf HaModiʿin*—AMAN) himself, Maj. Gen. Herzl Halevi, an orthodox Jew, stated in a cabinet meeting on November 1, 2015, that the feelings of rage and frustration, especially among the young, were "part of the reason for the wave of terror attacks in Jerusalem and the West Bank."[76] He explained that young people were throwing themselves at terrorist attacks because they were in despair about the state of affairs "and felt that they had nothing to lose."[77] Contradicting what Prime Minister Netanyahu had claimed, Maj. Gen. Herzl Halevi stated that Maḥmūd ʿAbbās had tried to keep the calm in the West Bank and instructed his forces to thwart attacks against Israel, but it seemed that part of the youth escaped control of the Palestinian Authority.[78]

The Intifada which began in September and had not stopped in November reflected the feeling of revolt that had been incubating during more than half a century of oppression, discrimination, and occupation of the Palestinian territory by Israel. And just as former President Jimmy Carter, and the former prime minister of Israel, Shimon Peres of the Labor Party argued in an interview with the *Associated Press* that Netanyahu has never been sincere about peace and that his peace overtures "never escaped the domain of talking" when it came to the creation of another state alongside Israel. But the alternative to the existence of two states in Palestine was "continued war and nobody can maintain a war forever."[79] "Netanyahu says he is against a binational state, but admits we will have to live by the sword forever; that's

---

[75]"Israel raids and shuts down Palestinian radio station." *AAAJ and agencies. al-Araby*, November 3, 2015. Available at: <http://www.alaraby.co.uk/english/news/2015/11/3/israel-raids-and-shuts-down-palestinian-radio-station>; "Israeli military closes Palestinian radio station for inciting violence. Israel says it has shut down a Palestinian radio station on charges of incitement. The move comes after Prime Minister Benjamin Netanyahu accused Palestinian leaders of stoking the violence that has plagued the region." *Deutsche Welle—DW*, November 3, 2015. Available at: <http://www.dw.com/en/israeli-military-closes-palestinian-radio%2D%2Dstation-for-inciting-violence/a-18822859>. Accessed on November 5, 2015; "Radio West Bank Radio Destroyed." *Deep Dish Waves of Change*, November 3, 2015. Available at: <http://deepdishwavesofchange.org/blog/2015/11/west%2D%2Dbank-radio-destroyed>. Accessed on November 3, 2015.

[76]Barak Ravid, "IDF Intelligence Chief: Palestinian Despair, Frustration Are among Reasons for Terror Wave. Major General Herzi Halevi's assessment contradicts Prime Minister Benjamin Netanyahu's message which blames the attacks on incitement and ingrained hatred." *Háaretz*, November 3, 2015. Available at: <http://www.haaretz.com/israel-news/.premium-1.683860>.

[77]*Ibidem.*

[78]*Ibidem.*

[79]Aron Heller, "Peres: Netanyahu was never sincere about making peace. Ex-president says PM's overtures have never 'escaped the domain of talking,' and warns against his notion of continually 'living by the sword.'" *The Times of Israel*, November 2, 2015. Available at: <http://www.timesofisrael.com/peres-netanyahu-was-never-sincere-about-making-peace/?utm_source=dlvr.it&utm_medium=twitter>.

his vision, it is a nightmare," noted the political scientist Menachem Klein,[80] whose promotion at Bar-Ilan University was blocked because he was considered too far to the left.[81] Netanyahu's strategy was effectively to maintain Israelis in fear and anxiety.

24.5   Obama/Netanyahu Disagreements and Pentagon's Military Aid in 2016

The extent of the intolerance of Netanyahu's government was such that his press officer, Ran Baratz, mocked John Kerry by saying that the American secretary of state's "mental age didn't exceed that of a 12-year-old" as well as accusing President Obama of anti-Semitism for advocating a two-state solution.[82] Netanyahu didn't fire him and the official apology did not heal the wounds.[83] President Obama simply made a "realistic assessment" that it would not be possible to achieve peace in Palestine before the end of his mandate, and according to his National Security Advisor Benjamin Rhodes, he would like to hear from Netanyahu how he would avoid a one-state solution, stabilize the situation, and signal that he was committed to the two-state solution without peace talks.[84] The truth of the matter was that

---

[80]Ian Black (Kafr Qassem), "Israel's strategic position 'enhanced by chaos of Arab neighbourhood.' Netanyahu government reaps benefits of Middle Eastern mayhem but is set to maintain the status quo of occupation on the Palestinian front." *The Guardian*, June 11, 2015.

[81]Or Kashti. "Israeli University Lecturer Says Denied Promotion for Being 'Too Leftist'—Bar Ilan's promotions committee also ruled against elevating Dr. Menachem Klein to the rank of professor five years ago." *Há'aretz*, February 10, 2011. Available at: <http://www.haaretz.com/israel-news/israeli-university-lecturer%2D%2Dsays-denied-promotion-for-being-too-leftist-1.342355>.

[82]JPost.Com Staff. 'Kerry's mental age doesn't exceed that of a 12-year-old,' Netanyahu's new media czar wrote Bennett blasts Kerry for linking Israeli-Palestinian conflict to ISIS proliferation. *The Jerusalem Post*, November 5, 2015. Available at: <http://www.jpost.com/Israel-News/Politics-And-Diplomacy/Kerrys-mental-age-doesnt-exceed-that-of-a-12-year-old-Netanyahus-new-media-czar-wrote-432104>. *Times of Israel*. "Netanyahu's new media czar called Obama 'anti-Semitic'- Ran Baratz also in hot water for comments disparaging Rivlin, John Kerry; two Likud ministers oppose his appointment." *The Times of Israel*, November 5, 2015. Available at: <http://www.timesofisrael.com/netanyahus%2D%2Dnew-media-czar-called-obama-anti-semitic/?utm_source=The+Times+of+Israel+Daily+Edition&utm_campaign=55b79272ba-2015_11_05&utm_medium=email&utm_term=0_adb46cec92-55b79272ba-55318305>.

[83]Josef Federman (Jerusalém), "Netanyahu appointment casts cloud over US visit." *Associated Press—The Washington Post*, November 5, 2015.

[84]Steven Mufson, "Obama administration concedes that Mideast peace is beyond reach on his watch." *The Washington Post*, November 5, 2015. "Obama rules out Israeli-Palestinian peace deal before leaving office—US officials say president has made 'realistic assessment'; will discuss steps to prevent further violence with Netanyahu on Monday." *Times of Israel*, November 6, 2015, Available at: <http://www.timesofisrael.com/obama-rules-out-israeli-palestinian-peace-deal-before-leaving-office/?utm_source=The+Times+of+Israel+Daily+Edition&utm_campaign=ecd33f82de-2015_11_06&utm_medium=email&utm_term=0_adb 46cec92-ecd33f82de-55318305>.

Netanyahu had never been committed to this solution. Netanyahu's acceptance to create one more state in Palestine was nothing but empty rhetoric.

However, despite the disagreements and difficulties in the relationship between Netanyahu and Obama, mainly because of the Nuclear Agreement with Iran, the American president earmarked US$3.1 billion in the 2016 budget for military assistance to Israel. According to AIPAC, this was the "most tangible manifestation of American support" to Israel; it would allow for the purchase of F-35 squadrons, totaling 33 jets, and several other war toys, in addition to the accompanying profits for the arms industry.[85] And Israel remained the largest cumulative recipient of military aid from the United States since the Second World War, having received US $124.3 billion (in current, not-inflated dollars) from American taxpayers, in addition to bilateral assistance, i.e., military assistance, transforming the IDF into one of the most sophisticated armed forces in the world, superior to all the neighboring states.[86]

[85]"Support Security Assistance for Israel." *American Israel Public Affairs Committee—AIPAC*. Available at: <http://www.aipac.org/learn/legislative-agenda/agenda-display?agendaid=% 7B407715AF-6DB4-4268-B6F8-36D3C6F241AA%7D>.

[86]Jeremy M. Sharp (Specialist in Middle Eastern Affairs), "U.S. Foreign Aid to Israel June 10, 2015." *Congressional Research Service 7-5700 www.crs.gov RL33222*. Available at: <https://www.fas.org/sgp/crs/mideast/RL33222.pdf>.

Chapter 25
A New Cold War, a New Moscow–Beijing Axis, and the Decline of American Hegemony

25.1 John Q. Adams' Warning

The backdrop of the wars in Ukraine, Syria, Iraq, Yemen, Libya, Afghanistan, etc. was made up of some acute and extremely complex contradictions, a reflection of the deeply antagonistic interests of the major powers, such as the United States, Russia, China, the European Union, and other countries in the Middle East and Eastern Europe. These wars were proxy wars between the great powers fought in other countries, using third-party actors without those powers' direct involvement. President Obama had adopted the "more missionary" foreign policy of the neo-conservatives of the Republican Party, as Professor Henry Kissinger put it, stressing that in this policy, "America had a mission to bring about democracy—if necessary, by the use of force," demonstrating some or total intolerance in the face of any opposition.[1]

In his Independence Day speech before the House of Representatives on July 4, 1821, the future sixth president of the United States John Quincy Adams, then secretary of state, proudly declared that "she [America] has, in the lapse of nearly half a century, without a single exception, respected the independence of other nations, while asserting and maintaining her own."[2] Adams added that America had abstained from interfering in the affairs of other countries, even when the

---

[1]"The Interview: Henry Kissinger." *The National Interest's. National Interest*, September/October, 2015. Available at: <http://nationalinterest.org/print/feature/the-interview-henry-kissinger-13615?page=3>.

[2]"Speech on Independence Day—John Quincy Adams—United States House of Representatives," July 4, 1821. Available at: <http://teachingamericanhistory.org/>; "Ashbrook Center at Ashland University." Available at: <http://teachingamericanhistory.org/library/document/speech-on-independence-day/>.

© Springer Nature Switzerland AG 2019
L. A. Moniz Bandeira, *The World Disorder*,
https://doi.org/10.1007/978-3-030-03204-3_25

conflict was close to her heart, and stressed that while she wanted the "freedom and independence of all," "she goes not abroad in search of monsters to destroy."[3] "Her glory is not dominion, but liberty," he concluded.[4]

This is not how US history played out, however. The ever "more missionary" compulsion to impose what it saw as democracy, even by force, expressed in the policy of exporting democracy and regime change,[5] grew as the interests of Wall Street became more entangled with the military-industrial complex, until they formed an aberration. The international position of the United States as the symbol of freedom, advocated by the Founding Fathers, was undermined. The truth is that the United States not only sought foreign "monsters to destroy," i.e., regimes that didn't suit its economic and geopolitical interests, but also spawned its own monsters. Organizations like the CIA and NATO were responsible for some of the bloodiest fiascos and humanitarian disasters in Eurasia, the Middle East, and Africa, as attested by the war in Afghanistan, the attack on Iraq, the bombing of Libya, the emergence of Da'ish in the midst of the bloodshed in Syria, and the putsch that led to the partition of Ukraine and consequent civil war in the Donbass.

25.2   Psychological and Economic Warfare, Demonization of Putin, and Nazism in Ukraine

As President George W. Bush before him, President Obama persisted in extending NATO's war machine to Ukraine. This country would serve as bridge head to penetrate the rest of Eurasia until the Caspian Sea, the largest lake on the planet with the world's second richest oil and gas reserves after the Persian Gulf. In addition, it has a great importance as link between the West and many other areas of interest.[6] And after Russia's resurgence under President Vladimir Putin, the United States were losing more and more influence in this region of

---

[3] *Ibidem.*

[4] *Ibidem*; John Quincy Adams, *Speech to the U.S. House of Representatives on Foreign Policy* (July 4, 1821)—Transcript. Miller Center—University of Virginia. Available at: <http://millercenter.org/president/speeches/speech-3484>; Carl Cavanagh Hodge & Cathal J. Nolan, *US Presidents and Foreign Policy—1789 to the Present*. Santa Barbara (California): ABC-CLIO, pp. 58–59.

[5] Joshua Muravchik, *Exporting Democracy: Fulfilling America's Destiny—Fulfilling the American Destiny*. Washington: Aei Press, 1991, p. 81–83; Peter J. Schraeder, *Exporting Democracy: Rhetoric Vs. Reality*. Colorado: Lynne Rienner Publishers, 2002, p. 131, 217–220.

[6] Megan Munoz, "For Members Only: The Consequences of the Caspian Summit's Foreign Military Ban." *Modern Diplomacy*, July 30, 2015. Available at: <http://moderndiplomacy.eu/index.php?option=com_k2&view=item&id=890:for-members-only-the-consequences-of-the-caspian-summit-s-foreign-military-ban&Itemid=771>.

vital economic, military, and geopolitical importance.[7] This explains the efforts by the governments of the West (the United States and European Union) to demonize Putin with Crimea's reintegration as pretext, using an intense campaign through the international corporate media, outlets for psychological warfare (PSYOPS).

With good reason, the economist Paul Craig Roberts, former assistant secretary of the Treasury in the Reagan administration (1981–1989), levied the accusation that "the Obama regime and its neocon monsters and European vassals have resurrected the Nazi government and located it in Ukraine." The coup in Ukraine—Roberts explained—was an effort by Washington "to thrust a dagger into Russia's heart."[8] "The recklessness of such a criminal act has been covered up by constructing a false reality of a people's revolution against a corrupt and oppressive government," he remarked, and the world should be stunned to see that "bringing democracy has become Washington's cover for resurrecting the Nazi state." The western media—Roberts stated—"has created a fictional account of events in Ukraine," omitting that the coup was set up by the Obama administration, overthrowing a democratically elected government and ignoring the "Nazi symbols" carried by the militias.[9]

Russia had every right to react, of course. Crimea's reintegration had become inevitable after the putsch to topple President Viktor Yanukovych sponsored by the United States. It had to defend the strategic naval base of Sevastopol, built by Russia in 1783 and vital for its access to the Black Sea, in addition to the oil and gas transport corridors from the Caspian Sea that crisscrossed the Ukraine. It was folly to imagine that Moscow would somehow ignore the offensive.

---

[7]Richard Bidlack, *Russia and Eurasia 2015–2016*. Lanham (Maryland): Rowman & Littlefield, 2015. 46th Edition, pp. vii–viii; Seyyedeh Motahhareh Hosseine & Asghar Shokri Moqaddam, "US Presence in Eurasia and Its Impact on Security and Military Arrangements of This Region." *Geopolitica*, May 5, 2014. Available at: <http://www.geopolitica.ru/en/article/us-presence-eurasia-and-its-impact%2D%2Dsecurity-and-military-arrangements-region#.Vex_MJc-7_A>.

[8]Paul Craig Roberts, "Truth Has Been Murdered." *Institute for Political Economy*, April 28, 2015. Available at: <http://www.paulcraigroberts.org/2015/04/28/truth%2D%2Dmurdered-paul-craig-roberts/print/>; "Paul Craig Roberts: 'Bringing Democracy' Has Become Washington's Cover For Resurrecting a Nazi State." *Silver Doctors*, May 6, 2015. Available at: <http://www.silverdoctors.com/paul-craig-roberts-bringing%2D%2Ddemocracy-has-become-washingtons-cover-for-resurrecting-a-nazi-state>.

[9]*Ibidem.*

25.3   Oil from the Caspian Sea and Waning American Influence in Central Asia

According to the US Information Administration, in 2012–2013, the Caspian Sea and its surroundings had proven reserves of 48 billion barrels of oil and 292 trillion cubic feet (Tcf) of natural gas. Offshore fields accounted for 41% of total Caspian crude oil and lease condensate (19.6 billion barrels).[10] The US Geological Survey (USGS) estimated that even more undiscovered reserves existed, with 20 billion barrels of oil and 243 Tcf of natural gas.[11] In 2012, the basins of the Caspian Sea produced 2.6 million barrels of crude oil per day, on average, about 3.4% of world consumption, most of it (35%) extracted from fields along the coast.[12] And in 2015, Azerbaijan alone was producing 291 million barrels of oil and 1.07 Tcf of natural gas.[13] The total reserves had previously (1999) been estimated at over 100 billion barrels of oil, ten times more than the reserves in Alaska.[14] The total oil output from the Caspian Sea was estimated to exceed that of the North Sea,[15] where exploited fields decreased from 44 in 2008 to only 12 in 2015, although there were still 16 billion recoverable barrels off the coast of Aberdeen and west of the Shetland Islands.[16]

Russia and Kazakhstan controlled the largest part of the Caspian Sea and at the Fourth Caspian Summit in Astrakhan (Russia) on September 29, 2014, the five countries bathed by its waters—Russia, Iran, Azerbaijan, Turkmenistan, and Kazakhstan—unanimously decided they would maintain the security of the region and not permit the interference of foreign military forces.[17] This agreement sought to protect Central Asia from the penetration by NATO forces, whose 376th Air Expeditionary Wing at the Manas Transit Center in Kyrgyzstan, established in 2001 for the International Security Assistance Force (ISAF) operations in Afghanistan, had to be closed on June 4, 2014. Some of the reasons cited for this closure

---

[10]"Oil and natural gas production is growing in Caspian Sea region." Today in Energy, September 11, 2013. *U.S. Energy Information Administration*. Available at: <http://www.eia.gov/todayinenergy/detail.cfm?id=12911>.

[11]*Ibidem.*

[12]"Caspian Sea—Overview of oil and natural gas in the Caspian Sea region—*International energy data and analysis.*" EIA Beta—*U.S. Department of Energy*, August 26, 2013. Available at: <http://www.eia.gov/beta/international/regions%2D%2Dtopics.cfm?RegionTopicID=CSR>.

[13]Jon Mainwaring, "Caspian Conference: Azeri Oil, Gas Production Target Raised for 2015." *Rigzone*, June 4, 2015. Available at: <http://www.rigzone.com/news/oil_gas/a/138946/Caspian_Conference_Azeri_Oil_Gas_Production_Target_Raised_for_2015>.

[14]Vladimir Babak, "Kazaskstan Around Big Oil," 1999, pp. 182–183.

[15]*Ibidem*, p. 183.

[16]Andrew Critchlow (Commodities editor), "North Sea oil production rises despite price fall The UK offshore region is set for the first increase in total production for 15 years." *The Telegraph*, August 3, 2015. Available at: <http://www.telegraph.co.uk/finance/newsbysector/energy/oilandgas/11780648/North-Sea-oil-production-rises-despite-price-slump.html>.

[17]Julia Nanay, "Russia's role in the energy Eurasian market," 2010, pp. 109–115.

were the low and inadequate lease, corruption in oil contracts, and concerns about environmental damage,[18] but another factor certainly included the assurance Kyrgyzstan gave Russia that it would not renew the contract with the United States.[19] When President Barack Obama had to close Manas air base, he planned to transfer it to Kazakhstan. At the same time, he undertook to expand NATO even further in the Eastern European countries, under the pretext of the crisis in Ukraine and the reincorporation of Crimea by Russia. But the Agreement of the Fourth Caspian Summit in Astrakhan closed off the Caspian Sea to Obama's designs. The United States would now find it hard to advance in a region where it previously maintained close military relations with Azerbaijan, Turkmenistan, and Kazakhstan ever since Operation Enduring Freedom was deployed against the Taliban in 2001. President Obama, however, did manage to reach an agreement with the president of Kazakhstan, Nursultan Nazarbayev, which allowed for the quick transport of troops and non-lethal equipment through its air space in less than 12 h from the United States (over the North Pole) to the Bagram military base, 25 miles north of the International Airport in Kabul, Afghanistan.[20] And Kazakhstan, with 6846 km of continuous border with Russia and 1533 km with China, was a country of crucial geopolitical importance to American strategy.

The US air base in Karshi-Khanabad in Uzbekistan had already been closed in 2005, but Germany continued to maintain a small air force base in Termez, now the only base from the West still operational there, in the southeast. It was also used by NATO countries for the war in Afghanistan, where 12,500 soldiers were still stationed in mid-2015, including the 850 Germans and 10,000 Americans of Operation Freedom's Sentinel to fight the insurgents who continued to operate in the northeastern province of Kunduz, with the participation of many Tadzhiks and Uzbeks, militants of the Islamic Movement of Uzbekistan. The government of Uzbekistan, which received 12.4 million € from Germany for the lease of the base since 2005 and 15.2 million € after 2008, was now demanding 35 million € in April 2015 and 72.5 million € for the renewal of the contract until 2016.[21] President Islam

---

[18]John C. K. Daly, "After Ukraine, Russia Beefs Up Military in Armenia and Kyrgyzstan." *Silk Road Reporters*, October 24, 2014. Available at: <http://www.silkroadreporters.com/2014/10/24/ukraine-russia-beefs-military-armenia-kyrgyzstan/>.

[19]Lt. Col. Max Despain, 376th Air Expeditionary Wing Public Affairs. "The End of an Era: 376th Air Expeditionary Wing inactivation ceremony," June 4, 2014. *U.S. Air Force*. Available at: <http://www.af.mil/News/ArticleDisplay/tabid/223/Article/485254/the-end-of-an-era-376th-air-expeditionary-wing-inactivation-ceremony.aspx>.

[20]Rick Rozoff, "Kazakhstan: U.S., NATO Seek Military Outpost between Russia and China," *Global Research*, April 15, 2010. Available at: <http://www.globalresearch.ca/kazakhstan-u-s-nato-seek-military-outpost-between-russia-and%2D%2Dchina/18680>; see also: <http://www.globalresearch.ca/kazakhstan-u-s-nato-seek-military-outpost-between-russia-and-china/18680?print=1>.

[21]Alexander Cooley, *Great Games, Local Rules: The New Great Power Contest in Central Asia*. Oxford-New York: Oxford University Press, 2012. p. 168; "Germany negotiates air base lease with Uzbekistan." *NEOnline* I TB. Available at: <http://neurope.eu/article/germany-negotiates-air-base-lease-uzbekistan/>.

Karimov also forbade the stationing of troops at Termez base so that it would only be used as a logistics center for electronic surveillance and intelligence gathering in Central Asia—in Kazakhstan, southeast Russia, and the west of China, as well as possibly in Iran, Pakistan, and India. It also served to supply the German troops of Resolute Support Mission stationed in the Hindu Kush, Afghanistan, since the International Security Assistance Force (ISAF) had formally put an end to combat operations on December 28, 2014.[22] Along with the Air Force of Uzbekistan, Germany only kept 3 C-160 Transall aircraft and 160 operators in Termez, but between 17,000 and 18,000 troops from various nations still remained in Afghanistan.

25.4   Russia's Military Modernization, Defense Treaties, and Eurasian Economic Union

The United States had distorted the role of NATO. Initially the alliance was defensive and limited to partners of Western Europe. Now America attributed out-of-area offensive missions to it, such as the war in Afghanistan and the bombardment of Libya to overthrow the regime of Muammar Gaddafi, perverting UNSC Resolution 1.970 (2011).[23] The American objective was to ensure a permanent presence in Hindu Kush and the Pamir Mountains, some of the highest in the world, as well as in the steppes of Central Asia.

Within the framework of bilateral cooperation, the United States was providing modern equipment to the countries of Eastern Europe that joined NATO, including Bulgaria and Poland. This included the AGM-158 JASSM (Joint Air-to-Surface Standoff Missile), a low visibility cruise missile that could be launched from a distance and enabled tactical aircraft to strike targets in Russia without entering the area covered by its missile defense system.

President Vladimir Putin—faced with NATO's expansion to Russia's vicinity, bolstering up to penetrate Eurasia and corner his country[24]—had been working for some time on hardening a collective defense and security system in the Caucasus. The outline of an agreement had already been established with Armenia, similar to what he had done with Kyrgyzstan, Tajikistan, Kazakhstan, and Belarus, whose

[22]Zdzislaw Lachowski, "Foreign Military Bases in Eurasia." *SIPRI Policy Paper No. 18. SIPRI, Stockholm International Peace Research Institute.* Stockholm: CM Grup-pen, Bromma, junho de 2007. Available at: <http://books.sipri.org/files/PP/SIPRIPP18.pdf>.

[23]"Security Council Approves 'No-Fly Zone' over Libya, Authorizing 'All Necessary Measures' to Protect Civilians, by Vote of 10 in Favour with 5 Abstentions 17 March 2011 Security Council. 6498th Meeting (Night)." Available at: <http://www.un.org/press/en/2011/sc10200.doc.htm>.

[24]Seyyedeh Motahhareh Hosseini & Asghar Shokri Moqaddam, "US Presence in Eurasia and Its Impact on Security and Military Arrangements of This Region." *Geopolitica*, May 5, 2014. Available at: <http://www.geopolitica.ru/en/article/us-presence-eurasia-and-its-impact-security-and-military-arrangements-region#.Vex_MJc-7_A>.

combat and defense units would act in coordination with Russia, according to Lieutenant General Pavel Kurachenko, commander of the Russian Aerospace Forces.[25] Russia also intended to establish air bases within the framework of the Collective Security Treaty Organization (Organizatsiya Dogovora o Kollektivnoy Bezopasnosti, ODKB) in some of the signatory countries, including Belarus and probably Armenia, Kazakhstan, Kyrgyzstan, Tajikistan, and other Central Asian countries.[26] Russia was negotiating the opening of an air base and a joint defense system in September 2015 with Belarus, and Moscow planned to send 2250 units of modern equipment, Su-35 and Su-35S fighter jets, MI-8MTV51 helicopters, radars, new paratrooper equipment, infantry fighting vehicles, and complex drones (UAV).[27] If you want peace, prepare for war. The Baltic countries and Poland, previously some of the most hawkish, were startled. The presence of NATO forces on their territory was superfluous.

In 1997, while President Bill Clinton planned NATO's expansion to the Eastern European countries, Rear Admiral Eugene J. Carroll Jr. published an op-ed in the *Los Angeles Times*. In it, he reiterated the warning of the diplomat George F. Kennan, author of the containment doctrine, who said that "expanding NATO would be the most fateful error of American policy in the post-cold war era. Such a decision may be expected [...] to impel Russian foreign policy in directions decidedly not to our liking."[28] It was clear Russia had to react, reintegrating Ukraine and Sevastopol into its jurisdiction in order to preserve the naval base at Akhtiar (white stone) bay, founded between 1783 and 1784. For when the American State Department and other public and private institutions in the United States (NED, USAID, and NGOs) promoted the putsch against president Viktor Yanukovych, one

---

[25]"Russian Unified Air Defense for CIS Collective Security." *Russian Peacekeper*, September 9, 2015. Available at: <http://www.peacekeeper.ru/en/?module=news&action=view&id=27398>.

[26]"Russia is ready to establish airbases in neighboring countries—Russian PM." *RT*, September 9, 2015. Available at: <http://www.rt.com/news/314787-russia%2D%2Dair-bases-csto/06>. Accessed on September 10, 2015; Christopher Harress, "Amid NATO Threats, Russia New Air Bases Could Open Across Eastern Europe and Central Asia." *International Business Times*, 9 de setembro de 2015. Available at: <http://www.ibtimes.com/amid-nato-threats-russia-new-air-bases-could%2D%2Dopen-across-eastern-europe-central-asia-2088746>; John C. K. Daly, "After Ukraine, Russia Beefs Up Military in Armenia and Kyrgyzstan." *Silk Road Reporters*, October 24, 2014. Available at: <http://www.silkroadreporters.com/2014/10/24/ukraine-russia-beefs-military-armenia-kyrgyzstan/>.

[27]"Putin orders talks on Russian military base in Belarus." *RT*, September 19, 2015. Available at: <https://www.rt.com/news/315964-putin-military-base-belarus/>. Accessed on September 19, 2015.

[28]Eugene J. Carroll Jr. (retired Navy rear admiral, deputy director of the Center for Defense Information). "NATO Expansion Would Be an Epic 'Fateful Error'—Policy: Enlargement could weaken unity within the alliance. Denials of the potential threat to Russia are delusory." *Los Angeles Times*, July 7, 1997. Available at: <http://articles.latimes.com/print/1997/jul/07/local/me-10464>; George F. Kennan, "A Fateful Error." *The New York Times*, July 5, 1997. *Wargaming italia*. Available at: <http://www.netwargamingitalia.net/forum/resources/george-f-kennan-a-fateful-error.35/>.

of the implicit goals was to establish a new regime and extend NATO's war machine to Ukraine, about 490 km from Moscow.

General Joseph Dunford Jr. of the US Marine Corps, appointed by President Obama as Chairman of the Joint Chiefs of Staff, told the Senate Armed Services Committee in Washington that "Russia presents the greatest threat to our national security. [...] If you look at their behavior, it's nothing short of alarming."[29] But President Putin had also perceived the threat represented by the manufacture in the United States of new high-precision, long-range missiles—Patriot, Aegis/Standard, SLAMRAAM (Surface Launched Advanced Medium-Range Air-to-Air Missile), and AIM-120 AMRAAM (Advanced Medium-Range Air-to-Air Missile) missiles, among others—all of which capable of hitting strategic targets in Russia. And since a few years, Russia had started modernizing its armaments and producing a cruise missile that could be launched from submarines and warships and reduce American military power over a vast region, from Warsaw to Kabul and from Rome to Baghdad.[30] The United States, on the other hand, developed the system known as JLENS, a tethered aerial cruise missile defense system with a wide-range and precision radar, and integrated it in the Theater Air and Missile Defense (JTAMD).[31] The disarmament treaties between the United States and Russia had been eroding since the George W. Bush administration, which had no regard for international law or the UN, and adopted the doctrine of preemptive wars recklessly to invade Iraq, the first of several countries it would attack, including Syria.

President Putin had saved Russia from disintegration during a crucial period. A "historical deed," as Mikhail Gorbachiov, the former secretary of the Communist Party (1985–1991) and president of the Soviet Union, reminded the Russian people when he spoke out in support of Crimea's reintegration.[32] All Putin's efforts sought to restore the economic and political influence of the Soviet Union, even if partially and playing by the rules of capitalism, under the name of the Eurasian Economic

---

[29]"Obama's pick for Joint Chiefs sides with Romney on Russia." *New York Post*, July 9, 2015. Available at: <http://nypost.com/2015/07/09/russia-is-greatest%2D%2Dthreat-to-america-joint-chiefs-nominee/>; Francesca Chambers (White House Correspondent For Dailymail.com) & Reuters "The Cold War is back: Putin's Russia named as number one threat to U.S. by Obama's nominee to lead the Joint Chiefs of Staff." *MailOnline*, July 9, 2015. Accessed on July 22, 2015.

[30]"Russia—Politics Putin prepares bitter and hysterical missile surprise to 'American partners'." *Pravda*, January 16, 2015. Available at: <http://english.pravda.ru/russia/politics/16-01-2015/129540-putin_missile_surprise-0/>.

[31]Julian Borger (diplomatic editor), "U.S. and Russia in danger of returning to era of nuclear rivalry—American threats to retaliate for Russian development of new cruise missile take tensions to new level." *The Guardian*, January 4, 2015. Available at: <http://www.theguardian.com/world/2015/jan/04/us-russia-era-nuclear-rivalry>.

[32]"Gorbachev: Putin saved Russia from disintegration." *RT*, December 27, 2014. Available at: <http://rt.com/news/217931-gorbachev-putin-saved-russia/>; Tom Porter, "Mikhail Gorbachev claims Vladimir Putin 'saved' Russia from falling apart." *International Business Times*, December 27, 2014. Available at: <http://www.ibtimes.co.uk/mikhail-gorbachev-claims-vladimir-putin-saved-russia%2D%2Dfalling-apart-1481065>.

Union (EurAsEc-EEU). The EEU would restructure the countries of the Common-wealth of Independent States (CIS) created in 1991 during President Boris Yeltsin's government without any real organicity, customs union, trade relations, or mutual assistance, although it possessed a market of around 180 million people. But the restoration of Russia to the economic, geopolitical, and strategic dimensions of the defunct Soviet Union was something the United States didn't accept, and wished to obstruct, enacting sanctions under the pretext of Crimea's reintegration and the civil war in eastern Ukraine. This was essentially the justification for the putsch against the government of President Viktor Yanukovych, carried out by ultranationalist and neo-Nazi militias, funded by the United States and the rich oligarchs, fearful that competition would end the monopoly on the industrial sectors they commanded if Ukraine were to join the Eurasian Economic Union.

25.5 Russia–China Cooperation, Nord Stream Pipeline, and Sanctions Against Russia

The unipolarity of the United States in the international financial system, a factor that made it possible to impose sanctions according to its economic and geopolitical interests, spurred other countries to seek different instruments outside the sphere of the dollar to trade and make financial transactions.[33] And in order to expand the use of national currencies (Russian ruble, Belarusian ruble, dram, and tenge), President Putin planned for the elimination of the dollar and the euro in international com-mercial transactions within the EEU countries—Russia, Belarus, Armenia, and Kazakhstan—and perhaps in other countries like Kyrgyzstan, Tajikistan, and Uzbek-istan.[34] In addition, Russia's Prime Minister Dmitry Medvedev was negotiating Vietnam's adherence to the EEU with Prime Minister Nguyen Tan Dung.[35] And in 2014, the central banks of Russia and China signed an agreement to swap 150 billion yuan (US$23.5 billion) to strengthen financial cooperation between both countries. In August 2015, China's Central Bank initiated a pilot program

---

[33]Ariel Noyola Rodríguez, "Russia Precipitates the Abandonment of the SWIFT International Payments System among BRICS Countries." *Global Research*, October 6, 2015; UNISA (Univer-sity of South Africa)—Institute for Global Dialogue. Available at: <http://www.igd.org.za/index.php/research/foreign-policy-analysis/south-south-cooperation/11465-russia-precipitates-the-aban donment-of-the%2D%2Dswift-international-payments-system-among-brics-countries>.

[34]"Putin says dump the dollar." *RT*, September 1, 2015. Available at: <https://www.rt.com/business/313967-putin-says-dump-dollar/>. Accessed on September 3, 2015. Also in: <https://www.rt.com/business/313967-putin-says%2D%2Ddump-dollar/>.

[35]"Vietnam and Eurasian Economic Union free trade zone deal in 'home straight'—Russian PM." *RT*, April 6, 2015. Available at: <http://www.rt.com/business/247033-russia-vietnam-trade-coop eration/>. Accessed on April 6, 2015.

replacing the dollar by the ruble in the city of Suifenhe, in its northeastern province Heilongjiang.[36]

Within the context of the financial-economic war waged by the United States and the European Union against Russia, Gazprom and China's National Petroleum Corporation (CNPC) signed—and Presidents Vladimir Putin and Xi Jinping approved—a memorandum of understanding to build the Power of Siberia (Сила Сибири) pipeline through 2500 of the Siberian fields in Krasnoyarsk and Irkutsk. This agreement to supply liquefied natural gas (LNG) to China was valued at US $400 billion and would be transacted in rubles/yuan. Gazprom and China also negotiated the supply through Siberia's western route using the 1700-mile-long Altai pipeline transporting 30 billion cubic meters per year, with the prospect of increasing this volume to 100 billion per year.[37] Gazprom was exporting liquid natural gas for about US$10.19 per MMBtu in mid-2015, but analysts believed that China paid only around US$8 per MMBtu.[38] At this low price, the American corporations that planned to supply China with the more expensive shale gas, investing in the construction of terminals along the Pacific coast of the United States, were expected to experience "some epic capital destruction."[39] They would not be able to compete on the price with Russia.

Russia had been on the verge of abandoning the construction of the Nord Stream gas pipeline, given the tensions created by the European Union, following the United States. It tried to negotiate the South Stream gas pipeline project with Turkey's President Recep Tayyip Erdogan, which would cross the Black Sea to Bulgaria and Europe. But alleging that this configured a monopoly and violated competition laws, the European Commission obstructed the pipeline for political reasons. Brussels' submission to Washington was severely damaging the economy of the European Union, particularly in Germany. The chief analyst of Bremer Landesbank, the economist Folker Hellmeyer, revealed that as a result of the sanctions against Russia, exports from Germany declined by 18% in 2014 and 34% in the first 2 months of 2015. But the damage was much more severe than statistics could show, since the "first losses" where compounded by "secondary effects" that became

---

[36]*Ibidem.*

[37]"Gazprom and CNPC sign memorandum on gas deliveries from Russia's Far East to China—Russia's gas major Gazprom and the Chinese National Oil and Gas Company have signed a Memorandum of Understanding on natural gas supplies from Russia to China and to build a pipeline to the Far East." *TASS*, September 3, 2014. Available at: <http://tass.ru/en/economy/818493>; Kenneth Rapoza, "Russian Government Ratifies Huge China Gas Pipeline Deal." *Forbes*, May 3, 2015. Available at: <http://www.forbes.com/sites/kenrapoza/2015/05/03/russian-government-ratifies-huge-china-gas-pipeline-deal/5>.

[38]MMBTU/MBTU is the acronym for One Million of British Thermal Units, a measure used for natural gas.

[39]Kurt Cobb, "Russia-China Deal Could Kill U.S. LNG Exports." *OilPrice.com/CNBC*, November 18, 2014. Available at: <http://oilprice.com/Energy/Natural-Gas/Russia-China-Deal-Could-Kill-U.S.-LNG-Exports.html>.

much worse over time.[40] Mr. Hellmeyer pointed out that the lack in predictability forced Siemens out of a large project; that Alstom lost a contract for the railway line between Moscow and Beijing; and that the potential for damage was more massive than the current accounts indicated, and not only for Germany but the entire European Union.[41]

Faced with the prospect of huge losses, the German companies E.ON and BASF/Wintershall, along with the British-Dutch Royal Dutch Shell plc, the French ENGIE and the Austrian OMV, disregarded the sanctions against Russia and maintained the project to build the Nord Stream gas pipeline-2 with Gazprom (with 51% of the shares). This pipeline would have two maritime extensions under the Baltic Sea and bypass Ukraine, no longer considered a reliable route.[42] The losses of the government in Kiev, deprived of the energy transit fees for approximately 140 billion cubic meters of gas, were estimated to be least US$2 billion dollars, as Prime Minister Arseniy Yatsenyuk stated in the Verkhovna Rada, condemning the project as anti-European and anti-Ukrainian.[43]

25.6   China and Russia and the Creation of a New International Payment System

The understandings between Russia and China were based on the exchange of the ruble/yuan. Since April 2012, the People's Bank of China was designing a new architecture for international payments and created the China International Payment System (CIPS),[44] a super-fast transaction system with the yuan CHN=CNY=CFXS

---

[40]"Top-Banker ist sich sicher: Russland und China gewinnen gegen die USA." *Deutsche Wirtschafts Nachrichten*, June 6, 2010. Available at: <http://deutsche-wirtschafts-nachrichten.de/2015/06/06/top-banker-ist-sich-sicher-russland-und-china%2D%2Dgewinnen-gegen-die-usa/>.

[41]*Ibidem.*

[42]"Gazprom, BASF, E.ON, ENGIE, OMV and Shell sign Shareholders Agreement on Nord Stream II project." *Gazprom*, September 4, 2015. Available at: <http://www.gazprom.com/press/news/2015/september/article245837/>; Denis Pinchuk & Olesya Astakhova & Oleg Vulkmanovic, "Gazprom to offer more gas at spot prices via Nord Stream II." *Reuters*, October 13, 2015. Available at: <http://www.reuters.com/article/2015/10/13/us-russia-gazprom-spot-idUSKCN0S71XS20151013>; Elena Mazneva & Dina Khrennikova, "Putin Bets on Germany as Gas Ties with Turkey Sour on Syria." *Bloomberg*, October 13, 2015. Available at: <http://www.bloomberg.com/news/articles/2015-10-12/putin-bets-on-germany-as-gas-ties-with-turkey-go-sour-over-syria>.

[43]Filip Singer, "Ukraine's PM blames EU for lack of partnership over support of Nord Stream-2 project." *TASS*, September 18, 2015. Available at: <http://tass.ru/en/world/822175>.

[44]"Internationalisierung des Yuan—China startet internationales Zahlungssystem—Bisher war die Abwicklung grenzüberschreitender Geschäfte in Yuan teuer und langwierig. Das soll nun besser werden und die Internationalisierung der chinesischen Währung vorantreiben." *Zürcher Kantonalbank*, October 9, 2015. Available at: <http://www.nzz.ch/finanzen/devisen-und-rohstoffe/china-startet%2D%2Dinternationales-zahlungssystem-1.18626842>.

replacing the clearing system controlled by the United States through the National Security Agency (NSA). This cleared the path for the internationalization of the yuan and its transformation into a reserve currency.[45] By 2014, the yuan was already the fifth largest currency in world trade.[46] And in its first phase,[47] the CIPS[48] began operating in October of 2015,[49] while Russia was set to launch a prototype of a national credit card—Mir (peace or world)—which could extend to the BRIC countries (the acronym for Brazil, Russia, India, and China coined by Jim O'Neill of the investment bank Goldman Sachs).[50] And in November 2015, the yuan was included in the Special Drawing Rights (SDR), the basket of currencies of the International Monetary Fund.

This new international financial transaction system—the CIPS—was a frontal assault on SWIFT.[51] Similarly, with the goal of planting the seed of a new international economic and financial order, China had founded the Asian Infrastructure Investment Bank (AIIB) with US$100 billion in capital and the adherence of numerous countries. And as an alternative to the IMF and the World Bank, the New Development Bank was created on June 20, 2015, in partnership with Brazil, Russia, India, and South Africa, also with a capital of US$100 billion.[52] Excluding South Africa, the four original BRIC countries comprised 40% of the world's population, a quarter of its area and 35% of its GDP.[53]

---

[45]Michelle Chen & Koh Gui Qing, "China's international payments system ready, could launch by end-2015—sources." *Reuters*, March 9, 2015. Available at: <http://www.reuters.com/article/2015/03/09/us-china-yuan-payments-exclusive-idUSKBN0M50BV20150309>.

[46]"China's mega international payment system is ready will launch this year—report." *RT*, March 10, 2015. Available at: <https://www.rt.com/business/239189-china-payment-system-ready/>.

[47]"China launches RMB int'l interbank payment system." *English.news.cn*, August 10, 2015. Available at: <http://news.xinhuanet.com/english/video/2015-10/08/c_134692342.htm>.

[48]"Payment, clearing and settlement systems in China." Available at: <https://www.bis.org/cpmi/publ/d105_cn.pdf>.

[49]"Internationalisierung des Yuan—China startet internationales Zahlungssystem—Bisher war die Abwicklung grenzüberschreitender Geschäfte in Yuan teuer und langwierig. Das soll nun besser werden und die Internationalisierung der chinesischen Währung vorantreiben." *Zürcher Kantonalbank*, October 9, 2015. Available at: <http://www.nzz.ch/finanzen/devisen-und-rohstoffe/china-startet%2D%2Dinternationales-zahlungssystem-1.18626842>.

[50]Alexej Lossan (RBTH), "Russland stellt Alternative zu Visa und MasterCard vor—Die russische Regierung hat in Moskau den Prototypen einer nationalen Kreditkarte vorgestellt. Allerdings wird noch einige Zeit vergehen, bis das neue Zahlungssystem flächendeckend eingeführt wird." *Russia Beyond and the Headlines*, June 4, 2015. Available at: <http://de.rbth.com/wirtschaft/2015/06/04/russland_stellt_alternative_zu_visa_und_mastercard_vor_33869>.

[51]"Mehr Unabhängigkeit: BRICS-Staaten vs. Wall Street und City of London." *Pravda TV*, October 14, 2015. Available at: <http://www.pravda-tv.com/2015/10/mehr-unabhaengigkeit-brics-staaten-vs-wall-street-und-city-of-london>.

[52]Gabriel Wildau (Shanghai), "New Brics bank in Shanghai to challenge major institutions." *The Financial Times*, July 21, 2015. Available at: <http://www.ft.com/intl/cms/s/0/d8e26216-2f8d-11e5-8873-775ba7c2ea3d.html#axzz3lo8DME81>.

[53]*Ibidem.*

Meanwhile, Moscow wanted to create another interbank system. The Central Bank of Russia was tasked with building an alternative to Society for Worldwide Interbank Financial Telecommunication (SWIFT)[54] in order to confront any sanctions from the United States and the European Union that affected Russia's international payment orders. This involved more than US$6 trillion and 10,000 financial institutions in 210 countries.[55] ROSSWIFT was the second largest member of SWIFT after the United States. If the United States and the European Union were to bar Russia from SWIFT, the situation could deteriorate to the point of generating an international conflict of greater proportions and unpredictable consequences.[56]

Replacing the dollar as the dominant currency in world trade would reduce the ability of the United States to apply sanctions against other countries, and it would create the conditions for greater liquidity in the markets. In 2014, Russia decided to set the price of its commodities—oil and gas—in rubles. Moscow signed a memorandum of understanding on an oil-for-goods swap transactions with Tehran, which would have a value of US$20 billion and give Rosneft around 500,000 bbl/day in oil to sell in the international market. This news alarmed Washington. Congressman Edward Royce (Republican, CA), chairman of the House Foreign Affairs Committee, wrote a letter to Secretary of State John Kerry dated June 2, 2014, in which he expressed "serious concern" about the possibility that the deal would allow Iran to increase its oil exports in exchange for weapons and new nuclear installations provided by Russia.[57] In Washington's eyes, this agreement would also undermine America's efforts to isolate Russia "after it annexed Crimea in March and started destabilizing eastern Ukraine."[58] In October 2015, the Russian banks Sberbank, VTB, Gazprombank, Bank of Moscow, Rosselkhozbank, etc. were already using another payment system outside of SWIFT.[59]

---

[54]This society—the Swift network—was created in Brussels in 1973.

[55]"Russia to launch alternative to SWIFT bank transaction system in spring 2015." *RT*, November 11, 2014. Available at: <https://www.rt.com/business/204459-russia-swift-payment-alternative/>.

[56]Michelle Chen & Koh Gui Qing (Hong Kong/Beijing), "Exclusive: China's international payments system ready, could launch by end-2015—sources." *Reuters*, March 9, 2015. Available at: <http://www.reuters.com/article/2015/03/09/us%2D%2Dchina-yuan-payments-exclusive-idUSKBN0M50BV20150309>.

[57]"Iran and Russia Making a Deal? Chairman Royce." *Presses State Department for Information*, June 3, 2014. Available at: <http://foreignaffairs.house.gov/press-release/iran-and-russia-making-deal-chairman-royce-presses-state-department-information>.

[58]*Ibidem.*

[59]"Several big Russian banks already use SWIFT equivalent—banking official. It was reported earlier that Russia's SWIFT equivalent would be launched in fall 2015." *TASS—Russia & India Reports*, September 18, 2015. Available at: <http://in.rbth.com/news/2015/09/18/several-big-rusian-banks-already-use-swift-equivalent-banking-official_425941>.

25.7   American Hegemony and the Petrodollar Standard

These events tended to put an end to the hegemony of the dollar, which had started weakening when Presidents Lyndon Johnson (1963–1969) and Richard Nixon (1969–1974) disregarded the gold exchange standard agreed upon at Bretton Woods (1944). In this standard, an ounce of gold (28.35 g) should be worth US $35, but in order to finance the imports of the United States and the costs of the Cold War and the war in Indochina, the United States issued and put more dollars into circulation than it could back up with the existing gold in Fort Knox. In addition, the banks and big corporations in the United States began investing heavily in Europe. All the stored gold reserves were virtually depleted by 1970. Only 1000 tons remained of the 8500 supposedly deposited in Fort Knox. Meanwhile, the dollar reserves in possession of European banks, the Eurodollars, had jumped from US $23.8 billion to US$36 billion in July 1971 and to US$40 billion in the following month, three times more than the United States needed to honor their obligations based on the Bretton Woods agreements.[60]

At the same time, the federal budget deficits had been growing since 1960 by US $3 billion per year, on average, jumping from US$9 billion in 1967 to US$25 billion in 1968 as a result of the costs of war in Indochina. The obligations of the United States reached US$36 billion, and the gold reserves plunged from US$24 billion in 1945 to US$16 billion in 1962 and only US$13 billion in 1969.[61] The volume of Eurodollars on the London market was estimated to have reached US$1.3 trillion in 1970, a pool of hot money circulated offshore without control but returning to the United States and funding deficits in Washington through the purchase of treasury bonds. Between 1968 and 1971, these deficits accumulated to US$56 billion. This was a gravely ill economy. If the countries holding the Eurodollar reserves were to demand the conversion of paper currency on the parity of US$35 per ounce of gold, the United States would default.[62] And so President Nixon unilaterally suspended the direct convertibility of dollars into gold in August 1971.[63] The international economic and monetary order was severely shaken. Confidence in the dollar took a hit, and the influx of foreign currency to Europe and Japan increased even further. When faced with the worsening of the crisis 2 years later, in 1973, President Nixon had to devalue the dollar by 10%, both breaking the Smithsonian Agreement regarding the European Joint Float and paving the way for free-floating currencies. The dollar, which only the United States could print, became the international fiduciary currency. The IMF then adopted the Special Drawing Rights (SDR) regime to conceal the weakness of the dollar as a currency. The president of France at the

---

[60]William Bundy, 1998, p. 361.

[61]"New York FED stores third od gold. 80 countries keeps 13 billion in vault." *Chicago Tribune*, September 23, 1969. Available at: <http://archives.chicagotribune.com/1969/09/23/page/53/arti cle/new-york-fed-bank-stores-third-of-gold>.

[62]F. William Engdahl, 1993, pp. 133–137.

[63]Satyendra Nayak, 2013, pp. 105–108.

time, General Charles de Gaulle, accused the United States of seizing an "exorbitant privilege," since it could continue financing its deficits by issuing more dollars and putting them into circulation.[64]

Meanwhile, from 1971 to 1973, Secretary of the Treasury Jack F. Bennettt (later CEO of Exxon) and Professor Henry Kissinger, President Nixon's National Security Adviser, with the support of the powerful London bankers sir Sigmund Warburg, Edmond Rothschild, Jocelyn Hambro, etc., entwined with Wall Street and negotiated a deal with King Fayṣal ibn 'Abd al-'Azīz Āl Su'ūd and the Saudi Arabian Monetary Agency. This deal was subsequently consolidated with the creation of the United States–Saudi Arabian Joint Commission on Economic Cooperation. Oil transactions would now occur in dollars only, which would be reinvested through the purchase of treasury bonds from the United States, permitting Washington to fund its growing deficits. On October 6, 1973, during the celebrations of Yon Kippur (Day of Atonement), the holiest day in the Jewish calendar, Syrian and Egyptian troops crossed the Suez Canal and attacked Israel, advancing toward the Sinai Peninsula and the Golan Heights. Despite Israel's surprise and initial defeats, suffering heavy losses of about 2600 soldiers, the IDF turned the situation around, and, on October 28, Egypt, Syria, and Israel accepted a cease-fire. In order to boycott the United States and the West for supporting Israel, Egypt encouraged the rise in the price of crude from US$3 to US$12 per barrel in 1974. But the recycling of dollars had already been agreed with Saudi Arabia when the oil shock occurred, and with the big profits resulting from the price hike, Riyadh bought US$2.5 billion in US Treasury bonds.[65] The oil/dollar agreement was expanded in 1975 to the other OPEC members.[66] The petrodollar standard had been consolidated and replaced the gold exchange standard. Any country that wished to buy oil would have to get dollars and take short-term loans from banks in Europe and the United States. The Eurodollars mutated into petrodollars. Foreign demand enabled the continuous issuance of paper money, as a *fiat currency*, and the accumulation of huge debts without Washington running the risk of default. And the petrodollars mutated into one of the foundations of US economic power, reinforced by yet another oil shock in 1979, while countries in Latin America, Asia, and Africa were plunged into a severe foreign debt crisis.

Richard Benson, a former economist at Chase Manhattan Bank, pointed out that the level of prosperity in the United States depended in no small measure on the massive deficits its governments were running in trade relations with other countries,

---

[64]*Ibidem*, pp. 107–108, "Norte-Sur. Un programa para la supervivencia. Informe de la Comisión Independiente sobre Problemas Internacionales del Desarrollo presidida por Willy Brandt." *The Independente Comisión on International Development Sigues*. Bogotá: Editorial Pluma, 1980, p. 305.

[65]William R. Clark, 2005, pp. 20–22.

[66]Alexander Clakson, "The Real Reason Russia is Demonized and Sanctioned: the American Petrodollar." *Global Research*, September 18, 2014. Available at: <http://www.globalresearch.ca/the-real-reason-russia-is-demonized-and-sanctioned-the-american-petrodollar/5402592>.

importing up to US\$3 trillion without actually paying for the goods it acquired.[67] The central banks wanted to accept dollar holdings as investments, but the only thing that had value in the modern economy was oil. "In the real world (which is a long way from Hollywood and the Liberal Media), the one factor underpinning American prosperity is keeping the dollar the World Reserve Currency."[68] And this could only happen if the oil-producing countries maintained the price and all their foreign exchange reserves in dollars. "If anything put the final nail in Saddam Hussein's coffin, it was his move to start selling oil for Euros," Richard Benson noted, adding that "the US is the sole super power and we control and dictate to the Middle East oil producers. America has the power to change rulers if they can't follow the "straight line" the United States dictates. America's prosperity depends on this."[69]

25.8   The Moscow–Beijing Axis and a New Dominant Currency in World Trade

The United States, however, had for some time "lost its ability to dictate economic policy of other countries," declared Princeton University Professor and Nobel Prize-winning economist Paul Krugman in a press interview.[70] But the big banks that ruled the world economy through the Fed and Wall Street never admitted that the dollar, still surviving as a *fiat currency*, could lose its status as the only currency in international transactions and trade, especially in oil and gas. It was one of the factors leading to the invasion of Iraq in 2003, when Saddam Hussein planned to replace the dollar with the euro in oil sales, a measure other countries could certainly follow.[71] Not without good reason, John Chapman, a former assistant secretary in the British civil service, wrote in *The Guardian* that "there were only two credible reasons for invading Iraq: control over oil and the preservation of the dollar as the world's reserve currency. Yet the government has kept silent on these factors."[72] Indeed, the reliance on the dollar as a fiat currency was dissipating.[73] Washington

---

[67]Richard Benson, SFGroup. "Oil, the Dollar, and US Prosperity." *Information Clearing House*, August 8, 2003. Available at: <http://www.informationclearinghouse.info/article4404.htm>.

[68]*Ibidem.*

[69]*Ibidem.*

[70]Giuliana Vallone, "Economia global projeta cenário decepcionante, diz Nobel de Economia." *Folha de S. Paulo*, October 19, 2015. Available at: <http://www1.folha.uol.com.br/mercado/2015/10/1695575-economia-global-projeta-cenario-decepcionante-diz-nobel-de-economia.shtm>.

[71]William R. Clark, 2005, pp. 113–117.

[72]Sandy Franks & Sara Nunnally, 2011, pp. 135–138, 150–151.

[73]John Chapman, "The real reasons Bush went to war—WMD was the rationale for invading Iraq. But what was really driving the US were fears over oil and the future of the dollar." *The Guardian*, July 28, 2004. Available at: <http://www.theguardian.com/world/2004/jul/28/iraq.usa>; Rachel Evans, "Russia Sanctions Accelerate Risk to Dollar Dominance." *Bloomberg*, August 6, 2014. Available at: <http://www.bloomberg.com/news/2014-08-06/russia-sanctions-accelerate%2D%

could not indefinitely issue paper money without backing to import more than it produced, while other countries continued to buy treasury bonds with those same dollars without backing, financing the public deficit and prosperity of the American population. The federal debt grew year after year and reached US$18.1 trillion in 2014.[74] It was projected to rise to US$22.488 trillion (federal, state, and local) by the end of the fiscal year 2016,[75] while GDP was only US$17.42 trillion (2014 est.).[76]

China's creation of the CIPS as an alternative to SWIFT combined with a similar initiative from Russia, the establishment of the Asian Infrastructure Investment Bank (AIIB) and the New Development Bank in partnership with Brazil, Russia, India, and South Africa, was threatening Wall Street's preeminence. And this meant the erosion of American hegemony, exercised through the dollar as the only international reserve currency and the expansion of NATO's military machine, which subordinated the European Union and other countries to its economic and political interests. To a large extent, this was the background of the crises in such countries as Ukraine and Syria.[77] And in his speech delivered during the officers' graduation ceremony at the West Point Military Academy on May 28, 2014, President Obama singled out the countries he deemed hostile to the United States, saying that "Russia's aggression toward former Soviet states unnerves capitals in Europe, while China's economic rise and military reach worries its neighbors. From Brazil to India, rising middle classes compete with us, and governments seek a greater say in global forums."[78] These were exactly the so-called BRIC countries.

The conflict had been decided, however, and the West's dominion had been broken—foreshadowed the economist Folker Hellmeyer, chief analyst of Bremer Landesbank.[79] Interviewed by the *Deutsche Wirtschaftsnachrichten* in June 2015, he noted that in 1990, the BRIC countries accounted for only 25% of the world

---

2Drisk-to-dollar-dominance.html>; Finian Cunningham, "'Deal or War': Is doomed Dollar Really Behind Obama's Iran Warning?" *RT*, August 16, 2015. Available at: <https://www.rt.com/op-edge/312531-iran-kerry-us-dollar/>.

[74]Federal Debt Clock. Available at: <http://www.usgovernmentdebt.us/>.

[75]*Ibidem.*

[76]*CIA—World Fact Book.* Available at: <https://www.cia.gov/library/publications/the-world-factbook/geos/us.html>. Accessed on October 16, 2015.

[77]"Jim Rogers—Russia/China/Brazil Joining Forces to Avoid U.S. Dollar." *The Daily* Coin, November 3, 2014. Available at: <http://thedailycoin.org/?p=10593>; Andrew Henderson, "Russia vs. the petrodollar: the latest reserve currency meltdown." *Nomad Capitalist.* Available at: <http://nomadcapitalist.com/2014/08/08/russia-vs-petrodollar-latest-reserve-currency-melt down/>.

[78]"Remarks by the President at the United States Military Academy Commencement Ceremony." *The White House. Office of the Press Secretary*, May 28, 2014. Available at: <https://www. whitehouse.gov/the-press-office/2014/05/28/remarks-president-united-states-military-academy-commencement-ceremon>.

[79]"Top-Banker ist sich sicher: Russland und China gewinnen gegen die USA." *Deutsche Wirtschafts Nachrichten*, June 6, 2015. Available at: <http://deutsche%2D%2Dwirtschafts-nachrichten.de/2015/06/06/top-banker-ist-sich-sicher-russland-und-china-gewinnen-gegen-die-usa/>.

production, while in 2015, they accounted for 56%, representing 40% of the world's population and controlling 70% of its currency reserves.[80] And—Hellmeyer argued—since the United States was unwilling to share power, that is, change the voting shares in the IMF and the World Bank, these emerging countries had no choice but to build their own financial system. "There lies the future," he said. Without Moscow and Beijing, no problem in the world could be solved, and Hellmeyer predicted that the Moscow–Beijing axis (Achse Moskau-Peking) would undoubtedly prevail against the old hegemony of the United States.[81]

---

[80] *Ibidem.*
[81] *Ibidem.*

Chapter 26
Epilogue: US Military-Financial Oligarchy and the Exporting of "Democracy" through War and Terror

> *If politics must truly be at the service of the human person, it follows that it cannot be a slave to the economy and finance. [. . .] Why are deadly weapons being sold to those who plan to inflict untold suffering on individuals and society? Sadly, the answer, as we all know, is simply for money: money that is drenched in blood, often innocent blood. In the face of this shameful and culpable silence, it is our duty to confront the problem and to stop the arms trade.*
>
> Pope Francis to the United States Congress ("Full text of Pope Francis' speech to US Congress, 25 September 2015." Available at: <http://www.aljazeera.com/news/2015/09/full-text-pope-francis-speech%2D%2Dcongress-150924152204132.html>.)

The revolutionary Thomas Paine (1737–1809), born in Norfolk (England) and one of the Founding Fathers of the United States, wrote: "the American Constitution was to Liberty, what a grammar is to language"; it defined its discourse and constructed its syntax.[1] The Anglo-Irish philosopher Edmund Burke (1729–1797), an exponent of conservatism in England, ironically challenged this revolutionary zeal by pointing out: "the colonists assert to themselves an independent constitution and a free trade," but they understood military troops had to sustain these supposed virtues; "as the colonists rise on you, the negroes rise on them. Troops again—Massacre, torture, hanging! These are your rights of men."[2]

Slavery was the "peculiar institution" of the United States. Slaves had no human rights and when slaves rebelled and killed their lords, repression of the most brutal

---

[1]Thomas Paine, 1996, p. 58.
[2]Edmund Burke, 1986, pp. 344–345.

© Springer Nature Switzerland AG 2019
L. A. Moniz Bandeira, *The World Disorder*,
https://doi.org/10.1007/978-3-030-03204-3_26

and ferocious kind followed. So it was in 1831, in Southampton, Virginia, when more than 100 Africans were massacred after an uprising, and another 16 were hanged. As Jean-Jacques Rousseau stated, in the strict sense of the word, "there has never been a true democracy, and there never will be."[3] Indeed, as Baruch Spinoza wrote to his friend Jari Jelle in a letter dated June 2, 1674, "every determination is negation."[4] This is how things have unfolded throughout history, in which the negation of democracy has resulted from its own determination. Democracy has identified itself with capitalism and reflected the evolution of capitalism, especially in the United States, where the first monopolistic economic institutions emerged—trusts, cartels, and unions.

As the State is the main consumer of heavy industry, militarism is a special instrument for accumulating capital and obtaining surpluses. Such militarism has marked almost all the history of the American republic since its beginnings. However, the phenomenon intensified from the second half of the nineteenth century. And the *mutazione dello stato*—the transmutation of the *res publica* into a special type of regime—progressed further after the Second World War. Democratic formalities were mainly maintained out of fear that communism would spread with the emergence of the Soviet Union as a world power. Communism, then manifested as Stalinist totalitarianism, had to be confronted with something like democracy, which the United States strove to represent from its origins.

The Soviet Union's collapse between 1989 and 1991 didn't herald the triumph of either the United States or democracy, however. In a study for the American Political Science Association, the political scientists Martin Gilens (Princeton University) and Benjamin I. Page (Northwestern University) concluded that there was no democracy in America, but "economic elite domination," since "the majority does not rule—at least not in the causal sense of actually determining policy outcomes."[5] Political decisions were taken by "powerful business organizations and a small number of affluent Americans." Despite the regular elections in the United States, freedom of speech, and several other rights, there was little doubt the economic elites held disproportionate sway in Washington.[6] The people's preferences seemed to have "only a minuscule, near-zero, statistically nonsignificant impact upon public policy," Martin Gilens and Benjamin I. Page stressed. To put it more clearly, formally, the democratic regime continued to operate, but the interests of financial capital

---

[3]"*il n'a jamais existé de véritable démocratie, et il n'en existera jamais.*" Jean-Jacques Rousseau, 1992, p. 95.

[4]*omnis determinatio est negatio.*

[5]Martin Gilens & Benjamin I. Page, "Testing Theories of American Politics: Elites, Interest Groups, and Average Citizens." American Political Science Association 2014. Available at: <https://doi.org/10.1017/S1537592714001595>. *Perspectives on Politics*, September 2014 |Vol. 12/No. 3, pp. 576–777. See also: <https://scholar.princeton.edu/sites/default/files/mgilens/files/gilens_and_page_2014_-testing_theories_of_american_politics.doc.pdf>.

[6]*Ibidem.*

concentrated in Wall Street, entangled with the interests of the oil and gas corporations and the war industry and its production chain, were mostly conditioning political decisions in Washington. These interests were expressed not only through the lobbying industry but also through contributions to the campaigns for elected office. And once in office, elected officials were necessarily beholden to the interests of their benefactors.

Former President James Earl (Jimmy) Carter Jr. (1977–1981), an "ethical man" and "one of the most honorable presidents of the United States," according to Fidel Castro,[7] also believed that "an oligarchy instead of a democracy" had settled in America. "Unlimited political bribery" has created "a complete subversion of our political system as a payoff to major contributors,"[8] i.e., money had "excessive influence" on elections.[9] Both Democrats and Republicans "look upon this unlimited money as a great benefit to themselves," Carter stressed, adding that this was "the essence of getting the nominations for president or to elect the president," governors of congressmen.[10] Folker Hellmeyer, chief analyst at the German Bremer Landesbank, also remarked on the mutation of democracy into a *"Demokratur"* (a German word blending for Demokratie/democracy and Diktatur/dictatorship), as the regime in the United States mutated into an oligarchy.[11]

The American Constitution no longer was "to Liberty what a grammar is to language," as Thomas Paine put it during the American Revolution.[12] In the twentieth century, the written constitution of the United States barely differed from what Ferdinand Lassalle (1825–1864) called a piece of paper (*Blatt Papier*),

---

[7]Ramonet, Ignacio. Cien horas con Fidel Castro. Conversación con Ignacio Ramonet. Oficina de Publicaciones del Consejo de Estado. La Habana. 2006.

[8]"President Jimmy Carter: The United States is an Oligarchy." *Thom Hartmann Program*, July 28, 2015. Available at: <http://www.thomhartmann.com/bigpicture/president-jimmy-carter-united-states-oligarchy>. Accessed on November 10, 2015; Corey Charlton, "'U.S. is no longer a democracy, it's an oligarchy': Jimmy Carter says he would 'absolutely not' be able to be president today because candidates need at least \$300 m." *DailyMail*, September 23, 2015. Available at: <http://www.dailymail.co.uk/news/article-3245948/Jimmy-Carter-claims-absolutely-not-able-president-today-U-S-politics-oligarchy-requires-300m-backing.html>; Jon Levine, "Jimmy Carter Tells Oprah America Is No Longer a Democracy, Now an Oligarchy." *Like Mic on Facebook*, September 24, 2015. Available at: <http://mic.com/articles/125813/jimmy-carter-tells-oprah-america-is-no-longer-a-democracy-now-an-oligarchy>. Accessed on November 10, 2015; Gregor Peter Schmitz (Atlanta), "NSA-Affäre: Ex-Präsident Carter verdammt US-Schnüffelei." *Spiegel Online*. Mittwoch, July 17, 2013. Available at: <http://www.spiegel.de/politik/ausland/nsa-affaere-jimmy-carter-kritisiert-usa-a-911589.html>; Leonardo Blair (*Christian Post* Reporter), "Former U.S. President Jimmy Carter thinks Edward Snowden's NSA leak was a good thing for America and believes the organization's intelligence gathering methods are undemocratic." *Christian Post*, July 19, 2013. Available at: <http://www.christianpost.com/news/america-has-no-functioning-democracy-says-former-pres-jimmy-carter-100503/>.

[9]*Ibidem.*

[10]*Ibidem.*

[11]"Top-Banker ist sich sicher: Russland und China gewinnen gegen die USA." *Deutsche Wirtschafts Nachrichten*, June 6, 2015. Available at: <http://deutsche-wirtschafts-nachrichten.de/2015/06/06/top-banker-ist-sich-sicher-russland-und-china-gewinnen-gegen-die-usa/>.

[12]Thomas Paine, 1996, p. 58.

since it reflected other distinct and real power relations (*die realen Machtverhältnisse*). That is, the de facto constitution (*die wirkliche Verfassung*)[13] was drafted by Wall Street, the Pentagon and the security apparatus, Congress, large banks, etc., constituting fundamental political fractions, whose interests, entwined with the military-industrial complex, determined the decisions of the Republican and Democratic parties. American democracy had virtually become what Eisenhower foreshadowed in 1961: "the insolvent phantom of tomorrow."[14] Or as America's 4th president, James Madison (1809–1817), predicted, "no nation could preserve its freedom in the midst of continual warfare."[15] And since its foundation in 1776 until December 2015, the United States has been at war for 218 out of 239 years, with only 21 years of peace during its existence as a nation.

26.1   Mutazione Dello Stato

Mutazione dello stato, the transformation of democracy into an oligarchy, into the dictatorship of financial capital, was no new phenomenon. But it was accelerated by the increasing concentration of wealth and social inequality in the United States, where the dominant class accumulated more wealth than at any other time since the Great Depression triggered by the crash of 1929. By 2013, the holdings of JPMorgan Chase, the largest bank in the world, totaled approximately US$4 trillion, US$1.53 trillion of which in derivatives.[16] These holdings were equivalent to one-third of USA GDP and then estimated at US$16.1 trillion.[17]

According to a study by economists Lawrence Mishel, Elise Gould, and Josh Bivens, the United States has suffered from rising income inequality and chronically slow growth in the living standards of low- and moderate-income Americans. This phenomenon preceded the Great Depression of the 1930s and occurred again after

---

[13]Ferdinand Lassalle, 1991, pp. 94–95.

[14]"Military-Industrial Complex Speech, Dwight D. Eisenhower." In: *Public Papers of the Presidents, Dwight D. Eisenhower, 1960–1961*, pp. 1035–1040. Available at: <http://quod.lib.umich.edu/p/ppotpus/4728424.1960.001/1087?rgn=full+text;view=image>.

[15]James Madison, "Political Observations, Apr. 20, 1795," *in: Letters and Other Writings of James Madison*, vol. 4. Philadelphia: J. B. Lippincott & Co., 1865, p. 491.

[16]Andrew Gavin Marshall (Occupy.com.), "Meet the Elites Inside the $4 Trillion Global Powerhouse Bank of JPMorgan Chase. JPMorgan Chase is one of the most powerful banks in the world, embedded within a transnational network of elite institutions and individuals." *Alternet*, July 4, 2013. Available at: <http://www.alternet.org/economy/jp-morgan-chase-bank-4-trillion-global-powerhouse-meet-elites-charge>.

[17]"U.S. Department of Commerce—Bureau of Economic Analysis. Current-Dollar and 'Real' Gross Domestic Product." Available at: <http://www.bea.gov/national/index.htm>. Accessed on February 1, 2016; "Gross domestic product (GDP) of the United States at current prices from 2010 to 2020 (in billion U.S. dollars)." *Statista—Statisc Portal*. Available at: <http://www.statista.com/statistics/263591/gross-domestic-product-gdp-of-the-united-states/>. Accessed on: February 2, 2016.

1970. One of the greatest challenges faced by the United States revolved around the lack of understanding of the root of income inequality and of the slow growth of living standards (the practically stagnating hourly wages of the vast majority of American workers).[18] *Financial Times* columnist Martin Wolf also pointed out that despite the complicated factors of technological innovation, trade liberalization, financial deregulation, and changes in corporate governance, the fruits of development were unquestionably accruing to the top of the social pyramid in the United States, and to a lesser extent in other high-income countries.[19] In fact, by 2015, about 1% of the world's population, living mainly in the United States and Europe, had accumulated 50% of the planet's wealth,[20] estimated at US$250 trillion. In 2007, before the financial crisis further worsened inequality, this share had been 2%.[21] In the United States alone, about US$63.5 trillion, the largest pool of money in the world, more than four times its GDP at the time of US$14.1 trillion,[22] was concentrated in private hands.[23] And according to Jesse Drucker of *Bloomberg Businessweek*, the United States was becoming a new tax haven where wealthy foreign oligarchs could hide their fortunes. It resisted in adopting the "new global disclosure standards" of bank accounts, creating "a hot new market and becoming

---

[18]Lawrence Mishel & Elise Gould & Josh Bivens, "Raising America's Pay." *An initiative of the Economic Policy Institute*, January 6, 2015. Available at: <http://www.epi.org/publication/charting-wage-stagnation/>.

[19]Martin Wolf, "Nativist populists must not win. We know that story: it ends very badly indeed." *Financial Times*, January 26, 2016. Available at: <http://www.ft.com/cms/s/0/135385ca-c399-11e5-808f-8231cd71622e.html#axzz3yYqNWs9U>. Accessed on January 28, 2016; Lawrence Mishel & Elise Gould & Josh Bivens, "Raising America's Pay." *An initiative of the Economic Policy Institute*, January 6, 2015. Available at: <http://www.epi.org/publication/charting-wage-stagnation/>.

[20]Richard Kersley (Head Global Thematic and ESG Research, Credit Suisse Investment Banking) & Markus Stierli (Head of Fundamental Micro Themes Research, Credit Suisse Private Banking & Wealth Management), "Global Wealth in 2015: Underlying Trends Remain Positive." *Credit Suisse Research Institute's Annual Global Wealth Report*, October 13, 2015. Available at: <https://www.credit-suisse.com/de/en/about-us/research/research-institute/news-and-videos/articles/news-and-expertise/2015/10/en/global-wealth-in-2015-underlying-trends-remain-positive.html>;   Jill Treanor, "Half of world's wealth now in hands of 1% of population—report. Inequality growing globally and in the UK, which has third most 'ultra-high net worth individuals,' household wealth study finds." *The Guardian*, October 13, 2015. Available at: <http://www.theguardian.com/money/2015/oct/13/half-world-wealth-in-hands-population-inequality-report>.

[21]António Sousa Lara, 2007, p. 13.

[22]"U.S. Department of Commerce—Bureau of Economic Analysis. Current-Dollar and 'Real' Gross Domestic Product." Available at: <http://www.bea.gov/national/index.htm>. Accessed on February 1, 2016.

[23]Graeme Wearden, "Oxfam: 85 richest people as wealthy as poorest half of the world. As World Economic Forum starts in Davos, development charity claims growing inequality has been driven by 'power grab'." *The Guardian*, January 20, 2014. Available at: <http://www.theguardian.com/business/2014/jan/20/oxfam-85-richest-people-half-of-the-world>. Accessed on January 28, 2016.

the go-to place to stash foreign wealth," even while it pressured other countries like Switzerland to do otherwise.[24]

At a Davos meeting in January 2016, Oxfam, a UK-registered institution, released a new report revealing that the world's 62 richest billionaires—mostly from the United States—owned as much wealth as the poorest half of the world's population, i.e., 1% of the world population had more wealth than the other 99%. This concentration of income accelerated after 2010, and while the number of richest billionaire oligarchs dwindled, the fortunes amassed by the rest went from US$500 billion (£350 billion) to US$1.76 trillion in 2015.[25, 26]

The accumulation of wealth in the hands of the financial oligarchy, which began in the second half of the nineteenth century, when the Panic of 1857 occurred, became more pronounced throughout the twentieth century and further accelerated after 1970 and the first decade of the twenty-first century. More and more political power was concentrated in the great Wall Street firms, especially the banks, atrophying democracy in the United States. Former Republican Senator Barry M. Goldwater, a famous exponent of conservatism in the United States, wrote in his memoirs that "the Wall Street banks contributed the financial muscle to elect Woodrow Wilson President in 1912."[27] And he added that international bankers made money by granting credit to governments and that these large state debts returned to lenders as huge interest payments. General Smedley Butler, who had denounced the fascist Wall Street plot against President Roosevelt in the 1930s, recalled that President Woodrow Wilson was reelected President in 1916 with the slogan "keep us out of war." Five months later, he asked congress to declare war on Germany. "Then what caused our government to change its mind so suddenly?" General Smedley Butler asked, to which he replied: "Money."[28] If France, Britain, and Italy lost the war, they would not be able to afford the US$5–US$6 billion they owed US banks and arms manufacturers.[29] US foreign policy since the end of the Soviet Union, guided by the interests of large banking, oil, and military corporations, engaged more and more in the international deployment of full-spectrum dominance

---

[24]Jesse Drucker (Bloomberg Businessweek), "US has become world's favorite new tax haven." Available at: <http://www.royalgazette.com/article/20160128/BUSINESS/160129700>.

[25]Richard Kersley (Head Global Thematic and ESG Research, Credit Suisse Investment Banking) & Markus Stierli (Head of Fundamental Micro Themes Research, Credit Suisse Private Banking & Wealth Management), "Global Wealth in 2015: Underlying Trends Remain Positive." *Credit Suisse Research Institute's Annual Global Wealth Report*, October 13, 2015. Available at: <https://www.credit-suisse.com/de/en/about-us/research/research-institute/news-and-videos/articles/news-and-expertise/2015/10/en/global-wealth-in-2015-underlying-trends-remain-positive.html>;   Jill Treanor, "Half of world's wealth now in hands of 1% of population—report. Inequality growing globally and in the UK, which has third most 'ultra-high net worth individuals,' household wealth study finds." *The Guardian*, October 13, 2015, <http://www.theguardian.com/money/2015/oct/13/half-world-wealth-in-hands-population-inequality-report>.

[26]António Sousa Lara, 2007, p. 13.

[27]Barry M. Goldwater, 1979, pp. 295–296, 308.

[28](Gen.) Smedley Butler, 2012, pp. 18–19.

[29]*Ibidem*, p. 9.

and full-spectrum superiority on land, sea, and air. Its strategic objective consisted in creating a unitary economic space, under the pretext of promoting democracy in the most diverse countries, thus spreading America's total superiority through the international dictatorship of financial capital. The larger the economic space, the greater the political power of the financial oligarchy based in Wall Street. This is why President Obama did everything to sign the Transatlantic Trade and Investment Partnership and Trans-Pacific Partnership (TTIP and TPP) treaties, surrounding the European Union on the one hand and China and Russia on the other. At the same time, the Pentagon sought once again to elevate Russia to the status of national security threat, just as China, Iran, and Da'ish, so it could maintain military control over NATO, especially Germany, and extract more budgetary resources for the fiscal year 2016.[30]

In his testimony before Congress, Jonathan Turley, a professor of public law at George Washington University, pointed to the dangers of concentrating power in the executive branch, as occurred particularly in the George W. Bush and Barack Obama administrations, which started wars in Iraq and Libya without legislative authorization.[31] While a "perpetual war" represented "perpetual profits" for extensive and complex businesses and government interests, it also constituted "perpetual losses for families."[32] And the working class was especially hard hit, providing about 78% of the fallen in Afghanistan between 2001, when the war began, and 2011, according to a study by Professor Michael Zweig, director of the Center for Study of Working Class Life at the State University of New York at Stony Brook.[33] But presidential powers were not the only thing enhanced; the budgets of military and internal security agencies also swelled. And this new coalition of corporations, agencies, and lobbyists overpowered the system, just as President Dwight Eisenhower had foreseen in 1961, when he warned American governments to guard against "the acquisition of unwarranted influence . . . by the military-industrial complex."[34]

---

[30]"Intervista con Vladimir Putin di Paolo Valentino, nostro inviato a Mosca—Putin al *Corriere della Sera*: 'Non sono un aggressore, patto con l'Europa e parità con gli Usa' Il presidente russo: 'Svilupperemo il nostro potenziale offensivo e penseremo a sistemi in grado di superare la difesa antimissilistica degli Usa. L'Italia spinge il dialogo tra Russia e Europa: ciò crea rapporti speciali'." *Corriere della Sera*, June 6, 2015. Available at: <http://www.corriere.it/esteri/15_giugno_06/intervista-putin-corriere-non-sono-aggressore-patto-europa-ab5eeffe-0c0a-11e5-81da-8596be76a029.shtml>.

[31]Jonathan Turley, "Big money behind war: the military-industrial complex. More than 50 years after President Eisenhower's warning, Americans find themselves in perpetual war." *Al Jazeera*, January 11, 2014. Available at: <http://www.aljazeera.com/indepth/opinion/2014/01/big-money-behind-war-military-industrial-complex-20141473026736533.html>.

[32]*Ibidem.*

[33]*Ibidem*, "America's Longest War: New Study Examines Demographics of U.S. Casualties in Afghanistan." *Democracy Now*, October 10, 2011, Available at: <http://www.democracynow.org/2011/10/10/americas_longest_war_new_study_examines>.

[34]Jonathan Turley, "Big money behind war: the military-industrial complex. More than 50 years after President Eisenhower's warning, Americans find themselves in perpetual war." *Al Jazeera*, January 11, 2014. Available at: <http://www.aljazeera.com/indepth/opinion/2014/01/big-money-

History confirmed his prediction. The military-industrial complex captured and held hostage all administrations, whether Republican or Democratic. And military expenditures continued to grow to support the war industry and its productive chain, generating the need for permanent war as well as real or perceived threats to the national security of the United States in order to consume the produced armaments and reproduce capital. No administration could really roll back the war industry without profound political implications, since this would increase the number of unemployed and disrupt the economic activities of several states (California, Texas, Missouri, Florida, Maryland, and Virginia) where it was located. This was especially the case for capital-intensive weapon manufacturers, whose interest consisted in experimenting these weapons in real wars so that the Pentagon could empty its stockpiles, promote armaments, sell them to other countries, and place new orders, generating huge commissions and dividends.

This is one of the reasons why the United States still had around 800 military installations around the world in 2013, 23 of which in Europe, most of them in Germany, which was home to the US Army Europe (USAREUR) command and the US Satellite Relay Station in Ramstein. The latter is crucial for the extrajudicial targeted killings with drone strikes against terrorist suspects in the Middle East, Africa, and Southeast Asia. There were also 23 facilities in Japan, 15 in South Korea, and 7 in Italy, in addition to hundreds scattered over more than 70 countries, including Bulgaria, Colombia, Aruba, Australia, Bahrain, Kenya, and Qatar,[35] at a cost of US$85 billion to US$100 billion, with another US$160 billion to US$200 billion being spent in war zones throughout the fiscal year 2014.[36] And President Obama was also planning to keep nine bases operational in Afghanistan until after 2014, Kabul, Bagram, Mazar, Jalalabad, Gardez, Kandahar, Helmand, Shindand, and Herat,[37] in addition to supplying Poland and other Eastern European countries with modern war equipment, including the AGM-158 JASSM (Joint Air-Surface Standoff Missile), and sending more troops to the Baltic countries under the cover of NATO.

---

behind-war-military-industrial%2D%2Dcomplex-20141473026736533.html>;   Eisenhower Dwight D., "Dwight D. Eisenhower: 1960–61: containing the public messages, speeches, and statements of the president, January 1, 1960, to January 20, 1961." *In*: *Public Papers of the Presidents, Dwight D. Eisenhower, 1960–1961*, pp. 1035–1040. Available at: <http://quod.lib. umich.edu/p/ppotpus/4728424.1960.001/1087?rgn=full+text;view=image>.

[35]David Vine, *How U.S. Military Bases Abroad Harm America and the World*. New York: Metropolitan Books—Henry Holt and Company, 2015; Chloe Fox, "The 15 Most Amazing Places Uncle Sam Could Send You." *The Huffington Post*, April 29, 2014. Available at: <http://www. huffingtonpost.com/2014/04/29/best-military-bases-around-the-world_n_5216682.html>.

[36]"David Vine Where in the World Is the U.S. Military?" *Politico Magazine*, July/August 2015. Available at: <http://www.politico.com/magazine/story/2015/06/us-military-bases-around-the-world-119321>.

[37]Tom Engelhardt, "America's Invisible Empire of Bases." *The Huffington Post*, May 14, 2013. Accessed on September 7, 2015. <http://www.huffingtonpost.com/tom-engelhardt/americas-invisible-empire_b_3272352.html>.

Thousands of lobbyists in Washington have secured uninterrupted increases in budget allocations for the Defense, Homeland Security, and Justice departments. Hundreds of billions of dollars flow from the public coffers every year to the 16 civilian and military security agencies, employing more than 107,035 people and with an estimated black budget of more than US$52 billion in 2013, and to military contractors, who continued to push for a constant war footing with a constant war budget.[38] And ironically, Professor Jonathan Turley noted, the heydays of this influence occurred under President Obama, who radically expanded drone strikes at his own discretion, with trillions of dollars flowing to military and security corporations during his 8 years in office.[39]

In a speech to the US Congress, Pope Francis frankly asked why lethal armaments were sold to those who planned "to inflict untold suffering on individuals and society." He quite rightly concluded that, "sadly, the answer, as we all know, is simply for money: money that is drenched in blood, often innocent blood."[40] Indeed, the United States remained the world's leading arms exporter, according to the Stockholm International Peace Research Institute (SIPRI), and the volume of its transfers to other countries grew by 23% between 2005–2009 and 2010–2014.[41] Its largest markets were the Gulf Cooperation Council countries, whose imports of war material—representing 54% of all imports by the Middle East—increased 71% between 2005–2009 and 2010–2014. During this same period (2010–2014), Saudi Arabia increased its purchases fourfold compared to 2005–2009 and stood out as the world's second largest importer of armaments.[42] "The United States has long seen arms exports as a major foreign policy and security tool," said Aude Fleurant, director of the SIPRI Arms and Military Expenditure Program, but he added that "in recent years exports are increasingly needed to help the USA arms industry maintain production levels at a time of decreasing USA military expenditure."[43]

Sales of the top 100 weapons manufacturers—42 of which based in the United States, accounting for 58% of the arms trade and supplying the Pentagon—had

---

[38]Jonathan Turley, "Big money behind war: the military-industrial complex. More than 50 years after President Eisenhower's warning, Americans find themselves in perpetual war." *Al Jazeera,* January 11, 2014. Available at: <http://www.aljazeera.com/indepth/opinion/2014/01/big-money-behind-war-military-industrial-complex-20141473026736533.html>.

[39]*Ibidem.*

[40]"Full text of Pope Francis' speech to US Congress." Available at: <http://www.aljazeera.com/news/2015/09/full-text-pope-francis-speech-congress-150924152204132.html>. Accessed on: September 25, 2015.

[41]"16 Mar. 2015: The United States leads upward trend in arms exports, Asian and Gulf states arms imports up, says SIPRI." *Stockholm International Peace Research Institute.* Available at: <http://books.sipri.org/files/FS/SIPRIFS1503.pdf>.

[42]*Ibidem.*

[43]*Ibidem.*

declined sharply, about 60%, after the 2011 troop withdrawal from Iraq.[44] In essence, however, President Obama made little to no change in George W. Bush's foreign policy, except for restoring relations with Cuba and reaching an agreement with Iran on the nuclear issue. He continued to frame the United States in the light of "exceptionalism," the "indispensable power," a variation on "God's chosen people" and "superior race." But when financial capital was no longer able to maintain world equilibrium through the rules of international law, the democracy America sought to export was exposed and its imperial authoritarianism laid bare. And when President George W. Bush invaded Iraq on the pretext of wiping out (the no-longer-existing) weapons of mass destruction and establishing democracy there and throughout the Middle East, he committed a strategic mistake. Bush was trying to shape realities beyond his control, Gen. William E. Odom, a former NSA director, told the Senate Foreign Relations Committee.[45] "In fact," he added, "the policy of spreading democracy by force of arms has become the main source of regional instability."[46]

26.2 Big Brother

Just as President George W. Bush before him, President Obama played the part of Big Brother from George Orwell's famous novel 1984, revealing that in his vocabulary "War is Peace; Freedom is Slavery & Ignorance is Strength."[47] The new international order of "peace and security, freedom, and the rule of law" President George H.W. Bush (1989–1993) had announced to the US Congress in 1991[48] was fading more and more. Order was fragmenting, weakened and disfigured, and the principle of national sovereignty virtually disappeared as the foundation of international law. It was eroded through such ruses as the Responsibility to Protect (R2P or RtoP) and the "right of humanitarian intervention," according to which sovereignty was a privilege, not an absolute right. If a state violated the precepts of good governance in this context, the international community (read: the United States and its vassals of the European Union) would be obliged to revoke its sovereignty and militarily overthrow its regime. This is why the United States escalated conflicts

---

[44]"Sales by largest arms companies fell again in 2012 but Russian firms' sales increased sharply." *Stockholm International Peace Research Institute (SIPRI)*. 2014. Munich, January 31, 2014. Available at: <http://www.sipri.org/media/pressreleases/2014/top100_january2014>.

[45]Lt. Gen. William E. Odom, "Strategic Errors of Monumental Proportions. What Can Be Done in Iraq?: Text of testimony before the Senate Foreign Relations Committee, 18 January 2007." *Antiwar.com*, January 26, 2007. Available at: <http://www.antiwar.com/orig/odom.php?articleid=10396>.

[46]*Ibidem.*

[47]George Orwell, 1977, pp. 4, 16, and 104.

[48]"Address Before a Joint Session of the Congress on the State of the Union." *The American Presidency Project*, January 29, 1991. Available at: <http://www.presidency.ucsb.edu/ws/?pid=19253>.

rather than trying to find a solution, and its attempt to dictate and unilaterally impose its model of democracy on other countries has only opened the door to chaos, terror, and the emergence of those President Vladimir Putin called neofascists (Ukraine) and radical Islamists (Middle East and elsewhere).[49]

According to the Conflict Barometer 2014 of the Heidelberg Institute for International Conflict Research (HIIK), led by Professor Frank R. Pfetsch, the global number of conflicts increased from 414 cases in 2013 to 424 in 2014 during the Obama administration, although the number of highly violent conflicts declined to 21 wars and 25 limited wars.[50] And between 2013 and 2014, the wave of refugees around the world reached unprecedented levels, according to information from the United Nations High Commissioner for Refugees. By the end of 2014, the number had grown to 59.5 million as a result of the escalation of wars, conflicts, widespread violence, and human rights violations.[51] By November 2015, the total had already surpassed 60 million, millions of them fleeing to Europe and Germany, in particular, which to them looked like El Dorado.

The number of terrorist attacks also increased in 2014 compared to 2013. According to a State Department report, 13,463 terrorist attacks occurred around the world in 2014, resulting in 32,700 deaths and more than 34,700 injuries.[52] This was an increase of 35% in the number of attacks and of 81% in total deaths, especially in Iraq, Afghanistan, and Nigeria. Attacks remained a frequent occurrence in Syria, where the number of victims of cruel methods, including crucifixions and decapitations, increased by 57%.[53] In Afghanistan alone—the country where President George W. Bush had unleashed his war on terror—the number of terrorist attacks grew by 38% between 2013 and 2014, while the death toll rose by 45%.[54]

---

[49]"Meeting of the Valdai International Discussion Club." *Official site of the* President of Russia, October 24, 2014. Available at: <http://en.kremlin.ru/events/president/news/46860>. Accessed on October 12, 2015.

[50]"Global Conflict Panorama. Highly Violent Conflicts in 2014 Limited Wars (25) Wars (21)." *Conflict Barometer 2014. Heidelberg Institute for International Conflict Research (HIIK), 2015.* Available at: <http://www.hiik.de/en/konfliktbarometer/pdf/ConflictBarometer_2014.pdf>.

[51]World at War Global—UNHCR Trends Forced Displacement in 2014. *2014 in Review—Trends at a glance.* Available at: <http://www.unhcr.org/556725e69.html>; Teresa Welsh, "UN Report: In New Record, 60 Million Displaced Worldwide, A wealth of global conflicts have contributed to the staggering refugee crisis across the world." *U.S. News*, June 18, 2015. Available at: <http://www.usnews.com/news/articles/2015/06/18/un-report-in-new-record-60-million-displaced-worldwide>.

[52]"Country Reports on Terrorism 2014." *U.S. Department of State, Bureau of Counterterrorism, June 2015.* Available at: <http://www.state.gov/documents/organization/239631.pdf>.

[53]"Statistical Information On Terrorism in 2014—Annex of Statistical Information Country Reports on Terrorism 2014. June 2015." *National Consortium for the Study of Terrorism and Responses to Terrorism.* START—A Department of Homeland Security Science and Technology Center of Excellence. Based at the University of Maryland. Available at: <http://www.state.gov/documents/organization/239628.pdf>.

[54]*Ibidem.*

These numbers confirmed the resounding defeat of the United States and Britain in the global war on terror, launched by George W. Bush with his attack on first Afghanistan and then Iraq, conflicts in which the United States, Britain, and its allies suffered 8331 casualties until early 2016.[55] President Obama feared the useless loss of more American lives but nevertheless continued the war under the name *Overseas Contingency Operation*, primarily by using "remotely piloted aircraft commonly referred to as drones."[56] But he also didn't win any battles, except for the execution of Osama bin Laden by a Navy SEAL team in Abbottabad (Pakistan) on May 2, 2011.

Obama could claim no other great achievement in the fight against terrorism. Iraq, Afghanistan, Pakistan, and Nigeria were some of the countries where the attacks by jihadists intensified most. And these were exactly the countries most frequently targeted by CIA drones launched from stations in Africa and, above all, Ramstein Air Base in Germany. Da'ish stood out as the organization most frequently involved in attacks (others included Boko Haram, Taliban and al-Shabaab, all extremist Sunnis, Salafi-Wahhabis), and by December 2014, it was wreaking havoc in Syria and Iraq with the participation of about 16,000 foreigners from 90 countries.[57]

Most of these Arab or European foreigners, just as the jihadists from the Caucasus (Russia, Uzbekistan, and Chechnya) and Syria, presenting themselves as "moderate rebels," were certainly trained by the US Special Forces in Turkey and Jordan. They actually belonged to several currents of 7000 radical Islamic groups, including Jabhat al-Nusrah, Ansar al-Shariah, and others,[58] which later openly allied themselves with Da'ish or deserted. "The so-called moderates had evaporated," the journalist Seymour Hersh noted.[59]

---

[55]iCasualties.org—Operation Iraqi Freedom—Operation Enduring Freedom/Afghanistan. Available at: <http://icasualties.org>.

[56]Scott Wilson & Al Kamen (*Washington Post* Staff Writers), "'Global War On Terror' Is Given New Name." *The Washington Post*, March 25, 2009. Available at: <http://www.washingtonpost.com/wp-dyn/content/article/2009/03/24/AR2009032402818.html>; "Obama's Speech on Drone Policy." *The New York Times*, May 23, 2013. Available at: <http://www.nytimes.com/2013/05/24/us/politics/transcript-of-obamas-speech-on-drone-policy.html?_r=0>.

[57]"Statistical Information On Terrorism in 2014—Annex of Statistical Information Country Reports on Terrorism 2014. June 2015." *National Consortium for the Study of Terrorism and Responses to Terrorism. START*—A Department of Homeland Security Science and Technology Center of Excellence. Based at the University of Maryland. Available at: <http://www.state.gov/documents/organization/239628.pdf>.

[58]"Who Has Gained Ground in Syria Since Russia Began Its Airstrikes—The full impact of Russian airstrikes on the Syrian war has yet to be realized, but some shifts have occurred in recent weeks." *The New York Times*, October 29, 2015. Available at: <http://www.nytimes.com/interactive/2015/09/30/world/middleeast/syria-control-map-isis-rebels-airstrikes.html?_r=0>.

[59]Seymour Hersh, "Military to Military." Seymour M. Hersh on US intelligence sharing in the Syrian war. *London Review of Books*, Vol. 38 No. 1, January 7, 2016, pp. 11–14. Available at: <http://www.lrb.co.uk/v38/n01/seymour-m-hersh/military-to-military>.

It is one of the reasons why President Obama suspended the training program, after wasting more than US$50 million to prepare jihadists to fight the Syrian regime, despite the resistance of a significant number of his army's chiefs of staff since mid-2013, when he received top secret estimates from the Defense Intelligence Agency (DIA), then headed by General Martin Dempsey, predicting that the fall of Bashar al-Assad would produce chaos, just as in Libya, and that the extremist Jihadists of Da'ish would seize power in Syria.[60] General Michael Flynn, then head of the DIA, confirmed to the renowned journalist Seymour Hersh that he had sent several warnings to the Joint Chiefs of Staff between 2012 and 2014 that Assad's fall would mean chaos and that terrorists would take power in Syria.[61] The Chiefs of Staff of the Armed Forces were divided, however, conducting a contradictory policy, and President Obama didn't listen, obsessed with the idea of the Cold War against Russia and his goal of overthrowing its ally Assad and eliminating the naval base of Tartus.

Major-General Igor Konashenkov, a spokesman for Russia's defense minister, said that President Obama was dividing the opposition in Syria between "moderate or immoderate," terrorists between "bad and very bad." He noted that this reminded him of the "theater of the absurd based on double standards and quibbling."[62] And the previous fiasco notwithstanding, the United States still spent US$136 million on the purchase of armaments for its "moderate rebels" in June 2015, and it used US$367 million out of the US$500 million approved by Congress to send them machine guns, grenades, and self-propelled rockets, dropped in northern Syria by a US Air Force C-17 plane in October 2015.[63] President Obama and everyone in Washington knew that most weapons sent through Saudi Arabia and Qatar to the so-called "secular opposition" fell into the hands of the radical terrorist jihadists who would form Da'ish. *The New York Times* had reported as much in 2012.[64] The truth of matter was that serving the interests of the war industry was one of the objectives.

---

[60] *Ibidem.*

[61] *Ibidem.*

[62] "US recent statements remind of theatre of the absurd—Russia's Defence Ministry." *TASS,* December 5, 2015. Available at: <http://tass.ru/en/politics/841839>.

[63] Thomas Gibbons-Neff. "Pentagon airdrops ammunition to groups fighting the Islamic State." The *Washington Post,* October 12, 2015. Available at: <https://www.washingtonpost.com/news/check point/wp/2015/10/12/pentagon-airdrops-ammunition-to-groups-fighting-the-islamic-state/>;
"With Obama's new plan for Syrian rebels, new worries. *Reuters/Jerusalem Post,* October 21, 2015. Available at: <http://www.jpost.com/Middle-East/With-Obamas-new-plan-for-Syrian-rebels-new-worries-427566>.

[64] David E. Sanger (Washington), "Rebel Arms Flow Is Said to Benefit Jihadists in Syria." *The New York Times,* October 14, 2012. Available at: <http://www.nytimes.com/2012/10/15/world/middleeast/jihadists-receiving-most-arms-sent-to-syrian-rebels.html>.

26.3   The Democracy of Chaos

In many respects, President Obama's foreign policy was disastrous. The NATO bombings he authorized devastated Libya, one of the richest nations in Africa. The fall of Gaddafi's regime hurled the country into economic and political chaos and transformed into a stateless territory. Two fragile governments—one based in Tripoli and the other in Tobruk—controlled nothing, since power had dispersed among the tribes, rival groups, and terrorists, in constant conflict, armed and in possession of sources of revenue, such as airports and oil fields.[65] International law continued to be violated on a daily basis with abductions, tortures, killings and executions, bombings of civilian areas, the destruction of property, and other abuses, according to a report from the UN Support Mission in Libya (UNSMIL) in collaboration with the UN Human Rights Office, released in November 2015.[66] And Libya—divided and its oil industry crippled—became the second largest transit country for migrants to Europe. Da'ish dominated the city of Derna in eastern Libya with 100,000 inhabitants and set up its headquarters in Sirte, between Benghazi and Tripoli, on the shores of the Mediterranean Sea. From there it recruited jihadists from the West through social media, who arrived from Rome and were dispatched in Toyota pickup trucks across the Sahara to Syria (Shaam), along with the smuggled weapons, ammunition, food, electronics, and other goods.[67] So the jihadists of the al-Battar brigade and other groups began focusing on the gates to Europe.[68] Who was responsible for this situation? The United States, France, and Britain under NATO's facade. Where was democracy in Libya? Maybe in the desert sands.

---

[65]Missy Ryan & Hassan Morajea, "In Libya, trying to make one government out of two." *The Washington Post*, September 18, 2015. Available at: <https://www.washingtonpost.com/world/national-security/in-libya-trying-to-make-one-government-out-of-two/2015/09/18/4c50627e-5d6b-11e5-9757-e49273f05f65_story.html>.

[66]"Deadly violence and abuses continue to grip Libya with civilians bearing the brunt." UNSMIL—United *Nations Support Mission in Libya*, Genebra/Tunis, November 16, 2015. Available at: <http://unsmil.unmissions.org/Default.aspx?tabid=3561&ctl=Details&mid=8549&ItemID=2099353&language=en-US>;   <http://www.ohchr.org/Documents/Countries/LY/UNSMIL_OHCHRJointly_report_Libya_16.11.15.pdf>; "Libya conflict: breaches of international law by all sides, says UN. United Nations reports widespread abductions, torture and killing of civilians by Islamic State and opponents." *The Guardian*, November 17, 2015.

[67]Missy Ryan, "Libya's political dysfunction enters uncharted territory." *The Washington Post*, October 20, 2015. Available at: <https://www.washingtonpost.com/world/national-security/after-key-expiration-libya-has-no-western-recognized-government/2015/10/20/792e1a9c-773e-11e5-b9c1-f03c48c96ac2_story.html>; Jack Moore, "'Libya Needs You Too': ISIS Social Media Drive Encourages Jihadis to Travel to North African Base." *Newsweek*, September 28, 2015. Available at: <http://europe.newsweek.com/libya-needs-you-too-isis-social-media-drive-encourages-jihadis-travel-north-african-base-333740>.

[68]Hassan Hassan, "Isis is expanding its international reach. That is hardly a sign of weakness." *The Guardian*, December 6, 2015. Available at: <http://www.theguardian.com/world/2015/dec/06/isis-expansion-libya-not-sign-of-weakness>.

The coup in Ukraine, coordinated by Assistant Secretary of State Victoria Nuland and the American ambassador in Kiev, Geoffrey R. Pyatt, resulted in yet another fiasco: President Putin reincorporated Crimea into Russia to secure the naval base of Sevastopol in the Black Sea as soon as the neo-Nazis and ultranationalists seized power in Kiev, triggering a civil war with the Russian-speaking provinces of the Donbass—Donetsk and Luhansk—where hostilities, however intermittent, were still ongoing in February 2016, already costing US$8 million per day.[69] Without Crimea and the Sevastopol base, and with the secession of the east and southeast, the richest regions of the country, Ukraine became economically less attractive to the West. By sending new lethal weapons to Kiev in November 2015, however, Washington appeared to have no desire for peace in Ukraine, whose monetary reserves had dropped to only 6 billion €, insufficient for 1 month of imports.

Ukraine was bankrupt. Its currency—the hryvnia—had lost 70% of its value against the dollar since February 2014, and its foreign debt would exceed 94.4% of GDP in December 2015.[70] According to the IMF, GDP would drop 11%, much worse than previously predicted. And according to the World Bank, the fall would be 12%,[71] which is what ended up happening. Even so, the IMF Executive Board changed its own rules about not providing financial assistance to countries about to go into default and at war. In December 2015 it renewed the credit line to Ukraine, in default with Russia, which it owed more than US$3 billion, without any conditions whatsoever to pay off its private creditors.[72]

And instability lingered. On February 3, 2016, Economy Minister Aivaras Abromavičius and his entire team resigned, accusing the government of President Poroshenko and Prime Minister Arseniy Yatsenyuk of obstructing the reforms of the economy and state-owned enterprises, in addition to covering up and promoting widespread corruption, especially in the energy sector.[73] The oligarchs maintained

---

[69]Benoît Vitkine, "Ukraine: une aide du FMI éloigne le risque de défaut." *Le Monde*, March 12, 2015. Available at: <http://www.lemonde.fr/economie/article/2015/03/12/ukraine-une-aide-du-fmi-eloigne-le-risque-de-defaut_4591777_3234.html>.

[70]IMF: Ukraine's public debt to exceed 94% of GDP. *UNIAN.NET*, October 7, 2015. Available at: <http://www.unian.info/economics/1145944-imf-ukraines-public-debt-to-exceed-94-of-gdp.html>.

[71]"IMF worsens Ukraine's GDP fall forecast to 11% in 2015." *KyivPost*, October 5, 2015. Available at: <https://www.kyivpost.com/article/content/ukraine-politics/imf-worsens-ukraines-gdp-fall-forecast-to-11-in-2015-399319.html>; "World Bank sharply downgrades Ukraine's GDP forecast." *RT*, October 5, 2015. Available at: <https://www.rt.com/business/317664-ukraine-gdp-world-bank/>. Accessed on October 6, 2015.

[72]Marine Rabreau. "Le FMI modifie ses règles pour aider l'Ukraine, Moscou enrage." *Le Figaro*, December 11, 2015. Available at: <http://www.lefigaro.fr/conjoncture/2015/12/11/20002-20151211ARTFIG00010-le-fmi-modifie-ses-regles-pour-aider-l-ukraine-moscou-enrage.php>.
Benoît Vitkine. "Ukraine: une aide du FMI éloigne le risque de défaut"—*Le Monde*, March 12, 2015. Available at: <http://www.lemonde.fr/economie/article/2015/03/12/ukraine-une-aide-du-fmi-eloigne-le-risque-de-defaut_4591777_3234.html>.

[73]Alec Luhn (Moscou), "Economic minister's resignation plunges Ukraine into new crisis. Aivaras Abromavičius and his entire team quit complaining of ingrained corruption, a major blow to

their hold on power and kept taking advantage of the state's largesse. And the impasse surrounding the implementation of the Minsk accords was not resolved. The Verkhovna Rada, controlled by neo-Nazis and ultranationalists, resisted approving the autonomy of the republics of Donetsk and Luhansk. The secession of the Donbass had meant the loss of a region responsible for 15% of GDP and a quarter of Ukraine's exports. The civil war, which until December 2015 had claimed about 9100 victims, continued, intermittently.[74] And in early 2016, Ukraine was bogged down in a deep economic and political crisis. It failed to carry out all the reforms required by the IMF for the release of the remainder of the US$17.5 billion in credit. Corruption continued to prevail. And the resistance in the Verkhovna Rada of neo-Nazis and ultranationalists, as well as of Prime Minister Arseniy Yatsenyuk, prevented the approval of the clauses of the Minsk accords to decentralize power and grant a special status to the provinces of the Donbass, particularly to the republics of Donetsk and Luhansk, in order to reunify Ukraine.

Prime Minister Yatsenyuk, however, was caught in a power struggle with President Poroshenko, and his unpopularity was growing in the midst of the severe economic crisis.[75] He had survived a vote of no confidence, but he then lost the majority in the Verkhovna Rada when the coalition led by President Poroshenko fell apart. He did not resign, despite the pressures and corruption scandals. Victoria Nuland, the Assistant Secretary of State close to Yatsenyuk, feared that chaos in Kiev would cast doubt on the continued support for Ukraine and lead the European Union to suspend sanctions against Russia.[76] Indeed, the European Union was keen to restore normal relations with Russia. European Commission President Jean-Claude Juncker declared that Ukraine would not become a member of NATO for the next two decades,[77] which could well mean never. The European Union was in no mood for a confrontation with Russia because of Ukraine, with the possibility of a war with unforeseeable results. Kiev would have to bite the bullet and implement the Minsk accords, whether it liked it or not. The geopolitical reality was that Ukraine

president and government." *The Guardian*, February 4, 2016. Available at: <http://www. theguardian.com/world/2016/feb/04/economic-minister-resignation-ukraine-crisis-aivaras-abromavicius>; Lydia Tomkiw, "Ukraine Economic Crisis 2016: As IMF Loan Stalls, Young Politicians Struggle to Push Through Reforms." *International Business Times*, February 9, 2016. Available at: <http://www.ibtimes.com/ukraine-economic-crisis-2016-imf-loan-stalls-young%2D %2Dpoliticians-struggle-push-through-2300131>.

[74]Tom Batchelor, "Ukraine civil war claims 9100 lives as UN warns Russian weapons are inflaming conflict. UKRAINE'S civil war has claimed the lives of more than 9000 people, a United Nations report has found." *Daily Express*. December 9, 2015. Available at: <http://www.express.co.uk/ news/world/625514/Ukraine-civil-war-deaths-9100-killed-conflict>.

[75]Lydia Tomkiw, "New Ukraine Political Crisis? Amid War with Russia, Economic Support Called into Question." *International Business Times*, April 2, 2016. Available at: <http://www.ibtimes. com/new-ukraine-political-crisis-amid-war-russia-economic-support-called-question-2293818>.

[76]"Bite the bullet. The Minsk peace deal is going nowhere." *The Economist*, March 19, 2016. Available at: <http://www.economist.com/news/europe/21695060-minsk-peace-deal-going-nowhere-bite-bullet?zid=307&ah=5e80419d1bc9821ebe173f4f0f060a07>.

[77]*Ibidem.*

could not be separated from Russia, with which it was economically integrated from the outset. But by March 2016, the deadlock still persisted, and Finance Minister Natalie Jaresko, former CEO of the investment bank Horizon Capital and the United States-funded private equity fund WNISEF, was already seeking to replace Arseniy Yatsenyuk in the post of prime minister. Jaresko was a Chicago-born Ukrainian and enjoyed the full confidence of the US State Department, for which she had worked as head of the economic section of the US Embassy in Kiev in the early 1990s. And so Ukraine had to remain under the control of the Western shadow bankers—Carlyle Group LP Emerging Sovereign Group LLC, Greylock Capital Management LLC, LNG Capital LLP, and GoldenTree Asset Management LP—hedge funds with highly risky, speculative investments that suffered huge losses amid the crisis triggered by the Maidan Square coup in 2014 and the ensuing reintegration of Crimea by Russia.

26.4   Proxy Wars

In the Middle East, meanwhile, the rise of Da'ish and its ever-progressing march into Iraq drove President Obama to order some strikes to contain it and later to operate illegally in Syria with French President François Hollande, who was one of the most assertive actors in the campaign to remove Assad. The air forces of both countries influenced the situation on the ground with jets from the United States, France, and other allies. But they were attacking minor, secondary targets instead of Da'ish itself, so that its contingents could continue the fight against the Assad regime. Da'ish would be easier to destroy later was probably their thinking. Operation Inherent Resolve, launched on August 8, 2014, didn't achieve any major success in the war against Da'ish until November 15, 2015, although it cost the United States US$5.2 billion with an average daily cost of US$11 million during 465 days of operations.[78]

And it certainly wouldn't be easy for Operation Inherent Resolve to achieve any resounding success. On November 16, 2015, approximately 45 minutes before bombarding the ISIS (Da'ish) oil infrastructure and transportation trucks in al-Bukamal, in eastern Syria near the Iraqi border, the United States issued a notice: "Warning, Airstrikes are coming, oil trucks will be destroyed. Get away from your oil trucks immediately. Do not risk your life."[79] The pretext was avoiding civilian

---

[78]"Operation Inherent Resolve—Targeted operations against ISIL terrorists. Cost of Operations."

[79]*U.S. Department of Defense.* Available at: <http://www.defense.gov/News/Special-Reports/0814_Inherent-Resolve>; "Department of Defense Press Briefing by Col. Warren via DVIDS from Baghdad, Iraq Press Operations:—Operation Inherent Resolve Spokesman Colonel Steve Warren." *Department of Defense*, November 18, 2015. Available at: <http://www.defense.gov/News/News-Transcripts/Transcript-View/Article/630393/department-of-defense-press-briefing-by-col-warren-via-dvids-from-baghdad-iraq>; Tyler Durden, "How Turkey Exports ISIS Oil to The World: The Scientific Evidence." *Zero Hedge*, November 28, 2015. Available at: <http://www.zerohedge.com/news/2015-11-27/how-turkey-exports-isis-oil-world-scientific-evidence>;

casualties, but the United States had never taken such care to save civilians. The supposed civilians in the target area were evidently the Da'ish terrorists and oil smugglers, and they clearly got the message, got out of their trucks, and ran away. American war planes destroyed only 116 trucks, proclaiming this feat as a great victory in the media, but hundreds still remained. The same notice was given in another strike on oil trucks with the machine guns and cannons of A-10 Warthogs and AC-130 aircraft.[80] Once more "moderate" and non-moderate terrorists certainly wouldn't want to stay and die. They slipped out, as they surely did in other occasions. The US Air Force nevertheless reported that it had destroyed 280 oil trucks along the Syrian–Iraq border.

It was clear that actually defeating ISIS or implementing any democracy in Syria wasn't the Leitmotiv of American intervention. Instead, the United States wanted the victory of "moderate" jihadists (as if such a thing existed) and institute a regime willing to close the naval base in Tartus—a similar reason as for the coup in Ukraine, targeting the Sevastopol base. Ultimately, this would block Russia's access to the Mediterranean and the warm waters of the Atlantic. And so, faced with the tortuous and cloaked politics of Presidents Obama, François Hollande, and Erdoğan, as well as Prime Minister Cameron, President Putin did not hesitate to intervene militarily in Syria.

He had previously met with the governments of several countries in the Middle East, including Saudi Arabia and Israel. Putin proposed to Prime Minister Netanyahu that Moscow take responsibility for guarding Israel's Mediterranean gas fields and also offered a Russian investment of $7–10 billion for developing Leviathan, the largest well, and the construction of a pipeline to Turkey for exporting the gas to Europe,[81] a multibillion dollar investment that neither Syria nor Hizballah would dare attack, even if it belonged to Israel.[82]

After the diplomatic work in pursuit of alliances and to reassure potential adversaries in the region, President Putin declared at the UN General Assembly on September 28, 2015, that the "power vacuum" in some countries of the Middle East and North Africa "obviously resulted in the emergence of areas of anarchy, which

"US airstrikes destroy more than 100 ISIS oil trucks in Syria." *RT*, November 16, 2015. Available at: <https://www.rt.com/usa/322330-isis-oil-trucks-destroyed/>; Lucas Tomlinson & Jennifer Griffin, "US military: Air strikes destroy 116 ISIS fuel trucks, sharing target info with France." *FoxNews.com*, November 16, 2015. Available at: <http://www.foxnews.com/politics/2015/11/16/us-military-sharing-intelligence-with-france-on-isis-targets-in-syria.html>.

[80]Jim Miklaszewski, "U.S. Destroys 280 ISIS Oil Trucks in Syrian City of Deir al-Zor." *NBC News*, November 23, 2015, Available at: <http://www.nbcnews.com/storyline/isis-terror/u-s-destroys-280-isis-oil-trucks-syrian-city-deir-n468126>. Accessed on December 9, 2015.

[81]"Putin's offer to shield & develop Israel's gas fields predated Russia's military buildup in Syria"; *DEBKAfile*, September 13, 2015. Available at: <http://www.debka.com/article/24885/Putin%E2%80%99s-offer-to-shield-develop-Israel%E2%80%99s-gas-fields-predated-Russia%E2%80%99s-military-buildup-in-Syria>. Accessed on September 13, 2015.

[82]*Ibidem*.

were quickly filled with extremists and terrorists."[83] He added that the so-called Islamic State had been joined by tens of thousands of militants, including former soldiers of the Iraqi army who were abandoned on the streets after the 2003 invasion, and many recruits from Libya, whose sovereignty was destroyed "as a result of a gross violation of UN Security Council Resolution 1973."[84] President Putin also denounced that the members of the Syrian opposition, labeled as "moderate" by the West, were joining the Islamic State with the weapons and training they had received. He warned that the situation was "extremely dangerous" and that in such circumstances it was "hypocritical and irresponsible to make declarations about the threat of terrorism and at the same time turn a blind eye to the channels used to finance and support terrorists, including revenues from drug trafficking, the illegal oil trade and the arms trade."[85] "To flirt with terrorists," he warned, was both shortsighted and dangerous.[86] And with their underhanded support to Ahrar al-Sham (Harakat Ahrar al-Sham al-Islamiyya), or the Islamic Movement of the Free Men of the Islamic Levant, and other groups, all terrorist allies of ISIS, this was exactly what Presidents Obama, Hollande, and Erdoğan were doing for the sake of Assad's fall in Syria. President Putin was fully aware that NATO aircraft continued to arrive at Iskenderun air base on the Turkish border with Syria, carrying war material from Muammar Gaddafi's arsenal captured after his fall as well as jihadists from the Libyan National Transitional Council.

26.5 Russia's Intervention

President Putin's speech seemed to convince the West that giving ultimatums to President Bashar al-Assad for him to step aside had not and would not produce any results.[87] And days later, on September 30, 2015, Russia openly intervened in Syria at the behest of President Bashar al-Assad. Sukhoi 12, Sukhoi-24M2s, Sukhoi Su-25s, Sukhoi Su-30SMs, and Sukhoi Su-34s war planes took off from Hmeymim air base in Latakia province and bombed Da'ish strongholds in northwestern Syria. Six warships from the Caspian Sea fleet—including a Gepard-class frigate and three Buyan-M class corvettes—fired supersonic 3M-14T Kalibr NK (Klub-N) VLS

---

[83]"Vladimir Putin in the plenary meeting of the 70th session of the UN General Assembly in New York." New York, "70th session of the UN General Assembly. September 28, 2015." *Presidential Executive Office* 2015. Available at: <http://en.kremlin.ru/events/president/news/50385>.

[84]*Ibidem.*

[85]*Ibidem.*

[86]*Ibidem.*

[87]"Putin's UN speech made West reconsider its reaction to developments in Syria—Lavrov. According to the Russian foreign minister, the West has realized there's no point in demanding Syrian President, Bashar al-Assad's stepping down." *TASS*, November 19, 2015. Available at: <http://tass.ru/en/politics/837793>.

cruise missiles, capable of flying between 1500 and 2500 km before hitting targets with the highest accuracy. They flew over Iranian and Iraqi airspace and destroyed the positions of Da'ish and other groups in Raqqa, Idlib, and Aleppo.[88] The Russian jet sorties and the 3M-14T Kalibr NK cruise missiles launched from the Caspian Sea were coordinated with a ground offensive by the Syrian Arab Army, Hizballah, and the Iranian Revolutionary Guards and Quds forces, which advanced and liberated Kuweires air base, surrounded by Da'ish in the province of Aleppo for 2 years.

The intervention in Syria showcased Russia's enormous and advanced military power, such as its supersonic 3M-14T Kalibr NK cruise missiles. The international scenario, and especially the evolution of the war, was changed both quantitatively and qualitatively. Not only did the intervention safeguard and consolidate Russia's position in the Middle East, it also complicated the political and strategic objectives of the United States, Turkey and some NATO partners, which consisted in deconstructing Syria, fragmenting it into several autonomous areas, with perhaps a modest federal government to reduce disagreements between such insurgent sponsors as Saudi Arabia and Turkey.[89] The American economist Paul Craig Roberts wrote, "Putin has launched a revolution that will overthrow the world's subservience to Washington."[90] And the intervention frustrated and hampered Ankara's attempts, backed by the United States and Western countries, to actually establish a no-fly zone on the Syrian–Turkish border to protect the supply of Da'ish terrorists and other groups, in addition to securing the passage of more jihadists to fight against Assad's regime.

On October 30, 2015, representatives from 29 countries, led by Russia and the United States, met in Vienna to discuss a solution to the war in Syria. The most important decisions—victories for Russia's Foreign Minister Sergey Lavrov—were aimed at not dividing the Syrian state or dismantling President Bashar al-Assad's army, as the United States had done in Iraq, enabling Da'ish to ultimately recruit the unemployed Sunni soldiers. No conclusion was reached on the fate of President Bashar al-Assad, whom Russia and Iran supported, but whom the United States, Turkey, Saudi Arabia, and other Gulf emirates wanted to overthrow at any cost. The situation in the Middle East was of the most complex and difficult kind. The deep-seated and radical rivalries involved more than the economic, political, and geopolitical conflicts between greater and smaller powers but also regional, tribal, ethnic, and religious animosity. Saudi Arabia, a Wahhabi tyranny, the Gulf emirates, and Turkey, whose president Erdoğan supported the Turkmen rebels and other terrorist groups in Syria, including Jabhat al-Nusra and Ahrar al-Sham, all Sunnis, in addition

---

[88]Farzin Nadimi, "Russia's Cruise Missiles Raise the Stakes in the Caspian." *The Washington Institute*, October 8, 2015. Available at: <http://www.washingtoninstitute.org/policy-analysis/view/russias-cruise-missiles-raise-the-stakes-in-the-caspian>.

[89]Michael E. O'Hanlon, "Deconstructing Syria: A new strategy for America's most hopeless war." The Brookings Institution, June 30, 2015. Available at: <http://www.brookings.edu/blogs/order-from-chaos/posts/2015/06/30-deconstructing-syria-ohanlon>.

[90]Paul Craig Roberts, "Putin Calls Out Washington." *Institute for Political Economy*. Available at: <http://www.paulcraigroberts.org/2015/10/02/putin-calls-washington-paul-craig-roberts/>.

to Israel, a Jewish state, were opponents of Iran, a Shia country, and Syria, the only secular regime still existing in the Middle East led by President Bashar al-Assad, a personal follower of the Alawite sect. Several state and non-state actors were active in the Levant.

On October 31, 2015, while the possibility of a cease-fire in Syria was being discussed in Vienna, flight 9268 (Metrojet Airbus A321-200) of the Russian company Kogalymavia departed with destination St. Petersburg from Sharm el-Sheikh Airport, where ten million passengers (mostly tourists) passed each year. It exploded 20 minutes into its flight over Wadi al-Zolomat in the Sinai Peninsula. All 224 on board perished. Da'ish claimed the attack as a retaliation for Russia's intervention in Syria. Alexander Bortnikov, head of the Russian Federal Security Service (Федеральная служба безопасности Российской Федерации), revealed that the bomb smuggled on Kogalymavia 9268 had a capacity of 1 kg of TNT. And the Da'ish terrorists published information (dubious to some experts) that the homemade bomb and detonator were held in a Schweppes Gold can.[91]

While several terrorist attacks occurred almost daily in the most different cities in Africa and Asia, resulting in hundreds of deaths that were reported by the corporate media without much emphasis, the bloody attacks in Paris of November 13, 2015, alarmed the West and shook France, where another massacre had already occurred in January 7, 2015, with the killing of the journalists of the humorous weekly Charlie Hebdo. The focus of the Syrian campaign, until then aimed at removing Bashar al-Assad, was for some time diverted to the effective combat of Da'ish. In addition, Washington, Paris, and London now understood the need to coordinate efforts with Russia, whose bombardments they had previously criticized for targeting "moderate" opposition groups, such as Jaish al-Muhajireen wal-Ansar, Harakat Sham al-Islam, Junud al-sham, and Fatah al-Islam. In reality, they were all Islamic terrorists who wanted to demolish President Bashar al-Assad's secular regime. On November 15–16, 2 days after the attack in Paris, the G20 met in Antalya, Turkey, where President Putin also saw President Obama separately. Putin presented these colleagues with Russian intelligence: photos of oil trucks smuggling oil to Turkey and a list of people funding Da'ish, living in 40 countries, including some members of the G-20.[92] The names of these countries were not released to the press, but it is safe to assume that they included Turkey, Saudi Arabia, Qatar, Kuwait, and the United Arab Emirates. Their millionaires made compulsory donations (Zakah), one of the five pillars of Islam, and voluntary donations (Sadaqah) to Islamic charities masquerading "as humanitarian aid organizations." Their real purpose was to fund

---

[91] Ahmed Aboulenein & Lin Noueihed (Cairo), "Islamic State says 'Schweppes bomb' used to bring down Russian plane." *Reuters*, November 19, 2015. Available at: <http://www.reuters.com/article/2015/11/19/us-egypt-crash-islamicstate-photo-idUSKCN0T725Q20151119#GUFrtPZ6HqUzyBMe.97>.

[92] Jackie Salo, "Putin Claims ISIS Receives Financing from 40 Countries at G-20 Summit Following Paris Attacks." *International Business Times*, November 16, 2015. Available at: <http://www.ibtimes.com/putin-claims-isis-receives-financing-40-countries-g-20-summit-following-paris-attacks-2187222>.

Da'ish and other terrorist groups in Syria.[93] Some of the terrorists' major sponsors included Tariq bin al-Tahar al-Harzim in Qatar and, in Kuwait, the millionaire and parliamentarian Muhammad Hayef al-Mutairi and the Sunni cleric Shafi al-Ajmi, who raised funds for the jihad in Syria.[94]

Washington had actually always known that prior to the capture of the oil fields in Syria and Iraq by Da'ish, the main source of terrorist funding had welled in Saudi Arabia and the emirates of the Gulf Cooperation Council. In secret cable #131,801, dated December 30, 2009, released by WikiLeaks, Secretary of State Hillary Clinton pointed out that "Saudi Arabia remains a critical financial support base for al-Qa'ida, the Taliban, LeT, and other terrorist groups, including Ḥamās, which probably raise millions of dollars annually from Saudi sources, often during Hajj and Ramadan."[95] Yet the United States and its EU vassals continued to sell huge quantities of armaments to Saudi Arabia and the emirates of the Gulf Cooperation Council (GCC), many of which passed on to terrorists. Washington was clearly also aware that President Erdoğan was instrumentalizing Da'ish. The Turkish National Intelligence Organization MİT (Millî İstihbarat Teşkilatı) was not only supplying them with ammunition, explosives, medicines, and counterfeit Turkish passports (£500 each) but also provided medical assistance to the wounded terrorists in the town of Gaziantep, 120 km from Aleppo, in addition to facilitating the entry into Syria of other fighters from various countries.[96] At least 1000 people of Turkish nationality were reported to be helping foreign jihadists—Chechens and other Caucasians—to penetrate into Syria and Iraq.[97] The crossing usually took place from the strategic border town of Akcakale, in southeast Turkey, to the town of Tell Abyad, 60 miles north of Raqqa, the headquarters of Da'ish, which controlled the region.[98]

---

[93] Janine di Giovanni & Leah McGrath Goodman, & Damien Sharkov, "How Does ISIS Fund Its Reign of Terror?" *Newsweek*, November 6, 2014. Available at: <http://www.newsweek.com/2014/11/14/how-does-isis-fund-its-reign-terror-282607.html>.

[94] *Ibidem.*

[95] "US embassy cables: Hillary Clinton says Saudi Arabia 'a critical source of terrorist funding'." *The Guardian*, December 5, 2010. Available at: <http://www.guardian.co.uk/world/us-embassy-cables-documents/242073>.

[96] Gary K. Busch (Londres), "Turkey's Complicated Relations with its Neighbours and Allies." *Dance with Bears*, December 3, 2015. Available at: <http://johnhelmer.net/?p=14723&print=1>; Nafeez Ahmed, "NATO is harbouring the Islamic State." *Insurge Intelligence*, November 19, 2015. Available at: <https://medium.com/insurge-intelligence/europe-is-harbouring-the-islamic-state-s-backers-d24db3a24a40#.8qqr59a74>.

[97] Guler Vilmaz, "Opposition MP says ISIS is selling oil in Turkey." *Al-Monitor*, June 13, 2014. Available at: <http://www.al-monitor.com/pulse/business/2014/06/turkey-syria-isis-selling-smuggled-oil.html>. Accessed on December 12, 2015.—"IŞİD, Türkiye'de petrol satıyor." *Taraf*, 13 Haziran 2014 Cuma 06:25.

[98] Tom Rayner (Middle East Reporter, Turkey-Syria border), "Foreign IS Recruits Using Fake Syrian Passports.—Smugglers highlight the difficulties faced by Turkey in identifying the true nationality of those entering Syria." *Sky News*, February 25, 2015. Available at: <http://news.sky.com/story/1433658/foreign-is-recruits-using-fake-syrian-passports>; Rebecca Perring, "Foreign fighters seeking to join Islamic State are 'using fake passports' to enter Syria." *Daily Express*, February 25, 2015. Accessed on March 1, 2015.

Mehmet Aşkar was one of the 11 arrested in Turkey on suspicion of belonging to Da'ish. During his trial at the Niğde, the country's High Criminal Court, he confessed that the Turkish National Intelligence Organization (MİT) had helped him smuggle armaments to the opposition in Syria since 2011, when the fighting began.[99] His companion, Haisam Toubalijeh, aka Keysem Topalca, also stated that he was able to bring in 100 NATO rifles for jihadists in 2013, escorted and without any inspection, thanks to his contacts inside MİT.[100]

On October 21, 2015, representatives Eren Erdem and Ali Şekerda of the opposition's Republican People's Party (CHP) held a press conference in Istanbul. They revealed that investigations by the prosecutor's office in Adana had confirmed that MİT had supplied Da'ish with sarin gas, which killed 1300 civilians in Ghouta on August 21, 2013, and that the attack had in fact been a false flag operation, orchestrated to blame President Bashar al-Assad of chemical warfare, violating the "red line" established by President Obama for the United States' intervention in Syria.[101] The representatives accused government officials of instructing prosecutor Mehmet Arikan to put an end to the investigation and not to take any action without the knowledge of Justice Minister Bekir Bozdag. The MİT's close collaboration with Da'ish could not be occurring without the consent and knowledge of then Prime Minister Erdoğan, especially when the news came out in Turkish newspapers. Erdoğan was playing all his cards to depose President Assad, and the operation with the Sarin gas imported by the Turkish company Zirve Import Export Ltd.,[102] according to a Defense Intelligence Agency report, was possibly carried out by the MİT in collaboration with Al Mukhabarat Al A'amah/Ri'āsat al-Istikhbārāt al-'Āmah, the General Intelligence Directorate of Saudi Arabia, which has always been active in Syria.

---

[99]"ISIL suspect: MİT helped us smuggle arms to radical groups in Syria." *Today's Zaman*. Istanbul, February 9, 2015. Available at: <http://www.todayszaman.com/anasayfa_isil-suspect-mi-t-helped-us-smuggle-arms-to-radical-groups-in-syria_372141.html>; "Turkish Intel provided weapons to ISIS, terror suspect says." *The Jerusalem Post*, October 2, 2015. Available at: <http://www.jpost.com/Middle-East/Turkish-Intel-provided-weapons-to-ISIS-terror-suspects-says-390571>.

[100]*Ibidem.*

[101]"Turkey's Main Opposition Party CHP Accuses AKP Government of Crimes Against Humanity: Says 2013 Chemical Attack in Syria Was Carried Out by ISIS With Sarin Gas Supplied By Turkey; Turkish Government Closed Investigation Into This Affair, Released Suspects Into Syria." *Special Dispatch No. 6195. The Middle East Media Research Institute, MEMRI*, October 22, 2015, Available at: <http://www.memri.org/report/en/0/0/0/0/0/0/8812.htm>; Christina Lin, "NATO, Turkey, annexation of north Syria like north Cyprus?" *The Times of Israel*, November 24, 2015. Available at: <http://blogs.timesofisrael.com/nato-turkey-annexation-of-north-syria-like-north-cyprus/>; Peter Lee, "Hersh Vindicated? Turkish Whistleblowers Corroborate Story on False Flag Sarin Attack in Syria!." *Counterpunch*, October 23, 2015. Available at: <http://www.counterpunch.org/2015/10/23/hersh-vindicated-turkish-whistleblowers-corroborate-story-on-false-flag-sarin-attack-in-syria/>.

[102]"The Red Line and the Rat Line: Seymour M. Hersh on Obama, Erdoğan and the Syrian rebels." *London Review of Books*, Vol. 36, N° 8, April 17, 2014, pp. 21–24; "Saudi black op team behind Damascus chem weapons attack—diplomatic sources." *RT*, October 4, 2013. Available at: <https://www.rt.com/news/syria-sarin-saudi-provocation-736/>. Accessed on October 6, 2013.

26.6   The Financial Resources of Terror

President Putin knew Da'ish was unlike any other non-state actor that had previously existed. None had the same financial resources (about US$2.5 billion), sophisticated weaponry—including US-made TOW missiles with a range of 2.33 miles (3350 m)—and the ability to dominate such a vast territory, a territory that included most of the oil fields in eastern Syria, with a production of about 50,000 bpd, and oil fields in Iraq, near Mosul, with an output of 30,000 bpd. The total production in the entire territory occupied by Da'ish would have been in the order of 34,000–40,000 bpd until October/November, before Russia's bombing campaign. The selling price per barrel hovered between US$20 and US$45, giving terrorists a daily profit of US $1.5 million.[103]

In June 2014, the lawmaker Mehmet Ali Ediboğlu of the Republican People's Party in Hatay province already claimed that Da'ish was smuggling and selling US $800 million worth of oil to Turkey from the fields of Rumeilan, in northern Syria, and Mosul, in Iraq.[104] Da'ish had also laid pipes in the border regions of Kilis, Urfa, and Gaziantep. The Rand Corporation estimated that Da'ish militants dominated dozens of fields, with a production capacity of more than 150,000 bpd, in addition to mobile refineries.[105] And according to the Iraqi Energy Institute, the oil explored in the fields of Deir ez-Zor (Dayr al-Zawr) in Syria and other fields in Iraq was transported to Zakho near the border with Turkey, where jihadists sold the barrels at the lowest price, earning about US$50 million a month.[106] Israeli and Turkish intermediaries transported the barrels to the Turkish city of Silopi, where the barrels were marked as originating from Kurdistan (Iraq) and sold at US$15–US$18 b/d (WTI and Brent Crude, at US$41 and US$45 b/d) to a Greek–Israeli merchant known as Dr. Farid, who exported them through ports in Turkey to other countries,

---

[103]Erika Solomon (Beirut) & Guy Chazan & Sam Jones (Londres), "Isis Inc.: how oil fuels the jihadi terrorists." *Financial Times*, October 14, 2015. Available at: <http://www.ft.com/intl/cms/s/2/b8234932-719b-11e5-ad6d-f4ed76f0900a.html#axzz3tNdaNsKF>; Markus C. Schulte von Drach & Benedikt Peters & Christoph Meyer, "Terrororganisation IS Der neue Feind der Bundeswehr." *Süddeutsche Zeitung*, Freitag, December 4, 2015.

[104]Guler Vilmaz, "Opposition MP says ISIS is selling oil in Turkey." *Al-Monitor*, June 13, 2014. Available at: <http://www.al-monitor.com/pulse/business/2014/06/turkey-syria-isis-selling-smuggled-oil.html>. Accessed on December 12, 2015.—"IŞİD, Türkiye'de petrol satıyor." *Taraf*, 13 Haziran 2014. Cuma 06:25.

[105]"A Dark Pool in the Mideast: The Problem of ISIS Oil Sales." Prepared by Minority Staff for Ranking Member Lisa Kurkowski—U.S. Senate Committee on Energy & Natural Resources, September 24, 2014. Available at: <http://www.energy.senate.gov/public/index.cfm/files/serve? File_id=005f682a-cc3f-4bd2-91b6-d68e0527439d>.

[106]Zeina Karam & Susannah George (Associated Press), "US, Russian airstrikes target ISIS oil business. But some say bombings may not totally halt trade." *Boston Globe*. Available at: <https://www.bostonglobe.com/news/world/2015/11/20/airstrikes-hurt-but-don-halt-isis-oil-smuggling-operations/2AnBYNGM2Z2F143iHjla5K/story.html>.

mainly Israel.[107] About 150 oil trucks and small containers lined up daily, each containing about US$10,000 worth of oil.[108] *"Quam verum, quod nervi belli sint pecuniae."*[109] This is why when Russia started its campaign in Syria, it massively intensified the bombing not only of the oil fields but also of the vehicles carrying the oil from Deir ez-Zor, in Syria, and Kirkuk and Mosul, in northern Iraq, to Turkey.

The Da'ish terrorists built a complex, tortuous, and far-reaching chain outside the normal financial system, through which they received between 10% and 25% of the value for the smuggled crude oil in cash, armaments, ammunition, medicines, and food. There were a number of ways they could receive the payments for the oil smuggled by a gang operating on the Turkish border, with branches in Raqqa, in Syria, and Mosul, in Iraq. According to the London newspaper *The Guardian*, oil sales (Iraq had the world's fifth largest reserve) on the black market quickly became Da'ish's main source of funding (43%), with the Turks as its main customers.[110] They also received large donations, extortion money, ransoms for the release of journalists or other hijacked civilians, revenue from robberies, and the contraband of antiquities from Babylon, in addition to other criminal acts.[111]

"As a result, the oil trade between the jihadis and the Turks was held up as evidence of an alliance between the two," *The Guardian* noted, stating that this collusion provoked protests in Washington and Europe—both worried that Turkey's border with Syria, extending 1448.41 km (900 miles), would transform into a gateway for jihadists from various countries.[112] On the night of May 15–16, 2015,

---

[107]"Israel buys most oil smuggled from ISIS territory—report." *Globe—Israel's Business Arena*. Available at: <http://www.globes.co.il/en/article-israel-buys-most-oil-smuggled-from-isis-terri tory-report-1001084873>; "Raqqa's Rockefellers: How Islamic State oil flows to Israel." *Al-Araby*, November 26, 2015. Available at: <http://www.alaraby.co.uk/english/features/2015/11/26/raqqas-rockefellers-how-islamic-state-oil-flows-to-israel>.

[108]Erika Solomon (Beirut) & Guy Chazan & Sam Jones (London), "Isis Inc.: how oil fuels the jihadi terrorists." *Financial Times*, October 14, 2015. Available at: <http://www.ft.com/intl/cms/s/2/b8234932-719b-11e5-ad6d-f4ed76f0900a.html#axzz3tNdaNsKF>.

[109]"The truth is that money is the lifeblood of war," *in*: BACON, *Francis (1561–1626). Sermones Fideles Sives Interiora Rerum XXIX—De Preferendis Finibus Imperii 4. The works of Francis Bacon, baron of Verulam, viscount St. Albans, and lord high chancellor of England.* Harvard College Library. London: Printed by W. Baynes and Sons, Paternoster Row, 1824, vol. 10, p. 80.

[110]Martin Chulov, "Turkey sends in jets as Syria's agony spills over every border—Turkish air strikes in Syria last week signaled a new phase in a conflict that has left its bloody mark on every country in the region. But will the Turks now agree to US demands to cease all clandestine dealings with Islamic State?" *The Guardian*, July 26, 2015. Available at: <http://www.theguardian.com/world/2015/jul/26/isis-syria-turkey-us>.

[111]Janine Di Giovanni & Leah McGrath Goodman & Damien Sharkov, "How Does ISIS Fund Its Reign of Terror?" *Newsweek*, November 6, 2014. Available at: <http://www.newsweek.com/2014/11/14/how-does-isis-fund-its-reign-terror-282607.html>.

[112]Martin Chulov, "Turkey sends in jets as Syria's agony spills over every border—Turkish air strikes in Syria last week signaled a new phase in a conflict that has left its bloody mark on every country in the region. But will the Turks now agree to US demands to cease all clandestine dealings with Islamic State?" *The Guardian*, July 26, 2015. Available at: <http://www.theguardian.com/world/2015/jul/26/isis-syria-turkey-us>.

however, Delta Force commandos (Combat Applications Group, CAG) raided Deir ez-Zor and killed the Tunisian-born Abu Sayyaf (Fathi ben Awn ben Jildi Murad al-Tunisi), the coordinator and manager of Da'ish's revenue administration.[113]

26.7   Turkey

Turkey has always been a key country of the utmost geopolitical and strategic importance because it controls the entry and exit of vessels to the Black Sea through the Bosporus and Dardanelles straits, both inside its territory. The confluence of the waters from the Tigris-Euphrates basin, on which Syria and Iraq depended, also fell under its jurisdiction, as did the junction of the Kirkuk-Ceyhan and Baku-Tbilisi-Ceyhan (BTC) pipelines, which carried oil and gas from the Caspian Sea to be exported by the state-owned companies BOTAŞ Petroleum Pipeline Corporation and Türkiye Petrolleri Anonim Ortaklığı (TPAO). And fearing that Gazprom would cut off its power supply, Turkey was also engaged in the construction of the Qatar–Saudi Arabia–Jordan–Syria–Turkey gas pipeline in opposition to the Iran–Iraq–Syria option, which is why it didn't respect the sovereignty of Iraq and sent troops to the Mosul region.

With the aid of the Kurdish Mafia, all this smuggled oil—about 80,000 bpd—was crossing 100 km of border between Cobanbey, Jarabulus, and Kilis, in eastern Syria, to Zakho in Turkey, controlled by Da'ish jihadists. Profits were estimated at US$40 million a month, or a total of US$500 million per year, according to Iraqi intelligence.[114] The Kurds used the same route to sell the oil extracted from their semiautonomous region in Iraq, without paying anything to Baghdad. And it was the same old route and underground pipeline network Saddam Hussein had used in 1998 to evade the UN embargo, according to Masoud Barzani, then head of Intelligence of the Kurdistan Regional Government,[115] and President Bill Clinton did not stop him, despite the sanctions on Iraq.[116]

The newspaper *Al-Araby* (the Arab), published in London with resources from the Qatari Fadaat Media and directed by the Palestinian scholar Azmi Bishara, founder of the Arab Center for Research and Policy Studies, published such

---

[113]Lucas Tomlinson & Jennifer Griffin, *The Associated Press*. "Army's elite Delta Force kills top ISIS official, Abu Sayyaf, in daring Syria raid." *FoxNews.com*, May 16, 2015. Available at: <http://www.foxnews.com/politics/2015/05/16/us-conducts-raid-on-isis-in-syria-kills-top-official.html>.

[114]"Saddam-style: ISIS oil exports worth $500 m a year 'conducted through Turkey'." *RT*, October 30, 2015. Available at: <https://www.rt.com/news/320190-isis-oil-saddam-turkey/>.

[115]Janine di Giovanni & Leah McGrath Goodman & Damien Sharkov, "How Does ISIS Fund Its Reign of Terror?" *Newsweek*, November 6, 2014. Available at: <http://www.newsweek.com/2014/11/14/how-does-isis-fund-its-reign-terror-282607.html>.

[116]James Risen, "Iraq Is Smuggling oil to The Turks under Gaze of U.S." *The New York Times*, 19 de junho de 1998. Available at: <http://www.nytimes.com/1998/06/19/world/iraq-is-smuggling-oil-to-the-turks-under-gaze-of-us.html?pagewanted=all&pagewanted=print>.

information on Da'ish's oil smuggle routes based on intelligence sources in Iraq. The oil was sold at a substantial discount to intermediaries, some from Turkey, and was bringing in around US$1 million per day, as David S. Cohen, US Under Secretary for Terrorism and Financial Intelligence, had already declared to the Carnegie Endowment for International Peace in October 2014.[117] Days earlier, Vice President Joe Biden himself said at a conference in Harvard University that the United States had a problem with its allies—the United Arab Emirates and Turkey—because they "poured hundreds of millions of dollars and thousands of tons of weapons into anyone who would fight against Assad," including "al-Nusra and al-Qaeda and the extremist elements of jihadis coming from other parts of the world."[118] Biden subsequently apologized, but the fact remains that he revealed that Washington was very well aware of President Erdoğan's endorsement of terrorists in Syria.

Philip Giraldi, a former CIA agent and military intelligence expert, confirmed in an interview to Sophie Shevardnadze of the TV show *Russia Today* (RT) that Washington had always known that the Islamic State (ISIS/ISIL or Da'ish) maintained friendly relations with Ankara and that Turkey was the main consumer of the illegal oil smuggled from Syria and Iraq, a trade in which President Erdoğan and his family were directly involved. This is why American airplanes had until then avoided bombing the oil truck convoys and only actually began to do so after President Putin spoke in Antalya with President Obama and Russia entered the war.[119]

The involvement of Bilal Erdoğan, the president's son, and his entire family went much further. In 2013, Bilal Erdoğan was accused of corruption and of receiving illegal donations, along with former government officials and businessmen, when he held a seat at the Board of Türkiye Gençlik ve Eğitime Hizmet Vakfı—TÜRGEV

---

[117]"Remarks of Under Secretary for Terrorism and Financial Intelligence David S. Cohen at The Carnegie Endowment for International Peace, 'Attacking ISIL's Financial Foundation'." *Department of the Treasury—Press Center*, October 23, 2014. Available at: <https://www.treasury.gov/press-center/press-releases/Pages/jl2672.aspx>.

[118]"Vice President Biden Delivered Remarks on Foreign Policy." On Thursday, October 2, 2014, the 47th; "Vice President of the United States, Joseph R. Biden Jr., delivered a public address on foreign policy to the JFK Jr. Forum. He spoke of the importance of America's international role, discussing conflicts in the Middle East, Russia and Asia. He also emphasized the need for a stronger American economy and greater trade. The Forum was moderated by David Ellwood, the Scott M. Black," 3 de outubro de 2014; "Professor of Political Economy and the Dean of the Harvard Kennedy School. Institute of Politics—Harvard University." Available at: <https://www.youtube.com/watch?v=dcKVCtg5dxM>; "Francesca Chambers for White House dances around questions about truth behind Biden's claims that Turkey and the UAE inadvertently armed terrorist groups." *MailOnline*, October 6, 2014. Available at: <http://www.dailymail.co.uk/news/article-2782891/White-House-dances-questions-truth-Biden-s-claim-Turkey-UAE-inadvertently-armed-terrorist-groups.html>.

[119]"Erdogan wants to turn Turkey into Islamist state, bets on uneducated masses—CIA veteran." *RT*, December 14, 2015. Available at: <https://www.rt.com/shows/sophieco/325829-syria-isis-us-allies/>. Accessed on December 22, 2015. "US 'Aware' Turkey Gets Daesh Oil, Wants to Keep Ties With Erdogan." *Sputnik*, Available at: <http://sputniknews.com/middleeast/20151210/1031554896/us-turkey-oil-daesh.html>. Accessed on December 22, 2015.

(Turkey Youth and Education Service Foundation). He was also summoned to provide clarifications to the attorney's office under the suspicion of laundering the bribes his father received. The suspicion had emerged from a dossier with photos and recordings of telephone conversations with his father, then prime minister, in which he warned his son to make all the money he kept at home disappear.[120] Subsequently, in early 2014, another recording was leaked about a US$10 million payment, without directly naming the reason, but some newspapers pointed out that it referred to a bribe for the construction of an oil pipeline. President Erdoğan denied. In any event, according to Syrian Information Minister Omran al-Zoubi, there was evidence that Bilal Erdoğan's transport company was receiving oil extracted from Deir ez-Zor in Syria and Mosul in Iraq, conquered by the jihadists, in order to export it to Asia. And this is why the Turkish media had nicknamed him "Da'ish Oil Minister."[121]

In October 2015, the French, American, and Russian air forces heavily bombed the fields and refineries in the province of Deir ez-Zor, home to the largest oil reserves in Syria, the Omar oil field, which yielded US$1.7 million to US$5.1 million per month. This was the province conquered by Da'ish in July 2014, but its output of about 383,000 bpd and 316 million cubic feet a day (Mmcf/d) of natural gas was virtually halted with the war, although the jihadists continued to produce 1000 bpd in a makeshift way. This oil was transported to Turkey in a variety of ways, but the coalition bombings of the United States and Russia had begun destroying the entire oil smuggling infrastructure and eliminating the oil trucks on the way to Turkey.

In September 2015, Bilal Erdoğan's BMZ Group purchased two more tankers from the Palmali Shipping and Transportation Agency for a value of US$36 million and registered by the Oil Transportation and Shipping Services Co Ltd. in Malta.[122] Soon after, however, his businesses began to suffer heavy damage as a result of the bombings by Russia, which ravaged the caravans, over 500 Da'ish oil trucks, and teared open a path for the advance of the Syrian Arab Army, the Iranian forces, and Hizballah toward Aleppo and Raqqa.

The destruction of the trucks transporting oil to Erdoğan's BMZ Group, with the consequent financial loss, was one of the factors that probably led Prime Minister Ahmet Davutoğlu to authorize an F-16 jet of the Turkish Air Force to attack a Russian Sukhoi Su-24M near the Syrian border on November 24, 2015. Turkey's president no doubt knew of this attack. Both pilots—Lieutenant Colonel Oleg

---

[120]Ozan Demircan, "Russland versus Türkei. Ist Erdogans Sohn der Ölminister des IS? Ein Sohn des türkischen Präsidenten soll mit Öl und anderen Gegenständen handeln, die der IS erbeutet. Die Vorwürfe wiegen schwer. Manches wirkt übertrieben—und manches ergibt verdächtig viel Sinn." *Handelsblatt*, December 5, 2015. Available at: <http://www.handelsblatt.com/politik/international/russland-versus-tuerkei-ist-erdogans-sohn-der-oelminister-des-is/12680606.html>.

[121]*Ibidem.*

[122]"Bilal Erdoğan's firm purchases two new tankers at cost of $36 million." *Today's Zaman*, Ankara, September 15, 2015. Available at: <http://www.todayszaman.com/anasayfa_bilal-erdogans-firm-purchases-two-new-tankers-at-cost-of-36-million_399209.html>.

Peshkov and Captain Konstantin Murakhtin, the Weapon Systems Officer (WSO)—were automatically ejected with parachutes. Militants of the Ankara-financed Syrian–Turkmen terrorist militias killed Lieutenant Colonel Oleg Peshkov with a missile while he was still airborne and then struck down a Typ Mi-8 helicopter on a rescue mission, killing the soldier Aleksandr Pozynich of the Russian naval infantry. Captain Konstantin Murakhtin survived by falling among the soldiers of the Syrian Arab Army, who took him to Hmeymim air base.

President Erdoğan claimed that the Sukhoi Su-24M had penetrated Turkey's airspace for 17 s. If it had indeed entered Turkey's airspace for 17 s, which certainly wasn't true, so much so that the Sukhoi Su-24M crashed in Syrian territory, this was no reason to shoot it down. It posed no threat to Turkey. It appears that the Sukhoi Su-24M was the target of a premeditated ambush. The United States had even sent six F-15C Eagle jets on November 6, 2015, to the Incirlik Air Base on the pretext of defending Turkey's airspace.[123] And when President Obama told the press that he trusted Erdoğan and that he had the right to defend his territory,[124] he was spouting nonsense, as always. A similar position was taken by NATO Secretary-General Jens Stoltenberg, who stated that the Atlantic Alliance was "indivisible, and we stand in strong solidarity with Turkey."

General Tom McInerney, former assistant vice chief of staff of the Air Force, rightly told *Fox News* that Turkey's attack on the Russian aircraft had been a "very bad mistake and showed poor judgment." It had been "overly aggressive" and he concluded that the incident "had to be preplanned."[125] Indeed, it was a prepared provocation, so much so that the short-tempered President Erdoğan refused to apologize. And Prime Minister Ahmet Davutoğlu justified the attack by stating that the Sukhoi Su-24M was bombing the militias of the Syrian–Turkmen ethnic minority. These militias were trained by the Turkish special forces (Özel Kuvvetler Komutanlığı) and operated in the Latakia region in Syria, near the Russian air base. They were a kind of fifth column, employed by President Erdoğan with the backing of the United States to establish a free zone on the border with Syria and protect the oil truck caravans tasked with the oil smuggling. Like the so-called Free Syrian Army, created with Sunni soldiers who had deserted, also the Syrian–Turkmen militias are in this region with the help of Saudi mercenaries and special security

---

[123]Terri Moon Cronk, DoD News, Defense Media Activity. "American Fighter Jets Sent to Help Protect Turkish Airspace." *U.S. Department of Defense*. Available at: <http://www.defense.gov/News-Article-View/Article/628558/american-fighter-jets-sent-to-help-protect-turkish-airspace>.

[124]"NATO meets as Russia confirms one of two pilots dead after jet shot down—as it happened." *The Guardian*, November 24, 2015. Available at: <http://www.theguardian.com/world/live/2015/nov/24/russian-jet-downed-by-turkish-planes-near-syrian-border-live-updates>.

[125]"McInerney: Turkey Shooting Down Russian Plane Was a 'Very Bad Mistake'." *Fox News Insider*, November 25, 2015. Available at: <http://insider.foxnews.com/2015/11/24/lt-gen-mcinerney-turkey-shooting-down-russian-plane-was-very-bad-mistake>; Conn Hallina, "Why Did Turkey Shoot Down That Russian Plane?" *Counterpunch*, December 11, 2015. Available at: <http://www.counterpunch.org/2015/12/11/why-did-turkey-shoot-down-that-russian-plane/>.

forces, who in 2012 had trained the recruits in Idlib province. And the terrorists of Jabhat al-Nusra and other groups could be found among these "moderates."[126]

Russia's severe bombings, however, were thwarting Turkey's efforts to establish a free zone in northern Syria, since President Obama, certain he could not get the support of the UN Security Council, had not agreed to the no-fly zone proposed by the Turkish president. And President Erdoğan's objective wasn't to clear the border from Da'ish terrorists. In addition to liquidating Bashar al-Assad's regime, he certainly meant to involve NATO in Turkey's defense (Article 5 of the Atlantic Alliance Treaty)[127] and oppose the actions of the Kurdish People's Protection Units (YPG), the Peshmerga militias in Syria and Iraq, thus pulverizing the Kurds and exterminating the Kurdistan Workers' Party (PKK).

Since President Putin's talks with President Obama and President François Hollande on the sidelines of the G20 meeting of November 2015, the Russian, American, and French air forces had also eliminated 1300 oil transport vehicles, inflicting even greater losses on the illicit oil trade between Bilal Erdoğan and Da'ish. Until November 23, one day before the Sukhoi Su-24M was shot down, Russia's air force had launched 141 sorties and destroyed 471 targets, oil fields, refineries, and depots seized by the terrorists, including the largest oil depot 15 km southwest of Raqqa and more than 1000 oil trucks in northern and eastern Syria.[128] President Erdoğan was—no doubt—enraged by the damage Russia was inflicting on his son's business and his plans to annex Aleppo and all of northern Syria, just as Turkey had done with the north of Cyprus.[129]

In a press interview, Lieutenant-General Sergey Rudskoy, Russia's defense minister, revealed aerial photos of the routes used by Da'ish to smuggle oil into Turkey. The convoy of about 8000 vehicles stretched beyond the horizon for 4–5 km from the Deir en-Zor fields in Syria, where they refueled oil. The vehicles

---

[126]Ruth Sherlock (Idlib Province, Syria), "Saudi millions and special forces expertise turn Syria's rebels into a fighting force.—Syria's ragtag rebel army is being turned into a disciplined military force, with the help of tens of millions of dollars of funding from the Middle East and under the watchful gaze of foreign former special forces." *The Telegraph*, September 21, 2012. Available at: <http://www.telegraph.co.uk/news/worldnews/middleeast/syria/9559151/Saudi-millions-and-special-forces-expertise-turn-Syrias-rebels-into-a-fighting-force.html>.

[127]"Article 5. The Parties agree that an armed attack against one or more of them in Europe or North America shall be considered an attack against them all and consequently they agree that, if such an armed attack occurs, each of them, in exercise of the right of individual or collective self-defense recognized by Article 51 of the Charter of the United Nations, will assist the Party or Parties so attacked by taking forthwith, individually and in concert with the other Parties, such action as it deems necessary, including the use of armed force, to restore and maintain the security of the North Atlantic area." *The North Atlantic Treaty*. Washington D.C. April 4, 1949. Available at: <http://www.nato.int/cps/en/natolive/official_texts_17120.htm>.

[128]"Russian airstrikes destroy 472 terrorist targets in Syria in 48 hours, 1000 oil tankers in 5 days." *RT*, November 23, 2015. Available at: <https://www.rt.com/news/323065-syria-airstrikes-terrorists-russia/>.

[129]Christina Lin, "NATO, Turkey, annexation of north Syria like north Cyprus?" *The Times of Israel*, November 24, 2015. Available at: <http://blogs.timesofisrael.com/nato-turkey-annexation-of-north-syria-like-north-cyprus/>.

transported about 200,000 bpd to the large Tüpraş business complex, which operated four refineries,[130] located at a distance of 100 km, in the province of the Batman River, the largest tributary of the Tigris in Turkey. There, it was probably mixed with oil from the Caspian Sea to be exported to the port of Ashdod in Israel from the Mersin, Dortyol, and Ceyhan maritime terminals.[131] The Malta-based shipping company BMZ Group Denizcilik handled this export. Its main shareholder was Bilal Erdoğan, the president's son, in association with Mustafa Erdoğan and Ziya İlgen.[132]

Faced with these facts, US Army Capt. Joseph R. John addressed a letter to Congress, dated December 2, 2015, asking why President Obama trusted Erdoğan when daily CIA reports had been informing him that:

1. Turkey's special forces were training terrorists on secret bases in Konya province.
2. Sümeyye Erdoğan, the daughter of the Turkish President, was running a secret hospital camp inside Turkey, just over the Syrian border, to treat the wounded Da'ish, until they were well enough to return to the Islamic State and continue their genocide against Syrian and Assyrian Christians.
3. Bilal Erdoğan, the president's son, was involved in the illegal oil trade and selling plundered Iraqi oil from the captured Mosul oil fields for billions of dollars to Turkish, Syrian, Japanese, and possibly Lebanese oil trading companies.
4. The smuggled oil generated billions of dollars to fund Da'ish against the Syrians and Assyrian Christians, in addition, of course, to enriching Recep Erdoğan and his son Bilal Erdoğan.

---

[130]The previously state-owned Tüpraş business complex was privatized through its sale to the Koç-Shell Joint Venture Group for US$4.14 billion in 2005.

[131]Martin Gehlen (Die Presse), "Wie der Erdölhandel des IS funktioniert. Russland wirft der Türkei vor, in den Ölhandel des IS verstrickt zu sein. Ankara weist das erbost zurück. Doch die Türkei ist tatsächlich ein Transitland." Die Presse.com, December 1, 2015. Available at: <http://diepresse. com/home/politik/aussenpolitik/4878738/Wie-der-Erdolhandel-des-IS-funktioniert? parentid=5786643&showMask=1>; Martin Gehlen, "Krieg der Worte zwischen Putin und Erdogan Die zwielichtige Rolle Ankaras beim Ölschmuggel des IS. Moskau beschuldigt die Türkei, den illegalen Rohölhandel mit den Terroristen zu schützen. Der IS-Ölschmuggel und wie er funktioniert ist in den Fokus geraten. Erdogan reagierte gereizt auf die Vorwürfe." Kölner Stadt-Anzeiger, December 1, 2015. Available at: <http://www.ksta.de/politik/krieg-der-worte-zwischen-putin-und-erdogan-die-zwielichtige-rolle-ankaras-beim-oelschmuggel-des-is,1518 7246,32680330.html>.

[132]"Turkish President's daughter heads a covert medical corps to help ISIS injured members, reveals a disgruntled nurse." *AWDNews*, July 15, 2015. Available at: <http://awdnews.com/top-news/turkish-president%E2%80%99s-daughter-heads-a-covert-medical-corps-to-help-isis-injured-members,-reveals-a-disgruntled-nurse>; "Bilal sessiz sedasız iki yeni gemi aldı. Cumhurbaşkanı Recep Tayyip Erdoğan'ın oğlu Bilal, kardeşi ve eniştesine ait BMZ Group Denizcilik şirketine inşa edilen. YARDIMCI 81 ve TURKTER 82 inşa numaralı nehir tankerleri, dün sesiz sedasız denize indirildi." *Cumhuriyet*, 11 Aralık 2015 Cuma. Available at: <http://www.cumhuriyet.com.tr/haber/ turkiye/369143/Bilal_sessiz_sedasiz_iki_yeni_gemi_aldi.html>.

5. Bilal Erdoğan provided terrorists with weapons and ammunition through his trading company, the BMZ Group.[133]

26.8   The Great Game

In the Great Game (Bolshaya Igra), the Russian Empire (Rossiyskaya Imperiya) had fought for control of Eurasia with the British Empire. Now the game was repeating itself with the participation of the United States, but on an even grander scale. And by the end of 2015, the prospects were blurred and the signs contradictory. Financial capital had penetrated all borders, and the United States, leading its ultra-imperialist cartel with the European Union, sought to consolidate dominance on a global scale. As such, it attempted to undermine a system it never actually respected: the principles of national sovereignty, of the equality of States and of nonintervention in internal affairs, instituted in 1648 by the Treaty of Westphalen. This system, which Immanuel Kant (1724–1804) considered crucial for perpetual peace (zum ewigen Frieden),[134] was confirmed by UN Charter, Article 1.2. Its violation, Kant wrote, constituted a *scandalum acceptum*, the bad example given by a nation that others followed,[135] such as intervening in other states to export democracy, protect the population, and so on. This was what the United States was doing with the passive or active backing of the European Union. And one of the many consequences of the war, Islamic terrorism, and sanctions plaguing Syria, blocking even the entry of food, was to force more than one million people, adults as well as children, not only from their own country but also from others, flooding all of Europe.

President Obama, playing under win–win terms to impose a "benevolent global hegemony," the Pax Americana, had only obtained fiascos, such as the putsch in Ukraine and the proxy wars in Libya, Syria, and elsewhere. President Putin, meanwhile, was playing on multidimensional, zero-sum terms, seeking a multipolar world, ordered on the prevalence of the principle of national sovereignty. He was winning all his moves and had not yet entered his end game. And one of the unfolding possibilities was certainly that Russia would never again give up Crimea, and that even if the provinces of Donetsk and Luhansk remained within Ukraine, transformed into a federation, they would achieve their autonomy and right to self-determination. Either the Minsk II Accords would take effect or the conflict would continue. As for Syria, the UN Security Council adopted Resolution 2254 (2015)

---

[133](Capt.) Joseph R. John, "The Son of Turkey's President is Funding ISIS with Obama's Knowledge." *Combat Veterans For Congress*—PAC, December 2, 2015. Available at: <http://combatveteransforcongress.org/story/son-turkeys-president%2D%2Dfunding-isis-obamas-knowledge>.

[134]Kant, Immanuel. Zum ewigen Frieden. Ein philosophischer Entwurf. Königsberg. Wortgetreuer Neudruck der Erstausgaben (Zweitdruck) von 1795. Her. von Julius Rodenberg. 1946.

[135]*Ibidem*, p. 8.

establishing a road map to peace[136] with the first negotiations for a transitional government scheduled for January. First, however, Russia and the coalition led by the United States would have to eliminate Da'ish and other terrorist groups over the course of 18 months.

Peace talks were suspended in early February, however, due to a number of contradictions and other factors, including the refusal of the opposition to negotiate with the government of President Assad and Saudi Arabia's intent to take representatives of the terrorist groups Jaysh al-Islam, Ahrar al-Sham, and the al-Nusra front (al-Qa'ida franchise) to the meetings in Geneva, which Russia did not accept. Nor could it accept this condition, as this went against the UN Security Council Resolution. In addition, Syrian Arab Army troops and the Iranian Quds forces, supported by Russian jets, including the most powerful and deadly Sukhoi Su-35S, liberated several villages in the north and were advancing on Aleppo, the second largest city in Syria, near the border with Turkey and a vital supply route for the Da'ish terrorists and other groups that destroyed many historic sites and other buildings there since 2011. From February 6–8, Bashar al-Assad's troops, in an advantage because of Russian aviation, occupied the hills of Barlahin, east of Aleppo, after exterminating the Da'ish forces assembled there.

Culminating successive tactical victories, the conquest of Aleppo would probably devastate all opposition fomented by the West, Turkey, and Saudi Arabia. It would cut off the route through which this opposition received supplies from Turkey across the borders at Bab al-Salama in the province of Aleppo and Bab al-Hawa in Idlib province. This would mean Bashar al-Assad had virtually recovered the entire territory occupied by Da'ish and the other terrorist opposition groups, establishing the conditions to remain in power for at least 2 years during a transition process. This was what the United States and its allies didn't want and hence the calls for Russia to stop the bombings. But Russia was not prepared to accept any cease-fire before the troops of the Syrian Arab Army had completed the siege of Aleppo and closed Syria's borders with Turkey in Bab al-Salama. And on February 10, 2016, they were very close to doing so. Without militarily blocking supplies from Turkey to the terrorists in Aleppo and Raqqa, a cease-fire would become almost impossible.

With the prospect of victory in Syria bolstering the position of President Assad, Russia gained decisive influence in the Middle East and significant bargaining power with the United States. The scenario in the region, however, was far more complex and adverse because of the profound and intractable ideological disputes between Sunnis and Shia, intertwined with a geopolitical struggle for hegemony involving Israel, Turkey, and Saudi Arabia and aligning 36 Islamic nations under the dubious pretext of fighting Da'ish. Together with Turkey, Saudi Arabia threatened to invade Syria, almost certainly with the real objective of countering Iran and Lebanon's Hizballah, who were backing the Bashar al-Assad regime. And war would escalate if

---

[136]"Security Council Unanimously Adopts Resolution 2254 (2015), Endorsing Road Map for Peace Process in Syria, Setting Timetable for Talks." *United Nations Security Council*. Available at: <http://www.un.org/press/en/2015/sc12171.doc.htm>.

these countries—Turkey and Saudi Arabia—would substantiate what they were already announcing to do, desperate with the imminent retaking of Aleppo and Raqqa by the Syrian Arab Army and its allies.

The United States, however, seemed to realize that they did not have the means and conditions to play global cop, as the neocons had imagined. The US/NATO interventions in Afghanistan and Iraq had demonstrated both the reach and the limitations of its military force. The war in Afghanistan, triggered in 2001 by President George W. Bush as the starting point for the war on terror, which President Obama maintained as a "necessary war,"[137] was draining the people of his country and sucking up US$4 million per hour (US$1.7 trillion from 2001 to 2015)[138] of US taxpayer money, with no prospect of success. There was no security or stability in Kabul, and the Taliban kept attacking and attacking. And around 1000–3000 Da'ish jihadists had already entered in Afghanistan, according to Ashton Carter, Secretary of Defense of the United States.[139]

Despite Bush's war on terror, which Obama rebranded as the Overseas Contingency Operations, terrorist attacks continued to occur all over the world since 2011.[140] In 2014 alone, 13,463 terrorist attacks took place, resulting in more than 32,700 deaths and leaving more than 34,700 injured.[141] The total number of victims of terrorism had risen by 81% compared to 2013.[142] And in 2015, the Report on Protection of Civilians in Armed Conflict, drafted by the United Nations Assistance Mission in Afghanistan (UNAMA) and the Office of the United Nations Human Rights Office (UNHRO), recorded 11,002 civilian victims in Afghanistan (3545 civilian deaths and 7457 injuries), 9% more than in 2014.[143] The terrorist attacks continued in 2016. In February 28, attacks were perpetrated in Ankara by either (the culprit's identities were still in doubt) the outlawed Kurdish Workers' Party (PKK) or Da'ish, which President Erdoğan and his son had until then propped up with the

---

[137]"Obama's Address on the War in Afghanistan." *The Washington Post*, December 1, 2009. Available at: <http://www.nytimes.com/2009/12/02/world/asia/02prexy.text.html?_r=0>.

[138]Niall Mccarthy, "The War On Terror Has Cost Taxpayers $1.7 Trillion [Infographic] Feb 3, 2015." *Forbes/Business*, February 3, 2015. Available at: <http://www.forbes.com/sites/niallmccarthy/2015/02/03/the-war-on-terror-has-cost-taxpayers-1-7-trillion-infographic/>.

[139]Yeganeh Torbati, "U.S. Defense Secretary, in Afghanistan, warns of IS threat." *Reuters*, December 18, 2015. Available at: <http://news.yahoo.com/defense-secretary-makes-surprise-visit-afghanistan-084956115.html>.

[140]*TheReligionofPeace.com.* Available at: <http://www.thereligionofpeace.com/>.

[141]*U.S. Department of State*—National Consortium for the Study of Terrorism and Responses to Terrorism: Annex of Statistical Information. Bureau of Counterterrorism—Country Reports on Terrorism 2014. Report. Available at: <http://www.state.gov/j/ct/rls/crt/2014/239416.htm>.

[142]"START—Annex of Statistical Information Country Reports on Terrorism 2014. June 2015. National Consortium for the Study of Terrorism and Responses to Terrorism." *A Department of Homeland Security Science and Technology Center of Excellence Based at the University of Maryland.* Available at: <http://www.state.gov/documents/organization/239628.pdf>.

[143]David Jolly, "Afghanistan Had Record Civilian Casualties in 2015, U.N. Says." *New York Times*, February 14, 2016. Available at: <http://www.nytimes.com/2016/02/15/world/asia/afghanistan-record-civilian-casualties-2015-united-nations.html?_r=0>.

purchase of oil, now practically interrupted by Russia's bombings. Istanbul was also hit several times, including in March, when two other bomb attacks by Da'ish made hundreds of victims at two subway stations and Zaventem Airport in Brussels. Brussels was a terrorist stronghold, especially the Molenbeek district, where some of those responsible for the simultaneous attacks against restaurants and clubs (such as Bataclan) in Paris on November 13, 2015, had been arrested. These atrocious attacks did not occur in a vacuum. According to estimates of the Pew Research Center, in 2016, Belgium had a population of 700,000 Muslims (6.2% of the country's total population), and 300,000 of them were concentrated in Brussels. Most lived in ghettos, such as the Molenbeek district, where poverty, unemployment (around 40%), and discrimination created the fertile conditions for Salafist indoctrination and the recruitment of young people to the jihad, revolted as they were by the US/NATO interventions in Arab countries.[144]

26.9   The Democratization of Terror

Da'ish was the creature that had escaped from the Americans' control. They had fed it in Syria with the complicity of Saudi Arabia and Turkey in order to fight the Bashar al-Assad regime. Now some countries in Europe suffered the blowback. But the terror was not limited to abominable bomb blasts and the killing of innocent civilians in France, Belgium, and other countries, such as Britain and Spain years before. The cruel and bestial bombings by the Saudi-led coalition of the (Shia) Houthis in Yemen, the only forces fighting Da'ish and the al-Qa'ida jihadists, also were nothing less than acts of terror. And they were carried out with President Obama's endorsement and jets bought in the United States. These attacks destroyed schools, hospitals, and hundreds of nonmilitary targets and left more than 7500 dead and more than 14,000 wounded in 9 months in 2015.[145] The number rose by many thousands by March 2016, and the scenario in Yemen was a humanitarian catastrophe. The West turned a blind eye.

Likewise, Turkey was massacring the Kurdish population. And not only on its own territory, it was also bombing the Kurds living in northern Syria and Iraq. It seemed to be fighting a civil war in the southeast against militants of the Kurdish Workers' Party (PKK) and was behaving practically as a rogue state. Not only did it shoot down Russia's Su-24M on November 24 and dispatch armed battalions to Ba'shiqa near Mosul in Iraq, insisting on keeping them in the region despite Prime

---

[144]Soeren Kern, "Why Belgium is Ground Zero for European Jihadis." *Gatestone Institute—International Policy Council*, March 23, 2016. Available at: <http://www.gatestoneinstitute.org/7677/belgium-jihadists>.

[145]"Slaughterer Saudi forces bombing Yemeni kids: Amnesty International." *Islamic Invitation Turkey*, December 11, 2015. Sábado—8 Rabi al-Awwal. Available at: <http://www.islamicinvitationturkey.com/2015/12/11/slaughterer-saudi-forces-bombing-yemeni-kids-amnesty-international/21,2015>. Accessed on October 19, 2015.

Minister Haider al-Abadi's ultimatum to withdraw them; it also bombed the positions of the Kurdish People's Protection Units (YPG) in northern Syria.

The two-state project in Palestine had gone up in smoke amid the advance of Jewish settlements in the West Bank. President Obama achieved nothing with Prime Minister Binyamin Netanyahu. Israel didn't halt the illegal colonization of the entire territory of Judea and Samaria, and the Palestinians retaliated by stepping up the terrorist attacks, killings with daggers and/or other weapons, further escalating Tel Aviv's repression. Gaza was left in ruins, unable to rebuild itself, and Palestine became an example of Thomas Hobbes' "perpetual war."[146]

In Iraq, the prospects of peace were also remote. On May 1, 2003, after destroying Saddam Hussein's regime in a matter of weeks, President George W. Bush stood on the deck the aircraft carrier USS Abraham Lincoln and boasted: "Mission Accomplished." Main combat operations had ended, he said, and "in the battle of Iraq, the United States and our allies have prevailed."[147] Iraq was ruined, and the state had been completely demolished. The war, however, had actually just begun, despite the signing of the Status of Forces Agreement (SOFA) between Bush and Prime Minister Nuri al-Maliki on December 14, 2008, to maintain US bases in the country. The resistance to the permanent occupation by foreign forces, especially in Basra and other cities, never went away.[148] And on December 31, 2011, Obama declared the end of Operation New Dawn. He had no alternative but to withdraw his troops from Iraq. At 2:30 a.m. in the morning of December 18, 2011, the last convoy with 100 vehicles and carrying 500 soldiers had already left to Kuwait from the Contingency Operating Base Adder near Nasiriya, a city in southern Iraq. This withdrawal was carried out in secret and under maximum security, so that the insurgents, the security officers aligned with the militias, and even the interpreters and government officials were kept in the dark: an inglorious, melancholy retreat. There was a strong fear that these last military units would be attacked, even though farewell ceremonies had occurred weeks before in Baghdad and other cities, with visits by Vice President Joseph R. Biden Jr. and Secretary of Defense Leon Panetta.[149] The war had not been won, however. It continued.

Despite the official removal of troops, a contingent of 16,000 Americans stayed behind in Iraq, mercenaries (about 200 for the defense of the embassy) and civilians employed by the large corporations hired for billions of dollars since the Bush administration, responsible for rebuilding Baghdad and other cities, among other tasks, such as restoring the country's infrastructure, devastated by years of sanctions

---

[146]Thomas Hobbes, 2002, p. 149.

[147]"Operation Iraqi Freedom—President Bush Announces Major Combat Operations in Iraq Have Ended." Remarks by the President from the USS Abraham Lincoln at Sea Off the Coast of San Diego, California. Office of the Press Secretary—For Immediate Release—May 1, 2003. Available at: <http://georgewbush-whitehouse.archives.gov/news/releases/2003/05/20030501-15.html>.

[148]James DeFronzo, 2010, pp. 246–249.

[149]Tim Arango & Michael S. Schmidt, "Last Convoy of American Troops Leaves Iraq." *International New York Times*, December 18, 2011. Available at: <http://www.nytimes.com/2011/12/19/world/middleeast/last-convoy-of-american-troops-leaves-iraq.html?_r=01>.

and war. These companies were receiving at least US$138 billion from American taxpayers, and only ten of them—Halliburton, Bechtel, DynCorp, Kellogg Brown & Root Services, Inc., and others—swallowed up 52% of this sum.[150] And at least US $31 billion was implicated in fraud, corruption, and waste during the operations in Afghanistan and Iraq, an amount that could potentially reach more than US$60 billion according to estimates by the Commission on Wartime Contracting in Iraq and Afghanistan, of the US Congress.[151]

In 2005, the US government noted the disappearance of US$9 billion, allocated for the reconstruction of Iraq during the 14-month administration of the diplomat Lewis Paul Bremer III, who sovereignly ruled over the country as head of the Coalition Provisional Authority after the invasion in 2003.[152] His responsibility in the disappearance of this vast sum was never proven. But the fact remains that he dismantled the Iraqi state with the approval of the White House and 10 Downing Street. Through Order No. 2, dated May 23, 2003, the Coalition Provisional Authority dissolved all entities of Iraq, including the Ba'ath Party, whose members were banned from public office, the Armed Forces, and the entire military and security structure in Iraq. This was one of the many and serious strategic mistakes that destabilized and fertilized the country for the flourishing of the Sunni insurgency. And later, when Da'ish penetrated Iraq from Syria, it would swell its ranks with Saddam Hussein's soldiers and army officers.

About 4 years after the withdrawal from Iraq, however, the United States had to redeploy the 26th Marine Expeditionary Unit (26th MEU) in order to reinforce a contingent operating in the 2nd Division Combat Operations Center for Nineveh Operations Command,[153] a small secret base in Makhmur in the north of the country, near Mosul, after a Marine was killed in a Da'ish attack. This return of American troops revealed that the Iraqi government still could not control the entire situation

---

[150]Angelo Young, "And The Winner for The Most Iraq War Contracts Is... KBR, With $39.5 Billion in A Decade." *International Business Times*, March 19, 2013. Available at: <http://www. ibtimes.com/winner-most-iraq-war-contracts-kbr-395-billion-decade-1135905>.

[151]"Wartime Contracting Commission releases final report to Congress. Pegs waste, fraud in Iraq, Afghanistan at >$30 billion. Sees threat of more waste in unsustainable projects. Faults both government officials and contractors. Offers 15 recommendations for contracting reform—Arlington, VA, 31 2011. *Commission on Wartime Contracting in Iraq and Afghanistan*. Available at: <http://cybercemetery.unt.edu/archive/cwc/20110929213900/http://www.wartimecontracting. gov/docs/CWC_nr-49.pdf>; R. Jeffrey Smith, "Waste, fraud and abuse commonplace in Iraq reconstruction effort $60 billion fueled pipe dream of a Western-style economy in the Middle East." *Center for Public Integrity*, March 14, 2013. Accessed on September 9, 2014. Available at: <http://www.publicintegrity.org/2013/03/14/12312/waste-fraud-and-abuse-commonplace-iraq-reconstruction-effort>.

[152]Paul Martin, "Paul Bremer on Iraq, ten years on: 'We made major strategic mistakes. But I still think Iraqis are far better off'. Ten years on, Paul Bremer recalls Iraq's descent into chaos and the fight to restore order." *The Independent*, March 18, 2013. Available at: <http://www.independent. co.uk/news/world/middle-east/paul-bremer-on-iraq-ten-years-on-we-made-major-strategic-mis takes-but-i-still-think-iraqis-are-far-8539767.html>.

[153]Malcolm W. Nance, 2014, 2a revised edition, p. 307.

and that it had not retaken Mosul, the second largest city in the country and occupied by Da'ish. But the war against Da'ish in Iraq was an offshoot and the other face of the war in Syria: Russia, the United States, and key European countries had reached an agreement during the 52nd Munich Security Conference held on February 12–14, 2016, in order to establish a cease-fire between the forces of Damascus and the Syrian Democratic Forces (SDF), a coalition of those opposition groups deemed non-terrorist. The main objective of the cease-fire, which did not include Da'ish, al-Nusra, and other terrorist factions, was to provide humanitarian aid to the various cities besieged by the Syrian Arab Army. It was a fragile truce. Bashar al-Assad's regime, backed by Russian aviation, Hizballah forces, and Iran's al-Quds brigades, had succeeded in restoring control over much of Syria's territory with a series of coordinated offensives in the northwest, advancing against Aleppo and Hama, one of the factors disrupting the Geneva negotiations. Assad now occupied a position of strength in his negotiations with the political opposition groups the West continued to support.

On March 14, 2016, President Putin surprised the West by announcing the withdrawal of troops from Syria on the grounds that the objectives had been achieved. Russia's military intervention had in fact changed the course of the conflict. It stabilized and invigorated Bashar al-Assad's regime, frustrating the dismantling of his state, as the West had done in Iraq and Libya. It also eliminated more than 2000 combatants from Da'ish, al-Nusra, and even the United States-backed Syrian Democratic Forces, and it destroyed most of the oil refineries Da'ish had conquered and the routes it used to illegally export oil to Turkey, smuggling operations that continued after the bombings, according to Minister Sergey Lavrov.[154] In any case, the intervention contained the veiled maneuvers in favor of Da'ish and the ambitions of President Erdoğan and Ahmet Davutoğlu, prime minister of Turkey. On the other hand, President Putin demonstrated Russia's great political relevance as an international superpower and its advanced military might, in addition to compelling the West to seriously consider and accept, albeit gracelessly, its geopolitical interests in not only Syria but in the Mediterranean. Putin's intervention against the terrorists could count on the support of the majority of Syria's people, according to the apostolic vicar of Aleppo, Georges Abou Khazen, who emphasized its special importance since it was accompanied by a peace process encouraging dialogue among various opposition groups,[155] some of which—the Nur al-Din Zinki Movement, the Mujahideen Army, the al-Fateh Brigades, the Sultan

---

[154]"Russian FM Lavrov: ISIS Terrorists Continue Smuggling Oil to Turkey." *Alalam-Al-Alam News Network Thursday*, March 24, 2016. Available at: <http://en.alalam.ir/news/1801802>; "ISIS, oil & Turkey: What RT found in Syrian town liberated from jihadists by Kurds (EXCLUSIVE)." *RT*, March 24, 2016. Available at: <https://www.rt.com/news/336967-isis-files-oil-turkey-exclusive/>.

[155]Ruth Gledhill (*Christian Today* Contributing Editor), "Russian action in Syria offers hope, claims Catholic bishop." *Christian Today*, February 19, 2016. Available at: <http://www.christiantoday.com/article/russian.action.in.syria.offers.hope.claims.catholic.bishop/80213.htm>.

Murad Brigades, and the Furqan Brigades—joined the fight to recapture Aleppo, occupied by terrorists.

Russia, meanwhile, couldn't and didn't intend to end the war in Syria, not without negotiating with the United States and its allies. A war that according to a report of the Syrian Center for Policy Research (SCPR) had already directly and indirectly claimed about 470,000 lives in 5 years (March 2011 to February by 2016), almost twice the number the UN had counted 18 months earlier (250,000), leaving 1.9 million injured, a total of 11.5% of the population, of which 45% have taken refuge in other countries.[156] In the course of 5 years, the war had resulted in a monumental humanitarian catastrophe. Syria's infrastructure was practically obliterated; most cities were reduced to rubble, amid chaos and carnage; priceless historical relics were destroyed by Da'ish terrorists; and Syria's economic losses were estimated at US$255 billion (£175 billion) or more.

Russia's Syrian campaign costs US$480 million, according to President Putin.[157] The troop withdrawal was only partial, however. Military and training advisors stayed behind. Colonel-General Aleksandr Dvôrnikov, who commanded operations in Syria and received the Hero of Russia medal, did not hide the fact that Spetsnaz special forces continued to operate in Syria.[158] They were surrounding the city of Aleppo in coordination with the Damascus troops, who used the most modern Russian T-72 and T-90 tanks. Their mission was to perform reconnaissance tasks for Russian air strikes, pointing out targets in remote regions, in addition to carrying out other missions. The Tartus naval base continued to operate normally. And the air sorties did not cease. From the Khmeimim Air Base in Latakia, the SU-35 and SU-30 jets continued their bombardment of Da'ish and Jabhat al-Nusra positions; the missile platforms in the Caspian and Mediterranean Sea remained operational to protect the ground forces of Damascus and Tehran. And in Khmeimim, President Putin had set up the powerful electronic warfare system Krasukha-4, a mobile, multifunctional jamming station capable of interfering, scrambling, and jamming

---

[156]Anne Barnard, "Death Toll from War in Syria Now 470,000, Group Finds." *International New York Times*, February 11, 2016. Available at: <http://www.nytimes.com/2016/02/12/world/middleeast/death-toll-from-war-in-syria-now-470000-group-finds.html?_r=0>; Ian Black (Middle East editor), "Report on Syria conflict finds 11.5% of population killed or injured—Exclusive Syrian Centre for Policy Research says 470,000 deaths is twice UN's figure with 'human development ruined' after 45% of population is displaced." *The Guardian*, February 11, 2016.

[157]Sviatoslav Ivanov & Ekaterina Zguirôvskaia, "Identidade de comandante de tropas na Síria é revelada. Anúncio veio à tona dias após fim da operação militar no país. Em cerimônia no Kremlin, coronel-general Aleksandr Dvôrnikov foi condecorado com medalha de Herói da Rússia." *Gazeta Russa*, March 28, 2016. Available at: <http://gazetarussa.com.br/defesa/2016/03/28/identidade-de-comandante-de-tropas-na-siria-e-revelada_579685>.

[158]*Ibidem*; Tom Batchelor, "Russian 'Spetsnaz' commandos on the ground in Syria to crush ISIS as 70,000 refugees flee. Russian 'Spetsnaz' special forces troops have surrounded the Syrian city of Aleppo amid fierce fighting in the besieged city, according to reports." *Daily Express*, February 6, 2016. Available at: <http://www.express.co.uk/news/world/641550/Syria-war-Russian-spetsnaz-Aleppo-ISIS-70000-refugees-flee>.

Da'ish's communications as well as preventing NATO from spying on what Russia was about to do.[159]

This electronic war station, mounted on a BAZ-6910-022 four-axle chassis, was already being used to great effect in the Donbass war. It was capable of intruding, interrupting, and scrambling enemy communications, in addition to neutralizing espionage by low-Earth orbit (LEO) satellites, such as the Lacrosse/Onyx series, aerial surveillance radars, and guided radars with a range of 150–300 km. Together with the Revolutionary Guards forces and the Hizballah militias, the Krasukha-4 system was an important factor in the Syrian Arab Army's retaking of the historic city of Palmira, a UNESCO World Heritage site. Da'ish had tried to demolish it completely by detonating numerous explosives implanted in the ruins, but it failed.

According to General Sergey Rudskoy, head of the Russian General Staff Main Operations Department, Russian aircraft carried out 5240 strikes on the camps and facilities of Da'ish and other opposition groups from September to December 2015.[160] And between December 2015 and early January 2016, the Syrian Arab Army troops, backed by Hizballah militias and thousands of Iraqi and Afghan soldiers, reconquered more than 150 cities and towns, securing important strategic regions on the border with Jordan and Turkey, advancing to close off Syria in all its dimension. Meanwhile, Russian airplanes assisted the Syrian Democratic Forces in the struggle to retake Raqqa, which was supported by the United States.

With the reconquest of Palmira, Bashar al-Assad's regime expanded its dominance over the country's territory and further strengthened its position, while Moscow and Washington maintained their understandings about Syria's fate throughout the peace process in Geneva, based on the principle that the institutions of the Syrian State would remain intact whatever the transitional government. In any case, Russia avoided regime change as had happened in Libya.

Since the dissolution of the Soviet Union, all US presidents—George H.W. Bush, Bill Clinton, George W. Bush, and Barack Obama—promoted conventional and unconventional wars in the Balkans and the Middle East and fomented subversion in the Caucasus, always under the pretext of making the world "safe for democracy."[161] What democracy? Wherever the United States intervened, with the "specific goal of bringing democracy," this meant bombing, destruction, terror, massacres, chaos, and humanitarian catastrophes. This is what the facts reveal. And as Oswald Spengler pointed out, the truth is there are no ideals in history, only facts; no truths, only facts; no reason, honesty, fairness, etc., only facts.[162] And throughout history, the facts have shown that the United States and the great capitalist powers have never actually

---

[159]Mary-Ann Russon, "Russia using electronic warfare to cloak its actions in Syria from Isis and NATO." *International Business Times*, October 10, 2015. Available at: <http://www.ibtimes.co.uk/russia-using-electronic-warfare-cloak-its-actions-syria-isis-nato-1523328>.

[160]"Russian Aviation in Syria Completed 5,240 Sorties Since Operation Beginning." *Sputnik*, December 25, 2015. Available at: <http://sputniknews.com/middleeast/20151225/1032286200/russia-syria-operation-targets.html>.

[161]John Prados, 2006, p. 641.

[162]Oswald Spengler, 1980, p. 1015.

gone to war for democracy and freedom or to protect civilians or human rights. They marched merely to defend their economic and geopolitical needs and interests, their imperial interests. And words do not change the reality of facts.[163]

St. Leon, March 2016.

---

[163]This lesson I learned from a young age from my uncle, a second father to me, Professor Edmundo Ferrão Moniz de Aragão.

References

"10 more questions Russian military pose to Ukraine". U.S. over MH17 crash. *RT*, 21 July 2014. Available at: <http://www.rt.com/news/174496-malaysia-crash-russia-questions/>. Accessed 22 July 2014.

10 "U.S.C. United States Code, 2006 Edition — Title 10 — ARMED FORCESSubtitle A — General Military Law — PART I — Organization and General Military Powers Chapter 15 — Enforcement of the Laws to Restore Public Order from the U.S. Government Printing Office". Available at: <http://www.gpo.gov/fdsys/pkg/USCODE-2006-title10/html/USCODE-2006-title10-subtitleA-partI-chap15.htm>.

"15 June 2016: Nuclear force reductions and modernizations continue; peace operations increase". *New Stockholm International Peace Research Institute 2015 (SPRI)*. Yearbook out now. Available at: <http://www.sipri.org/media/pressreleases/2015/yb-june-2015/>.

"1936 Constitution of the USSR. Adopted December 1936". Available at: <http://www.departments.bucknell.edu/russian/const/36cons01.html#article14>.

"2008 Presidential Election. Center por Responsive Politics". OpenSecrets.org. Available at: <https://www.opensecrets.org/pres08/>.

"2014 UNHCR country operations profile — Afghanistan". *United Nations High Commissioner for Refugees*. Available at <http://www.unhcr.org/pages/49e486eb6.html>.

"2016 rapeseed harvest in Ukraine is imperiled". *World News Report — Ukrainian Biofuel Portal —* 21 September 2015. Available at: <http://world.einnews.com/article/287393651/P1Iu7e-i9RjcBYu4>.

"334. Instruction From the Department of State to the Embassy in Syria". *Foreign Relations of the United States*, 1955–195. vol. XIII, Near East: Jordan-Yemen, Document 334. Office of the Historian, Bureau of Public Affairs, United States Department of State. Available at: <https://history.state.gov/historicaldocuments/frus1955–57v13/d334>.

"39 people die after radicals set Trade Unions House on fire in Ukraine's Odessa". *RT*, 2 May 2014. Available at: <http://www.rt.com/news/156480-odessa-fire-protesters-dead/>. Accessed 2 August 2014.

"5 facts you need to know about Ukraine-EU trade deal". *RT,* 27 June 2014. Available at: <http://rt.com/business/168856-ukraine-europe-trade/>.

"95.7% of Crimeans in referendum voted to join Russia — preliminary results". *RT —* 17 March 2014. Available at: <http://www.rt.com/news/crimea-vote-join-russia-210/>.

"A/HRC/31/CRP.3". *Human Rights Council — Thirty-first session*, 23 February 2016.

ABDULLAH II OF JORDAN, King. *Our Last Best Chance*: *The Pursuit of Peace in Time of Peril*. New York: Penguin Group, 2011, pp. 131, 196 e 200.

© Springer Nature Switzerland AG 2019
L. A. Moniz Bandeira, *The World Disorder*,
https://doi.org/10.1007/978-3-030-03204-3

ABDULLAH, Khaled. "UN 'conservative estimates' show 700 children among 6,000 Yemen fatalities" *RT*, 17 February 2016. Available at: <https://www.rt.com/news/332710-yemen-humanitarian-catastrophe-fatalities/>.

ABLAZE, Georgia. *War and Revolution in Caucasus* (Edited by Stephan F. Jones). London/New York: Routledge, 2010, pp. 63–75.

"About 300 Ukrainian mercenaries from Syria fighting in south-eastern Ukraine — source — Most of the mercenaries are from western regions of Ukraine, a source in the General Staff of the Russian Armed Forces says". *TASS*, 29 May 2014. Available at: <http://tass.ru/en/world/733865>.

"Above 6,000 German companies to be hit by sanctions on Russia — export body." *RT*, 21 March 2014. Available at: <http://rt.com/business/germany-russia-sanctions-businesses-365/>.

"Academics and scientists on preventing war", 15 May 2014. *Scientists as Citizens.* Available at: <http://scientistsascitizens.org/tag/public-health/#sthash.urQJHF51.KP101NB6.dpuf>. Directly in: <http://scientistsascitizens.org/2014/05/15/academics-and-scientists-on-preventing-war/>. Accessed 27 November 2018.

ADAMS, John Quincy. *Speech to the U.S. House of Representatives on Foreign Policy (4 July 1821)* — Transcript. Miller Center — University of Virginia. Available at: <http://millercenter.org/president/speeches/speech-3484>.

"Administration on December 1, 2013, and on the parliament in the end of January and on February 18, 2014. Shortly after midnight on February 20, Dmytro Yarosh". Available at: <https://newcoldwar.org/wp-content/uploads/2015/02/The-%E2%80%9CSnipers%E2%80%99-Massacre%E2%80%9D-on-the-Maidan-in-Ukraine-revised-and-updated-version-Feb-20–2015.pdf>.

"Adrian Croft European Union signs landmark association agreement with Ukraine". *Reuter* — World. Brussels, 21 March 2014. Available at: <http://www.reuters.com/article/2014/03/21/us-ukraine-crisis-eu-agreement-idUSBREA2K0JY20140321>.

"Afghan heroin major factor for destabilization in Russia — official". *ITAR-TASS,* 19 August 2014. Available at: <http://en.itar-tass.com/russia/745640>.

"Agenda items 2 and 10" — *Annual report of the United Nations High Commissioner for Human Rights* and reports of the *Office of the High Commissioner and the Secretary-General Technical* assistance and capacity-building — Investigation by the Office of the United Nations High Commissioner for Human Rights on Libya: detailed findings. Available at: <http://www.ohchr.org/en/hrbodies/hrc/pages/hrcindex.aspx>.

AHMED, Nafeez. "How the West Created the Islamic State". Part 1 — Our Terrorists. *Counterpunch. Weekend Edition*, 12–14 September 2014. Available at: <http://www.counterpunch.org/2014/09/12/how-the-west-created-the-islamic-state/print>.

_____. "Syria intervention plan fueled by oil interests, not chemical weapon concern". *The Guardian*, 30 August 2013. Available at: <http://www.theguardian.com/environment/earth-insight/2013/aug/30/syria-chemical-attack%2D%2Dwar-intervention-oil-gas-energy-pipelines>.

"AI — HRW im Solde der Giftgas Terroristen: Barak Obama: UN Bericht, der Gift Gas Angriff in Syrien, durch die Terroristen". *Geopolitiker's Blog,* 26 December 2013. Available at: <http://geopolitiker.wordpress.com/?s=chemical+atta-cks+syria>.

AJAMI, Fouad. *The Syrian Rebellion*. Califórnia: Hoover Institution Press/Stanford University, 2012, p. 52.

AKKOC, Raziye; WINCH, Jessica; SQUIRES, Nick. "Mediterranean migrant death toll '30 times higher than last year': as it happened. More than 1,750 migrants perished in the Mediterranean since the start of the year — more than 30 times higher than during the same period of 2014, says the International Organisation for Migration". *The Telegraph*, 21 April 2015. Available at: <http://www.telegraph.co.uk/news/worldnews/europe/italy/11548995/Mediterranean-migrant-crisis-hits-Italy-as-EU%2D%2Dministers-meet-live.html>.

AL-ASSAD, Bashar. "All contracts signed with Russia are implemented". *Izvestia*, 26 августа 2013 (26 August 2013), |Политика|Izvestia|написать авторам — Читайте далее: <http://izvestia.ru/news/556048#ixzz3FBxhnBKi>.

AL-KHATTEEB, Luay (Special to CNN). "How Iraq's black market in oil funds ISIS". *CNN*, 22 August 2014. Available at: <http://edition.cnn.com/2014/08/18/business/al-khatteeb-isis-oil-iraq/>. Accessed 2 October 2015.

AL-MAGHAFI, Nawal. "Yemen is becoming the new Syria — and Britain is directly to blame. Our support for the brutal Saudi Arabian intervention is creating a lawless wasteland where extremist groups like ISIL can thrive". *The Telegraph*, 24 February 2016. Available at: <http://www.telegraph.co.uk/news/worldnews/middleeast/yemen/12171785/Yemen-is-becoming-the-new-Syria-and-Britain-is-directly-to-blame.html>.

AL-MASRI, Munib. "United, the Palestinians Have Endorsed 1967 Borders for Peace. Will Israel? Now Ḥamās has indicated its recognition of the 1967 borders, the main Palestinian players all seek an historic agreement with Israel. But is Netanyahu's government strong enough to respond?" *Há'aretz*, 7 May 2014. Available at: <http://www.haaretz.com/opinion/1.589343>.

"Al-Qaida als Franchise-System — Lose verbunden, unabhängig finanziert, zu Ad-hoc-Kämpfern ausgebildet: Die neue Terroristen-Generation ist nicht kontrollierbar". *Die Welt*, 8 July 2014.

AL-SHISHANI, Murad Batal. "Islamist North Caucasus Rebels Training a New Generation of Fighters in Syria". *Terrorism Monitor,* v. 12, 3 February 2014. Available at: <http://www.jamestown.org/programs/tm/single/?cHash=ae2a2cd5f15746b0534e5bb000c9ceff&tx_ttnews[tt_news]=41927#.VolBKVJ0f_A-GuidoSteinberg>.

ALBEGRIN, Bertil (Uppsala University) *et al. The Viking.* Gotheburg (Sweden): AB Nprdbok, 1975, pp. 132–133.

"Albert Einstein — Interview with Alfred Werner", *Liberal Judaism* (April-May 1949). Available at: <http://wist.info/einstein-albert/25402/>.

"Aleppo, la collera del vescovo" *La Stampa*, 3 February 2016. Available at: <http://www.lastampa.it/2016/02/03/blogs/san-pietro-e-dintorni/aleppo-la-collera-del-vescovo-kXa49OUOjrxEj6lr2CjsUI/pagina.html?zanpid=2132932023625905153/>.

"Aleppo, na ira de um Bispo". *Fratres in Unum.Com — Ecce quam bonum et quam incundum habitare fratres in unum.* 11 February 2016. Por Marco Tosatti — *La Stampa* | Translation: Gercione Lima. Available at: <http://fratresinunum.com/>.

ALESSI, Christopher; RAYMUNT, Monica. (Reuters). "Germans wary of Merkel's tough line on Russia". *Chicago Tribune*, 25 April 2014. Available at: <http://articles.chicagotribune.com/2014–04-25/news/sns-rt-us-germany-russia-20140424_1_germans-economic-sanctions-gregor-gysi>.

ALOUF, Rushdi Abu (Gaza City). "Ḥamās and Fatah unveil Palestinian reconciliation deal". *BBC News,* 23 April 2014. Available at: <http://www.bbc.com/news/world-middle-east-27128902>. Accessed 29 October 2015.

"Ambassador to Hungary: Who Is Colleen Bell." *AlllGov*. Monday, 2 June 2014. Available at: <http://www.allgov.com/news/appointments-and-resignations/ambassador-to-hungary-who-is-colleen-bell-140602?news=853292>.

AMBROSE "Saudis offer Russia secret oil deal if it drops Syria". *The Telegraph, 27* 2013. "Schmutzige Deals: Worum es im Syrien-Krieg wirklich geht." *Deutsche Wirtschafts Nachrichten* 31 August 2013. Available at: <http://deutsche-wirtschafts-nachrichten.de/2013/08/31/schmutzige-deals-worum-es-im-syrien-krieg-wirklich-geht/>.

AMBROSE, Stephen E. *Rise to Globalism — American Foreign Policy since 1938.* New York/London: Penguin Books, American 4th Revised Edition, 1985, pp. 63–64.

AMER, Adnan Abu. "Ḥamās denies link to murders of Israeli students". *Al Monitor*, 3 July 2014. Available at: <http://www.al-monitor.com/pulse/originals/2014/07/palestine-Ḥamās-links-murder-israeli-teens-unclear.html>.

"An attempted American coup d'État: 1934". *What Really Happened — The History the Government hopes you don't learn.* Available at: <http://whatreallyhappened.com/WRHARTICLES/coup.htmlDouglasa>.

AN Overview of Growing Income Inequalities in OECD Countries: *Main Findings — Divided We Stand — Why Inequality Keeps Rising* © *OECD 2011.* Available at: <http://www.oecd.org/els/soc/49499779.pdf>.

"An W. M. Molotow *et al.*", 21 November 1921 *in*: LENIN, W. I. *Briefe — Band IX* — November 1921 —March 1923. Institut für Marxismus-Leninismus bei der SED. Berlin: Dietz Verlag, 1974, p. 32.

"Analysis of the causes of the crash of Flight MH17 (Malaysian Boeing 777)". *Informational Briefing from the Russian Union of Engineers* — *15/08/2014*. Available at: <http://www. globalresearch.ca/wpcontent/uploads/2014/09/MH17_Report_Russian_Union_of_Engi neers140818.pdf>.

"Analysis: Ukraine's and Russia's aerospace industries will be hit hard by deteriorating relations". London — *Flightglobal,* 23 September 2014.

ANDERSON, Jenny. "Goldman to Disclose Profit It Made on Libyan Trades". *The New York Times,* 24 November 2014. Available at: <http://dealbook.nytimes.com/2014/11/24/goldman-to-disclose-profit-it-made-on-libyan-trades/?_r=0>.

ANDERSON, Perry. "American Foreign Policy and its Thinkers". London: *New Left Review*, 83 Sept/Oct 2013, p. 152.

ANDREW, Christopher; GORDVIETSKY, Oleg. *KGB — Inside Story*. New York: Harper Perennial, 1991, pp. 464–465.

"Angeblicher Bush-Hitler-Vergleich". *Der Spiegel*, 20 September 2002. Available at: <http://www. spiegel.de/politik/deutschland/angeblicher-bush-hitler-vergleich-daeubler-gmelin-fuehlt-sich-voellig-falsch-verstanden-a-215061-druck.html>.

"Angeblicher Hitler-Vergleich Schröder schreibt an Bush / Ministerin spricht von Verleumdung" — *Frankfurter Allgemeine Zeitung*, 20 September 2002.

"Annual Report. Israel and Occupied Palestinian Territories." *Amnesty International Report 2014/ 15*. Available at: <https://www.amnesty.org/en/countries/middle-east-and-north-africa/israel-and-occupied-palestinian-territories/report-israel-and-occupied-palestinian-territories/>.

"Anti-Russian sanctions hurt Europe harder than expected, threaten 2.5mn jobs — study". *RT*, 19 June 2015. Available at: <http://rt.com/news/268336-russian-sanctions-hurt-europe/>.

"Arábia Saudita — Reino da Arábia Saudita — Chefe de Estado e de governo: Rei Abdullah bin Abdul Aziz Al Saud. 62". *O Estado Dos Direitos Humanos no Mundo*: Anistia Internacional. Informe 2014/15, pp. 63–64. Available at: <https://anistia.org.br/wp-content/uploads/2015/02/ Informe-2014–2015-O-Estado-dos-Direitos-Humanos-no-Mundo.pdf>.

ARBUTHNOT, Felicity. "Ukraine: US Ambassador to Moscow's 2008 Cable — 'Nyet, Means Nyet: Russia's NATO Engagement's Red Line.' *Global Research*, 9 May 2014. Available at: <http://www.globalresearch.ca/ukraine-us-ambassador-to-moscows-2008-cable-nyet-means-nyet-russias-nato-engagements-red-line/5381475>.

ARCHER, Jules. *The Plot to Seize the White House*: *The Shocking True Story of the Conspiracy to Overthrow FDR*. New York: Skyhorse Publishing Inc., 2007, pp. 20–34.

ARENDT, Hannah. *On Revolution*. London: Penguin Books, 1965, pp. 35–36.

_____. *The Revolution*. London: Penguin Books, 1993, p. 104.

"Argentina ambassador pick, and Obama bundler, has never been to Argentina". FoxNews.com, 7 February 2014. Available at: <http://www.foxnews.com/politics/2014/02/07/nominee-for-argentina-ambassador-and-obama-bundler-has-never-been-to-argentina/>.

ARIS, Ben (Berlin); CAMPBELL, Duncan (Washington). "How Bush's grandfather helped Hitler's rise to power". *The Guardian*, Saturday, 25 September 2004.

ARMSTRONG, Martin. "The US did not cause the fall of the Soviet Union — that is a False Belief on Both Sides". *Armstrong Economics,* 18 March 2014. Available at: <http:// armstrongeconomics.com/2014/03/18/the-us-did-not-cause-the-fall-of-the-soviet-union-that-is-a-false-belief-on-both-sides/>.

"Arrested Oil Tycoon Passed Shares to Banker Rothschild". *The Washington Times*, 2 November 2003.

ARSENIY Yatsenyuk Foundation Open Ukraine. Available at: <http://openukraine.org/en/about/ partners>.

ARSUOCT, Sebnem. "Biden Apologizes to Turkish President". *The New York Times*, 4 October 2014.

"Article 18. The territory of a Union Republic may not be altered without its consent". *1936 Constitution of the USSR*. Bucknell University, Lewisburg, PA 17837. Available at: <http://www.departments.bucknell.edu/russian/const/1936toc.html>.

"Ashbrook Center at Ashland University". Available at: <http://teachingamericanhistory.org/library/document/speech-on-independence-day/>.

ASLAN, Reza. *Zelota. A vida e a época de Jesus de Nazaré*. Rio de Janeiro: Jorge Zahar Editor, 2013, pp. 74–76.

ÅSLUND, Anders; MFAUL, Michael (Editors). *Revolution in Orange — The Origins of Ukraine's Democratic Breakthrought*. Washington D.C.: Carnegie Endowment for International Peace, 2006, pp. 184–188.

ÅSLUND, Anders. "How oligarchs are losing out". *KyivPost*, 29 May 2015. Available at: <http://www.kyivpost.com/opinion/op-ed/how-oligarchs-are-losing-out-390953.html>. "Associated Press — AP (Artemivsk, Ukraine) "Embattled Debaltseve falls to Ukraine rebels; troops retreat"— *Mail Online*. Available at: <http://www.dailymail.co.uk/wires/ap/article-2958163/Ukraine-says-rebels-continue-onslaught-Debaltseve.html>.

ATTIÉ, Caroline. *Struggle in the Levant: Lebanon in the 1950s*. London/New York: I. Ib. Tauris/Center for Lebanese Studies-Oxford, 1004. pp. 140–144.

AUTORENKOLLEKTIV. *Der Zweite Welt Krieg — 1939–1945*. Berlin: Dietz Verlag, 1985.

AVERIN, Sergey. "One Year of Civil War in Ukraine: Timeline and Facts". *Sputnik*, 7 March 2015. Available at: <http://sputniknews.com/europe/20150407/1020582134.html>.

BABAK, Vladimir. "Kazaskstan Around Big Oil", *in*: CROISSANT, Michael P.; ARAS, Bülent (Editores). *Oil and Geopolitics in the Caspian Sea Region*. Westport (Connecticut): Praeger, pp. 182–183.

BACEVICH, Andrew J.: *America's War — For the Greater Middle East: A Military History*. New York: Random House, 2016.

"Back in the USSR — How could the Kremlin keep them down, after they'd seen our farms?" *Boston College — Winter Magazine* 2004. Available at: <http://bcm.bc.edu/issues/winter_2004/ll_ussr.html>. Accessed 21 September 2014.

BACZYNSKA, Gabriela (Moscow). "Missile maker says Russia did not shoot down Malaysian plane over Ukraine". *Reuters*, 2 June 2015. Available at: <http://www.reuters.com/article/2015/06/02/us-ukraine-crisis-mh17-russia-idUSKBN0OI1S620150602>. Accessed 14 August 2015.

_____. (Urzuf, Ucrânia). "Ultra-nationalist Ukrainian battalion gears up for more fighting". *Reuters*, 25 May 2015. Available at: <http://www.reuters.com/article/2015/03/25/us-ukraine-crisis-azov-idUSKBN0ML0XJ20150325>.

BADDELEY, John F. *The Russian Conquest of the Caucasus*. New York: Russel & Russel, 1969, pp. 42–43.

BAKER, Aryn. "The Failed Saudi-Russian Talks: Desperate Diplomacy as Syria Implodes, Saudi Arabia's intelligence chief reportedly offered Russian President Vladimir Putin a multibillion-dollar arms deal to curb Moscow's support for the Syrian regime". *Time*, 9 August 2013.

BAKER, Peter. "As World Boils, Fingers Point Obama's Way". *The New York Times*, 15 August 2014.

_____. "Obama Says 'World Set a Red Line' on Chemical Arms. *The New York Times*, 4 September 2013.

BAKER, Russ; LARSEN, Jonathan Z. "CIA Helped Bush Senior in Oil Venture". *Real News Project*, 8 January 2007. Available at: <http://www.ctka.net/zapata.html>.

BALDOR, Lolita C. (Associated Press). "ACLU reports 21 homicides in U.S. custody". Uruku.net. Last update 21/11/2014. Available at: <http://www.uruknet.info/?p=17119>.

_____ (Associated Press). "Russian jet passes near US warship". *Boston Globe*, 14 April 2014. Available at: <http://www.bostonglobe.com/news/world/2014/04/14/russian-jet-passes-near-warship/FK75kdLyhVJfOpC5eWdFRL/story.html>.

BANGKOK Post, 17 December 2013. Available at <http://www.bangkokpost.com/lite/local/385256/pressure-mounts-on-ukraine-leader-ahead-of-russia-visit>.

BAR-ELI, Avi. "Ya'alon: British Gas natural gas deal in Gaza will finance terror. Former IDF Chief of Staff accuses Gov't of not Ordering Military action in Gaza so as not to Damage BG Deal." Haaretz.com, 21 October 2007. Available at: <http://www.haaretz.com/misc/article-print-page/ ya-alon-british-gas-natural-gas-deal-in-gaza-will-finance-terror-1.231576?trailingPath=2. 169%2C2.216%2C>.

BAR'EL, Zvi; RAVID, Barak. "Gaza Prohibitions Were 'Too Harsh,' Livni Tells TurkelLivni said the Defense Ministry was responsible for banning numerous food products from entering Gaza, such as pasta, coriander, spices and even ketchup". Há'aretz, 26 October 2010. Available at: <http://www.haaretz.com/print-edition/news/gaza-prohibitions-were-too-harsh-livni-tells-turkel-1.321157>. Accessed 3 November 2015.

BAR'EL, Zvi. "Has ISIS Infiltrated the West Bank? — The pamphlet claiming responsibility for the kidnappings doesn't seem to have come from the Salafi group now terrorizing Iraq and Syria. But maybe a local cell decided to claim affiliation with ISIS to inspire fear." Há'aretz, 14 June 2014. Available at: <http://www.haaretz.com/israel-news/.premium-1.598648>. Accessed 31 October 2014.

"Barack Obama's Bundlers. Bundlers are people with friends in high places who, after bumping against personal contribution limits, turn to those friends, associates, and, well, anyone who's willing to give, and deliver the checks to the candidate in one big bundle". OpenSecrets — The Center for Responsive Politics. Available at: <http://www.opensecrets.org/pres12/bundlers. php?id=N00009638>.

BARCHENKO, Anastasia. "The price of divorce for Russian oligarchs". Russia Beyond the Headlines, 23 March 2014.Available at: <http://rbth.com/business/2014/03/23/the_price_of_ divorce_for_russian_oligarchs_35297.html>.

BARFI, Barak. "Khalifa Haftar: Rebuilding Libya from the Top Down". The Washington Institute, August 2014. Available at: <http://www.washingtoninstitute.org/policy-analysis/view/khalifa-haftar-rebuilding-libya-from-the-top-down>.

BARNES, Julian E.; ENTOUS, Adam; LEE, Carol E. "Obama Proposes $500 Million to Aid Syrian Rebels — Program to Train and Equip Moderate Opposition Would Expand U.S. Role in Civil War". The Wall Street Journal, 26 June 2014.

BARTLETT, Eva. "Distorting the story of Syria's Heritage destruction". Crescent International, February 2015. Available at: <http://www.crescent-online.net/2015/02/distorting-the-story-of-syrias-heritage-destruction-eva-bartlett-4815-articles.html>.

BASSET, Laura. "Rand Paul: We Created 'Jihadist Wonderland' In Iraq". Huffpost Politics, 23 June 2014. Available at: <http://www.huffingtonpost.com/2014/06/22/rand-paul-iraq_n_ 5519287.html>.

BEAUMONT, Peter (Jerusalem); CROWCROFT, Orlando (El Ad). "Bodies of three missing Israeli teenagers found in West Bank — Naftali Frankel, Gilad Shaar and Eyal Yifrach were kidnapped while hitchhiking back from their religious schools". The Guardian, 30 June 2014.

BECKER, Jo; SHANE, Scott. "Secret 'Kill List' Proves a Test of Obama's Principles and Will". The New York Times, 29 May 2012.

_____. "The Libya Gamble Part 1. Hillary Clinton, 'Smart Power' and a Dictator's Fall". International New York Times, 27 February 2016. Available at: <http://www.nytimes.com/2016/02/28/ us/politics/hillary-clinton-libya.html?mabReward=A6&action=click&pgtype=Homepage& region=CColumn&module=Recommendation&src=rechp&WT.nav=RecEngine>.

_____. "The Libya Gamble Part 2. A New Libya, With 'Very Little Time Left'". International New York Times, 27 February 2016. Available at: <http://www.nytimes.com/2016/02/28/us/ politics/libya-isis-hillary-clinton.html?_r=1>.

BECKER, Markus. "Beitrag in US-Zeitung — Merkels Bückling vor Bush — Angela Merkel hat für einen handfesten Eklat gesorgt: In einem Beitrag für die Washington Post stimmte die CDU-Chefin in den Kriegsgesang der US-Regierung ein, wetterte gegen die Bundesregierung — und brach damit nach Ansicht der SPD eine Tradition deutscher Politik". Spiegel Online, 20 February 2003. Available at: <http://www.spiegel.de/politik/ausland/beitrag-in-us-zeitung-merkels-bueckling-vor-bush-a-237040-druck.html>.

BEDNARZ, Dieter *et al.* (Spiegel Staff). "A Country Implodes: ISIS Pushes Iraq to the Brink". *Spiegel Online*, 17 June 2014. Available at: <http://www.spiegel.de/international/world/the-implosion-of-iraq-at-the-hands-of-the-isis-islamists-a-975541.html>.

BEEVOR, Antony. *Stalingrad — Fateful Siege: 1942–1943*. New York: 1999, p. 396.

BEN-MEIR, Alon (Senior Fellow, Center for Global Affairs, NYU). "The Fallacy of the Gaza Withdrawal", *in*: *HuffPost News,* 13 November 2014. Available at: <http://www.huffingtonpost.com/alon-benmeir/the-fallacy-of-the%2D%2Dgaza-w_b_6152350.html>. Accessed 25 October 2015.

BENNET, James. "Israel Attacks Arafat's Compound in Swift Response After a Bombing Kills 17". *The New York Times*, 6 June 2002. Available at: <http://www.nytimes.com/2002/06/06/international/middleeast/06MIDE.html>.

BENSON, Richard. SFGroup. "Oil, the Dollar, and US Prosperity". *Information Clearing House*, 8 August 2003. Available at: <http://www.informationclearinghouse.info/article4404.htm>.

BENZ, Wolfgang. *Handbuch des Antisemitismus — Judenfeindschaft in Geschichte und Gegenwart — Organisationen, Institutionen, Bewegungen*. Band 5, De Gruyter, 2013, pp. 468–471.

BERGEN, Peter. "Drone Wars — The Constitutional and Counterterrorism Implications of Targeted Killing" — Testimony presented before the U.S. Senate Committee on the Judiciary Subcommittee on the Constitution, Civil Rights and Human Rights. *New America Foundation,* 24 April 2013. Available at: <http://www.newamerica.net/publications/resources/2013/drone_wars>.

BERGER, Marilyn. "Boris N. Yeltsin, Reformer Who Broke Up the U.S.S.R., Dies at 76". *The New York Times*, 24 April 2007.

BERNHARD, Michael; KUBIK, Jan (Ed.). *Twenty Years After Communism: The Politics of Memory and Commemoration*. Oxford/New York: Oxford University Press, 2014, p. 157–158, 166.

BERTSCH, Gary K., POTTER, William C. (Editors). *Dangerous Weapons, Desperate States: Russia, Belarus, Kazakstan and Ukraine*. New York: Routledge, 1999, p. 65.

BERTSCH, Gary K.; GRILLOT, Suzette Grillo (Editors). *Arms on the Market — Reducing the Risk of Proliferation in the Former Soviet Union*. New York: Routledge, 1998, p. 73.

BEYME, Klaus von. *Die Russland Kontroverse — Eine Analyse des ideologischen Konflikts zwischen Russland-Verstehern und Russland-Kritikern*. Wiesbaden: Spring 2016.

"Biden blames US allies in Middle East for rise of ISIS". *RT*, 3 October 2014. Available at: <http://rt.com/news/192880-biden-isis-us-allies/>.

BIDLACK, Richard. *Russia and Eurasia 2015–2016*. Lanham (Maryland): Rowman & Littlefield, 2015. 46th Edition, pp. vii-viii.

"Billionaire No More: Ukraine President's Fortune Fades With War". *Bloomberg*. Available at: <http://www.bloomberg.com/news/articles/2015–05-08/billionaire-no-more-ukraine-president-s-fortune-fades-with-war>.

BIRNBAUM, Michael *et al.* "Vladimir Putin says Russia will respect result of Ukraine's presidential election". *The Washington Post*, 23 May 2014.

BIRNBAUM, Michael; KUNKLE, Fredrick; HAUSLOHNER, Abigail. "Vladimir Putin says Russia will respect result of Ukraine's presidential election". *The Washington Post*, 23 May 2014.

"Black Sea Fleet Stirs Controversy Between Russia And Ukraine' From: Russia Moscow To: Central Intelligence Agency | Defense Intelligence Agency | National Security Council | Russia Moscow Political Collective | Secretary of Defense | Secretary of State Date: 2008 June 4, 03:47 (Wednesday) Canonical ID: 08MOSCOW1568_a Original Classification: Unclassified, for official use only". Available at: <https://wikileaks.org/plusd/cables/08MOSCOW1568_a.html>.

BLACK, Edwin. "How IBM Helped Automate the Nazi Death Machine in Poland" Week of March 27-April 2, 2002 [Postado em 26 March 2002]. Available at: <http://emperors-clothes.com/analysis/ibm.htm>.

_____. "The Nazi Party: General Motors & the Third Reich". Jewish Virtual Library. American-Israeli Cooperative Enterprise. Available at: <http://www.jewishvirtuallibrary.org/jsource/Holo caust/gm.html>.

_____. *IBM and the Holocaust: The Strategic Alliance between Nazi Germany and America's Most Powerful Corporation*. Dialog Press, 2002

BLACK, Ian (Kafr Qassem). "Israel's strategic position 'enhanced by chaos of Arab neighbourhood'. Netanyahu government reaps benefits of Middle Eastern mayhem but is set to maintain the status quo of occupation on the Palestinian front". *The Guardian*, 11 June 2015.

BLACK, Jan K. *Sentinels of Empire — The United States and Latin American*. New York: Greenwood Press, 1986, pp. 13–14.

"Blackwater lässt grüßen. Kämpfen US-Söldner in der Ukraine?", *N — TV*, Sonntag, 11 May 2014. Available at: <http://www.n-tv.de/politik/Kaempfen-US-Soeldner-in-der-Ukraine-arti cle12808976.html>.

BLAIR, David (Chief Foreign Correspondent). "Capture of Debaltseve shreds the latest Ukraine ceasefire deal — The pro-Russian rebels must now decide whether to press on with their advance — but Ukraine's president is out of options, writes David Blair". *The Telegraph*, 18 February 2015. Available at: <http://www.telegraph.co.uk/news/worldnews/europe/ukraine/ 11421390/Capture-of-Debaltseve-shreds-the-latest-Ukraine-ceasefire-deal.html>.

BLAKE, Mariah (Correspondent of *The Christian Science Monitor*). "Guantánamo ex-detainee tells Congress of abuse — Murat Kurnaz, who testified in a landmark hearing Tuesday, says he spent days chained to the ceiling of an airplane hangar. He was determined innocent in 2002, but held until 2006." *The Christian Science Monitor*. 22 May 2008. Available at: <http://www. csmonitor.com/World/Europe/2008/0522/p01s06-woeu.html>.

BLANCHARD, Christopher M. (Specialist in Middle Eastern Affairs). "Saudi Arabia: Background and U.S. Relations". *Congressional Research Service — Informing legislative debate since 2014. September 8, 2015. 7- 5700* www.crs.gov *-RL33533*. Available at: <http://fas.org/sgp/crs/ mideast/RL33533.pdf>. Accessed 8 January 2014.

BLANFORD, Nicholas (Beirut). "The Next Big Lebanon-Israel Flare-Up: Gas". *Time*, 6 April 2011. Available at <http://content.time.com/time/world/article/0,8599,2061187,00.html>.

BLOG at WordPress.com. *The Quintus Theme*. Available at: <https://pietervanostaeyen.wordpress. com/2015/04/19/libya-situation-map-mid-april-2015>.

BLUM, William. *Killing Hope: US Military and CIA Interventions Since World War II*. Monroe, ME: Common Courage Press, pp. 84–89.

BLUMENTHAL, Max. "Is the US backing neo-Nazis in Ukraine? — John McCain and other State Department members have troubling ties to the ultra-nationalist Svoboda party". (VIDEO) — *Salon*, 25 February 2014. Available at: <http://www.salon.com/2014/02/25/is_the_us_backing_ neo_nazis_in_ukraine_partner/>.

BOCQUET, Greg. "Who Owns the U.S.?" *Yahoo Finance*, 28 February 2011. Available at: <http:// finance.yahoo.com/news/pf_article_112189.html>.

BODNER, Matthew e EREMENKO, Alexey. "Russia Starts Building Military Bases in the Arctic". *The Moscow Times*, 8 September 2014. Available at: <http://www.themoscowtimes.com/busi ness/article/russia-starts-building-military-bases-in-the-arctic/506650.html>.

BOECKH, Katrin. *Stalinismus in der Ukraine: die Rekonstruktion des sowjetischen Systems nach dem Zweitem Welt Krieg*. Wiesbaden: Harrassowizt Verlag, pp. 190–191.

BOGA, Sandra. "Ukraine 2015/16 rapeseed exports seen down 18%". *Informa — Public Ledger*, 04 August 2015. https://www.agra-net.net/agra/public-ledger/commodities/oils-oilseeds/rape seed/ukraine-201516-rapeseed-exports-seen-down-18%2D%2D1.htm. Accessed 21 September 2015.

BOOTH, William. "Israel announces new settlement construction in occupied West Bank, East Jerusalem". *The Washington Post*, 10 January 2014. Available at: <https://www. washingtonpost.com/world/middle_east/israel-announces-new-settlement-construction-in-occu pied-west-bank-east-jerusalem/2014/01/10/166c9db6–7a0b-11e3-a647-a19deaf575b3_story. html>.

BORGER, Julian (Brussels); LUHN, Alec (Moscow); NORTON-TAYLOR, Richard. "EU announces further sanctions on Russia after downing of MH17". *The Guardian*, Tuesday 22 July 2014. Available at: <http://www.theguardian.com/world/2014/jul/22/eu-plans-further-sanctions-russia-putin-mh1>.

_____. (Diplomatic editor). "CIA mock executions alleged in secret report". *The Guardian*, 23 August 2009.

_____. (diplomatic editor). "U.S. and Russia in danger of returning to era of nuclear rivalry — American threats to retaliate for Russian development of new cruise missile take tensions to new level". *The Guardian*, 4 January 2015. Available at: <http://www.theguardian.com/world/2015/jan/04/us-russia-era-nuclear-rivalry>.

_____. (Washington); WHITE, Michael; MACASKILL, Ewen (Kuwait City); WATT, Nicholas. "Bush vetoes Syria war plan". *The Guardian,* 15 April 2003.

_____. (Washington). "Bush says Arafat must go". *The Guardian*, 25 June 2002. Available at: <http://www.theguardian.com/world/2002/jun/25/usa.israel>.

BORKIN, Joseph. *The Crime and Punishment of I.G. Farben*. New York: The Free Press (A Division of Macmillan Publishing Co., Inc.), 1978.

BOTA, Alice; KOHLENBERG, Kerstin. "Ukraine: Haben die Amis den Maidan gekauft? Die USA gaben in der Ukraine über Jahrzehnte Milliarden aus. Wohin floss das Geld?". *Die Zeit*, n$^{\underline{o}}$ 20/2015, 17 May 2015. Available at: <http://www.zeit.de/2015/20/ukraine-usa-maidan-finanzierung/komplettansicht>.

"BOWLER, Tim (Business reporter). 'Falling oil prices: Who are the winners and losers?" *BBC News*, 19 January 2015. Available at: <http://www.bbc.com/news/business-29643612>.

BRADSHER, Keith. "Some Chinese Leaders Claim U.S. and Britain Are Behind Hong Kong Protests." *The New York Times*, 10 October 2014.

BRANCH, Taylor. *The Clinton Tapes — Wrestling History with the President*. New York: Simon & Schuster, 2009, p. 168. William J. Clinton: "The President's News Conference with President Kučma of Ukraine", 22 November 1994. Online by Gerhard Peters and John T. Woolley. *The American Presidency Project*. Available at: <http://www.presidency.ucsb.edu/ws/?pid=49507>.

BRANDON, Ray; LOWER, Wendy (Editores). *The Shoa in Ukraine — History, Testimony, Memoralization*. Bloomington, Indianapolis: Indiana University Press, 2008.

_____. (Editores). *The Shoa in Ukraine — History, Testimony, Memoralization*. Bloomington, Indianapolis: Indiana University Press, 2008, pp. 55–56. 274–275, 291–310.

BRAUDEL, Fernand. *Écrits sur l'Histoire*. Paris: Flammarion, 1969, pp. 104–105,

BRAUN, Stephen (Associated Press). "Ukrainian energy firm hires Biden's son as lawyer". *The Washington Times*, 7 June 2014. Available at: <http://www.washingtontimes.com/news/2014/jun/7/ukrainian-energy-firm-hires-biden-as%2D%2Dlawyer/?page=all>.

BRESSER-PEREIRA, Luiz Carlos. "A crise financeira de 2008". *Revista de Economia Política*, vol. 29 n°. 1. São Paulo, January/March 2009. ISSN 0101–3157. Available at: <http://www.scielo.br/scielo.php?pid=S0101–31572009000100008&script=sci_arttext>.

BROAD, William J.; SANGER, David E. "U.S. Ramping Up Major Renewal in Nuclear Arms". *The New York Times*, 21 September 2014.

BRØNDSTED, Johannes. *The Vikings*. New York: Penguin Books, 1986.

BROOK, Kevin Alan. *Jews of Khazaria*. New York: Rowman & Littlefield Publishers Inc, 2010.

BROWN, Nathan J. "Five myths about Ḥamās". *The Washington Post*, 18 July 2014.

BRZEZINSKI, Zbigniew. *Game plan: how to conduct the US*: *Soviet contest*. New York: Atlantic Monthly, 1986, p. 226.

_____. *The Grand Chessboard — America Primacy and its Geostrategic Imperatives*. New York: Basic Books, 1997.

BUCHANAN, Pat. "A U.S.-Russia War Over Ukraine?" Creators.com. 17 April 2015. Available at: <http://www.creators.com/opinion/pat-buchanan/a-us-russia-war-over%2D%2Dukraine.html>. Accessed 2 September 2015.

BUCHANAN, Patrick J. "Address to the Republican National Convention". Houston, Texas: delivered 17 August 1992. *American Rhetoric. Online Speech Bank.* Available at: <http://www.americanrhetoric.com/speeches/patrickbuchanan1992rnc.htm>.

"Budapest Memorandums on Security Assurances, 1994", in: *Council of the Foreign Relations,* 5 December 1994. Available at: <http://www.cfr.org/nonproliferation-arms-control-and-disarmament/budapest-memorandums-security%2D%2Dassurances-1994/p32484>.

BUGRIY, Maksym. "The Cost to Ukraine of Crimea's Annexation". *Eurasia Daily Monitor,* vol. 11, Issue: 70. April 14, 2014. *Jamestown Foundation.* Available at: <http://www.jamestown.org/regions/europe/single/?tx_ttnews[tt_news]=42227&tx_ttnews[backPid]=51&cHash=5bd3d36f8fd90bb8c050304f4aff136a#.VS0P0JM-7_A>.

BUNDY, William. *A tangled web: the making of foreign policy in the Nixon presidency.* New York: Hill and Wang — Farrar, Straus and Giroux, 1998, p. 361.

BURAKOVSKY, Igor *et al.* "Costs and Benefits of FTA between Ukraine and the European Union". *Institute for Economic Research and Policy Consulting* — Kyiv 2010, pp. 32–35. УДК 339.54: 339.56: 339.924 ББК 65,58Б91 — Recommended for publication by the Academic Board's Decision of Diplomatic Academy of Ukraine under the Ministry of foreign affairs of Ukraine (Protocol n° 1 as of October 13, 2010). Available at: <http://www.ier.com.ua/files/Books/Ocinka_vytrat/ocinka_vitrat_eng.pdf>.

BURKE, Edmund. *Reflections on the Revolution in France.* London: Penguin Books, 1986, pp. 332–333 e 345.

BUSH, George W. *The National Security Strategy of the United States of* America — White House, Washington, 17 September 2002. Available at: <http://www.informationclearinghouse.info/article2320.htm>.

Bushology Interactive: 2000–2004 — The Bush dynasty. Available at: <http://www.moldea.com/bushology3.html>.

BUTLER, General Smedley Darlington. *War Is as Racket.* Dragon Nikolic (Editor), 2012, p. 1.

BYMAN, Daniel L. "Why Drones Work: The Case for Washington's Weapon of Choice". *Brookings,* July/August 2013. Available at: <http://www.brookings.edu/research/articles/2013/06/17-drones-obama-weapon-choice-us-counterterrorism-byman>.

BYRON, George Gordon, (Lord). "Mazeppa", *in: Poems,* vol. I. London: J-M. Dent & Sons Ltd., 1948, pp. 397–457.

BYSHOK, Stanislav; KOCHETKOV, Alexey. *Neonazis & Euromaidan — From democracy to dictatorship.* (North Charleston United States): CreateSpace Independent Publishing Platform (www.kmbook.ru), 2ª edição, 2014.

CAMERON, David R. "Putin's Gas-Fueled Bailout of Ukraine — Europe may have given up too quickly on bailout and potential trade agreement for Ukraine". *YaleGlobal Online,* 2 January 2014. Available at: <http://yaleglobal.yale.edu/content/putin%E2%80%99s-gas-fueled-bailout-ukraine>.

"Campaigners urge States to stop selling billions of dollars in weapons to Saudi Arabia that are killing civilians in Yemen", 26 February 2016. Available at: <http://controlarms.org/en/news/campaigners-urge-states-to-stop-selling-billions-of-dollars-in-weapons-to-saudi-arabia-that-are-killing-civilians-in-yemen/>.

CAMPBELL, Duncan (Washington). "How Bush's grandfather helped Hitler's rise to power". *The Guardian,* 25 September 2004.

"Capitalist crisis and European defense industry". Stop Wapenhandel. Available at: <http://www.stopwapenhandel.org/node/751>.

"Capture of U.S.-Trained Fighters in Syria Sets Back Fight Against ISIS — Lieutenant Farhan al-Jassem spoke to the Center for Public Integrity before he was taken". *Syrian Observatory for Human Rights,* 3 August 2015. Available at: <http://www.syriahr.com/en/2015/08/capture-of-u-s-trained-fighters-in-syria-sets-back-fight-against-isis/>.

CARLISLE, Tamsin. "Qatar seeks gas pipeline to Turkey". The National — Business. August 26, 2009. Available at: <http://www.thenational.ae/business/energy/qatar-seeks-gas-pipeline-to-turkey>.

CARROLL JR. Eugene J. (retired Navy rear admiral, deputy director of the Center for Defense Information). "NATO Expansion Would Be an Epic 'Fateful Error' — Policy: Enlargement could weaken unity within the alliance. Denials of the potential threat to Russia are delusory". *Los Angeles Times*, 7 July 1997. Available at: <http://articles.latimes.com/print/1997/jul/07/local/me-10464>.

_____. *Deputy Director Center for Defense Information*. Washington, 1 May 1998, To the Editor.

"Carta de Osvaldo Aranha, embaixador dos Estados Unidos em Washington, ao presidente Getúlio Vargas", Wash., 2–12-1952, pasta de 1952

CARTALUCCI, Anthony. "'IS' supply channels through Turkey". (Video) — *Deutsche Welle (DW)* — 28 November 2014. Available at: <http://www.dw.com/en/is-supply-channels-through-turkey/av-18091048>.

CARTALUCCI, Tony. "US-Turkey "Buffer Zone" to Save ISIS, Not Stop Them". *NEO (New Eastern Outlook)*. Available at: <http://journal-neo.org/2015/10/24/us-turkey-buffer-zone-to-save-isis-not-stop-them/>.

"Carter: Zero Chance for Two-state Solution — Netanyahu decided 'early on to adopt a one-state solution, but without giving the Palestinians equal rights', former U.S. president accuses in interview". *Há'aretz*, 13 August 2015. Available at: <http://www.haaretz.com/israel-news/1.671056>.

"Caspian Sea — Overview of oil and natural gas in the Caspian Sea region — *International energy data and analysis*". *EIA Beta — U.S. Department of Energy,* 26 August 2013. *Available at:* <http://www.eia.gov/beta/international/regions-topics.cfm?RegionTopicID=CSR>.

"Cause of Syrian civil war, ISIS & Western propaganda: Assad interview highlights". *RT*, 18 September 2015. Available at: <http://www.rt.com/news/315848-assad-syria-isis-interview/>.

CENCIOTTI, David. "According to an authoritative source, two Su-27 Flankers escorted the Boeing 777 Malaysian minutes before it was hit by one or more missiles". *The Aviationist*, 21 July 2014. Available at: <http://theaviationist.com/2014/07/21/su-27s-escorted-mh17/>.

"Center for Advanced Holocaust Studies United States Holocaust Memorial Museum, 2013". Available at: <http://www.ushmm.org/m/pdfs/20130500-holocaust-in-ukraine.pdf>.

CHAMBERS, Francesca (White House Correspondent For Dailymail.com) & Reuters "The Cold War is back: Putin's Russia named as number one threat to U.S. by Obama's nominee to lead the Joint Chiefs of Staff." *MailOnline*, 9 July 2015. Accessed 22 July 2015.

CHAPMAN, John. "The real reasons Bush went to war — WMD was the rationale for invading Iraq. But what was really driving the US were fears over oil and the future of the dollar". *The Guardian*, 28 July 2004. Available at: <http://www.theguardian.com/world/2004/jul/28/iraq.usa>.

CHASSANY, Anne-Sylvaine. "Ukraine talks in Paris end on positive note", 2 October 2015. Available at: <http://www.ft.com/intl/cms/s/0/0b24a898–693f-11e5-a57f-21b88f7d973f.html#axzz3ntbj5Ujy>.

CHAULIA, Sreeram. "Democratisation, Colour Revolutions and the Role of the NGOs: Catalysts or Saboteurs?" *Global Research*, 25 December 2005. Available at: <http://www.globalresearch.ca/democratisation-colour-revolutions-and-the-role-of-the-ngos-catalysts-or-saboteurs/1638>.

CHELLEL, kit. "Libyan Investment Authority Sues Goldman Sachs in London". *Bloomberg News*, 22 January 2014. Available at: <http://www.bloomberg.com/news/2014–01-22/libyan-investment-authority-sues-goldman-sachs-in-london-court.html>.

CHEN, Michelle; QING, Koh Gui. (Hong Kong/Beijing). "Exclusive: China's international payments system ready, could launch by end-2015 — sources". *Reuters*, 9 March 2015. Available at: <http://www.reuters.com/article/2015/03/09/us-china-yuan%2D%2Dpayments-exclusive-idUSKBN0M50BV20150309>.

_____. "China's international payments system ready, could launch by end-2015 — sources". *Reuters*, 9 March 2015. Available at: <http://www.reuters.com/article/2015/03/09/us-china-yuan-payments-exclusive-idUSKBN0M50BV20150309>.

CHERNENKO, Elena; GABUEV, Alexander (Kommersant — Russian daily). "Stratfor Chief's "Most Blatant Coup in History". Interview Translated in Full. *Insider Russia*, 20 January 2015. Available at: <http://russia-insider.com/en/2015/01/20/256>.

CHETERIAN, Vicken. "The August 2008 war in Georgia: from ethnic conflict to border wars", *in*: CHIVERS, C. J.; SCHMITT, Eric. "Arms Airlift to Syria Rebels Expands, With Aid From C.I. A." *The New York Times*, 24 March 2013.

"China confirms new generation long range missiles. China's ownership of a new intercontinental ballistic missile said to be capable of carrying multiple nuclear warheads as far as the United States is confirmed by state-run media". *AFP — The Telegraph*, 1 August 2014.

China launches RMB int'l interbank payment system". *English.news.cn*, 10 August 2015. Available at: <http://news.xinhuanet.com/english/video/2015–10/08/c_134692342.htm>.

China's mega international payment system is ready will launch this year — report". *RT*, 10 March 2015. Available at: <https://www.rt.com/business/239189-china-payment-system-ready/>.

"China" — *Nuclear Threat Initiative* (NTI). Available at: <http://www.nti.org/country-profiles/china/nuclear/>.

CHOMSKY, Noam; HERMAN, Edward S. *The Washington Connection and Third World Fascism — The Political Economy of the Human Rights*: vol. I. Boston: South End Press, 1979, pp. 252–253.

CHORVATH, Karolina (Special to CNBC.com). "Why Ukraine needs Russia — for now, anyway". Wednesday, 4 Jun 2014. CNBC.com. Available at: <http://www.cnbc.com/id/101727421>.

CHOSSUDOVSKY, Michel. "The U.S. has installed a Neo-Nazi Government in Ukraine". *Global Research*, 26 February 2015. Available at: <http://www.globalresearch.ca/the-u-s-has-installed-a-neo-nazi-government-in-kraine/5371554?print=1>.

CHOURSINA, Kateryna; SAZONOV, Alexander. "Russia Seizes Candy Factory Owned by Ukraine Leader Poroshenko". *Bloomberg*, 29 April 2015. Available at: <http://www.bloomberg.com/news/articles/2015–04-29/russia-seizes-candy-factory-owed-by-ukraine-presi dent-poroshenko>.

CHOURSINA, Kateryna; VERBYANY, Volodymyr; SAZONO, Alexander. *Billionaire No More*: *Ukraine President's Fortune Fades With War*. Bloomberg, 8 May 2015.

CHRISTEN, Elisabeth; FRITZ, Oliver; STREICHER, Gerhard. "Effects of the EU-Russia Economic Sanctions on Value Added and Employment in the European Union and Switzerland". Reports (*work in progress*), June 2015. *Austrian Institute of Economic Research*. Available at: <http://www.wifo.ac.at/jart/prj3/wifo/main.jart?rel=en&reserve-mode=active&content-id=1424976969312&publikation_id=58195&detail-view=yes>.

CHURCHILL, Winston S. *Memórias da Segunda Guerra Mundial*. São Paulo: Nova Fronteira, 2nd print, 1995, pp. 722–724.

_____. *The Second World War — The Grand Alliance*. London: Guild Publishing — Book Club Associates, vol. III.

CIA — *Country Comparison*: *GDP — Per Capita* (PPP). Available at: <https://www.usaid.gov/sites/default/files/documents/1863/USAID_Ukraine_CDCS_2012–2016.pdf>.

CIA — *The World Fact Book* — Fact. Available at: <https://www.cia.gov/library/publications/the-world-factbook/geos/up.html>.

CIA — *World Fact Book*. Available at: <https://www.cia.gov/library/publications/the-world-factbook/geos/us.html>. Accessed 16 October 2015.

CICERO, Marcus Tullius. *De re publica — Vom Gemeinwesen* (Lateinisch/Deutsch). Stuttgart: Phillip Reclam, June 1979, p. 230.

CIENSKI, Jan (Warsaw). "Russia's reliance on Ukraine for military hardware raises fears". *The Financial Times*, 20 April 2014. Available at: <http://www.ft.com/cms/s/0/9cc89022-c87b-11e3-a7a1-00144feabdc0.html#axzz3QtFrdlkm>.

CLAKSON, Alexander. "The Real Reason Russia is Demonized and Sanctioned: the American Petrodollar". *Global Research*, 18 September 2014. Available at: <http://www.globalresearch.ca/the-real-reason-russia-is-demonized-and-sanctioned-the-american-petrodollar/5402592>.

CLARCK, Wesley K. *L'Irak, le Terrorisme et l'Empire American*. Paris: Editions du Seuil, 2004.

CLARK, William R. *Petrodollar Warfare*: *Oil, Iraq and the Future of the Dollar*. Gabriola Island — British Columbia (Canadá), 2005.

CLEMENT, Scott. "Most in U.S. oppose Syria strike, Post-ABC poll finds". *The Washington Post*, 3 September 2013.

CLINTON, Bill. *My Life*. London: Hutchinson, 2004, p. 570.

Coalland — Faces of Donetsk — Zoï Environment Network and UNEP/GRID-Arendal, ISBN: 978–82-7701–090-8. France: Global Publishing Services, 2011, p. 12.

COALSON, Robert. "Ukraine's Choice: East or West?" *Israel* Military.net, 15 November 2013. Available at: <http://www.rferl.org/content/ukraine. . ./25169110.html>.

COBB, Kurt. "Russia-China Deal Could Kill U.S. LNG Exports". OilPrice.com/CNBC, 18 November 2014. Available at: <http://oilprice.com/Energy/Natural-Gas/Russia-China-Deal-Could-Kill-U.S.-LNG-Exports.html>.

COHEN, Gili. "Two Soldiers Killed by Gaza Militants Who Breached Border — Two more wounded; Palestinian militants launch anti-tank missile at IDF unit". *Há'aretz*, 19 July 2014. Available at: <http://www.haaretz.com/israel-news/.premium-1.606012>.

COHEN, Josh (Reuters). "Putin says Ukraine being overrun by fascists — and he may be right — Kiev has now handed the Kremlin 'evidence' for Putin's claim that Russia is facing off against fascists." *The Jerusalem Post*, 16 May 2015. Available at: <http://www.jpost.com/International/Putin-says-Ukraine-being-overrun-by-fascists-and-he-may-be-right-4032>.

COHEN, Max. "Angela Merkel schreibt in der *Washington Post*: 'Schroeder Doesn't Speak for All Germans' By Angela Merkel", *The Washington Post*, 20 February 2003, p. A39. Available at: <http://www.ariva.de/forum/Angela-Merkel-schreibt-in-der-Washington-Post-153840>.

COHLAND, Tom; KESHIK, Norhan. "West bankrolls Free Syrian Army fightback". *The Times — The Australian*, 8 February 2014. Available at: <http://www.theaustralian.com.au/news/world/west-bankrolls-free-syrian-army-fightback/story-fnb64oi6–1226820979028?nk=7f805021fdbcc30f4ca8b9d3cd537c47#>.

COHN, Gary; THOMPSON, Ginger; MATTHEWS, Mark. "Torture was taught by CIA; Declassified manual details the methods used in Honduras; Agency denials refuted". *The Baltimore Sun*, 27 January 1997, edição final. Available at: <http://articles.baltimoresun.com/1997–01-27/news/1997027049_1_training-manual-torture-methods-counterintelligence-interrogation. Cf. also in: <http://www.hartford-hwp.com/archives/40/055.html>.

Collapse of Ukrainian exports to Russia and Europe in first six months of 2015". *Introduction by New Cold* War.org — *The New Cold War*: *Ukraine and beyond*, 20 August 2015. Available at: <http://newcoldwar.org/collapse-of-ukrainian-exports-to-russia-and-europe-in-first-six-.months-of-2015/>.

COMERFORD, Vincent (Herausgegeben). *Holodomor and Gorta Mór*: *Histories, Memories and Representations of Famine*. London: Anthen Press, 2012, pp. 40–45.

Concern mounts for refugees and asylum-seekers in Libya". *UNHCR*, Briefing Notes, 5 August 2014. Available at: <http://www.unhcr.org/53e0c0a09.html>.

CONETTA, Carl. "America's New Deal With Europe: NATO Primacy and Double Expansion, Project on Defense Alternatives Commentary". *Cambridge, MA*: *Commonwealth Institute*, October 1997. Available at: <http://www.comw.org/pda/eurcom.htm>.

Conference on Security and Co-operation in Europe Final Act" — Helsinki 1975, p. 4. Available at: <https://www.osce.org/mc/39501?download=true>.

COOK, Fred J. *O Estado Militarista*. Rio de Janeiro: Civilização Brasileira, 1964, pp. 84–85, 88–89.

COOK, Steven A.; MATTEI, Eni Enrico (Senior Fellow for Middle East and Africa Studies). How to Get Egypt's Generals Back on Our Side. ForeignPolicy.com, 5 January 2015. Available at: <http://www.cfr.org/egypt/get-egypts-generals-back%2D%2Dour-side/p35922>.

COOLEY, Alexander. *Great Games, Local Rules*: *The New Great Power Contest in Central Asia*. Oxford-New York: Oxford University Press, 2012. p. 168.

COPELAND, Miles. *The Game Player. Confessions of the CIA's original political operative.* London: Aurum Press, pp. 92–194.

COPSEY, Nathaniel. "Ukraine", *in*: Ó BEACHÁIN, Donnacha; POLESE, Abel (Editors). *The Colour Revolutions in the Former Soviet Revolutions. Successes and Failures.* London/New York: Routledge, 2010.

CORN, David. "WATCH: Rand Paul Says Dick Cheney Pushed for the Iraq War So Halliburton Would Profit. As the ex-veep blasts Paul for being an isolationist, old video shows the Kentucky senator charging that Cheney used 9/11 as an excuse to invade Iraq and benefit his former company". *Mother Jones/Foundation for National Progress,* 7 April 2014. Available at: <http://www.motherjones.com/politics/2014/04/rand-paul-dick-cheney-exploited-911-iraq-halliburton>.

Corporate Interests behind Ukraine Putsch". Consortiumnews.com, 16 March 2014. Available at: <https://consortiumnews.com/2014/03/16/corporate-interests-behind-ukraine-putsch/>.

Correio Braziliense, 16 June 1991, p. 22.

CORSI, Jerome R. "Generals conclude Obama backed al-Qaida, Probe of military experts finds U.S. 'switched sides' in terror war". *WND,* 19 January 2015. Available at: <http://www.wnd.com/files/2012/01/Jerome-R.-Corsi_avatar-96x96.jpg>.

Council Fails to Uphold its Responsibility to Protect in Syria". International Coalition for the Responsibility to Protect (ICRtoP) — *The Canadian Centre for the Responsibility to Protect,* 7 October 2011. Available at: <http://icrtopblog.org/2011/10/07/un-security-council-fails-to-uphold-its-responsibility-to-protect-in-syria/>.

Countries outside the United States — June 2013". Executive — Summary, Table 5. *U.S. Energy Information Administration,* 13 June 2013. Available at: <http://www.eia.gov/analysis/studies/worldshalegas/pdf/fullreport.pdf?zscb=84859470>.

COYNASH, Halya. "Poroshenko grants Belarusian Neo-Nazi Ukrainian citizenship". *Kyiv Post,* 9 December 2014. Available at: <http://www.kyivpost.com/opinion/op-ed/halya-coynash-poroshenko-grants-belarusian-neo-nazi-ukrainian-citizenship-374562.html>.

CRAMER, Clayton. "An American Coup d'État?" *History Today,* vol. 45, issue: 11, 1995. Available at: <http://www.historytoday.com/clayton-cramer/american-coup-detat>.

CRIDER, Cori. "Guantánamo children". *The Guardian,* 19 July 2008. Available at: <http://www.theguardian.com/world/2008/jul/19/humanrights.usa>.

CRIENGLISH News, 26 June 2015. Available at: <http://english.cri.cn/12394/2015/06/26/2982s884702_5.htm>.

CRITCHLOW, Andrew (Commodities editor). "North Sea oil production rises despite price fall The UK offshore region is set for the first increase in total production for 15 years". *The Telegraph,* 3 August 2015. Available at: <http://www.telegraph.co.uk/finance/newsbysector/energy/oilandgas/11780648/North-Sea-oil-production-rises-despite-price-slump.html>.

CROOK, Sabine. "Slow sowing pace raises concern for Ukraine's rapeseed crop — Ongoing dryness during the current sowing window is likely to cut Ukraine's rapeseed harvest to between 1–1.5 million tonnes compared with 1.7 mln for this year's harvest, analyst UkrAgroConsult said today". *Informa — Public Ledger,* 15 September 2015. Available at: <https://www.agra-net.net/agra/public-ledger/commodities/oils-oilseeds/rapeseed/slow-sowing-pace-raises-concern-for-ukraines-rapeseed-crop-1.htm>. Accessed 21 September 2015.

CROWLEY, Sean. "(Not) Behind Enemy Lines I: Recruiting for Russia's War in Ukraine". *LEKSIKA,* 25 June 2015. Available at: <http://www.leksika.org/tacticalanalysis/2015/6/24/not-behind-enemy-lines-i-recruiting-for-russias-war-in-ukraine>.

CUNNINGHAM, Finian. "'Deal or War': Is doomed Dollar Really Behind Obama's Iran Warning?" *RT,* 16 August 2015. Available at: <https://www.rt.com/op-edge/312531-iran-kerry-us-dollar/>.

_____. "Washington's Cloned Female Warmongers", *in*: *Information Clearing House,* 9 February 2014. Available at: <http://www.informationclearinghouse.info/article37599.htm>.

CUNNINGHAM, Nick. "Russia Eyes Crimea's Oil and Gas Reserves". *Oil Price*, 16 March 2014. Available at: <http://oilprice.com/Energy/Energy-General/Russia-Eyes-Crimeas-Oil-and-Gas-Reserves.html>.

D'ANIERI, Paul J. *Economic Interdependence in Ukrainian-Russian Relations*. New York: New York University Press, 1999, pp. 17, 20–205.

D'ORNELLAS, Charlotte (Journaliste indépendante). "La sainte colère de l'archevêque d'Aleppo. Les médias européens n'ont cessé d'étouffer le quotidien de ceux qui souffrent en Syrie". *Boulevard Voltaire*, Available at: <http://www.bvoltaire.fr/charlottedornellas/sainte-colere-de-larcheveque-dalep,235328>.

Daily updates from the Special Monitoring Mission to Ukraine". *OSCE Special Monitoring Mission to Ukraine*. Available at: <http://www.osce.org/ukraine-smm/daily-updates>.

Dairy woes to shrink Ukraine cattle herd to 14% of Soviet levels". *Blackseagrain,* 18 September 2015. Available at: <http://www.blackseagrain.net/novosti/dairy-woes-to-shrink-ukraine-cattle-herd-to-14-of-soviet-levels>. Accessed 21 September 2015.

DALBY, Chris. "Who Is Buying The Islamic State's Illegal Oil?" OilPrice.com, 30 September 2014. Available at: <http://oilprice.com/Energy/Crude-Oil/Who-Is-Buying-The-Islamic-States-Illegal-Oil.html>. Accessed 2 October 2015.

DALE SCOTT, Peter. *Drugs, Oil, and War: The United States in Afghanistan, Colombia, and Indochina*. Lanham, Maryland: Rowman & Littlefield Publishers, Inc., 2003 p. 35.

DALY, John C. K. "After Ukraine, Russia Beefs Up Military in Armenia and Kyrgyzstan". *Silk Road Reporters*, 24 October 2014. Available at: <http://www.silkroadreporters.com/2014/10/24/ukraine-russia-beefs-military-armenia-kyrgyzstan/>.

_____. "After Ukraine, Russia Beefs Up Military in Armenia and Kyrgyzstan". *Silk Road Reporters*, 24 October 2014. Available at: <http://www.silkroadreporters.com/2014/10/24/ukraine-russia-beefs-military-armenia-kyrgyzstan/>.

DALY, John. "Ukraine's Yulia Timoshenko — Victim or Crook?" OilPrice.com, 12 October 2011. Available at: <http://oilprice.com/Energy/Energy-General/Ukraines-Yulia-Timoshenko-Victim-Or-Crook.html>.

DAN, Uri (Ariel Sharon's companion of combat). "Der Feind: Er ist ein Mörder — Im Todesbett ist Arafat dort, wo er hingehört". Die *Weltwoche*, Ausgabe 46/2004. Available at: <http://www.weltwoche.ch/ausgaben/2004–46/artikel-2004–46-er-ist-ein-moerder.html>.   Accessed 23 October 2015.

DAN, Zhang (Editor) "Failure of Hong Kong version of 'Color Revolution' would be a bliss". CCTV.com, 22 October 2014. Available at: <http://english.cntv.cn/2014/10/22/ARTI1413962823597930.shtml>.

DAVENPORT-HINES, Richard (Editor). *Capital Entrepreneurs and Profits*. London, 1990, pp. 145–146.

DAVIES, Nick. *Flat Earth News — An Award-winning Reporter Exposes Falsehood, Distortion and Propaganda in the Global Media*. London: Chatto & Windus, 2008, pp. 214, 230–231, 241–243.

Davos 2015: Nouriel Roubini says Income Inequality Creates U.S. Plutocracy". *Bloomberg Business*. Available at: <https://www.youtube.com/watch?v=t1Vv13XZ5Us>.

DAWISHA, Karen; PARROT, Bruce. *Russia and the New States of Eurasia: The Politics of Upheaval*. Cambridge: Press Syndicate of the University of Cambridge, 1995, pp. 210–211.

DEARDEN, Lizzie. "Jabhat al-Nusra seizes control of major Syrian government stronghold with rebel coalition — The city of Jisr al-Shughur lies on a strategic motorway from the capital to coast". *The Independent*, 25 April 2015. Available at: <http://www.independent.co.uk/news/world/middle-ast/jabhat-al-nusra-seizes-control-of-major-syrian-government-stronghold-with-jihadist-coalition-10203764.html>.

_____. "MH17 crash: Fragments of Russian missile BUK launcher found at crash site". *The Independent*, 11 August 2015. Available at: <http://www.independent.co.uk/news/world/europe/mh17-crash-investigators-find-parts-of-buk-missile-possibly-used-to-shoot-plane-down-10450053.html>. Accessed 12 August 2015.

Declaration of Establishment of State of Israel — 14 May 1948". *Israel Ministry of Foreign Affairs.* Available at: <http://www.mfa.gov.il/mfa/foreignpolicy/peace/guide/pages/declaration%20of%20establishment%20of%20state%20of%20israel.aspx>.

DEHGHAN, Saeed Kamali; NORTON-TAYLOR, Richard. "CIA admits role in 1953 Iranian coup — Declassified documents describe in detail how US — with British help — engineered coup against Mohammad Mosaddeq". *The Guardian,* 19 August 2013.

DELACENSERIE, Katie L.; (professor) OBERLY, James W.; WISCONSIN, Eau Claire. "Wall Street's Search for a Man on a White Horse: The Plot to Overthrow Franklin Delano Roosevelt". For Presentation to History 489. University of Wisconsin — Eau Claire. Spring 2008, p. 29.

DELLA PERGOLA, Sergio. "Jewish Demographic Policy Population Trends and options in Israel and in the diaspora". The Hebrew University of Jerusalem Editors Barry Geltman, rami Tal. *The Jewish People Policy Institute* (ppi) (established by the Jewish agency for Israel, Ltd). Available at: <http://jppi.org.il/uploads/Jewish_Demographic_Policies.pdf>.

DEMBITSKI, Alexander (CEIC Analyst). "The Economic Implications of Ukraine-Russia Trade Relations". *CEIC Russia Data Talk,* 8 July 2014. Available at: <http://www.ceicdata.com/en/blog/economic-implications-ukraine-russia-trade-relations.> And also in: <http://www.ceicdata.com/en/blog/economic-implications-ukraine-russia-trade-relations#sthash.bdvfLVlj.dpuf>.

Democratic vote, govt. without fascists needed in Ukraine before any talks". *RT,* 25 de March 2014. Available at: <http://rt.com/news/ukraine-government-fascists-gysi-997/>.

DEMPSEY, Judy. "Victory for Russia as the EU's Nabucco Gas Project Collapses". — *Carnegie Europe,* Monday, July 1, 2013. Available at: <http://carnegieeurope.eu/strategiceurope/?fa=52246>.

DENTON, Sally. *The Plots against the President — FDR, a Nation in Crisis, and the Rise of the American Right.* New York: Bloomsbury Press, 2012.

DESILVER, Drew. "5 facts about economic inequality". *Fact Tank — Pew Research Center,* 7 January 2014. Available at: <http://www.pewresearch.org/fact-tank/2014/01/07/5-facts-about-economic-inequality/>.

_____. "Who's poor in America? 50 years into the 'War on Poverty,' a data portrait". *PewResearch Center,* 13 January 2014. Available at: <http://www.pewresearch.org/fact-tank/2014/01/13/whos-poor-in-america-50-years-into-the-war-on-poverty-a-data-portrait/>.

DEUTSCHER, Isaac. *O judeu não-judeu e outros ensaios.* Rio de Janeiro: Civilização Brasileira, 1970, p. 30.

DEYOUNG, Karen. "Commander of U.S.-backed rebels captured by al-Qaeda militants in Syria". *The Washington Post,* July 30, 2015. "West suffers new Syria setback as US-trained rebels arrested". *The Times,* 21 September 2015. Available at: <http://www.thetimes.co.uk/tto/news/world/middleeast/article4562713.ec>.

DIAMOND, Jeremy. "Rand Paul skips hearing on State funding, hits Clinton on Benghazi". *CNN,* 22 April 2015. Available at: <http://www.nationalreview.com/corner/414500/hillary-clintons-top-aides-knew-first-minutes-benghazi-was-terrorist-attack-e-mails>.

DICKEL, Ralf *et al.* "Reducing European Dependence on Russian Gas: distinguishing natural gas security from geopolitics". *Oxford Institute for Energy Studies.* October 2014 OIES PAPER: NG 92. ISBN 978–78467-014–6. Available at: <http://www.oxfordenergy.org/wpcms/wp-content/uploads/2014/10/NG-92.pdf>.

DICKEY, Christopher. "Yulia Tymoshenko: She's No Angel". *The Daily Beast,* 23 February 2014. Available at: <http://www.thedailybeast.com/articles/2014/02/23/yulia-tymoshenko-she-s-no-angel.html>.

DIEHL, OLE. *Kiew und Moskau — Die ukrainisch-russischen Beziehung als zentrales Problem deutscher und europäischer Sicherheit.* Bonn: Forschungsinstitut der Deutschen Gesellschaft für Auswärtige Politik e. V., April 1994.

Diplomatische Bewegung in der Ukraine-Krise". *Tagsspiegel,* 20 February 2014. Available at: <http://www.tagesspiegel.de/politik/eu-aussenminister-in-kiew-diplomatische-bewegung-in-der-ukraine-krise/9513942.html>.

DOBBS, Michael (*Washington Post*). "In Bid to Support Yeltsin, IMF Lends Russia $10.2 Billion". *The Seattle Times*, 27 March 1996. Available at: <http://community.seattletimes.nwsource.com/archive/?date=19960327&slug=2321108>.

Document Office of Naval Intelligence Report on Russian Navy: The following is the Office of Naval Intelligence (ONI) report, The Russian Navy: A Historic Transition. U.S. Naval Institute". *USNI News.htm*, 18 December 2015. Available at <http://news.usni.org/2015/12/18/document-office-of-naval-intelligence-report-on-russian-navy>.

Documents: Bush's Grandfather Directed Bank Tied to Man Who Funded Hitler", 17 October 2003. Associated Press. Available at: <http://www.foxnews.com/story/2003/10/17/documents-bush-grandfather-directed-bank-tied-to-man-who-funded-hitler/>.

Dodd interview: Federated Press, January 7, 1938". *Apud* SELDES, George. *Facts and Fascism*. New York: In Fact, Inc., Fifth Edition, 1943, pp. 122–123.

DODD, JR William E.; DODD, Martha (Editors). *Ambassador Dodd's Diary*. London: Victor Gollancz Ltd., 1943.

DOLAN, Kerry A.; KROLL, Luisa. "Inside the 2014 Forbes Billionaires List: Facts And Figures". *Forbes*, 3 March 2014. Available at: <http://www.forbes.com/sites/luisakroll/2014/03/03/inside-the-2014-forbes-billionaires-list-facts-and-figures/>.

DOLGOV, Anna. "Russia's Igor Strelkov: I Am Responsible for War in Eastern Ukraine". *The Moscow Times*, 21 November 2014. Available at: <http://www.themoscowtimes.com/news/article/russias-igor-strelkov-i-am-responsible-for-war-in-eastern-ukraine/511584.html>.

Domestic Operational Law: The Posse Comitatus Act and Homeland Security. COL (Ret) John R. Brinkerhoff. Reprinted with permission from the *Journal of Homeland Security*. Newsletter 10–16 — December 2009. *Center for Army Lessons Learned*. Available at: <http://usacac.army.mil/cac2/call/docs/10–16/ch_12.asp>.

DORRIL, Stephen. *MI6 — Insaide the Covert World of Her Majesty's Secret Intelligence Service*. New York/London: The Free Press, 2000.

DOSTAL, Jörg Michael. "Post-independence Syria and the Great Powers (1946–1958): How Western Power Politics Pushed the Country Toward the Soviet Union". Paper Prepared for the 2014 Annual Meeting of the Academic Council on the United Nations System, June 19–21, 2014, Kadir Has University, Istanbul, Panel 14: Understanding and Responding to Crisis, Resistance and Extremism. Available at: <http://acuns.org/wp-content/uploads/2013/01/Syria-Paper-1946–1958-for-ACUNS-Conference-Website-12-June-2014.pdf>.

DREYFUSS, Bob. "The CIA Is Training Syria's Rebels: Uh-Oh, Says a Top Iraqi Leader". *The Nation*. 1 March 2013. Available at <http://www.thenation.com/blog/173149/cia-training-syrias-rebels-uh-oh-says-top-iraqi-leader#>.

DREZNER, Daniel W. *The Sanctions Paradox: Economic Statecraft and International Relations*. Cambridge Studies in International Relations — Economic Statecraft and International Relations. Cambridge University Press, pp. 203–205.

DROBNY, Sheldon. "Bob Novak Thinks Prescott Bush Was A Liberal". *Huffington Post*, 27 July 2007. Available at: <http://www.huffingtonpost.com/sheldon-drobny/bob-novak-thinks-prescott_b_58119.html>.

DUJARRIC, Stéphane. "Daily Press Briefing by the Office of the Spokesperson for the Secretary-General", 21 April 2015. Available at: <http://www.un.org/press/en/2015/db150421.doc.htm>.

DURHAM, Robert B. *False Flags, Covert Operations & Propaganda*. Raleigh, North Carolina: Lulu.com, 2014, p. 392.

DYER, Emily; KESSLER, Oren; WATERMAN, Kit; ABBOTT, Samuel James. *Terror in the Sinai*. London: The Henry Jackson Society, 2014, p. 4. Available at: <http://henryjacksonsociety.org/wp-content/uploads/2014/05/HJS-Terror-in-the-Sinai-Report-Colour-Web.pdf>.

DZARASOV, Rusland. "Cómo Rusia volvió al capitalismo". *Nueva Sociedad*, 253, Buenos Aires: Friedrich Ebert Stiftung, September/October 2014, pp. 120–135.

EAVIS, Peter. "Executive Pay: Invasion of the supersalaries". *The New York Times*, 12 April 2014.

EcoFinanças. Available at: <http://www.ecofinancas.com/noticias/moody-s-rebaixa-rating-soberano-ucrania-para-caa2/relacionadas>.

"Editors Christians Massacred by 'Free' Syrian Army Terrorists (Rebels)". OrtodoxNet.com.*Blog.* 24 August 2013. Available at: <http://www.orthodoxytoday.org/blog/2013/08/christians-massa cred-by-free-syrian-army-terrorists%2D%2Drebels/>.

EDWARDS, Maxim. "Symbolism of the Donetsk People's Republic". *OpenDemocracy,* 9 June 2014. Available at <https://www.opendemocracy.net/od-russia/maxim-edwards/symbolism-of-donetsk-people%E2%80%99s%2D%2Drepublic-flag-novorossiya>.

EIL — Kiew entsendet Blackwater-Söldner zur Unterdrückung der Proteste im Osten der Ukraine". *Sputnik* (RiaNovosti), 7 April 2014. Available at: <http://de.sputniknews.com/politik/ 20140407/268223480.html>.

EINHORN, Catrin; FAIRFIELD, Hannah; WALLACE, Tim. "Russia Rearms for a New Era". *The New York Times,* 24 December 2015. Available at: <http://www.nytimes.com/interactive/2015/ 12/24/world/asia/russia

_____. "Russia Rearms for a New Era". *The New York Times,* 24 December 2015. Available at: <http://www.nytimes.com/interactive/2015/12/24/world/asia/russiaarming.html?hp& action=click&pgtype=Homepage&clickSource=story-heading&module=photo-spot-region& region=top-news&WT.nav=top-news>.

Einsatz gegen Separatisten: Ukrainische Armee bekommt offenbar Unterstützung von US-Söldnern" *Spiegel Online,* 11 May 2014. Available at: <http://www.spiegel.de/politik/ ausland/ukraine-krise-400-us-soeldner-von-academi-kaempfen-gegen-separatisten-a-968745. html>.

"El PAK-FA tendrá un sistema que dejará indefenso cualquier objetivo". *RT* — 25 April 2014. Available at: <http://actualidad.rt.com/actualidad/view/126348-pak-fa-sistema-guerra-radioelectronica-guimalai?print=1>.

El-TABLAWY, Tarek. "Tripoli Clashes Toll Rises by 22 as Libya Crisis Deepens". *Bloomberg News,* 3 August 2014. Available at: <http://www.businessweek.com/news/2014–08-03/tripoli-fighting-death-toll-rises-by-22-as-libya-crisis-deepens>.

ELLIOTT, Larry (economics editor); PILKINGTON (editor). "New Oxfam report says half of global wealth held by the 1%". *The Guardian,* 19 January 2015.

EMERSON, Michael *et al. The Prospect of Deep Free Trade between the European Union and Ukraine.* Brussels: Centre for European Policy Studies (CEPS), 2006, pp. 150, 154 e 206.

EMMOTT, Robin (Brussels). "Q&A-What is Ukraine's association agreement with the EU?" *Reuters,* 26 June 2014. Available at: <http://www.reuters.com/article/2014/06/26/eu-ukraine-idUSL6N0P61N720140626>.

_____. *World News Report.* Available at: <http://world.einnews.com/article_detail/287643883/ 3njHxBQ7N2T1sbWX?n=2&code=P21DsWBPJxF7hfqq>.

ENGDAHL, F. William. *A Century of War — Anglo-American Oil Politics and the New World War.* Ebner Ulm (Germany): Dr. BöttingerVerlag GmbH, 1993, pp. 133–137.

ENTOUS, Adam; MALAS, Nour; COKER, Margaret. "A Veteran Saudi Power Player Works To Build Support to Topple Assad". *Wall Street Journal — Middle East News,* 25 August 2013. Available   at: <http://online.wsj.com/news/articles/ SB10001424127887323423804579024452583045962>.

"Entrevista de Eric Hobsbawm a Martin Granovsky". *Page 12*, Buenos Aires, 29 March 2009.

EPA/Sergey Dolzhenko. "According to the General Staff, there are also facts of participation of private military companies in the Ukrainian events". *TASS,* 23 May 2014. Available at: <http:// tass.ru/en/world/732817>.

"Erdogan usa a al-Qaeda para encobrir sua invasão à Síria". *Pravda,* 30 May 2014, (Edição em português). Available at: <http://port.pravda.ru/busines/30–03-2014/36510-erdogan-0/>.

ERDOĞDU, Erkan. "Bypassing Russia: Nabucco project and its implications for the European gas security". MPRA Paper from University Library of Munich, Germany. Published in *Renewable and Sustainable Energy Reviews*, 9.14(2010): pp. 2936–2945. Available at: <http://econpapers. repec.org/paper/pramprapa/26793.htm>.

ERLANGER, Steven; MYERS, Steven Lee. "NATO Allies Oppose Bush on Georgia and Ukraine". *The New York Times*, 3 April 2008.

"Alt-Kanzler Schröder macht EU für Ukraine-Krise verantwortlich." Welt am Sonntag. Available at: <http://deutsche-wirtschafts-nachrichten.de/2014/05/11/alt-kanzler-schroeder-macht-eu-fuer-ukraine-krise-verantwortlich>.

EU-Ukraine Association Agreement — the complete texts. Available at: <http://eeas.europa.eu/ukraine/assoagreement/assoagreement-2013_en.htm>.

"Europe's boat people — The EU's policy on maritime refugees has gone disastrously wrong". *The Economist. Europe in Trouble*, 11 April 2015. Available at: <http://www.economist.com/news/leaders/21649465-eus-policy-maritime-refugees-has-gone-disastrously-wrong-europes-boat-people>.

European Commission — Monitoring Agri-trade Policy (MAP — 2014) — Agricultural trade in 2013: EU gains in commodity exports. Available ate: <http://ec.europa.eu/agriculture/trade-analysis/map/2014–1_en.pdf>.

EVANS-PRITCHARD, Ambrose. "Saudis offer Russia secret oil deal if it drops Syria Saudi Arabia has secretly offered Russia a sweeping deal to control the global oil market and safeguard Russia's gas contracts, if the Kremlin backs away from the Assad regime in Syria". *The Telegraph*, 27 August 2013.

EVANS, Rachel. "Russia Sanctions Accelerate Risk to Dollar Dominance". *Bloomberg*, 6 August 2014. Available at: <http://www.bloomberg.com/news/2014–08-06/russia-sanctions-acceler ate-risk-to-dollar-dominance.html>.

Everything you need to know about Crimea. Why is the Crimean peninsula part of Ukraine? Why does Russia have military presence there? Here is a short guide for the perplexed". *Há'aretz*, 11 March 2014. Available at: <http://www.haaretz.com/world-news/1.577286>.

"Ex-PM da Alemanha. 'Culpa do que se passa na Ucrânia é da EU', diz Schroeder". Diário de Notícias/Globo, 11 May 2014. Available at: <http://www.dn.pt/inicio/globo/interior.aspx?con tent_id=3856448&seccao=Europa&page=-1>.

"Ex-U.S. President Jimmy Carter Says Situation in Gaza Is 'Intolerable'. Speaking at a press conference in Ramallah, Carter lamented that 'not one destroyed house has been rebuilt' in Gaza since the war last summer". *Há'aretz & The Associated Press,* 2 May 2015. Available at: <http://www.haaretz.com/israel-news/1.654622>.

"Experts clash over Palestinian demographic statistics on eve of 2015, Israel's population hits 8.3 million — Data predicted equal Jewish, Arab population in Israel and territories by 2016". *The Jerusalem Post,* 22 October 2015 I 9 Heshvan, 5776. Available at: <http://www.jpost.com/Middle-East/Experts-clash-over-Palestinian-demographic-statistics-386443>.

"Factbox: Russia's S-400 Air-Defense Missile System". *The Moscow Times*, 26 November 2014. Available at: <http://www.themoscowtimes.com/business/article/factbox-russia-s-s-400-air-defense-missile-system/511884.html>.

"Factsheet: Russia Europe liquid relationship often overlooked". *Clingendael International Energy Programme (CIEP).* Available at: <http://www.clingendaelenergy.com/files.cfm?event=files. download&ui=9C1E06F0–5254-00CF-FD03A39927F34043>.

"Factsheet: The Case against Shell". Consortiumnews.com. Available at: <https://ccrjustice.org/learn-more/faqs/factsheet%3A-case-against-shell-0>.

FAHIM, Kareem. "Saudis Face Mounting Pressure over Civilian Deaths in Yemen Conflict". *The New York Times,* 29 September 2015.

FAQs: The Military Commissions Act". *Center for Constitutional Rights.* Available at: <http://ccrjustice.org/learn-more/faqs/faqs%3A-military-commisions-act>.

Fareed Zakaria: During the revolutions of 1989, you funded a lot of dissident activities, civil society groups in eastern Europe; Poland, the Czech Republic. Are you doing similar things in Ukraine? Soros: I set up a foundation in Ukraine before Ukraine became independent of Russia. And the foundation has been functioning ever since and played an important part in events now", "Soros on Russian ethnic nationalism". *CNN*, 25 May 2014. Available at: <http://cnnpressroom.blogs. cnn.com/2014/05/25/soros-on-russian-ethnic-nationalism/>.

FARIS, Hani A. *The Failure of the Two-State Solution*: *The Prospects of One State in the Israel-Palestine Conflict*. New York: I.B.Tauris & Co Ltd, 201.

FARREL, Nicholas. "Libya's boat people and Italy's tragic folly. The 'mare nostrum' policy has acted as a magnet for boat people; the crisis is only growing". *The Spectator,* 6 September 2014. Available at: <http://www.spectator.co.uk/features/9303722/italys-decriminalising-of-illegal-immigration-has-acted-as-a-green-light-to-boat-people/>.

FARSAKH, Leila (Research fellow at the Trans-Arab Research Institute, Boston). "The Palestinian Economy and the Oslo Peace Process". *Trans-Arab Institute (TARI)*. Available at: <http://tari.org/index.php?option=com_content&view=article&id=9&Itemid=11>.

Federal Debt Clock. Available at: <http://www.usgovernmentdebt.us/>.

FEDERMAN, Josef (Jerusalem). "Netanyahu appointment casts cloud over US visit". *Associated Press — The Washington Post*, 5 November 2015.

FELGENHAUER, Tyler. "Ukraine, Russia, and the Black Sea Fleet Accords". *WWS Case Study 2/99*. Available at: <http://www.dtic.mil/dtic/tr/fulltext/u2/a360381.pdf>.

FERGIANI, Mohammed Bescir. *The Lybian Jamahiriya*. London: Darf Publishers Ltd., 1983, pp. 46–70, 102–109.

FERREIRA, Argemiro — "Documentos secretos revelam mais truques sujos planejados nos EUA para derrubar Fidel", *in*: *Tribuna da Imprensa*, Rio de Janeiro, 5 January 1998.

FEST, Joachim C. *Hitler*. London: Penguin Books, 1974, p. 653.

FEYGIN, Yakov. "Ukraine is stuck in a post-Soviet condition". *OpenDemocracy*, 12 March 2014. Available at: <https://www.opendemocracy.net/od-russia/yakov-feygin/ukraine-is-stuck-in-post-soviet-condition-east-vs-west-ukrainian-economy>.

"Final Report of the Task Force on Combating Terrorist and Foreign Fighter Travel". *Homeland Security Committee — U.S. House of Representatives*, 29 September 2015. Available at: <https://homeland.house.gov/wp-content/uploads/2015/09/TaskForceFinalReport.pdf>, pp. 11–12. Accessed 28 September 2015.

"Final Report of the Task Force on Combating Terrorist and Foreign Fighter Travel". *Homeland Security Committee — U.S. House of Representatives*, 29 September 2015. Available at: <https://homeland.house.gov/wp-content/uploads/2015/09/TaskForceFinalReport.pdf, pp. 11–12>.

FIORI, Jose Luís. "A Lenda dos Peregrinos". *Valor Econômico*, São Paulo, 13 September 2006.

FISCHBACH, Michael R. *Records of Dispossession*: *Palestinian Refugee Property and the Arab-Israeli Conflict*. New York: Columbia University Press, 2003.

FISHER, Alan W. *The Crimean Tatars*. California: Hoover Institution on Revolution and Peace — Stanford University — Hoover Institution Press, 1978, pp. 37–38.

FISHER, Matthew. "Canadians take part in NATO war games aimed at sending message to Russia over Ukraine aggression". *National Post*, 25 May 2015. Available at: <http://news.nationalpost.com/news/world/canadians-take-part-in-nato-war-games-aimed-at-sending-message-to-russia-over-ukraine-aggression>. Accessed 2 September 2015.

FISHER, Max. "Ḥamās is not ISIS. Here's why Netanyahu says it is anyway". *Vox — Israel-Palestine Conflict,* 25 August 2014. Available at: <http://www.vox.com/2014/8/25/6064467/no-netanyahu-Ḥamās-is-not-isis-isis-is-not-Ḥamās>.

_____. "This one map helps explain Ukraine's protests". *The Washington Post*, 9 December 2013. Available at: <https://www.washingtonpost.com/blogs/worldviews/wp/2013/12/09/this-one-map-helps-explain-ukraines-protests/>.

FLAMINI, Roland. "Crimea: Putin's War for Oil and Gas?" — *World Affairs — Corridors of Power*, 20 May 2014. Available at: <http://www.worldaffairsjournal.org/blog/roland-flamini/crimea-putins-war-oil-and-gas>.

"Flashback 2011: Hillary Clinton Laughs About Killing Moammar Gaddafi: 'We Came, We Saw, He Died!'". *Real Clear Politics* (Video), 19 June 2015. Available at: <http://www.realclearpolitics.com/video/2015/06/19/flashback_2011_hillary_clinton_laughs_about_killing_moammar_gaddafi_we_came_we_saw_he_died.html>.

Focus Economics — Economic Forecasts from the World's Leading Economists, 6 October 2015. Available at: <http://www.focus-economics.com/countries/ukrain>.

"Follow the Enron Money". *CBS,* 12 January 2002. Available at: <http://www.cbsnews.com/news/follow-the-enron-money/>.

FONER, Eric. *The Story of American Freedom.* New York/London: W. W. Norton & Company, 1998, pp. 327–332.

"Forbes Billionaires 2015: Which Billionaires Lost The Most Money — Rinat Akhmetov on Forbes Lists". Available at: <http://www.forbes.com/profile/rinat-akhmetov/>.

"Former Policy-Makers Voice Concern over NATO Expansion". *Open Letter to President Clinton,* 26 June 1997. Available at: <http://www.bu.edu/globalbeat/nato/postpone062697>.

FOWLER, Don. *Lucretius on Atomic Motion*: *A Commentary on De Rerum Natura.* Book Two — Lines 1–332. Oxford: Oxford University Press, 2002, p. 10.

FOX, Steve. "Libya burns as politicians and militia groups vie for control". *Middle East Eye,* 24 August 2014. Accessed 2 December 2014. Available at: <http://www.middleeasteye.net/news/politicians-and-militia-groups-vie-control-battle-torn-libya-99372368>.

FRANKS, Sandy; NUNNALLY, Sara. *Barbarians of Oil*: *How the World's Oil Addiction Threatens Global Prosperity and Four Investments to Protect Your Wealth.* Hoboken-New Jersey: John Wiley & Sons Inc, United States, 2011, pp. 135–138, 150–151.

"Free Syrian Army will not join US-led coalition against IS". *Nairaland,* 14 September 2014. Available at: <http://www.nairaland.com/1902522/free-syrian-army-not-join>.

FREELAND, Chrystia. "Lunch with the FT — Tea with the FT: Yulia Tymoshenko". *The Financial Times,* 16 August 2008. Available at: <http://www.ft.com/cms/s/0/f4b1341a-6a58–11dd-83e8–0000779fd18c.html>.

FRÈRE, Jacques. "Ukraine / Donbass: Debaltsevo est libérée!" *NationsPresse,* 17 February 2015. Available at: <www.nationspresse.info/. . ./ukraine-donbass-debaltsevo>.

"Friedensprozess: Scharon spricht von historischer Wende". *Spiegel Online,* 11 November 2004. Available at: <http://www.spiegel.de/politik/ausland/friedensprozess-scharon-spricht-von-historischer-wende-a-327352.html>.

FRIEDGUT, Theodore H. *Iuzovka and Revolution, vol. I*: *Life and Work in Russia's Donbass, 1869–1924.* Studies of the Harriman Institute at Columbia — University Princeton / New Jersey: Princeton University Press, 1989.

FRIEDMAN, George. "Kosovar Independence and the Russian Reaction". *Stratfor — Geopolitical Weekly,* 20 February 2008. Available at: <http://www.stratfor.com/weekly/kosovar_independence_and_russian_reaction#axzz3DObNowiM>.

_____. "Russia Examines Its Options for Responding to Ukraine". *Stratfor — Geopolitical Weekly,* 18 March 2014. Available at: <http://www.stratfor.com/weekly/russia-examines-its-options-responding-ukraine#axzz38IEGZtks>.

FRIEDMAN, Thomas L. "Foreign Affairs: Now a Word From X". *The New York Times,* 2 May 1998. Available at: <http://www.nytimes.com/1998/05/02/opinion/foreign-affairs-now-a-word-from-x.html>.

_____. "President Obama Talks to Thomas L. Friedman about Iraq, Putin and Israel". *The New York Times,* 8 August 2014.

"Frigid fighting: Russian Arctic war games top off new base voyage". *RT,* 29 September 2014. Available at: <http://rt.com/news/191536-arctic-mission-drills-missile/>.

FUKUYAMA, Francis. *Political Order and Political Decay — From the Industrial Revolution to the Globalization of Democracy.* New York: Farrar, Straus & Giroux, 2014, pp. 461–462, 487.

_____. *The End of History and the Last man.* London: Penguin Books, 1992.

"Full Text of 'Netanyahu's Foreign Policy Speech at Bar Ilan'". *Há'aretz,* 14 June 2009. Available at: <http://www.haaretz.com/news/full-text-of-netanyahu-s-foreign-policy-speech-at-bar-ilan-1.277922>.

"Full Text of 'U.N. report on the alleged use of chemical weapons in Syria'". United Nations Mission to Investigate Allegations of the Use of Chemical Weapons the Syrian Arab Republic Report on the Alleged Use of Chemical Weapons in the Ghouta Area of Damascus on 21 August

2013. *Internet Archive*. Available at: <https://archive.org/stream/787426-u-n-report-on-the-alleged-use-of-chemical/787426-u-n-report-on-the-alleged-use-of-chemical_djvu.txt>.

"Full text of the 'interview of President Assad to Izvestia — President of the Syrian Arab Republic told about threat of US invasion, about his relationship with Putin and about common fate of Russian and Syrian people'". All in exclusive interview in *Izvestia,* 26 August 2013. *The Saker's 2nd blog. Monthly Archives*: August 2013. Available at: <http://thesaker.wordpress.com/2013/08/page/2/>.

FULLER, Graham E. (ex-vice-presidente do National Intelligence Council at the CIA). "Bush Must See Past the Acts of Terror to the Root Causes". *Los Angeles Times,* 29 January 2002. Available at: <ttp://articles.latimes.com/2002/jan/29/opinion/oe-fuller29>.

GALBERT, Simond de. *A Year of Sanctions against Russia — Now What?: A European Assessment of the Outcome and Future of Russia Sanctions*. Washington: Center for Strategic and International Studies, 2015, pp. 8–9.

GAMIO, Lazaro; JOHNSON, Richard; TAYLOR, Adam. "The crisis in Gaza". *The Washington Post,* 1 August 2014. Available at: <http://www.washingtonpost.com/wp-srv/special/world/the-gaza-crisis/>. Accessed 3 November 2012.

GANSER, Daniele. *NATO — Geheimarmeen in Europe. Inszenierter Terror und verdeckte Kriegsführung*. Zürich: Orell Füsli Verlag AG, 2014, pp. 42–55, 96–97, 102–110.

GARAMONE, Jim. "Russian Aircraft Flies Near U.S. Navy Ship in Black Sea". *American Forces Press Service — US Department of Defense,* Washington, 14 April 2014. Available at: <http://www.defense.gov/news/newsarticle.aspx?id=122052>.

GARAUDY, Roger. "The Myth of a Land without People for a People without land". *The Holocaust Historiography (Project)*. Available at: <http://www.historiography-project.com/jhrchives/v18/v18n5p38_Garaudy.html>.

GARB, Paula. "The View from Abkhazia and South Ossetia Ablaze", *in*: ABLAZE, Georgia. *War and Revolution in Caucasus* (Edited by Stephan F. Jones). London/New York: Routledge, 2010, pp. 140–149.

GATES, Robert. *Duty — Memoirs of a Secretary at War*. New York: Alfred A. Knopf, 2014.

GAVLAK, Dale; ABABNEH, Yahya. "Exclusive: Syrians in Ghouta Claim Saudi-Supplied Rebels behind Chemical Attack. Rebels and local residents in Ghouta accuse Saudi Prince Bandar bin Sultan of providing chemical weapons to an al-Qaida linked rebel group". *MintPress News,* 29 August 2013. Available at: <http://www.mintpressnews.com/witnesses-of-gas-attack-say-saudis-supplied-rebels-with-chemical-weapons/168135/>.

"Gaza crisis: Toll of operations in Gaza". *BBC News,* 1 September 2014. Available at: <http://www.bbc.com/news/world-middle-east-28439404>. Accessed 1 November 2015.

"Gaza Economy on the Verge of Collapse, Youth Unemployment Highest in the Region at 60 Percent". *World Bank,* 21 May 2015. Available at: <http://www.worldbank.org/en/news/press-release/2015/05/21/gaza-economy-on-the-verge-of-collapse>.

"Gazprom and CNPC sign memorandum on gas deliveries from Russia's Far East to China — Russia's gas major Gazprom and the Chinese National Oil and Gas Company have signed a Memorandum of Understanding on natural gas supplies from Russia to China and to build a pipeline to the Far East". *TASS,* 3 September 2014. Available at: <http://tass.ru/en/economy/818493>.

Gazprom Export — Transportation. Available at: <http://www.gazpromexport.ru/en/projects/transportation/>.

"Gazprom, BASF, E.ON, ENGIE, OMV and Shell sign Shareholders Agreement on Nord Stream II project". *Gazprom,* 4 September 2015. Available at: <http://www.gazprom.com/press/news/2015/september/article245837/>.

GEARAN, Anne. "In recording of U.S. diplomat, blunt talk on Ukraine". *The Washington Post,* 6 February 2014.

GEBRIAL, Dalia. "Unrecovered and Unremembered: Gaza One Year After Operation Protective Edge". *Egyptian Streets,* 31 July 2015. Available at: <http://egyptianstreets.com/2015/07/31/unrecovered-and-unremembered-gaza-one-year-after-operation-protective-edge/>.

Gefechte im Osten: 730.000 Ukrainer wandern nach Russland aus. Seit Jahresbeginn sind rund 730.000 Menschen aus der Ukraine nach Russland ausgewandert. Das Uno-Flüchtlingswerk hält die Zahlen aus Moskau für glaubwürdig". *Spiegel Online,* Dienstag, 5 August 2014. Available at: <http://www.spiegel.de/politik/ausland/kaempfe-im-osten-730–000-ukrainer-fliehen-nach-russland-a%2D%2D984567.html>.

GEHA, Rani. "Russian President, Saudi Spy Chief Discussed Syria, Egypt". *Al-Monitor*, 22 August 2013. Available at: <http://www.al-monitor.com/pulse/politics/2013/08/saudi-russia-putin-bandar-meeting-syria-egypt.html#>.

GEHLEN, Reinhard. *Dee*herbund, 1971.

GENESIS — Kapitel 15:18–21 — Die Heilige Schrift des Alten und Neuen Testaments. Aschaffenburg: Paul Pattloch Verlag, 17. Auflage, 1965, p. 15.

GEODAKYAN, Artyom. "Lavrov: trends of color revolutions and democracy export can be changed. The Russian foreign minister said the Ukrainian conflict also erupted under outside pressure on Kiev". *ITAR-TASS*, 12 December 2014. Available at: <http://tass.ru/en/world/766611>.

George Bush, Address Before a Joint Session of Congress (September 11, 1990)". *Miller Center — University of Virginia*. Available at: <http://millercenter.org/president/bush/speeches/speech-3425>.

"George Friedman Viewing Russia from the Inside Stratfor — Global Intelligence". *Geopolitical Weekly*, 16 December 2014. Available at: <https://www.stratfor.com/weekly/viewing-russia-inside#>.

GERLACH, Thomas; SCHMIDT, Gert. *Ukraine: zwischen den Karpaten und dem Schwarzen Meer*. Berlin: Trescher Verlag, pp. 448–449.

German trade group BGA warns sanctions 'life-threatening' to Russia, hurting Germany". *DW (Deutsche Welle)*, 12 March 2014). Available at: <http://www.dw.de/german-trade-group-bga-warns-sanctions-life-threatening-to-russia-hurting-germany/a-17492056>.

German-Foreign-Policy.com. 10 April 2014. Available at: <http://www.german-foreign-policy.com/en/fulltext/58837/print>.

"Germany Government Debt to GDP 1995–2015 I Data I Chart I Calendar". *Trading Economics*. Available at: <http://www.tradingeconomics.com/germany/government-debt-to-gdp>.

"Germany negotiates air base lease with Uzbekistan". *NEOnline* I TB. Available at: <http://neurope.eu/article/germany-negotiates-air-base-lease-uzbekistan/>.

GIACOMO, Carol. "Joe Biden Apologizes for Telling the Truth". *The New York Times — The Opinion Pages*, 6 October 2014.

GLABERSON, William. "Obama Faces Court Test over Detainee". *The New York Times*, 28 July 2009.

GLEDHILL, Ruth. "Russian action in Syria offers hope, claims Catholic bishop". *Christian Today*, 19 February 2016. Available at: <http://www.christiantoday.com/article/russian.action.in.syria.offers.hope.claims.catholic.bishop/80213.htm>.

GOLDBERG, Jeffrey. "How Much Does It Cost to Be Ambassador to Hungary?" *Bloomberg*, Feb 11, 2014. Available at: <http://www.bloombergview.com/articles/2014-02-11/how-much-does-it-cost-to-be-ambassador-to-hungary->.

GOLDWATER, Barry M. *With No Apologies — The Outspoken Political Memoirs of America's Conservative Conscience*. New York: Berkley Books, 1979.

GONZÁLEZ, Francisco J. Ruiz. "La Arquitectura de Seguridad Europea: Un Sistema Imperfecto e Inacabado" — De la Caída del Muro de Berlín (1989) a la Guerra De Georgia (2008). Tesis Doctoral. Universidad Nacional de Educación a Distancia. Instituto Universitario General Gutiérrez Mellado, 2012 pp. 168–160. Available at: <http://e-spacio.uned.es/fez/eserv/tesisuned:IUGM-Fjruiz/Documento.pdf>.

"Gorbachev: Putin saved Russia from disintegration". *RT*, 27 December 2014. Available at: <http://rt.com/news/217931-gorbachev-putin-saved-russia/>.

GORDON, Michael R. "Anatomy of a Misunderstanding". *The New York*, 25 May 1997.

_____. "U.S. Steps Up Aid to Syrian Opposition, Pledging $60 Million". *The New York Times*, 28 February 2013.

GORMAN, Siobhan; ENTOUS, Adam. "CIA Plans Yemen Drone Strikes — Covert Program Would Be a Major Expansion of U.S. Efforts to Kill Members of al Qaeda Branch". *The Wall Street Journal*, 14 June 2011.

GORODETSKY, Gabriel. *Grande Delusion. Stalin and the German Invasion of Russia*. New Haven, London: Yale University Press, 1999, pp. 299–300.

Governance — Presidential Approval Ratings — George W. Bush. *Gallup Poll*. Available at: <http://www.gallup.com/poll/116500/presidential-approval-ratings-george%2D%2Dbush. aspx>.

GRESSEL, Gustav. "Russia's post-Cold War borders. Russia's Quiet Military Revolution, and What It Means For Europe". *European Council on Foreign Relations (ECFR)*, 143, pp. 1–17. Available at: <http://www.ecfr.eu/page/-/Russias_Quiet_Military_Revolution.pdf>.

GRETA LYNN, Uehling. *Beyond Memory: The Crimean Tatars' Deportation and Return*. New York: Palgrave Macmillan, 2004, pp. 3–4.

"Gross Domestic Product (GDP) in Ukraine — GDP of Ukraine, 1990–2013". *World macroeconomic research*. Available at: <http://kushnirs.org/macroeconomics/gdp/gdp_ukraine.html>.

"Gross Domestic Product & Corporate Profits: Second Quarter 2008 (Preliminary)". *US Bureau of Economic Analysis*. Available at: <http://bea.gov/newsreleases/national/gdp/2008/gdp208p. htm>.

"Gross Domestic Product: Fourth Quarter 2008 (Final) Corporate Profits: Fourth Quarter 2008 (Final)". *US Bureau of Economic Analysis*. Available at: <http://www.bea.gov/newsreleases/ national/gdp/2009/pdf/gdp408f.pdf>.

GUIMARÃES, Leonam dos Santos (Diretor de Planejamento, Gestão e Meio Ambiente — Eletrobrás Termonuclear SA — Eletronuclear). "O Retorno de Giges à Caverna Nuclear". *DefesaNet*, 10 July 2015. Available at: <http://www.defesanet.com.br/nuclear/noticia/19703/ O-Retorno-de-Giges-a-Caverna%2D%2DNuclear/>.

GUIMOND, DanleMiel. "UKRAINE — Crimes de guerre de l'OTAN à Debaltsevo? Joe Biden redessine la carte de Lvov à Kahrkiv". ESC_Niouze, 9 February 2015. Available at: <https:// entretiensentresoi.wordpress.com/2015/02/09/ukraine-que-peut-bien-cacher-lotan-a-debaltsevo/>.

GUNEEV, Sergey. "German Businesses Suffer Losses Due to EU Anti-Russia Sanctions: Official. *Sputnik*, 14 January 2015. Available at: <http://sputniknews.com/business/20150114/ 1016894488.html>.

HAINES, John. "Ukraine — Still Here After Autumn?" *The Foreign Policy Research Institute* (FPRI), May 2014. Available at: <http://www.fpri.org/articles/2014/05/ukraine-still-here-after-autumn>.

HALL, John (for *MailOnline*). "Meet the Peshmerga's International Brigade: From IT workers to ex-soldiers, the men from the West teaming up with Kurdish forces to fight ISIS." *MailOnline*, 21 April 2015. Available at: <http://www.dailymail.co.uk/news/article-3049019/Peshmerga-s-foreign-legion-fighting-alongside-defeat-ISIS-workers-ex-soldiers-brave-men-world-teaming-Kurdish-forces.html>.

Hamburger Abendblatt. Available at: <http://www.abendblatt.de/politik/article126202086/Gregor-Gysi-Sanktionen-gegen-Russland-verschaerfen-die-Krise.html>.

HANNA, Jason; REBAZA, Claudia. "MH17 investigators: Possible missile parts found". *CNN*, 11 August 2015. Available at: <http://edition.cnn.com/2015/08/11/europe/mh17-investigation/ index.html>. Accessed 12 August 2015.

HARDING, Luke (Luhansk). "Ukraine's government has lost control of east, says acting president — Oleksandr Turchynov says security forces are unable to control situation in Donetsk and Luhansk regions". *The Guardian*, 30 April 2014. Available at: <http://www.theguardian.com/ world/2014/apr/30/ukraine-government-lost-control-east-acting-president — Alec Luhn>.

_____. "Russian aid convoy heads for Ukraine amid doubts over lorries' contents — Kiev says it will turn back shipment which Moscow describes as humanitarian but which west says could be prelude to invasion". *The Guardian*, 12 August 2014.

_____. "Ukraine extends lease for Russia's Black Sea Fleet. Deal with new President Viktor Yanukovych to cut Russian gas prices sees Ukraine tilt backs towards Moscow". *The Guardian*, 21 April 2010.

HARDISTY, Jean; BERLET, Chip. Exporting Right-Wing Christianity. *Jean Hardisty*. Available at: <http://www.jeanhardisty.com/writing/articles-chapters-and-reports/exporting-right-wing-christianity/>.

HARNDEN, Toby (Washington). "Bush sees Arafat as irrelevant". *The Telegraph*, 6 June 2002. Available at: <http://www.telegraph.co.uk/news/worldnews/middleeast/israel/1396455/Bush-sees-Arafat-as-irrelevant.html>.

HARRESS, Christopher. "Amid NATO Threats, Russia New Air Bases Could Open Across Eastern Europe And Central Asia". *International Business Times*, 9 September 2015. Available at: <http://www.ibtimes.com/amid-nato-threats-russia-new-air-bases-could-open-across-east ern-europe-central-asia-2088746>.

HARTMANN, Thom. "Reaganomics killed America's middle class. This country's fate was sealed when our government slashed taxes on the rich back in 1980". *Salon*, 19 April 2014. Available at: <http://www.salon.com/2014/04/19/reaganomics_killed_americas_middle_class_partner/>.

HASSAN, Amro (Cairo). "Libya's parliament ducks fighting to meet in eastern city of Tobruk". *Los Angeles Times*, 2 August 2014. Available at: <http://www.latimes.com/world/middleeast/la-fg-libya-parliament-tobruk-20140802-story.html>.

HASSEL, Florian (Donezk). "Igor Strelkow, Kommandeur in der Ostukraine, der Mann hinter der Schreckensherrschaft". *Süddeutsche Zeitung*, 12 May 2014. Available at <http://www. sueddeutsche.de/politik/igor-strelkow-kommandeur-in-der-ostukraine-der-mann-hinter-der-schreckensherrschaft-1.1958675>. Accessed 14 February 2016.

HATCHETT, Ronald. "Yeltsin: Fighting To Stay On Top". JOC.com, 18 August 1992. Available at: <http://www.joc.com/yeltsin-fighting-stay-top_19920818.html>.

HAWRYLYSHYN, Bohdan. *Ten years of work on behalf of Ukraine*: notable highlights. Part II. A Washington dinner. Available at: <http://www.ukrweekly.com/old/archive/1999/099921. shtml>.

HECKER, Siegfried S. "For U.S. and Russia, Isolation Can Lead to Nuclear Catastrophe". *The New York Times*, 18 November 2014.

HEDGES, Chris. *American Fascists — The Christian Right and the War on America*. New York: Free Press, 2006.

HEGEL, George Wilhelm Friedrich. *Wissenschaft der Logik:Die Lehre von Sein (1832)*. (Neu herausgegeben von Hans-Jürgen Gawoll). Hamburg: Felix Meiner Verlag, 1990, pp. 198–203, 241–244.

HEILBRUNN, Jacob. "The Interview: Henry Kissinger". *The National Interest*, September/October 2015. Available at <http://nationalinterest.org/print/feature/the-interview-henry-kissin ger-13615>.

HELLER, Aron. "Peres: Netanyahu was never sincere about making peace. Ex-president says PM's overtures have never 'escaped the domain of talking', and warns against his notion of contin-ually 'living by the sword'". *The Times of Israel*, 2 November 2015. Available at: <http://www. timesofisrael.com/peres-netanyahu-was-never-sincere-about-making-peace/?utm_source=dlvr. it&utm_medium=twitter>.

HENDERSON, Andrew. "Russia vs. the petrodollar: the latest reserve currency meltdown". *Nomad Capitalist*. Available at: <http://nomadcapitalist.com/2014/08/08/russia-vs-petrodollar-latest-reserve-currency-meltdown/>.

HENDERSON, Dean. *The Federal Reserve Cartel*. Estados Unidos: Jill Henderson, 2010, pp. 28–30.

HENNINGSEN, Patrick. "Saudi Prince Bandar's second attempt at bribing Russia to drop support of Syria". *21st Century Wire*, 27 August 2013. Available at: <http://21stcenturywire.com/2013/08/27/saudi-prince-bandars-second-attempt-at-bribing-russia-to-drop-support-of-syria/>.

HERRIDGE, Catherine; BROWNE, Pamela (Fox Business). "Exclusive: The Arming of Benghazi — The United States supported the secret supply of weapons to Libyan rebels while Hillary Clinton was Secretary of State according to federal court documents obtained by Fox News. In a sworn declaration". *Benghazi Accountability Coalition,* 29 June 2015. Available at: <http://benghazicoalition.org/>.

HERSH, Seymour M. "Annals of National Security — The Redirection. Is the Administration's new policy benefitting our enemies in the war on terrorism?" *The New Yorker,* 5 March 2007 Issue. Available at: <http://www.newyorker.com/magazine/2007/03/05/the-redirection?currentPage=all>.

_____. "The Red Line and the Rat Line". *London Review of Books*, 6 April 2014. Available at: <http://www.lrb.co.uk/2014/04/06/seymour-m-hersh/the-red-line-and-the-rat-line>.

_____. "Whose sarin?" *London Review of Books*, 19 December 2013, Vol. 35, no. 24, pp. 9–12.

HERSZENHORN, David M. "I.M.F. Criticizes Ukraine Plan for Economy". *The New York Times*, 19 December 2013.

HIGGINS, Andrew; KRAMERFEB, Andrew E. "Archrival Is Freed as Ukraine Leader Flees". *The New York Times*, 22 February 2014.

"High court judge orders Goldman Sachs to disclose Libya profits — Libyan sovereign wealth fund, which is suing Goldman, estimates the US investment bank made $350m in upfront profit on nine derivatives products". *The Guardian*, 24 November 2014.

HIGHAM, Charles. *Trading with the Enemy — How the Allied Multinationals supplied Nazi Germany through World War Two — An Expose of the American Money Plot — 1933–1949*. London: Robert Hale, 1983.

HILL, Henryk. *Second Polish Republic-The Book. Chapter 20: War crimes and atrocities*. Available at: <https://sites.google.com/a/secondpolishrepublic.net.pe/second-polish-republic-the-book/chapter-20 —>.

HILLE, Kathrin (Moscow). "The pursuit of Yukos' wealth". *Financial Times*, 12 January 2014. Available at: <http://www.ft.com/cms/s/0/d4658d96–7b7d-11e3–84af-00144feabdc0.html#axzz3EWrKjn6p>.

_____. "Ukrainian port is key to Russia's naval power". *The Financial Times*, 27 February 2014. Available at: <http://www.ft.com/cms/s/0/1f749b24–9f8c-11e3-b6c7–00144feab7de.html#axzz3X7DJLGGh>.

HIRSH, Michael; OLIPHANT, James. "Obama Will Never End the War on Terror — The president stands to leave an open-ended conflict to his successor". *National Journal*, 27 February 2014. Available at: <http://www.nationaljournal.com/magazine/obama-will-never-end-the-war-on-terror-20140227>.

HODGE, Carl Cavanagh; NOLAN, Cathal J. *US Presidents and Foreign Policy — 1789 to the Present*. Santa Barbara (California): ABC-CLIO, pp. 58-59.

HOEFLE, John. "LaRouche: Return to FDR's Glass-Steagall Standard Now!" *Executive Intelligence Review,* 16 October 2009. Available at: <http://www.larouchepub.com/other/2009/3640return_glass-steagall.html>.

HOFT, Jim. "More Emails Prove Hillary Clinton & Obama KNEW Benghazi Terror Attack Was Planned by Al-Qaeda Group — *FOX News* confirmed Monday that the US ran guns from Benghazi to Syria before the attack on the US consulate on September 11, 2012". *Gateway Pundit,* 21 May 2015. Available at: <http://www.thegatewaypundit.com/2015/05/more-emails-prove-hillary-clinton-obama-knew-benghazi-terror-attack-was-planned-by-al-qaeda-group/#ixzz3fOnqw6Rm>.

HOSENBALL, Mark. "Bush: 'We're At War'. *Newsweek*, 24 September 2001.

HOSSEINE, Seyyedeh Motahhareh; MOQADDAM, Asghar Shokri. "US Presence in Eurasia and Its Impact on Security and Military Arrangements of This Region". *Geopolitica*, 5 May 2014.

Available at: <http://www.geopolitica.ru/en/article/us-presence-eurasia-and-its-impact-secu rity-and-military-arrangements-region#.Vex_MJc-7_A>.

HUAN, Major General Yang (ex-comandante-adjunto do Segundo Corpo de Artilharia — Forças de Mísseis Estratégicos). "China's Strategic Nuclear Weapons". *Institute for National Strategic Studies*. Available at: <http://fas.org/nuke/guide/china/doctrine/huan.htm.China>; See also: <http://www.nti.org/country-profiles/china/nuclear/>.

"Human Rights Council — Twenty Second Session — Agenda items 2 and 7Annual report of the United Nations High Commissioner for Human Rights and reports of the Office of the High Commissioner and the Secretary General Human rights situation in Palestine and other occupied Arab territories — Report of the United Nations High Commissioner for Human Rights on the implementation of Human Rights Council resolutions S 9/1 and S-12/1 — Addendum Concerns related to adherence to international human rights and international humanitarian law in the context of the escalation between the State of Israel, the de facto authorities in Gaza and Palestinian armed groups in Gaza that occurred from 14 to 21 November 2012". Avance version Distr.: General 6 March 2013 — pp. 6–11. Available at: <http://www.ohchr.org/Documents/ HRBodies/HRCouncil/RegularSession/Session22/A.HRC.22.35.Add.1_AV.pdf>.

HUNTER, Shreen T. *Islam in Russia — The politics of Identity and Security*. New York/London: M.E. Sharpe — Center for Strategic and International Studies, 2004, p. 9.

HUSSEIN, M.A.; ABRAHAM, R. "ISIS, Not Ḥamās, Claimed Responsibility For Kidnapping Three Israeli Teens". *Counter Current News*, 22 August 2014. Available at: <http:// countercurrentnews.com/2014/08/isis-in-the-west-bank-not-Ḥamās-first-claimed-responsibil ity-for-kidnapping-those-israeli-teens/>. Accessed 31October 2014.

HYDE, Lily (Kiev). "Ukraine to rewrite Soviet history with controversial 'decommunisation' laws — President set to sign measures that ban Communist symbols and offer public recognition and payouts for fighters in militias implicated in atrocities". *The Guardian*, 20 April 2015. Available at: <http://www.theguardian.com/world/2015/apr/20/ukraine-decommunisation-law-soviet>.

"Ilegal Israeli Settlements". *Council for European Palestinian Relations*. Available at: <http:// thecepr.org/index.php?option=com_content&view=article&id=115:illegal-israeli-settle ments&catid=6:memos&Itemid=34>.

"IMF Board Approves $15.2 Billion Loan to Ukraine". *Bloomberg News*, 29 July 2010. Available at: <http://www.bloomberg.com/news/articles/2010–07-28/imf-approves-15–2-billion-loan-to-ukraine-on-fiscal-adjustment-pledge>.

"Immigration to Israel: Total Immigration, by Year (1948 — Present 2014)". *Jewish Virtual Library*. Available at: <https://www.jewishvirtuallibrary.org/jsource/Immigration/Immigra tion_to_Israel.html>.

"In first, Ḥamās official takes credit for kidnap and murder of Israeli teens". *The Jerusalem Post*, 20 August 2014. Available at: <http://www.jpost.com/Arab-Israeli-Conflict/In-first-Ḥamās-offi cial-takes-credit-for-kidnap-and-murder-of%2D%2DIsraeli-teens-371703>.

"In His Own" — Bill Clinton — Speaking yesterday in Detroit. *The New York Times*, 23 October 1996. Available at: <http://www.nytimes.com/1996/10/23/us/in-his-own-words-939471.html>.

"In Ukraine, U.S interests are incompatible with the interests of the Russian Federation". Stratfor chief George Friedman on the roots of the Ukraine crisis Interview by Elena Chernenko & Alexander Gabuev — us-russia.org, 17 January 2015. Available at: <http://us-russia.org/2902-in-ukraine-us-interests-are-incompatible-with-the-interests-of-the-russian-federation-stratfor-chief-george-friedman-on-the-roots-of-the-ukraine-crisis.html>.

"Influencing the SARG in the end of 2006", 13 December 2006. Available at: <https://wikileaks. org/cable/2006/12/06DAMASCUS5399.html>.

"Informational Briefing from the Russian Union of Engineers, 15/08/2014 — Analysis of the causes of the crash of Flight MH17 (Malaysian Boeing 777). Ivan A. Andrievskii, First Vice-President of the All-Russian Public Organization Russian Union of Engineers — Chairman of the Board of Directors of the Engineering Company 2K". *Global Research*. Available at: <http://www.

globalresearch.ca/wp-content/uploads/2014/09/MH17_Report_Russian_Union_of_Engi
neers140818.pdf>.

Informationen zur politischen Bildung, 2015, Nr. 28 Quellentext Bevölkerungsstatistik: Die
Ukraine – ein Land zwischen West und Ost / Geschichte der Ukraine im Überblick.
Informationen zur politischen Bildung aktuell Nr. 28/2015. https://www.bpb.de/izpb/209719/
geschichte-der-ukraine-im-ueberblick?p=all, accessed: 16.6.2018

"International Military Review — Syria-Iraq battlespace, Dec. 29, 2015". *International Military
Review*, 29 December 2015. Available at: <http://southfront.org/international-military-review-
syria-iraq-battlespace-dec-29–2015/>.

"Internationalisierung des Yuan — China startet internationales Zahlungssystem — Bisher war die
Abwicklung grenzüberschreitender Geschäfte in Yuan teuer und langwierig. Das soll nun besser
werden und die Internationalisierung der chinesischen Währung vorantreiben". *Zürcher
Kantonalbank*, 9 October 2015. Available at: <http://www.nzz.ch/finanzen/devisen-und-
rohstoffe/china-startet-internationales-zahlungssystem-1.18626842>.

"Intervention en Syrie: derniers développements" — *Agora Dialogue*, 1 September 2013. Available
at: <http://agora-dialogue.com/intervention-en-syrie-derniers-developpements/>.

"Intervention en Syrie: Hollande sous la pression de l'opposition". *Le Parisien*, 31 August 2013.

"Interview to German TV channel ARD". Vladivostok, 17 November 2014. *President of Russia*.
Available at: <http://eng.kremlin.ru/news/23253>.

"Interview With Reza Moghadam — Ukraine Unveils Reform Program with IMF Support" — *IMF
Survey*, 30 April 2014. Available at: <http://www.imf.org/external/pubs/ft/survey/so/2014/
new043014a.htm>.

"Investigation of un-American propaganda activities in the United States. Hearings before a Special
Committee on Un-American Activities, House of Representatives, Seventy-fifth Congress, third
session-Seventy-eighth Congress, second session, on H. Res. 282, to investigate (1) the extent,
character, and objects of un-American propaganda activities in the United States; (2) the
diffusion within the United States of subversive and un-American propaganda that is instigated
from foreign countries or of a domestic origin and attacks the principle of the form of
government as guaranteed by our Constitution; and (3) all other questions in relation thereto
that would aid Congress in any necessary remedial legislation". *United States Congress House.
Special Committee on Un-American Activities (1938–1944)*. vol.: Appendix pt.7. Washington,
U.S. Govt. Printing Office. National Archive. Available at: <https://archive.org/stream/
investigationofu07unit/investigationofu07unit_djvu.txt>.

IOFFE, Julia. "Kiev Chameleon". *New Republic*, 5 January 2010. Available at: <http://www.
newrepublic.com/article/world/kiev-chameleon>.

"Iran accuses Saudis of hitting Yemen embassy". *BBC: Middle East*, 7 January 2016. Available at:
<http://www.bbc.com/news/world-middle-east-35251917>.

"Iran and Russia Making a Deal? Chairman Royce". *Presses State Department for Information*,
3 June 2014. Available at: <http://foreignaffairs.house.gov/press-release/iran-and-russia-mak
ing-deal-chairman-royce-presses-state-department-information>.

"Iran to double gas production at South Pars largest Phase". *PressTV*, 30 May 2014. Available at:
<http://www.presstv.ir/detail/2014/05/30/364764/iran-to-boost-south-pars-gas-output/>.

"Iran's South Pars phases to be completed by 2017: Official". *PressTV*, 30 May 2014. Available at:
<http://www.presstv.ir/detail/2014/05/30/364764/iran-to-boost-south-pars-gas-O output/>.

"Irregular Migrant, Refugee Arrivals in Europe Top One Million in 2015: IOM". *International
Organization for Migration*, 22 December 2015. Available at: <https://www.iom.int/news/
irregular-migrant-refugee-arrivals-europe-top-one-million-2015-iom>.

"ISIS told Yazidi sex slaves that rape is part of their twisted corruption of Islam". *Mirror*, 14 August
2015. Available at: <http://www.mirror.co.uk/news/world-news/isis-told-yazidi-sex-slaves-
6251415>.

"Israel raids and shuts down Palestinian radio station". *AAAJ and agencies. al-Araby*, 3 November
2015. Available at: <http://www.alaraby.co.uk/english/news/2015/11/3/israel-raids-and-shuts-
down-palestinian-radio-station>.

"Israeli jets strike 34 targets in Gaza Strip — Air force hits Ḥamās, Islamic Jihad structures; 4 reported wounded; 2 rockets explode in Israel causing damage, hours after discovery of kidnapped teens' bodies". *The Times of Israel*, 1 July 2014. Available at: <http://www. timesofisrael.com/palestinians-israeli-jets-strike-over-30-targets-in-gaza/>.

"Israeli military closes Palestinian radio station for inciting violence. Israel says it has shut down a Palestinian radio station on charges of incitement. The move comes after Prime Minister Benjamin Netanyahu accused Palestinian leaders of stoking the violence that has plagued the region". *Deutsche Welle — DW*, 3 November 2015. Available at: <http://www.dw.com/en/ israeli-military-closes-palestinian-radio-station-for-inciting-violence/a-18822859>. Accessed 5 November 2015.

"Israelis Stand to Gain $120 Billion, Palestinians $50 Billion in Two-State Solution Over Next Decade". *Rand Corporation*, 8 June 2015. Available at: <http://www.rand.org/news/press/ 2015/06/08.html>.

"It started in a mood of eerie calm, but then 2008 exploded into a global financial earthquake." *The Guardian — The Observer*, 28 December 2008. Available at: <http://www.theguardian.com/ business/2008/dec/28/markets-credit-crunch-banking-2008>.

"It's a dead end': German FM joins chorus of discontent over Russia sanctions rhetoric". *RT*, 18 May 2014. Available at: <http://rt.com/news/159716-germany-sanctions-russia-criticism/>.

ITO, Suzanne. "Despite U.N. Objections, U.S. Continues to Detain Children at Guantánamo". *American Civil Liberties (ACLU)*, 22 July 2008. Available at: <https://www.aclu.org/print/blog/ human-rights-national-security/despite-un-objections-us-continues-detain-children- guantanamo>.

IVRY, Bob; KEOUN, Bradley; KUNTZ, Phil. "Secret Fed Loans Gave Banks $13 Billion Undisclosed to Congress". *Bloomberg*, 28 November 2011. Available at: <http://www. bloomberg.com/news/2011–11-28/secret-fed-loans-undisclosed-to-congress-gave-banks-13-bil lion-in-income.html>.

IWAŃSKI, Tadeusz. "The collapse of Ukraine's foreign trade", 18 March 2015. Available at: <http://www.osw.waw.pl/en/publikacje/analyses/2015–03-18/collapse-ukraines-foreign- trade>.

JAFFE, Greg. "U.S. model for a future war fans tensions with China and inside Pentagon". *The Washington Post*, 1 August 2012. Available at: <http://www.washingtonpost.com/world/ national-security/us-model-for-a-future-war-fans-tensions-with-china-and-inside-pentagon/ 2012/08/01/gJQAC6F8PX_story.html>.

"James S. Brady Press Briefing Room" — *White House President Obama*. Available at: <http:// www.whitehouse.gov/the-press-office/2012/08/20/remarks-president-white-house-press- corps>.

JAMES, Lawrence. *The Golden Warrior: the life and legend of Lawrence of Arabia*. London: Scribner, 1970.

JASPER, William F. "George Soros' Giant Globalist Footprint in Ukraine's Turmoil". *The New American*. Available at: <http://www.thenewamerican.com/world-news/europe/item/17843- george-soros-s-giant-globalist-footprint-in-ukraine-s-turmoil>.

Jerusalem's al-Aqsa mosque sees Israeli-Palestinian clashes". *BBC News*, 13 September 2015. Available at: <http://www.bbc.com/news/world-middle-east-34237219>.

"Jim Rogers — Russia / China / Brazil Joining Forces to Avoid U.S. Dollar". *The Daily Coin*, 3 November 2014. Available at: <http://thedailycoin.org/?p=10593>.

JOHANEVICH, Milla. "Serbia: Clinton, billionaire Muja and Soros to get $1 trillion dollars deal in Kosovo". *Digital Journal*, 5 December 2011. Available at: <http://digitaljournal.com/blog/ 14219>.

"John McCain tells Ukraine protesters: 'We are here to support your just cause'". *The Guardian*, 15 December 2013. Available at: <http://www.theguardian.com/world/2013/dec/15/john- mccain-ukraine-protests-support-just-cause>.

JOHN, Josh Dorner; WILLETT, David. "McCain's Million Dollar Big Oil *Quid Pro Quo* Cam- paign Cash from Big Oil Flows In After Offshore Drilling Flip-Flop". *Sierra Club*. Available at:

<http://action.sierraclub.org/site/MessageViewer;
jsessionid=9C3A870C38955027BEF958DFC1084DC5.app207a?em_id=65021.0>.

JOHNSON, Ian. *A Mosque in Munich: Nazis, the CIA, and the Rise of the Muslim Brotherhood in West*. Boston/New York: Houghton Mufflin Harcourt, 2000. p. 127.

JONES, Seth G. "A Persistent Threat — The Evolution of al Qa'ida and Other Salafi Jihadists (Prepared for the Office of the Secretary of Defense)". *RAND National Research Institute. RAND Corporation*, 2014, p. x. ISBN: 978–0-8330–8572-6. Available at: <http://www.rand.org/content/dam/rand/pubs/research_reports/RR600/RR637/RAND_RR637.pdf>.

"Jordan hosts 900 U.S. troops to shield against Syria". *Daily Star* (Lebanon) — *Associated Press*, 22 June 2013. Available at <http://www.dailystar.com.lb/News/Middle-East/2013/Jun-22/221243-us-military-presence-in-jordan-expands-to-1000-soldiers.ashx#axzz3CMsQVR3F>.

JOSCELYN, Thomas. "Jihadist front established to represent foreign fighters in Syria". *The Long War Journal — Foundation for Defense of Democracies*. Available at: <http://www.longwarjournal.org/archives/2015/07/jihadist-front-established-to-represent-foreign-fighters-in-syria.php>.

JP Sottile for Buzzflash at Truthout. "The Business of America Is Giving Countries Like Ukraine the Business", Wednesday, 12 March 2014. Available at: <http://www.truth-out.org/buzzflash/commentary/the-business-of-america-is-giving-countries-like-ukraine-the-business>.

JPost.Com Staff. 'Kerry's mental age doesn't exceed that of a 12-year-old', Netanyahu's new media czar wrote Bennett blasts Kerry for linking Israeli-Palestinian conflict to ISIS proliferation". *The Jerusalem Post*, 5 November 2015. Available at: <http://www.jpost.com/Israel-News/Politics-And-Diplomacy/Kerrys-mental-age-doesnt-exceed-that-of-a-12-year-old-Netanyahus-new-media-czar-wrote-432104>.

Judicial Watch — Documents Archive. — pp. 1–3 (2–3) from JW v DOD and State 14–812. Available at: <http://www.judicialwatch.org/wp-content/uploads/2015/05/pp.-1–3-2–3-from-JW-v-DOD-and-State-14–812-DOD-Release-2015–04-10-final-version1.pdf>.

"Judicial Watch: Defense, State Department Documents Reveal Obama Administration Knew that al Qaeda Terrorists Had Planned Benghazi Attack 10 Days in Advance", 18 May 2015. Available at: <http://www.judicialwatch.org/press-room/press-releases/judicial-watch-defense-state-department-documents-reveal-obama-administration-knew-that-al-qaeda-terrorists-had-planned-benghazi-attack-10-days-in-advance/>.

"Julia Tymoshenko: The iron princess". *The Independent*, 28 October 2007. Available at: <http://www.independent.co.uk/news/people/profiles/julia-tymoshenko-the-iron-princess-397875.html>.

KALENIUK, Daryna; SENYK, Halyna. "Who will get stolen Lazarenko money?" *Kyiv Post*, 12 September 2013. Available at: <http://www.kyivpost.com/opinion/op-ed/who-will-get-stolen-lazarenko-money-329296.html>.

KALMAN, Aaron. "Israel used 17 tons of explosives to destroy Syrian reactor in 2007, magazine says, Mossad agents stole key information on Assad's nuclear project from Vienna home of Syrian atomic agency head, New Yorker claims". *The Times of Israel*, 10 September 2012. Available at: <http://www.timesofisrael.com/israel-uses-17-tons-of-explosives-to-destroy-syrian-reactor/>.

KANAT, Kilic Bugra. *A Tale of Four Augusts*: *Obama's Syria Policy*. Ankara (Turquia): Seta Publications, 2015, pp. 11, 77 e 83–84.

KANT, Immanuel. Zum ewigen Frieden. Ein philosophischer Entwurf. Königsberg. Wortgetreuer Neudruck der Erstausgaben (Zweitdruck) von 1795. Her. von Julius Rodenberg. 1946

KARON, Tony. "Israel Violence Means Big Trouble for Sharon, Arafat and Bush". *Time*, 6 August 2001. Available at: <http://content.time.com/time/world/article/0,8599,170235,00.html>.

KATCHANOVSKI, Ivan. "The 'Snipers' Massacre" on the Maidan in Ukraine". Available at: <http://www.scribd.com/doc/244801508/Snipers-Massacre-on-the-Maidan-in-Ukraine-Paper-libre>.

KATZ, Emily Tess. "Matt Taibbi: America Has A 'Profound Hatred Of The Weak And The Poor'". *HuffPost Live, HuffPost Businnes*, 1 December 2014. Available at: <http://www.huffingtonpost. com/2014/04/16/matt-taibbi-the-divide_n_5159626.html>.

KECK, Zachary. "Is China Preparing MIRVed Ballistic Missiles?" *The Diplomat*, 8 August 2014. Available at: <http://thediplomat.com/2014/08/is-china-preparing-mirved-ballistic-missiles>.

_____. "The Buzz — Russia's Massive Military Buildup Abroad: Should NATO Worry?" *The National Interest*, 17 June 2015. Available at: <http://www.nationalinterest.org/blog/the-buzz/ russias-massive-military-buildup-abroad-should-nato-worry-13132>.

KELLEY, Matt (*Associated Press*) "Bush Administration Spent $65 Million to Help Opposition in Ukraine" — *Associated Press* — *Fox News*, 10 December 2004. Available at: <http://www. foxnews.com/story/2004/12/10/us-spent-65m-to-aid-ukrainian-groups/>.

KELLEY, Michael B. "Al-Qaeda Jihadists Are The Best Fighters Among The Syria Rebels". *Business Insider* — *Military & Defense*, 31 July 2012. Available at: <http://www. businessinsider.com/al-qaeda-jihadists-are-among-the-best-fighters-among-the-syria-rebels-2012-7?IR=T>.

———. "There's A Reason Why All of The Reports about Benghazi Are So Confusing". *Businness Insider — Military & Defense*, 3 November 2012. Available at: <http://www.businessinsider. com/benghazi-stevens-cia-attack-libya-2012–11?IR=T>.

KENEZ, Peter. *Civil war in South Russia 1919–1920*: *The defeat of the Whites*. Hoover Institution on War, Revolution, and Peace Berkeley (Califórnia): University of California Press, 1977, pp. 162–163.

KENNAN, George F. "'A Fateful Error.' *The New York Times*, February 5 1997" *in: Wargaming italia*. Available at: <http://www.netwargamingitalia.net/forum/resources/george-f-kennan-a-fateful-error.35/>. Accessed 27 November 2018.

KENNEDY JR., Robert. "Middle Eastern Wars Have ALWAYS Been About Oil". *WashingtonsBlog*, 26 February 2016. Available at: <http://www.washingtonsblog.com/2016/ 02/middle-eastern-wars-always-oil.html>. Also: https://www.globalresearch.ca/middle-eastern-wars-have-always-been-about-oil/5510640. Accessed 27 November 2018.

_____. "Syria: Another Pipeline War". *EcoWatch*, 25 February 2016. Available at: <http:// ecowatch.com/2016/02/25/robert-kennedy-jr-syria-pipeline-war/>.

KERSHNERJAN, Isabel. "Netanyahu Says Some Settlements to Stay in Israel". *The New York Times*. 24, 2010. Available at: <http://www.nytimes.com/2010/01/25/world/middleeast/ 25mideast.html?_r=0>.

KESSLER, Glenn. "Netanyahu: 'America is a thing you can move very easily'". *The Washington Post*, 16 July 2010.

_____. "President Obama and the 'red line' on Syria's chemical weapon". *The Washington Post*, 6 September 2013.

KIERKEGAARD, Søren. *Fucht und Zittern*. Munique: Güterloher Verlaghaus, 1993, pp. 58–59, 140–141.

"Kiev and Babi Yar". *Holocaust Encyclopedia*. Available at: <http://www.ushmm.org/wlc/en/ article.php?ModuleId=10005421>.

"Kiev fights in Ukraine's southeast for shale gas deposits to be controlled by US — Pushkov-Russia". *Itar-TASS*, 16 August 2014. Available at: <http://tass.ru/en/russia/745305>.

KIM, Lucian. "Debaltseve debacle puts Ukraine's leader in jeopardy. That suits Vladimir Putin just fine". *Reuters*, 19 February 2015. Available at: <http://blogs.reuters.com/great-debate/2015/02/ 19/debaltseve-debacle-put-ukraines-leader-in-jeopardy-and-that-suits-vladimir-putin-just-fine/ >. Accessed 27 February de 2015.

_____. "Debaltseve debacle puts Ukraine's leader in jeopardy. That suits Vladimir Putin just fine". *Reuters*, 19 February 2015. Available at: <http://blogs.reuters.com/great-debate/2015/02/19/ debaltseve-debacle-put-ukraines-leader-in-jeopardy-and-that-suits-vladimir-putin-just-fine/>. Accessed 27 February 2015.

KINCAID, Cliff. "Clinton's Kosovo Whopper". *Free Republic*, 28 September 2006. Available at: <http://www.freerepublic.com/focus/f-news/1709979/posts>.

KING, Charles. "The Five-Day War — Managing Moscow after the Georgia Crisis". *Foreign Affairs*, November/December 2008 Issue. Available at: <http://www.foreignaffairs.com/articles/64602/charles-king/the-five-day-war>.

KINGSLEY, Patrick (Cairo); STEPHEN, Chris; ROBERTS, Dan (Washington). "UAE and Egypt behind bombing raids against Libyan militias, say US officials". Available at: <http://www.theguardian.com/world/2014/aug/26/united-arab-emirates-bombing-raids-libyan-militias>.

KINZER, Stephen. *Overthrow. America's Century of Regime Change from Hawaii to Iraq.* New York: Times Books — Henry Hold & Company, 2006, p. 321.

KIRICHUCK, Sergey. "Ukraine: far-right extremists at core of 'democracy' protest — As violent scenes play out on the streets of Kiev, we look at the major role extremist right-wing movements have played in Ukraine's 'pro-democracy' movement". *Channel 4 News* (*Ukraina*), 24 January 2014. Available at: <http://www.channel4.com/news/kiev-svoboda-far-right-protests-right-sector-riot-police>.

KIRTIKAR, Margo. *Once Upon a Time in Baghdad: The Two Golden Decades The 1940s and 1950s.* Crossways, Dartford (U. K.); Xlibris Corporation, 2011, pp. 270–271.

KISSINGER, Henry A. "How the Ukraine crisis ends". *The Washington Post*, 5 March 2014.

_____. "Syrian intervention risks upsetting global order", *The Washington Post*, 2 June 2012.

_____. *Diplomacy.* New York: A Touchstone Book — Simon & Schuster, 1995, p. 607.

_____. *World Order.* New York: Penguin Press, 2014, p. 336.

"Klitschko erzählt von der Todes-Nacht auf dem Maidan". *Focus Online.* Available at: <http://www.focus.de/politik/ausland/news-ticker-zur-eskalation-in-der-ukraine-25-tote-busse-karren-demonstranten-vom-land-nach-kiew_id_3625618.html>.

KLOSTERMAYR, M. "Syria: Mother Agnes on the Chronology of Chemical Attack near Damascus — Mother Agnes speaks about the fabricated videos of the chemical attack near Syria's capital, Damascus". *SyriaNews*, 26 September 2013. Available at: <http://www.syrianews.cc/syria-mother-agnes-chemical-attack-damascus/>.

KLUßMANN, Uwe; SCHEPP Matthias Schepp; WIEGREFE, Klaus. "NATO's Eastward Expansion — Did the West Break Its Promise to Moscow?" *Spiegel Online*, 26 November 2009. Available at: <http://www.spiegel.de/iMargaretanternational/world/nato-s-eastward-expansion-did-the-west-break-its-promise-to-moscow-a-663315-2.html>.

KOESTLER, Arthur. *The Thirteenth Tribe.* New York: Random House, 1976, pp. 13–19, 154–166. 223–226.

KOZY, John. "Mother Russia". *Nueva Sociedad* — 253, Buenos Aires: Friedrich Ebert Stiftung. September / October 2014, pp. 131–137.

KRAMAR, Oleksandr. "Back on the Ground — Agribusiness becomes the biggest component of Ukraine's economy. What will it take for the growth to continue?". *Ukrainain Week*, 25 August 2015. Available at: <http://ukrainianweek.com/Economics/144123>.

KRAMER, Andrew E.; GORDON, Michael R. "U.S. Faults Russia as Combat Spikes in East Ukraine". *The New York Times*, 13 February 2015.

_____. HERSZENHORN, David M. (Artemivsk, Ukraine). "Retreating Soldiers Bring Echoes of War's Chaos to a Ukrainian Town". *The New York Times*, 19 February 2015. Available at: <http://www.nytimes.com/2015/02/20/world/europe/leaders-speak-by-telephone-to-try-to-impose-ukraine-cease-fire.html>.

KRAMER, Mark. "Why Did Russia Give Away Crimea Sixty Years Ago?" *Cold War International History Project.* Available at: <http://www.wilsoncenter.org/publication/why-did-russia-give-away-crimea-sixty-years-ago>.

KRAMIM, Mitzpe (West Bank); LUBELL, Maayan. "In Netanyahu's fourth term, what's next for Israeli settlements?" *Reuters*, 6 April 2015. Available at: <http://www.reuters.com/article/2015/04/06/us-israel-palestinians-settlements-insig-idUSKBN0MX0T220150406>. Accessed 1 November 2015.

KRANISH, Michael. "Powerful alliance aids 'Bushes' rise". (Part One), *Boston Globe*, 22 April 2001.

_____. "Prescott Bush & Nazis", *Boston Globe*, 4 July 2001. The Mail Archive, Available at: <https://www.mail-archive.com/ctrl%40listserv.aol.com/msg71122.htm>.

"Krim-Krise — Altkanzler Schmidt verteidigt Putins Ukraine-Kurs". *Spiegl Online*, 26 March 2014. Available at: <http://www.spiegel.de/politik/ausland/helmut-schmidt-verteidigt-in-krim-krise-putins-ukraine-kurs-a-960834-druck.html>.

KRUSHCHEV, Nikita. *Memoirs of Nikita Khruschev*, vol. I Comissar (1918–1945), edited by Sergey Khruschev. Pennsylvania: Pennsylvania State University Press, 2004.

KUBICEK, Paul. *The History of Ukraine*. London: Greenwoods Press, 2008.

KUDELIA, Sergiy. "Ukraine's 2014 presidential election result is unlikely to be repea-ted". *The Washington Post*, 2 June 2014.

KULS, Norbert; KNOP, Carsten. "Goldman-Sachs-Chef Blankfein: Ich bin ein Banker, der Gottes Werk verrichtet". *Frankfurter Allgemeine Zeitung*, 9 November 2009.

KURNAZ, Murat. *Five Years of my Life — An Innocent Man in Guantanamo*. New York: Palgrave Macmillan, 2009, p. 224.

KUROMIYA, Hiroaki. *Freedom and Terror in the Donbas: A Ukrainian- Russian Borderland, 1870s-1990s*. New York/Cambridge: Cambridge University Press, 1998.

KUZIO, Taras. "Comments on Black Sea Fleet talks". *The Ukrainian Weekly,* 19 February 2006, p. 8. Available at: <http://ukrweekly.com/archive/pdf3/2006/The_Ukrainian_Weekly_2006–08.pdf>.

_____. "The Crimea: Europe's Next Flashpoint? — November 2010". Washington, *The Jamestown Foundation*, p. 4. Available at: <http://www.peacepalacelibrary.nl/ebooks/files/372451918.pdf>.

"L'Armée syrienne accusée d'avoir utilisé du gaz toxique, l'ONU sommée de réagir". *Le Figaro*, 21 August 2013.

"L'Évolution des inégalités de revenus dans les pays riches". *Inequality Watch*, 6 February 2012. Available at: <http://inequalitywatch.eu/spip.php?article58&lang=fr>.

LACHOWSKI, Zdzislaw. "Foreign Military Bases in Eurasia". *SIPRI Policy Paper No. 18. SIPRI, Stockholm International Peace Research Institute*. Estocolmo: CM Gruppen, Bromma, June 2007. Available at: <http://books.sipri.org/files/PP/SIPRIPP18.pdf>.

LAFRANIERE, Sharon. "Stepashin Confirmed as Russian Premier". *Washington Post — Foreign Service,* 20 May 1999, p. A19. Available at: <http://www.washingtonpost.com/wp-srv/inatl/longterm/russiagov/stories/stepashin052099.html>.

LAMONICA, Barbara. "The Attempted Coup against FDR". *Probe*. March-April 1999 issue (vol. 6, n°. 3). Available at: <http://www.ctka.net/pr399-fdr.html>.

LAMOTHE, Dan. "How U.S. weapons will play a huge role in Saudi Arabia's war in Yemen". *The Washington Post*, 26 March 2015. Available at: <https://www.washingtonpost.com/news/check point/wp/2015/03/26/how-u-s-weapons-will-play-a-large-role-in-saudi-arabias-war-in-yemen/>.

LANGER, Gary. "Six in 10 Oppose U.S.-Only Strike on Syria; A Closer Division if Allies are Involved". *ABC News*, 3 September 2013. Available at <http://abcnews.go.com/blogs/politics/2013/09/six-in-10-oppose-u-s-only-strike-on-syria-a-closer-division-if-allies-are-involved/>.

LARSON, Leslie. "Senate sneers as soap opera exec is confirmed Ambassador to Hungary". *Daily News*, New York, 3 December 2014. Available at: <http://www.nydailynews.com/news/poli tics/soap-opera-producer-confirmed-ambassador-hungary-article-1.2031496>.

LASSALLE, Ferdinand. *Ausgewählte Reden und Schriften — 1849–1864*. Berlin: Dietz Verlag, 1991, pp. 94–97.

LATSCH, Gunther. "Die dunkle Seite des Westens". *Der Spiegel*, 11 April 2005.

LAUB, Karin. "Libya: Estimated 30,000 Died in War; 4,000 Still Missing". *Huffpost World Post — The Huffington Post,* 8 September 2011. Available at: <http://www.huffingtonpost.com/2011/09/08/libya-war-died_n_953456.html>.

"Laut Zeitungsbericht: amerikanische Söldner sollen in Ostukraine kämpfen" *Frankfurter Allgemeine Zeitung,* 11 May 2014. Available at: <http://www.faz.net/aktuell/politik/ausland/laut-zeitungsbericht-amerikanische-soeldner-sollen-in-ostukraine-kaempfen-12933968.html>.

LAYMAN, Geoffrey C.; HUSSEY, Laura S. "George W. Bush and the Evangelicals: Religious Commitment and Partisan Change among Evangelical Protestants, 1960–2004". *University of Maryland*. This paper originally was prepared for presentation at the University of Notre Dame conference on "A Matter of Faith? Religion in the 2004 Election," Notre Dame, In, December 2–3, 2005. — Department of Government and Politics, 3140 Tydings Hall, College Park, MD 20742.

LAZAR, Alex. "Oslo Mayor Unhappy With Obama's Norway Ambassador Nominee". *The Huffington Post*. Available at: <http://www.huffingtonpost.com/2014/07/08/george-tsunis-norway_n_5567351.html>.

LAZARE, Daniel. "Climbing into Bed with Al-Qaeda". *Information Clearing House*, 2 May 2015. Available at: <http://www.informationclearinghouse.info/article41742.htm>.

LAZAROFF, Tovah. "Has Netanyahu been boom or bust for Israel's West Bank settlement enterprise?" *The Jerusalem Post*, 17 March 2015. Available at: <http://www.jpost.com/Israel-Elections/Has-Netanyahu-been-boom-or-bust-for-Israels-West-Bank-settlement-enterprise-394135>.

LE TELLIER, Alexandra. "After MH17, questions of trust from Ron Paul and others". *Los Angeles Times*, 21 July 2014. Available at: <http://www.latimes.com/opinion/opinion-la/la-ol-malaysia-airlines-flight-17-mh17-ron-paul-mainstream-media-20140721-story.html>. Accessed 11 August 2015.

LENIN, W. I. "The Ukraine", *in*: Collected Works. London: Lawrence & Wishart, 1964, vol. 25 (June - September de 1917).

_____. "Rede bei der Öffnung des Parteitags 27 März 1922", *in*: LENIN, W. I. *Werke*. August 1921 —March 1923. Berlin: Dietz Verlag, 1962, Band 33, pp. 285–287.

_____. "VII Moskauer Gouvernement-Parteikonferenz", Oktober 1921, pp. 29–31, *in*: LENIN, W. I. *Werke*. August 1921 —March 1923. Berlin: Dietz Verlag, 1962, Band 33, pp. 75–76.

LEPETYUK, Vadym. "Hyperinflation in Ukraine" — Econ1102 — Guest Lecture — *University of Minnesota*. Available at: <http://www.econ.umn.edu/~dmiller/GLhyperinflation>.

Letters of Henry Adams (1892–1918) — Edited by Worthington Chauncey Ford — Boston/New York: Houghton Mifflin Company, 1938, vol. II, p. 99. Available at: <http://archive.org/stream/lettersofhenryad008807mbp/lettersofhenryad008807mbp_djvu.txt>.

LEVY, Adrian; SCOTT-CLARK, Cathy. "'He won, Russia lost' — Roman Abramovich, Britain's richest man, has lavished millions and millions upon Chelsea Football Club". *The Guardian*, 8 May 2004.

LEVY, Clifford J. Levy. "'Hero of Ukraine' Prize to Wartime Partisan Leader Is Revoked". *The New York Times*, 12 January 2011.

LEVY, Gideon. "Tricky Bibi — Israel has had many rightist leaders since Menachem Begin promised 'many Elon Morehs', but there has never been one like Netanyahu, who wants to do it by deceit". *Há'aretz*, 15 July 2010. Available at: <http://www.haaretz.com/misc/article-print-page/tricky-bibi-1.302053?trailingPath=2.169%2C2.225%2C2.227%2C>.

"Libya — Overview — Libya is a member of the Organization of the Petroleum Exporting Countries, the holder of Africa's largest proved crude oil reserves, and an important contributor to the global supply of light, sweet crude oil". *Energy Information Administration (EIA)*, 25 November 2014. Available at: <http://www.eia.gov/countries/cab.cfm?fips=LY>.

"Libya death toll rises as clashes in Benghazi continue". *Al Arabya*, 2 October 2014. Available at: <http://english.alarabiya.net/en/News/africa/2014/10/02/Seven-Libyan-soldiers-killed-in-Benghazi-bombs-and-clashes-army-official-says.html2014>. Accessed 3 December 2014.

"Libya: US and EU say Muammar Gaddafi must go". *BBC* — Seccion Africa, 11 March 2011. Available at: <http://www.bbc.com/news/world-europe-12711162>.

"Libyan Army General Khalifa Haftar a CIA operative: Analyst". *Press TV*, 6 September 2014. Available at: <http://www.presstv.ir/detail/2014/06/09/366288/gen-khalifa-haftar-cia-man-in-libya/>.

"Libyan rebels 'receive foreign training'. Rebel source tells Al Jazeera about training offered by US and Egyptian special forces in eastern Libya". *Al Jazeera*, 3 April 2011. Available at: <http://www.aljazeera.com/news/africa/2011/04/201142172443133798.html>.

"L'est, les Nazis de hier sont réhabilités. En Ukraine et ailleurs dans líex-URSS: honneur aux anciens SS". Available at: <http://www.resistances.be/ukraine.html>.

"Life in the Gaza Strip". *BBC News*, 14 July 2014. Available at: <http://www.bbc.com/news/world-middle-east-20415675?print=true>.

LIND, Michael. *The American Way of Strategy — U.S. Foreign Policy and the American Way of Life.* Oxford: Oxford-New York: University Press, 2006, p. 134.

LIPKA, Michael. "The continuing decline of Europe's Jewish population". *Pew Research Center*. Available at: <http://www.pewresearch.org/fact-tank/2015/02/09/europes-jewish-population/>.

LISTER, Charles R. *The Islamic State — A Brief Introduction*. Washington, D.C., Brooking Institution Press, 2015, p. 5.

LITTLE, Alan. "Business; Economy — Parliament calls on Yeltsin to resign". *BBC News*, 21 August 1998. Available at: <http://news.bbc.co.uk/2/hi/business/155494.stm>.

LLOYD, Henry Demarest. *Wealth against Commonwealth*. Englewood Cliffs (New Jersey): Prentice Hall, Inc., 1965, pp, 5, 10 e 163.

LOBE, Jim. "CEOs at Big U.S. Companies Paid 331 Times Average Worker". *Inter Press Service (IPS)*, Apr 16, 2014. Available at: <http://www.ipsnews.net/2014/04/ceos-big-u-s-companies-paid-331-times-average-worker/>.

"Looking behind the Bushes — Great moments in a great American family". *The Progressive Review. An Online Journal of Alternative News & Information*. Available at: <http://prorev.com/bush2.htm>.

LOSSAN, Alexej (RBTH). "Russland stellt Alternative zu Visa und MasterCard vor — Die russische Regierung hat in Moskau den Prototypen einer nationalen Kreditkarte vorgestellt. Allerdings wird noch einige Zeit vergehen, bis das neue Zahlungssystem flächendeckend eingeführt wird". *Russia Beyond and the Headlines*, 4 June 2015. Available at: <http://de.rbth.com/wirtschaft/2015/06/04/russland_stellt_alternative_zu_visa_und_mastercard_vor_33869>.

LÜDERS, Alexander. "Polnische Spezialisten". *Focus*, Samstag 13 September 2014. Available at: <http://www.focus.de/politik/ausland/polnische-spezialisten-ukraine-krise-kommentar_id_5967578.html>.

LUHN, Alec (Artemivsk); GRYTSENKO, Oksana (Luhansk). "Ukrainian soldiers share horrors of Debaltseve battle after stinging defeat — Thousands of Ukrainian soldiers retreat from strategic town taken by pro-Russia separatists, leaving their dead and wounded comrades behind." *The Guardian*, 18 February 2015. Available at: <http://www.theguardian.com/world/2015/feb/18/ukrainian-soldiers-share-horrors-of-debaltseve-battle-after-stinging-defeat>.

_____. (Moscow); HARDING, Luke. "Russian aid convoy heads for Ukraine amid doubts over lorries' contents — Kiev says it will turn back shipment which Moscow describes as human-itarian but which west says could be prelude to invasion". *The Guardian*, 12 August 2014.

LUSTICK, Ian S. "Israel's Migration Balance — Demography, Politics, and Ideology", pp. 33–34. *Israel Studies Review*, Vol. 26, Issue 1, Summer 2011: 33—65 © Association for Israel Studies doi: 10.3167/isr.2011.260108. Available at: <https://www.sas.upenn.edu/polisci/sites/www.sas.upenn.edu.polisci/files/Lustick_Emigration_ISR_11.pdf>.

LUTSEVYCH, Orysia. "How to Finish a Revolution: Civil Society and Democracy in Georgia, Moldova and Ukraine", pp. 4–7. Briefing paper Russia and Eurasia | January 2013 | REP BP 2013/01. *Chatham House*. Available at: <http://www.chathamhouse.org/sites/files/chathamhouse/public/Research/Russia%20and%20Eurasia/0113bp_lutsevych.pdf>.

LUXEMBURG, Rosa. "Fragment über Krieg, nationale Frage und Revolution", *Ibidem*, p. 369.

_____. "Zur russischen Revolution", *in*: LUXEMBURG, Rosa. *Gesammelte Werke*. Berlin: Dietz Verlage, 1990, Band 4, p. 355.

LYNCH, Dennis. "Russian Next-Gen 100-Ton Nuclear Missile Could Be Test-Fired By 2017, Says Russian News Wire". *International Business Times*, 29 January 2015. Available at: <http://

www.ibtimes.com/russian-next-gen-100-ton-nuclear-missile-could-be-test-fired-2017-says-rus sian-news-1799970>.

LYNGAR, Edwin. "Christian right's rage problem: How white fundamentalists are roiling America. Far-right Christians like Todd Starnes think their nation's in danger. You won't believe what they want to do next". *Salon*, 1 December 2014. Available at: <http://www.salon.com/2014/12/01/far_right_christian_haters_rage_and_cruelty_from_white_fundamentalist_amer ica/?source=news-letter>.

LYSENKO, Andriy. "Ukrainian Armed Forces de-mine Kominternove". *Ukraine Crisis Media Center*. Kyiv, 16 March 2015. Available at: <http://uacrisis.org/20074-andrijj-lisenko-59>.

MACASKILL, Ewen. "Bush: 'God told me to end the tyranny in Iraq' — President told Palestinians God also talked to him about Middle East peace". *The Guardian*, 7 October 2005. Available at: <http://www.theguardian.com/world/2005/oct/07/iraq.usa>.

MACFARQUHAR, Neil. "A Russian Convoy Carrying Aid to Ukraine Is Dogged by Suspicion". *The New York Times*, 12 August 2014. "Ukraine officially recognizes Russian aid convoy as humanitarian". *RT*, 16 August 2014. Available at: <http://www.rt.com/news/180844-ukraine-recognizes-russia-humanitarian-aid/>. Accessed 17 August 2014.

MACHIAVELLI, Niccoló. *Discorso sopra la prima deca di Tito Livio*. Milão: Rizzoli Editore — BUR Classici, 9ª edição, 2013, pp. 491–492.

MADDOX, Bronwen. "Jimmy Carter: there is zero chance for the two-state solution. The US has withdrawn from tackling the Middle East's most intractable problem, says the former President". *Prospect*, 13 August 2015. Available at: <http://www.prospectmagazine.co.uk/world/jimmy-carter-there-is-zero-chance-for-the-two-state-solution>.

MADHANI, Aamer. "White House — Obama Says Libya's Qaddafi Must Go". *National Journal*, 3 March 2011. Available at: <http://www.nationaljournal.com/obama-says-libya-s-qaddafi-must-go-20110303>.

MADI, Mohamed. "Profile: Libyan ex-General Khalifa Haftar". *BBC News*, 16 October 2014. Available at: <http://www.bbc.com/news/world-africa-27492354>.

MADISON, James. "Political Observations", 20, 1795. In: *Letters and Other Writings of James Madison*, vol. 4, 1865, p. 491.

MADSEN, Wayne. "Nuland attempts Kiev Version 2.0 in Skopje". *Strategic Culture Foundation*, 16 February 2015. Available at: <http://m.strategic-culture.org/news/2015/02/16/nuland-attempts-kiev-version-2-skopje.html>.

MAGOCSI, Paulo R. *A History of Ukraine — The Land and its People*. Toronto: University of Toronto Press, 2ª ed., 2010, pp. 64–67.

MAINWARING, Jon. "Caspian Conference: Azeri Oil, Gas Production Target Raised for 2015". *Rigzone*, 4 June 2015. Available at: <http://www.rigzone.com/news/oil_gas/a/138946/Caspian_Conference_Azeri_Oil_Gas_Production_Target_Raised_for_2015>.

MAKHNO, Nestor. *A "revolução" contra a revolução*. São Paulo: Cortez Editora, 1988, pp. 70–71 e 261–262.

MALGAVKO, Alexei. "Lawrow: Eine Million Flüchtlinge aus Ukraine 2014 in Russland eingetroffen". *Sputnik*, 1 June 2014. Available at: <http://de.sputniknews.com/panorama/20150601/302576655.html>. Accessed 7 June 2014.

MALIK, Shiv; MCCARTHY, Tom. "Syria: US sees 'no avenue forward' to 'meaningful action' by UN — as it happened". *The Guardian*, 28 August 2013.

MALISHEVSK, Nikolai. "Polish Death Squads Fighting in Ukraine. CIA Covert Operation?" *Global Research*, 28 May 2014. Strategic Culture Foundation. Available at: <http://www.globalresearch.ca/polish-death-squads-fighting-in-ukraine-cia-covert-operation/5384210>.

MALLOF, F. Michael. "Saudis Pressure Russians to Drop Syria — Effort coordinated with U.S., Europe". *WND*, 26 August 2013. Available at: <http://www.wnd.com/2013/08/saudis-pressure-russians-to-drop-syria/>.

MANGASARIAN, Leon. "Ukraine Crisis Echoes 1914, German Ex-Leader Schmidt Says". *Bloomberg*, 16 May 2014. Available at: <http://www.bloomberg.com/news/articles/2014-05-16/ukraine-crisis-resembles-europe-1914-says-helmut-schmidt>.

"Many Ukraine soldiers cross into Russia amid shelling". *BBC Europe,* 4 August 2014. Available at: <http://www.bbc.com/news/world-europe-28637569>. Accessed 6 August 2014.

MARANTO, Robert; LANSFORD, Tom; JOHNSON Jeremy (Editors). *Judging Bush (Studies in the Modern Presidency).* California: Stanford University Press, 2009, p. 233.

MARCHAK, Darina; GORCHINSKAYA, Katya. "Russia gives Ukraine cheap gas, $15 billion in loans". Gazprom will cut the price that Ukraine must pay for Russian gas deliveries to $268 per 1,000 cubic metres from the current level of about $400 per 1,000 cubic metres. *KyivPost,* 17 December 2013. Available at: <http://www.kyivpost.com/content/ukraine/russia-gives-ukraine-cheap-gas-15-billion-in-loans-333852.html>.

MARPLES, David R. "The Ethnic Issues in the Famine of 1932–1933", *in:* NOACK Christian; JANSSEN, Lindsay; COMERFORD, Vincent (Herausgegeben). *Holodomor and Gorta Mór: Histories, Memories and Representations of Famine.* London: Anthen Press, 2012, pp. 40–45.

MARX, Karl; ENGELS, Friedrich. *Die deutsche Ideologie, in:* MARX, Karl; ENGELS, Friedrich. *Werke,* Band 3. Berlin: Dietz Verlag, 1981, pp. 26–27 e 40.

MASTERS, Jonathan (Deputy Editor). "Targeted Killings". *Council of Foreign Relations,* 23 May 2013. Available at: <http://www.cfr.org/counterterrorism/targeted-killings/p9627>.

MATHIASON, Nick; STEWART, Heather. "Three weeks that changed the world". *The Guardian.* Available at: <http://www.theguardian.com/business/2008/dec/28/markets-credit-crunch-banking-2008>.

MATISHAK, Martin. "$42 Million for 54 Recruits: U.S. Program to Train Syrian Rebels Is a Disaster". *The Fiscal Times,* 10 September 2015. Available at: <http://www.thefiscaltimes.com/2015/09/10/42-Million-54-Recruits-US-Program-Train-Syrian-Rebels-Dud>.

MATLACK, Carol. "Losing Crimea Could Sink Ukraine's Offshore Oil and Gas Hopes". *Bloomberg,* 11 March 2014. Available at: <http://www.bloomberg.com/bw/articles/2014–03-11/losing-crimea-could-sink-ukraines-offshore-oil-and-gas-hopesatlack>.

_____. "Ukraine Cuts a Deal It Could Soon Regret". *Bloomberg.* Available at: <http://www.bloomberg.com/news/articles/2013–12-17/yanukovych-and-putin-russia-will-invest-15-billion-in-ukraine>.

MATTHEWS, Alan. "Russian food sanctions against the EU". *CAP Reform.EU,* 15 August 2014. Available at: <http://capreform.eu/russian-food-sanctions-against-the-eu/>.

MAULDIN, William. "Europeans Face Export Losses as Sanctions Bite Russian Ruble". *The Wall Street Journal,* 19 December 2014. Available at: <http://blogs.wsj.com/economics/2014/12/19/europeans-face-export-losses-as-sanctions-bite-russian-ruble/>.

MAUPIN, Caleb. "Nazis to Enforce Neoliberalism: 'Operation Jade Helm' and the Ukrainian National Guard". *Neo Eastern Outlook (NEO),* 20 July 2015. Available at: <http://journal-neo.org/2015/07/20/nazis-to-enforce-neoliberalism-operation-jade-helm-and-the-ukrainian-national-guard/>.

MAZNEVA, Elena; KHRENNIKOVA, Dina. "Putin Bets on Germany as Gas Ties with Turkey Sour on Syria". *Bloomberg,* 13 October 2015. Available at: <http://www.bloomberg.com/news/articles/2015–10-12/putin-bets-on-germany-as-gas-ties-with-turkey-go-sour-over-syria>.

MAZZETTI, Mark. "Panel Faults C.I.A. Over Brutality and Deceit in Interrogations". *The New York Times,* 10 December 2014.

MCALLISTER, Ian; WHITHE, Stephen. 'Rethinking the Orange Revolution', *in:* LANE David; WHITE, Stephen (Editors). *Rethinking the 'orange Revolution'.* London/New York: Routledge, 2010, pp. 138–139.

"McCormack-Dickstein Committee". U.S. House of Representatives, Special Committee on Un-American Activities, Investigation of Nazi Propaganda Activities and Investigation of Certain Other Propaganda Activities United States Congress. Available at: <http://www.archives.gov/legislative/guide/house/chapter-22-select-propaganda.html>.

MCKILLOP, Andrew. "Did Natural Gas Debt Trigger the Ukraine Crisis? The Market Oracle". *Politics / Eastern Europe,* 28 February 2014. Available at <http://www.marketoracle.co.uk/Article44628.html>.

MCLEES, Alexandra; RUMER, Eugene. "Saving Ukraine's Defense Industry", 30 July 2014. *Carnegie Endowment for International Peace*. Available at: <http://carnegieendowment.org/2014/07/30/saving-ukraine-s-defense-industry>.

"Media Blacks Out Pentagon Report Exposing U.S. Role In ISIS Creation". *MintPress*. Available at: <http://www.mintpressnews.com/media-blacks-out-pentagon-report-exposing-u-s-role-in-isis-creation/206187>.

MEEK, James. "The millionaire revolutionary". *The Guardian*, 26 November 2004. Available at: <http://www.theguardian.com/world/2004/nov/26/ukraine.gender>.

"Mehr Unabhängigkeit: BRICS-Staaten vs. Wall Street und City of London". *Pravda TV*, 14 October 2015. Available at: <http://www.pravda-tv.com/2015/10/mehr-unabhaengigkeit-brics-staaten-vs-wall-street-und-city-of-london>.

MELLOY, John (Investing Editor of CNBC.com). "Goldman, Morgan Stanley May Shed 'Bank' Status: Analyst". *CNBC*, 12 October 2011. Available at: <http://www.cnbc.com/id/44875711>.

MELNIKOV, Valeriy; RIA Novosti. "Kiev official: Military op death toll is 478 civilians, outnumbers army losses". *RT*, 10 July 2014. Available at: <http://www.rt.com/news/171808-eastern-ukraine-civilians-killed/s>.

MEMOLI, Michael A.; MASCARO, Lisa (Washington). "Obama donor George Tsunis ends his nomination as Norway ambassador". *Los Angeles Times*, 13 December 2014. Available at: <http://www.latimes.com/world/europe/la-fg-norway-ambassador-nominee-withdraws-20141213-story.html>.

"Merkel und der Irak-Krieg — Ein Golfkriegssyndrom ganz eigener Art". *Süddeutsche Zeitung*, 17 May 2010. Available at: <http://www.sueddeutsche.de/politik/merkel%2D%2Dund-der-irak-krieg-ein-golfkriegssyndrom-ganz-eigener-art-1.747506>.

METZEL, Mikhail (TASS). "West's support for state coup in Ukraine prime cause of crisis in Ukraine — Putin". *TASS*, 19 June 2015. Available at: <http://tass.ru/en/world/802418>.

MEYSSAN, Thierry. "Ukraine: Poland trained putchists two months in advance". *Voltaire Network* | Damascus (Syria) | 19 April 2014. Available at: <http://www.voltairenet.org/article183373.html>. Accessed 25 August 2015.

"MH17 investigators to RT: No proof east Ukraine fragments from 'Russian' Buk missile". *RT*, 11 August 2015. Available at: <http://www.rt.com/news/>.

"Middle East: Palestinian refugee numbers/whereabouts". *IRIN — Humanitarian news and analysis*. Available at: <http://www.irinnews.org/report/89571/middle-east-palestinian-refugee-numbers-whereabouts>.

"Milieudefensie / FoE Netherlands: Harmful shale gas deal between Shell and Yanukovych must be halted". *Friends of the Earth International*. Available at: <http://www.foei.org/news/milieudefensie-foe-netherlands-harmful-shale-gas-deal-between-shell-and-yanukovych-must-be-halted-2/>.

"Military Balance 2014", *The International Institute for Strategic Studies (IISS)*. Available at: <https://www.iiss.org/en/publications/military%20balance/issues/the-military-balance-2014-7e2c>.

"Military cooperation with Russia important for Belarusian security — defense minister". *TASS*, 17 June 2015. Available at: <http://tass.ru/en/world/801299>.

"Military-Industrial Complex Speech", Dwight D. Eisenhower, 1961. *Public Papers of the Presidents, Dwight D. Eisenhower, 1960*, pp. 1035–1040.

MILLEGAN, Kris, *Prescott Union Banking Corporation and the Story*. Available at: <http://www.fleshingoutskullandbones.com/P.Bush-Union_Banking/NYTH.html#>.

———. "Triumph, troubles shape generations". (Part Two), *Boston Globe*, 23 April 2001.

MILLER, Jake. "Kerry: 'Definitive' U.N. report confirms Assad behind chemical attack". *CBS News*, 19 September 2013. Available at: <http://www.cbsnews.com/news/kerry-definitive-un-report-confirms-assad-behind-chemical-attack/>.

MILNE, Seumas. "If the Libyan war was about saving lives, it was a catastrophic failure NATO claimed it would protect civilians in Libya, but delivered far more killing. It's a warning to the Arab world and Africa". *The Guardian*, 26 October 2011

Ministry of Defence of Ukraine. Available at: <https://en.wikipedia.org/wiki/Battle_of_Debaltseve>.

Minnəhar miṣrayim 'a-hannāhār haggāōl nəhar-pərāṯ" (rio: Nāhār). Genesis (Bərēšīṯ), 15:18. Biblia Hebraica Stuttgartensia, editio quinta emendata, Stuttgart: Deutsche Bibelgesellschaft, 1997, p. 21.

"Minsk agreement on Ukraine crisis: text in full". *The Telegraph*, 12 February 2015. Available at: <http://www.telegraph.co.uk/news/worldnews/europe/ukraine/11408266/Minsk-agreement-on-Ukraine-crisis-text-in-full.html>.

MITCHELL, Jon. "Libya — War in Libya and Its Futures — Tribal Dynamics and Civil War (1)" *The Red (Team) Analysis Society*, 13 April 2015. Available at: <http://www.google.de/imgres? imgurl=https%3A%2F%2Fwww.redanalysis.org%2Fwp-content%2Fuploads%2F2015% 2F04%2FTribes-Map.jpg&imgrefurl=https%3A%2F%2Fwww.redanalysis.org%2F2015% 2F04%2F13%2Fwar-libya-futures-tribal-dynamics-civil-war%2F&h=477&w=550& tbnid=LZASOPFCv39wlM%3A&zoom=1&do-cid=MzM39PpnHvjhWM& ei=xqyjVeKhFarNygOGhIXoCQ&tbm=isch&iact=rc&uact=3&dur=1719&page=1& start=0&ndsp=42&ved=0CDAQrQMwBQ>.

MITCHELL, Lincoln A. *The Color Revolutions*. Philadelphia: Pennsylvania Press, 2012.

MITCHELL, Thomas G. *Likud Leaders: The Lives and Careers of Menachem Begin, Yitzhak Shamir, Benjamin Netanyahu and Ariel Sharon*. Jefferson-North Carolina: McFarland & Company Inc. Publishers, 2015, p. 179.

Modern Jewish History: Pogroms. Jewish Virtual Library. 2ª ed., pp. 71–73. Available at <http:// www.jewishvirtuallibrary.org/jsource/History/pogroms.html>.

"Mohammed Jawad —Habeas Corpus". *American Civil Liberties (ACLU)*, 24 August 2009. Available at: <https://www.aclu.org/national-security/mohammed-jawad-habeas-corpus>.

MOMMSEN, Margareta. *Wer herrscht in Rußland? Der Kreml und di Schatten der Macht.* Munique: Verlag C. H. Beck, 2003, pp. 56–57, 63–70 *passim*; WEST, Darrel M. *Billionaires — Reflections on the Upper Crust*. Washington, D.C: Brookings Institution Press, 2014, p. 7, 103–104.

MONAGHAN, Angela. "Ukraine bailout of $17bn approved by IMF who warns reforms are at risk. Kiev agrees to a sweeping economic programme but may need to extend bailout if the unrest in east of country escalates". *The Guardian*, 1 May 2014.

MONIZ BANDEIRA, Luiz Alberto. "Um mestre do direito e da vida", prefácio ao ensaio do professor Alberto da Rocha Barros, *Que é o fascismo?* Rio de Janeiro-Guanabara, Editora Laemmert, 1969, pp. 7.

_____. *A reunificação da Alemanha — Do ideal socialista ao socialismo real.* São Paulo: editora UNESP, 3ª. Edição revista e aumentada, 2009.

_____. *A segunda guerra fria — geopolítica e dimensão estratégica dos Estados Unidos — Das rebeliões na Eurásia à África do Norte e ao Oriente Médio.* Civilização Brasileira, 2ª. ed., 2014.

_____. *De Martí a Fidel — A Revolução Cubana e a América Latina.* Rio de Janeiro: Civilização Brasileira, 2ª edição revista e ampliada, 2009, pp. 769–784.

_____. *Formação do império americano — Da guerra contra a Espanha à guerra no Iraque.* Rio de Janeiro: Civilização Brasileira, 4ª ed. revista e atualizada, 2014.

MONIZ DE ARAGÃO, Antônio Ferrão. *Classificação methódica e enciclopédica dos conhecimentos humanos — Introdução Geral — 1ª parte.* Salvador: Typ. Constitucional, 1871, p. 378 *passim*.

MORELL, Michael; HARLOW Bill. *The Great War of our Times — The CIA fight against Terrorism and Al Qa'ida.* New York/Boston: Twelve, 2015.

MORRIS, Benny. "For the record". *The Guardian*, 14 January 2004. Available at: <http://www. theguardian.com/world/2004/jan/14/israel/print>.

_____. "Palestinian Identity: The Construction of Modern National Consciousness (review)". *Israel Studies* — vol. 3, Number 1, Spring 1998, pp. 266–272. Available at: <https://muse.jhu.edu/ login?auth=0&type=summary&url=/journals/israel_studies/v003/3.1morris.html>.

_____. *The Birth of the Palestine refugee problem, 1947–1949*. Cambridge: Cambridge University Press, 1987, pp. 89–96, 101–111.

"Moscow rejects Saudi offer to drop Assad for arms deal". *Agence France-Presse — Global Post* 8 August 2013. Available at: <http://www.globalpost.com/dispatch/news/afp/130808/moscow-rejects-saudi-offer-drop-assad-arms-deal.

"Moscow will respond to NATO approaching Russian borders 'accordingly' — Putin". *RT*, 16 June 2015. Available at: <http://rt.com/news/267661-russia-nato-border-weapons/>.

MOSK, Matthew (Washington Post Staff Writer). "Industry Gushed Money after Reversal on Drillin". *The Washington Post*, 27 July 2008. Available at: <http://www.washingtonpost.com/wp-dyn/content/article/2008/07/26/AR2008072601891.html>.

"Mother Superior presents a 50 pages report to the Human Rights Commision regarding the gas attacks". Available at: <http://www.abovetopsecret.com/forum/thread972253/pg1>.

MOYER, Elizabeth. "Washington's $5 Trillion Tab". *Forbes*, 12 November 2008. Available at: <http://www.forbes.com/2008/11/12/paulson-bernanke-fed-biz-wall-cx_lm_1112bailout.html>.

MOZGOVAYA, Natasha. "U.S. Finalizes $30 Billion Weapons Deal With Saudi Arabia: White House says agreement — under which 84 F-15 fighter jets will be sold to the kingdom, will help U.S. economy and strengthen regional security". *Há'aretz*, 29 December 2011. Available at: <http://www.haaretz.com/middle-east-news/u-s-finalizes-30-billion-weapons-deal-with-saudi-arabia-1.404461>.

MUFSON, Steven. "Obama administration concedes that Mideast peace is beyond reach on his watch". *The Washington Post*, 5 November 2015. "Obama rules out Israeli-Palestinian peace deal before leaving office — US officials say president has made 'realistic assessment'; will discuss steps to prevent further violence with Netanyahu on Monday". *Times of Israel*, 6 November 2015, Available at: <http://www.timesofisrael.com/obama-rules-out-israeli-pales tinian-peace-deal-before-leavingoffice/?utm_source=The+Times+of+Israel+Daily+Edition& utm_campaign=ecd33f82de-2015_11_06&utm_medium=email&utm_term=0_adb46cec92-ecd33f82de-55318305>.

MUGHRABI, Magda "Five years ago, an initially peaceful uprising in Libya quickly developed into armed conflict involving Western military intervention and eventually ended when Colonel Mu'ammar al-Gaddafi was killed in October 2011. Successive governments then failed to prevent newly-formed militias of anti al-Gaddafi fighters from committing serious crimes for which they never faced justice. The country remains deeply divided and since May 2014 has been engulfed in renewed armed conflict". *Amnesty International*, London, 16 February 2016. Available at: <https://www.amnesty.org/en/latest/campaigns/2016/02/libya-arab-spring-7-ways-human-rights-are-under-attack/>.

_____. "Libya since the 'Arab Spring': 7 ways human rights are under attack". *Amnesty International* — LibyaArmed Conflict, London, 16 February 2016. Available at: <https://www.amnesty.org/en/latest/campaigns/2016/02/libya-arab-spring-7-ways-human-rights-are-under-attack/>.

MULLINS, Eustace. *The Secrets of Federal Reserve*. s/ed. Print on Demand, 2010, pp. 21–26.

MUNOZ, Megan. "For Members Only: The Consequences of the Caspian Summit's Foreign Military Ban". *Modern Diplomacy*, 30 July 2015. Available at: <http://moderndiplomacy.eu/index.php?option=com_k2&view=item&id=890:for-members-only-the-consequences-of-the-caspian-summit-s-foreign-military-ban&Itemid=771>.

MURAVCHIK, Joshua. *Exporting Democracy: Fulfilling America's Destiny — Fulfilling the American Destiny*. Washington: Aei Press, 1991, p. 81–83.

"Must Watch: 20.11.2013!! (pre-Maidan!): Ukraine Deputy has proof of USA staging civil war in Ukraine". Transcript — *Investment Watch*. 27 January 2015. Available at: <http://investmentwatchblog.com/proof-of-us-sponsored-coup-in-ukraine-ukrainian-politician-before-the-violent-demonstrations-on-maidan-us-embassy-in-kiev-ran-a-project-called-techcamp-to-train-activists-in-organizing-protests/>.

"Must watch: Ukrainian Deputy: US to stage a civil war in Ukraine! This was 20.11.2013!! Before Maidan". *The Vineyard of the Saker,* 28 January 2015. Available at: <http://vineyardsaker. blogspot.de/2015/01/must-watch-ukrainian-deputy-us-to-stage.html>.

MYERS, Steven Lee; SCHMITT, Eric. "Russian Military Uses Syria as Proving Ground, and West Takes Notice". *The New York Times,* 14 October 2015. Available at <http://www.nytimes.com/ 2015/10/15/world/middleeast/russian-military-uses-syria-as-proving-ground-and-west-takes-notice.html?_r=0>.

"Nach dem Bush-Hitler-Vergleich — Ministerin Däubler-Gmelin tritt ab". *Der Spiegel,* 23 September 2002. Available at: <http://www.spiegel.de/politik/deutschland/nach-dem-bush-hitler-vergleich-ministerin-daeubler-gmelin-tritt-ab-a-215291-druck.htm>.

NAGLE, Chad. "Ukraine's pro-Russian separatists claim Bolshevik legacy". *The New Hetmanate,* 7 February 2015. Available at <http://newhetmanate.net/2015/02/07/ukraines-pro-russian-sepa ratists-claim-bolshevik-legacy/>.

NAGOURNEY, Adam. "'Cultural War' of 1992 Moves In From the Fringe". *The New York Times,* 29 August 2012.

NANAY, Julia. "Russia's role in the energy Eurasian market", *in*: PEROVIC, Jeronim; ORTTUNG, Robert W.; WENGER, Andreas (Editores). *Russian energy power and foreign relations: Implications for conflit and cooperation.* Abingdon, Oxford: Taylor Francis Ltda., 2010, pp. 109–115.

NARVSELIUS, Eleonor. *Ukrainian Intelligentsia in Post-Soviet L'viv: Narratives, Identity, and Power.* Lanham/Maryland: Lexington Books-Rowman & Littlefield, s./d. pp. 343–344.

National Bank of Ukraine. Balance of Payments and External Debt of Ukraine in the First Quarter of 2014. Available at: <http://www.bank.gov.ua/doccatalog/document; jsessionid=D3E06465B2108ABB86DD04A0A4677539?id=10132249>.

"NATO countries are trying to take away 15% of the Serbian territory. Why?!". *Live Leak.* Available at: <http://www.liveleak.com/view?i=861_1365352907>.

"NATO countries have begun arms deliveries to Ukraine: defense minister". *Reuters,* 14 September 2014. Available at: <http://www.reuters.com/article/2014/09/14/us-ukraine-crisis-heletey-idUSKBN0H90PP20140914>. Accessed 30 August 2015.

"NATO countries have begun delivering weapons to Ukraine to help fight pro-Russian separatists, the country's defence minister claimed last night". *The Times,* 15 September 2014. Available at: <http://www.thetimes.co.uk/tto/news/world/europe/article4206727.ece>.

"NATO leaders pledge support to Ukraine at Wales Summit". *NATO/OTAN — North Atlantic Treaty Organization,* 4 September 2014. Available at: <http://www.nato.int/cps/de/natohq/ news_112459.htm>.

"NATO to give Ukraine 15mn euros, lethal and non-lethal military supplies from members". *RT,* 4 September 2014. Available at: <http://www.rt.com/news/185132-nato-ukraine-aid-support/>. Accessed 5 July 2014.

NAYAK, Satyendra. *The Global Financial Crisis: Genesis, Policy Response and Road Ahead.* New Delhi, 2013, pp. 105–108.

NEEF, Christian (Kiev). "Yanukovych's Fall: The Power of Ukraine's Billionaires". *Spiegel Online International,* 25 February 2014. Available at: <http://www.spiegel.de/international/europe/ how-oligarchs-in-ukraine-prepared-for-the-fall-of-yanukovych-a-955328.html>.

NERUDA, Pablo. "Nuevo canto de amor a Stalingrado", *in: Tercera Residencia.* Buenos Aires: Editorial Losada, 1951, pp. 83–87.

NESBIT, Jeff: Poison Tea — How Big Oil and Big Tobacco Invented the Tea Party and Captured the GOP. New York: Thomas Dunne Books — S. Martins's Press, 2016.

"Netanyahu's new media czar called Obama 'anti-Semitic' — Ran Baratz also in hot water for comments disparaging Rivlin, John Kerry; two Likud ministers oppose his appointment". *The Times of Israel,* 5 November 2015. Available at: <http://www.timesofisrael.com/netanyahus-new-media-czar-called-obama-anti-semitic/?utm_source=The+Times+of+Israel+Daily+Edi tion&utm_campaign=55b79272ba-2015_11_05&utm_medium=email&utm_term=0_ adb46cec92-55b79272ba-55318305>.

NEVINS, Sean. "2011 NATO Destruction of Libya Has Increased Terrorism Across Region". "From Libya to Mali, Nigeria and Somalia, NATO's 2011 intervention against Moammar Gadhafi has had an undeniable domino effect — but when do the dominoes stop falling?" *MintPress News*, 20 May 2015. Available at: <http://www.mintpressnews.com/2011-nato-destruction-of-libya-has-increased-terrorism-across-region/205801/>.

"New York FED stores third od gold. 80 countries keeps 13 billion in vault". *Chicago Tribune*, 23 September 1969. Available at: <http://archives.chicagotribune.com/1969/09/23/page/53/article/new-york-fed-bank-stores-third-of-gold>.

NEWMAN, Alex. "What is the Obama-backed Free Syrian Army?" *New American,* 17 September 2013. Available at: <http://www.thenewamerican.com/world-news/asia/item/16550-what-is-the-obama-backed-free-syrian-army>.

NIMMO, Kurt. "Russia Says U.S. Mercenaries in Eastern Ukraine — Coup government in Kyiv moves to quell separatism as civil war brews". Infowars.com, 10 March 2014. Available at: <http://www.infowars.com/russia-claims-greystone-mercenaries-team-up-with-right-sector-in-eastern-ukraine/>.

_____. "Sen. Feinstein: 'There Will Be Plots to Kill Americans'". Infowars.com On June 23, 2014. *In*: *Featured Stories, Infowars Exclusives, Tile*. Available at: <http://www.infowars.com/sen-feinstein-there-will-be-plots-to-kill-americans/print/>.

No war plans for Syria: U.S." *CNN*, 16 April 2003. Available at: <http://edition.cnn.com/2003/WORLD/meast/04/15/sprj.irq.int.war.main/index.html>.

N° 1014–3 — On Amendments to Certain Laws of Ukraine Concerning Ukraine's Abolishment of the Policy of Neutrality. Verkhovna Rada abolished Ukraine's neutral status Denys Kolesnyk". *Info-News,* 23 December 2014. Available at: <http://info-news.eu/verkhovna-rada-abolished-ukraines-neutral-status/#sthash.O9KFKoxv.i4tIzVYC.dpuf>.

NOLAN, Cathal J. (Editor). *Notable U.S. Ambassadors since 1775*: *A Biographical. Dictionary*. Westport, Connecticut: Greenwood Press, 1997, p. 90. Tamara Keith. "When Big Money Leads To Diplomatic Posts". *NPR*, 3 December 2014. Available at: <http://www.npr.org/2014/12/03/368143632/obama-appoints-too-many-big-donors-to-ambassadorships-critics-say>.

"Norte-Sur. Un programa para la supervivencia. Informe de la Comisión Independiente sobre Problemas Internacionales del Desarrollo presidida por Willy Brandt". *The Independente Comisión on International Development Sigues*. Bogotá: Editorial Pluma, 1980, p. 305.

"Northwestern Mutual Voice Team, Northwestern Mutual. Who Wins And Who Loses As Oil Prices Fall?" *Forbes — Investing*, 16 December 2014. Available at: <http://www.forbes.com/sites/northwesternmutual/2014/12/16/who-wins-and-who-loses-as-oil-prices-fall/>.

NORTON-TAYLOR, Richard. "US weapons to Ukraine 'would be matched by Russian arms to rebels' — International Institute for Strategic Studies warns that Moscow could arm separatists more quickly than US could reinforce Ukraine's forces". *The Guardian*, 11 February 2015. <https://www.theguardian.com/world/2015/feb/11/us-weapons-to-ukraine-would-be-matched-by-russian-arms-to-rebels>. Accessed 3 December 2018.

NOVICHKOV, Nikolai (Moscow). "Country Risk — MH17 'shot down by Ukrainian SAM', claims Almaz-Antey". *IHS Jane's Defence Weekly*, 4 June 2015. Available at: <http://www.janes.com/article/52019/mh17-shot-down-by-ukrainian-sam-claims-almaz-antey>. Accessed 14 August 2014.

"Nuclear War's Impact on Global Climate". Available at: <http://www.aasc.ucla.edu/cab/200706140013.html>.

"Number of foreign fighters in Syria has doubled in past year — report". *RT*, 27 September 2015. Available at: <https://www.rt.com/news/316644-jihadists-flow-double-syria/>. Accessed 28 September 2015.

Nyet Means Nyet: *Russia's NATO Enlargement*. Cable 08MOSCOW265 Reference ID — 2008–02-01- Confidential — Moscow 000265 — FM Amembassy Moscow — Ref: A. Moscow 147 ¶B. Moscow 182 — Classified By: Ambassador William J. Burns. Reasons 1.4 (b) and (d). Available at: <http://wikileaks.org/cable/2008/02/08MOSCOW265.html>.

"Obama Pledges to Push Trans-Pacific Partnership In State Of The Union The Roundup for January 21st, 2015.", "Taken For Granted At Davos That US Government Run On 'Legalized Corruption'". *DSWright*, 21 January 2015. Available at: <http://news.firedoglake.com/2015/01/21/taken-for-granted-at-davos-that-us-government-run-on-legalized-corruption/>.

"Obama's pick for Joint Chiefs sides with Romney on Russia". *New York Post*, 9 July 2015. Available at: <http://nypost.com/2015/07/09/russia-is-greatest-threat-to-america-joint-chiefs-nominee/>.

"Obama's Top Fund-Raisers". *The New York Times*, 13 September 2012. Available at: <http://www.nytimes.com/interactive/2012/09/13/us/politics/obamas-top-fund-raisers.html?_r=0>. Accessed 18 April 2014.

Observatory of Economic Complexity. Available at: <http://atlas.media.mit.edu/profile/country/ukr/. See also: http://atlas.media.mit.edu/profile/country/ukr/>.

ODOM, Lt. Gen. William E. "Strategic Errors of Monumental Proportions. What Can Be Done in Iraq? Text of testimony before the Senate Foreign Relations Committee, 18 January 2007". AntiWar.com, 26 January 2007. Available at: <http://www.antiwar.com/orig/odom.php?articleid=10396>.

"OECD Income Distribution Database: Gini, poverty, income, Methods and Concepts. Social policies and data". Available at: <http://www.oecd.org/els/soc/income-distribution-database.htm>.

Of Russian origin: *Cossacks — Russiapedia*. Available at <http://russiapedia.rt.com/of-russian-origin/cossacks/>.

"Office of the United Nations High Commissioner for Human Rights Report on the human rights situation in Ukraine". 15 July 2014. Available at: <http://www.ohchr.org/Documents/Countries/UA/Ukraine_Report_15July2014.pdf>. Accessed 8 August 2014.

"Oil and natural gas production is growing in Caspian Sea region". *Today in Energy*, 11 September 2013. *U.S. Energy Information Administration*. Available at: <http://www.eia.gov/todayinenergy/detail.cfm?id=12911>.

OLEARCHYK, Roman (Kiev); MEYER, Gregory (New York). "Cargill acquires stake in Ukraine agribusiness". *Information Clearing House*, 13 March 2014. Available at: <http://www.informationclearinghouse.info/article37931.htm>.

_____. (Kiev). "Ukraine offers to guarantee Naftogaz debt". *Financial Times,* 21 September 2009. Available at: <http://www.ft.com/intl/cms/s/0/f04c0740-a6b8–11de-bd14–00144feabdc0.html#axzz37w0928mV>.

_____. "Ukraine's Naftogaz battles to avert default". *Financial Times*, 30 September 2009. Available at: <http://www.ft.com/intl/cms/s/0/6efad0e2-add7–11de-87e7–00144feabdc0.html#axzz37w0928mV>.

OLIPHANT, Roland (Odessa). "Ukraine crisis: death by fire in Odessa as country suffers bloodiest day since the revolution". *The Telegraph,* 3 May 2014. Available at: <http://www.telegraph.co.uk/news/worldnews/europe/ukraine/10806656/Ukraine-crisis-death-by-fire-in-Odessa-as-country-suffers-bloodiest-day-since-the-revolution.html>.

"On NATO, How Will Russia React? Kennan's Warning". *The New York Times*, 4 May 1998.

"One Hundred Ninth Congress of the United States of America at the Second Session Begun and held at the City of Washington on Tuesday, the third day of January, two thousand and six H. R. 5122". Available at: <https://www.govtrack.us/congress/bills/109/hr5122/text>.

"Operation Mongoose Priority Operations Schedule — 21 May — 30 June 1962, Washington, May 17, 1962". *Foreign Relations of the United States* (FRUS), vol. X, 1961–1962, Cuba, pp. 810-820.

OPPEL JR, Richard A.; NATTA JR, Don Van. "Enron's Collapse: The Relationship; Bush and Democrats Disputing Ties to Enron". *The New York Times*, 12 January 2002.

OR KASHTI. "Israeli University Lecturer Says Denied Promotion for Being 'Too Leftist' — Bar Ilan's promotions committee also ruled against elevating Dr. Menachem Klein to the rank of professor five years ago". *Há'aretz*, 10 February 2011. Available at: <http://www.haaretz.com/israel-news/israeli-university-lecturer-says-denied-promotion-for-being-too-leftist-1.342355>.

ORCUTT, Mike (Technology Review). "Shale gas has become the geopolitical energy that can change ruling power globally. Kiev fights in Ukraine's southeast for shale gas deposits to be controlled by US". *Gunnars tankar och funderingar.* Available at: <http://gunnarlittmarck. blogspot.de/2014/08/shale-gas-has-become-geopolitical.html>.

ORENSTEIN, Mitchell A.; ROMER. "George Putin's Gas Attack — Is Russia Just in Syria for the Pipelines?" *Foreign Affairs*, 14 October 2015. Available at: <https://www.foreignaffairs.com/ articles/syria/2015–10–14/putins-gas-attack>.

"Orthodox public concerned for threat of neo-nazism in Ukraine". *Interfax*, 27 October 2006. Available at: <http://www.interfax-religion.com/?act=news&div=2192>.

OSIPIAN, Ararat L. *The Impact of Human Capital on Economic Growth: A Case Study in Post-Soviet Ukraine — 1989–2009.* London: Palgrave Macmillan, 2009, pp. 123–124.

OSWALD, Vivian. *Com vistas para o Kremlin — A vida na Rússia pós-soviética.* São Paulo: Editora Globo, 2011, p. 75.

"Overview: Bush and Public Opinion. Reviewing the Bush Years and the Public's Final Verdict". *Pew Research Center,* 18 December 2008. Available at: <http://www.people-press.org/2008/ 12/18/bush-and-public-opinion/#.

OZHIGANOV, Edward. "The Crimean Republic: rivalries concepts". *In*: ARBATOV, Alekseĭ; CHAYES, Abram; CHAYES, Antônio Handler (Editors). *Managing Conflict in the Former Soviet Union: Russian and American Perspectives.* Center for Science and International Affair — John Kennedy School of Government, Harvard University, 1997, p. 123.

PA, Tatyana Zenkovich. "Poroshenko's fortune estimated at $750 million — Forbes-Ukraine — Ukrainian president ranks eighth in the ranking, which is topped by Rinat Akhmetov ($6.9 billion), Viktor Pinchuk ($1.5 billion) and ex-Dnipropetrovsk region governor Igor Kolomoysky ($1.4 billion)". *TASS*, 27 March 2015. Available at: <http://tass.ru/en/world/ 785423>.

"Package of Measures for the Implementation of the Minsk Agreements". *Présidence de la République française* — Élysée.fr. Available at: <http://www.elysee.fr/declarations/article/pack age-of-measures-for-the-implementation-of-the-minsk-agreements/>.

PAGE, Jeremy (Kabul). "Mohammed Jawad: 'I was 12 when I was arrested and sent to Guantanamo'." *The Times*, 27 August 2009. Available at: <http://www.thetimes.co.uk/tto/ news/world/asia/afghanistan/article1843471.ece>.

Palestinians at the End of 2015", *Palestinian Central Bureau of Statistics (PCBS)*, 30 December 2015. Available at: <http://www.pcbs.gov.ps/site/512/default.aspx?tabID=512&lang=en& ItemID=1566&mid=3171&wversion=Staging>.

PANETTA, Leon. NEWTON, Jim. *Worthy Fights*. New York: Penguin Press, 2014, p. 396.

_____. *Worthy Fights*. New York: Penguin Press, 2014.

PARFITT, Tom (Urzuf, Ucrânia). "Ukraine crisis: the neo-Nazi brigade fighting pro-Russian separatists — Kiev throws paramilitaries — some openly neo-Nazi — into the front of the battle with rebels". *The Telegraph*, 11 August 2014. Available at: <http://www.telegraph.co.uk/ news/worldnews/europe/ukraine/11025137/Ukraine-crisis-the-neo-Nazi-brigade-fighting-pro-Russian-separatists.html>.

PARRY, Hannah (Dailymail.com). "Yazidi sex slave claims she was raped by 'white American ISIS jihadi' in Syria". *Daily Mail*, 24 September 2015. Available at: <http://www.dailymail.co. uk/news/article-3248173/Yazidi-sex-slave-claims-raped-American-teacher-turned-ISIS-jihadi-testify-Congress.html>. Accessed 29 September 2015.

PARRY, Nat. "Beneath the Ukraine Crisis: Shale Gas". Consortiumnet.com, 24 April 2014. Available at: <https://consortiumnews.com/2014/04/24/beneath-the-ukraine-crisis-shale-gas/>.

PARRY, Robert. "UN Investigator Undercuts New York Times on Syria. Assad Government not Responsible for August 21 Chemical Attack". Available at: https://www.globalresearch.ca/ uninvestigator-undercuts-new-york-times-on-syria-assad-government-not-responsible-for-august-21-chemical-attack/5362559. Accessed 28 November 2018.

"Party of Regions MP Tsariov accuses US Embassy in Ukraine of training revolutionaries for street protests". *KyivPost,* 20 November 2013. | Politics–*Interfax-Ukraine* Available at: <http://www.

kyivpost.com/content/politics/party-of-regions-mp-tsariov-accuses-us-embassy-in-ukraine-of-training-revolutionaries-for-street-protests-332162.html>.

"Paul Craig Roberts: 'Bringing Democracy' Has Become Washington's Cover For Resurrecting a Nazi State". *Silver Doctors*, 6 May 2015. Available at: <http://www.silverdoctors.com/paul-craig-roberts-bringing-democracy-has-become-washingtons-cover-for-resurrecting-a-nazi-state>.

PAUL, Ron. "After a Twelve Year Mistake in Iraq, We Must Just March Home". *The Ron Paul Institute for Peace & Prosperity*, 22 March 2015. Available at: <http://www.ronpaulinstitute.org/archives/featured-articles/2015/march/22/after-a-twelve-year-mistake-in-iraq-we-must-just-march-home/>.

"Paulo Craig Roberts Interviewed by the *Voice of Russia*", 27 June 2014US war against Russia is already underway. PaulCraigRoberts.org. Available at: <http://www.paulcraigroberts.org/2014/07/01/us-war-russia-already-underway-pcr-interviewed-voice-russia/>.

PAUWELS, Jacques R. "Profits über Alles! American Corporations and Hitler". *Global Research*, 15 May 2014 — *Global Research*, 8 June 2004. *Centre for Research on Globalization*. Available at: <http://www.globalresearch.ca/profits-ber-alles-american-corporations-and-hitler/4607>.

"Payment, clearing and settlement systems in China". Available at: <https://www.bis.org/cpmi/publ/d105_cn.pdf>.

PELLERIN, Cheryl. DoD News, Defense Media Activity. "DoD Moves Forward on Ukraine National Guard Training". *U.S. Department of Defence. Washington*, 20 March 2015. Available at: <http://www.defense.gov/News-Article-View/Article/604322>.

PERLEZ, Jane. "Expanding Alliance: THE OVERVIEW; Poland, Hungary and the Czechs Join NATO". *The New York Times,* 13 March 1999.

PERRY, Dan; FEDERMAN, Josef. "Netanyahu years continue surge in settlement". *Associated Press*, 15 December 2014. Available at: <http://news.yahoo.com/netanyahu-years-see-surge-west-bank-settlements-075922371.html>.

PESSOA, Fernando. *Sobre Portugal — Introdução ao Problema Nacional.* (Recolha de textos de Maria Isabel Rocheta e Maria Paula Morão. Introdução organizada por Joel Serrão.). Lisboa: Ática, 1979, p. 19. Available at: <http://multipessoa.net/labirinto/portugal/12>.

PETRAS, James. "The Kiev Putsch", *in*: LENDMAN, Stephen (Ed.). *Flashpoint in Ukraine — How US drive for Hegemony Risks World War III*. Atlanta, GA: Clarity Press, Inc., 2014, pp. 228–229.

PIFER, Steven. "The Trilateral Process: The United States, Ukraine, Russia and Nuclear Weapons". Paper I May 2011. *Brooking*. Available at: <http://www.brookings.edu/research/papers/2011/05/trilateral-process-pifer>.

PIKETTY, Thomas. *L'Économie des inegalités*. Paris: La Découverte. Septième édition, 2015.

_____. *Le Capital aux XXIe*. Paris: Seuil, 2013.

PINCHUK, Denis; ASTAKHOVA, Olesya; VULKMANOVIC, Oleg. "Gazprom to offer more gas at spot prices via Nord Stream II". *Reuters*, 13 October 2015. Available at: <http://www.reuters.com/article/2015/10/13/us-russia-gazprom-spot-idUSKCN0S71XS20151013>.

PIPES, Daniel. "Imperial Israel: The Nile-to-Euphrates Calumny". *Middle East Quarterly,* March 1994. Available at: <http://www.danielpipes.org/247/imperial-israel-the-nile-to-euphrates-calumny>.

PITALEV, Ilya. "Serious meetings needed to settle situation around Ukraine — Gorbachev". *Itar—Tass,* Moscow, 26 December 2014. Available at: <http://itar-tass.com/en/russia/769544>.

PIVEN, Ben; WILLERS, Ben. "Infographic: Ukraine's 2014 presidential election". *Al Jazeera*, 23 May 2014. Available at: <http://america.aljazeera.com/multimedia/2014/5/ukraine-presidentialelectioninfographic.html>. Accessed 5 August 2015.

PIZZI, Michael. "Libya's rogue general, an ex-CIA asset, vaunts his anti-extremism services. Khalifa Haftar wants to rid Libya of the Muslim Brotherhood — something many regional powers may rally behind". *Al Jazeera*, 24 July 2014.

"Plünderung der Welt — Ukraine: US-Investment-Bankerin ist neue Finanzministerin". *Deutsche Wirtschafts Nachrichten*, 2 December 2014. Available at: <http://deutsche-wirtschafts-nachrichten.de/2014/12/02/ukraine-us-investment-bankerin-ist-neue-finanzministerin/>.

PODOLS, Anatoly. "Collaboration in Ukraine during the Holocaust: Aspects of Historiography and Research". *The Holocaust in Ukraine — New Sources and Perspectives — Conference Presentations*, pp. 187–195.

POHL, J. Otto. "The Deportation and Fate of the Crimean Tatars". International Committee for Crimea. Washington, DC, 2003. Esse paper foi apresentado na 5th Annual World Convention of the Association for the Study of Nationalities: "Identity and the State: Nationalism and Sovereignty in a Changing World". New York: Columbia University, 13–15 April 2000. Foi parte do painel "A Nation Exiled: The Crimean Tatars in the Russian Empire, Central Asia, and Turkey." Available at <http://www.iccrimea.org/scholarly/jopohl.html>.

"Política Externa Norte-americana — Análise de Alguns Aspectos", Anexo 1 e único ao Ofício n° 516/900.1 (22), secreto, embaixada em Washington ao Ministério das Relações Exteriores, Washington, 13.06.1963, Arquivo do Ministério das Relações Exteriores-Brasília, 900.1 (00), Política Internacional, de (2) a (98), 1951/66.

POLLACK, Norman. "Obama's Foreign Policy — Militarization of Globalism". *Counterpunch*, 18 August 2014. Available at <http://www.counterpunch.org/2014/08/18/militarization-of-globalism/print>.

PONS, Silvio. *The Global Revolution*. Oxford: Oxford University Press, 2014, pp. 318–320.

POORT, David; SILVERSTEIN, Ken. "Swiss study: Polonium found in Arafat's bones — Scientists find at least 18 times the normal levels of radioactive element in late Palestinian leader". *Al Jazeera*, 7 November 2013. Available at: <http://www.aljazeera.com/investigations/killing-arafat/swiss-study-polonium-found-arafats-bones-201311522578803512.html>.

POP, Valentina. "Multi-billion losses expected from Russia sanctions". *EuObserver*, Brussels, 28 July 2014. Available at: <https://euobserver.com/economic/125118>.

POPE FRANCIS. Speech to US Congress, 25 september 2015". Available at: <http://www.aljazeera.com/news/2015/09/full-text-pope-francis-speech%2D%2Dcongress-150924152204132.html>.

"Poroshenko sold ROSHEN to Yanukovych — via the Rothschilds". *Seemorerocks,* 2 September 2014. Available at: <http://robinwestenra.blogspot.de/2014/09/poroshenkos-chocolate-empire.html>.

PORTER, Gareth. *Manufactured Crisis — Untold Story of the Nuclear Scare*. Charlotteville, Virginia: Just World Books, 2015.

PORTER, Tom. "Mikhail Gorbachev claims Vladimir Putin 'saved' Russia from falling apart". *International Business Times*, 27 December 2014. Available at: <http://www.ibtimes.co.uk/mikhail-gorbachev-claims-vladimir-putin-saved-russia-falling-apart-1481065>.

POWELL, Colin L. *The Military Strategy of the United States — 1991–1992*. Washington: US Government, Printing Office, ISBN 0–16-036125-7, 1992, p 7. Draft Resolution — 12 Cooperation for Security in the Hemisphere, Regional Contribution to Global Security — The General Assembly, recalling: Resolutions AG/RES. 1121 (XXX- 091 and AG/RES. 1123 (XXI-091) for strengthening of peace and security in the hemisphere, and AG/RES. 1062 (XX090) against clandestine arms traffic.

PRADOS, John. *Safe for Democracy: The Secret Wars of the CIA*. Chicago, Ivan R. Dee, 2006, 163–164

Pravda.ru, 23 August 2015. Available at: <http://port.pravda.ru/mundo/23–08-2015/39316-maidan_donbass-0/#sthash.l0BIcUeA.dpuf>.

"Premier Stalin to Prime Minister — 4 Sept. 41" *in*: CHURCHILL, Winston. *The Second World War — The Grand Alliance*. London: Guild Publishing — Book Club Associates, vol. III, pp. 405–406.

"Presentation of foreign ambassador's letters of credence: Vladimir Putin received letters of credence from 15 foreign ambassadors. By tradition, the ceremony marking the official start of the ambassador's mission in the Russian Federation, took place in the Grand Kremlin

Palace's Alexander Hall". *President of Russia. The Kremlin, Moscow.* 26 November 2015. Available at <http://en.kremlin.ru/events/president/news/50786>.

"President Bush Addresses the Nation: Following is the full text of President Bush's address to a joint session of Congress and the nation", 20 September 2001. *eMediaMillWorks — The Washington Post.* Available at: <http://www.washingtonpost.com/wp-srv/nation/specials/attacked/transcripts/bushaddress_092001.html>.

"President Bush Calls for New Palestinian Leadership" — The Rose Garden — Office of the Press Secretary for Immediate Release — June 24, 2002. *White House — Presidente George W. Bush.* Available at: <http://georgewbush-whitehouse.archives.gov/news/releases/2002/06/20020624-3.html>.

"President confers posthumous title Hero of Ukraine to Stepan Bandera — President Victor Yushchenko awarded Ukrainian politician and one of the leaders of Ukrainian national movement Stepan Bandera a posthumous title Hero of Ukraine and the Order of the State". *Official Website of President of Ukraine — Press office of President Victor Yushchenko*, 22 January 2010. Available at: <http://www.president.gov.ua/en/news/16473.html>.

"President Obama's Second-Term Ambassadorial Nominations. Updated April 17, 2015". *American Foreign Service Association.* Available at: <http://www.afsa.org/secondterm.aspx>.

"President Signs Authorization for Use of Military Force bill. Resolution 23, Statement by the President. 'Today I am signing Senate Joint Resolution 23, the 'Authorization for Use of Military Force'". *George W. Bush — The White House*, 18 September 2001. Available at: <http://georgewbush-whitehouse.archives.gov/news/releases/2001/09/20010918-10.html>. Accessed 26 November 2018.

"President Welcomes Palestinian President Abbas to the White House". The Rose Garden. *The White House — President George W. Bush.* Office of the Press Secretary, 26 May 2005. Available at: <http://georgewbush-whitehouse.archives.gov/news/releases/2005/05/print/text/20050526.html>.

"President's New Conference with President Leonid Kravchuck of Kiev, January 12, 1994", *in:* CLINTON, William J. *Public Papers of the Presidents of the United States: William J. Clinton, 1994,* pp. 43–46. Available at: <https://books.google.de/books?id=NCThAwAAQBAJ&pg=PA46&lpg=PA46&dq=Clinton+Partnership+For+peace+Ukraine&source=bl&ots=xAVnTwVIs-&sig=rnoNdxUxlugp_6qfOJFYzP0D97Q&hl=de&sa=X&ei=gd_pVLiHOsb9UOGRgtAN&ved=0CFMQ6AEwBQ#v=onepage&q=Clinton%20Partnership%20For%20peace%20Ukraine&f=false>.

PRIEST, Dana (*Washington Post* Staff Writer). "CIA Holds Terror Suspects in Secret Prisons — Debate Is Growing Within Agency about Legality and Morality of Overseas System Set Up After 9/11". *The Washington Post*, 2 November 2005.

PRINS, Nomi. *All the Presidents — Bankers.* The Hidden Alliances that Drive American Power. New York: Nation Books, 2014.

"Profile: Ukraine's ultra-nationalist Right Sector". *BBC Europe*, 28 April 2014. Available at: <http://www.bbc.com/news/world-europe-27173857>.

"Prominent Russians: Nestor Makhno (October 26, 1888 — July 6, 1934)". *Russiapedia.* Available at: <http://russiapedia.rt.com/prominent-russians/history-and-mythology/nestor-makhno/>.

"Protesters Declare Independent People's Republic in Ukraine's Luhansk", *Sputnik* (RIA Novosti), 28 April 2014. Available at: <http://sputniknews.com/world/20140428/189420422.html#ixzz3h677L7fE>.

"PROTOCOL on the results of consultations of the Trilateral Contact Group (Minsk, 05/09/2014". Available at: <http://mfa.gov.ua/en/news-feeds/foreign-offices-news/27596-protocolon-the-results-of-consultations-of-the-trilateral-contact-group-minsk-05092014>.

"Public Attitudes toward the War in Iraq: 2003–2008". *Pew Research Center*, 19 March 2008. Available at: <http://www.pewresearch.org/2008/03/19/public-attitudes-toward-the-war-in-iraq-20032008/>.

Public Papers of the Presidents of the United States. George W. Bush (In Two Books) Book I: January 1 to June 30, 2005. Washington: US Government Printing Office, p. 880. Available at: <https://books.google.de/books?id=5VVC1YI72DoC&pg=PA880&lpg=PA880& dq=George+W.+Bush+%E2%80%9Cmust+remove+unauthorized+outposts+and+stop+settle ment+expansion.#v=onepage&q=George%20W.%20Bush%20%E2%80%9Cmust% 20remove%20unauthorized%20outposts%20and%20stop%20settlement%20expansion.& f=false>.

PUSHKOVA, Darya (RT correspondent). "Prominent Russians: Vladimir Potanin". *RT*, 1 February 2010. Available at: <http://russiapedia.rt.com/prominent-russians/business/vladimir-potanin/>.

"Putin explained why he decided to return Crimea to Russia". *Itar-TASS.* Available at: <http://tass. ru/en/russia/781790>.

"Putin orders talks on Russian military base in Belarus". *RT*, 19 September 2015. Available at: <https://www.rt.com/news/315964-putin-military-base-belarus/>. Accessed 19 September 2015.

"Putin reveals secrets of Russia's Crimea takeover plot". *BBC News — Europe,* 9 March 2015. Available at: <http://www.bbc.com/news/world-europe-31796226?print=true>.

"Putin says dump the dollar". *RT*, 1 September 2015. Available at: <https://www.rt.com/business/ 313967-putin-says-dump-dollar/>. Accessed 3 September 2015. Also in: <https://www.rt.com/ business/313967-putin-says-dump-dollar/>.

PUTIN, Vladimir. "The World Order: New Rules or a Game without Rules". Meeting of the Valdai International Discussion Club. 24 October 2014, 19:00, Sochi. *Official site of the President of Russia.* Available at: <http://en.kremlin.ru/events/president/news/46860>. Accessed 12 October 2015.

"Putin: 40+ ICBMs targeted for 2015 nuclear force boost". *RT*, 16 June 2015. Available at: <http:// rt.com/news/267514-putin-ballistic-missiles-army/>.

"Putin's Gambit: How the EU Lost Ukraine". *Der Spiegel,* 25 November 2013. Available at: <http://www.spiegel.de/international/europe/how-the-eu-lost-to-russia-in-negotiations-over-ukraine-trade-deal-a-935476.html>.

"Q&A: Mikhail Khodorkovsky and Russia". *BBC News — Europe*, 22 December 2013. Available at: <http://www.bbc.com/news/world-europe-25467275>.

"R-36 (SS-18 Satan) — Intercontinental ballistic missile Military-Today". *Military* Today.com. Available at: <http://www.military-today.com/missiles/ss18_satan.htm>.

RABINOVICH, Itamar. "The Devil We Knew". *The New York Times*, 18 November 2011.

RACHKEVYCH, Mark. "50 Richest Ukrainians". *Kyiv Post,* 11 June 2009. Available at: <http:// www.kyivpost.com/content/ukraine/50-richest-ukrainians-43241.html>.

RADIA, Kirit *et al.* "US Contractor Greystone Denies Its 'Mercenaries' in Ukraine". *ABC News*, 8 April 2014. Available at: <http://abcnews.go.com/Blotter/greystone-firm-accused-disguising-mercenaries-ukrainians/story?id=23243761>.

————; MEEK, James Gordon; FERRAN, Lee; WEINBERG, Ali. "US Contractor Greystone Denies Its 'Mercenaries' in Ukraine". *ABC News*, 8 April 2014. Available at: <http://abcnews. go.com/Blotter/greystone-firm-accused-disguising-mercenaries-ukrainians/story? id=23243761>.

"Radicals stage disorder at May Odessa massacre trial in southern Ukraine". *TASS*, 22 January 2015. Available at: <http://tass.ru/en/world/772769>. Accessed 2 August 2015.

"Radio West Bank Radio Destroyed." *Deep Dish Waves of Change*, 3 November 2015. Available at: <http://deepdishwavesofchange.org/blog/2015/11/west-bank-radio-destroyed>. Accessed 3 November 2015.

RADWAN, Tarek. "Top News: Syrian Antiquities and the ISIS Billion-Dollar Economy". *Atlantic Council*, 26 August 2015. Available at: <http://www.atlanticcouncil.org/en/blogs/menasource/ top-news-syrian-antiquities-and-the-isis-s-billion-dollar-economy>.

RAINSFORD, Sarah (Artemivsk, Ukraine). "Ukraine civilians stranded as shells pound Debaltseve". *BBC News*, 30 January 2015. Available at: <http://www.bbc.com/news/world-europe-31055060>. Accessed 27 August 2015.

RAMONET, Ignacio. Cien horas con Fidel Castro. Conversación con Ignacio Ramonet. Oficina de Publicaciones del Consejo de Estado. La Habana. 2006

RANKING, Jennifer & agencies. "Russia responds to sanctions by banning western food imports". *The Guardian*, 7 August 2014.

RAO, Sujata. "Big debts and dwindling cash — Ukraine tests creditors' nerves". *Reuters*, 17 October 2013 — Available at: <http://uk.reuters.com/article/2013/10/17/uk-emerging-ukraine-debt-idUKBRE99G06P20131017>. *Trading Economics*. Available at: <http://www.tradingeconomics.com/ukraine/external-debt>.

RAPOPORT, Louis. *Shake Heaven & Earth: Peter Bergson and the Struggle to Rescue the Jews of Europe*. Jerusalem: Gefen Publishing House, 1999.

RAPOZA, Kenneth. "Russian Government Ratifies Huge China Gas Pipeline Deal". *Forbes*, 3 May 2015. Available at: <http://www.forbes.com/sites/kenrapoza/2015/05/03/russian-government-ratifies-huge-china-gas-pipeline-deal/5>.

RASMUS, Jack. "Who Benefits From Ukraine Economic Crisis", *in*: LENDMAN, Stephen (Edit.) — *Flashpoint in Ukraine. How the US Drive for Hegemony Risks World War III*. Atlanta: Clarity Press, 2014, pp. 120–121.

RAVID, Barak. "IDF Intelligence Chief: Palestinian Despair, Frustration Are among Reasons for Terror Wave. Major General Herzi Halevi's assessment contradicts Prime Minister Benjamin Netanyahu's message which blames the attacks on incitement and ingrained hatred". *Há'aretz*, 3 November 2015. Available at: <http://www.haaretz.com/israel-news/.premium-1.683860>.

RAY, Lada. "7 Million People, 30% of GDP Say Goodbye to Ukraine: Donetsk and Lugansk Vote to Secede", 11 May 2014. *Futurist TrendCast*. Available at: <https://futuristtrendcast.wordpress.com/2014/05/11/live-voting-now-donetsk-peoples-republic-independence-referendum/>. Accessed 1º August 2015.

RAYMAN, Noah. "Leaked Audio Depicts U.S. Diplomat Cursing E.U. Diplomacy. Americans pointed the finger at Russia for the leak". *Time*, 6 February 2014. Available at: <http://world.time.com/2014/02/06/victoria-nuland-leaked-audio-european-union/>.

REAGAN, Ronald. *An American Life*. London: Arrow Books, 1991, p. 550.

REED, Stanley; KRAMER, Andrew E. "Chevron and Ukraine Set Shale Gas Deal". *The New York Times*, 5 November 2013.

"Regime Change in Kiev — Victoria Nuland Admits: US Has Invested $5 Billion In The Development of Ukrainian, 'Democratic Institutions'" Video — International Business Conference at Ukraine in Washington — National Press Club — December 13, 2013 — Victoria Nuland — Assistant Secretary of State for Europe and Eurasian Affairs. Postado em 9 February 2014.

"Regional Nuclear War Could Devastate Global Climate". Rutgers, the State University of New Jersey. *ScienceDaily*, 11 December 2006. Available at: <http://www.sciencedaily.com/releases/2006/12/061211090729.htm>.

"Remarks — Victoria Nuland, Assistant Secretary, Bureau of European and Eurasian Affairs. Washington, DC, December 13, 2013". *U.S. Department of State*. Available at: <http://www.state.gov/p/eur/rls/rm/2013/dec/218804.htm>.

"Remarks by the President at the United States Military Academy Commencement Ceremony". U.S. Military Academy-West Point, New York. *The White House — Office of the Press Secretary*, 28 May 2014. Available at: <http://www.whitehouse.gov/the-press-office/2014/05/28/remarks-president-west-point-academy-commencement-ceremony>.

"Remarks by the President in Address to the Nation on Syria East Room". *The White House Office of the Press Secretary For Immediate Release*, 10 September 2013. Available at: <http://www.whitehouse.gov/the-press-office/2013/09/10/remarks-president-address-nation-syria>.

"Remarks by the President to the White House Press Corps". *The White House — Office of the Press Secretary*, 20 August 2012.

"Remarks Following Discussions with Prime Minister Ariel Sharon — February 7", *Public Papers of the Presidents of the United States — George W. Bush — Book I — January 1 to June 30 2002*. Washington: United States Printing Office, 2004, pp. 190–192. Available at: <https://

books.google.de/books?id=f_vhrnvPUqwC&pg=PA191&lpg=PA191&dq=George+W.
+Bush+on+Arafat&source=bl&ots=-dNb0FG8py&sig=VZFu2d1XF-CaQvIUoxjR-
4zesV0&hl=de&sa=X&ved=
0CEoQ6AEwCWoVChMI6N_VyZzWyAIVxdssCh2G8A54#v=onepage&q=
Jordan&f=false>.

"Remarks Prior Discussions with King Abdullah II of Jordan and an Exchange with Reporters —
February 1 2002". *Public Papers of the Presidents of the United States — George W. Bush —
Book I* — January 1 to June 30 2002. Washington: United States Printing Office, 2004,
pp.   160–162.   Available   at: <https://books.google.de/books?
id=f_vhrnvPUqwC&pg=PA191&lpg=PA191&dq=George+W.+Bush+on
+Arafat&source=bl&ots=-dNb0FG8py&sig=VZFu2d1XF-CaQvIUoxjR-
4zesV0&hl=de&sa=X&ved=0CEoQ6AEwCWoVChMI6N_
VyZzWyAIVxdssCh2G8A54#v=onepage&q=Jordan&f=false>.

*Report of the Senate Select Committee on Intelligence — Committee Study of the Central Intelli-
gence Agency's Detention and Interrogation Program together with Foreword by Chairman
Feinstein and Additional and Minority Views.* December 9, 2014 — Ordered do be printed.
Approved December 13, 2012 — Updated for Release April 3, 2014, Desclassification Revisions December 3, 2014. United States Senate, 113th 2nd Session, S. Report 113–288,
pp. 96, 105–107, 429 *passim. Justice Campaign.* Available at: <http://thejusticecampaign.
org/?page_id=273>. Accessed 17 November 2014.

"Report: U.S. officials say Israel would need at least 100". *Ha'aretz,* Israel, 20 February 2012.
Available at: <http://www.haaretz.com/news/diplomacy-defense/report-u-s-officials-say-israel-
would-need-at-least-100-planes-to-strike-iran-1.413741>.

REUTER, Lise (Staff Writer). "NNSA completes move to new $687M manufacturing plant".
Kansas City Business Journal, 8 July 2014. Available at: <http://www.bizjournals.com/
kansascity/news/2014/07/08/national-nuclear-security-administration.html?page=all>.

RINGHAUSEN, Jeffrey. "Refuting the Media: Punishment and the 2005–06 Gas Dispute",
pp. 3–33. University of North Carolina at Chapel Hill — Department of Slavic, Eurasian, and
East European Studies. 2007- UMI Number: 1445454. Available at: <http://media.proquest.
com/media/pq/classic/doc/1372035111/fmt/ai/rep/NPDF?_
s=E21sZ9Yq1ee87kdZ1Xdh24phC7U%3D>.

RISEN, James. *State of War. The Secret History of the CIA and the Bush Administration.*
New York: Free Press, 2006, pp. 157–159.

ROBERTS, Paul Craig. "Washington Orchestrated Protests Are Destabilizing Ukraine". February
12, 2014. Institute for Political Economy. Available at: <http://www.paulcraigroberts.org/2014/
02/12/washington-orchestrated-protests-destabilizing-ukraine/>.

_____. "The Next Presidential Election Will Move the World Closer to War". 16 November 2014.
Institute for Political Economy. Available at: <http://www.paulcraigroberts.org/2014/11/16/
next-presidential-election-will-move-world-closer-war-paul-craig-roberts/>.

_____. "Truth Has Been Murdered". *Institute for Political Economy,* 28 April 2015. Available at:
<http://www.paulcraigroberts.org/2015/04/28/truth-murdered-paul-craig-roberts/print/>.

ROCHA BARROS, Alberto da. *Que é o Fascismo?* Rio de Janeiro-Guanabara: Editora Laemmert,
1969.

RODRÍGUEZ, Ariel Noyola. "Russia Precipitates the Abandonment of the SWIFT International
Payments System among BRICS Countries". *Global Research,* 6 October 2015.

Roland Dumas: deux ans avant le début de la guerre, l'Angleterre préparait l'invasion des rebelles
en Syrie". *Wikileaks Actu Francophone.* Available at: <https://wikileaksactu.wordpress.com/
category/syrie/>.

Romanian President Traian Basescu (R) speaks with Cmdr. Scott Jones (L) and Cmdr. Charles
Hampton during his visit to the ship on April 14 in Constanta, Romania. **Stratfor",** *Global
Intelligence,* 8 May 2014. Available at: <http://www.stratfor.com/image/romanian-president-
traian-basescu-r-speaks-cmdr-scott-jones-l-and-cmdr-charles-hampton-during>.

Ron Paul CG #23 Opening the Secret 9/11 Records". Interview — Money and Markets: Podca. Available at: <http://www.moneyandmarkets.com/podcasts/ron-paul-cg-23-opening-the-secret-911-records>.

"Ron Paul: Government Had Foreknowledge of 9/11 Terror Attacks. Paul argues U.S. gov't more destructive than Osama Bin Laden". *Washington Free Beacon*, 30 August 2014 — *ICH — Information Clearing House*. Available at: <http://www.informationclearinghouse.info/arti cle39542.htm.docx>.

ROSS, Anthony, C. *et al.* "The Costs of the Israeli-Palestinian Conflict: Executive Summary". *Rand Corporation*, 18 June 2015. Available at: <http://www.rand.org/pubs/research_reports/RR740–1.html>.

ROSS, Andreas (New York). "Kampf gegen IS — Amerikas nächster Kriegspräsident". *Frankfurter Allgemeine Zeitung*, 24 September 2014.

ROSS, Brian (*ABC News* Chief Investigative Correspondent); ESPOSITO, Richard. "CIA's Harsh Interrogation Techniques Described". *ABC News*. 18 November 2005. Available at: <http://abcnews.go.com/Blotter/Investigation/story?id=1322866>.

ROSS, Sonya; AGIESTA, Jennifer. "AP poll: Majority harbor prejudice against blacks". *AP Big Story*, 27 October 2012. Available at: <http://bigstory.ap.org/article/ap-poll-majority-harbor-prejudice-against-blacks>.

ROSSOLIŃSKI-LIEBE, Grzegorz. *Stepan Bandera — The Life and Afterlife of a Ukranian Nationalist — Fascism, Genocide, and Cult.* Stuttgart: *Ibidem*-Verlag, 2014.

ROSTIZKE, Harry. *CIA's Secret Operations — Espionage, Counterespionage and Covert Actions.* New York: Reader's Digest Press, 1977.

"Rota: de Maidan até a guerra no Donbass". [22/8/2015, Alexey Zotyev / (ru. Cassad.net; esp. em slavyangrad), traduzido]. *Vila Vudu* — Samstag, 22. August 2015. Original russo: Закон об особом порядке местного самоуправления в отдельных районах Донецкой и Луганской областей (Закон об особом статусе Донбасса), текст проекта №5081 от 16.09.2014. Закон и Бизнес. Available at: <http://zib.com.ua/ru/print/100900-zakon_ob_osobom_poryadke_mestnogo_samoupravleniya_v_otdelnih.html".

ROUSSEAU, Jean-Jacques. *Du Contrat Social.* Paris: GF Flammarion, 1992, p. 95.

ROZOFF, Rick. "Kazakhstan: U.S., NATO Seek Military Outpost between Russia and China", *Global Research*, 15 April 2010. Available at: <http://www.globalresearch.ca/kazakhstan-u-s-nato-seek-military-outpost-between-russia-and-china/18680>.

RT — Donetsk activists proclaim region's independence from Ukraine". *RT*, 7 April 2014. Available at: <http://www.rt.com/news/donetsk-republic-protestukraine-841/>.

RUDOREN, Jodi; ASHKENAS, Jeremy. "Netanyahu and the Settlements — Israeli Prime Minister Benjamin Netanyahu's settlement policy resembles his predecessors' in many ways, but it is a march toward permanence in a time when prospects for peace are few." *International New York Times*, 12 March 2015. Available at: <http://www.nytimes.com/interactive/2015/03/12/world/middleeast/netanyahu-west-bank-settlements-israel-election.html?_r=0>.

"Russia — an economy on the brink". *BBC News*, 24 August 1998. Available at: <http://news.bbc.co.uk/2/hi/business/150383.stm>.

"Russia — Overview, November 26, 2013 (Notes)". *U.S. Energy Information Administration*. Available at: <http://www.eia.gov/countries/country-data.cfm?fips=up>.

"Russia — Politics Putin prepares bitter and hysterical missile surprise to 'American partners'". *Pravda*, 16 January 2015. Available at: <http://english.pravda.ru/russia/politics/16–01-2015/129540-putin_missile_surprise-0/>.

"Russia and China veto UN resolution against Syrian regime". *Associated Press/The Guardian*, 5 October 2011.

"Russia crisis will cost EU up to 100 billion in value — Press". *Start your bag,* 19 June 2015. Available at: <http://startyourbag.com/germany/russia-crisis-will-cost-eu-up-to-100-billion-in-value-press/>.

"Russia is ready to establish airbases in neighboring countries — Russian PM". *RT*, 9 September 2015. Available at: <http://www.rt.com/news/314787-russia-air-bases-csto/06>. Accessed 10 September 2015.

"Russia losing $140 billion from sanctions and low oil prices." *CNN Money.* Available at: <http://money.cnn.com/2014/11/24/news/economy/russia-losing-140-billion-oil-sanctions/>.

"Russia rebuffs Saudi offer to drop Syria support for arms deal: Report". *PressTV*, 8 August 2013. Available at: <http://www.presstv.ir/detail/2013/08/08/317827/russia-snubs-saudi-bid-for-shift-on-syria/>.

"Russia says US rudely interfered, The US leadership ignored Moscow's repeated warning that shattering the fragile inter-political balance in Ukraine would result in the emergence of a serious hotbed of instability in Europe in Ukraine's affairs by backing coup". TASS-World, 7 May 2015. Available at: <http://tass.ru/en/world/793425>.

"Russia to carry out 10 test launches of Angara heavy carrier rocket by 2020". *TASS*, 28 July 2015. Available at: <http://tass.ru/en/non-political/811139>.

"Russia to create Angara rocket launch pad". *Business Standard.* Moscow, 28 July 2015. Available at: <http://www.business-standard.com/article/news-ians/russia-to-create-angara-rocket-launch-pad-115072801010_1.html>.

"Russia to launch alternative to SWIFT bank transaction system in spring 2015". *RT*, 11 November 2014. Available at: <https://www.rt.com/business/204459-russia-swift-payment-alternative/>.

"Russia to Open Military Base in Belarus". *The Moscow Times*, 26 June 2013. Available at: <http://www.themoscowtimes.com/news/article/russia-to-open-military-base-in-belarus/482355.html>.

"Russia won't quit nuclear forces treaty unless it faces 'serious threat' — Kremlin". *RT*, 23 September 2014. Available at: <http://rt.com/politics/189904-russia-inf-treaty-ivanov/>.

"Russia, China should jointly counter color revolutions — Russian Defense Ministry. The Russian and Chinese defense ministers focused on the recent Hong Kong protests and acknowledged that no country is immune from 'color revolutions'". *ITAR-TASS*, Beijing, 18 November 2014. Available at: <http://tass.ru/en/russia/760349>.

"Russia: Death of a Policeman". *Times*, 4 January 1954. Available at <http://content.time.com/time/magazine/article/0,9171,860194,00.html>.

"Russia's Black Sea port of Novorossiysk to house subs carrying long-range cruise missiles". *Itar-TASS- Russia* — 23 September 2014. Available at: <http://tass.ru/en/russia/750841>.

"Russia's economy under Vladimir Putin: achievements and failures". Analysis & Opinion — *RIA Novosti*, 3 January 2008. Available at: <http://en.ria.ru/analysis/20080301/100381963.html>.

"Russia's new military doctrine lists NATO, US as major foreign threats". *RT*, 26 December 2014. Available at: <http://rt.com/news/217823-putin-russian-military-doctrine/>.

"Russia's President Vladimir Putin has described the collapse of the Soviet Union as 'the greatest geopolitical catastrophe' of the 20th century". *BBC News,* 25 April 2005.

Russia's Road to Corruption — How the Clinton Administration Exported Government Instead of Free Enterprise and Failed the Russian People. "Chapter 8 — 1998: Years of Bad Advice Culminate in Russia's Total Economic Collapse". U.S. House of Representatives, Washington, D.C. Report Date: September 2000. Available at: <http://fas.org/news/russia/2000/russia/part08.htm>.

"Russian fighter jet ignored warnings and 'provocatively' passed U.S. Navy destroyer in Black Sea for 90 minutes, getting as close as 1,000 yards". *Daily Mail Online*, 15 April 2014. Available at: <http://www.dailymail.co.uk/news/article-2604590/Russian-fighter-jet-ignored-warnings-provocatively-passed-U-S-Navy-destroyer-Black-Sea-90-minutes-getting-close-1–000-yards.html>.

"Russian Foreign Minister calls Free Syrian Army 'phantom' group' — October 05". Available at: <http://tass.ru/en/politics/826244>. Accessed 5 October 2015.

"Russian Military Forum — Russian Armed Forces-Russian Air Force". Available at: <http://www.russiadefence.net/t2803p615-pak-fa-t-50-news>.

"Russian military plane shot down Ukrainian Su-25 aircraft in Ukraine". *KyivPost — Interfax-Ukraine*, 17 July 2014. Available at: <http://www.kyivpost.com/content/ukraine/russian-mili tary-plane-shot-down-ukrainian-su-25-aircraft-in-ukraine-356422.html>.

"Russian operation in Syria is our salvation' — top Syrian Catholic bishop to RT". *RT*, 18 February 2016. Available at: <https://www.rt.com/news/332922-aleppo-bishop-russia-support/>.

"Russian State takes bigger part in the economy, despite trumpeted privatization plans". *RT*, 6 November 2012. Available at: <http://rt.com/business/russia-state-economy-privatization-043/>.

"Russian Su-27 Airbase to Be Set Up in Belarus in 2016: Air Force Chief". *Sputnik*, 15 October 2014 Available at: <http://sputniknews.com/military/20141015/194098896.html>.

"Russian Unified Air Defense for CIS Collective Security". *Russian Peacekeper*, 9 September 2015. Available at: <http://www.peacekeeper.ru/en/?module=news&action=view&id=27398>.

"Russland-Sanktionen rächen sich: 500.000 deutsche Jobs in Gefahr". Available at: <http://www.t-online.de/wirtschaft/id_74428354/russland-sanktionen-raechen-sich-500–000-deutsche-jobs-in-gefahr.html>.

RYAN, Yasmine. "Russia's oligarchs guard political might — Under Putin, a new middle class has emerged, but socio-economic changes haven't yet translated into political clout". *Al Jazeera*, 4 March 2012. Available at: <http://www.aljazeera.com/indepth/features/2012/02/2012225212624758833.html>.

SAAR, Erik; NOVAK, Viveca. *Inside the Wire. A Military Intelligence Soldier's Eywitness Account of Life at Guantánamo*. New York: Penguin Press, 2005, p.114.

"Sabra and Shatila massacre: General info." *The WikiLeaks Supporters Forum*, 14 January 2014. Available at: <http://www.wikileaks-forum.com/sabra-and-shatila-massacre/613/sabra-and-shatila-massacre-general-info/26766/>.

SAGER, Gesche. "Henry Ford und die Nazis — Der Diktator von Detroit". *Spiegel Online*, 29 July 2008. Available at: <http://www.spiegel.de/einestages/henry-ford-und-die-nazis-a-947358.html>.

SAKWA, Richard. *Frontline Ukraine — Crisis in the Borderlands*. London: I.B. Tauris, 2015.

"Sales by largest arms companies fell again in 2012 but Russian firms' sales increased sharply". *Stockholm International Peace Research Institute (SIPRI). 2014*. Munique, 31 January 2014. Available at: <http://www.sipri.org/media/pressreleases/2014/top100_january2014/>.

SALHANI, Claude. "Islamic State's Ultimate Goal: Saudi Arabia's Oil Wells". OilPrice.com, 9 September 2014. Available at: <http://oilprice.com/Geopolitics/Middle-East/Islamic-States-Ultimate-Goal-Saudi-Arabias-Oil-Wells.html>.

SALMONI, Barak A.; LOIDOLT, Bryce; WELLS, Madeleine. "Regime and Periphery in Northern Yemen — The Huthi Phenomenon". *National Defense Research Institute — RAND*, 2010. pp. 264–265. Prepared for the Defense Intelligence Agency. Available at: <http://www.rand.org/content/dam/rand/pubs/monographs/2010/RAND_MG962.pdf>.

"Sandwiches Are Symbol of Sympathy to Ukrainians at Maidan: Nuland"- *Sputnik News — International*, 18 December 2014. Available at: <http://sputniknews.com/politics>.

SANGER, David E. "Rebel Arms Flow Is Said to Benefit Jihadists in Syria". *The New York Times*, 14 October 2012.

"Sanktionen dummes Zeug Schmidt verteidigt Putins Krim-Politik". *Frankfurter Allgemeine Zeitung*, 26 March 2014. Available at: <http://www.faz.net/aktuell/politik/inland/schmidt-verteidigt-putins-krim-politik-12864852.html>.

SARNA, Arkadiusz. "The transformation of agriculture in Ukraine: from collective farms to agroholdings". *OSW Commentary — Centre for Eastern Studies*. Number 127, 2 June 2014. Available at: <www.osw.waw.pl. Also in: http://aei.pitt.edu/57943/1/commentary_127.pdf>.

"Saudi Arabia has secretly offered Russia a sweeping deal to control the global oil market and safeguard Russia's gas contracts, if the Kremlin backs away from the Assad regime in Syria". *The Telegraph*, 27 August 2013.

"Saudi Arabia Sent Death Row Inmates to Fight in Syria in Lieu of Execution", *Assyrian International News Agency — AINA News*, 20 January 2013. Available at: <http://www.aina. org/news/20130120160624.htm>.

"Saudi Arabia tries to tempt Russia over Syria". *Al-Alam News Network*, 7 August 2013. Available at: <http://en.alalam.ir/print/1502972>.

SAUL, Jonathan (London). "Russia steps up military lifeline to Syria's Assad — sources". *Reuters*, Fri Jan 17, 2014. Syrian energy deal puts Russia in gas-rich Med". *UPI* —Beirut, Lebanon. Business News / Energy Resources, 16 January 2014.

SAUNDERS, Bonnie F. *The United States and Arab Nationalism The Syrian Case 1953–1960*. Praeger, 1996, pp. 48–50, 62, 70.

SAVKOVIĆ, Marko (Belgrade Centre for Security Policy (BCSP). "Europe's Defence in Times of Austerity: Spending Cuts as a One-Way Street?" *International Relations and Security Network (ISN)* ETH Zurich, 9 October 2012. Available at: <http://www.isn.ethz.ch/Digital-Library/ Articles/Detail/?id=154133>.

SCAHILL, Jeremy. "The CIA's Secret Sites in Somalia Renditions, an underground prison and a new CIA base are elements of an intensifying US war, according to a Nation investigation in Mogadishu". *The Nation*, 10 December 2014. Available at: <http://www.thenation.com/article/ cias-secret-sites-somalia/>.

SCHECK, Werner. *Geschichte Russlands — Von de Frühgeschichte bis zur Sowjetunion*. Munique: Wilhelm Heyne Verlag, 2. Aulage, 1980.

SCHIRRA, Bruno. *ISIS — Der globale Dschihad*, Berlin: Econ Verlag, 2015, pp. 174–180.

SCHLESINGER, Jr., Arthur M. *The Age of Roosevelt — The Politics of Upheaval*. Boston: Houghton Mifflin Company — The Riverside Press Cambridge, 1960.

SCHMEMANN, Serge. "Assassination in Israel: The Overview — Assassination in Israel: The Overview; Rabin Slain After Peace Rally in Tel Aviv; Israeli Gunman Held; Says He Acted Alone". *The New York Times*, 5 November 1995. Available at: <http://www.nytimes.com/1995/ 11/05/world/assassination-israel-overview-rabin-slain-after-peace-rally-tel-aviv-israeli.html? pagewanted=all>.

_____. "Netanyahu, Scorning Critics, Visits West Bank Settlement". *The New York Times*, 27 November 1996. Available at: <http://www.nytimes.com/1996/11/27/world/netanyahu-scorning-critics-visits-west-bank-settlement.html>.

SCHMID, Beat. "Obama, der Kriegspräsident". *Schweiz am Sonntag*, Samstag, 27 September 2014. Available at: <http://www.schweizamsonntag.ch/ressort/meinung/obama_der_ kriegspraesident/>.

SCHMITT, Eric; HUBBARD, Ben. "U.S. Revamping Rebel Force Fighting ISIS in Syria". *The New York Times*, 6 September 2015. Available at: <http://www.nytimes.com/2015/09/07/world/ middleeast/us-to-revamp-training-program-to-fight-isis.html>. Accessed 7 September 2015.

"Schmutzige Deals: Worum es im Syrien-Krieg wirklich geht". *Deutsche Wirtschafts Nachrichten*, 31 August 2013. Available at: <http://deutsche-wirtschafts-nachrichten.de/2013/08/31/ schmutzige-deals-worum-es-im-syrien-krieg-wirklich-geht/>.

"Schmutzige Deals: Worum es im Syrien-Krieg wirklich geht". *Deutsche Wirtschafts Nachrichten* | Veröffentlicht: 31 August 2013. Available at: <http://deutsche-wirtschafts-nachrichten.de/2013/ 08/31/schmutzige-deals-worum-es-im-syrien-krieg-wirklich-geht/>.

SCHOFIELD, Matthew (McClatchy Foreign Staff). "Rumors of American mercenaries in Ukraine spread to Germany — NATO flexes muscles as Combined Resolve II unfolds in Hohenfels". *Stars and Stripes*, 12 May 2014. Available at: <http://www.stripes.com/news/europe/nato-flexes-muscles-as-combined-resolve-ii-unfolds-in-hohenfels-1.282650>.

SCHOLL-LATOUR, Peter. *Die Flucht der bösen Tat. Das Scheitern des Westens im Orient*. Berlin: Propyläen, 2014.

SCHRAEDER, Peter J. *Exporting Democracy: Rhetoric Vs. Reality*. Colorado: Lynne Rienner Publishers, 2002, pp. 131, 217–220.

SCHUCHTER, Arnold. *Regime Change: National Security in the Age of Terrorism*. Bloomington, Indiana: iUniverse, 2004, p. 118.

SCHULBERG, Jessica (Foreign Affairs Reporter, *The Huffington Post*). "Benjamin Netanyahu's Latest Rejection of a Palestinian State. 'You think there is a magic wand here, but I disagree,' he told his political opponents, who have been pushing for peace talks." *TheWorldPost — The Huffington Post*, 27 October 2015. Available at: <http://www.huffingtonpost.com/entry/israel-benjamin-netanyahu-reject-palestinian-state_562e5f1be4b0c66bae58b878>.

SCHULLER, Konrad (Warschau). "Ukraine Der gestürzte Oligarch und der Rechte Sektor". *Franfurter Allgemeine Zeitung*, 26 March 2015. Available at: <http://www.faz.net/aktuell/politik/ausland/europa/ihor-kolomojskijs-entmachtung-inszenierte-abschiedszeremonie-13505871.html>.

SCHULTEN, Ralf. "Experte warnt vor Folgen einer Aufrüstung der UA!" *Focus Online*, 6 April 2015. Available at: <http://www.focus.de/politik/ausland/ukraine-krise/experte-warnt-vor-folgen-einer-aufruestung-der-ua-ukraine-krise-kommentar_id_6343836.html>.

SCOTT, Franklin D. *Sweden — The Nation's History*. Chicago — Illinois: University Minnesota Press/American Scandinavian Foundation. Distributed by Swedish American Historical Society, 4th Printing, 1983.

"Secretary of Defense Testimony — Statement on Syria before the Senate Armed Services Committee as Delivered by Secretary of Defense Chuck Hagel, Washington, D.C., 17 April 2013". *U.S. Department of Defense*. Available at <http://www.defense.gov/Speeches/Speech.aspx?SpeechID=1771>.

"Section 2. Limits Of The Territorial Sea Article 4 — Outer limit of the territorial sea — The outer limit of the territorial sea is the line every point of which is at a distance from the nearest point of the baseline equal to the breadth of the territorial sea". United Nations Convention on the Law of the Sea". Available at: <http://www.un.org/depts/los/convention_agreements/texts/unclos/unclos_e.pdf>.

"Security Council Approves 'No-Fly Zone' over Libya, Authorizing 'All Necessary Measures' to Protect Civilians, by Vote of 10 in Favour with 5 Abstentions 17 March 2011 Security Council. 6498th Meeting (Night)". Available at: <http://www.un.org/press/en/2011/sc10200.doc.htm>.

"Security Council Fails to Adopt Text Demanding That Israel Halt Settlement Activity as Permanent Member Casts Negative Vote". *United Nations — Security Council*. 6484th Meeting (PM) 18 February 2011. Available at: <http://www.un.org/press/en/2011/sc10178.doc.htm>.

SEELYE, Katharine Q. "A Nation Challenged: The Prisoners; First 'Unlawful Combatants' Seized In Afghanistan Arrive At U.S. Base In Cuba". *The New York Times*, 12 January 2002. Available at: <http://www.nytimes.com/2002/01/12/world/nation-challenged-prisoners-first-unlawful-combatants-seized-afghanistan-arrive.html?pagewanted=print>.

SEIFFERT, Jeanette. "The significance of the Donbas. The Donbas is Ukraine's industrial heartland. But its coal-based economy is a heavily-subsidized millstone for Ukraine, not a powerhouse, no matter how important its arms exports might be to the Russian military". *Deutsche Welle (DW)*, 15 April 2014. Available at: <http://www.dw.com/en/the-significance-of-the-donbas/a-17567049>. Accessed 1 August 2014.

SELDES, George. *Facts and Fascism*. New York: In Fact, Inc., Fifth Edition, 1943.

SÉNÈQUE (SENECAE, L. Annaei). *Phaedra*. Presses Universitaires de France, 1965, versos 165–170 e 906, pp. 51 e 132.

SENNOTT, Charles M. *The Body and the Blood: The Middle East's Vanishing Christians and the Possibility for Peace*. New York: Public Affairs — Perseus — Book Group, 2002, pp. 66–67.

SERLE, Jack; ROSS, Alice K. "Monthly Updates on the Covert War — July 2014 Update: US covert actions in Pakistan, Yemen and Somalia". All Stories, Covert Drone War, Monthly Updates on the Covert War. *The Bureau of Investigative Journalism,* 1 August 2014. Available at: <http://www.thebureauinvestigates.com/2014/08/01/july-2014-update-us-covert-actions-in-pakistan-yemen-and-somalia/>.

SERLE, Jack. "Drone strikes in Yemen — Analysis: What next for Yemen as death toll from confirmed US drone strikes hits 424, including 8 children". *The Bureau of Investigative Journalism,* 30 January 2015. Available at: <https://www.thebureauinvestigates.com/2015/01/30/analysis-death-toll-drone-strikes-yemen-crisis-what-next/>.

"Several big Russian banks already use SWIFT equivalent — banking official. It was reported earlier that Russia's SWIFT equivalent would be launched in fall 2015". *TASS — Russia & India Reports,* 18 September 2015. Available at: <http://in.rbth.com/news/2015/09/18/several-big-rusian-banks-already-use-swift-equivalent-banking-official_425941>.

SHABAD, Rebecca. "US-backed Rebels and Islamic State sign Ceasefire/Non-aggression Pact — ISIS, Syrian rebels reach ceasefire". *Information Clearing House,* 13 September 2014. Available at: <http://www.informationclearinghouse.info/article39665.htm. MEE staff>.

SHACKLE, Samira. "UAE-Egypt attack on Libya aimed at Islamists". *Memo — Middle East Monitor,* 27 August 2014. Available at: <https://www.middleeastmonitor.com/blogs/politics/13771-uae-egypt-attack-on-libya-aimed-at-islamists>.

"Shadow banking system a growing risk to financial stability — IMF Fund report says tightening of bank regulations may be driving shift to lending by hedge funds and private equity". *The Guardian,* 1 October 2014.

SHAH, Anup. "US Military Commissions Act 2006 — Unchecked Powers?" *Global Issues,* 30 September 2006. Available at: <http://www.globalissues.org/article/684/us-military-commissions-act-2006-unchecked-powers>.

SHAKDAM, Catherine. "Genesis: The real story behind the rise of ISIS", *RT,* 25 July 2015. Available at: <http://www.rt.com/op-edge/310731-isis-rise-support-terror/>.

SHAKESPEARE, William. "Timon of Athens", Act IV, Scene III, *in*: SHAKESPEARE, William. *Complete Works.* New York: Gramercy Books, 1975, p. 761.

SHALAIM, Avi. "It's now clear: the Oslo peace accords were wrecked by Netanyahu's bad faith — I thought the peace accords 20 years ago could work, but Israel used them as cover for its colonial project in Palestine". *The Guardian,* 12 September 2013.

"Shale gas reserves and major fields of Ukraine" — Projects in Ukraine — 14.06.2013 — *Unconventional Gas in Ukraine.* Available at: <http://shalegas.in.ua/en/shale-gas-resources-in-ukraine/>.

SHAMIR, Shlomo. "The UN Is Ripe for Advancing the Palestinian Agenda — The settlements have been defined as the number-one problem impeding peace, and no Israeli attempt to blame the stalemate on the Palestinians will be accepted at the UN". *Há'aretz,* 22 February 2011. Available at: <http://www.haaretz.com/print-edition/opinion/the-un-is-ripe-for-advancing-the-palestinian-agenda-1.344905>.

SHANE, Scott; LIPTAK, Adam. "Detainee Bill Shifts Power to President". *The New York Times,* 30 September 2006.

SHANKER, Thom; CHIVERS, C. J.; GORDON, Michael R. "Obama Weighs 'Limited' Strikes against Syrian Forces". *The New York Times,* 27 August 2013.

SHARIFULIN, Valery. "Russia's new military doctrine says use of protest moods typical for conflicts nowadays. The doctrine also stresses amassed combat employment of high-precision weaponry, drones and robots". *ITAR-TASS,* 26 December 2014. Available at: <http://tass.ru/en/russia/769513>.

SHARKOV, Damien. "Ukrainian Nationalist Volunteers Committing 'ISIS-Style' War Crimes". *Newsweek,* 9 October 2014. Available at: <http://europe.newsweek.com/evidence-war-crimes-committed-ukrainian-nationalist-volunteers-grows-269604>.

"Sharon Urges 'Elimination' of Arafat, Terrorist Leaders". *Deseret News,* 17 July 1989. Available at: <http://www.deseretnews.com/article/55557/SHARON-URGES-ELIMINATION-OF-ARAFAT-TERRORIST-LEADERS.html?pg=all>. Accessed 23 October 2015.

SHARP, Jeremy M. (Specialist in Middle Eastern Affairs). "U.S. Foreign Aid to Israel June 10, 2015". *Congressional Research Service 7–5700* www.crs.gov *RL33222.* Available at: <https://www.fas.org/sgp/crs/mideast/RL33222.pdf>.

SHELLEY, Mary. *Frankenstein.* New York: 1818 Edition 2015, pp. 106–107.

SHERIDAN, Kerry (*Agence France Press*). Iraq Death Toll Reaches 500,000 Since Start Of U.S. Led Invasion, New Study Says. TheHuffingtonPost.com, 15 October 2013. Available at: <http://www.huffingtonpost.com/2013/10/15/iraq-death-toll_n_4102855.html>.

SHERLOCK, Ruth. "Syria rebel quits after battlefield defeat — Syria rebel commander lashes out at his western patrons as he quits in protest at losses to regime". *The Telegraph*, 4 November 2013. Available at: <http://www.telegraph.co.uk/news/worldnews/middleeast/syria/10425001/ Syria-rebel-quits-after-battlefield-defeat.html>.

SHERMER, Michael. "Does deterrence prohibit the total abolishment of nuclear weapons?" *Scientific American,* Vol. 310, Issue 6. 1 June 2014. Available at: <http://www. scientificamerican.com/article/will-mutual-assured-destruction-continue-to-deter-nuclear-war/? print=true>.

SHERWOOD, Harriet; SMITH, Helena (Athens); DAVIES, Lizzy (Rome); GRANT, Harriet. "Europe faces 'colossal humanitarian catastrophe' of refugees dying at sea. UN considers Africa holding centres as 'boat season' is expected to bring sharp increase in migrants making treacherous crossing", *The Guardian*, 2 June 2014.

SHINKMAN, Paul D. "U.S., John Kerry Disgusted With Ukrainian Response to Protests. Response to protests not acceptable for democracy, Secretary of State John Kerry says". *U.S. News*, 11 December 2013. Available at: <http://www.usnews.com/news/articles/2013/12/11/us-john-kerry-disgusted-with-ukrainian-response-to-protests>.

SHIRER, William L. *The Rise and Fall of the Third Reich. A History of a Nazi German.* New York: Fawcett Crest, 1960, Book Five — Beginning of the End.

SHUTTLEWORTH, Kate (Jerusalem). "Ultraorthodox Jews at the Damascus gate in Jerusalem after a Palestinian man was shot dead by police after allegedly stabbing and injuring a 15-year-old Jewish youth". *The Guardian*, 4 October 2015. Available at: <http://www.theguardian.com/ world/2015/oct/04/israel-second-stabbing-just-hours-after-two-jewish-men-fatally-stabbed>.

SIDDIQUE, Haroon; MCCARTHY, Tom. "Syria crisis: US isolated as British MPs vote against air strikes — as it happened. Trouble for White House after UK parliamentary revolt. Doubts circulate about case tying Assad to chemical weapons". *The Guardian*, 30 August 2013.

SINGER, David; GROSSMAN, Lawrence. *American Jewish Year Book 2003*, Vol. 103. New York: America Jews Committee, pp. 210–211.

SINGER, Filip. "Ukraine's PM blames EU for lack of partnership over support of Nord Stream-2 project". *TASS*, 18 September 2015. Available at: <http://tass.ru/en/world/822175>.

SIPRI Yearbook 2015 (Oxford: Oxford University Press, 2015). Available at: <http://www.sipri. org/research/armaments/nuclear-forces>.

SISK, Richard. "Syrian Rebel Training Program Costs Millions and Counting". *DoD-Buzz — Military.com Network*, 9 September 2015. Available at: <http://www.dodbuzz.com/2015/09/ 09/syrian-rebel-training-program-costs-millions-and-counting/>.

SIVAN, Emmanuel. *Radical Islam: Medieval Theology and Modern Politics.* New York: Yale University Press, 1985, pp. 117–18.

SMITH, Truman. *Berlin Alert — The Memoirs and Report of Truman Smith.* Robert Hessen (Editor). Stanford — California: Hoover Institution/Stanford University, 1984, pp. 117, 143.

SNELBECKER, David. "The Political Economy of Privatization in Ukraine". *Center for Social & Economic Research: CASE Research Foundation*, Warsaw 1995: Paper was prepared for the project: "Economic Reforms in the former USSR". Reformy gospodarcze na terenie dawnego ZSRR, financed by the Committee of Scientific Research (Komitet Badań — Naukowych).

SNYDER, Timothy. "A Fascist Hero in Democratic Kiev". *The New York Review of Books*, 24 February 2010. Available at: <http://www.nybooks.com/blogs/nyrblog/2010/feb/24/a-fas cist-hero-in-democratic-kiev/>.

_____. "Who's Afraid of Ukrainian History?" *The New York Review of Books*, 21 September 2010. Available at: <http://www.nybooks.com/blogs/nyrblog/2010/sep/21/whos-afraid-ukrainian-his tory/?printpage=true>.

SOFFER, Ari. "Ḥamās Leader Objects: Don't compare us to ISIS. Khaled Meshaal objects to Netanyahu's comparison between Ḥamās and Islamic State, says Ḥamās 'isn't a violent religious group.'" *Arutz Sheva 7 — Israelnationalnews.com*, 23 August 2014. Available at: <http://www.israelnationalnews.com/News/News.aspx/184333#.VjoltCt0f_B>.

SOKOL, Sam. "Diaspora. Election results buoy Ukrainian Jews". *Jerusalem Post*, 27 October 2014. Available at: <http://www.jpost.com/Diaspora/Election-results-buoy-Ukrainian-Jews-379969>.

SOLOMON, Ariel Ben. "On eve of 2015, Israel's population hits 8.3 million. Experts clash over Palestinian demographic statistics. Data predicted equal Jewish, Arab population in Israel and territories by 2016". *The Jerusalem Post*, 1 January 2015. Available at: <http://www.jpost.com/Middle-East/Experts-clash-over-Palestinian-demographic-statistics-386443>.

"Some 400 killed over last 6 weeks in Libya clashes". *Press TV Wednesday*, 3 December 2014. Available at: <http://www.presstv.ir/detail/2014/11/30/388096/libyas-6-week-death-toll-reaches-400/>.

SORENSEN, Theodore C. "The star spangled shrug". *The Washington Post*, 2 July 1995.

SORKIN, Andrew Ross; BAJAJ, Vikas. "Shift for Goldman and Morgan Marks the End of an Era". *The New York Times*, 21 September 2008. Available at: <http://www.nytimes.com/2008/09/22/business/22bank.html?_r=0>.

SOURANI, Raji. "History is repeated as the international community turns its back on Gaza — As was the case in Operation Cast Lead, the international community is once again turning its back on Gaza." *Al Jazeera*, 17 November 2012. Available at: <http://www.aljazeera.com/indepth/opinion/2012/11/20121117115136211403.html>.

SOUSA LARA, António. "Crise, Geopolítica e Prospectiva", *in*: SOUSA LARA, António (Coord.). *Crise, Estado e Segurança*. Lisboa: Edições MGI, 2014, pp. 18 e 25.

_____. *Subversão e Guerra Fria*. Lisboa: Instituto Superior de Ciências Sociais e Políticas, 2011, p. 134.

SOUZA, Lucio Vinhas; LOMBARDE, Phillippe. *The Periphery of the Euro: Monetary and Exchange Rate Policy in CIS Countries*. Hants-Burlington: Ashgate, 2006, pp. 276–278.

"Soziales aus Rußland", *in*: MARX K.; ENGELS, F. *Werke*. Band 18, Berlin: Dietz Verlag, 1976, pp. 556–559.

Soziales aus Rußland", *in*: MARX, K.; ENGELS, F. *Ausgewählte Schriften*, Band II, Berlin: Dietz Verlag, 1976, p. 39.

SPARROW, Andrew. "MPs vote down military intervention in Syria: Politics live blog • Government intelligence on Syria • Government legal advice on attacking Syria • MPs vote down plan for military intervention in Syria. Government defeat — What it means". *The Guardian*, 30 August 2013.

"Speech on Independence Day — John Quincy Adams — United States House of Representatives", 4 July 1821. Available at: <http://teachingamericanhistory.org/>.

SPENCER, Robert. "U.S. training Free Syrian Army in Jordan — a group that violently targets Christians". *Jihad Watch*, 7 February 2014. Available at: <http://www.jihadwatch.org/2014/02/u-s-training-free-syrian-army-in-jordan-a-group-that-violently-targets-christians>.

SPRENG, Norman M. *Putin-Versteher: Warum immer mehr Deutsche Verständnis für Russland haben*. Essen: BrainBookMedia, 2015, pp. 285–286.

STAFF, Spiegel. "Summit of Failure — How the EU Lost Russia over Ukraine". *Spiegel Online*, 24 November 2014. Available at: <http://www.spiegel.de/international/europe/war-in-ukraine-a-result-of-misunderstandings-between-europe-and-russia-a-1004706-druck.html>.

STAHEL, Albert A. "Regime-change — fortwährende Fehlschläge der USA". *Strategische Studien*, 17 January 2015. Available at: <http://strategische-studien.com/2015/01/17/regime-change-fortwaehrende-fehlschlaege-der-usa-2/>.

STANLEY, Tim. "Obama has killed thousands with drones, so can the Nobel committee have their Peace Prize back?" *The Telegraph*, 10 October 2013.

STARR, Steven. "Senator Corker's Path to Nuclear War", 23 August 2014. Available at: <http://www.paulcraigroberts.org/2014/08/23/guest-article-steven-starr-senator-corkers-path-nuclear-war/print/>.

_____. "The Lethality of Nuclear Weapons: Nuclear War has No Winner". *Global Research — Centre for Research on Globalization*, 5 June 2014. Available at: <http://www.globalresearch.ca/the-lethality-of-nuclear-weapons-nuclear-war-has-no-winner/5385611>.

_____. "The Lethality of Nuclear Weapons: Nuclear War has No Winner". *Global Research — Centre for Research on Globalization,* 5 June 2014. Available at: <http://www.globalresearch. ca/the-lethality-of-nuclear-weapons-nuclear-war-has-no-winner/5385611>.

Starvation as warfare: Pro-Kiev forces 'block food, medicine, aid from reaching east" *RT,* 24 December 2014. Available at: <http://www.rt.com/news/217279-ukraine-aid-battalions-blockade/>.

Status of World Nuclear Forces 2014 — Federation of American Scientists. Available at: <http:// fas.org/issues/nuclear-weapons/status-world-nuclear-forces/>.

STEA, Carla. "Manipulation of the UN Security Council in support of the US-NATO Military Agenda — Coercion, Intimidation & Bribery used to Extort Approval from Reluctant Members". *Global Research — Global Research Center on Globalization,* 10 January 2012. Available at: <http://www.globalresearch.ca/manipulation-of-the-un-security-council-in-sup port-of-the-us-nato-military-agenda/28586>.

STEINBERG, Guido. "A Chechen al-Qaeda? Caucasian Groups Further Internationalise the Syrian Struggle". *Stiftung Wissenschaft und Politik: German Institute for International and Security Affairs (SWP). SWP Comments,* 31 June 2014, pp.1–7. Available at: <https://www.swp-berlin. org/fileadmin/contents/products/comments/2014C31_sbg.pdf>.

STEINHAUSER, Paul (CNN Deputy Political Director). "Poll: More disapprove of Bush than any other president". *CNN* Politics.com, 1 May 2008. Available at: <http://edition.cnn.com/2008/ POLITICS/05/01/bush.poll/Updated 0117 GMT (0917 HKT)>.

STEINHAUSER, Paul; HELTON, John. "CNN poll: Public against Syria strike resolution" *CNN,* 9 September 2013. Updated 1649 GMT (0049 HKT). Available at <http://edition.cnn.com/ 2013/09/09/politics/syria-poll-main/>.

STEPHEN, Chris. "War in Libya — the Guardian briefing — In the three years since Muammar Gaddafi was toppled by Libyan rebels and NATO airstrikes, fighting between militia has plunged the country into civil war and seen Tripoli fall to Islamists. The involvement of Qatar, Egypt and the UAE risks a wider regional war". *The Guardian,* 29 August 2014. Available at: <http://www.theguardian.com/world/2014/aug/29/-sp-briefing-war-in-libya>.

STERN, David. "Russia offers Ukraine major economic assistance". *BBC Europe,* 17 December 2013. Available at: <http://www.bbc.com/news/world-europe-25411118>.

_____. "Ukraine's revolution and the far right". *BBC News Europe,* 7 March 2014. Available at: <http://www.bbc.com/news/world-europe-26468720?print=true>.

STEWART, Dale B. "The Russian-Ukrainian Friendship Treaty and the Search for Regional Stability in Eastern Europe". December 1997. Thesis S714366. N PS Archive 1997, 12. Naval Postgraduate School — Monterey, California. Available at: <https://archive.org/stream/ russianukrainian00stew/russianukrainian00stew_djvu.txt>.

_____. "The Russian-Ukrainian Friendship Treaty and the Search for Regional Stability in Eastern Europe". December 1997. Thesis S714366. N PS Archive 1997, 12. *Naval Postgraduate School* — Monterey, California. Available at: <https://archive.org/stream/ russianukrainian00stew/russianukrainian00stew_djvu.txt>.

"Strategic Missile Forces" — *Ministry of Defence of the Russian Federation — Strategic Missile Forces.* Available at: <http://eng.mil.ru/en/structure/forces/strategic_rocket.htm>.

"Strikes said to be from planes flying out of Egyptian airbases signal step towards direct action in conflict by other Arab states". *The Guardian,* 26 August 2014.

SUBTELNY, Orest. *Ukraine — A History.* Toronto: Toronto University Press, 3ª ed., 2000, pp. 468–471.

SUDOPLATOV, Pavel; SUDOPLATOV, Anatoli; SCHECTER, Jerrol L.; SCHECTER, Leona P. *Special Tasks.* Boston: Little, Brown & Company, 1995.

"Sugonyako: Since 2005, we have accumulated the external debt from $14 to $74 billion. Our economy is unprofitable, and our government is inefficient". Gordon.com, 12 January 2015. Available at: <http://english.gordonua.com/news/exclusiveenglish/Sugonyako%2D% 2D60898.html>.

"Sumary 2010/2 — 22 July 2010 — Accordance with international law of the unilateral declaration of independence in respect of Kosovo. Summary of the Advisory Opinion, On 22 July 2010, The International Court of Justice gave its Advisory Opinion on the question of the Accordance with international law of the unilateral declaration of independence in respect of Kosovo". Available at: <http://www.icj-cij.org/docket/files/141/16010.pdf>.

SUN TZU; SUN PIN. *El Arte de la Guerra* (Completo). Buenos Aires: Editorial Distal, 1996, pp. 39 e 70.

"Support Security Assistance for Israel". *American Israel Public Affairs Committee — AIPAC*. Available at: <http://www.aipac.org/learn/legislative-agenda/agenda-display?agendaid=% 7B407715AF-6DB4–4268-B6F8–36D3C6F241AA%7D>.

SURDEM, Tyler. "American — 'War, Or Peace?'" Available at: <http://www.zerohedge.com/ news/2013-03-15/which-more-american-war-or-peace>.

SUSKIND, Ron. "Faith, Certainty and the Presidency of George W. Bush". *The New Yor Times — Magazine*, 17 October 2004. Available at: <http://www.nytimes.com/2004/10/17/magazine/ 17BUSH.html?_r=0>.

SUSSMAN, Gerald. *Branding Democracy: U.S. Regime Change in Post-Soviet Eastern Europe*. New York: Peter Lang Publishing, 2010, pp. 108–109.

SUTELA, Pekka. "The Underachiever — Ukraine's Economy Since 1991". Ukraine March 2012. *Carnegie Papers. Carnegie Endowment for International Peace*. Available at: <http:// carnegieendowment.org/files/ukraine_economy.pdf>.

SUTELA, Pekka. "Ukraine after Independence — The Underachiever — Ukraine's economy Since 1991". Paper — 9 March 2012. *Carnegie Endowment for International Peac*e. Available at: <http://carnegieendowment.org/files/ukraine_economy.pdf>.

SUTTON, Antony C. *Wall Street and de the Rise of Hitler*. United Kingdom: Clairview Books, 2011.

SUTYAGIN, Igor. "Russian Forces in Ukraine". *Briefing Paper — Royal United Services Institute for Defence and Security Studies*. March 2015. Available at: <https://www.rusi.org/downloads/ assets/201503_BP_Russian_Forces_in_Ukraine_FINAL.pdf>. Accessed 12 August 2014.

"Syria conflict: 75 US-trained rebels crossed into Syria from Turkey, monitoring group says", *ABC News*. Available at: <http://www.abc.net.au/news/2015–09-20/75-us-trained-rebels-enter-syria-monitoring-group-says/6790300>.

"Syria crisis: David Cameron makes case for military action". *BBC News UK Politics*, 29 August 2013. Available at <http://www.bbc.com/news/uk-politics-23883427>.

"Syria crisis: Foreign minister denies chemical attacks". *BBC News Middle East*, 27 August 2013. Available at: <http://www.bbc.com/news/world-middle-east-23850274>.

"Syria profile". BBC News — Middle East, 19 March 2014. Available at: <http://www.bbc.com/ news/world-middle-east-14703995>.

"Syria: Destruction and Murder Funded by Foreign Forces: Mother Agnes Mariam Challenges the UNHRC — Address by Mother Agnes Mariam of the Mussalaha Initiative given at the UNHCR in Geneva by Mother Agnes Mariam". *Global Research*, 16 March 2014. Available at: <http:// www.globalresearch.ca/syria-destruction-and-murder-funded-by-foreign-forces-mother-agnes-mariam/5373684>.

"Syria: Political Conditions and Relations with the United States After the Iraq War. Alfred B. Prados and Jeremy M. Sharp, Foreign Affairs, Defense, and Trade Division. Congressional Research Service Report RL32727 — February 28, 2005". *WikiLeaks Document Release*, 2 February 2009. Available at: <http://wikileaks.org/wiki/CRS-RL32727>.

"Syria: reported chemical weapons use — Joint Intelligence Committee letter. From: Cabinet Office — History: Published 29 August 2013. Part of: Working for peace and long--term stability in the Middle East and North Africa and Syria. Letter from Jon Day, the Chairman of the Joint Intelligence Committee (JIC), about reported chemical weapons use in Syria". *Gov. UK*. Available at <https://www.gov.uk/government/publications/syria-reported-chemical-weapons-use-joint-intelligence-committee-letter>.

"Syria's rebel fighters recruited to fight Isis, but captured and beaten by Jabhat al-Nusra for 'collaborating with crusaders'". *The Independent*, 28 September 2015. Available at: <http://www.independent.co.uk/news/world/middle-east/syrias-rebel-fighters-recruited-to-fight-isis-but-captured-and-beaten-by-jabhat-alnusra-for-collaborating-with-crusaders-10432686.html>.

"Syrian soldiers are fighting for their lives as well as their country". Robert Fisk, Middle East correspondent for the Independent discusses the current situation in Syria. Transcript. Reporter: Emma Alberici. *Lateline,* Broadcast: 10 November 2014. Available at: <http://www.abc.net.au/lateline/content/2014/s4125600.htm>.

"Syrie: David Cameron contraint par l'opposition d'attendre le rapport des inspecteurs de l'ONU". *Slate Afrique*, 30 August 2013. Available at <http://www.slateafrique.com/367024/syrie-david-cameron-contraint-par-l%E2%80%99opposition-d%E2%80%99attendre-le-rapport-des-inspecteurs-de-l%E2%80%99onu>.

"Syrie: Destruction et assassinats financés par des puissances étrangères. Discours de Mère Agnès pour "l' Initiative Moussalaha" [Réconciliation] en réponse aux déclarations du Haut commissariat aux réfugiés [UNHCR]". *Mondialisation.ca., Centre de Recherche sür la Mondialisation,* 24 March 2014. Available at: <http://www.mondialisation.ca/syrie-destruction-et-assassinats-finances-par-des-puissances-etrangeres/5375060>.

"Syrie: l'intervention militaire pourrait débuter le 4 septembre". *La Voix de la Russie,* 30 October 2013. Available at: <http://french.ruvr.ru/news/2013_08_30/Syrie-lintervention-militaire-pourrait-debuter-le-4-septembre-7767/>.

"Syrie: Obama veut un vote du Congrès, Hollande sous pression". *Le Parisien*, 1 September 2013. Available at: <http://www.leparisien.fr/recherche/recherche.php?q=sur+trois+%2864+%25%29+sont+oppos%C3%A9s+%C3%A0+une+intervention+militaire+en+Syrie+&ok=ok>.

"Syrie/attaque chimique: 'pas 100% de certitude' (Cameron) — Dossier: Situation politique en Syrie". *RIA Novosti*, 29 August 2015. Available at <http://fr.ria.ru/world/20130829/199146661.html>.

TANQUINTIC-MISA, Esther. "2/3 of Global Military Conflicts Instigated By U.S. — Russian Minister; Willing To Share with Asian Countries Army Modernization Experience". *International Business Times*, 28 November 2014. Available at: <http://au.ibtimes.com/articles/574282/20141128/military-conflicts-u-s-russia-asia-army.htm#.VHiV8LR3ucw>.

TARPLEY, Webster Griffin; CHAITKIN, Anton. *George Bush — The Unauthorized Biography.* Washington, D.C., 1982, pp. 28–34; ARIS, Ben (Berlin).

TARPLEY, Webster Griffin Tarpley: Obama — the Postmodern Coup — Making of a Manchurian Candidate. Joshua Tree (California): Progressive Press, 2008.

TAUBMAN, William. *Khrushchev: The Man and His Era.* New York, W. W. Norton & Company, 2003, p. 73.

TAYLOR, Guy. "Obama lied about Syrian chemical attack, 'cherry-picked' intelligence: report". *The Washington Times*, 9 December 2013. Available at: <http://www.washingtontimes.com/news/2013/dec/9/obama-lied-about-syrian-chemical-attack-cherry-pic/>.

"TechCamp Kyiv 2012". *Embassy of the United States — Kiyv — Ukraine.* Available at: <http://ukraine.usembassy.gov/events/tech-camp.html>.

TELLER, Hanoch. *A Midrash and Masseh.* Jerusalem: Marsi Tabak, 1990, p. 314.

"Text of newly approved Russian military doctrine. Text of report by Russian presidential website on 5 February" ("The Military Doctrine of the Russian Federation" approved by Russian Federation presidential edict on 5 February 2010). Available at: <http://carnegieendowment.org/files/2010russia_military_doctrine.pdf>.

"Text of the John Warner National Defense Authorization Act for Fiscal Year 2007. The John Warner National Defense Authorization Act for Fiscal Year 2007. This bill was enacted after being signed by the President on October 17, 2006. The text of the bill below is as of *Sep 30, 2006* (Passed Congress/Enrolled Bill). H.R. 5122 (enr) — An Act To authorize appropriations for fiscal year 2007 for military activities of the Department of Defense, for military construction, and for defense activities of the Department of Energy, to prescribe military personnel strengths for such fiscal year, and for other purposes". *U.S. Government Printing*

Office (GPO). Available at: <http://www.gpo.gov/fdsys/search/pagedetails.action?packageId=BILLS-109hr5122enr>.

"The Administration's Fiscal Year 2015 Overseas Contingency Operations (OCO) Request. The White House — President Barack Obama". *Office of the Press Secretary*, 26 June 2014. Available at: <http://www.whitehouse.gov/the-press-office/2014/06/26/fact-sheet-administration-s-fiscal-year-2015-overseas-contingency-operat>.

"The Associated Press. "Guantánamo Detainee Released". *The New York Times*, 24 August 2009. Available at: <http://www.nytimes.com/2009/08/25/world/asia/25gitmo.html>.

"The Business Plot (Takeover of the White House) 1933". 10 January 2009. Available at: <http://www.abovetopsecret.com/forum/thread426623/pg1>.

"The Elusive 'Bruce-Lovett Report'". *Cryptome — Center for the Study of Intelligence Newsletter*. Spring 1995 Issue n° 3. 3 August 2009. Available at: <https://cryptome.org/0001/bruce-lovett.htm>.

"The End of an Era: 376th Air Expeditionary Wing inactivation ceremony", 4 June 2014. *U.S. Air Force*. Available at: <http://www.af.mil/News/ArticleDisplay/tabid/223/Article/485254/the-end-of-an-era-376th-air-expeditionary-wing-inactivation-ceremony.aspx>.

The Fundamental Flaws of the Clinton Administration's Russia Policy. Russia's Road to Corruption — How the Clinton Administration Exported Government Instead of Free Enterprise and Failed the Russian People — Chapter 4. Speaker's Advisory Group on Russia. United States House of Representatives 106th Congress. U.S. House of Representatives, Washington, D.-C. Report Date: September 2000". Available at: <http://fas.org/news/russia/2000/russia/part04.htm>.

The Huffington Post, 7 August 2014. Available at: <http://www.huffingtonpost.com/2014/07/08/george-tsunis-norway_n_5567351.html>.

"The Interview: Henry Kissinger" *The National Interest*'s. *National Interest*, September/October 2015. Available at: <http://nationalinterest.org/print/feature/the-interview-henry-kissinger-13615?page=3>.

"The Israeli Information Center for Human Rights in the Occupied Territories". *B'Tselem*, 11 May 2015. Available at: <http://www.btselem.org/settlements/statistics>.

The Military Writings of Leon Trotsky. How the Revolution Armed, Vol. 2, 1919. The Southern Front III. *The Red Army's Second Offensive in the Ukraine. (August-December 1919)*. Available at <https://www.marxists.org/archive/trotsky/1919/military/ch108.htm>. Also in: <https://www.marxists.org/archive/trotsky/index.htm>.

The Myths of the 20th Century. *4* — The myth of a "land without a people for a people without a land". *Le Monde*, 15 October 1971. Source: Mrs. Golda Meir. Statement to *The Sunday Times*, 15 June 1969. Available at: <http://www.biblebelievers.org.au/zionmyth6.htm>.

The National Military Strategy of the United States of America 2015 (2015 NMS). Available at: <http://www.jcs.mil/Portals/36/Documents/Publications/National_Military_Strategy_2015.pdf>.

The National Security Strategy. White House, September 2002. Available at: <http://www.state.gov/documents/organization/63562.pdf>.

"The new Crimean war: how Ukraine squared up to Moscow". *The Independent*, 9 January 2006. Available at: <http://www.independent.co.uk/news/world/europe/the-new-crimean-war-how-ukraine-squared-up-to-moscow-522213.html>.

"The Outstanding Public Debt as of 28 Oct 2014 at 04:14:26 PM GMT". *In: U.S. National Debt Clock*. Available at: <http://www.brillig.com/debt_clock/>.

"The PAK-FA will have a system that will leave any target helpless. Why so much importance is given to this event?" *Royal Moroccan Armed Forces*: *Armement et matériel militaire*, 14 March 2014. Available at: <http://far-maroc.forumpro.fr/t1685p345-pak-fa>.

"The politics of Enron. Four committees in search of a scandal. As Congress cranks into action, there's not much sign of the dirt from Enron reaching the president". *The Economist*, 17 January 2002. Available at: <http://www.economist.com/node/940913>.

"The politics of Enron. Four committees in search of a scandal. As Congress cranks into action, there's not much sign of the dirt from Enron reaching the president". *The Economist*, 17 January 2002. Available at: <http://www.economist.com/node/940913. CBSNews.com staff>.

The real SyrianFreePress Network War Press Info, 13 August 2013. Available at: <https://syrianfreepress.wordpress.com/2013/08/09/russia-rebuffs-saudi-offer-to-drop-syria-support-for-arms-deal-report/>.

"The Rise of the Sun Belt (p. 197)". *Access to Social Studies.* Available at: <http://access-socialstudies.cappelendamm.no/c316289/artikkel/vis.html?tid=357420>.

"The transformation of agriculture in Ukraine: From collective farms to agroholdings". *OSW — Ośrodek waschodnich, in Marka Kapia,* 2 July 2014. Available at: <http://www.osw.waw.pl/en/publikacje/osw-commentary/2014–02-07/transformation-agriculture-ukraine-collective-farms-to>.

"The truth about Russia's new military doctrine". *RT Op-Edge,* 27 February 2015. Available at: <http://rt.com/op-edge/236175-president-putin-military-doctrine-document/>.

"The Ukrainian soldiers taking refuge in Russia". *BBC News,* 5 August 2014. Available at: <http://www.bbc.com/news/world-europe-28652096>. Accessed 6 August 2014.

"The United Nations — Human Rights Council holds interactive dialogue with Fact-finding Mission on Israeli Settlements Human Rights Council", 18 March 2013. Available at: <http://www.ohchr.org/EN/NewsEvents/Pages/DisplayNews.aspx?NewsID=13156&LangID=E>.

The Wikileak Files — The World According to U.S. Empire — With an Introduction by Julian Assange. London/New York.

"Thread: 'The Eight Families' — Why should everyone else except them be communists? The Federal Reserve Cartel: The Eight Families. So who then are the stockholders in these money center banks?" *Mail Online,* 6 September 2011. Available at: <http://boards.dailymail.co.uk/news-board-moderated/10233373.htm>.

"Timeline of U.S. Federal Debt since Independence Day 1776". Debt.org. Available at: <http://www.debt.org/blog/united-states-federal-debt-timeline/>. Disponível also in: <http://www.usgovernmentdebt.us/>.

"Times of Israel staff & AFP Carter says Ḥamās leader committed to peace, Netanyahu not". *The Times of Israel,* 2 May 2015. Available at: <http://www.timesofisrael.com/carter-says-Ḥamās-leader-committed-to-peace-netanyahu-not/>.

"Times of Israel staff text of UNHRC resolution on Gaza war probe — Motion passed on Friday by UN Human Rights Council welcomes findings of McGowan Davis commission". *The Times of Israel,* 3 July 2015. Available at: <http://www.timesofisrael.com/full-text-of-unhrc-resolution/>.

TOCQUEVILLE, Alexis. *De la Démocratie en Amérique.* Paris: Gallimard, 1968.

"Top Ten Questions on NATO". *Sheet released by the NATO Enlargement Ratification Office — U. S. Department of State — Archive,* 19 February 1998. Available at: <http://1997–2001.state.gov/www/regions/eur/fs_980219_natoqanda.html>.

"Top U.S. official visits protesters in Kiev as Obama admin. ups pressure on Ukraine president Yanukovych". *CBS/Wire Services,* 11 December 2013. Available at: <http://www.cbsnews.com/news/us-victoria-nuland-wades-into-ukraine-turmoil-over-yanukovich/>.

"Top-Banker ist sich sicher: Russland und China gewinnen gegen die USA". *Deutsche Wirtschafts Nachrichten,* 6 June 2010. Available at: <http://deutsche-wirtschafts-nachrichten.de/2015/06/06/top-banker-ist-sich-sicher-russland-und-china-gewinnen-gegen-die-usa/>.

TOPF, Andrew. "Did the Saudis and the US Collude in Dropping Oil Prices?" OilPrice.com, 23 December 2014. Available at: <http://oilprice.com/Energy/Oil-Prices/Did-The-Saudis-And-The-US-Collude-In-Dropping-Oil-Prices.html>.

Toujours plus d'inégalité: pourquoi les écarts de revenus se creusent. OECD. Available at: <http://www.oecd.org/fr/els/soc/49205213.pdf>. Accessed 24 May 2015.

TOYNBEE, Arnold J. *A Study of History.* Abridgement of vols. I-VI. London/New York/Toronto: Geoffrey Cumberlege/Oxford University Press, 1951, p. 364.

TRAYNOR, Ian (Europe editor); WALKER, Shaun (Donetsk); SALEM, Harriet (Slavyansk); LEWIS, Paul (Washington). "Russian president also calls for halt to Ukrainian military operations against pro-Russia activists in eastern towns". *The Guardian*, 8 May 2014. Available at: <http://www.theguardian.com/world/2014/may/07/ukraine-crisis-putin-referendum-autonomy-postponed>.

TREMBLAY, Rodrigue. "Bill Clinton's 'Neocon-inspired Decisions' Triggered Three Major Crises in our Times". *Global Research*, 13 August 2014. Available at: <http://www.globalresearch.ca/bill-clintons-neocon-inspired-decisions-triggered-three-major-crises-in-our-times/5395715?print=1>.

TROTSKY, Leon. "Problem of the Ukraine" (April 1939)". *Written*: 2 April 1939. *Originally published*: Socialist Appeal, 9 May 1939.*Source*: Arsenal of Marxism, Fourth International, Vol. 10, n° 10, November 1949, pp. 317–319. *Transcription/HTML Markup*: Einde O'Callaghan for the *Trotsky Internet Archive*. Available at <http://www.marxists.org/archive/trotsky/1939/04/ukraine.html>.

_____. *História da Revolução Russa*. Rio de Janeiro: Editora Paz e Terra, 1977, 3° vol., 1977, pp. 736–737.

_____. *La Revolución de 1905*. Barcelona: Editorial Planeta, 1975, p. 30.

_____. *La Révolution trahie*. Paris: B. Grasset, 1936.

TRUMAN, Harry. *Memoirs by Harry Truman — Years of Trial and Hope*. Vol. 2. New York: Doubleday y Company, 1956.

TSETSURA, Katerina; GRYNKO, Anastasia; KLYUEVA, Anna. "The Media Map Project — Ukraine — Case Study on Donor Support to Independent Media, 1990–2010", p. 14. Available at: <http://www.academia.edu/3295647/Media_Map_Project._Ukraine_Case_study_on_donor_support_to_independent_media_1990–2010>.

TUCÍDIDES. *Historia de la Guerra de Peloponeso*. Madrid: Casa Editorial Hernando S.S., Tomo Primeiro, Libros I e II, 1952, pp. 104–195.

TYLER, Patrick E. (Special to *The New York Times*). "U.S. Strategy Plan Calls for Insuring No Rivals Develop A One-Superpower World — Pentagon's Document Outlines Ways to Thwart Challenges to Primacy of America", *The New York Times*, 8 March 1992. Available at: <http://work.colum.edu/~amiller/wolfowitz1992.htm>.

U.N. Security Council Report. Monthly Forecast, March 2014. Available at: <http://www.securitycouncilreport.org/monthly-forecast/2014–03/libya_8.php>.

"U.S. Embassy Hosted TechCamp Kyiv 2.0 to Build Technological Capacity of Civil Society". *Embassy of the United States — Kyiv-Ukraine*. Available at: <http://ukraine.usembassy.gov/events/techcamp-2013-kyiv.html>.

"U.S. Operatives Killed Detainees during Interrogations in Afghanistan and Iraq". *American Civil Liberties Union*, 24 October 2005. Available at: <https://www.aclu.org/news/us-operatives-killed-detainees-during-interrogations-afghanistan-and-iraq>. Os documentos estão disponíveis em: <http://action.aclu.org/torturefoia/released/102405/3164.pdf>.

"U.S. secretly backed Syrian opposition groups, WikiLeaks reveals — $6 million for Syrian exiles to help", *Daily Mail*, 18 April 2011.

"U.S. Spent $65M to Aid Ukrainian Groups". *Associated Press — Fox* News.com, 10 February 2004. Available at: <http://www.foxnews.com/story/2004/12/10/us-spent-65m-to-aid-ukrainian-groups/print>.

"UAE 'behind air strikes in Libya'. Two US officials say United Arab Emirates carried out air raids against militias using bases in Egypt". Al Jazeera, 26 August 2014. Available at: <http://www.aljazeera.com/news/middleeast/2014/08/uae-behind-air-strikes-libya-201482523130569467.html>.

UEHLING, Greta Lynn. *Beyond Memory — The Crimean Tatars' Deportation and Return*. New York: Pallgrave MacMillan, 2004, pp. 30–34.

"UK planned war on Syria before unrest began: French ex-foreign minister". *Press TV*, 16 June 2013. Available at: <http://www.presstv.ir/detail/2013/06/16/309276/uk-planned-war-on-syria-before-unrest/>.

"Ukraine — Country Analysis Note" — *U.S. Energy Information Administration*. Available at: <https://www.eia.gov/beta/international/analysis.cfm?iso=UKR>

"Ukraine — manifestation monstre des pro-européens à Kiev". *Le Monde*.fr avec AFP, 15 December 2013. Available at: <http://www.lemonde.fr/europe/article/2013/12/15/ukraine-200–000-pro-europeens-rassembles-a-kiev_4334662_3214.html>:

"Ukraine and Russia. Why is Ukraine's economy in such a mess?" *The Economist*, 5 March 2014. Available at: <http://www.economist.com/blogs/freexchange/2014/03/ukraine-and-russia>.

"Ukraine bans Communism & Nazism, celebrates UPA nationalists as 'freedom fighters'." *RT*, 9 April 2015. Available at: <http://www.rt.com/news/248365-ukraine-bans-communism-nazism/>. Accessed 11 April 2015.

"Ukraine clashes: dozens dead after Odessa building fire — Trade union building set alight after day of street battles in Black Sea resort city". *The Guardian*, 2 May 2014. Available at: <http://www.theguardian.com/world/2014/may/02/ukraine-dead-odessa-building-fire>.

"Ukraine Crisis Endangers Exxon's Black Sea Gas Drilling: Energy". *Bloomberg*, 11 March 2014. Available at: <http://www.bloomberg.com/news/articles/2014–03-10/ukraine-crisis-endangers-exxon-s-black-sea-gas-drilling-energy>.

"Ukraine crisis sharpens focus on European shale gas". *Reuters*, London, 4 March 2014. Available at: <http://www.reuters.com/article/2014/03/14/europe-shale-ukraine-idUSL6N0MB1WI20140314>.

"Ukraine crisis: 'Don't arm Kiev' Russia warns US". *CNN News*, 10 February 2015. Available at: <http://www.bbc.com/news/world-europe-31356372>.

"Ukraine crisis: Transcript of leaked Nuland-Pyatt call". *BBC News* (From the section Europe) — A transcript, with analysis by *BBC* diplomatic correspondent Jonathan Marcus) — 7 February 2014. Available at: <http://www.bbc.com/news/world-europe-26079957>.

"Ukraine crisis: Viktor Yanukovych leaves Kiev for support base. US warns deal remains 'very, very fragile; as president visits eastern stronghold of Kharkiv". *The Telegraph*. London, 22 February 2014.

"Ukraine Cuts a Deal It Could Soon Regret". *Bloomberg*, 17 December 2013. Available at: <http://www.bloomberg.com/bw/articles/2013–12-17/ukraine-cuts-a-deal-it-could-soon-regret>.

"Ukraine External Debt 2003–2015" — *Trading Economics*. Available at: <http://www.tradingeconomics.com/ukraine/external-debt>.

"Ukraine External Debt 2003–2015". *Trading Economics*. Available at: <http://www.tradingeconomics.com/ukraine/external-debt>.

"Ukraine misses Gazprom's deadline to pay gas debt". *BBC News*, 8 April 2014. Available at: <http://www.bbc.com/news/business-26930998>.

"Ukraine must stop ongoing abuses and war crimes by pro-Ukrainian volunteer forces". *Amnesty International*, 8 September 2014. Available at: <https://www.amnesty.ie/news/ukraine-must-stop-ongoing-abuses-and-war-crimes-pro-ukrainian-volunteer-forces>.

"Ukraine president Viktor Yanukovych denounces 'coup d'État' after protesters take control in Kiev". *ABC News*. Available at: <http://www.abc.net.au/news/2014–02-22/ukraine-president-viktor-yanukovych-leaves-kiev-reports/5277588>.

"Ukraine pushes to 'ban communism' by 70th anniversary of victory over Nazism". *RT*, 6 April 2015. Available at: <http://www.rt.com/news/247009-ukraine-communism-ban-nazism/>. Accessed 6 April 2015.

"Ukraine Receives First Batch of US Humvees". *Agence France-Presse*, 25 March 2015. "Defense News". Available at: <http://www.defensenews.com/story/defense/international/europe/2015/03/25/ukraine-receives-first-batch-us-humvees/70445154/>. Accessed 26 March 2015.

"Ukraine Shale Gas: Shell Moves Forward While Chevron Stalled". *Natural Gas — Europe*, 20 January 2013. Available at: <http://www.naturalgaseurope.com/regional-ukraine-govern ments-approve-shell-shale-gas-production-sharing-agreement>.

"Ukraine wants help to build nuclear defence shield". *Ukraine Today Weekly Digest*, 22 September 2015. Available at: <http://uatoday.tv/politics/ukraine-wants-help-to-build-nuclear-defence-shield-arseniy-yatsenyuk-498674.html>.

"Ukraine world's 4th largest arms exporter in 2012, according to SIPRI". *Interfax-Ukraine Kiev Post*, 18 March 2013. Available at: <http://www.kyivpost.com/content/ukraine/ukraine-worlds-4th-largest-arms-exporter-in-2012-according-to-sipri-321878.html?flavour=full>.

"Ukraine-Konflikt — Schröder macht EU für Krim-Krise mitverantwortlich". *Spiegel Online*, 9 March 2014. Available at: <http://www.spiegel.de/politik/deutschland/krim-krise-ex-kanzler-gerhard-schroeder-kritisiert-eu-a-957728.html>.

"Ukraine-Krise NATO sichert Ukraine Hilfe gegen Russland zu — Das westliche Militärbündnis will die Regierung in Kiew im Konflikt mit Russland unterstützen. NATO-Generalsekretär Rasmussen hat Berater und andere Mittel zugesichert". *Die Zeit Online* (Ausland), 7 August 2014.

"Ukraine: Abuses and war crimes by the Aidar Volunteer Battalion in the north Luhansk region". *Amnesty International*, 8 September 2014, Index number: EUR 50/040/2014. Available at: <http://www.amnesty.org/en/documents/EUR50/040/2014/en/>.

Ukraine: Economy- Infoplease.com. Available at: <http://www.infoplease.com/encyclopedia/world/ukraine-economy.html#ixzz387gacUF3>.

"Ukraine: Nuland feeds hungry Maidan protesters and police." Video Id: 20131211–054. Available at: <https://ruptly.tv/vod/20131211–054>.

"Ukraine: Nuland feeds hungry Maidan protesters and police". *RT — Ruptly*, 11 December 2013. Available at: <http://ruptly.tv/site/vod/view/6876/ukraine-nuland-feeds-hungry-maidan-protesters-and-police>.

"Ukraine: Space Deal With Brazil Uncertain. Public Library of U.S. Diplomacy | Secretary of State". Available at: <https://wikileaks.org/plusd/cables/09KYIV2182_a.html>.

"Ukraine's 'Romantic' Nazi Storm Troopers". Consortiumnews.com, 15 September 2014. Available at: <https://consortiumnews.com/2014/09/15/ukraines-romantic-nazi-storm-troopers/>.

"Ukraine's Biggest Trading Partners: Countries". *Bloomberg Visual Data.* Available at: <http://www.bloomberg.com/visual-data/best-and-worst/ukraines-biggest-trading-partners-countries>.

Ukraine: Economy — Infoplease.com. Available at: <http://www.infoplease.com/encyclopedia/world/ukraine-economy.html#ixzz387gacUF3>.

"Ukraine's government and Shell sign operation agreement to develop shale deposit". Projects in Ukraine. *Unconventional Gas in Ukraine*, 12 September 2013. Available at: <http://shalegas.in.ua/en/uryad-ukrajiny-i-shell-pidpysaly-uhodu-pro-operatsijnu-diyalnist-z-vydobutku-vuhlevodniv/>.

"Ukraine's Nadra Yuzivska and Shell Entered into Shale Gas Production PSA" — *Oil Market Magazine*, 24 January 2013. Available at: <http://oilmarket-magazine.com/eng/shownews.phtml?id=221>.

"Ukraine's neo-Nazi leader becomes top military adviser, legalizes fighters". *RT*, 6 April 2015. Available at: <http://www.rt.com/news/247001-ukraine-army-adviser-yarosh/>. Accessed 6 April 2015.

"Ukraine's Oil and Natural Gas Reserves — A Pawn in Geopolitical Chess Game?" *Viable Opposition* — Sunday, March 16, 2014. Available at: <http://viableopposition.blogspot.fr/2014/03/ukraines-oil-and-natural-gas-reserves.html>.

"Ukraine's Orange Revolution Well and Truly Over". *Kiev Ukraine News Blog*, 30 April 2010.

"Ukraine's Poroshenko Says War Costing $8 Million Per Day". *The Moscow Times*, 5 February 2015. Available at: <http://www.themoscowtimes.com/business/article/ukraine-s-poroshenko-says-war-costing-8-million-per-day/515488.html>.

"Ukraine's war-torn east home to third of country's GDP — minister". *TASS*, 31 March 2015. Available at: <http://www.rt.com/business/245597-ukraine-donbass-third-of-gdp/>.

"Ukrainian Oligarchs and the — "Family", a New Generation of Czars — or Hope for the Middle Class?" *International Research and Exchange Board* (IREX) — Department of State — August 2013. Available at: <https://www.irex.org/sites/default/files/Holoyda%20EPS%20Research%20Brief.pdf>.

"Ukrainian Su-25 fighter detected in close approach to MH17 before crash — Moscow". *RT*, 21 July 2014. Available at: <http://www.rt.com/news/174412-malaysia-plane-russia-ukraine/>. Accessed 22 July 2014.

"Ukrainian troops 'demoralised' as civilians face down anti-terror drive. General Vasily Krutov says main force is security service with army as back-up, but analysts criticise lack of plan from

Kiev". *The Guardian*, 16 April 2014. Available at: <http://www.theguardian.com/world/2014/apr/16/ukrainian-troops-civilians-kiev-anti-terrorist-krutov>.

ULFKOTTE, Udo. *Gekaufte Journalisten — Wie Politiker, Geheimdienste und Hochfinanz Deutschlands Masssenmedien Lenken*. Rottemburg: Kopp Verlag, 2014, pp. 43–46, 146–150.

ULRICH, Bernd. "Die Deutschen und Russland: Wie Putin spaltet". *Die Zeit*, N° 16/2014, 10 April 2014. Available at: <http://www.zeit.de/politik/ausland/2014–04/germans-russia-media-putin/komplettansicht>.

UMBACH, Frank (Associate Director at the European Centre for Energy and Resource Security (EUCERS). "Russian-Ukrainian-EU gas conflict: who stands to lose most?" *NATO/OTAN*. Available at: <http://www.nato.int/docu/review/2014/NATO-Energy-security-running-on-empty/Ukrainian-conflict-Russia-annexation-of-Crimea/EN/index.htm>.

"UN Commission of Inquiry on Syria 'is acting to incite further Massacres'— Hands Off Syria — Australia, Press Release". *Global Research News,* 15 September 2013. Available at: <http://www.globalresearch.ca/hands-off-syria-un-commission-of-inquiry-on-syria-is-acting-to-incite-further-massacres/5349937>.

"UN General Assembly — Resolution 181 (Partition Plan), November 29, 1947." *Israel Ministry of Foreign Affairs*. Available at: <http://www.mfa.gov.il/mfa/foreignpolicy/peace/guide/pages/un%20general%20assembly%20resolution%20181.aspx>.

"Un navire de débarquement de la marine américaine est arrivé en Méditerranée". *Le Voix de Russe*. Available at: <http://french.ruvr.ru/news/2013_08_31/Un-navire-de-debarquement-de-la-marine-americaine-est-arrive-en-Mediterranee-2627/>.

"UN refugee agency warns of 'sharp rise' in people fleeing eastern Ukraine". United Nation High Commissioner for Refugees (UNHCR). *UN Centre*, 27 June 2014. Available at: <http://www.un.org/apps/news/story.asp?NewsID=48159#.VcYWd_k-7_A>.

"UN Report on Chemical Weapons Use in Syria". *Council on Foreign Relations*, 12 December 2013. Available at: <http://www.cfr.org/syria/un-report-chemical-weapons-use-syria/p31404>.

"UN: Gaza Could Become 'Uninhabitable' By 2020 — Israeli military action and economic blockade have rendered the coastal strip unfit for civilian life, report says." *MiniPress News*, 2 September 2015. Available at: <http://www.mintpressnews.com/un-gaza-could-become-uninhabitable-by-2020/209180/>.

"Unfassbare Unglücke. 290 Menschen sterben beim Abschuss eines iranischen Jet". *Focus*, Freitag, 18 July 2014. Available at: <http://www.focus.de/politik/ausland/flugzeugabschuesse-der-historie-nach-mh17-diese-fluege-wurden-ziele-von-flugzeugabschuessen_id_4001088.html>.

UNGER, Christian. "Krim-Krise Gregor Gysi: "Sanktionen gegen Russland verschärfen die Krise", 26 March 2014.

UNISA (University of South Africa) — Institute for Global Dialogue. Available at: <http://www.igd.org.za/index.php/research/foreign-policy-analysis/south-south-cooperation/11465-russia-precipitates-the-abandonment-of-the-swift-international-payments-system-among-brics-countries>.

"United States Government Debt to GDP 1940–2015 | Data | Chart | Calendar". *Trading Economics*. Available at: <http://www.tradingeconomics.com/united-states/government-debt-to-gdp>.

UNRWA — United Nations Relief and Works Agency for Palestine Refugees in the Near East. *Gaza Emergency*, 15 October 2015. Available at: <http://www.unrwa.org/gaza-emergency>.

"US blames Russia for rebel ceasefire violations in Ukraine — Joe Biden warns Moscow it will face 'costs' if Russian forces and separatists fail to respect the Minsk agreement and continue to attack Debaltseve". *The Telegraph*, 18 February 2015. Available at: <http://www.telegraph.co.uk/news/worldnews/europe/ukraine/11419309/US-condemns-rebel-ceasefire-violations-in-Ukraine.html>.

"US House urges Obama to send arms to Ukraine". *RT*, 24 March 2015. Available at: <http://www.rt.com/news/243417-us-house-weapons-ukraine/ — Accessed 24 March 2015.

"US responsible for two-thirds of all military conflicts — Russia's top brass". *RT*, 28 November 2014. Available at: <http://rt.com/news/209379-us-military-conflicts-antonov/>.

"US sends 300 troops to Ukraine to train forces fighting pro-Russian rebels — Russia criticized the arrival of US military personnel, saying the move could further destabilize Ukraine". *Al Jazeera*, 17 April 2015. Available at: <http://america.aljazeera.com/articles/2015/4/17/us-sends-300-troops-to-ukraine.html>.

"USA finanzieren offenbar syrische Opposition", *Focus Nachrichten*, 18 April 2011.

USAID — Ukraine Country Development Cooperation Strategy 2012–2016, p. 8. Available at: <https://www.usaid.gov/sites/default/files/documents/1863/USAID_Ukraine_CDCS_2012-2016.pdf>. Also: <https://www.cia.gov/library/publications/resources/the-world-factbook/geos/up.html>.

"USS Donald Cook Leaves Black Sea". *Naval Today*, 25 April 2014. Available at: <http://navaltoday.com/2014/04/25/uss-donald-cook-leaves-black-sea/>.

"USSR's Nikita Khrushchev gave Russia's Crimea away to Ukraine in only 15 minutes". *Pravda*, 19 February 2009. Available at: <http://english.pravda.ru/history/19–02-2009/107129-ussr_crimea_ukraine-0/>.

VALLONE, Giuliana. "Economia global projeta cenário decepcionante, diz Nobel de Economia". *Folha de S.Paulo*, 19 October 2015. Available at: <http://www1.folha.uol.com.br/mercado/2015/10/1695575-economia-global-projeta-cenario-decepcionante-diz-nobel-de-economia.shtm>.

VELLACOTT, Chris; KELLY, Lidia. "Russia can run on empty for a year if sanctions block new bonds". *Reuters*, 2 September 2014. Available at: <http://www.reuters.com/article/2014/09/02/ukraine-crisis-russia-bonds-idUSLN0R330720140902>.

"Vice President Joe Biden's son joins Ukraine gas company". BBC News, 14 May 2014. Available at: <http://www.bbc.com/news/blogs-echochambers-27403003>.

VIDAL, Dominique. "Ten years of research into the 1947–49 — WAR The expulsion of the Palestinians re-examined." *Le Monde diplomatique* (English Edition). December 1997. Available at: <http://mondediplo.com/1997/12/palestine>.

"Vietnam and Eurasian Economic Union free trade zone deal in 'home straight' — Russian PM". *RT*, 6 April 2015. Available at: <http://www.rt.com/business/247033-russia-vietnam-trade-coop eration/>. Accessed 6 April 2015.

VILMAZ, Guler. "Opposition MP says ISIS is selling oil in Turkey" — "The Islamic State of Iraq and al-Sham (ISIS) has been selling smuggled Syrian oil in Turkey worth $800 million, according to Ali Ediboglu, a lawmaker for the border province of Hatay from the main opposition Republican People's Party (CHP)". *Al-Monitor*, 13 June 2014. Available at: <http://www.al-monitor.com/pulse/business/2014/06/turkey-syria-isis-selling-smuggled-oil>.

"Vital Statistics: Latest Population Statistics for Israel — (Updated September 2015)". *Jewish Virtual Library*. Available at: <http://www.jewishvirtuallibrary.org/jsource/Society_&_Cul ture/newpop.html>.

"Vladimir Putin in the plenary meeting of the 70th session of the UN General Assembly in New York". *New York, Presidential Executive Office 2015*. Available at: <http://en.kremlin.ru/events/president/news/50385>.

VLASOVA, Anastasia (*Kyiv Post*); GRYTSENKO, Oksana. "Thousands of Ukrainian soldiers trapped as Debaltseve pocket closes". *Kyiv Post*, 18 February 2015. Available at: <http://www.kyivpost.com/content/kyiv-post-plus/thousands-of-soldiers-endangered-in-debaltseve-pocket-380978.html>.

VOLKOGONOV, Dmitri. *The Rise and Fall of Soviet Empire. Political Leaders from Lenin to Gorbachev*. London: HarperCollins/Publishers, 1999.

VOLTAIRE (François Marie Arouet). *Dictionaire Philosophique*. Paris: Garnier-Flammarion, 1964, p. 248.

"Völuspá. "Der Seherin Gesicht". *Die Edda — Götterdichtung Spruchweisheit Heldensängen der Germanen*. Munique: Dietrich Gelbe Reihe, 2004, p. 35. "Valans Spådom". *Eddan — De Nordiska Guda — Och Hjältesångerna*. Estocolmo: Norstedrs Förlag, 1998, p. 8.

WALKER, Shaun (Donetsk); LUHN, Alec (Kiev). "Petro Poroshenko wins Ukraine presidency, according to exit polls — 'Chocolate king' expected to secure 56% of vote and vows to restore peace following election billed as most important since independence". *The Guardian*, 25 May 2014.

_____. (Donetsk). "Russia will recognise outcome of Ukraine poll, says Vladimir Putin — Putin says Russia will 'respect the choice of Ukrainian people', but separatist authorities vow to disrupt weekend's presidential election". *The Guardian*, 23 May 2014.

_____. (Luhansk). "Despair in Luhansk as residents count the dead — The worst-hit city in eastern Ukraine is struggling with the aftermath of violence as a semblance of normality return". *The Guardian*, 11 September 2014. Available at: <http://www.theguardian.com/world/2014/sep/11/despair-luhansk-residents-count-dead>.

_____. (Mariupol). "Azov fighters are Ukraine's greatest weapon and may be its greatest threat — The battalion's far-right volunteers' desire to 'bring the fight to Kiev' is a danger to post-conflict stability". *The Guardian*, 10 September 2014. Available at: <http://www.theguardian.com/world/2014/sep/10/azov-far-right-fighters-ukraine-neo-nazis>.

_____. (Moscow) & agencies. "Vladimir Putin offers Ukraine financial incentives to stick with Russia — Moscow to buy $15bn of Ukrainian government bonds and cut gas price after Kiev resists signing EU deal amid mass protests". *The Guardian*, 18 December 2013.

_____. (Yalta). "Ukraine's EU trade deal will be catastrophic, says Russia — Kremlin claims neighbouring state faces financial ruin and possible collapse if integration agreement goes ahead". *The Guardian*, 22 September 2013.

WALLS, Seth Colter. "New Questions over McCain Campaign Chief's Ties to Ukraine". *The Huffington Post*, 06/27/2008. Available at: <http://www.huffingtonpost.com/2008/06/20/new-questions-over-mccain_n_108204.html>. Accessed 1 June 2015.

WALSH, Nick Paton; CAPELOUTO, Susanna. "Ukrainian protesters get visit from Sen. John McCain — McCain: America stands with Ukrainians". *CNN*, 15 December 2013. Available at: <http://edition.cnn.com/2013/12/14/world/europe/ukraine-protests/> (Accessed 10 March 2015).

_____. "Opposition source: Syrian rebels get U.S.-organized training in Jordan". *CNN*, 15 March 2013. Available at: <http://edition.cnn.com/2013/03/15/world/meast/syria-civil-war/index.html?hpt=hp_bn2>.

WARBURG, Sidney. *The Financial Sources of National Socialism*: *Hitler's Secret Backers*. Palmdale (CA): Omni Publications, 1995, pp. 14–16 e 44–47.

WATSON, Paul Joseph. "Former Nazi Bank to Rule the Global Economy". *Prison* Planet.com, 30 April 2010 / In Featured Stories, Old Infowars Posts Style. Available at: <http://www.infowars.com/former-nazi-bank-to-rule-the-global-economy/>.

WATSON, Steve. "Total Bailout Cost Heads Towards $5 TRILLION. Numbers becoming meaningless as Paulson defends government intervention". Infowars.net, 15 October 2008. Available at: <http://infowars.net/articles/october2008/151008Bailout_figures.htm>.

"Wealth: Having it all and wanting more". *Oxfam Issue Briefing January 2015* — WWW.Oxfam. Org. Available at: <http://policy-practice.oxfam.org.uk/publications/wealth-having-it-all-and-wanting-more-338125>.

WEAVER, Courtney (Artemivsk); OLEARCHYK, Roman (Kiev). "City of Debaltseve emerges as a tipping point in Ukraine's war". *Financial Times*, 9 February 2015. Available at: <http://www.ft.com/intl/cms/s/0/7fe1d32e-b047-11e4-92b6-00144feab7de.html#axzz3jwzpgTib>.

WEINER, Tim. *Legacy of Ashes — The History of the CIA*. New York/Toronto: Doubleday, 2007, pp. 138–14.

WEINSTEIN, Adam. "A Privately Owned Nuclear Weapons Plant in. . .Kansas City? In a last-ditch court hearing, activists seek to block a new Honeywell project", Mother Jones, 29 August 2011. Available at: <http://www.motherjones.com/politics/2011/08/nuclear-weapons-plant-kansas-city>.

WEISS, Michael; HASSAN, Hassan. *ISIS — Inside the Army of Terror*. New York. Regan Arts, 2015, pp. 166–167.

WERNER, Alfred (1911–1979). *Albert Einstein Archives* 30–1104. The Hebrew University of Jerusalem, Israel. Available at: <http://alberteinstein.info/vufind1/Search/Results?lookfor=%

22Albert+Einstein+Archives%2C+The+Hebrew+University+of+Jerusalem%2C+Israel%22&
type=Series&filter[]=enddate%3A%221949–03-31%22&sort=enddate+asc>.

WERTH, Nicolas. "Crimes and Mass Violence of the Russian Civil Wars (1918–1921)". *Online Encyclopedia of Mass Violence®* — ISSN 1961–9898. 3 April 2008. Available at <http://www.massviolence.org/crimes-and-mass-violence-of-the-russian-civil-wars-1918?artpage=3>.

WEST, Darrel M. *Billionaires: Reflexions on the Upper Crust.* Washington, D.C.: Brookings Institution Press, 2014, p. 4.

WEZEMAN, Pieter D.; WEZEMAN, Siemon T. "Trends in International Arms Transfers, 2014". *SIPRI Fact Sheet*, 25 de March. Stockhol International Peace Research Institute (SIPRI). Available at: <http://books.sipri.org/files/FS/SIPRIFS1503.pdf>.

WHITE, Stephen *et al. Developments in Soviet Politics.* London: MacMillan, 1990.

WHITE, Stephen; McALLISTER, Ian. "Rethinking the 'Orange Revolution'" *in*: LANE, David; WHITE, Stephen. *Rethinking the 'Orange Revolution'.* London/New York: Routledge, 2010.

WHITLOCK, Craig "U.S. secretly backed Syrian opposition groups, cables released by WikiLeaks show". *The Washington Post*, 17 April 2011. Available at: <https://www.washingtonpost.com/world/us-secretly-backed-syrian-opposition-groups-cables-released-by-wikileaks-show/2011/04/14/AF1p9hwD_story.html>.

WHITLOCK, Monica (BBC correspondent in Kabul). "Legal limbo of Guantanamo's prisoners". *BBC News*, 16 May 2003. Available at: <http://news.bbc.co.uk/2/hi/americas/3034697.stm>.

_____. "Legal limbo of Guantanamo's prisoners". *BBC News*, 16 May 2003. Available at: <http://news.bbc.co.uk/2/hi/americas/3034697.stm>.

WHITMORE, Brian. "Russia: The End of Loans-For-Shares — Nearly a decade ago in a move that reshaped Russia's political landscape, the ailing and embattled Kremlin leader Boris Yeltsin sold off the crown jewels of the country's economy to a select group of oligarchs. Russian President Vladimir Putin is now ready to buy them back". *Radio Free Europe/Radio Liberty*, 29 September 2005. Available at: <http://www.rferl.org/articleprintview/1061761.html>.

WHITNEY, Mike. "The University of Al-Qaeda? America's — 'Terrorist Academy' in Iraq Produced ISIS Leaders". *Counterpunch*, 6 October 2014. Available at <http://www.counterpunch.org/2014/10/06/americas-terrorist-academy-in-iraq-produced-isis-leaders/print>.

WIDMER, Fred. Forum: Politik Kämpfe in der Ostukraine: "Praktisch jedes Haus zerstört — Mär vom faschistischen Putsch". *Spiegel Online*, 30 August 2014. Available at: <http://www.spiegel.de/forum/politik/kaempfe-der-ostukraine-praktisch-jedes-haus-zerstoert-thread-141429–11.html>.

WIEGREFE, Klaus. "Germany's Unlikely Diplomatic TriumphAn Inside Look at the Reunification Negotiations". *Spiegel Online,* 29 September 2010. Available at: <http://ml.spiegel.de/article.do?id=719848&p=6>.

_____. "Germany's Unlikely Diplomatic Triumph an Inside Look at the Reunification Negotiations". *Spiegel Online*, 29 September 2010. Available at: <http://ml.spiegel.de/article.do?id=719848&p=6>.

WIEL Iris van de. "The Russian Crisis 1998". *Economic Report — Rabobank — Economic Research Department.* Available at: <https://economics.rabobank.com/publications/2013/september/the-russian-crisis-1998/>.

WILDAU, Gabriel (Shanghai). "New Brics bank in Shanghai to challenge major institutions". *The Financial Times*, 21 July 2015. Available at: <http://www.ft.com/intl/cms/s/0/d8e26216–2f8d-11e5–8873-775ba7c2ea3d.html#axzz3lo8DME81>.

WILKINSON, Richard; PICKETT, Kate. "Margaret Thatcher made Britain a less, not more, desirable place to do business". *The Guardian*, 10 April 2013. Available at: <http://www.theguardian.com/commentisfree/2013/apr/10/inequality-margaret-thatcher-britain-desirable-business>.

"William E. Dodd to Franklin D. Roosevelt". Franklin D. Roosevelt Presidential Library and Museum — Great Britain/German Diplomatic Files — Box 32 — Folder Titles List Dodd-->FDR 10/19/36. Germany: William E. Dodd: 1936–38 (i300) Index. Available at: <http://docs.fdrlibrary.marist.edu/psf/box32/a300l02.html>.

WILLIAM, Brian G. *The Crimean Tatars — The Diaspora Experience and the Forging of a Nation.* Leiden-Boston-Köln: Brill, 2001, pp. 10–13.

WILSON, Scott; WARRICK, Joby. "Assad must go, Obama says". *The Washington Post,* 18 August 2011. Available at: <http://www.washingtonpost.com/politics/assad-must-go-obama-says/2011/08/18/gIQAelheOJ_story.html>.

WINFIELD, Nicole (Associated Press). "Italy recovers more bodies of would-be refugees from Libya. Migrants fleeing in boats from unrest in Libya face deadliest few days, as more than 300 have drowned since Friday". *The star.com World,* 26 August 2014. Available at: <http://www.thestar.com/news/world/2014/08/26/italy_recovers_more_bodies_of_wouldbe_refugees_from_libya.html>.

"Winston Churchill's *Iron Curtain Speech* — Winston Churchill presented his *Sinews of Peace* (the *Iron Curtain Speech*), at Westminster College in Fulton, Missouri on March 5, 1946". *History Guide.* Available at: <http://www.historyguide.org/europe/churchill.html>.

WINTER, Michael. "Report: Saudis sent death-row inmates to fight Syria. Secret memo says more than 1,200 prisoners fought Assad regime to avoid beheading". *USA TODAY,* 21 January 2013. Available at: <http://www.usatoday.com/story/news/world/2013/01/21/saudi-inmates-fight-syria-commute-death-sentences/1852629/?siteID=je6NUbpObpQ-LvY5MH6LGuR644xcPiwBWQ>.

WITT, Howard (Washington Bureau). "Arafat's power to stop terror attacks debated". *Chicago Tribune,* 4 December 2001. Available at: <http://www.chicagotribune.com/chi-0112040122dec04-story.html>.

WITTNER, Lawrence S. "Despite protests Kansas City gets a new nuclear power plant". *LA Progressive — Alex Jones' Infowars,* 6 September 2011. Available at: <http://www.infowars.com/despite-protests-kansas-city-gets-a-new-nuclear-power-plant/>.

WOLCZUK, Kataryna; WOLCZUK, Roman. "What you need to know about the causes of the Ukrainian protests". *The Washington Post,* 9 December 2013.

WOLF, Naomi. "Fascist America, in 10 easy steps". *The Guardian,* 24 April 2007.

"World must help pull Libya out of human rights chaos five years since uprising that ousted al-Gaddafi". *Amnesty International — Libya Armed Conflict,* 16 February 2016. Available at: <https://www.amnesty.org/en/latest/news/2016/02/world-must-help-pull-libya-out-of-human-rights-chaos-five-years-since-uprising-that-ousted-al-gaddafi/>.

"Worldwide displacement hits all-time high as war and persecution increase". *UNHCR — Geneva. Annual Global Trends Report,* 18 June 2015. Available at: <http://www.unhcr.org/print/558193896.html>.

WURSTER, Linda. "Das Bataillon Asow — Schmutziger Kampf in der Ukraine: Neonazis im Dienst der Regierung". *FOCUS-Online,* Aktualisiert am Donnerstag, 14 August 2014. Available at: <http://www.focus.de/politik/ausland/das-bataillon-asow-schmutziger-kampf-in-der-ukraine-neonazis-im-dienst-der-regierung_id_4058717.html>.

Xinhua, 26 June 2015. Available at: <China.org.cn. http://www.china.org.cn/china/Off_the_Wire/2015–06/26/content_35915205.htm>.

YAAKOV, Yifa; NEWMAN, Marissa. "Israel's three murdered teens buried side-by-side amid national outpouring of grief. PM says Israel will expand action against Ḥamās if need be; missiles hit Eshkol region; tens of thousands mourn teens at joint burial service, separate funerals; Israel vows to apprehend killers 'dead or alive'; US warns Israel against 'heavy-handed' response". *The Times of Israel,* 1 July 2014. Available at: <http://www.timesofisrael.com/idf-hunts-for-two-suspects-in-teens-murder/>.

YAKOVENKO, Iryna; POLOSKOVA, Oleksandra; SOLONINA, Yevhen; SINDELAR, Daisy. "A Sticky Situation for Poroshenko As Russians Seize Candy Assets". *Radio Free Europe — Radio Liberty,* 29 April 2015. Available at: <http://www.rferl.org/content/ukraine-poroshenko-roshen-russia-seizes-candy-lipetsk/26985196.html>.

YAQUB, Salim. *Containing Arab Nationalism: The Eisenhower Doctrine and the Middle East.* Chapel Hill & London: University of North Carolina Press, 2004, pp. 48–52, 149.

YATSENYUK, Arseniy. Available at: <http://openukraine.org/en/about/partners>.

YAVLINSKY, Grigory. "Russia's Phony Capitalism". *Foreign Affairs — Council of Foreign Relations*, May/June 1998. Available at: <http://www.foreignaffairs.com/articles/54018/grigory-yavlinsky/russias-phony-capitalism>.

"Yazidi Slave Reveals: American Jihadi is 'Top ISIS Commander'". *AlulBayt News Agency (BNA)*, 29 September 2015. Available at: <http://en.abna24.com/service/middle-east-west-asia/archive/2015/09/29/712912/story.html>.

YBARRA, Maggie. "Russian fighter jet buzzes U.S. Navy destroyer in Black Sea amid Ukraine crisis". *The Washington Times*, 14 April 2014. Available at: <http://www.washingtontimes.com/news/2014/apr/14/russian-fighter-jet-buzzes-us-navy-destroyer-black/>.

Yearbook of the United Nations 2001. Vol. 55. Department of Public Information. United Nations, New York, 2003, pp. 408 e 648. Available at: <https://books.google.de/books?id=Yt3o624miKQC&pg=PA407&lpg=PA407&dq=Palestine+more+than+14+months222+Israelis+killed+compared+to+742+Palestinians&source=bl&ots=9vhs9RceFM&sig=KRN8BCZqK8FH6iwLi2cKyMsJHeE&hl=de&sa=X&ved=0CD8Q6AEwBWoVChMI1deIvdPYyAIVitYsCh1azAMq#v=onepage&q=Arafat&f=false>.

"Yemen needs peace, not more bombs February 29, 2016". Available at: <http://controlarms.org/en/>.

"Yemen: Yemen — Conflict (ECHO, UN, EP, Media) (ECHO Daily Flash of 29 February 2016) 29 February 2016. *UN Office for the Coordination of Humanitarian Affairs* Country: Iraq, Jordan, Nepal, Nigeria, Ukraine, World, Yemen — European Commission Humanitarian Aid Office Country: Saudi Arabia, United Arab Emirates, Yemen". Available at: <http://www.unocha.org/aggregator/sources/80>.

YERGIN, Daniel. *O Petróleo*. São Paulo: Scritta Editorial, 1990, pp. 335–337.

YOUNG, Angelo. "And The Winner For The Most Iraq War Contracts Is... KBR, With $39.5 Billion In A Decade". *International Business Times,* 19 March 2013. Available at: <http://www.ibtimes.com/winner-most-iraq-war-contracts-kbr-395-billion-decade-1135905>.

_____. "Cheney's Halliburton Made $39.5 Billion on Iraq War". *RSN*. Available at: <http://readersupportednews.org/news-section2/308–12/16561-focus-cheneys-halliburton-made-395-billion-on-iraq-war>.

"Yushchenko said he wants clarity on gas sector". *The Ukrainian Weekly,* 19 February 2006, p. 8. Available at: <http://ukrweekly.com/archive/pdf3/2006/The_Ukrainian_Weekly_2006–08.pdf>.

ZACEC, Jane Shapiro; KIM I. Ilpyong (Editors). *The Legacy of the Soviet Bloc*. Gainesville: Florida University Press, 1997, pp. 110–112.

"Zeid deplores mass execution of 47 people in Saudi Arabia". *United Nations of the Human Rights-Office of the High Commissioner for Human Rights*. Genebra, 3 January 2016. Available at: <http://www.ohchr.org/EN/NewsEvents/Pages/Media.aspx?IsMediaPage=true&LangID=E>.

ZHARKESHO, Yernar (Director of Research Institute). "Comparative analysis of trends and challenges to maintain adequate institutional and human resource capacities of public administrations in post-Soviet countries". Background discussion paper. *Academy of public Administration under the President of Kazakhstan*. Available at: <http://workspace.unpan.org/sites/Internet/Documents/UNPAN93486.pdf>.

ZHILIN et al. *La Gran Guerra Patria de la Unión Soviética — 1941–1945*. Moscow, 1985.

ZHUKOV, Yuri M. "Rust Belt Rising.The Economics behind Eastern Ukraine's Upheaval". *Foreign Affairs — Council of Foreign Relations*, 11 June 2014. Available at: <http://www.foreignaffairs.com/articles/141561/yuri-m-zhukov/rust-belt-rising>.

ZINETS, Natalia; PIPER, Elizabeth (Kiev). "Crimea cost Ukraine over $10 billion in lost natural resources". *Reuters*, Mon Apr 7, 2014.

ZONSZEIN, Mairav (Tel Aviv). "Jewish migration to Israel up 40% this year so far — Ukrainians and Russians account for surge as numbers leaving Western Europe in first three months remains steady despite Paris attacks in January, report shows". *The Guardian*, 3 May 2015.

ZUESSE, Eric. "MH-17 'Investigation': Secret August 8th Agreement Seeps Out — Perpetrator of the downing in Ukraine, of the Malaysian airliner, will stay hidden". *Infowars. Com*, 25 August 2014. Available at: <http://www.infowars.com/mh-17-investigation-secret-august-8th-agree ment-seeps-out/>.

Интересы РФ и США в отношении Украины несовместимы друг с другом". Глава Stratfor Джордж Фридман о первопричинах украинского кризиса- Коммерсантъ от 19 December 2014. Available at: <http://www.kommersant.ru/doc/2636177>.

Кајгана — Пресвртница за Украина. Available at: <http://forum.kajgana.com/threads/%D0%9F %D1%80%D0%B5%D1%81%D0%B2%D1%80%D1%82%D0%BD%D0%B8%D1%86% D0%B0-%D0%B7%D0%B0-%D0%A3%D0%BA%D1%80%D0%B0%D0%B8%D0%BD% D0%B0.71107/page-204>.

Марионетки Майдан. www.youtube.com/watch?v=MSxaa-67yGM04.02.2014. Hochgeladen von Re Post. "Victoria Nuland gaffe: Angela Merkel condemns EU insult". *BBC Europe*, 7 February 2014. Available at: <http://www.bbc.com/news/world-europe-26080715>.

"О временном порядке местного самоуправления в отдельных районах Донецкой и Луганской областей" (Закон об особом статусе). Закон об особом порядке местного самоуправления в отдельных районах Донецкой и Луганской областей (Закон об особом статусе Донбасса), текст проекта №5081 от 16.09.2014. Закон и Бизнес". Available at: <http://zib.com.ua/ru/print/100900-zakon_ob_osobom_poryadke_mestnogo_ samoupravleniya_v_otdelnih.html>.

"Росія захопила в Криму майна на 127 мільярдів — Мохник". Українська правда, Понеділок, 07 квітня 2014. Available at: <http://www.pravda.com.ua/news/2014/04/7/7021631/view_ print/>.

"Ситуационный а нализ гибели рейса МН17 (малайзийского Boeing 777), сделанный на основе инженерно — технического анализа от 15.08.2014 — Информационное сообщение от Российского союза инженеров", 13 November 2014. Available at: <http:// www.российский-союз-инженеров.рф/RSI_Boeing777_13.11.2014.pdf>.

Index

© Springer Nature Switzerland AG 2019
L. A. Moniz Bandeira, *The World Disorder*,
https://doi.org/10.1007/978-3-030-03204-3

CPSIA information can be obtained
at www.ICGtesting.com
Printed in the USA
LVHW080147060622
720567LV00003B/13